THE American Quilt SERIES

DESIGNS of the HEART

❋ The Pattern ❋ The Pledge ❋
❋ The Promise ❋

Three Bestselling Novels Complete in One Volume

JANE PEART

INSPIRATIONAL PRESS

NEW YORK

First Inspirational Press edition published in 1999.

Inspirational Press
A division of BBS Publishing Corporation
386 Park Avenue South
New York, NY 10016

Inspirational Press is a registered trademark of
BBS Publishing Corporation.

Published by arrangement with Zondervan Publishing House.

Library of Congress Catalog Card Number: 98-72401
ISBN: 0-88486-223-2

Interior design by Sherri Hoffman
Frontispiece illustration by Michael Ingle
Part title illustrations by Adam Bloom

Printed in the United States of America.

CONTENTS

The PATTERN

Part One

Chapter One

~❧~

Johanna Shelby, eighteen and recently having returned home from boarding school, stood looking out through the rain-smeared bedroom window. It had started raining early in the morning and had continued steadily all day. Now it was coming down in sheets.

Sighing impatiently, she turned back into the room. She gave a rueful glance at her new scarlet taffeta party dress hanging on the ledge of her armoire. She was looking forward eagerly to wearing it tonight at the first party of the holiday season, held at the home of her best friend, Liddy Chalmers. But if this kept up, it might be impossible to get there, country roads being what they were.

On her way across the room, she practiced a few dance steps, ending up by holding on to one of the bedposts, where she twirled around a couple of times before plopping down and bouncing onto the feather mattress. There she sighed again.

Although she had only been home a few days, she already felt restless, at loose ends. Why? At school, she couldn't wait to get home for Christmas. And now it certainly was not that she missed school! For a free-spirited girl like Johanna, the rules, regulations, routine, the tedious hours in needlework class, and the memorizing endless verses to recite in the weekly elocution programs were boring and meaningless. In fact, Johanna was determined not to go back. That is, if she could convince her parents that she was quite "finished" enough. After two and a half years at Miss Pomoroy's Female Academy in Winston, she had had enough!

No, it certainly wasn't the lack of boarding school schedule that made her feel so fidgety. It was that she couldn't seem to settle down now that she was home. She felt so betwixt and between. She had changed more than she realized while being away. She'd gone off to school when she was sixteen and didn't seem to fit back into the family nest so neatly.

Johanna didn't really know what made her feel so uncomfortable back in the Shelby family circle. Maybe it was her prickly relationship with her sister Cicely, the next oldest. After her first greeting, Cissy had slipped back into her old adversary role with Johanna. Of course, Elly, the youngest, was adorable and as loving and lovable as ever. It was something else Johanna couldn't define. Even though she tried, she had the uneasy feeling she didn't really belong here anymore.

That is why after only a few days, Johanna found herself strangely at odds with everyone. It wasn't that she didn't love them all. It was just that she had the strangest feeling, as if she were on the brink of something, something unknown, something that was both exciting and a little daunting.

Johanna walked over to the window again. Putting her palms up against the steaming panes, she pressed her face against the glass. Just then the sky seemed to split open with a jagged streak of lightning that zigzagged down through dark, purple-edged clouds, sending the bare trees outside into stark silhouettes in a blinding flash. This was followed by a loud crackle of thunder that caused Johanna to jump back from the window in alarm.

In a panic reaction, Johanna turned and ran out of the room and down the stairs into the parlor, where the rest of the family was gathered, in time to hear her mother declare, "My good gracious, that was quite a jolt. It's a regular downpour. The roads will be rivers of mud by evening. I've a mind not to set out in this weather—"

"Not *go?*" a chorus of protest came from both the other girls. Cissy ran to stand beside her mother, peering out the window. Elly jumped up from the hassock, dropping her cat, which she'd been holding in her lap, to exclaim, "Not go to the *party?*"

"Oh Mama, surely you don't mean *that!*" cried Johanna, looking at her father for support and mainly concerned about having another evening confined at home and about losing the opportunity to wear her new dress.

"Well, I don't know. . . ." Mrs. Shelby's voice trailed into uncertainty. "Just getting from the carriage to the house, we'll get drenched for sure."

"Oh, it will be all right, Mama. We can bundle up and wear boots and carry our slippers 'til we get inside," Cissy assured her. At fifteen, she was the practical one.

"I suppose." Mrs. Shelby's voice still sounded tentative.

"Please, Mama, don't say we can't go!" wailed Elly, who at nearly eleven had been promised this treat, her first time to attend a really "grown-up" party.

"Oh, come now, Rebecca," boomed Tennant Shelby, the girls' father, who had caught Johanna's pleading look. He laid aside the book he had been reading to say chidingly to his wife, "Can't let a little rain deprive these pretty young ladies of the first party of the holiday season."

His wife gave him a cautionary look. Tennant was so indulgent of their three daughters, especially Johanna, that it was *she* who sometimes had to exert discipline or take the stern parental role. However, she was already inclined to put

7

aside her own misgivings about the weather. The Chalmerses' party *was* the first of the holiday season. After all, she wasn't yet too old to remember what fun a dancing party could be. More to the point, with three daughters to eventually marry off, it was important that they get out socially. Particularly for Johanna, their oldest, home after her years out of circulation here in Hillsboro. Now eighteen, ready to be launched into society and ready for a serious courtship and marriage proposal. Not that it would be much of a problem. Johanna was pretty, vivacious, and bright. Any number of eligible young men would no doubt find her attractive. It was only a matter of choosing the right one.

Rebecca felt all three pairs of anxious eyes upon her. Waiting an appropriate length of time, she said slowly, "Well, I suppose it will be all right. If we leave early enough and you make sure Thomas drives carefully." This admonition was directed at her husband. Her decision was greeted by exclamations of relief and delight by her daughters.

By dark, the icy rain had turned to sleet, and once more Mrs. Shelby voiced her doubts about the wisdom of venturing out over rutted roads in the stormy night. Again she was the lone dissenter, and again she was coaxed, cajoled, persuaded. Finally, at half-past seven, swathed in hooded cloaks, shod in sturdy boots, their portmanteaus containing dainty slippers into which they could change upon their arrival, they were at last ready to leave. In high spirits, the three Shelby girls climbed into the family carriage. Inside the narrow interior, settling their crinolines, they seated themselves opposite their parents. As the carriage jolted along the country roads now running with streams of mud, the girls chattered merrily, giggling at whatever nonsensical things one or the other of them said. Elly, squeezed between her older sisters, was wildly

8

excited to have been allowed to come along. She was ecstatic at the prospect of the evening ahead.

Upon reaching the Chalmerses' house, Thomas, the Shelbys' coachman, pulled up as close to the covered side porch as possible. With Rebecca issuing warnings to be careful, the three girls, giggling with nervous excitement, descended from the carriage. Jumping over puddles, they ran through the pelting rain up the front steps of the house, through the door opened by the jovial Mr. Chalmers, and into the front hall.

The warm, candlelit house was already filled with the sound of fiddle music, lighthearted laughter, and happy voices. Someone took Johanna's cape, and as she stood there for a minute looking about, Liddy Chalmers, her closest friend from childhood, came rushing up to her. "Oh, Johanna! I'm so glad to see you! I was afraid you might not come! Isn't this weather dreadful?" She gave Johanna's arm an excited squeeze. "Come on. You can primp in my bedroom before we go in to dance." She lowered her voice significantly. "Burton Lassiter's been pacing up and down like a madman, waiting for you to arrive! I hid your dance card so he wouldn't fill up every slot."

Liddy propelled Johanna back through the narrow hall to her downstairs bedroom, chatting all the while. "I absolutely *love* your dress, Johanna! It's a perfect color for you."

Sitting on the mounting steps to the high, four-poster bed, Johanna bent to pull off her boots and get her dancing shoes out of her bag. Liddy continued to talk as Johanna took out the red satin slippers with the tiny silk roses on the toes and slipped them on her feet.

"It's going to be such a fun party. I wish you could spend the night so we could stay up till all hours and talk." Suddenly Liddy clapped her hands. "Maybe the weather will worsen and you'll have to! Anyway, come along. Papa's about to call the first reel."

At the entrance to the parlor, now cleared of furniture for dancing, the eager Burton Lassiter was quick to find Johanna and claim her as his partner for the Virginia Reel, which was usually the dance to open a party.

When they finally came to a breathless halt after the lively dance, Johanna's gaze swept the room. It was then she became aware of the young man leaning against the pilaster in the archway.

He was very tall and his dark shaggy hair needed a good trim. He was not handsome, and his features were too irregular, with a strong nose and a determined mouth. However, the combination was oddly attractive. His gray eyes, regarding her so steadily, were intelligent yet held a hint of humor.

As the stranger glanced at her, Johanna experienced the strangest sensation, as if somehow they knew each other, as if they'd met somewhere. Of course, that was impossible! Yet the strong feeling lingered.

She and Burton took their places with other couples lining up for the quadrille. The music struck up and she was swept into the promenade. Again Johanna caught sight of the stranger, and to her immediate confusion, found he was looking at her as well.

Who was he? she wondered curiously. In spite of her odd sense of recognition, she couldn't place him. In as small a town as Hillsboro, a stranger stood out. Surely Liddy would know. For some reason, Johanna felt an urgency to find out. Fanning herself briskly, she told Burton she was perishing from thirst and sent him off to fetch her a glass of punch.

Then she quickly darted to Liddy's side. Taking her by the wrist, she led her aside and whispered, "Come with me. I have to talk to you!"

Puzzled but compliant, Liddy followed Johanna's lead down the hall to her bedroom. Some of the other girls were already there, restoring hairdos and primping in front of the mirror as they came in.

"What is it?" Liddy asked.

"Who is that tall fellow standing beside Dr. Murrison? Is he new in town? A relative? A nephew? Who?"

"That's Dr. Murrison's new assistant."

"What's his name?"

"His name is Ross Davison. He's been with Dr. Murrison for a few months now. He came after you left for school in September."

"Where's he from?"

"If you heard him talk, you wouldn't have to ask where he's from," a voice behind them said with a snicker. Unaware that they'd been overheard, both girls turned around. Emily Archer, a girl Johanna had never liked very well, was standing in front of the full-length mirror. Her face in the glass had a know-it-all smirk. But at the moment, she had the information Johanna wanted, so Johanna swallowed her dislike to ask, "What do you mean? Is he a foreigner?"

Emily giggled shrilly. "No, silly, he's from the *mountains!*"

"Mountains?"

"From Millscreek Gap, for pity's sake!" Emily fluffed her corkscrew curls and patted her skirt, turning this way and that as she surveyed herself in the mirror. "I suppose he *must* be educated—I mean, to be a doctor and all," she remarked indifferently. "But he still has that hill twang." Emily mimicked, *"You kin jest tell."*

11

Johanna frowned. She suddenly remembered why she had never liked Emily very much. Emily had a sharp tongue. She was always quick with a snide remark, a mean comment, or a sly innuendo. For some reason, it made Johanna cross to hear Emily make fun of that young man with his serious expression and deep-set, thoughtful eyes. But Johanna let it pass, not wanting to appear too interested in the newcomer. Emily had a razor-like tongue, liked nothing better than to tease. Johanna was not about to become her target by giving her anything to turn into a joke.

"Come on," she said to Liddy. "Burton's waiting for me with punch." She slipped her hand into Liddy's arm and they made their escape.

"What a cat that Emily is!" commented Liddy as they hurried out into the hall. "Actually, Dr. Davison is very well mannered and pleasant. Dr. Murrison sent him over when my little brother Billy had croup, and he couldn't have been nicer."

Back in the parlor, Burton was nowhere in sight, and Johanna allowed her gaze to seek that of the young doctor. As her eyes met his, he turned and spoke to Dr. Murrison. Then, to her surprise, they both crossed the room. "Well, Johanna, my dear, it's nice to see you home from Winston and looking so well," Dr. Murrison said. "I don't believe you've met my new assistant, Ross Davison."

Johanna's heart gave a little leap. "No, Dr. Murrison, I've not had the pleasure. Good evening, Dr. Davison," she managed to say, fluttering her fan to cool her suddenly flushed face.

"Good evening, Miss Shelby. I trust you are having a pleasant time?"

His voice was deep. There *was* a trace of the mountain twang to it, as Emily had said. However, Johanna did not find it at all unpleasant.

"Yes, indeed. And you?" As she looked up at him, Johanna felt a tingling in her wrists and fingertips.

It was uncanny, Johanna thought, this feeling of recognition. As though somehow they had been parted a long time and were, at this very moment, seeing each other again. The sensation was bewildering.

"If you have not already promised it, may I have the next dance?" His question brought her back to the present moment.

Even though she *had* promised the next three, Johanna simply put her hand in Ross's, felt his fingers close over it. He bowed from his great height, and she moved with him out onto the polished dance floor as the first notes of the next set began. Out of the corner of her eye, she saw Burton, looking bewildered and a little indignant, glancing around in search of his missing partner. But she didn't care. She knew she was exactly where she wanted to be, dancing with this tall newcomer.

Ross was not the best of dancers. He was a little unsure and stiff, his height making him rather awkward. It did not matter to Johanna. She felt as if she were floating, her head spinning as fast as her feet. They circled, his hand firmly on her waist, her face upturned to his, and she could not remember ever feeling so happy. The piece ended and as they waited for the next one, they smiled at each other—as if they had danced together many times before.

The music started again, and again they seemed to move in perfect step. At length the melody ended. Yet, they remained facing each other. Mr. Chalmers's booming voice jovially announced, "Line up, ladies and gentlemen, for musical chairs."

Reluctantly Ross stepped back, bowed slightly, and relinquished Johanna. A row of chairs, numbering one less than the assembled guests, was placed down the middle of the long room.

The musicians started playing a lively march, and the company began moving in a circle around the room, giggling, shuffling a little, attempting to anticipate when the music would stop and they would have to rush for a seat. As one by one a chair was eliminated and one or more persons had to drop out, the circle grew smaller and the fun and hilarity of the suspense grew louder. Every once in a while Johanna would catch Ross's glance. He was so tall and lanky that watching him scramble for a chair was comical. What pleased her the most was that he seemed to be thoroughly enjoying himself and had lost that slight awkwardness. Although his shyness touched her, she was elated that he could enjoy such fun.

Soon there were only a handful of marchers left, Ross and Johanna among them. The musicians, enjoying the sight as much as the onlookers clustered around the periphery of the room, changed the tempo from fast to slow to trick the hopeful remaining players. Johanna was almost weak with laughter, and once when the music stopped abruptly, she and Ross landed unceremoniously on the same chair. In a gentlemanly manner, he shifted and stood up, leaving her seated while a more bois-terous young man slid into the only other chair left empty. Ross joined the spectators as Johanna stayed in the game. With two chairs and three people left, the room became noisier than ever, people cheering on their favorites. When the music halted, Johanna made a dash for a seat, and as she did she lost her balance and went crashing, sending the chair sliding, her-self collapsing in a heap with upturned crinolines and taffeta ruffles. One small dancing slipper, with its tiny heel, went skit-tering across the polished floor and out of sight.

Burton ran to help the laughing Johanna to her feet. Leaning on his arm, she hopped to the side of the room, where someone pushed a chair for her to collapse into. Johanna's laughter suddenly came to a swift halt when, from

14

across the room, she saw her mother's disapproving expression. Johanna felt a sinking sensation, which was quickly replaced by one of rebellion. What had she done that was so horrible? Just played a silly game to the fullest. What on earth was wrong with *that*? She turned away from the admonishing face just as Ross came up to her, bearing her small satin shoe in his open palm.

He knelt to slip it back on her foot. As his hand held the arch, Johanna felt a tingle running up from her foot all through her. Involuntarily she shivered. He glanced up at her, and for a single moment their gazes met and held, as if seeking an answer to an unspoken question. Then people gathered around, and their voices crowded out the sound of Johanna's heart beating so loudly she was sure everyone could hear it.

⚜

Hours later Johanna was sitting in front of her dressing table, dreamily brushing her hair, when her mother entered her bedroom.

Johanna had been reliving the evening. At least the part after she had been introduced to Ross Davison. Following that, the rest of the party had simply faded into a backdrop. She hardly remembered the carriage ride home, the excited voices of her sisters discussing the evening. She had seemed to float up the stairs and into her own bedroom on some kind of cloud. Now her mother was talking to her in a tone of voice that was edged with severity, chiding her about something. Johanna blinked, looked at her mother, and tried to concentrate on what she was saying.

"I simply cannot believe it, Johanna! I thought your years at Miss Pomoroy's had taught you some reticence, some proper behavior. I am shocked to see that—given the opportunity—you are as much a hoyden as ever!"

Johanna, outwardly submissive, listened to her mother's lecture while continuing to brush her hair. *Eighty-two, eighty-three, eighty-four,* she counted silently, wondering if her mother's tirade would end at the prerequisite one hundred strokes.

"I expect you to set a good example for your younger sisters, Johanna. This was Elly's first grown-up party, and she worships you, you know, imitates everything you do: your mannerisms, your likes, dislikes—unfortunately, your bad traits as well as any good ones you might exhibit. I am thoroughly ashamed of your lack of decorum tonight, Johanna. And with that—that rough-hewn young man, whose parlor manners also need a great deal of improvement." All at once Rebecca realized Johanna was not really listening. Hadn't she heard a word? Maybe the child was tired. Perhaps this could wait until tomorrow.

"You *do* understand, don't you, Johanna? Anything you do reflects on the family. People are ever ready to gossip or spread untrue rumors. I would not want anyone to get the idea—" Again Johanna's expression looked faraway. Her sweetly curved mouth was—smiling. Rebecca's voice sharpened. "Johanna!"

"Yes, Mama. I do. I didn't mean to—I was just having fun."

"I'm sure that was all there was to it, dear. But we can't give the wrong impression—you see?"

"Yes, Mama," Johanna replied demurely.

Rebecca leaned down and kissed the smooth brow, cupping her daughter's cheek for a moment with her hand. Her eyes swept over her daughter. Johanna was fulfilling her childhood promise of beauty. Her complexion was lovely, her eyes, with their sweeping lashes, truly beautiful, Rebecca thought fondly. *But we must be careful that her gaiety and vivaciousness aren't misunderstood.*

As soon as the door closed behind her mother, Johanna put down her hairbrush and studied her reflection in the mir-

16

ror. Was it possible? Did she really look different? Something had happened tonight, and she seemed changed somehow.

In a way, that shouldn't have surprised her. She *felt* different. Ever since she'd come home less than a week ago, she had felt oddly displaced. The familiar seemed unfamiliar. Even getting used to being with her parents and two younger sisters again had presented problems. However, Johanna knew it was something more than that. Deep inside, there was a heart hunger she couldn't explain or even understand. A need for something to give her life meaning and purpose.

Johanna blew out her lamp, climbed into bed, and pulled the quilt up to her chin. She shut her eyes, squeezing them tight, and the image of Ross Davison came into her mind. He was different from most of the young men she knew, the ones she'd smiled at and teased at picnics, flirted with and danced with at parties.

He might be a bit awkward and unsure of himself socially, perhaps not good at small talk or such. He was already into a man's life, a doctor, healing the sick and injured, saving lives. It made the lives of most of the other young men she knew seem shallow by comparison.

Up until recently Johanna's life had been that of a schoolgirl—simple, uncomplicated, filled with friends, fun, light flirtations. Now Ross Davison had stepped into her life. His eyes seemed to look into her very soul. It had been almost as if he recognized that longing within her she had not ever spoken of to anyone.

Suddenly Johanna saw a possibility of something deeper and more important. She wasn't exactly sure just what happened tonight. She only knew that something had and nothing would ever be the same again. It both excited and frightened her.

Chapter Two

*A*t breakfast the following day, Rebecca announced, "Johanna, I want you to take the fruitcakes around to the aunties. You may take the small buggy. If you don't dawdle or stay too long at each house, you should be back by noon. No later, because I shall need it myself this afternoon when I go to help decorate the church for Advent services."

Delivering fruitcakes to her cousins was Rebecca's holiday custom. Since she used a secret Shelby family recipe handed down to her by her mother-in-law, she knew that this was one thing none of them could duplicate. Fond as they all were of each other, nonetheless an unspoken but very real rivalry existed among the cousins.

"Yes, Mama, I'll be happy to." Johanna cheerfully accepted the errand, glad of the opportunity to get out of the house and thus escape some of the household chores Rebecca daily allotted to each daughter.

Immediately Cissy protested. "Why does Johanna get to do all the fun things?"

The difference in their ages always rankled Cissy. It was something she had not had to deal with while Johanna was away. After her first welcome to Johanna at her homecoming, Cissy had reverted to petty jealousy. Rebecca sent her a disapproving glance. "Because Johanna can drive the trap, for one reason. For another, the aunties haven't seen her since she came home." Then she added, "And stop frowning. Your expression is as unbecoming as your attitude." To Johanna she said, "I'll put the fruitcakes in a basket and then have Thomas bring the trap around."

Her mother's reprimand subdued whatever else Cissy might have argued. At least temporarily. However, when Rebecca left the table, Cissy stuck out her tongue at Johanna, who ignored her and went to get her hooded cape. She was pulling on her leather driving gloves as Rebecca emerged from the kitchen area carrying a willow basket packed with the gaily beribboned rounded molds of fruitcakes. Johanna drew a long breath, relishing the combined smells of brandied fruit, cinnamon, nutmeg. "Umm, smells delicious, Mama."

"Take care, and try to be back on time," her mother's voice followed her as Johanna took the basket and started out.

"Yes, Mama," Johanna promised as she opened the front door. She gave a cheery wave to her sisters, a pouting Cissy and a resigned Elly, both assigned to polishing silver.

Outside, Thomas, the Shelbys' "man of all work," waited beside the small, one-seated buggy at the front of the house, holding the mare's head. Thomas was husband to their cook, Jensie, brother to Bessie, the maid. All three had worked for her family as long as Johanna could remember.

"Morning, Thomas," Johanna greeted him, then paused to rub Juno's nose and pet her neck before climbing into the driver's seat.

"You be careful now, Miss Johanna. She's feelin' mahty frisky this mawnin'," Thomas cautioned, handing her the reins.

"Thank you. I will," she said. She gave the reins a flick and started down the winding drive out onto the county road.

The morning was bright, sunny, the air crisp and clear, and Johanna felt lighthearted and free. She was glad to be home, back in Hillsboro, after the long months away. At boarding school, her independent, happy-go-lucky spirit felt hopelessly surpressed by the strict rules. She had the secret intention that during this Christmas vacation, she would persuade her indulgent father to let her stay home rather than go back to the academy. She felt she'd had enough education and enough of the restrictive life at school. Cissy could go in her place!

As they moved along at a brisk pace in the winter sunshine, Johanna enjoyed traveling over the familiar roads, breathing deep of the pine-scented air. She was actually looking forward to having a visit with each auntie as she delivered her mother's special holiday gift.

Johanna's "aunties" were not *really* her aunts. They were her mother's first cousins. And they all had the same first name: Johanna. Their grandmother, Johanna Logan, had five daughters and one son. Each daughter named their first daughter Johanna in honor of her. The only one not named Johanna was Rebecca, the daughter of the son. *His* wife, the only daughter-in-law in the family, had refused to have *her* daughter christened Johanna. All the first cousins named Johanna were called by other names to distinguish them from each other. Thus there was Aunt Hannah, Auntie Bee, Aunt Jo McMillan, Aunt Honey, Aunt Johanna Cady.

Thinking of the aunties, Johanna often wondered if her mother ever resented the fact that *her* mother had broken with tradition and not named her Johanna. She never said and somehow Johanna had resisted asking. Her mother rarely talked about her childhood or her life before marrying. It was as if everything began for her when she became Mrs. Tennant Shelby. It seemed she had become part of his life and left her own completely, proud of her husband's prominence, their place in Hillsboro society.

Families were funny things, Johanna mused as she turned off the main road and took the rutted lane that led to the Breckenridges' home, the one closest to the Shelbys', her first stop. She and her sisters were the only girls in the family. The other relatives on both sides who had children had boys. Johanna had never given it much thought, but recently she had noticed that her mother quite bristled when the other aunties talked—or the better word was *bragged*—about their male offspring. Would her mother have rather had sons? Johanna wondered. However, she'd heard several of the aunties sigh and verbally declare they pined for a daughter, making such remarks as, "such comfort, so companionable, considerate in old age." So maybe it all evened out in the end, Johanna decided as she pulled up in front of her Auntie Bee's. She knew this would be a happy reunion. Auntie Bee, childless herself, doted on the Shelby girls, and secretly Johanna was her favorite "niece."

Winding the reins around the hitching post, Johanna ran up the porch steps. She raised the brass knocker and banged it a few times before Auntie Bee, who was somewhat hard of hearing, opened the door. "Why, Johanna, how lovely to see you! Come in, dear!" she said, beckoning her inside. "My, you get prettier every time I see you."

Johanna gave her a hug, relishing the familiar fragrance of violet eau de cologne she always associated with this aunt. "I've brought you Mama's Christmas fruitcake!"

Looking as surprised as if receiving it weren't an annual event, Auntie Bee declared, "How dear of her! And I know it's delicious. Let's slice a piece and have some tea. You can stay for a visit, can't you?"

"I probably shouldn't. Mama wants the trap back by noon."

"Not just for a wee bit?"

"Well, I guess—why not!"

"Why not, indeed! Come along inside. No mistake about its being December, is there? Lots of frost this morning when your Uncle Radford set out for his office." Auntie Bee took Johanna's cape and hung it up, saying, "Now you go right on in the parlor, where I've a nice fire going. That'll take the chill off you after being out in the cold air. I'll get our tea and slice the cake."

"Can I help you, Auntie?"

"No, dearie, you just go on in and make yourself comfortable. I won't be but a minute." Auntie Bee bustled out to the kitchen.

Auntie Bee's quilting frame was set up in the cozy parlor, and Johanna went over to examine the one she was working on. When her aunt came back in carrying the tray with tea things, Johanna told her, "This is very pretty, Auntie, and I like the colors—what's the pattern called?"

"It's called the Tree of Life. In the Bible, a tree is the symbol of all the good things of life: plenty, goodness, and wisdom. All God's gifts to humankind we're to enjoy on this earth—our families, our home, what he provides—the abundant life the Scripture speaks about."

Johanna regarded her aunt's serene expression, the sincerity with which she spoke. Surely she never had a doubt or an uncertainty, unlike Johanna, who always questioned everything. "You really believe that, don't you, Auntie?"

"Of course, dearie. What's not to believe?" Bee put one hand on the open Bible on its stand beside her quilting frame. "As it is written in Proverbs 3, 'Happy is the man that findeth wisdom. She is a *tree of life* to them that lay hold upon her.'"

22

After consuming a large piece of fruitcake and a cup of tea, Johanna turned down her aunt's urging for a second helping of each and departed for her next stop.

As she drove away, waving her hand to her plump aunt standing on the porch waving back, Johanna wondered: had her aunt never had a rebellious thought, a longing for something different than a placid existence? Was she always so at peace, as perfectly content as she appeared? Johanna sighed. She herself had so many unfulfilled dreams, so many romantic fantasies and desires. Perhaps her aunt's kind of serenity came eventually with age? She didn't really know. In her own heart a restlessness stirred, a deep yearning for an experience that did not even have a name. Was she to constantly search for something she might never find?

***

As she approached Aunt Hannah Mills's house, Johanna hoped she would not have to listen to a prolonged recital of her aunt's ailments. Aunt Hannah tended to complain at length of various aches. The consensus of family opinion was that most of them were imaginary. Today Johanna was in luck. At her knock, the door was opened impatiently, and Johanna got the immediate impression she had come at an inopportune time. The household was in the midst of holiday cleaning. Behind Aunt Hannah, through the door to the parlor, Johanna saw Suzy, the maid, kneeling at the hearth, polishing the brass fender, the fire tools, and the andirons. The frown on her aunt's face faded at once when she saw Johanna.

"Why, Johanna, child! What a surprise!" she spoke, trying not to sound irritated by the unexpected visit. This aunt was known in the family as a fuss-budget about her home—for her, cleanliness was truly next to godliness—and twice a year the entire house was scrubbed, cleaned, polished to a fare-thee-well. Christmas was one of those times. Yet since hospitality was a cardinal rule practiced by all the family, she welcomed Johanna inside.

"One of your mother's lovely fruitcakes!" she exclaimed with feigned surprise as Johanna handed it to her. "My, my, I don't see how your mother manages to do all she does. A houseful of girls to look after, a large household to run, all the entertaining she does, besides her charitable activities. Of course, *she* has been blessed with good health!" Aunt Hannah sighed lugubriously. "Not like some of us." She drew her small bottle of smelling salts from her apron pocket and inhaled. "I have felt quite unwell since . . . well, I believe I overdid it when—"

"I'm sorry to hear that, Aunt Hannah," Johanna said brightly, determined not to be an unwilling audience to a long list of Aunt Hannah's hypochondriac complaints. "I do hope you will take care so that you won't miss the holiday festivities. New Year's dinner is at our house this year."

Aunt Hannah looked aghast. "Miss our family dinner? Of course not! I wouldn't miss *that* even if—"

Before she could add the phrase "if I were on my deathbed," which Johanna anticipated might be next, Johanna said quickly, "I must be on my way, Aunt Hannah. I have the other fruitcakes to deliver, and Mother explicitly told me to be back home by noon. She is expected to be at the church to help decorate."

"Go along then, child. How I wish I had the strength to volunteer for such active things, too, but I just haven't felt up to it—"

Johanna moved to the door. One hand on the knob, she said, "Do give Uncle Roy my love. We shall see you on Christmas Day at Aunt Honey's." The door was open now.

"Yes. That is, if—"

Before her aunt could finish her sentence, Johanna stepped outside onto the porch, into the crisp, cold morning.

Aunt Hannah gasped, saying, "Oh, I must shut the door quickly, Johanna, or I'll catch my death—"

"Sorry, Auntie," apologized Johanna, then she ran down the porch steps and climbed back into the buggy. Glad to escape, she picked up the reins with a long sigh of relief. Next stop was Aunt Cady's. Johanna Cady was what Johanna called her "fashionable aunt." She was exceptionally attractive and youthful looking, with fine hazel eyes, silvery blond hair. She had a distinct style, impeccable taste, and a rather superior air. As Johanna arrived, she saw her aunt's carriage in front of the house, and when her aunt answered the knock at her door, she was dressed and ready to leave. Her peacock blue faille ensemble was elegant, and her bonnet sported curled plumes and velvet ribbon.

"Oh, dear me, Johanna, I'm just about to depart," Aunt Cady said. "With the holidays upon us, I moved up my visiting day so as to get all my calls in before I get caught up in the season. Munroe and Harvel will be home from college day after tomorrow, you know—and then there'll be no end to it!" She threw up her hands in mock dismay, but Johanna knew her aunt was looking forward with great pleasure to the arrival of her two handsome sons.

"It's all right, Aunt Cady. I just came to leave Mama's gift."

"Oh, how nice." Her aunt accepted it distractedly, placing it on the polished Pembroke table in the hall behind her. "When the boys come, we shall have to have some kind of party, invite all their friends—I don't know just when, but we shall of course let you know. They shall be so pleased to see you, Johanna." Her aunt's gaze traveled approvingly over her. "The boys will be amazed to see how pretty and grown up you are since last year!"

Johanna wasn't so sure. Her older boy cousins had always rather ignored her, being busy with their own social activities. Years ago it might have mattered to her to be noticed by her two attractive cousins, but somehow now at the mention of them, she mentally shrugged.

"Do tell them hello for me, and of course, tell Uncle Madison," she said as she went back out to the buggy.

"We'll see you at church on Christmas Day and at dinner afterward. And be sure to thank Rebecca for me, won't you, dear?" Aunt Cady called after her.

Johanna had one more stop to make before heading home. She had purposely saved this one till last, because Aunt Johanna Hayes was her favorite. She was called Aunt Honey, because that was the name her husband Matt called her in his loud, jovial voice. He was a large man, measuring at least two feet taller than his petite wife. That name suited this aunt perfectly, Johanna thought as she approached the fieldstone and frame house surrounded by tall pines at the end of a lane. Honey had remained a great deal like the lighthearted girl she had been, frivolous, charming, fun-loving, the pampered pet of her husband and three strapping sons.

Up to her elbows in flour, Aunt Honey was making the decorated Christmas cookies of all sorts of shapes and sizes for which she was famous in the family.

"Darling girl, how happy I am to see you! But you've just missed Jo," Honey told Johanna. Her plump face showed dismay. "She'll be sorry to miss you. But she would go out riding! I told her I thought it was too cold, but you know how she is!"

Aunt Jo was spending Christmas with the Hayeses. Johanna knew Aunt Jo was an excellent horsewoman and no matter what the weather, she would go riding. "Yes, I know. I'll leave her fruitcake from Mama anyway and see her another time."

26

"Ah yes, there'll be plenty of family get-togethers during the holidays," Aunt Honey agreed. "Want to sample one of my cookies?"

"I can't stay, Aunt Honey, but I'll take one along to munch on."

"Of course. Come along into the kitchen with me. I have a batch almost ready to take out of the oven."

Suddenly a startled look crossed Aunt Honey's face, and she sniffed the air suspiciously. "Oh, my! I'd better get them out quick, or they'll be burned."

Johanna followed her into the deliciously fragrant kitchen. Aunt Honey scurried over to the stove and slipped out the tray of bell- and tree-shaped Christmas cookies. "Uh-oh, they're a bit brown at the edges!"

"They'll be fine, Aunt Honey," Johanna consoled. "Once you've covered them with colored sugar."

"What a clever girl, you are, Johanna," her aunt declared happily. "That's just the thing."

"I really must go, Auntie."

"Do tell your mama thank you for our cake. Matt always looks forward to Rebecca's fruitcake," Aunt Honey said as she walked to the door with Johanna. "Your mother is so organized, no one can keep up with her! And here I am, not finished with my baking, not by half. I'm hopeless, it seems, no matter how early I start."

"You're just right, Aunt Honey." Johanna gave her a hug and went out the door. "And we'll see you on Christmas!"

Her errands done, Johanna decided to ride through town on her way home. With only a half-formed thought in her mind, she slowed her horse to a walk as she went by Dr. Murrison's house. Ever since the Chalmers' party, Johanna had spent a great deal of time thinking about the tall, young doctor with his slow smile and disturbingly penetrating eyes.

However, as she passed the brown-shingled house, there was no one in sight. She felt disappointed, but then, what she had hoped for? A chance to talk to him again? There was just something about Ross Davison. . . .

In no hurry to get home, where household chores awaited her, Johanna decided to do a little shopping. She had a good half hour before her mother expected her back. Why not stop at the little notions shop that carried ribbons and lace and look around for a bit? She had started making handkerchief cases in needlework class months ago as Christmas gifts for both her sisters. As usual with such things, she had lost interest in the project, and she had brought them home with her, unfinished. With Christmas only a few days away, maybe she could find some lace or trim to add a finishing touch.

She found a space in front of the shop and, hitching Juno to the post, went inside. It didn't take long to find what she wanted. Her purchases made, she was just leaving the store when she saw him crossing the street, coming straight toward her!

At the exact same time, Ross Davison saw *her*. Her scarlet cape, caught by a sudden wind, swirled up behind her like a bright fan, framing her dark, flying hair. He thought Johanna the loveliest thing he had ever seen.

"Miss Shelby," he greeted her. "What luck!"

"Luck?"

"Yes, quite a coincidence."

Or a hopeful wish come true, Johanna thought, amazed. Trying to conceal her pleasure, she teased, "Don't tell me you just happened to be thinking of me!"

"As a matter of fact, I *was*."

Johanna was taken aback. Most young men of her acquaintance were not so frank expressing their feelings. In her social circle, an unwritten law was never to say what you

28

meant—a game played equally by ladies and gentlemen. Johanna had always thought it ridiculous nonsense. Ross's frankness was as refreshing as it was startling.

"Yes," he said, "I *was* thinking about what a good time we had at the Chalmerses' party—"

"Musical chairs, you mean? Yes, it was fun." She laughed and Ross thought Johanna was prettier even than he had remembered, her face all glowing and rosy, her smiling mouth showing small white teeth.

"I hope we may enjoy other such times, or"—he frowned suddenly—"will you be returning to school after the holidays?"

Although she had not launched her planned campaign to persuade her parents to let her stay home instead of going back to the academy, she hesitated. "I may not be going back. I hope to be through with all that—"

"With boarding school? Or learning in general?" he grinned.

"Oh, there are lots of things I want to learn—*outside* the schoolroom." Her eyes sparkled with mischief.

"I see." Ross regarded her so seriously, she began to feel uncomfortable. Recalling her mother's recent lecture on deportment, she hoped that her remark did not sound too flippant, too flirtatious. An awkward silence stretched between them. To break it, Johanna asked, "And why are you not going about doing good, curing illnesses, and that sort of thing, Dr. Davison?"

"At the moment, it seems most of Hillsboro's citizens are in good health or too busy with Christmas preparations to be sick."

For a minute, they simply stood smiling at each other. Since she could think of no plausible reason to delay longer, Johanna shifted and moved as if to go. "Well, I must be on my way, Dr. Davison."

"May I help you with your packages, Miss Shelby?"

There were so few, it seemed an almost ridiculous suggestion. But grasping at anything to prolong this chance meeting, Johanna just as ridiculously replied, "Why, thank you, Dr. Davison."

"Where's your buggy?"

It was right in front of them, a matter of a few steps. "Over there."

"I'll see you to it," Ross said quite solemnly. His hand slipped under her elbow, and they walked over to where Juno patiently waited. Ross helped her climb in, then said with obvious reluctance, "Well, I have patients to see—"

"Yes, and I'd better get home."

Before relinquishing her small parcels, he asked, "When may I hope to see you again?"

"Perhaps at church on Sunday," Johanna blurted out impulsively, then blushingly amended, "—that is, *if* you attend?"

"Not always, but"—he looked amused—"*this* Sunday I will."

She picked up the reins. Their gaze still held. Johanna was amazed that so much had been said, and yet so much remained unspoken but somehow understood. At last she said, "Good-bye, then. Until Sunday."

"Yes, 'til Sunday. Good-bye."

Feeling unreasonably happy, Johanna started for home.

The following Sunday, Johanna was already up when her mother came into her bedroom to awaken her with a cup of hot chocolate. In fact, Johanna was standing in front of the mirror trying on her new bonnet while still in her nightie. Surprised, Mrs. Shelby raised her eyebrows but said nothing.

Johanna was usually the hardest of the three girls to get up and moving in the morning. What had prompted this early rising? Surely it wasn't sudden religious fervor? Rebecca regarded her oldest daughter curiously.

Rebecca was inordinately proud of her three pretty daughters, and this morning as they made their way to church, she noted that Johanna looked especially attractive. Her new bonnet of russet velvet, with a cluster of silk bittersweet berries nestled on green velvet leaves on the band, and wide brown satin ribbons tied under her chin, was most becoming. She was also being extremely amiable and sweet-tempered, moving over at Cissy's demand for more room in the carriage, looking demure with folded hands over her prayer book. Something was stirring, Rebecca felt sure, but she could not pinpoint what it might be.

As for Johanna, when they reached the churchyard, her heart was pumping as fast as if she were on her way to a ball. When they all got out of the carriage, she saw Dr. Murrison and his tall assistant mounting the church steps. She dared not look to the right or left to try to locate where they were seated as she followed her parents down the aisle to their family pew, indicated by the small brass identifying marker engraved SHELBY.

Before she sat down, she glanced around as casually as possible and saw that the two were seated toward the back of the church. Then she remembered it was well known that Dr. Murrison always sat in the rear near the door in case a medical emergency called him away from divine service. She ducked her head, studying the hymn book. After reading the same line over at least three times, none of it making sense, she realized she was much too aware of the young man three pews behind her. It became suddenly hard to breathe, much less sing.

Somehow Johanna got through *this* Sunday's seemingly endless service. When her mother stopped to chat with

31

friends on the way out of church, she had to curb her irritation. *Oh, please don't let him leave,* she prayed. Stepping outside onto the church steps, to her delight she saw her father
engaged in conversation with Dr. Murrison, and Ross stood
quietly beside him. She heard her father saying, "But of
course, you both must join us. Am I right, my dear?" He
turned to Rebecca as she and Johanna approached them.
"Wouldn't we be pleased to have Dr. Murrison and his assistant join us for dinner on New Year's?"

Dr. Murrison, a ruddy-cheeked, gray-whiskered man with
a gruff manner that his small, twinkly blue eyes belied,
demanded, "But wouldn't we be intruding? A family occasion, surely?"

"Not at all, my good fellow," Mr. Shelby denied heartily.
"Holidays are no time to be alone. Now, we'll say no more
about it. But expect you both."

Rebecca murmured something appropriate. Johanna
shyly smiled at Ross. His eyes seemed to light up, replacing
his serious expression with one of pleasure. A few more pleas-
antries were exchanged, then good-byes were said.

Once in the family carriage, her father announced, as if
in explanation of his impromptu invitation, "Couldn't let
Alec spend the most festive day of the holidays alone, could
we? He used to spend the holidays with his sister over in
Clayton County. But she passed away last summer—and that
young fellow, Davison, he'd never get to his home in the
mountains in this weather. Snow's made the road up to
Millscreek impassable."

Johanna did not listen to the rest of her parents' discussion. She was too happy planning what she would wear when
Ross Davison came to the house for dinner. Ten days seemed
a long time to wait.

Chapter Three

I don't want to go!" pouted Elly at the breakfast table. "I don't want to have my music lesson. Why do I have to do it during the holidays? I didn't think I'd have to go to lessons at all, with Johanna just come home."

"That will do, Elly," Mrs. Shelby said sternly. "You will take your music lessons as usual. Miss Minton is paid for each pupil's lesson. If you don't go, she doesn't get paid. She is the sole support of her invalid mother, and it is only right and proper that you go. Besides, I heard you practicing yesterday, and you certainly *need* the instruction. You fumbled quite badly on your piece. Now, that's all I have to say. Go and get ready."

Elly's lower lip trembled and tears filled her eyes.

"I'll take Elly over to Miss Minton's, Mama," offered Johanna. "And maybe we can go have a little treat afterward. You'd like that, wouldn't you, Elly?"

Her little sister's face brightened. "Oh, yes!" She jumped up from her chair.

"That's very generous of you, Johanna." Mrs. Shelby looked approvingly at her but added, "Still, I believe, Elly must learn responsibility without the promise of reward. *This* time, however, it will be all right."

Within twenty minutes Johanna and Elly were on their way. Elly took Johanna's hand, swinging it happily.

"I've missed you, Johanna. It's really lonely at home without you."

"I missed you, too, punkin." Johanna smiled down at the rosy, upturned face.

"I hate taking piano lessons. But Mama insists. She says every young lady should play a musical instrument and must have accomplishments." Elly had some trouble with the word. "When I ask *why*, Cissy says, 'So that suitable gentlemen will want to marry you.' As if I cared about *that*," she sniffed disdainfully. "But Cissy *does*. She plays the flute and *she* likes it. She can't wait 'til she's old enough to have beaux." Elly looked sideways at Johanna. "Do you have beaux, Johanna? I mean, someone special you want to marry?"

"Not really, Elly," Johanna laughingly replied, but a small, secret smile played around her mouth as she thought of Ross Davison. Although she couldn't as yet consider him a beau—or even a would-be suitor, there was something tucked deep inside her heart that whispered "possibility."

Caught up in thoughts of the mysterious, unknown future, Johanna was surprised when they reached Miss Minton's house in what seemed to her like no time at all. Elly yanked the leather thong, setting the pewter doorbell clanging and bringing a flustered-looking Miss Minton.

When she saw Johanna, she gave a her head a little jerk. Johanna had not been one of her best students nor a favorite. Too restless, too uninterested, and one who had not progressed much, in spite of all Miss Minton's efforts. In her opinion, *she* had not been at fault—it was simply that Johanna had not applied herself.

"Well, Johanna, I see you're back from school. Were *they* able to give you some appreciation of the value of a musical education?"

Trying to keep a straight face, Johanna replied, "I *was* in choir, Miss Minton, but that's about all."

"Humph. Let's hope they were more successful than I at teaching you to sing on key," was Miss Minton's rejoinder. "Come along, Elinor. I hope you're prepared today. Go in the front room. I have another student in the parlor." From inside the house, the scratchy sound of a squeaky violin could be heard. Johanna suppressed a wince. She certainly didn't intend to remain here listening to Elly's stumbling fingers on the piano, accompanied by the agonizingly dreadful rendition of the violin student. Helping Elly off with her coat and bonnet, she whispered, "I'll go do some errands and be back for you in an hour. Then we'll go have our treat."

Elly threw Johanna a hopeless look. No prisoner on the way to the gallows could have looked more desperate. Before Elly reluctantly followed Miss Minton's rigid back down the narrow hall, Johanna gave her a little wave and a sympathetic smile.

Outside in the crisp winter morning, Johanna walked briskly toward the center of town. She had no particular place in mind to wile away the hour Elly was enduring her music lesson. Johanna window-shopped at the milliner's and manteau maker's, then went to the stationer's. Browsing the displays of handsome desk sets, she wished she could buy one for her father as a Christmas gift. Of course, they were all much too expensive, some elaborate silver ones consisting of inkwells, sealing stamps, quill holders. She sighed. She would probably have to finish embroidering the spectacle case she had started and never completed, for his birthday, and give it to him for his Christmas present.

Outside again, she walked slowly down the street, in the direction of Dr. Murrison's residence. A wooden sign with his name and the words "Physician and Surgeon" underneath swung on the gate. In smaller letters, another name—Dr. Ross Davison—had been painted by a different hand. She put out a tentative hand and traced the name over a couple of times with her gloved finger.

"Miss Shelby!" a deep male voice called and she whirled around. Ross Davison was running out from the side entrance of the house, without his coat, his hair tousled by the wind. Johanna felt her face flood with color.

When he reached her, Johanna saw obvious happiness in his face. He leaned forward on the gateposts. His eyes shone, his smile wide.

"Miss Shelby, what brings you out this chilly morning?"

"Yes, it is chilly." She raised her eyebrows, noting he was in his shirtsleeves, as if he had come flying out when he saw her, in too much of a hurry to put on his jacket.

To her amazement he stated, "I saw you from the window and was afraid you might pass by without my having a chance to speak to you."

What honesty! What lack of pretense or guile! Johanna thought of all the silly chitchat most young gentlemen dealt out in conversing with young ladies. Ross Davison was certainly different.

"As to what I'm doing out," she replied, "I'm on my way to fetch my youngest sister from her music lesson." Johanna laughed. "Actually, I should say *rescue* her. She was very reluctant to go, and only the promise of a treat afterward would persuade her."

Ross was spellbound. Just looking at her, her lovely eyes sparkling with merriment and her cheeks as glowing as twin roses, listening to her voice, her laughter, made his heart happy. As a doctor, he was aware of his own physical reaction at the sight of her. His heart rate had quickened alarmingly, and probably his blood pressure rose as well. Diagnosis: decidedly unmedical. He knew he was in fine health, so there must be another explanation.

A little uneasy under his steady gaze, Johanna said, "I must be on my way. It should be nearly time for the prisoner's release."

"Can you wait until I get my coat?" he asked. "I'd like to accompany you, if I may? Maybe buy both of you a treat?"

"Why, thank you, Dr. Davison. That would be very nice." Johanna was too delighted to dissemble.

"Good. Then, I'll be right back," Ross promised and, turning, ran back to the house. A minute later he emerged, still thrusting his arms into his coat sleeves. He twisted a long knitted scarf around his neck and fell into step alongside her, breathless.

"My goodness, Dr. Davison, you could win a marathon!"

"I'm what town folks call a 'ridge runner,'" he laughed heartily, turning the word used often as a derogatory name for mountain folk into a matter of pride.

On the short walk over to Miss Minton's, they talked and laughed easily, as if they had known each other a long time. Being with Ross was so natural, Johanna felt relaxed and happy. Elly, her snub nose pressed against the window next to the front door, was already anxiously awaiting Johanna's arrival. Her coat was buttoned crookedly, her bonnet jammed on her head, its strings tied carelessly into a crooked bow.

Miss Minton stood behind her, arms folded. Seeing that Johanna had not returned alone but accompanied by a young man, her eyes sharpened disapprovingly behind her spectacles.

Johanna made quick work of the introductions, then took Elly's hand, and the three of them hurried down the path and out the gate. "Dr. Davison has kindly offered to stand for our treat, Elly," Johanna explained.

"What would you say to a candied apple on a stick, Miss Elly?" Ross asked. "When I was in the bakeshop earlier, they were making them. And the smell of brown sugar, cinnamon, and apples was almost too much."

"Sounds wonderful, doesn't it?" Johanna squeezed Elly's hand.

Elly's eyes lit up and she smiled shyly, nodding her head.

The trio were blissfully ignorant that behind a stiff, lace curtain, the watchful gaze of Miss Minton was following them.

Miss Minton's mouth pressed in a straight line. What a bold baggage Johanna was! And that young assistant of Dr. Murrison. Shouldn't he be tending sick folks instead of gallivanting around with that Shelby girl? Miss Minton intended to pass on her opinion to the next mother who showed up today with one of her pupils.

Outside, the subjects of Miss Minton's negative consideration were having a merry time. They stopped to get their candy apples, then walked down to the duck pond while they ate, the sweet, sticky coating blending deliciously with the tart taste of the juicy apples. The three of them carried on a jolly conversation. Both Johanna and Ross included Elly, giving her attention as an equal.

Finally Ross said he had to go back to his office. "But I've had a wonderful morning, thanks to you two. You don't know how much it means to a doctor to be with healthy, happy folks for a change."

Elly looked wistfully at the tall departing figure and sighed. "Isn't he nice? I'd like him for a beau, wouldn't you, Johanna?"

Out of the mouths of babes! But Johanna didn't dare admit her wholehearted agreement with Elly's opinion. The little girl might just pop out with something at the wrong moment. For now, Johanna wanted to keep her still uncertain feelings about Ross Davison to herself. So not answering, she just gave her a quick hug and said, "Come on, Elly, I'm cold. I'll race you home." Then picking up her skirt, she started to run, forgetting altogether that she was now a young lady and this was unseemly behavior for someone who was eighteen.

⁂

For the next few days, Johanna's thoughts swirled, circled, and whirled around Ross Davison. It was a delicious secret that she hugged close, too precious to share with anyone. Was it real, had it truly happened? Her inner happiness softened and sweetened her, touching everything she said and did with a remarkable gentleness.

Rebecca thoughtfully noted this "weather change" in her oldest daughter. Perhaps some of Miss Pomoroy's influence had taken its hoped-for effect on Johanna. Usually when Johanna was home, she created all sorts of small tempests. Frequent spats between her and Cissy, careless neglect of household duties, a general disregard for anything but her own pleasurable activities. Maybe all the trouble and expense she and Tennant had lavished on Johanna was at last reaping some benefits. Johanna certainly seemed to be maturing. Of course, she had always been generous, cheerful, maybe too fun-loving but certainly a joy to be around. Now if she could just become more interested in the womanly skills that would be necessary assets when she married. Of course, there was still time for that. Johanna had another year to complete at the academy. . . .

Unaware of her mother's concern, Johanna was fully enjoying her vacation, free from ringing bells, boring lessons, required stitchery classes. Every day, she received fistfuls of invitations to holiday parties. Each one a potential chance of seeing Ross Davison, now a part of the social circle of Hillsboro's young people. Whatever people like the snobbish

39

Archers might say, an eligible bachelor was always welcome, and as the respected Dr. Murrison's assistant, Ross had an assured acceptance.

As she wrote her replies to these invitations, Johanna could never have guessed that her next meeting with Ross would be pure "happenstance" or that it would have such unexpected repercussions.

Two days before Christmas it snowed. Snow in Hillsboro was unusual. Snow of this depth and of such lasting quality was really rare. The temperature dropped and the foot or more of snow that blanketed the town formed an icy crust, perfect for sledding. Elly was beside herself with glee, and Johanna was still young enough to love the snow and see its possibilities for enjoyment.

Excitedly they got out the seldom-used wooden sled and waxed the runners. Bundled up with scarves and mittens, Johanna and Elly went to join some other adventurous ones who had made a sliding track on the hillside.

The air was as keen and stimulating as chilled wine, stinging the eyes and turning noses and cheeks red as ripe cherries. Up and down the winding hill the girls went, swooping down the slopes and shouting at the top of their voices as they sped to the bottom.

It was when they reached the bottom for about the fourth time and were starting the slow climb back up to have another spinning ride that Johanna spotted Ross coming along the street. Holding on to the brim of his tall hat with one hand and his doctor's bag with the other, his head bent against the wind, he plowed along the path through high drifts on either side.

Unable to resist the impulse, Johanna bent over, quickly scooped a handful of snow, formed it into a ball, and sent it winging through the air. It hit its target exactly, knocking

Ross's hat clear off. Startled, he halted and spun around, looking for the culprit. Then he saw Johanna and Elly holding on to each other as they convulsed with laughter. His first puzzled expression instantly broke into a wide grin. "You rascals!" he shouted. Dropping his bag, he swiftly rounded a ball of snow with both hands and threw it. It landed on Johanna's shoulder as she turned to avoid being his target. There followed a fierce snowball fight, two against one. Elly and Johanna alternately fashioned snowballs and pelted Ross while he struggled valiantly to return as good as he was getting. Finally it ended in a laughing truce, with Ross pulling out a large white handkerchief and waving it. He retrieved his hat, dusted the snow off its brim, and picked up his medical bag. Smiling broadly, he approached the two girls, who were still laughing merrily.

"Enough! I surrender. I have sick people who are down with the croup, chills, and fever!" Ross pleaded submissively. "How can you two justify delaying me on my rounds of mercy, waylaying me and attacking me so viciously?"

For an answer, Johanna reached down and molded another snowball and tossed it with all her might, only to be hit by one herself as she turned her back and started running out of range. Her laughter was ringing out in the air when unexpectedly she heard her name spoken admonishingly. She whirled around to see Emily and Mrs. Archer approaching along the side of the street. Emily's mother had a shocked look on her face. Johanna blushed scarlet, feeling like a child caught with a hand in the forbidden cookie jar. Not only was she positive Mrs. Archer would relay *this* escapade she had observed to everyone, including Johanna's mother and aunties, but Johanna knew Emily was delighted to have a spicy tidbit to pass along to her chosen friends. Johanna Shelby and the young doctor carrying on in broad daylight on the street!

Emily's eyes were wide with curiosity as she and her mother came to a stop within a few feet of both Johanna and Ross.

Johanna attempted a semblance of poise and started to make introductions but did not have a chance. With lifted eyebrows Mrs. Archer said coolly, "Oh, we've met Dr. Davison, Johanna. I wasn't aware *you* two were acquainted."

Emily interjected too sweetly, "Don't you remember, Mama? Johanna and Dr. Murrison were the last left playing musical chairs at the Chalmerses' party." She glanced over at Johanna with the look of a tabby cat licking a bowl of cream.

Johanna flushed, gritting her teeth. That Emily! What a spiteful person she was. However, Ross, unaware or undisturbed by the fact that Emily was trying to embarrass them, bowed slightly, acknowledging Mrs. Archer. Then he laughingly declared, "That was the most fun I've had since I was a tadpole."

Mrs. Archer gave him a cold look that might have chilled a lesser individual. "*Really?* How odd, Dr. Davison." Then, turning to her daughter, she said, "Come along, Emily. We must get on with our errands." She added pointedly, "Johanna, do give your dear mother my kind regards." With that parting jab they walked off. Johanna bit her lip in frustration, knowing for certain she would hear about this later.

Ross seemed hardly to notice their departure. His mind was too taken up with Johanna. Did she have any idea how pretty she was? Her dark curls escaping from the red knitted cap tumbled onto her shoulders. The rosy laughing mouth. The blue, blue eyes shining with fun.

After exchanging a few more silly jests, Ross set his hat straight and gave them a small salute. "Good day, Miss Shelby, Miss Elly. Regrettably, I have work to do while *others* may play!" He made an exaggerated bow. "And may I take this opportunity to wish you both a very happy Christmas."

"I like him," Elly declared as she and Johanna started back up the hill.

"I do, too," said Johanna, knowing it was much more than that.

"He doesn't seem at all like a stuffy old doctor, does he?"

"No," replied Johanna. They went back to sledding, the playful incident with Ross part of a happy day. A day when Johanna had seen yet another side of Ross Davison. A side that appealed to her own fun-loving self.

❧

This year Christmas dinner was at Aunt Bee and Uncle Radford's home. Since it was also their twentieth wedding anniversary, the whole family was in an especially festive mood for the double celebration. As they gathered around the table for dinner, Aunt Hannah's husband, Uncle Roy, who was an elder in church, was asked to say the blessing. All heads bowed as it was ponderously intoned, and afterward the light buzz of conversation resumed as plates and platters were passed.

Then something happened that startled Johanna. During one of those lulls that sometimes occur even in the most congenial company when everyone is simply enjoying the good food, Aunt Hannah remarked, "By the way, Johanna, Emily Archer's mother said the strangest thing to me when I saw her the other day." Aunt Hannah pierced her with a sharp look. "She mentioned that she had seen you and Dr. Murrison's assistant in quite a rowdy display, throwing snowballs at each other in broad daylight on the street! I told her she must be mistaken, that I thought it unlikely that a girl with your background and breeding and so recently come from Miss Pomoroy's establishment would be making a spectacle of herself in public!"

The silence that followed was so absolute that one could have heard the proverbial pin drop. Johanna felt her cheeks flame as everyone either looked at her or avoided doing so. Worst of all, she felt her mother's gaze rest upon her. What could she say in her own defense? Besides, it was true. It had happened, there was no use denying it. Johanna opened her mouth to explain, but as it turned out, it was Elly who did.

"Oh yes, Aunt Hannah. It is true! Johanna and I both did. It was ever so fun! Dr. Davison is so kind and jolly. Johanna and I had such a good time."

Aunt Hannah looked a trifle sheepish at the little girl's enthusiastic explanation, but she still had the last word. Giving a little clucking sound of disapproval, she said, "One would hardly expect a *physician* to engage in such sport."

"And why not?" boomed Uncle Matt. "He's a young fella, even though a man of medicine! I admit to feeling like frolicin' myself sometimes in the snow!" he chuckled heartily.

There was a murmur of amusement at this around the table, then a general, noncontroversial conversation continued.

Johanna cast her uncle a grateful look, then glanced at Aunt Hannah. Known in the family for a talent of turning a joyous occasion into something else, she had certainly been true to form today. Thankfully, Uncle Matt, was jolly enough to make up for it.

Johanna avoided her mother's questioning eye, knowing she would have some explaining to do later. Inwardly she fumed. The Archers had wasted no time carrying their tidbit of gossip to willing ears. However, evidently Aunt Hannah's *informant*, Mrs. Archer, had failed to tell her that her younger sister was there, too.

Although the meal proceeded without further ado, Aunt Hannah's acid remark about Ross had spoiled the family holiday dinner for Johanna. Auntie Bee's lemon meringue pie could have been cardboard for all Johanna could tell.

At least her little sister had saved the day. And Uncle Matt's comment had dashed some cold water on Aunt Hannah's criticism. But only temporarily. Back at home, as Johanna had known she would, Rebecca came into Johanna's bedroom. "Why didn't you mention seeing Dr. Davison and having a snowball fight the day you took your sister sledding?"

"I didn't think it was important." Johanna shrugged. "It was just a silly game—"

"It seemed important enough to Mrs. Archer for her to speak of it to Hannah. You know how it upsets me to have my daughters the subject of criticism or comment."

"Oh Mama, you know Emily's mother is a terrible gossip. She was just trying to find something to talk about. Why is she so interested in what other people do? I say she's much too inquisitive. She should mind her own affairs."

"Don't be disrespectful of your elders, Johanna," her mother corrected sharply, then added with a raised eyebrow, "Besides, the only people who mind others being inquisitive are those who have something to hide." She paused. "Do you have anything you'd like to tell me, Johanna?"

"No, Mama, I don't." Johanna pressed her lips together stubbornly.

Rebecca sighed and went to the door. Her hand touched the knob and was about to turn it, when she glanced again at Johanna.

"Remember, Johanna, anything you girls do or say reflects on us—your parents, your home, your upbringing."

Without looking at her, Johanna replied, "Yes, Mama, I know."

Chapter Four

❦

Coming as it did at the end of the festive holiday season, New Year's Day had always been rather a letdown for Johanna. After the round of parties and festivities, it used to mean her reluctant return to the strict regime of Miss Pomoroy's. This year was different. After much pleading, she had received parental permission to remain at home.

Johanna, jubilant with that victory, had other reasons to be happy. This year it was the Shelbys' turn to host the traditional family gathering, and the fact that Dr. Murrison and his assistant had been invited to share it with them made it special.

Since this was Rebecca's first time in six years to have everyone at Holly Grove for the holiday dinner, everything had to be perfect. Right after Christmas, preparations began to ready the Shelby house for the occasion. Ordinarily Johanna dreaded the uproar of housecleaning. However, this year she pitched in with energy and enthusiasm that surprised Rebecca. The fact that Ross would be a guest was, of course, the spur.

Rebecca directed the work, allotting certain tasks and jobs to everyone. Their cook, Jensie, asked her sister, Aster, to come over and help Bessie with the heavier work of cleaning. Every nook and cranny had to be thoroughly dusted, every piece of furniture polished, the pine floors waxed. The

Shelby girls were all put to work as well. All the silver had to be shined, brass candlesticks polished, the Christmas greenery refreshed, and the red bayberry candles replaced on the mantel sconces and windowsill lamps.

Cissy frequently complained of fatigue, of being overworked, and begged to rest. Elly sighed and dawdled over every task assigned. However, Johanna's mood was merry as she hummed at any job she was asked to do. Her cheerful attitude made her sisters alternately resentful or suspicious and mystified her mother. Even so, Rebecca appreciated her willingness to help with everything. For the time being, Rebecca's mind was concentrated on the result of her efforts: perfection. The annual New Year's Day dinner was an unadmitted competition among the ladies, each one trying to outdo the others when it was her turn. Secretly Johanna thought the beginning of a new decade was terribly exciting. *1840!* What would the next year hold? The next *ten*? She had been a mere child at the beginning of the last—now she was a young woman with everything to look forward to. The possibilities seemed endless. Johanna's imagination went soaring. Heavens, she would be twenty-eight at the end of another decade. All sorts of things would have happened to her by then.

At last all was in readiness. The house sparkled and shone. The smell of lemon wax, almond paste, the fragrance of balsalm potpourri from bowls set about the rooms, the spicy aroma of cinnamon, ginger, and nutmeg from baking pies, mingled with the scent of cedar boughs and evergreen pine wreaths still hanging at the windows.

New Year's Day dawned with overcast skies. Gray clouds hovered with the promise of more snow. Before leaving for the special New Year's Day services at noon, Rebecca made a last-minute survey of her domain, satisfying herself that all was in perfect order. She anticipated that her cousins would give the

Shelby household a polite yet precise appraisal. At length, everything met her approval, and the family went off to church.

Johanna hoped she would see Ross there. Although the shape of her bonnet kept her eyes reverently toward the pulpit, precluding any possible sidelong glances, under her jade velvet pelisse trimmed with beaver, her heart raced. He might be there observing *her*! But there was no sign of him, either in the back pews as they left or in the churchyard. An emergency of some sort? A sick child? A dying patient? A doctor's life was full of such unexpected happenings. What might have prevented his attendance at church could also cause him not to come to dinner. Such a possibility dismayed her.

Johanna had no time to dwell on such a catastrophe, because no sooner had the Shelbys reached home than the aunties and their husbands began to arrive.

Each lady brought her very best culinary effort to add to the veritable feast Rebecca and Jensie had prepared. Each cousin prided herself on being a fine cook, so each dish presented was to be profusely praised. By the time everyone gathered in the parlor for a holiday libation, all were in a good mood, ready to see the old year out and welcome in the new.

Although she circulated among her relatives, chatting with each in turn as her mother would have her do, Johanna kept stealing surreptitious glances at the grandfather clock in the hall. Each time she passed a window, she glanced out hopefully, longing to see Ross coming through the gate. Even while trying to respond to some of the parlor conversation, she strained her ears for the sound of the knocker on the front door.

She knew dinner was planned for five o'clock. *Please don't be late,* she prayed. Delaying dinner would upset her mother, and she wanted Ross's first visit to come off well. Even a medical emergency would not be an excuse if her mother's sweet potato soufflé collapsed.

❦

In an uncharacteristic state of mind, Ross Davison walked through the gathering winter dusk on his way out to Holly Grove. This would be the first time he would see Johanna in her own home, one he knew was far different from his own. During his time in Hillsboro, he had been in enough homes of people like the Shelbys to realize just how different their backgrounds were.

Ever since he'd met Johanna, his feelings both daunted and excited him. Every time he saw her, his pulse rate was erratic, his heartbeat accelerated. He had to ask himself a dozen times a day what kind of madness this was. His hopes were probably impossible. All week he had debated whether or not to find some way to get out of the invitation Dr. Murrison had accepted for them both. He had argued both sides, vacillating. It would be wiser not to go, something told him. However, the thought of missing a chance to see her, be with her again, proved too much. Now here he was, on his way.

Holly trees lined the curving driveway up to the impressive house of pink brick with white columns and black shutters. Standing at the gate, Ross looked up at the Shelby home. In the twilight, all the windows, adorned with scarlet-bowed wreaths, were lit with candles.

He swallowed hard, then opened the gate and went forward, up the porch steps. At the paneled door, there was another moment of hesitation. Then resolutely he raised his hand to the gleaming brass knocker in the shape of a pineapple, the traditional symbol of southern hospitality.

When Johanna opened the door for him herself, Ross was caught off guard. In a red and green plaid dress that rustled crisply, she looked so enchanting that it quite took his breath away. "Oh Ross, I'm so glad!" she said impulsively, then attempted to regain a proper manner. "Good evening. Do come in." She stepped back so he could enter.

Feeling tongue-tied. Ross struggled for words. He fumbled to take off his hat, held it awkwardly until he realized she was holding out her hand to take it so she could place it on the rack by the door. "Where's Dr. Murrison?" she asked.

"He'll be along soon," Ross assured her. "Just as we were leaving, an old patient stopped by to bring him a Christmas present, and nothing would do but that he come in for some cheer. You know how it is at holiday time."

A burst of laughter and the sound of voices floated out from the parlor. Ross glanced in that direction, an unmistakable look of alarm on his face. Johanna caught it and realized how shy he was. Immediately she sought to put him at ease. "Don't look so startled. It's only family. Of course, there *are* quite a lot of them," she laughed gaily. "But they're all quite harmless." She lowered her voice conspiratorially. "Just try not to sit down by Aunt Hannah, or she'll regale you with all her symptoms. I'll seat you by Auntie Bee. She's a dear and will want to know all about you." Smiling encouragingly, she took his arm and led him into the parlor.

To Ross the elegantly furnished room seemed filled with dozens of pairs of eyes, all turned to him. Johanna began to introduce him. The names went in one ear and out the other, the faces all became blurred. Ross was grateful to sit down at last. A jovial, gray-whiskered gentleman handed him a cup of eggnog. Later he unobtrusively placed it on the small pie crust table at his elbow. He was sure it contained spirits, and he was not a drinking man.

Seated across the room, between Uncles Matt and Radford, Johanna looked at Ross fondly. Even his awkwardness touched her. However, Johanna tried to see him through the appraising eyes of her mother, her aunties. Johanna knew they would probably not consider him handsome in the slightest. However, to her there was such strength in his rugged features, sensitivity in his expression, depth of intelligence in his eyes, that she thought him one of the finest-looking men she had ever seen.

Within twenty minutes the front door knocker sounded and Dr. Murrison arrived. He and Tennant Shelby were old friends and he knew the others, so he was completely at ease. At once he was drawn into the general conversation of the group. The Shelbys, Millses, Hayeses, Cadys, McMillans, and Breckenridges never lacked for topics to discuss, debate, or argue about. The fact that the young doctor was sitting quietly, observing Johanna, went quite unnoticed—*except* by her mother.

Rebecca had excused herself to give her beautifully set table a last critical look before inviting the company to come into the dining room. Pleased that her best china, with its sculptured edge of flowers, gleamed in the glow of candles in two six-branched silver holders, she gave a final touch to the centerpiece, an artistic arrangement of fruit and pinecones. Then Rebecca returned to the parlor. She stood at the threshold, waiting for the appropriate moment to invite everyone to come in and be seated. It was then, with a sudden sharpeninging of her senses, that she saw Ross unabashedly staring at Johanna.

It struck her with that alertness one recognizes as impending threat or danger. Immediately she glanced at her daughter. Her face illuminated by firelight, Johanna was indeed lovely. Her dark hair, parted in the middle, with bunches of curls on either side of her face, was tied with crimson ribbons. A fluting of ruffles framed her face and slender neck. However, it was her expression that caused Rebecca's intake of breath. Johanna was gazing across the room at the young doctor, with the same raptness in her eyes as *his!*

Johanna's eyes held nothing back. Their glance was softly melting. Rebecca knew her daughter so well. *Why, the girl's in love!* Rebecca felt heat rising into her face. *How in the world did that happen?* There was only time for those fleeting thoughts. No time for her awareness to do more than register. Just then, Tennant caught her attention lifting eyebrows in a silent question. At her nod, he got to his feet, announcing, "Well, ladies and gentlemen, I believe my dear wife has come to fetch us in to dinner."

Seated across the table from him, Johanna watched Ross from under the fringe of her lashes. She felt a tenderness she had never known for anyone, along with the realization that he was feeling uncomfortable. He moved the lined-up silverware at his place nervously as he tried to pay close attention to what Uncle Madison Cady was expounding. Ross seemed so stiff, so different from the joking, laughing young man she had danced with, pummeled with snowballs, and talked with so freely at other times. Of course, it was meeting all her relatives. That must be hard on a stranger. Her sympathy came to the surface as she watched how he remained mostly silent after answering a few questions politely put to him. But to Johanna, everything about him seemed somehow so endearing and sweet. For example, how he had bent his head considerately to speak to Auntie Bee so that her deafness would not demand his repeating.

Rebecca's practiced glance passed over the table, her hostess's eye making sure everyone was enjoying the meal. Her gaze rested upon Johanna and, alerted, moved quickly across to young Dr. Davison, then back to her daughter. Neither of them were eating! Johanna had hardly touched her food! Where was her normal hearty appetite, an appetite that Rebecca had often claimed was *too* hearty, unladylike? She was only nibbling, pushing her carrots around her plate with her fork.

Something was going on between those two. Rebecca remembered she had felt that same little dart of alarm watching them together at the Chalmerses' party earlier in the month. But she thought her word of caution to Johanna about her frivolous behavior had settled it. Even as that thought passed through her mind, she saw an exchange of glances between Johanna and the young doctor. Rebecca knew that look, recognized it for what it was. Surely not *love* but certainly romantic *infatuation*. A twinge of possible problems pinched Rebecca. No question about it, she must speak to Johanna *again*.

Dinner finally came to an end, with everyone declaring they had eaten too much and enjoyed it immensely. They all returned to the parlor and settled back into chairs, on sofas, and a kind of desultory conversation ensued. For a few minutes Rebecca lost track of the topic everyone seemed to be discussing. She was distracted by the sight of Johanna and the young doctor sitting together at the other end of the room, conversing. Johanna's attitude was that of someone intently listening to Dr. Davison's every word. The scene had the look of intimacy Rebecca felt inappropriate. If she could have overheard their conversation, she would have been even more upset.

Ross was saying, "There are some things I've been wanting to talk to you about—some things I'd like you to know about me. Maybe I'm speaking out of place—I don't know. I don't have all the social graces I know you're accustomed to—I know your family, your background, is a great deal different from mine." He hesitated. "But Miss Shelby, I come from good folks, honest, hardworking, God-fearing folks with a lot of pride. I am the oldest in my family. My father died— was killed logging, actually. I didn't get much schooling after that. That is, until a friend of Dr. Murrison's, a teacher, saw something in me—a hunger to learn, maybe—and talked my mother into letting me come with him into town, live with his family, go to school. I always wanted to be a doctor—I don't know why—always wanted to help things that were hurt, animals, children, anyone who was sick." Ross halted. "I wanted most of all to learn doctoring so I could go back to the mountains and minister to my people. I've seen children die that didn't need to, men die from blood poisoning, women—well, all kinds of sicknesses and disease nobody knew how to treat or cure. And since I got *my* chance, I want to give something back. Can you understand that?"

"Oh, yes!" Johanna said breathlessly, completely entranced by his earnestness. No young man had ever spoken to her like this, about serious things, important things, things that counted. She was amazed and touched and thrilled that Ross Davison wanted to share these things—evidently so dear to his heart—with her.

"You may wonder why I'm telling you all this. I don't usually talk so much, not about myself anyway. But I needed to tell you. I felt you'd understand, Miss Shelby—"

"Oh, please, call me Johanna!"

Ross looked doubtful. "I've never known anyone like you before. I haven't had much time for socializing. When I was at college, I had to work, and then there were my studies. I'm not much at dancin'"—his eyes twinkled—"as you found out!"

"You did quite well," Johanna smiled, "experienced or not!"

Ross paused for a moment. "I was looking forward very much to coming to your home tonight. Your mother was very kind to include me. She didn't have to just because Dr. Murrison is an old family friend."

"But you couldn't be alone on New Year's Day!" exclaimed Johanna. "It's such a special occasion."

"Yes, I suppose it is. We never made much of holidays at home—" He then stopped. "Anyway, it was very gracious—"

"It was lovely to have you."

Rebecca decided it was time to interrupt. The two were completely absorbed in each other. Someone was bound to notice, then there'd be questions. She would ask Johanna to go to the kitchen, bring back fresh coffee to replenish everyone's cup. Before she could put idea to action, Dr. Murrison rose, declaring he must take his leave. Immediately his assistant also got to his feet. Reluctantly, Rebecca was sure, from the way his gaze lingered on Johanna.

After bidding everyone good-bye and thanking Rebecca for her hospitality, the two physicians went toward the hall. Mr. Shelby accompanied them, and before Rebecca could invent some excuse to stop her, Johanna quickly followed.

While Dr. Murrison and her father finished up their conversation, Ross asked her shyly, "I wondered if you'll be going to the taffy pull at the Chalmerses' next Wednesday?"

"Yes! Will you?"

"Miss Liddy was kind enough to invite me."

"Then we shall see each other there," Johanna said brightly.

"Yes," Ross replied solemnly. "I shall look forward to it."

When the door closed behind them and her father returned to the parlor, Johanna spun around a couple of times in an impromptu dance. She felt her spirits soaring outrageously. Spinning to a stop, she suddenly *knew*. Why, *this* was falling in love!

The night of the Chalmerses' party, Johanna had felt something happen between them. She hadn't quite known what. Startled, her lips formed the words: I love him! To her own astonishment, she knew it was true.

Chapter Five

❧

The evening of the taffy pull, Johanna was invited to stay overnight with her friend Liddy.

Winter taffy pull parties were one of the most popular kinds of social get-togethers for young people. Although it was not openly admitted, the romantic potential of such an evening was widely accepted. At least, the young people themselves regarded it as romantic. If their parents did not, it was only because their memories were short. Often such a casual, spontaneous evening of two-by-two candy making developed into a more serious courtship. Under the laughter and gaiety and visible adult supervision, it afforded a means for couples to pair off without raised eyebrows. Within the guise of making candy, there was the chance for a quick hug and kiss in an alcove or corner. In fact, it was one of those well-circulated sayings, part joke and part truth, that a winter night of pulling taffy often resulted in a June wedding.

For that reason alone, knowing Ross had been included in the guest list, Johanna was particularly looking forward to the evening. Without being closely observed by chaperones, there was a real possibility of having another private conversation with Ross.

She was thrilled he'd confided in her about his family, his life, his hopes, his ideas of being a doctor. None of the other young men she knew had ever talked to her that way; as if she were an equal, as if she had intelligence to understand serious things.

As Johanna was about to leave on the afternoon of the party, Rebecca had a moment's uneasiness. Johanna had been to dozens of taffy pulls, and Liddy had been her friend since childhood. Why was she acting so excited, so eager to be on her way?

Although, ever since gaining permission not to return to Miss Pomoroy's, Johanna had been a shining example of obedience, cheerfulness, and helpfulness. She did her chores without complaining, was tolerant of Cissy and kind to Elly. Then, why did Rebecca feel troubled? It was the dreamy look she sometimes saw in Johanna's eyes, how she went about smiling as if she were listening to music. Instead of the volumes of history her father had assigned for her to study in order to continue her education in lieu of going back to school, Rebecca had found an open book of poetry on Johanna's bedside table! Poetry, indeed! Still, she did not see any tangible evidence that there was anything to chastise Johanna about.

Of course, Rebecca had no idea of how many "happenstance" meetings there had been with the young doctor on the days Johanna had eagerly volunteered to do errands for her mother.

So Johanna kissed her mother's cheek and went gaily off in the buggy that had been sent for her, neither of them dreaming that this evening would be a turning point in both their lives.

A big iron pot filled with sorghum was already boiling and bubbling on the stove in the Chalmerses' kitchen when

Johanna arrived. She knew almost everyone there, and there was much chatter, everyone exchanging news and telling each other about their Christmases. They gathered around the stove, waiting for when the sugary mixture reached the proper consistency, while Liddy's father, red-faced, perspiring, shirtsleeves rolled up to his elbows, kept stirring. Suddenly he bellowed, "Get your plates buttered, folks!"

Mrs. Chalmers and the other mothers in attendance stood by the kitchen table, handing out solid white ironstone plates on which butter had been slathered. One by one, people filed up to the stove, and Mr. Chalmers ladled out dipperfuls of the syrupy liquid onto the greased plates, where it had to cool. When it was cool enough to be lifted off with the hands, the fun of pulling began.

With much laughter and conversation, everyone rubbed their hands with lard. Then the boys selected a partner and the pulling started. At first the molasses was stiff and hard to handle, but once it got started, it was easier to work, and it would be stretched into a kind of rope. The boy would grab the rope in the middle and pass the end on to his girl partner. Of course, sooner or later a few of the girls managed to get all mixed up in the rope of taffy. When this happened, the boy had to get his arms around the girl, standing behind her to free her hands from a wad of taffy. The point of the pulling was *supposed* to be to make the taffy more brittle and tasty. The longer it was pulled, the whiter it got. This was done with a great deal of giggling, squealing, and laughter, the hilarious "shenanigans" all taking place under tolerant chaperonal surveillance.

When Mrs. Chalmers felt the "tomfoolery" had gone as far as it should, she called for the taffy to be coiled onto the buttered plates. There was provided a second round of fun as people twirled and swirled the candy, making designs of hearts and links, and fashioning a fancy final assortment of the hardening taffy. When the taffy was ready for breaking up, couples took their pieces and, pairing off, went to find a place to chat, eat, and enjoy.

As it turned out, Johanna didn't have the worry of wondering how Ross would get into all the playing around. For the first part of the evening, she kept watching for him. Her distraction annoyed her partner, Burton Lassiter. "Pay attention, Johanna! Pull! Stretch it before it hardens," he told her in vain.

Johanna was finally rewarded when Ross arrived. She saw him before he saw her. He stood in the doorway with Liddy, appearing to listen to whatever she was saying while his gaze searched the room. When he saw Johanna, he distractedly excused himself from their hostess and came straight across the room to her. Suddenly everyone else in the crowded room simply disappeared for her. He was standing right in front of her, his thick hair and his shoulders glistened with raindrops. Had he come out in this storm without a coat, forgotten his hat? Johanna wondered.

"Good evening, Johanna. I'm sorry to be late and I cannot stay, but I must speak to you." Ross held out his hand and she put hers into it. He looked around and, seeing an unoccupied corner in the crowded room, led her over to it.

They sat down. Still holding her hand, he said, "I have to leave soon. The Barlow children are pretty sick. I saw them earlier today, but I'm uneasy about them. I want to check on them again."

"I understand," Johanna said, nodding her head.

Neither of them cared if curious eyes were upon them as Ross covered both her hands with his and leaned toward her, saying earnestly, "But even if it were only for a few minutes, I didn't want to miss the chance of seeing you. You see, Johanna, there is something I must say to you. Something important. In fact, I can't think of anything else." He paused. "I know this isn't the proper time or place—could you possibly meet me tomorrow? Say about two in the afternoon? I should be finished with office hours by then—"

"Yes. Where? You didn't say."

Ross's heavy brows drew together. "Someplace where we can talk without—what about the bandstand in the park near the skating pond past the stone bridge? You know where I mean?" His hands tightened on hers. "And if anything should delay me, will you wait?"

"Of course I'll wait," she said. "No matter how long." She was already planning what excuse she'd use to get out of the house that time of day. She felt wildly happy. Secret meetings, the stuff of romance novels. Johanna reveled in the excitement of it.

For a full minute they simply gazed into each other's eyes. What she saw in his told her what she had longed to know. Johanna was suddenly breathless.

Reluctantly Ross said, "I have to go. It may seem impolite to Liddy, but I don't want to disturb the Barlows by coming by too late."

"I'll walk out with you," Johanna offered, rising. She waited while he made his apologies to Liddy, then, ignoring Liddy's puzzled glance and Mrs. Chalmers's soaring eyebrows, she followed Ross out the front door.

They came out onto the porch. It had stopped raining but the night was cold and damp. Johanna shivered. Immediately Ross was concerned. "You shouldn't be out here. You'll get chilled."

"I wanted to come."

They moved closer to each other. She half turned toward him, and the moment was vibrant with all that was between them yet undeclared. Then, in a low voice, Ross spoke.

"I love you, Johanna."

That was what she had hoped, wished for in her heart, but now that it had been said, it startled her. She drew in her breath, then with something like relief whispered, "I love you, too, Ross."

"Oh, Johanna." He held out his arms and she went into them. He drew her close, held her tight. Her cheek rubbed against the scratchy texture of his rough wool coat. Her ear was pressed hard against his chest so that she could hear his pounding heart. "Oh Johanna, I love you so much—" Then, almost in a groan, he said, "But it's impossible."

She pulled back, looked up at him. "*Impossible?* What do you mean, impossible?"

"How can I make you happy?"

"You already have."

"I mean—what have I to offer someone like you?"

"Yourself. That's all I'll ever want," she replied softly.

Ross put his hands on either side of her face, raising it so he could look deeply into her eyes. Then he gently lifted her chin, leaned down, and kissed her mouth. His lips were warm in the cold air and the kiss was sweet. There was a kind of desperation in his voice when he asked, "What are we going to do, Johanna?"

❧

When Ross left, Johanna went back into the party. For the rest of the evening, Johanna moved as if in a daze. She spoke to others, laughed, pulled taffy, and chatted merrily with everyone. She felt as if she were in a puppet show, mouthing lines spoken by someone else, with somebody pulling the strings. She didn't remember what she said once the words were out of her mouth. Liddy kept glancing at her curiously, Burton sulked, and Mrs. Chalmers gave her several disapproving looks. It didn't matter. Johanna knew now that what was between her and Ross was no mere flirtation. It wasn't only her own dreams and fantasies about him. Ross Davison was in love with her.

Ross had asked, "What are we going to do, Johanna?"

Do? What did he mean, *do?*

～❧～

In the Chalmerses' guest room, Johanna propped the lavender-scented pillows behind her and sat up in bed. She was not the least sleepy, even though, with an exaggerated yawn, she had discouraged Liddy from coming in to gossip and chitchat as they usually did after a party. Liddy had gone away miffed, and although Johanna was sorry about that, she needed to be alone. Something important had happened between her and Ross tonight, and she wanted to think about it, sort out her feelings.

Everything she felt was so new. Yet there was a sweet familiarity about Ross. The odd feeling that they had known each other for a long time lingered. It was as if she had been waiting for him all her life.

She heard the steady patter of rain on the windowpanes. Where was Ross? Was he home yet? Or driving back to town along some country road? Or was he still with those sick children? Her heart felt tender as she thought of what a good doctor he must be. Was he thinking of her, as she was of him?

How conscientious Ross was. Her heart softened further as she contemplated his innate nobility. Yes, nobility. That best described him.

It made her feel humble that such a man *loved her*! She still couldn't quite believe it. She must change, become *worthy* of his love. She needed to mold herself into something better, stronger. Johanna closed her eyes in remembered

62

delight of his kiss. She hugged her knees and smiled. Being in love was so wonderful!

Again Ross's question came into her mind.

"What are we going to do, Johanna?"

Do? Although she wanted to keep this happy secret to herself for a little while, of course in time they would tell everyone, share their happiness. That's all they would *do*. She couldn't imagine what else Ross meant.

Johanna slid down into the pillows, shutting her eyes at last and, with a happy sigh, went to sleep.

Chapter Six

Hurrying through the blustery January afternoon, Johanna hugged her happiness close. Oh, how wonderful it was to at last be free to say "I love you" and mean it! Ross was everything she had ever dreamed of in a lover—more, even! How had she been so lucky? She had never been so happy in her life. She had gone to meet him today from Liddy's house, where she had stayed overnight after the taffy pull party. She had invented an errand so that she could go alone. Liddy had seemed suspicious. Johanna could not share her secret—at least, not yet. Promising she would return so that she would be there when Mr. Chalmers arrived from town to drive her back to Holly Grove, she had rushed out without further explanation.

Ross was waiting for her at the appointed place. Johanna rushed toward him, but instead of looking happy, Ross looked worried. He hadn't slept, he told her. He had been wrong to speak of love to her as he had last night, he began. But she would not let him finish.

"No, no, it wasn't! I love you, too, Ross. And I know it's right."

"But what can we do, Johanna?" The words seemed wrung from the depths of his heart.

His question puzzled her. What would they do? What did any two people in love do? They got married.

He acted as if there were insurmountable problems. She wouldn't listen to any he tried to tell her about. He had house calls to make, and nothing was really settled as he hurried away.

She was so happy, she felt her heart might burst. She couldn't wait to tell her parents. Of course, they did not know Ross very well, but they knew Dr. Murrison. He was an old family friend. They certainly knew and respected Dr. Murrison and must realize he would not have chosen Ross from among all the medical students he could have brought in as his assistant, if he had not been convinced of his character and ability.

And of course, her parents would probably be surprised, call theirs a whirlwind romance, but what was wrong with that? After their first surprise, they would be happy for her. She was sure.

Johanna could not have been more wrong.

❦

The minute the words were out of her mouth, Johanna knew she had made a mistake. She saw the stricken expression on her mother's face. Immediately Johanna was contrite. She was furious with herself for having upset her mother so much. But even though she realized she had not picked the right moment, she hadn't expected this intense opposition.

"It's out of the question. You're much too young and I won't hear of it."

Her mother's reaction chilled Johanna with its cold vehemence. Perhaps it was mostly because she would be the first one to leave the nest. At first Johanna did not realize that the real problem regarded her choice.

Though her father was surprised, his objections were milder. "Well, Johanna, I thought it was young Burton Lassiter you were interested in. He certainly has hung about here looking at you with calves' eyes long enough. What's wrong with Burton? Good family, nice fellow."

"Oh, Burton!" Johanna scoffed. "I don't love Burton. I never could. You can't make me love someone I don't. You certainly can't make me marry someone I don't love."

"Who was talking marrying?" Tennant protested. "Anyway, I agree with your mother. You're far too young to be thinking about marrying anyone."

"Mama was seventeen when she married *you*, Papa. And I'm eighteen and will soon be nineteen."

"That's quite enough, Johanna," her mother interrupted sharply. "We'll speak no more about it. And we will certainly make our wishes plainly known to Dr. Murrison that we do not appreciate Dr. Davison's attentions to our daughter without our permission."

Johanna turned pale. "Oh Mama, you wouldn't! That would humiliate Ross, and he is so sensitive."

Rebecca looked at her coldly. "He should have had the good manners to address your father before he spoke to you of love, Johanna—assuredly before he spoke of marriage. It is just more evidence that he has neither the breeding nor background that we would accept in a prospective husband for our daughter—any of our daughters. And as I have told you many times, as the oldest it is up to you to set the example for your younger sisters. Now, that is all. I suggest you go to your room and give some thought to your rash, reckless behavior and the upset you have caused your parents."

Mute with misery, speechless with frustration and resentment, Johanna turned and went out of the room, ran upstairs and into her bedroom, letting the door slam behind her. She flung herself down and, in a torrent of tears, wept into her pillow for some time.

She knew she had done everything wrong, had approached her parents in the worst way. She'd ruined everything! She had foolishly hoped they would be happy for her. She had not thought of all the objections her mother had listed. It seemed so petty, so cruel, to judge Ross on such shallow measurements. What could she now do to put things right? To make Ross acceptable to her parents?

She woke the next morning with a blotched complexion, eyelids puffy from her frequent bursts of tears during the sleepless night. When her mother sent Cissy to call her down for breakfast, she pleaded a headache and said that she was going to stay in bed. When her mother peeked in the door later in the day, Johanna pretended to be asleep. She had lain there through the hours trying to come up with a new way to present Ross to her parents, to ask them to try to get to know him, to discover his fine qualities. If they did, she knew they could not help but be impressed with the same things she saw and loved in him.

The winter afternoon darkened, and Johanna knew her father would soon be home. When she heard the front door open and her father call out "Rebecca!" as he always did when he entered the house, she tiptoed out of her bedroom, leaned over the banister, and heard the murmur of her parents' voices. She felt sure they were discussing her. She crept downstairs, in her nightie and barefooted, and huddled on the steps, straining to hear what her father and mother were talking about.

She heard her mother say, "She's buried herself in her room all the day, won't eat a bite, determined to be stubborn. She has upset the whole household over this foolish thing. She won't listen to me. She won't listen to anybody!"

"It's her fondness for melodrama, that's all. It will all be over in a few weeks, I'm sure."

At her father's rejoinder, Johanna stiffened indignantly. If there was anything that infuriated her, it was indulgent amusement, that her earnest pleading could be dismissed as a whim not worth considering.

Her father was always inclined to be amused at whatever Johanna did. All her life, when she had popped up with something she had just discovered or thought, he had looked at her indulgently. She could remember numerous times when he had done exactly the same as he had last night when she broke her news about Ross. He had smiled at her, stood up, and patted her on the head as if she were a recalcitrant child who needed to be pacified and reassured that somehow, in time, she would get over her silly notion.

Well, *this* time he was wrong. He'd see. They'd both see. She was serious. She loved Ross Davison, and in spite of anything they said, she was going to keep on loving him and someday they would marry.

Then she heard her mother say firmly, "You must speak to Alec Murrison, Tennant. That's all there is to it. I am sure he would not countenance his assistant pursuing a courtship that was unwelcome. Even if it is only a matter of our friendship, I am sure he will see that our wishes are respected."

Johanna's hands balled into fists and she pressed them against her mouth. Oh, no! That would hurt Ross so dreadfully. He revered and admired Dr. Murrison so much. To have him rebuke him for—what? For loving her! It was too awful. Johanna crept back upstairs and into her room, choking back new sobs.

❧

Across town in the house of the town's physician, another conversation was taking place. Remembering that this was the man who had taken him in, treated him like a son, rendered the hospitality of his home, given him the benefit of his own knowledge and skill, been his mentor and his instructor, Ross hesitated. Perhaps it was too much to ask for Dr. Murrison to champion his cause. Perhaps Dr. Murrison would be risking his friendship with the Shelbys if he gave his blessing to Ross's asking for Johanna's hand in marriage. But how else could this ever come about? At least he could ask Dr. Murrison if he should try.

"I want to marry Johanna Shelby. Do you think there is any hope? I don't want to take advantage of you, sir, but I do need your opinion."

Dr. Murrison pursed his mouth as if giving the statement considerable thought. He knocked his pipe ashes on the stone edge of the fireplace, took his time refilling it and lighting it again before answering Ross's question.

"Have you addressed the young lady herself as yet?"

"Not formally asked her to marry me. However, truthfully, I have told her I love her." He paused in anguished embarrassment. "I couldn't help myself. But I didn't speak of marriage. I wanted to talk to you first, and if you think it would be all right, I would then, of course, approach her father and ask his permission."

"Well, that certainly is the usual way of things," Dr. Murrison agreed, but there was a degree of hesitancy in his words that sent a cold chill through Ross. Something more was coming, and instinctively he braced himself for it.

Then Ross suddenly decided that whatever it was—and he suspected what it *might* be—he didn't want to hear it. Abruptly he got to his feet and said, "I shouldn't have taken advantage of our relationship. I was wrong to place you in an awkward position. Forgive me." Without waiting for Dr. Murrison's reply, Ross left the room.

He went quickly upstairs to his room. He sank into the one chair in the sparsely furnished space and stared at the flickering light shining through the door of his small stove. Why had he been so stupid? Why hadn't he seen what should have been obvious to him from the first? The Shelbys, one of the most prominent families in Hillsboro, accepting a poor, backwoods doctor with no future for the husband of their daughter? He gave a short, harsh laugh. For that's what it was—laughable! Ridiculous. Impossible. How could he have been foolish enough to entertain such a thought—to dream?

―――

At church the following Sunday, Johanna was sitting in the family pew, beside her mother. Rebecca's head was bowed in private prayer before the service. Johanna bowed her head also. She wasn't praying, exactly—she was pleading in anguish and fear. Fear that what she wanted most in the world would not be allowed her. *Please, please, God.*

While her mother stopped after the service to compliment the minister on his sermon, Johanna stepped outside, looking for Ross or Dr. Murrison in any of the groups of men gathered in the churchyard, talking. But the tall figure she hoped to see was nowhere in sight.

It was bitterly cold and frosty, and when Johanna's mother joined her on the church steps, she took her arm, urging sharply, "Come along, Johanna. Get into the carriage. It's too cold to stand around in this wind."

Chapter Seven

~☙❧~

*R*ebecca, her back very straight, sat at her quilting frame in the parlor. Seven stitches to the inch, in her hand the needle, poised daintily, moved expertly in and out. She had placed a lot of hope in Johanna. Much careful thought and consideration had been given to her rearing. Expense too, sending her to a fine female academy for the kind of education necessary for a girl who would assume the role of a wife in a prestigious marriage. Johanna had shown little interest in housewifely skills. She had acquired exquisite manners and social graces, could set a beautiful table, and was a graceful dancer and a gracious conversationalist. Of course, if she married someone from a wealthy family, such as Burton Lassiter, she would have plenty of servants. However, a woman still needed to master all sorts of tasks to enable her to teach her servants, show them how the work was to be done.

Rebecca gave a small shudder. Although her face was expressionless, she was concerned about her oldest daughter. Through the years, Rebecca had learned to conceal her emotions—disappointment, hurt, anxiety. Pride might be her besetting sin, but it was also her shield.

One deep wound she had suffered and tried to conceal was that she was the *only* one of all Grandmother Logan's granddaughters not to bear her name—Johanna. As if that weren't humiliation enough, then there was her own failure to produce a son for her husband. After two miscarriages and one stillborn, with much difficulty she had delivered Johanna. Three years later Cissy, and five years after that, Elly. But no male to carry on the family name.

Thinking of her own mother, Rebecca had to suppress her resentment. Why had she refused to follow the tradition of the family she married into? Rebecca had hardly known the rebellious young woman who had been her mother. She had died when Rebecca was only four. But of course, the story of her own christening had been told to Rebecca by anxious "do-gooders" and busybodies. It was a family scandal that could not be hushed up, because it had been witnessed by so many. A whole churchful, as a matter of fact. Possibly the whole congregation. The time had come for the minister to ask the question, "And by what name shall this child be known?" and instead of replying as expected, "Her name shall be Johanna," her mother, dark eyes flashing, had responded in a clear voice, audible to the very rafters of the small stone church, "Rebecca." There had been, Rebecca was told, a collective gasp of shock.

The story had been repeated many times to Rebecca over the years, and she grew to dislike hearing it. She'd had to live with the legacy she had been left. It had, in a way, made her the outcast. She had tried to make up for it by excelling in many ways, always competing for attention among her cousins, for her grandmother's affection. But in the end, no one really seemed to care. Bee and Honey and Jo McMillan and Johanna Cady and even Hannah never mentioned it.

The Pattern

Was blood thicker than water? Had somehow Johanna, her carefully taught daughter, inherited the wildness of her maternal grandmother? The rebellious spirit? Flaunting what was expected, falling foolishly in love with an unsuitable man? Ross Davison might be a fine young man—certainly Alec Murrison thought the world of him. Still, he was not the right husband for *her* daughter. Johanna Shelby had been reared to marry a man of wealth, society, good family, refined background.

Well, it would not be. She would not allow it. Not let all her dreams, hopes, plans, go amiss because of a foolish girl's fancy.

Rebecca bent her head again over her work. This quilt, on which she was spending hours of meticulous care, tiny stitches outlining the lovely pattern, was for Johanna. Her wedding quilt. Rebecca had carefully traced the pattern from the ancient design, adding some of her own creative inter-pretations. It was called the Whig Rose by most, although the more romantic name was Rose of Sharon, which was taken from the beautiful Scripture in Song of Songs, the love song of Solomon to his bride, a part of the Bible that was now taught to describe Christ's love for the church.

As the Rose of Sharon, the pattern was a dazzling decla-ration of human love, the joy and passion between man and woman, honoring the sacredness of marriage. Secretly that is how Rebecca thought of it as she appliquéd the delicate scrolls, the buds, stems, and leaves, white thread on white. To her it represented all those hidden expectations she had brought to her own wedding, the special dreams of happiness she had hoped would be fulfilled. Now, years later, she was a mature woman who had survived the cares and concerns, the sorrows and losses, the disenchantments of life. As she sewed, Rebecca reflected on her own memories. If all those hopes and dreams had never been fully realized, still she had experienced a satisfying life, once she had faced realities, put away fanciful dreams. As she stitched into this quilt for her daughter renewed promises that yet might be for her happiness, Rebecca's mouth tightened. Rebecca rapped her thimbled finger on the edge of her quilting frame resolutely. *I won't let her make some stupid mistake, throw her life away.*

The following afternoon was the cousins' weekly quilting session. Alternating homes, the ladies of the family gathered to work on each other's quilts. Each cousin had her own special quilt in progress on which the others sewed. Of course, this was more than simply a sewing session. It was a time to exchange events and town gossip, discuss relatives and friends and upcoming plans, or contribute a bit of interesting news. Dessert and coffee and tea were served, perhaps a new recipe to be tasted, commented upon, and enjoyed. It was always a congenial time, and Rebecca always looked forward to it with pleasure. However, in her present state of mind, she was tempted to promote her slightly scratchy throat into a full-fledged cold to avoid going.

These get-togethers had started before they all had married, at the time all were working on quilts for their hope chests. Now it had become a weekly ritual in their lives. Nothing but a serious illness or a life-and-death crisis was an acceptable excuse for not attending. To not go was bound to cause concern of one kind or another.

Only the most unobservant person could have missed the effect of Hannah's remark at Christmas about Johanna's snow frolic with Dr. Davison. Since not one of her cousins could be qualified as that, Rebecca was also sure her canny relatives had noticed Johanna's obvious gaiety brought on by the arrival of the young doctor on New Year's Day. Surely one of them had guessed her high spirits were prompted by something other than a family gathering.

Nothing in the family was ever a private matter. Although kept within the family enclave, everything that happened or was about to happen or needed to be decided was always discussed at length among the cousins. Rebecca was sure someone, some way or other, would mention Johanna's escapade, her interest in Dr. Murrison's assistant.

Although Rebecca felt ill-prepared to answer any probing questions, at length she decided she had to go. There was no possible way out. However, she was determined to maintain a discreet silence on the subject, no matter what the provocation. She anticipated that if there were any, it would most probably come from Hannah. With no children of her own to make excuses for or explanations about, Hannah had an insatiable curiosity about others' offspring.

Resignedly Rebecca hooked the braided fastenings of her mauve pelisse, settled her bonnet on her head, tying its brown satin ribbons firmly under her chin, and set out. Today's meeting was at Johanna Cady's house, only a short distance from the Shelbys'. The brisk walk would clear her head for whatever lay ahead.

As she stepped inside her cousin's door, she was greeted by the usual buzz of conversation from the already assembled ladies, which only halted briefly as she was welcomed. The hostess for the day, Johanna Cady—called Josie by her cousins—rose to take Rebecca's cape, compliment her bonnet, and relieve her of her muff.

"You're late, Rebecca. I thought something might have happened."

"I'm sorry. A little delay, that's all."

"Well, you're here now, and that's all that matters." Josie lowered her voice. "You missed all the discussion about the new pattern we're starting. Of course, Hannah had to have her say, which took a while. So we got started later than usual."

Rebecca took her place at the quilting frame, between Honey and Hannah, and threaded her needle. The pattern stretched out was called Caesar's Crown. It was an array of geometric shapes forming an intricate design, on which Hannah was unfavorably commenting, "Why ever did you pick such a complicated one, Josie?"

"Because it's beautiful. Why else?" Josie retorted; adding tartly, "When it's done properly."

Honey, always the conciliator, spoke up. "I've seen one or two of these finished, and they're outstanding."

"Did Munroe or Harvel use drafting tools to cut your material from?" Hannah persisted.

"No. As a matter of fact, I did it all myself. I used bowls and teacups and folded paper," Josie said with a little toss of her head. "It just takes a little imagination."

"Well, I prefer the Double Wedding Ring pattern to this—it's every bit as handsome and much simpler," sniffed Hannah, anxious to have the last word. Then, in order to keep Josie from another sharp rejoinder, Hannah turned her attention to Rebecca, asking, "Has Johanna finished her twelve quilt tops yet, Rebecca?"

Traditionally, a young woman completed twelve quilt tops for her hope chest. A quilt was supposedly finished by the time she was ready to be engaged. Before Rebecca could think of a noncommittal answer, Bee appeared with the tray of cakes and the tea service. "Let's take a break, ladies," she suggested, and the ladies left their sewing for a welcome time of refreshment. Hannah's question was left dangling.

Rebecca had always been provoked by Johanna's lack of interest in quilting and needlework of any kind. Cissy was much more amenable in every way toward the womanly arts

76

so necessary in a genteel woman's preparation for marriage. If only Johanna were more diligent and less imaginative and adventurous. If she *were*, there would certainly not be this need to worry over her.

Josie used Hannah's comment to introduce a subject she wanted to bring up. "Speaking of the Double Wedding Ring pattern, I think we should start working on one soon," she smiled smugly and sat back, waiting for her cousins' eager curiosity.

"What do you mean, Josie?" asked Bee.

"Well, it isn't official," she began tantalizingly, "but I think Harvel is about to propose to Marilee Barrington. He's just spoken to her father over in Cartersville, and—"

She was immediately the target of enthusiastic inquiries, demands for a description of the young lady, the possible date of the nuptials, and other pertinent questions. Of course, it was Hannah who had to put a chill into the happy conversation. She pierced Rebecca with a long look and pursed mouth, remarking morosely, "What a shame we couldn't be planning a lovely quilt for Johanna!"

Every eye, albeit tactful ones, turned expectantly toward Rebecca. She could easily have said something scathing to silence her cousin, but that would only have revealed her own inner upset. Instead, keeping her voice even, a tolerant smile in place, she replied, "No news from that corner, I'm afraid." Inside she was indignant at her cousin's bluntness. Somehow Hannah always managed to strike a sour note.

For the rest of the afternoon, Rebecca sewed quietly, not adding much to the hum of conversation that flowed around her. Her mind was busily plotting a sure way to remove Johanna from the dangerous ground on which she was treading because of her foolish infatuation with the young doctor. Johanna was always drawn to the different, the out of the ordinary, the unusual. And Ross Davison certainly fit all those criteria.

If only Tennant hadn't given into Johanna's pleas not to be sent back to Miss Pomoroy's. Rebecca had been against it and yet had allowed herself to be persuaded. Privately she had decided Johanna was as "finished" as she need be. They could apply the saved fee to Cissy's turn to go next year. Rebecca had to admit that the thought of enjoying Johanna's company at home had influenced her decision. Now she regretted her quick capitulation.

How cleverly Johanna had managed to manipulate her parents for her own purpose. Rebecca could but wonder how she herself had been taken in by Johanna's persuasiveness. All Johanna had ever wanted was to stay in Hillsboro, near the young doctor. It's my own fault, Rebecca chided herself. I saw it on New Year's Day! They only had eyes for each other. Johanna attempted to hide it, but *he* was too honest to try. Rebecca sighed. Even then it was probably too late. It had gone too far by then.

But of course, this courtship was impossible. And now it was up to *her* to do something, Rebecca decided.

Quite unexpectedly she was handed the opportunity she had been searching for. She was brought back from her own troubling thoughts into the present when she heard Honey announce, "I'm planning to go to Winston with Jo when she returns home."

Winston! Of course! Rebecca thought immediately. Winston, where the McMillans lived, was a lovely place with two colleges and a seminary, a cultured atmosphere. It was a hospitable and friendly town. What a perfect solution! Get Johanna out of town. Her cousin had a wide circle of friends, most of whom had children Johanna's age who could introduce her into their lively social life. Johanna could accompany Honey on her trip. Honey adored Johanna, and if Johanna could be persuaded—

No, not persuaded—*told* she must go. Rebecca was through with indulging her. They would have to be firm. Johanna must be kept from a mistake that might ruin her life.

Rebecca decided to have a private word with Honey. As soon as Honey got up to leave, Rebecca quickly followed. Once outside walking together, she tucked her arm through her cousin's and outlined her plan, confiding the reasons she had not wanted to share with the others.

Honey was delighted with the idea. Encouraged by this response, Rebecca felt led to open up more about her concerns, about how unsuitable she felt Johanna's interest in Ross Davison was and how anxious she was to remove Johanna even temporarily from an impulsive attachment.

Honey looked doubtful. "Well, of course, I'm sure Jo will be happy to introduce Johanna and perhaps even give a party or two for her while we're there, but I've never seen parental interference do more than intensify a romance, sometimes even making it the reason to flourish."

"Be that as it may, Honey, it's a risk I shall have to take. You know how impulsive Johanna is, and I just cannot take the chance of her rushing headlong into something as disastrous as this match could be."

❧

Johanna had heard her mother leave and knew she would be gone several hours for the weekly quilting session. She could not remember at which auntie's house it was being held this week. It didn't matter. She knew that sooner or later her situation would be circulated on the family grapevine. Johanna expected this, anticipated it, both dreading and looking forward to the opinions they would express. All would be different, she was sure. She wasn't counting on allies because, despite their contrasting views, the cousins usually stood together on such things. All she could hope for was some understanding.

The house was empty. Now that the holidays were over, her sisters had started back to the dame school they attended in town, and she was alone.

It had been a horrible week. She had stubbornly refused to join the family for meals since the terrible scene with her parents two nights before. Johanna was not proud of the chaos she had brought into the usual harmonious atmosphere of the Shelby home. But they were being so unreasonable. They were refusing to even allow Ross to come and talk to them, ignoring all his fine qualities in an unyielding assertion that he was "unsuitable."

Her parents were giving her a studied silent treatment, maintaining a rare period of unity about the issue. That her father was as adamant as her mother was a bitter pill to swallow. Always before, he had been willing to let Johanna present her case, whatever it was. It especially hurt that this time he stuck with her mother, and her mother was entirely inflexible.

They had forced her to be deceitful, she justified, slipping out of the house on the chance that she would meet Ross as he went about making house calls in town. By some sort of unspoken agreement, they had found that the curved stone bridge near the churchyard was an easy place for their paths to cross by "happenstance." That's where she hurried on her way today. She felt a little uneasiness, a kind of nervous apprehension. She had not yet told him of her parents' reaction to telling them they were in love. She knew how deeply wounding it would be to his pride to learn they did not approve of him as a prospective husband for their daughter.

At the little bridge, Johanna looked anxiously for the familiar figure she hoped to see. She had only a few minutes to wait. Soon she saw Ross, his head bent against the wind, striding toward her.

As soon as she saw his expression, she knew something was very wrong. There were circles under his deep-set eyes, as if he had not slept. He looked drawn and there was a vulnerability about him she had never noticed before. Something had happened. Had someone in her family gone to him, told him they considered his courtship unacceptable? Her father? No, not him. Her mother? One of her uncles?

Perhaps they had even gone to Dr. Murrison? She had been foolish to think they could keep their love secret—not in *this* family, she thought with some bitterness. Not when everyone lived in everyone else's pockets. Her heart felt heavy and she felt almost sick. Ross's step slowed as he approached her, almost as if he were reluctant to see her, to tell her what she felt in her heart of hearts he had come to say.

Shivering with cold and nervousness, Johanna wasted no time. She had already broken so many rules of so-called ladylike deportment as related to him, it would be better to know at once what was the matter. It was too important. She had to know.

"What is it, Ross? You look so troubled."

"Johanna, we cannot go on meeting like this. Your parents would be angry if they knew. We must not see each other again."

"Not see each other? What do you mean? Not ever?" How did he know about her mother and father's disapproval? "Ross, why? Is this your idea? But you said—" She hesitated. Then she had no pride left and finished, "you said that you loved me."

"I shouldn't have, Johanna. It was wrong of me."

"*Wrong?* How is it wrong? You did say you loved me, didn't you? Or did I imagine it? Dream up the whole thing?" Her voice trembled, tears glistening in her eyes.

"No, of course not. I do love you, Johanna. Maybe I should never have told you, because it was wrong—"

"I don't understand." She shook her head.

"The fact is, Dr. Murrison himself has discouraged me from pursuing my courtship. He says I should never have spoken to you about love—or anything—without first speaking to your parents. Dr. Murrison pointed out that this was probably the first thing they hold against me. That I don't know the proper thing to do, that I don't have the manners or the right background for—"

"Oh, for pity's sake, Ross, has he threatened you? Would he dismiss you?"

"No, of course not. He just pointed out the simple truth. You come from a home, a family, a life, so different from mine or what I have to offer—"

"Does love mean nothing? That we love each other—did you tell him *that?*"

Looking abject, Ross slowly shook his head. "No, I didn't. Because in my heart, I know they're right."

"No, they're not. They're very, very wrong. I love you. I won't hear any more of this." Johanna placed her fingers on his lips to keep him from saying more.

Ross pulled them gently away from his mouth and went on speaking.

"We must be sensible, Johanna. What *do* I have to offer you? A doctor without a practice of my own. I'm going back this summer when my apprenticeship with Dr. Murrison is over. Back to the mountains—you don't know what living there would be like. There'll be hardly any money, because most of the folks I'll be caring for don't have any. They'll pay in potatoes or corn or firewood, most likely. Johanna, how can a man ask his wife—a girl like you, who's been used to so much more—"

"I don't care about that!" she protested.

"But *I* do. And if I were your father, I would. Dr. Murrison's right. He told me he worked years before he could get married. I have nothing to offer you—"

"That's not true, Ross. You have everything to offer me. Your life, your love, your whole heart—that's all I want, all I'll ever want."

She put her gloved hand on his arm. His head was turned from her, and she longed to see his face, to try to read what he was thinking in his eyes. "Look at me, Ross." Her voice was low, urgent, sweet to his ears. He turned, took both her hands in his, brought them to his chest, looked down into her upturned face.

"Oh, Johanna. I love you, but I want to do the right thing."

"This is the right thing," she whispered. "Let me talk to my parents. Surely they want me to be happy."

"I believe they want your happiness, but I also believe they don't think I would be part of the happiness they want for you."

"I think it was a surprise—even a shock—but when I tell them how I feel, how I really feel about you, I think they'll understand."

Ross did not look so sure. "I don't want you to be alienated from your parents, Johanna—" His voice deepened with determination. "I won't go against your parents' wishes. I respect them too much for that."

A shaft of wind blew Johanna's bonnet back, her hair about her face, and she pushed it back impatiently, tucking the strands behind her ears, then straightened her bonnet.

"I've always been able to convince my parents when I really and truly wanted something. *This* time it's the most important thing in my life." Johanna tried to sound convincing. However, Ross's expression, the uncertainty in his eyes, shook her confidence.

When they parted, she felt cold and a little afraid. It was beginning to get dark as she walked home. The damp, gusty wind blew wet leaves, scattering them, plastering them on gates and fences along the way. The glow of being with Ross, the warmth of his kiss on her lips, began to fade. She shivered. She had never before felt like this. The loving closeness of her family had always protected her, sheltered her. No one could understand how miserable she was, how desolate, how totally alone she felt. There was no one to comfort her, support her. She was in this by herself. It would take all her courage to see it through, to stand fast. Even Ross doubted the wisdom of what they were doing. He was even willing to give her up—for what? For people to whom wealth, privilege, and standing in society meant more than love?

Her mother was already home when Johanna returned red-eyed from her walk, hoping she could blame it on the cold wind. She halted briefly at the door of the parlor, made some comment about the weather to her mother, then went upstairs.

Johanna seemed oddly subdued, Rebecca thought. The suspicion that she might be hiding something confirmed her own decision. She had made the wise choice, done the right thing. The sooner Johanna was out of harm's way, the better.

In her room, Johanna paced agitatedly. She must get this over, get everything out into the open. The sooner, the better. She would wait until after supper, after both her younger sisters were in bed. Then when both parents were together, she would go to them. The only way she could hope to make her parents understand that she was serious was to tell them in clear, brave, simple language, "I love Ross Davison and intend to marry him." Over and over she rehearsed just what she would say. But she never got to say those fiercely independent words.

Johanna worked herself up to such hope that she never imagined she could fail to convince them. She did not take into account that her parents were just as determined not to let their daughter "throw herself away" on a penniless doctor from the hills.

Chapter Eight

The following evening during dinner, the atmosphere was strained. Even the two younger girls seemed affected by the hovering storm. Finally everyone finished and as Johanna rose, preparing to do her assigned job of clearing the table, Rebecca spoke, "Leave that, Johanna. Cissy and Elly can do it tonight. Your father and I want to speak to you in the parlor."

Johanna followed, half glad that although this was unexpected, it might be the chance she was waiting for. She drew a long breath and followed her parents across the hall.

Her mother stood at the door and closed it after Johanna entered. Rebecca moved to stand at her husband's side, and they both turned to face her. Johanna felt a premonition—of what, she wasn't quite sure. Then her mother spoke.

"We have been shocked and saddened by your rebellious spirit, your unfilial behavior, your unwillingness to obey us as your parents, who are wiser and far more competent to judge what is best for you. This unsuitable attachment must be ended at once. Since you do not see fit to obey us out of love and submission, we are sending you away from the occasion of your willful disregard of parental guidance until you come to your senses. Tomorrow you are leaving with Aunt Honey for an extended stay at Aunt Jo's in Winston. We hope this will give you the opportunity to examine your recent behavior, come to your senses, and once more trust that we know what is best for you."

Stunned, Johanna gasped. "You can't mean that! You wouldn't! How could you, Mama?" Her voice broke into a sob. "To send me away like this—like I've done something wicked! I don't deserve to be treated like a child!"

"You *are* little more than a child, Johanna—a foolish, stubborn one, we have to concede. However, you are still under our supervision, and we are responsible for your actions, certainly for your future. You will do as you are told."

"Papa, do you agree?" Johanna turned in desperation to her usual advocate. But Tennant's face was averted. He stared into the fire and did not turn to look at Johanna. But her mother spoke, drawing Johanna's attention back to the one who was the real originator of the idea to exile her.

"Your clothes and other things are packed, and you will leave first thing in the morning."

Unable to speak, blinded by tears, Johanna whirled around and ran out of the room, tripping on the hem of her dress as she stumbled up the stairs to her room. She let the door slam behind her, then stood there for a moment looking wildly around as if for some escape. Then her gaze found her small, humpbacked trunk at the foot of the poster bed. The lid was raised but it was neatly packed, just awaiting a few last minute belongings to be placed in the top layer.

A sob rose and caught in Johanna's throat. So it was true. They were sending her away. Well, if they thought that would make her forget Ross or change her mind about him— they were wrong. Johanna's jaw clenched.

❦

Later, coming upstairs, Rebecca paused on the landing. From behind Johanna's closed bedroom door, she heard muffled sounds. One hand gripped the banister. Her sobs were pathetic, heartrending to hear. Consciously Rebecca stiffened, stifling her maternal urge to go in, to comfort. Then her sensible nature took over. No, Johanna needed to learn that life wasn't simply a matter of choices. There was a reason. She could not allow her daughter to throw away her life, all she'd been groomed and trained for, on a nobody—a man from who knows what kind of family? Slowly Rebecca mounted the rest of the stairs and passed her daughter's door without stopping.

※

The next morning when Aunt Honey's coach was sent around for her, Johanna came downstairs to find her father had already left the house for his law office. Puzzled, she asked, "Didn't Papa even wait to tell me good-bye?"

"You have hurt your father deeply," Rebecca replied tightly.

Her words stung Johanna as much as if she had been slapped in the face. She stepped away from her mother, feeling both guilty to have caused her beloved father unhappiness and wounded by this rebuke. She knew she had behaved impulsively, spoken disrespectfully. Much she wished she could retract. She was remorseful and if he had been there, she might have begged her father's forgiveness. But to let her leave like this seemed too cruel a punishment.

"It's time to go, Johanna. Matthew and Honey want to get an early start, and you still have to pick up Aunt Jo."

Her mother turned a cool cheek for Johanna to kiss, and dutifully Johanna bid her good-bye. She prayed that someday all this hurt between them would be healed. She dearly wanted this, but not if it meant giving up Ross.

The night before, she had committed one last rebellious act. She had written to Ross, planning to post it somehow on the way. In her letter, she told him of her departure, adding,

Ross, I am doing what my parents wish by going to my aunt's without complaint, if only to prove that this imposed separation will not change my feelings toward you. In fact, I believe the old adage "Absence makes the heart grow fonder." I trust that you feel the same as I do. I trust that when you said you loved me, you meant it and are willing to wait and hope that this forced parting will have been worth it when my parents give their consent.

After writing those lines, Johanna had put her pen aside for a moment. She knew she had laid her heart bare and it may have been reckless to do so. But Johanna knew Ross was a man to trust—his word was his bond. He had told her he loved her, and that was enough for her. Both of them knew that the feeling between them was too strong to be denied. It wasn't as simple a matter as her parents thought. What was between her and Ross was deeper than that.

A future together seemed threatened, but Johanna felt that whatever the future held, she wanted to share it with Ross. No matter what price she had to pay. Otherwise, she foresaw for herself a life of bitter regret, a loss that nothing else would ever fill.

Now as she looked through the oval window in the back of Uncle Matthew's carriage and saw the house she had left grow smaller and smaller as they went down the lane, Johanna's heart was wrenched. Home, with all it implied, meant a great deal to Johanna. She had often been homesick when away at school, had longed to be back in the warm, harmonious atmosphere with her parents and sisters. But now it was almost a relief to be going. The strain between her and her parents had become unbearable. On the other hand, leaving Hillsboro meant that even a chance encounter with Ross was impossible.

Well, she would have to make the best of it. Ross would know she had not given up, and however long her exile would be, her parents would see it had not achieved its goal. When it was over and she came back, surely they could work things out.

Aunt Jo and Aunt Honey were companionable fellow travelers, and the daylong trip was not too arduous at all. Even though Johanna was sure her aunties had been advised of the reason she was accompanying them, they did not mention a word, and the day passed pleasantly. Uncle Matthew fell asleep almost as soon as they had passed the town limits, and he slept most of the way.

The McMillan's house was a rambling fieldstone-and-clapboard structure a little distance from town. Aunt Jo's husband, Mac, as everyone called him, came out on the porch to greet them heartily as the carriage came to a stop in front. His warm welcome was the key to the rest of Johanna's visit.

There was an assortment of relatives from odd branches of all the families that were merged with the Logan clans, and all of them outdid themselves to entertain the visiting cousins. Everyone contrived to make Johanna's visit pleasant. There were parties of all kinds, dancing, skating, suppers, and teas. Aunt Jo had many friends with sons and daughters Johanna's age. Most of the young men attended the local college and always came with two or three classmates to any sort of gathering to which they were invited. Johanna never lacked for dance partners at any of the events, even though she felt less like dancing and partying than she ever had. She missed Ross terribly. In the midst of any party, her thoughts would stray to the one person who wasn't there, and her vivaciousness would visibly fade, her attention span falter, her conversation become distracted.

The days passed, one after the other, until Johanna had been in Winston almost two weeks. One morning she woke up close to despair. She felt so helpless. If only she could do something instead of sit it out and drearily wait for her parents to alter their decision. She had no idea what her mother had arranged with Aunt Honey about how long she was to stay at Aunt Jo's. She was getting very weary of the seemingly endless round of Winston social life—it struck her as inconsequential and meaningless.

Her forced "exile," as Johanna privately termed her visit, did provide a chance for some rare introspection, something she had little time for at home. In Rebecca's well-run household, every chore was assigned, checked upon, every moment of the day accounted for. But here Johanna often lay awake at night after the rest of the house was quiet, its occupants asleep. Then most often her thoughts flew to Ross. She wondered what he was doing, tried to imagine him meeting with patients or perhaps sitting at his study table at night, his dark head bent over his huge medical books.

In the long nights before sleep overtook her, Johanna examined her reasons for her strong attraction for this man, who had come as a stranger into the town where *she* had grown up. Yet there had been an immediate bonding. It was as if heart spoke to heart, soul to soul, as if they had looked deeply into each other's eyes and found life's meaning there.

It must be unusual, it must not happen often. She readily understood why her parents found it bewildering. She did, too. Even though she didn't fully understand it herself, she knew it was real.

Johanna decided to confide in Aunt Honey. She had always been easy to talk to, quick to sympathize, ready to understand. There was a disarming innocence about her, maybe due in part to Uncle Matt's take-charge attitude toward her. He treated her with such caring affection, almost as if she were a child. But Honey was far from childish. She was a keen observer of and had a tolerance for human behavior, its foibles and failings. She never seemed critical nor surprised by anyone's failures.

One afternoon Johanna came into the parlor when Aunt Jo had gone riding, and she found Aunt Honey was alone. Her aunt raised her eyes from her knitting. "Well, dearie, are you enjoying your visit?"

Johanna walked over to the window, fiddled with the drapery tassel, staring disconsolately out the window for a few minutes. Then spinning around, she faced her aunt. "It's not working, you know," she said bluntly.

Honey surveyed her niece warily. "What do you mean, dearie?"

"Oh, I know you had to join in the conspiracy," Johanna blurted out. "And I don't blame *you*, Aunt Honey. I know my parents think they're doing the right thing, separating me from Ross. They think I'm going to change. But I'm not."

Aunt Honey lowered her knitting and looked at Johanna. "You think not, eh?"

"I know not!" replied Johanna firmly. "I love him and he loves me. And they should just accept that."

"Can't you try to see this from your parent's viewpoint?" Aunt Honey suggested mildly.

"I can't. How can I?"

"I suppose you're right, dear. How could anyone expect you to?"

"You do understand, don't you, Aunt Honey?" Johanna sighed. "It's so unfair. They won't even let him come to the house, let themselves get to know him." She paused, then turned to her aunt eagerly. "When we get back to Hillsboro, would you let Ross visit me at your house?"

Startled, Honey looked at Johanna, then slowly shook her head. "Johanna, dear, I couldn't possibly go against your parents' wishes. It would be wrong—"

"But it's wrong of *them* to keep us apart. All I want to do is be happy! Why don't they want me to be happy?"

"Don't be so harsh on your parents, Johanna. They *are* thinking of your happiness. They just don't think what you want to do will make you happy."

"Ross *will* make me happy."

Aunt Honey looked pensive. Her eyes rested thoughtfully on her niece.

"No other person can guarantee you happiness, Johanna. Much as you think they can. Life isn't a fairy tale with everyone's story having a happy ending."

But she saw that Johanna wasn't really listening. There was a bemused expression on her face, a faraway look in her eyes. She was gazing somewhere into the future, a future with Ross. Honey realized she might have been talking to a stone for all the good her warning was doing. A fairy-tale romance was what Johanna was living, what she wanted. All true love, glorious sunsets, moonlit nights, music, eternal bliss. Honey sighed, perhaps she'd better write a letter to her cousin Rebecca.

However, Honey procrastinated. Maybe it would just take more time. After all, Johanna seemed to be trying to enter into the social activities Jo arranged for her.

At least for another week or so. Then came a day when Johanna did not come down to breakfast. She complained of a headache. When her aunt took her up a tray of tea and toast, she found Johanna's eyes swollen from crying. The next day she remained in bed. She refused to eat, no matter what dainties or delicacies the McMillan's cook fixed for her. She grew pale and wan. The aunties became concerned, then worried.

"This won't do," Aunt Jo said severely to her cousin. "It won't do at all." So Honey sat down and wrote the letter she had put off writing to Rebecca and Tennant.

My Dear Cousins,

I hesitate to write this letter, but both Jo and I feel it is necessary to apprise you of the rather alarming decline in Johanna's physical condition, which causes a great deal of concern. We know the reason you felt a change of scene from Hillsboro would be beneficial (her interest in Ross Davison, whom you consider an unacceptable suitor). However, we must inform you that her interest in him has not diminished, nor has her determination wavered. Her symptoms would seem grave if we all did not know their source to be emotional. To put it quite plainly, Johanna is "heartsick" and fading fast like a flower deprived of sunlight. She is without energy, enthusiasm, takes little food or liquids—in other words, she is gravely depressed. We are really concerned that she may be moving into melancholia. She no longer takes any interest in the social life here in Winston, although she has been both welcomed and sought after by the young people of Jo's acquaintance. We therefore have come to the conclusion that it would be best if she came home, where she can have parental care.

Your devoted cousin,
Honey

Within a week word came back that Johanna was to return to Hillsboro on the next stagecoach.

Chapter Nine

❦

Johanna arrived back home looking considerably thinner and quite pale. Her first look at her daughter gave Rebecca a start. Gone were the rosy cheeks, the sparkle in her eyes, the lilt in her voice. Even if Johanna were dramatizing herself, the result was effective. Determined not to soften her attitude to her recalcitrant daughter, Rebecca simply saw to it that she ate every bite of the nourishing food placed before her, got plenty of rest and a daily walk in fresh air.

For her part, Johanna was glad to be home, glad that her parents seemed reasonably happy to see her. Things settled back to the normal routine of life Johanna knew before she had disrupted it with her rebellion. Elly, of course, was delighted to have her adored older sister home, while Cissy seemed aloof. During Johanna's absence, she had strenuously played the dutiful daughter, in contrast to Johanna. It amused Johanna somewhat to see her sister take advantage of the situation. It also saddened her, because although no one spoke of it, she could tell her own place in the family was not quite what it had been.

Secretly Johanna was biding her time, trying to find some way to contact Ross or prevail on her parents to change their minds about allowing them to see each other.

Liddy Chalmers, her first visitor, seemed shocked at her appearance. "My goodness, Johanna! What's wrong? You look so thin and pale! Have you been ill? What has happened?"

Tears welled up in Johanna's eyes at the sympathy in Liddy's voice. "*Everything's* happened!" she wailed. "Everything in the world. My heart is breaking. I'm in love with Ross Davison, and I don't know what I'm going to do about it."

Liddy's eyes widened. "Ross Davison? *Really?* I mean, I noticed you only had eyes for each other at the taffy pull, but then you went away, and—"

Johanna poured out her heart. Liddy was titillated by the details of Johanna's description of her secret meetings with Ross, which to Liddy's imagination had all the elements of one of the romantic novels she devoured about star-crossed lovers. But sympathetic as she proved to be, Liddy still was shocked that Johanna had defied her parents. It just wasn't done. Not in their ordered world. Johanna soon sensed that her friend was not as supportive as she had hoped she might be and that it would be wiser to keep her own council rather than confide in her.

During the days after her homecoming, Johanna spent a great deal of time in her room. Ostensibly, she was working on her album quilt or otherwise putting her time to good use. Actually, she was doing much soul searching.

Johanna knew that her parents' purpose in sending her away to forget Ross had been a failure. It had confirmed her feelings for him, deepened her conviction that their two lives were meant to be joined.

Johanna felt that with Ross her life would take on new depth. None of the young men her parents deemed eligible had stirred her heart, her imagination, her spirit, as Ross Davison had done. Observing the lives of the women in her family, Johanna found them a tedious round of shallow pleasures and rigid duties, restricted by limiting social rules. Johanna desperately wanted something else. She wanted her life to have meaning, to have it matter that she even existed.

She believed strongly that by sharing Ross's life, she would find the meaning she was searching for in her own. Johanna was convinced this was her chance. She even dared to think it was God's purpose for her life, if she just had the courage to grasp it.

On the brink of despair, deep in her heart she believed that if they were *not* allowed to marry, the rest of her life would be lonely, dissatisfied, unfulfilled.

At length she came to the important decision to take matters into her own hands. She would send a note to Ross asking him to meet her at the bridge near the churchyard. That would be easily enough arranged, since her mother insisted on her daily "constitutional." Whether he answered or met her or not, Johanna would accept it as God's will. She was willing to risk leaving the result to God.

She wrote only a few lines.

My Dear Ross,

I am home again and must see you so we can talk. Please meet me at the bridge near the churchyard.

Ever your Johanna

❧

A little before the hour she was to meet Ross, Johanna hurried past the steepled church and, winding through the graveyard, to the arched stone bridge. The day was gray and overcast, and the willows bending over the river were bare. Johanna arrived breathless with anticipation and anxiety. What if Ross did not come? Not showing up could be his way of telling her he was not going to defy her parents' disapproval. As she came in sight of the bridge, to her relief she saw Ross already there. She saw his tall figure, the shoulders hunched slightly, folded arms on the ledge, staring down into the rushing water below.

She ran the last few steps toward him. At the click of her boots on the bridge, he turned, and as he did, Johanna remembered how at their first meeting she'd had the strange sensation that they were being reunited again after a very long separation. What she had felt before was some kind of mysterious precognition. Only this time it was true. This time it was *really* happening.

Johanna halted and there were a few seconds of hesitation before either of them moved. Then simultaneously they both rushed forward. He caught her hands tightly in his. His gaze embraced her hungrily.

"Oh Ross, I missed you so!" Johanna cried.

Ross did not reply. His eyes said so much more. He simply drew her to him, holding her so close that she could feel the thud of his heart next to her own. Then, his arm around her waist, they walked down closer to the water.

"Johanna, was this wise? I feel so guilty deceiving your father and mother by meeting you. And Dr. Murrison too. But when I got your note, I couldn't *not* come. I never meant to cause such . . . trouble."

"It's not your fault, Ross. I had to see you. I had to be sure. . . ." Johanna paused and looked at him anxiously.

Ross shook his head sadly. "It's wrong to meet like this when your parents have made it clear that—"

"Ross, don't say that. Just listen. *Listen!*" she begged. "I love you. Nothing else matters if you love me, too. You *do* love me, don't you?"

98

"You know I do, Johanna, but I had no right to speak without first—"

"If you love me, Ross, I have no intention of forgetting you or giving you up. I shall go to my parents, tell them. And if they still—"

"No, Johanna." Ross's tone was firm, decisive. "That's not your place. It is mine. I have given this a great deal of thought. In fact, I have thought of scarce else since you went away. I will go to your father like any honorable man would do, ask him to give me, to my face, the reasons they consider me unworthy to . . . court you." The corners of his mouth lifted slightly at the use of the old-fashioned word. "I love you, Johanna, and I intend to fight for you."

During the next few days, the March weather was as unpredictable as Johanna's emotional seesaw. One day she would awaken to gusty winds, rain dashing against the windows—the next morning sunshine would be drenching her bedroom. Johanna's mood vacillated from hope to despair. Had Ross acted as he had told her he intended to? Had he gone to see her father? Written him? Life in the Shelby household seemed to go on its usual smooth way, neither parent giving Johanna any indication that Ross had taken the step he had promised.

Then one late afternoon Johanna's father came home earlier than usual. He came to the door of the room where Rebecca sat at her quilting frame, beckoned her to follow him into his study, then closed the door.

Johanna had been in the room with Rebecca, dusting her mother's collection of porcelain figures. Evidently her father had not seen her. As her parents disappeared, Johanna put the Dresden shepherdess back on the mantelpiece and tiptoed across the hall. She paused briefly at the closed study door, straining to hear some of their conversation. But all she could hear was the steady flow of her father's deep voice, interrupted occasionally by her mother's. However, she could not tell anything from the tones of their voices.

Johanna's heart beat a staccato. She felt sure she and Ross were under discussion. Had there been a meeting? Had Ross been dismissed, his suit rejected? Had he been humiliated? No, her father was first and foremost a gentleman. He was also a compassionate, understanding man, a gentle father.

In an agony of uncertainty, Johanna crept past the closed room, up the stairway, and into her bedroom. There she flung herself on her knees and prayed. She tried to pray as she had been taught, a submissive, surrendered kind of prayer, the kind she had been told was most pleasing to God. However, such learned prayers were in conflict with the desperate ones of her heart. Even as she murmured, "If it be your will . . .," deep down it was *her* will she wanted done. Her stubborn, rash, reckless will to have Ross no matter what the cost.

Johanna was not sure how long she had prayed when there was a brisk knock at her bedroom door. Quickly she scrambled to her feet, just as Cissy poked her prim little face in, saying importantly, "Johanna, Mama and Papa want to see you right away." She delivered this message with the unspoken implication, *You're in trouble!*

❦

Johanna entered the room with a sinking feeling. Her mother was seated at her quilting frame and did not look up. Her father stood, his back to the door, staring into the fire blazing on the hearth. At her entrance he turned. His expression was unreadable.

"You wanted to see me, Papa?" Johanna asked in a voice that trembled slightly.

"Yes. Your mother and I want to talk with you, Johanna. Come in, please, and take a seat."

Johanna wasn't prepared for the gentleness in her father's voice. In fact, she had been half afraid they had discovered her secret meetings with Ross and she was about to receive a stern lecture on deceitfulness and disobedience. She came in and closed the door behind her and walked across the room to the chair he'd indicated.

Her knees were shaking, so she was glad to sit down. However, she perched on the edge of the chair, clasping her hands tightly together on her lap. Holding her breath, she looked from one to the other of her parents. Her mother continued stitching and did not meet her daughter's gaze. Johanna then looked toward her father expectantly. There was a tenseness in his posture unlike his usual relaxed attitude when at home.

"First, I want you to know, Johanna," he began in a rather lawyerly manner, "that we respect you, admire you even, for your courage to withstand our persuasion—yes, our attempts to influence you from making what we deem an unwise decision. It shows character—"

Her mother stirred as if in disagreement, and Mr. Shelby glanced over at her. He paused a few seconds before he continued, amending his statement. "At least a determination that, while perhaps misguided, is nevertheless commendable."

Johanna braced herself for whatever was forthcoming.

"As your parents, we feel it our responsibility to guide you in matters that your youth, inexperience, may not give you the wisdom to decide for yourself. When someone is young and in love, clarity is often blurred." He paused again. "Your mother and I have spent many hours in prayerful discussion of this situation." He spoke slowly and very deliberately. "We feel that as your parents, we should point out to you that with such a man as Ross Davison, his lifework, which he intends to pursue in a remote, very poor mountain community, will always come first. The needs of the people he serves will always be his priority. Much like that of a dedicated minister of the gospel. A wife and family will always have to take second place, even though that might not be his conscious choice. Do you understand what I mean?"

"Yes, sir, I think I do."

"You and this young man, Ross Davison, have very different backgrounds, as you must know. You have been reared in a comfortable home, provided with all the necessities—and what's more, some of the luxuries. You have been sheltered, privileged. From what I understand, he was raised in poverty, hardship, but through his own efforts and those of some who believed in him, he has managed to get an education and is now a skilled physician."

Mr. Shelby turned, picked up one of the fire tools from beside the hearth, poked at the logs. The sizzling hiss of a breaking log filled the temporarily silent room. It was a full minute before he began to speak again.

Johanna pressed her palms together in suspense. Where was all this leading?

Slowly her father turned back, and in a voice thick with emotion, he said, "We have met with our trusted friend Dr. Murrison, who told us that Dr. Davison is a man of unquestioned integrity and honor as well as being a fine doctor. The young man you have chosen and wish to marry is one of remarkable intelligence, character. Still, I feel I must tell you, Johanna, that if you marry this man, you will be going into a kind of life for which you have no preparation. It will be a hard life, a life of work, privation—" He halted, as though he felt it difficult to go on.

"Yes, Papa?" Johanna prodded breathlessly.

He looked at her and she saw on his face infinite resignation, sadness. Then he said, "We have agreed nothing is worth the stress and discord that have been constant in this household of late." He cleared his throat. "So we want you to know that if you truly believe that a marriage to Ross Davison will bring you fulfillment and happiness—then we consent to it."

Stunned, Johanna glanced at her mother, then back to her father.

"Oh, Papa, do you really mean it?"

"Yes, my dear. I would not say so if I did not. We give our consent." He shook his head. "That is not to say that we approve of it or have reconsidered the obstacles we see in such a marriage. What we are saying is that we give our permission for you and Dr. Davison to see one another and"— Mr. Shelby shrugged—"the rest is up to you."

Johanna jumped up and rushed over to him. "Oh Papa, thank you, thank you!" She spun around toward her mother. Rebecca held up a hand as if to ward off a hug.

"No, Johanna, don't thank *me*! You have had your way in this matter. Over my disapproval, my objections. I hope it won't bring you unhappiness."

Johanna was too relieved to let even her mother's coldness dampen her joy. "I'm sorry if I've hurt you, Mama, but I know it's the right thing." She paused. "May I have permission to let Ross know your decision?"

She glanced at her mother, whose mouth tightened as a flush of anger rose into her face. Johanna turned to her father for the answer.

"Dr. Davison has already been told. Through Dr. Murrison. It was Alec Murrison who came to see me at my office to plead the young man's cause. His arguments were valid, convincing. I told him he should have become a defense lawyer instead of a doctor." Mr. Shelby smiled but it was a tight, rather grim smile. "I'm sure Dr. Davison now knows he can pursue his . . . courtship."

Johanna moved to the parlor door. Tears of happiness sprang into her eyes. Her hand on the knob, she turned back into the room. "Thank you," she said again, then went out and started up the stairs. She saw her two sisters leaning over the balcony at the top of the stairway. She recognized by their guilty faces that they had been doing their best to eavesdrop on the conversation in the parlor. But too happy to be cross, she laughed. Running the rest of the way to the top, she grabbed each girl by one hand and spun them around, pulled them with her down the upstairs hall in a merry, exultant dance.

The next morning, in the cold light of day, her euphoria wore off.

She had dashed off a note to Ross informing him of her parents' decision, hoping he would call upon her that evening. That done, Johanna's soaring spirits had suddenly departed. The impact of what had taken place began to filter through her elation of the night before. Reality flooded Johanna.

The full impact of what her parents had done hit her. They were not forbidding her to see Ross. They were giving her the freedom to make up her own mind. It was to be her choice, her decision. It was overwhelming and a little frightening.

It was rather like, she remembered, how she had struggled with the doctrine of free will when she had attended confirmation classes. "But why did God give us free will when he knows we will sin and might lose heaven? I'd much rather God made us be good and be *sure* I was going," she had argued with the baffled young assistant minister who had taught the young applicants.

She had rushed headlong into this exciting experience of falling in love. Perhaps she had not thought long or far enough ahead. All she had been aware of was that she loved Ross, wanted to be with him, was thrilled he loved her.

Her parents had given her permission to exercise her free will and marry him. Now she could make her own choice. As she fully realized this, she felt some trepidation at being told she was responsible for her own life.

She had won her fight to have her own way. But what had she lost? Somehow Johanna had always known that she was her father's favorite, his chosen companion for walks in the woods, where he had pointed out to her the flora and fauna. Botany was one of his many interests. And he had a love of words, of Shakespeare's plays and poetry, which he shared with Johanna. However, in the past few months their old easy camaraderie had disappeared.

Johanna desperately wanted it back, wanted to be reconciled with her father. Yet truthfully she felt it was too late to regain what was lost. Ever since Ross had become an issue, Johanna's father had kept his distance from her. Certainly he'd been influenced by her mother's disapproval. But the look on his face the night before, even as he gave Johanna her "heart's desire," had been a mixture of sorrow, regret.

She hadn't meant to hurt anyone. Especially not her beloved father. Was there always a shadow side to happiness?

~❧~

Within the week, Ross arrived at Holly Grove in the evening to begin what was to be his formal courtship of Johanna.

Johanna waited upstairs in her bedroom, its door half open, listening for the brass knocker on the front door to announce Ross's arrival. When it came, her heart echoed its clanging. Next she heard footsteps on the polished floor of the downstairs hall, the murmur of male voices, and knew Ross was being greeted by her father. Breathlessly she prayed, *Oh, dear Lord, let it go well.*

Then, at the rustle of taffeta skirts on the stairway, Johanna shut her bedroom door quietly, holding her breath until there came a tap and her mother appeared in the doorway. Her expression was bland. Whatever she was feeling, she concealed it well.

"Johanna, Dr. Davison is speaking with your father now. In ten minutes you may go down and join them."

Johanna nodded, smiling at her mother, a smile that was not returned. Rebecca left and Johanna stood, hands clasped against her breast, feeling the pounding of her heart. She went out into the hall and remained at the top of the steps, counting silently to herself until the clock struck ten minutes past the hour. Then she slowly walked down the stairway.

Her father held open the door to the parlor for her. Beyond him she saw Ross standing, his back to the fireplace.

"I'll leave you two now—I am sure you have much to say to each other," her father murmured and went across the hall to his study, leaving the door slightly ajar, as was only proper.

Johanna started toward Ross just as he took a few steps forward, holding out both his hands to her. "Johanna, Johanna—"

Tears of joy sprang into her eyes. Her tongue tried to form his name, but her throat was too tight to speak. They stood inches apart, simply looking at each other. Then Ross took one of her hands and kissed her fingertips. "At last, Johanna, at last," he whispered. "Your father has given us his permission." He did not say "his blessing," and Johanna wondered if Ross realized the difference. However, at the moment she was too consumed with happiness to pursue the thought. She had won—*they* had won—and that was all that was important for *now*.

She moved closer and lifted her face.

"I love you, Johanna," he said, almost in a sigh, then leaned down and kissed her softly.

With a small indrawn breath she returned his kiss. A sensation of pure joy swept over her. This was it, the answer to all her prayers, hopes, and dreams.

⁓⁊⁊⁓

Each evening thereafter, unless some medical emergency prevented him, Ross appeared at the Shelby home to spend some time with Johanna. Johanna lived for those moments alone with him, albeit the parlor door was always discreetly left ajar.

One evening, Ross was delayed and Johanna waited impatiently for him to come. A family had come down with some kind of fever and he'd had to attend them, he explained when she rushed to welcome him. In the parlor, his arm around her waist, Ross led her over to the sofa. "I have something to show you, Johanna. Something I've had for a long time. Something I had made while you were in Winston, with only my faith that this time would come, that this would happen."

Ross held out his hand, and in its palm lay something round, shiny, a circlet of gold, her wedding ring!

"Look inside," he urged her. Johanna held the small band up to the light shining out from the glowing fire.

"Love, Fidelity, Forever. JS-RD," she read aloud.

She looked up at Ross with eyes glistening with tears. For a minute emotion made her unable to speak. She remembered Ross once saying, "What do I have to offer you, Johanna?"

Here lay the answer in the palm of her hand. A circle of love, embracing, enveloping, protecting love, that's what he was offering her now and forever, as long as they both should live and on afterward into eternity.

Chapter Ten

❦

Once the aunties and other family members were told and her engagement was formally announced, Johanna—her heart's desire granted—became the daughter Rebecca had always dreamed of. She could not have been more docile, more open to suggestions, directives, plans. Johanna was ready to compromise on any detail. Rebecca found this new side of her oldest daughter remarkable. Though easier to deal with than the one that had balked at so much Rebecca had wanted in the past, it was a little difficult to get used to and somewhat unnerving.

The plans for Johanna's marriage to Ross went forward smoothly, at least on the surface. Rebecca was still given to moments of deep doubt. She would think that if she and Tennant had simply held out longer, not given in to Alec Murrison's championship for his young assistant nor to Johanna's alarming melancholy, perhaps—*perhaps*—it all might have eventually resolved itself. But Rebecca was too pragmatic to spend much time in vain self-reproach. There were too many details to be attended to, too much to be accomplished and completed to waste any time in useless regret.

The wedding was to be a quiet one, not in church but in the Shelby's parlor, with only the immediate family attending, which in their case made up quite a crowd. To Rebecca's secret relief, Ross informed her—without seeming embarrassment—that none of his family would be able to come. His mother never traveled, he told her, and his sisters were too young. Spring planting would keep his younger brother Merriman and his family from coming as well. Although Rebecca accepted his explanation and assured him she understood, privately she had not been sure if the Davisons would be comfortable among the Hillsboro people. Of course, they would have been welcomed graciously. Still, it was one less problem to worry about, she told herself complacently.

⁂

Johanna could hardly wait to tell her best friend, and a few days following the Shelbys' acceptance of the inevitable, Liddy was invited over so that Johanna could share her news.

"Oh Johanna, are you *sure?*" Liddy's eyes were wide, marvels of ambiguity. She was both excited and sad. A romantic, she was thrilled at the happy ending of this star-crossed love story, and yet she felt uneasy about her friend's future.

"I've never been more sure of anything in my life!" declared Johanna. The two girls were sitting on Johanna's quilt-covered bed a few days after the Shelbys had given their consent to Ross's marriage request. "Ross is everything I ever dreamed of, Liddy, and so much more. I am beside myself with happiness." Johanna's smile and eyes radiated joy. Her whole expression glowed.

"But to go live up in the mountains, Johanna, miles away from everyone you know, from everything you're used to." Liddy's voice held doubt.

"I've been away from Hillsboro before, for goodness' sake, Liddy! Almost three years at Miss Pomoroy's. And if *that* wasn't different from what I'm used to, nothing is! I love Ross and we're going to have a wonderful life together. And it will all work out. Don't worry about me." Johanna reached over and squeezed Liddy's arm.

"I don't know, Johanna. I heard Mama talking to one of your aunts, and—"

"I hope you didn't pay any attention to any of that? Who was it, Aunt Hannah? She always takes the gloomy side of everything."

"Well, Mama agreed with it, Johanna. She said when love is blind, there's a rude awakening."

"Oh, fiddle! That's one of those typical old wives' tales ladies say to each other when they don't agree about something. I just hope *I* never get old and narrow and view anything that is different as bad. Of course, Ross is different from most of the insipid men we know here, Liddy."

"Not all of them. Take Burton, for instance—"

"*You* take him, Liddy!" Johanna said indignantly, then giggled.

"I *would* if I could!" Liddy retorted snappishly. "The problem is, he's brokenhearted over *you*, miss!"

"I'm sorry, Liddy. I was teasing. Burton is a dear, lovable fellow. I just don't love him. Not all his persuading would ever change that. You can't just decide to love someone. It just happens. Like it did with Ross and me. Neither of us was expecting it or even looking for it. But we *knew* when it *did* happen, and that's what makes me so sure."

"Johanna, be serious for a minute, please. I just have to talk to you!" Liddy suddenly burst out. She began to sniff and her eyes filled. "It's all wrong. You must give it some more thought before you go and do something you'll regret for the rest of your life! I just hope you won't be sorry. As Mama agreed with your auntie, 'Marry in haste, repent in leisure.'"

Johanna looked at her, startled.

110

"Oh Johanna, he's just not right for you!"

"What do you mean, *not right?*" Johanna echoed, bewildered.

"I mean—well, it's not that he isn't fine, honorable, and a good doctor, but to *marry* him, Johanna, and go so far away to live, on the edge of nowhere, in the hills, with people you don't even know, will have nothing in common with. . . . Oh Johanna, you just *can't!*" Liddy's eyes filled with tears that began to stream down her face.

"I don't see what you mean, Liddy."

"That's because you're not willing to look, Johanna."

"Pish tush!" Johanna said scornfully. "You're a regular old lady, Liddy. Where's your sense of romance?" She teasingly tossed a small embroidered pillow at her friend.

Liddy tossed it back, pretending to pout. "Well, don't say you weren't warned."

"Not warned? No, I'd never say *that*. If you only knew how many times I've had to listen to the same sort of thing you've been saying. I think every one of the aunties, one way or another, have delivered such warnings." Johanna smiled. "And I'm going to prove them all wrong! So there!" She stuck out a small, pink tongue.

Her friend ignored Johanna's attempt at comedy. "Mama says Millscreek Gap is real backwoods, Johanna. You're not just going to move everything from your home up there like it was a paper cutout and fit it in there and everything will be the same. Don't you understand how *primitive* mountain people's lives are? You've never even met his folks, never been to his home, seen how they live—my goodness, some of those mountain people that come down to town to sell their baskets and chairs . . . why, they're just not like *us*, Johanna. I mean, some of them don't even know how to read or write, Johanna, do you realize that?"

Indignantly Johanna stared at her. "I can't believe you're saying this, Liddy. You sound like Emily Archer! Place Ross beside any other man in all of Hillsboro, and he'd stand head and shoulders above them all. Ross is a *doctor*, an educated man. You should hear him discuss things—all sorts of things. Not just about medicine and all. Even Papa had to admit that he is very intelligent."

"Maybe. But that's a man's world, Johanna. You're going to miss things you don't even realize now."

"Like what?" Johanna demanded.

"Well, like things you take for granted. Things we all take for granted, everyday things as well as special things. Up in the hills, there are no shops or stores or theater or—"

"None of that matters." Johanna's eyes grew dreamy. "Don't you understand that, Liddy? Not when you're in love the way Ross and I are. The question isn't, Is he good enough for *me*? but, Am I good enough for *him*?"

"Johanna, will you just listen?" begged Liddy.

"No, I don't think I will," retorted Johanna, getting up from the bed on which the two had been seated. "I thought you were different, Liddy. I thought you would understand, be glad for me. Not come here talking to me as though I'm some half-wit that doesn't know what she's doing. Telling me that I'm making a mistake. What kind of a friend are you?" Johanna was getting choked up as the words rushed up on her. "I'm so lucky that Ross loves me. I have to pinch myself at times to make sure I'm not dreaming." Johanna turned her back on Liddy and went over and stood at the window, her shoulders stiff with anger.

At length the sound of sobbing caused her to turn back into the room. Liddy was bent over, her head in her hands, crying brokenheartedly. Johanna's soft heart melted. She went over to her weeping friend, put her arms around her.

"It's all right, Liddy. Don't cry anymore. I know you just said what you thought you should. But believe me, I'm going to be so happy."

"Oh Johanna, I'm sorry," Liddy sobbed, her arms tightening around Johanna. "I'm just going to miss you so terribly."

"And I will miss *you*! We've been friends *so* long! But you will be one of my bridesmaids, won't you? I'd ask you to be the maid of honor, but Mama says I must have Cissy—it's only proper for the sister of the bride and all that. But I do want you specially, so will you?"

"Of course!" Liddy said and the two girls hugged.

During the rest of the visit, the two girls discussed colors, material, and design of the bridesmaids dresses. By the time Liddy left, things had smoothed out between them. At least on the surface. But Liddy's criticism had wounded Johanna, and she knew that somehow their friendship would never be quite the same.

❧❦❧

One afternoon just a few days later Johanna had another visitor, an unexpected one. Bessie stuck her head in Johanna's bedroom door and announced, "Miss Johanna, dere's a young gemun to see you."

"Dr. Davison?" Johanna asked excitedly, jumping up from her desk and dropping the quill pen with which she was addressing wedding invitations.

"No'm, it's Mr. Lassiter."

"Oh, dear!" Johanna's exclamation was dismayed. She had not seen Burt since her engagement had become common knowledge in Hillsboro. She wasn't looking forward to this, she thought as she gave a quick peek in her mirror, smoothed her hair, and straightened her lace collar. But there was no help for it. She had to see him, even if it turned out to be unpleasant.

Burton had never made a secret of his feelings toward her, at least as much as she would allow him to. Johanna had consistently tried to avoid his getting serious. She knew it was only her efforts that had delayed his proposing. She knew Burton had planned to talk to her father as soon as he completed his year of reading law with his uncle. Well, it was all neither here nor there now, she sighed and went downstairs.

As she entered the parlor, Burton turned from where he stood staring moodily out the window. Johanna had no trouble reading his expression. His face was a mixture of disappointment and indignation.

"Johanna, how could you have done this? You hardly know the fellow. No one does!" were the first words out of his mouth.

This declaration immediately infuriated Johanna, and she lost no time indicating that to Burton.

"*I* know him. *Dr. Murrison* certainly knows him. And who are you to make such a statement?" She drew herself up, attempting to look both angry and dignified, a hard combination to achieve.

"But *I* love you, Johanna. I always have. I always intended to ask you to marry *me*! You must have known that."

"I'm sorry, Burton. I knew you were fond of me. Why, we've been friends since—since we were children almost. At least from the time we went to Mrs. Clemens's dancing classes. And we shall always be friends. But I never led you to believe there would be anything else between us. I certainly never *meant* to, if you somehow got that impression."

"That's beside the point, Johanna. We have everything to make a really good marriage. We have the same background, we grew up at the same time, we go to the same church, we know all the same people. I am my parents' only son, and I will get all the family silver, seventeen acres of land

114

on which to build you a beautiful house, provide you with a home, a life that you're used to—there's no reason at all why you wouldn't accept my proposal."

"The most important reason of all, Burt," Johanna said softly. "I don't love you—not the way a woman should love the man she marries. I'm sorry, but that's the truth. Hard as that may be for you to accept."

Burton shook his head vigorously and went over to her.

"Johanna, you've got to listen to sense. This is a foolhardy thing you're doing. Marrying a man who's practically a stranger, going off into the mountains, to who knows what kind of a life? It's ludicrous. Everyone agrees."

Anger rushed up in Johanna. The idea that Burton's family and, as he indicated, *everyone* in Hillsboro, were talking about her, discussing her decision, infuriated her.

"Burton, I'm sorry if you're hurt. I'm sorry if you think I'm making some kind of terrible mistake, but there it is. And despite what you or anybody else—*anybody* at all—has to say about it, I'm going to marry Ross Davison, and I'm more proud and happy about that than anything I've ever done in my entire life."

Burton looked crestfallen. He threw out his hands in a gesture of helplessness.

"I always knew you were stubborn, Johanna, but mark my words, what you're doing is beyond reason." His mouth tightened into a straight line. Then quite suddenly his expression changed into one of inconsolable regret. "I *know we* could have been happy, Johanna. If you'd just given me a chance. . . ."

Johanna's sympathetic heart softened at the sheer dismay in his face, the sadness in his voice.

"Oh Burt, if it were as easy as that. Someday you'll understand. I mean, I genuinely hope that someday you'll find someone and feel the way I feel about Ross. You'll recognize it *then*. You'll understand what I'm saying and know you can't settle for anything less."

Burton shook his head again. "How can you be sure that isn't the way I already feel about *you*, Johanna?"

Johanna took a step back, moved toward the parlor door leading into the hallway. "I'm sorry, Burt, I truly am. I never meant to make you unhappy." She knew there was really nothing else to say. She wanted him to leave, to have this painful confrontation over.

Head down, Burton crossed the room and, without looking back, walked past Johanna into the front hall. There he picked up his hat and cloak, opened the door, and went out.

Johanna sighed. It had been a difficult half hour. But what else could she have said or done? Truthfully she did hope Burton would find someone to love. Someone he could love as much as he thought he did Johanna. As much as she loved Ross.

However, much as she tried to dismiss it, Burton's words hung like a shadow over her own happiness. He had said a great many things that she didn't want to agree with but knew were true. Of course, the conventional wisdom was that you married someone from a similar background, someone with whom you had much in common.

She and Ross *did* come from different worlds, but a strong love could bridge those differences. And the one thing of which Johanna was sure was that their love was strong enough.

⚜

Burton's emotional plea for her to reconsider her decision to marry Ross was not the only such experience Johanna had after her engagement was announced. A visit from her paternal grandmother proved even more difficult. The old lady had arrived one morning, earlier than she usually went out anywhere. Johanna was called down to the parlor to find her father's formidable mother seated by the fireplace, one hand clutching the top of her gold-headed cane. Her small, bright eyes pierced Johanna as she entered the room.

Hardly before Johanna had kissed her withered cheek and greeted her, Melissa Shelby demanded, "What's this I hear about you, young lady? I couldn't believe my ears when your father came to inform me that you were to be married to someone I never heard of!"

Johanna had tried to explain that Ross was Dr. Murrison's assistant and a doctor, but her grandmother waved her ringed hand in a dismissing gesture.

"Tut, tut. Alec Murrison, what does *he* know? I've known *him* since he was a lad, and never did think him too bright!" she had said sharply. "Being a doctor don't give him insight or the ability to make a good match." She shook her head, making the silver corkscrew curls under the black lace widow's cap bob. "*His* say-so don't make it the right thing for *you*." She glanced over at Rebecca. "Neither does your mother and father's *reluctant* approval of this engagement. In *my* day, daughters married whomever their parents picked out for them. Not just any Johnny-come-lately that happened along."

Patiently Johanna attempted to placate the indignant old lady. "Grandmother, I truly believe that if you met Ross, you'd change your mind."

The old lady's chin had risen disdainfully. "Well, young lady, I'd planned that you would have my Georgian silver tea set when you married, but I thought you would choose someone from one of the Hillsboro families I know. What's wrong with some young man from among your parents' friends?" She turned to Johanna's mother accusingly. "I just don't understand young people these days—*or* their parents, for that

117

matter. My papa ruled with an iron hand, and we all snapped to, I'll tell you." She tapped her cane sharply on the floor.

"We certainly intended to bring Johanna's young man to call on you, Mama-in-law," Rebecca had replied. "It did all come up rather unexpectedly. We thought—" She never got to finish what she might have said, because Melissa interrupted.

"*Intended?* What good does that do *now?* As I told my son, everyone knows what is paved with good *intentions*."

"I'm sorry," Rebecca had murmured, then sent Johanna an angry glance that said, Now, see what you've done?

Impulsively Johanna had gone over to her grandmother, knelt down in front of her, and looked up into the frowning face.

"You want me to be happy, don't you, Grandmother? I'm sure if you allowed yourself to know Ross, you'd see how very kind and good he is and you'd see that I was making a good choice, the *right* choice for *me*. Please, may I bring him over?"

Rebecca had looked at her daughter, mentally shaking her head. There she goes, turning on the charm. And she'll have her way. She always does! In front of her eyes, she saw her daughter wield the magic she had seen her use so often on her father.

In the end, Johanna had received a grudging invitation from Grandmother Shelby to bring Ross for tea the following Sunday afternoon.

⁓≫⁓

That evening while waiting for Ross's usual, often brief visit, Johanna wondered if all the opposition they were getting had made her more stubborn or strengthened her love. It was a toss-up. The more people told her she was making a mistake, the more she dug her heels in, declaring they were wrong. Ross often seemed distracted, and she worried that he might have the same kind of doubts. They had stepped onto this path together, and there was no turning back now. The question was, Was it true love or pride? Johanna quickly dismissed these troublesome thoughts. Of course she loved Ross. Of course she wanted to marry him. When they were together, nothing like that entered her mind. She basked in the love she saw shining in his eyes. The clasp of his hand on hers, his kiss on her lips, thrilled her, and then she knew she wanted nothing more than to spend the rest of her life with him.

During the next few weeks, the Shelby household was as busy as the proverbial beehive. The local seamstress had all but moved in to work on Johanna's gown and the bridesmaids' dresses.

Concentrating on filling a suitable hope chest for Johanna, Rebecca often asked herself in frustration, What in the world would the girl need for a log cabin in the mountains? If Johanna were marrying a young man from Hillsboro and doing things properly, there would have been at least a six-month engagement and they would have spent a year embroidering and monogramming linens. Rebecca sighed. So much for that. What was expected of a bride in town had nothing to do with what her housekeeping requirements in Millscreek Gap might be.

Johanna did not appear at all troubled by whatever doubts others had with her marriage plans. As she basked in her love, her days passed in a kind of euphoric daze. She would soon have her heart's desire. However, she *was* sensitive enough to realize that Cissy was jealous of all the attention she was getting. For weeks the wedding had been the center of activity at Holly Grove, and Cissy's attitude had become increasingly noticeable. Johanna did not want her sister to be unhappy, even if only because her pouting face sometimes intruded on Johanna's own happiness. She decided to do something. One night at bedtime she crossed the hall, tapped gently at the door of the bedroom Cissy shared with Elly, and entered.

Elly was already asleep. Cissy was perched on the bed, brushing her hair their mother's required one hundred strokes. She looked up in surprise at Johanna's entrance. Cissy neither smiled nor gave Johanna an opening. Probably brooding over some imagined slight or something that had happened that made her feel neglected, Johanna thought. However, she continued with her intended mission. She held out her hand, in which she held a folded, lace-trimmed hankie.

"Cissy, I'll soon be gone and you'll be the oldest one," she began. Cissy gave her head a little "So what?" toss. Undaunted, Johanna continued, "And I want you to have something special to remember me. Here."

Cissy's eyes widened in surprise. "What is it?"

"Take it and see."

Looking cautious, Cissy took it into her own hands and slowly unfolded the dainty linen handkerchief. Lying within the folds was a pair of earrings, small garnet drops surrounded by tiny pearls.

"Oh, Johanna!" Cissy exclaimed. "Thank you. I've always loved these."

"I'm glad."

"Are you sure? I mean, do you really want *me* to have them?"

"Yes. And you're to wear them on my wedding day. They'll look perfect with your dress." Cissy's gown was to have pink draped puffs over rose taffeta.

Impulsively Cissy hugged her. "Thank you, Johanna!"

Suddenly Johanna felt sorry for all the spats, all the spiteful words they'd carelessly flung at each other in the midst of small tiffs and little arguments. She wished she and Cissy had been closer all these years. She wished she could have loved this sister as easily as she had Elly.

For now, anyway, their particular bridge of built-up resentment and disharmony had been crossed. Johanna was satisfied she'd responded to her inner nudging to make amends with her sister. She was going on to a new, wonderful life with Ross, and she didn't want to have any regrets about unmended fences left behind.

⚜

The aunties had combined their talents and many hours to make their niece a beautiful quilt in record time, to give as a wedding present. Although Rebecca knew what they were doing and why they were meeting more frequently, she used the explanation that her demanding duties as mother of the bride-to-be prevented her from coming to the regular weekly sessions. This left her cousins free to discuss the situation regarding what was commonly agreed to be an "unsuitable" match.

"Johanna's marriage is a terrible blow to both Rebecca and Tennant," Hannah declared.

"If that's so, Rebecca is holding up very well under the circumstances," remarked Jo McMillan.

"Of course. Rebecca's got too much pride to admit it," snapped Hannah, bristling that her opinion would be contradicted.

"But I think Dr. Davison is a fine young man," Honey ventured mildly.

"If he's Johanna's choice, what difference should it make to anyone else?" demanded Jo McMillan.

"That's fine for *you* to say, Jo—*you* don't have a daughter. I'm sure Rebecca hoped Johanna would do her proud and make a prestigious marriage. That Lassiter boy, for example. Or Judd Sellers," persisted Hannah.

"'Love laughs at locksmiths in spite of parents' plans,' to misquote Shakespeare. Didn't Rebecca and Tennant try locking Johanna up, so to speak?" demanded Jo. "Wasn't that what the trip to visit us after Christmas was all about?"

Hannah pursed her lips. "Well, even if they gave in, it has still all happened too fast. A proper engagement should last at least one year." Hannah gave a definitive nod. "And as long as we're quoting or misquoting, 'Marry in haste, repent in leisure.' That's all I have to say."

Honey and Jo exchanged an amused look, sharing their doubt that it was all Hannah had to say.

"It's really not for us to judge. If Johanna is happy, what else matters? She's the one who will suffer if it's a mistake," commented Bee.

"I agree, and when you come right down to it, I've never seen anyone look happier. Why, Johanna's become quite beautiful in the last few weeks, haven't you noticed?" Josie asked.

"The two of them absolutely adore each other. He can't keep his eyes off her. The way he looks at her ..." Bee's voice trailed off, and a dreamy expression passed over her plump, pink face. "Humph—" *was* all Hannah seemed to be able to say after that.

～❦～

The wedding was set for a Tuesday, the first week in June. It was a far cry from the wedding Rebecca had wished for her oldest daughter. It had always been her hope to put on an elaborate wedding reception appropriate for the Shelbys' standing in the community. But if Johanna noticed the lack of what would have been extravagant preparations had there been another type of celebration, another bridegroom, she was too blissful to care.

The ritual service would be read by Reverend Moresby, and the couple would respond standing in front of the fireplace, which was to be decorated with simple arrangements of flowers and candles. Afterward, cake and wine would be served to the company.

The morning promised as pretty a day as anyone could have wished for a June wedding. The first thing Johanna saw upon awakening was her gown, which was hanging on the pine armoire opposite her bed. It was of oyster white faille and, touched by the sunlight flooding in from the window, seemed to sparkle with iridescent light.

Elly was her first visitor. She came into Johanna's bedroom proudly bearing a tray with hot chocolate and biscuits. "Mama said I could bring you your breakfast this morning, Johanna," she announced. "See, I picked this myself for you." She pointed with one chubby finger to a single white rose, drops of dew still sparkling like diamonds on its velvety petals faintly blushed with pink.

They were soon interrupted by a quick tap on the door, and Cissy came in, her hair still wrapped in paper curlers, to sit beside Elly on the foot of the bed while Johanna sipped her cocoa.

Cissy had dropped the superior air she had maintained while Johanna was in their parents' disfavor. After Johanna's gift, she had changed and had entered into the wedding preparations helpfully and happily. She gloried in the position of being the maid of honor as well as in knowing that once Johanna had departed, *she* would be the oldest daughter in the home. Privately she intended to learn by her sister's folly and only have beaux her parents approved. In the meantime, there was no harm in being close to her sister again. In fact, down deep Cissy knew she would miss Johanna. Terribly. Throughout their childhood, Johanna had always been the lively center of fun games and merriment and mischief. Cissy realized that something sparkling and delightful would disappear out of all their lives with Johanna's departure from their home.

Elly too was caught up in the general prewedding excitement and anticipation, but Johanna had always been especially sweet to her little sister Elly, her pet. There was enough difference in their ages that there had never been any competitive rivalry between them as had existed between Cissy and Johanna, Cissy and Elly. When she realized that Johanna would actually be leaving them, going off to live with Ross far away, Elly felt very sad. And she was quite fond of the tall, gentle man who, Johanna had explained, was going to be her "brother." Having them both leave together would be hard for Elly to take.

The entrance of Rebecca soon sent the two younger girls scuttling to get dressed. "Hurry now. I'll be in later to tie your sashes," she told them. "And do your hair, Cissy." Cissy was the only one of the three who did not have natural curls.

When they had left, Rebecca turned to Johanna. "Come, Johanna, it's time," she said briskly. Her daughter's glowing eyes and radiant face brought sudden, unexpected tears stinging into Rebecca's eyes. To hide them, she quickly turned her back, went over to the armoire, making a pretense of smoothing the shimmering folds of the wedding dress.

When Johanna was bathed, her hair brushed, braided, and wound into a coronet, with four ringlets on either side, bunched and tied with white ribbon, Johanna stood in front of the mirror while her mother buttoned the twenty tiny buttons down the back of her bodice.

Where was Ross? Johanna wondered. Was he getting himself into a white shirt, uncomfortably submitting to the requisite fastening of a high, stiffly starched collar, a silk cravat, getting some last-minute advice from Dr. Murrison, who was to stand up with him at today's ceremony? Dear Ross, she thought with a tender sympathy—it will only be for a few hours. One can withstand anything for a few hours. And then—a lifetime of happiness together.

Johanna was so preoccupied by her own happy thoughts that she missed the expression on her mother's face reflected in the mirror as she stood behind her. Rebecca looked at her with a mingling of sadness and hopelessness. *If only . . . If only . . .* were the errant thoughts flowing restlessly through her mind.

But Johanna was unaware of such maternal regrets. Her heart was singing. At last! At last, all her dreams were coming true.

"Now the skirt, Johanna," her mother said, and the silk overskirt slid over her taffeta petticoat with a delightful whispering swish.

Throughout the morning, the aunties had arrived one by one, peeking their bonneted heads in the bedroom door, whispering, "Could I be of any help?" Only Aunt Honey's offer was accepted, as she had brought the bridal bouquet Johanna was to carry, lilies of the valley, picked fresh that very morning from Aunt Honey's garden, then encircled in a paper lace ruffle and tied with satin ribbons.

Cissy came in next, looking very grown-up in her maid of honor gown, gazing at herself in the mirror as she moved her head back and forth to make her new garnet earrings swing. Next Liddy and Elly were admitted, looking like two spring flower fairies in their pastel dresses, wreaths of fresh flowers on their heads. Finally Johanna was ready, just as there came a discreet knock on the door, and her father stood on the threshold.

When Johanna turned to greet him, she was caught off guard by what she saw in her father's eyes as he gazed upon her in her bridal gown. For perhaps the first time in her life, she grasped the intensity of his love. Mingled there also was something she could not quite discern. It was a moment filled with a depth of emotion she had never plumbed. Her instinct was to lighten it. Affecting a coyness she had often mimed on other occasions to amuse him, Johanna put her forefinger under her chin and curtsied, asking, "How do I look?"

Tennant cleared his throat, said huskily, "Beautiful, my dear." They had survived the emotional moment, and Johanna moved swiftly across the room and placed her hand on his arm. He patted her hand and asked, "Ready?" She nodded and together they went into the hall to the top of the stairway, then slowly descended the steps. At the bottom, they turned to enter the parlor, where the preacher and Johanna's bridegroom waited.

The familiar parlor had been transformed into a bower of fragrant loveliness. All the aunties had contributed the choicest flowers from their individual gardens, and arranged them in milk glass vases on the mantelpiece and in baskets fanning out from the fireplace.

For Johanna, who was seeing it all with starry eyes, the room shimmered with light from hundreds of candles, although actually there were only two four-branched candelabra behind Reverend Moresby, creating an angelic haloed aura around his head. Then her gaze met Ross's, and her breath was taken away by the impact. All nervousness left her. Never before in her life had she felt so calm, so confident, so sure, as she did going forward to take his outstretched hand.

All past tragedies were forgotten in that one triumphant moment. Having one's dream come true was a very satisfactory state of affairs.

As her father took her hand and placed it in Ross's extended one, Johanna felt the symbolism of the act, which signified a transfer of responsibility, protection, and caring between the two men. Up to this moment Tennant had been her "cover." From this day forward it would be Ross's duty to love, honor, and cherish her.

Johanna was fully aware that in the exchange of vows, she was not only giving herself into Ross's care but promising to hold him in esteem, give him reverence and obedience, "as long as you both shall live." It was the most solemn, sacred pledge she had ever taken, and she intended to carry it out with all her mind, soul, spirit.

She held her breath as the minister intoned the closing admonition of the marriage ritual. "The sacrifices you will be called upon to make, only love can make easy—perfect love can make them joy." *Sacrifices?* she thought, glancing up at Ross's serious profile. All she could think of was the *joy*.

A smile played at the corners of her mouth. Of course she promised to "love, honor, and obey." She pushed back the lace mitt on her third finger, left hand, so that Ross could slip on her wedding band. Then she heard the thrilling words before the benediction. "I now pronounce you man and wife."

A long moment of quiet followed that pronouncement, then suddenly it was broken by a rush of voices. Hugs, kisses, and congratulations followed as the assembled family crowded around the couple.

Soon after the ceremony, other guests began arriving for the reception. The Shelby parlor had been too small to accommodate all their acquaintances and friends for the actual ceremony. In a daze of pure happiness, Johanna took her place beside Ross and her parents to greet them.

As the guests came through the receiving line, Johanna read in their glances—although they were all too polite to say anything—a startling message. It was the same look that had puzzled her when she saw it in her father's eyes earlier.

Now she understood it clearly. *Pity!* She could almost hear the whispers of some of the wedding guests, the comments. "Imagine! A pretty, popular, accomplished young woman throwing herself away to marry a penniless doctor and go live in a remote mountain community."

Even as it made her furious, she felt a slight chill slide through her veins.

If she had not been so completely in love with Ross Davison, it might have caused her deep anger. Or worse still, fear. But just then she felt his hand clasp hers in a reassuring squeeze. Looking up at him, she saw in *his* eyes all that mattered—unabashed, unconditional, unswerving love.

❦

Auntie Bee, young in heart and a romantic, had offered her home for the newlyweds to stay in for the three days before they left for their home in the mountains. She and her husband, Radford, were leaving right after Johanna's wedding for a long-planned visit to her husband's ninety-four-year-old mother in Pennfield. Therefore their house would be empty and thus provide the young couple privacy for a short "honeymoon."

In a flurry of rice and rose petals, Johanna and Ross, hand in hand, left the reception in the buggy lent by Dr. Murrison, drove the short distance to the Breckenridge house. Auntie Bee's housekeeper of many years, Tulie, met them at the door.

"Evenin', Miss Johanna. Evenin', Doctor," she greeted them, her wrinkled brown face creased in a wide, toothless smile.

Tulie had known Johanna since she was a little girl, so the curtsey was in deference to Johanna's husband the doctor and her new status as a "married lady."

"Miss Bee and me got the guest room all ready," she told them. "And Miss Bee thought you-all would like to eat your supper on de balcony oberlookin' de garden."

"That sounds lovely, Tulie." Johanna smiled and, still holding Ross's hand, followed the old woman up the winding stairway to the second floor.

At the top, Tulie turned as if to be sure they were behind her, then waddled down the corridor to the end and opened a door, gesturing them to enter. They stepped inside the spacious, high-ceilinged room scented with lilac and rose potpourri, and the door clicked shut behind them, signaling Tulie's quiet departure.

Johanna had been in and out of her aunt's house dozens of times, she realized, but she had never been in the guest room. She looked around with pleasure. Everything—colors, fabrics, and furnishings—was in exquisite taste. In the white-paneled fireplace, a fire had been laid, ready for the touch of a match should the evening turn cool. A golden maple tester bed was covered by Auntie Bee's prize Double Wedding Ring quilt.

Johanna walked over and opened the French windows to the balcony, where a round table covered with white linen cloth and set with sparkling crystal goblets and fine china awaited them. To one side was a wheeled cart on which were placed several silver-domed serving dishes and a coffee urn.

"Come look, Ross," she called.

He followed her out and stood behind her.

"Isn't it perfect?" she said.

He slipped his arms around her waist, leaned down and kissed her cheek. "Yes, perfect," he whispered.

Johanna turned in his arms. Ross's hands smoothed over her ringleted curls, causing Johanna's ornamented hair combs to drop with a plink to the polished floor, loosening masses of lustrous hair to tumble onto her shoulders. She lifted her face for his kiss. This was the kiss they had waited for, the kiss that expressed a love they both knew would be forever.

～❧～

At Holly Grove, in the master bedroom, Rebecca stood at her window looking out into the moon-drenched night. A tumult of emotions had kept her awake. This was her daughter's wedding night. Oh, Johanna! Dear child, foolish child. Rebecca closed her eyes, twisted her hands together, and leaned her forehead against the glass.

Her heart was full of pain, yet hope mingled with anxiety, resignation with prayer. Could she have done anything more to prevent this marriage? That thought still anguished Rebecca's mind. Was the premonition she felt just imagination gone wild? Didn't Paul exhort his followers to bring vain imagination into captivity? She must not borrow trouble but hope the best for a marriage that, in her opinion, was doomed to bring unhappiness to her beloved daughter.

She heard a stirring in the bed behind her, then Tennant's concerned voice. "My dear, is anything wrong?"

She half turned toward him, shook her head. "No, nothing. Just couldn't sleep."

How could she tell him how her thoughts of the past had rushed over her, overwhelming her with echoes of another love—someone whom she had weighed and found wanting, contrasted to *him?* In Tennant Shelby she had seen what she wanted in life. Tennant had never known that Rebecca had made so difficult a choice. She had already met Tennant when this other young man entered her life, and love—spontaneous, impulsive, unexpected—had flamed up between them. But she had let him go. His last words, flung at her in anger, still haunted....

130

Rebecca shuddered, drew her shawl closer about her shoulders. There are two tragedies in life, the old Arabic proverb says. One is not getting what you wish for—the other is getting it.

Tennant's voice came again. "Come to bed, love. You must be exhausted. It's been quite a day. . . ."

Part Two

Chapter Eleven

❧❦❧

A second-day reception was held at Holly Grove for friends of the family who had not been invited the day of the ceremony. A glowing Johanna, in a dress of red-and-white dotted swiss, its eyelet-ruffled neckline edged with narrow red velvet ribbons, stood beside her new husband and her parents to receive guests. Her pride was apparent as she introduced Ross to those who had not yet met him. She was all smiles, sweetness, and gaiety.

Rebecca observing her, thought with mild irony, *Of course, now that you've got what you wanted, my girl, butter would melt in your mouth. Let's hope that it doesn't turn to sour cream.*

The aunties were in full force, darting here and there, seeing that the refreshment table and punch bowl were kept replenished, buzzing like happy bees, murmuring among themselves, nodding and smiling as they gazed fondly at the newlyweds.

Ross, never all that at ease at social occasions, was glad when it was over. While Johanna, her sisters, and relatives gathered to ooh and aah over the many wedding gifts, Ross sought the respite of the side porch.

It was approaching evening and the breeze was cool, refreshing on his hot cheeks. He had been acutely aware of the curiously speculative looks of the Shelbys' friends who were meeting him for the first time. He could guess some of the comments being made, such as "What can a girl like Johanna see in *him?*" or "What can the Shelbys be thinking of to let their daughter marry him?" Perhaps he was oversensitive. However, even as strongly as he loved Johanna, he'd had moments of deep uncertainty himself. He had been brought up to respect his elders, to listen to their advice, heed their warnings, which had often been right. He hoped, for Johanna's sake, he had not allowed good judgment to be swayed by his emotion. He hoped he could make her happy—even though he wasn't sure just how.

⟞⟝

Early the morning of the third day after the wedding, Ross and Johanna started out from Hillsboro for the mountains. The farewells to her parents and sisters were blessedly brief. Happy and excited as she was to begin her new life with the husband she adored, Johanna did not trust herself to say good-bye without tears. Leaving her childhood home was hard enough. Leaving her parents, knowing that the hurt and disappointment she had caused them had not completely healed, was even harder.

Saying good-bye to Cissy, who had already assumed her coveted role as the oldest Shelby daughter at home, amused Johanna more than it saddened her. However, when it came to Elly, the dam of tears broke. The little girl hugged Johanna tight around her waist, wailing, "Don't go, Johanna, or take me with you!"

Kissing the child's wet cheeks, Johanna cuddled her, saying in a choked whisper, "You can come visit me, honey, if Mama will let you! But I have to go with Ross now." Finally she had to almost pry the little girl's fingers away from her clinging hold. Rebecca stepped forward and took Elly by the shoulders.

"That will do, Elly. Shame for being such a crybaby. Johanna is married now and must go with her husband." Almost the same words Johanna had used, but they sounded so different in her mother's voice. Startled at the hard edge to Rebecca's usually melodious voice, for a moment Johanna looked at her mother. But her expression was composed, controlled. Johanna started to say something. Something foolish, like "Mama, do you love me?" But the words caught in her throat. She felt Ross's hand on her arm.

"Come, Johanna," he said gently. "We must get started if we want to get there before dark."

With another kiss and hug for Elly, Johanna put her hand through Ross's arm and turned to go.

To her surprise, at the last minute Cissy came running down the porch steps after them. "Wait, Johanna, wait!" she called. Johanna turned and Cissy flung herself into her arms. "Oh Johanna, we're going to miss you." Johanna could feel Cissy's tears against her cheek. Surprised at this show of emotion from the sister who usually kept her distance, Johanna hugged her hard and whispered back, "Take care of Elly. Be sweet to her, won't you?"

Cissy nodded. Then they heard their mother's voice. "Come, Cissy. Don't delay them. They must be on their way."

They would be riding on the two horses that were the McMillan's wedding gift to them. Some of Johanna's belongings had already been sent ahead to the cabin where they were to live in Millscreek Gap. Later Johanna's trunk and other belongings would follow in a wagon.

"Come, Johanna," Ross said again.

The sisters' embrace loosened. For one long minute they looked into each other's eyes. Johanna wished she had taken time to become closer to Cissy, tried to understand her better. But now it was too late. Her real parting with family had come.

"Good-bye," she said over the hard lump in her throat.

Ross handed her up into her sidesaddle and tightened the straps of her small traveling bag behind her, then mounted his own horse. With one last look and wave to the group standing on the veranda, Johanna turned her horse's head and followed Ross down the drive. They rode side by side but were silent as they passed through town. Johanna was dealing with a myriad of emotions that had suddenly rushed up inside her. Ross was sensitive enough to understand that she was saying good-bye to what she was leaving behind.

At the town limits, they took the narrow, rutted road that led through the dense woods and upward into the mountains. It was nearly a day's journey to reach Ross's homeland. Johanna had never seen the sky so blue. A rising mist shimmered with the golden sunlight. The farther they got up into the hills, the sweeter the air, which was fragrant with the mingled scents of wild honeysuckle, sunbaked pine needles on the trail, ferns, spicy spruce. All along the paths and deep into the forest that flanked them on both sides, were masses of mauve and purple rhododendron, orangey azalea, and delicate pink mountain laurel, more beautiful in their random profusion than the arranged bouquets in church.

The deeper they went, the more the silence surrounded them, yet it was alive with all sorts of sounds. They heard the rustle of meadowlarks rising out of the brush, startled by the noise of their horses' hooves, muffled as they were by the carpeted trail. There were butterflies hovering over the blue-purple violets, half hidden by the shiny-leafed galax on the forest floor. Graceful sprays of white flowers hung from the sourwood, with clusters resembling the more cultivated wisteria on her Grandmother Shelby's porch. High in the treetops, there came the song of birds and the humming of bees. The singing of the creek could be heard far below them as they climbed higher. It was June in the high country in all its glory. Ross turned in his saddle and smiled at her. Johanna felt her heart melt with happiness. After all this time, all this waiting, hoping, and praying, she and her husband were on their way to their own home high in the mountains—could anything be more wonderful?

Soon Johanna noticed a wooden board nailed to a tree, on which was crudely painted the words MILLSCREEK GAP with an arrow pointing north. A little farther along, they passed through what could only be described as a wide place in the trail. There on one side was a slightly listing wooden building with a sign over the door that read GENERAL STORE AND POST OFFICE.

Was this it? Johanna wondered. Was this all there was to the town of Millscreek? Had Liddy been right? Johanna remembered that her friend had called it something like the far side of nowhere.

Ross turned again and smilingly pointed to the sagging, weathered structure but didn't even bother to stop. Is that where she would come to buy supplies and get her mail? A small frisson of anxiety stirred in the pit of her stomach, but she quickly quelled it. Everything was going to be all right, everything was going to be fine. Just different, Johanna reassured herself.

The trail began to climb now, and every so often they would pass a weather-beaten, gray house perched on the side of a hill. Sometimes they would see a sunbonneted woman with a couple of children out in a garden. As they passed she would lean on her hoe for a few minutes, watching them go by. Ross would always shout, "Howdy!" and Johanna would wave tentatively. Rarely were these greetings acknowledged or returned, except by the children, who would run forward at the sight of the two on horseback, then stand staring, their fingers in their mouths. Perhaps they were shy of strangers. *Not that we will be strangers for long,* Johanna thought optimistically. *Once Ross takes his place here as the only, much-needed doctor, these people will lose their shyness and become my friends, too. I'll visit and they'll visit. . . .*

This was her first chance since the wedding to give serious thought to what her new life with him might be like. Of course, Ross had spoken about his family at length, told her about his stalwart father, killed felling a tree when Ross was only fourteen. His mother, Eliza, was left a widow with four children and forced to scratch a living on the small plot of land to provide food, clothing, for her family. Johanna could tell Ross was proud of how Eliza Davison had kept the small farm going, reared the four children by herself, with only young Ross to help.

His brother, Merriman, had been just twelve when Ross had gone to live with the schoolteacher in town and get his education. His mother had been fiercely insistent on this. "I was torn," Ross had confided to Johanna, "thinkin' I oughta stay and be the man of the family, but she wouldn't hear of it. She told me, 'Son, the Good Lord give you a brain, hands to heal, and it would be like throwing away a gift if you didn't take this chance Teacher Gibbs is offerin' you.' I was determined then and there to come back. I'd do what she expected me to do, then give Merriman his chance."

"And did he take it?" Johanna had asked.

A kind of sadness had come into Ross's expression at her question. "No, he's married now and got two young'uns. I reckon he knew what he wanted. Sis Jenny is a sweet girl, and they have a home and a farm just up the hill from Ma. Merriman still helps her as much as he can. I guess folks do what they think will make them happy. You can't give something to someone if they don't want to take it."

Johanna had sensed Ross's regret that his younger brother had passed up on the opportunity Ross had been prepared to give him. It had also probably left Ross feeling sort of lonely as the only member of the family who'd furthered himself, she thought. That left his two little sisters, Sue and Katie, now eight and ten, still at home.

Johanna was both looking forward to and dreading meeting them all. What kind of a mental picture did they have of *her*? she wondered.

They climbed steadily upward, twisting back and forth along the winding trail. The forest was silent, beautiful, but Johanna found it rather foreboding with its impenetrable shadows even on this sunny morning. Just then Ross turned and called back, "We're almost there, honey. Up over this next rise and Ma's cabin is right on the ridge."

At the prospect of meeting Ross's mother for the first time, Johanna felt slightly apprehensive. She knew Eliza Davison must be a woman of strength and courage to have reared such a man as Ross. How proud she must be that he'd become a doctor! Johanna wanted desperately for Ross's mother to accept her, to think she was worthy of her fine son. And Johanna wanted to be a loving daughter to *her*. Ross had tried to tell her not to expect too much show of emotion at this first meeting. "You know, mountain folk are different. Not that they aren't as hospitable as, say, people in Hillsboro are. Ma is as kindhearted and generous as you'd find anywhere. She's just not talkative." In spite of his reassurance that his mother was looking forward to her coming and would welcome her, Johanna felt a little ripple of nervousness as they approached the rambling, weathered log house.

Ross turned his horse under the shade of a drooping pine tree, tethered him to the rustic fence, then came over to lift Johanna down from her saddle. His hands spanned her waist and he held her for a minute, smiling down at her.

"Don't look so scared," he teased. "Nobody's gonna bite you."

"Don't tell *me* that! You said you were shaking in your boots when you went to see *my* parents for the first time. Anyway, who said I was nervous?" Johanna demanded with mock severity. "Do I look all right?" She adjusted the brim of her tricorne.

"You look just right," Ross grinned.

"Really?" Johanna tugged at her jacket and fluffed out the lacy jabot of her blouse. She hoped her blue, braid-trimmed riding habit didn't look too fancy.

Before Ross had a chance to reassure her again, a tall woman stepped out from the house and came to the edge of the porch and said, "Well, howdy!"

"Ma!" Ross waved one hand. "This is Johanna, Ma." Turning to Johanna, he held out his hand. "Come on, honey." They walked toward the porch. "This is my mother, Eliza."

"How do you do, Mrs. Davison. I'm so happy to be here."

Holding Ross's hand tightly, Johanna went with him up the steps. At the top, Johanna debated whether she should kiss her new mother-in-law or not.

Eliza Davison was thin as a reed, with dark hair heavily peppered with gray. Her calico dress was crisp, covered by a spotless cotton apron. Immediately Johanna saw Ross in his mother's strong features—the firm mouth and chin, the deep-set, slate gray eyes under dark, straight brows. Under their searching gaze, Johanna felt exposed, disconcerted. The woman seemed to be staring right into her, taking her measure. In spite of the sun on her back, Johanna felt chilled.

Face to face with Ross's mother, she wondered how Eliza Davison, born and raised in these mountains, *really* felt about her oldest son marrying a girl from town.

However, Eliza's greeting was warm and friendly enough. "Well, Johanna, I'm right pleased to meet you. My son has shure spoke highly of you. Now, do come inside and out of the day's heat."

Ross held the door so that Johanna could follow his mother into the house. The interior was dim and cool, smelled of wood shavings, soap, and some delicious cooking aromas emanating from the kitchen area at the far end of the room.

"These are Ross's sisters, Sue and our baby, Katie." Eliza gestured to two skinny little girls standing in the shadows. Both were dressed in starched calico dresses, the hems of which they were twisting. Their hair was plaited in tight braids, but Johanna could hardly see their faces, because they'd ducked their heads at her entrance.

"Sue, Katie. Come on over and meet your brother's wife," their mother beckoned them. Heads still down, they took a few steps forward, then stopped a few feet from Johanna, bare toes wiggling.

"Hello!" Johanna bent toward them, smiling. "I have two younger sisters, too," she said. "I hope we'll be great friends."

The two smiled shyly but didn't speak. Ross stepped over and swung one up in each arm, and they burst into giggles. Johanna could see at once that they adored their older brother. It made her feel a little more at ease to see how quickly he acted completely at home and didn't appear anxious or uneasy. It was as though he were trying to show her that this was a place where one could act naturally, not have to put on airs of any kind or be especially mannerly.

"You must be hungry, comin' sech a long way, startin' out 'fore dawn. Sit ye down." Eliza indicated the long, rectangular, scrubbed pine table, with half-sawn log benches on either side, their surface worn smooth. "I asked Merriman and Jenny to come for dinner, but he was gettin' his garden in and not shure he'd be done by supper. But I reckon they'll both be here 'fore too long. And bring their young'uns. They've two boys, Johanna. Three and five, and they're a handful." She shook her head and a slight smile touched her thin lips. She looked at Ross. "Puts me in mind of Ross and Merriman at their ages." Then she motioned to the two girls. "Come on, you two, help me put things on the table." Over her shoulder, she said to Ross, "Do you want to show Johanna where she can wash up?"

Johanna was glad to be taken to the side of the porch, where a basin of fresh water, a clean towel, and a cake of soap were set on a wooden table under a small mirror. She took off her hat and unwound the veil, smoothing back her hair, tightening the ribbon that held it. She rinsed her face and hands. Then, as it was getting very warm, she took off her snug jacket.

Ross was waiting by the front door. "Merriman and Jenny just came," he told her and led her back inside.

Merriman was a head shorter than Ross but had the same lean good looks. He was very tan, however, and the bronzed skin made his eyes seem very blue. His wife, Johanna decided, would have been exceptionally pretty if she weren't painfully thin and pale-skinned. Her light brown hair was drawn severely back from her face into a plain knot at the back of her head. She seemed very shy and kept her remarkably lovely eyes downcast. She mumbled her hello, then immediately scooted over to help Eliza in the kitchen area.

"All right now, gather round, folks. Everything's ready," Eliza said as she brought two large platters to the table, one of fried chicken, one of roasted ribs. Jenny and Sue followed with bowls of sweet potatoes, hominy, greens, and an apple pie. Jenny and Merriman's two small, towheaded boys scram-

bled up on the benches on either side of the long table just as
their grandmother set a black iron skillet of cornbread from
right off the stove onto the table.

Once everyone was seated, a silence fell. It lengthened.
Johanna felt her stomach tense. No one moved or spoke. Was
this a kind of silent grace? Like the Quakers', maybe? She had
never thought to ask Ross. At home, the Shelbys held hands
around the table while Papa said the blessing. Under lowered
lashes, she looked around warily. To her surprise, both of Ross's
little sisters were watching her gravely. Eliza's head was bowed.
The silence seemed to stretch. Johanna stirred uncomfortably.
She felt Ross's hand squeeze hers gently, and she raised her
head cautiously. Eliza was looking at her and said quietly, "If
you'll do the honors, Johanna." Suddenly she realized that as
the guest at the table, *she* was supposed to say the blessing. She
glanced at Ross for confirmation. He nodded, smiling slightly.
Quickly she bowed her head, trying frantically to remember
the one so often said at home. In a low voice that sounded
more like a mumble, she recited it. A moment later plates were
being passed, and she let out a breath of relief.

It took her a few moments to regain herself. She ventured two or three attempts to engage Jenny in conversation
but failed. She did notice, however, that once or twice Merriman's wife glanced at her furtively. Actually, Jenny was
looking at her blouse! Given the plain gray calico Jenny was
wearing, Johanna understood. It was only natural. Jenny
couldn't be more than nineteen. Like any young girl, she
loved pretty things. Probably she had nothing of her own like
Johanna's Cluny lace-trimmed blouse.

Johanna tried hard to think of some comment to make,
but all she could think of was to compliment Eliza on the food.
It seemed insane. She had never before felt so tongue-tied. She
wanted to please Ross by being friendly to his family, but

everything she said seemed to fall flat. She ended up being quiet while Ross and Merriman talked about mutual friends, the crops planted, the weather. Maybe the Davisons didn't talk much at meals, unlike her own family, who always entered into a lively discussion at mealtimes. She should stop trying so hard, she decided. It wasn't that Ross's family disliked her, she assured herself. *It's just that I'm a stranger, an outsider, that I don't belong here yet. It will take time for them to get to know me, for me to know them.*

Johanna had heard somewhere that to find out what kind of a husband a man would be, watch how he treats his mother. She was touched by the gentle way Ross spoke to Eliza, the respect he showed her.

Johanna was relieved when Ross got to his feet, saying they must go if they were to reach their own home before dark. Johanna thanked Eliza, said good-bye to Merriman and Jenny, urging her new sister-in-law and brother-in-law to come see them as soon as they were settled. She gave the little girls a special invitation to come up and visit. Ross kissed his mother's cheek, hugged his sisters, then brought the horses around and helped Johanna mount, and they started back up the hillside.

In spite of the fact that she had wanted it so much, that first meeting, brief as it was, put Johanna off slightly, put her on her guard. Although she had not known exactly what to expect, it had not been the welcoming she had hoped for.

Ahead of them the mountains loomed, clouds, wreathing the summits, or opened to reveal peaks crowned with a glorious golden light. The path zigzagged upward. In the clear evening light, the mountain was bathed in sunlit isolation. "There it is, honey." Ross pointed and Johanna saw the peaked roof of a log cabin with a wide stone chimney just ahead. "That's *our* place."

Johanna's heart lifted. "Our place," Ross had said. The place where they would live as husband and wife. After all these months of longing and waiting, here at last they would begin their life together.

When she stepped inside the cabin, it seemed dark after coming in from the brilliant sunset. She looked around. One large room with a stone fireplace at one end. Ross was behind her, waiting for her reaction. He had spent the previous week getting it ready for her. Then she saw the rocking chair. She walked over to it, admiring its smooth finish.

"It's a wedding present from Uncle Tanner," Ross said. He gave it a gentle push and stood there smiling as it moved back and forth without a sound, without a creak. His hand smoothed the gleaming arms caressingly.

"Who is Uncle Tanner?" Johanna asked.

Ross smiled. "You'll find out soon enough. I reckon they'll be by to visit 'fore too long. He and Aunt Bertie—"

"Your aunt and uncle?" Johanna was curious because she'd never heard Ross mention them.

"Not really, but we've always called them 'Aunt and Uncle.' I think actually they're Ma's cousins."

"Oh, I see, like my 'aunties' are *my* mother's first cousins."

"That's right," Ross agreed, then said, "Now I'll show you the spring." He took her hand and led her outside. He guided her up a little rise to a clump of poplar trees, over to a ledge, and pointed, "There it is." Johanna looked to see a natural bowl of water standing clear as glass, surrounded on three sides with a ledge of rock and a tangled web of roots. Around the spring and beside the stream that flowed from it were beds of moss, and galax, and vines of other plants that bloom in summer. On the far side, overhanging the spring, were a dozen wild blackberry stalks. As they drew nearer, Ross said, "This is the lifeblood of our place, Johanna. The purest, sweetest water you'll ever taste." He reached down and picked up a dipper lying on the stone, filled it, and handed it to her to drink. It was just as he said, icy, delicious. She closed her eyes as she swallowed, and then she felt his lips warm on hers.

He took the dipper from her, laid it back on the stone, put his arm around her waist, and together they walked back down the path.

On the porch, Ross turned and pointed. "Look there, Johanna." A summer moon was rising slowly over them. Arms around each other, waiting, they watched until it hung, a great silver dollar, above the trees. It was so exquisitely beautiful, Johanna drew in her breath.

Then Ross swung her up into his arms and carried her into the house, saying softly, "Welcome home, Johanna."

Chapter Twelve

Johanna stirred slowly out of sleep. Not fully awake, without quite opening her eyes, she was aware of brightness under her closed lids. She felt warmth. Sunlight. *It's morning,* she thought drowsily. She felt a floating sensation, almost like flying. *This is happiness! What I'm feeling is real, true, and it's me and I'm happy!*

She stretched and reached out to the pillow next to hers. She opened her eyes, blinking. The bed beside her was empty. Raising herself on her elbows, she looked around.

From the alcoved bed, she could see across the center room into the kitchen. She smelled the unmistakable aroma of freshly made coffee. Ross, she smiled. He must have got up early and made it. Just then the cabin door opened and he walked in.

He looked over at the bed and, seeing her, asked, "Sleep well?"

"Perfect!"

He came over and stood at the foot of the bed. "I love you, Mrs. Davison."

She held out her arms to him. "Say that again."

"Which? I love you? Or Mrs. Davison?"

"Both!"

He laughed, came over to the side of the bed, and took her into his arms. He buried his face in her tangled curls, and for a moment they just held on to each other. Then Johanna leaned back and smiled up at him.

"What shall we do today?"

"We could go pay Aunt Bertie a visit," Ross suggested as Johanna threw back the covers and got out of bed. "I saw Uncle Tanner yesterday when I went down to Ma's, and he asked me if the 'honey was still on the moon.'" He grinned. "Folks figure a new couple need a few weeks alone to get used to each other or find out they've made a mistake."

"Mistake?" Johanna pretended indignation. "Well, at least not *me*." She tossed her head. "I don't know whether your kin think *you're* the one that might have made one."

She slid her bare feet into the small velvet slippers, reached for her dressing gown. Ross held it for her to put on, then wrapped his arms around her.

"No, ma'am, no mistake. Best thing that ever happened to me." He leaned down, kissed her cheek, her neck, until she wiggled around laughing and turned, hugged him.

"Oh Ross, I'm so happy!" she sighed.

"Well, so am I."

Aunt Bertie and Uncle Tanner's cabin was nestled among shaggy rhododendron bushes as big as trees, and shadowed by balsams. Aunt Bertie was a treat. Just as Ross had told her, Johanna liked her right away. Who could not?

She was spare, straight backed, her movement as brisk as a much younger woman. Daily use of hoe, shears, washboard, and skillet had made her hands strong. Her wrinkled face had a rosy tan, and her snapping dark eyes held a twinkle. There was a youthful lilt in her voice. Cocking her head to one side like an inquisitive bird, she asked Johanna, "How old do you take me for?"

Afraid to offend if she guessed wrong, Johanna hesitated, and Aunt Bertie laughed, "Goin' onto seventy-nine next January. I 'spect to go on jest as I've been doin' 'til the Good Lord takes me home. I been working a garden and spinning wheel since I was eight years old. My mama had a passel of young'uns, and I was the oldest girl, so I took over a lot of the chores. I've been workin' all my life, and I don't want to end my days in a rockin' chair, although Tanner makes the best ones." She pointed to the two on the porch and urged Johanna, "Sit over there and try it."

"Uncle Tanner made one for us, Aunt Bertie," Ross said. "It was sitting in our cabin when we came. Figured it was a wedding present."

"Of course it were! I plum forgot. When he heard you were gittin' married, Ross, he started on it." She fixed Johanna with bright eyes. "Don't it rock nice and smooth?"

"Yes, ma'am. It's beautiful."

"Now, you-all sit down and we'll have a nice visit. Ross, Tanner's out there gittin' his cider press cleaned up, ready for when our apples are ripe." She glanced at Johanna. "Wait 'til you taste Tanner's sweet cider. But first you gotta try my pie," she chuckled. She bustled into the cabin.

Ross gave Johanna a "Didn't I tell you?" look just as a tall man came from around the house.

"Reckon I heard voices," the man said.

Ross went down the steps and greeted him. "Uncle Tanner, we just wanted to pay you and Aunt Bertie a call, thank you for the chair. Come meet my bride."

"Don't mind if I do," Uncle Tanner said, a grin cracking his weathered, tan face. He was thin as a whip, rather stooped in the shoulders, but moved with a lively gait. If Aunt Bertie was almost eighty, Johanna thought, Uncle Tanner must be that old or maybe older.

Uncle Tanner took the steps spryly. "Mahty pleased to meet you. Looks like Ross got not only what he needed and wanted but somethin' fine and purty, too," he chuckled and held out his hand to Johanna.

Johanna extended her own, and the old man grasped it and gave it a good, strong shake. Under his steady gaze, she felt herself weighed, measured, and not found wanting.

Johanna was pleased to feel she'd passed muster of someone she knew her new husband held in high regard.

Aunt Bertie appeared at the door. "Y'all come on in now." After the three of them were seated at the scrubbed pine table, Aunt Bertie came in from the kitchen, carrying a pie plate in one hand and a jar of honey in the other. She put the pie on the table and the jug of honey beside it, then started cutting generous wedges, lifting them one by one onto the plain, cream-colored pottery plates beside the tin.

"Now, if you want something tasty, spread some of this here honey over the top," she said as she handed around the plates. The pie was hot and its flaky crust a golden brown. The honey looked like clear liquid sunshine. Hesitantly but afraid she might offend Aunt Bertie if she didn't follow her suggestion, Johanna tentatively drizzled the honey over the top of her piece of pie.

A smile twitched Aunt Bertie's lips. "Never tried that before, I reckon?" Watching Johanna take a bite, Aunt Bertie said, "See? Good, ain't it?" With satisfaction, she turned to Ross. "How about you, Ross? You ever tried it?"

"No, ma'am, not that I can remember."

Aunt Bertie looked shocked. "You're funnin' me, ain't you? Can't believe you've lived this long and never had apple pie with honey."

When Johanna and Ross left, nothing would do but that they carry away with them a willow basket loaded with goodies from Aunt Bertie's larder—jars of strawberry jam, peach preserves, apple butter. "My apple butter's known in these parts," she told Johanna. "Come fall when the apple crop is in, I'll teach you how to make it with my recipe," she promised.

❧❦

"So what do you think of Aunt Bertie and Uncle Tanner?" Ross asked.

"I think they're wonderful!" Johanna answered.

"Good." Ross seemed satisfied. "I could tell *they* liked *you*."

What Johanna didn't say, afraid she might be misunderstood, was what she had found so surprising and so refreshing—their lack of artifice of any kind. They spoke, acted, responded, in such a natural, unaffected way. Johanna found it utterly charming. She was used to society's polite shallowness, especially in a first meeting with someone, when people tended to be somewhat formal. Aunt Bertie and Uncle Tanner had just taken her in, showing her the same warmth they bestowed upon Ross, whom they'd known all his life. Of course, she was sure they would have welcomed her just because she was Ross's wife. Still, Johanna hoped to win her own place within his family circle before too long.

Chapter Thirteen

❦

$\mathcal{J}$ohanna woke up and even before she opened her eyes, she knew she was alone. The cabin was quiet. Ross must have already left. She sat up feeling somehow bereft, deserted, even though she'd known this day was coming. She recalled their conversation of the night before, while Ross had been packing his medicine bag.

"Well, darlin' mine, I have to be about my doctoring. I've got people who've been waiting for me, and I had a whole passel of messages passed on to me—the Henson's baby has colic, Molly Renner needs a tonic, Tobias's leg is actin' up again, all kinds of ailments to see to up and down the mountainside."

Johanna had sighed, "I guess so. That's what we came up here for, wasn't it? For you to be a doctor and for me to be your wife! But what shall *I* do without you all day!"

"I don't know." Ross had looked puzzled. "Ma always found something that needed doing."

Johanna had felt somehow rebuked and said no more. As they kissed good night, Ross told her, "I'll be up and off at the crack of dawn, most probably. Got a lot of mountain to cover tomorrow."

Still, Johanna wished he had wakened her so that she could have fixed him breakfast, seen him off like a proper wife. She got up and looked around the small cabin. Here there were not the kind of household tasks she had been assigned at home—polishing silver, arranging flowers, or practicing her music. Or the social calls or visits from friends for tea in the afternoon, such as there had been in Hillsboro.

The long day stretched ahead of her emptily. Oh, there were chores enough to do, but Johanna did not feel like tackling any of them. She longed for—what?

She did not even want to admit that what she missed was the very thing she had run away from. Used to the activity of her busy home, Johanna was not accustomed to spending a great deal of time alone. Even at Miss Pomoroy's, there had been her classmates and the set pattern of the day.

There wasn't even anything really to do. Housekeeping, with no mahogany furniture to dust or polish, no brass candlesticks to shine, was simple.

When they arrived here, Johanna had found their shelves stocked with home-canned fruits and vegetables, deer jerky, and there had been a cured ham, a side of bacon, fresh eggs, butter, and milk in the springhouse. At the foot of the bed, a cedar box had been supplied with coarse sheets, homespun blankets.

Johanna's own belongings, her trunk of clothes, boxes of wedding presents, and her hope chest had not yet come. Perhaps when they did, she would have more to do, placing them, arranging things, putting her own touch on their home.

She poured herself a cup of the coffee Ross had made and left on the stove, then went over to stand at the open front door, looking out. An unwanted thought came into her mind. What would she do with the rest of her life, here on this isolated hillside with no family, no friends? Surely the novelty of marriage or coming here had not worn off so quickly.

Their cabin was surrounded by the tall pines, and suddenly she had a feeling of being closed in. Frightened, she turned back into the room. Maybe she should go down and visit Ross's mother. That would probably be a good thing to do, get better acquainted. Getting out in the open in the fresh air and sunshine would ease that strange feeling of being up here by herself, cut off from the world.

Johanna put on a fresh dress and did up her hair. She felt a little shy about just showing up at Eliza's with no invitation. But wasn't that foolish? She was sure that mountain folk didn't stand on any sort of ceremony, especially not among family members. As Ross's wife, Eliza's daughter-in-law, *she* was family now, wasn't she? She tied on a wide-brimmed straw hat and set out. She thought she remembered the way, although the last two times they had been there, they were on horseback. She had only to follow the path, and she would soon be at Eliza's house. However, the path had several forks winding in different directions, some quite overgrown with brush, laurel bushes, sweeping pine branches. Soon Johanna became confused and wondered if somehow she had taken a wrong turn.

At a little clearing she stopped, trying to orient herself. Suddenly she heard the sound of childish voices. Within a few minutes two little girls came into sight. Sue and Katie, Ross's sisters! Recognizing them, Johanna was filled with relief. They would show her the way, of course, even take her there themselves. "Good morning! I'm so glad to see you," she began, waving her hand to them. But their reaction stunned her. Immediately their smiles disappeared. The smaller of the two slipped behind the older, her finger in her mouth, while the other girl looked startled.

Knowing they were shy, Johanna smiled and took a few steps toward them, saying, "I'm on my way down to see your mother. Am I on the right path? I felt lost."

They stared back at her, eyes wide, but said nothing.

Johanna tried again. "Is this the right way?"

They nodded in unison and then spun around and ran, stumbling over their bare feet in their hurry to get away, running back the way they had come. Left so unceremoniously, Johanna felt bewildered and hurt. Was it just shyness or didn't they like her? She had always been good with children. Elly adored her and so did all her little friends. Johanna sighed. She probably had a lot to learn about mountain people, children as well as grownups.

All desire to visit with her mother-in-law vanished. She was unsure of her welcome in the middle of the day, when Eliza might be busy with many chores and wonder why *she* wasn't similarly occupied. It might be an interruption or, worse still, an intrusion. Not willing to risk another rejection, Johanna turned around and retraced her steps back up to their own cabin.

That evening when she told Ross about her encounter with his sisters, he brushed it off casually. "They're just shy. Not used to talking to strangers."

"*Strangers?* I'm their sister-in-law," she protested.

Seeing Johanna's expression, Ross quickly said, "You won't always be a stranger, honey. But right now they don't know you, and to them you *are* a stranger. It'll work out in time. You'll see."

In spite of his reassurance, Johanna still felt uncertain. Day after day, she kept putting off going down to see Eliza. That is, until Ross brought up the subject himself, saying, "I stopped by Ma's on my way home today, Johanna, and she was wonderin' if you were poorly? I said, 'No, she's fit as a fiddle.' I think that was her way of asking why you hadn't been down to see her. Better go tomorrow, honey. Else she might feel slighted."

The next day, Johanna went down to see Ross's mother, and it was a pleasant enough visit, although she still found Eliza rather standoffish. That too could be shyness—or was it wariness of *strangers*? However, it made Johanna determined to win her over. She wanted desperately for Ross's mother to love her.

The weeks of summer went by. Still Johanna had to fight the feeling of being an outsider. She did not know how to break through the wall they had put up. She was longing to be friends. She couldn't summon the courage to bring up the subject again to Ross. At length she decided that all she could do was be herself, whatever the mixture was that made her who she was. Whether his family liked it or not, liked *her* or not, Ross had found that mixture exciting, desirable. Certainly enough to stand up to her father and, against all odds, ask for her hand in marriage.

Sometimes Johanna would stand on the porch of their cabin after Ross had left for the day and look down into the valley. She saw plumes of thin blue smoke rising over the treetops and knew they came from the piled stone chimneys in the dozens of log cabins scattered all along the way, up and down the hillside. Each of those cabins had people, families, women who would possibly be her friends. All she had to do was reach out. It was a new experience. Johanna had always been open to people, had always had friends. Why not now? Was she *really* that different that they didn't want to know her? As the weeks passed, she became even more reluctant to try.

One day, she saw Ross's little sisters come by on the trail below the cabin, carrying buckets. Johanna ran out onto the porch and invited them to come in. However, they shyly shook their heads. Sue, the older of the two, said, "No'm, we cain't. It's blackberry-pickin' time. Ma's goin' to make jelly, and we best get on with pickin'." She held up her bucket. "Ma don't like us gone too long."

Johanna was tempted to offer them some cookies and lemonade, cool from the springhouse, but then decided she wouldn't. Watching them go on down the path with their buckets, Johanna realized she missed her own sisters. More than she expected to, more than she had when she was away at school. The fact was that there were more and more times during the day when Johanna's thoughts flew home to Hillsboro.

❧

The tiny twinge of homesickness Johanna had consciously tried to push away surfaced when her trunks finally arrived. They were brought up the hill by mule, delivered by the taciturn Jake Robbins, the postmaster in charge of the small post office in back of the general store. As soon as he deposited them with the few words Johanna could wrest from him, she eagerly started to unpack them.

The first trunk contained the wedding presents that, before the ceremony, Johanna had been too excited to really appreciate. She put those beside the gifts of linen and china to wait so that she and Ross could look at them and enjoy them together. It was unpacking the second trunk that caused her first excitement and delight to vanish. An unexpected depression swept over her when she saw the contents. Her mother had seemingly emptied her bedroom of all traces of *her*. As if she had never lived there at all! Her books, vases, throw pillows, knickknacks. Her mother had sent Johanna her childhood, her girlhood, her life at home! As though she were never coming back! The emotional blow was stunning. It cut a deep wound. Johanna sank to the floor, her knees having suddenly gone weak.

Holding a small pair of blue Delft candlesticks that had once graced the little fireplace in her room, Johanna felt as though she had been cut adrift from everything dear and

159

familiar. She glanced around the cabin. Where would these go? Where would any of these things fit into her new environment, these surroundings? For the first time since she had come with Ross to the mountains, Johanna felt a sense of loss, a void that nothing came quickly to fill. Had she cut herself off from home, family, as completely as it seemed?

Chapter Fourteen

❧❧❧

*B*y the end of the summer, Johanna had organized herself to accomplish certain everyday chores, although there were still ones she hadn't got the hang of yet. Johanna realized she had a lot to learn about housekeeping.

She had no one to teach her the considerable skills necessary for her to learn if she was to keep house properly here, make a home for Ross. She wanted it to be a haven of warmth, comfort, and peace after a long day on horseback visiting the sick.

She was hesitant to ask Eliza, fearing that her mother-in-law would be scornful of her inadequacy. She didn't want to impose on Aunt Bertie, who had already been more than friendly and who was always busy and never seemed to know an idle minute. Why, Aunt Bertie would think Johanna plum daft not to be able to find enough to do to fill her days.

What Johanna did not understand was that far from being unfriendly, the mountain people were hesitant to intrude on someone they considered smarter, more accomplished than themselves. They would never offer help or advice that wasn't requested.

Ironically, Johanna discovered that among the books her mother had packed in her trunk was the well-thumbed dictionary her father had given her when she was ten. There was a needlepoint marker in the P's, the last section in which she had looked up a word, memorized the definition. She smiled, a trifle nostalgically. Her father's admonition was still a good one. She would continue to learn a new word every day, even if there was no one to test her on it.

"Perseverance," "persistence," "patience," were all good goals to pursue in this new life she had taken on. She needed them all as she tried to "perfect" her wifely skills. All had been badly employed as she groaned over lumpy rice, burned biscuits, scorched cornbread.

But Johanna was determined she would learn. And slowly, gradually, painfully, she did.

～୨୧～

Johanna's inner doubts were transitory, usually lasting only the length of a long day spent alone when Ross was late coming home from "doctoring." She *was* happy, Johanna told herself over and over. She loved Ross and she tried to keep her moments of melancholy well hidden from him.

One night Ross was out very late. He'd been called to tend the children of the storekeeper, who all had bad earaches. The Millscreek Gap store also housed the post office, and while there, Ross had been given a letter addressed to Johanna.

When he got home, he found Johanna asleep in the rocker by the fire. Ross placed the letter on the mantelpiece, then gently wakened Johanna and carried her to bed. She sleepily acknowledged his presence but went right back to sleep. It wasn't until morning that he told her about the letter.

For some reason, she waited until Ross left to open it. She recognized her mother's fine penmanship and opened the letter at once. As she read it, she felt a rush of unexpected emotion. Pictures of Holly Grove flooded into her mind. She could almost smell the scent of potpourri, flowers from her mother's garden, the mingled smells of polished wood, baking apples, and beeswax candles. Turning page after page, other familiar images came. Things she hadn't realized she cared much about or missed, now became cherished memories. Johanna had left all of this happily for "love and the world well lost." A dear, familiar world, as it turned out.

Johanna read on.

> *Cissy is growing into a very pretty young woman and is agreeable in every way. We had a length of silk, striped in pale blue and cerise, made into a lovely gown for her to wear to the Pettigrew's party, at which she was quite the belle of the ball.*

Impatiently Johanna put the letter down for a minute. She could just imagine how Cissy was "toeing the mark" to her mother's satisfaction. She could read between the lines her mother had written, could almost hear all the same things her parents had tried to tell her. If she had listened . . .

Johanna got up and walked restlessly around the room. Why should news of the social life in Hillsboro bother her now? She didn't really miss it, *did* she?

When she had first come to the mountains, the possibility of unhappiness had seemed *impossible*, but now . . .

Suddenly the cabin door opened and Ross stood there. Startled, Johanna winked back her tears and got to her feet.

"Why, Ross! What are you doing back?"

He remained standing there for a full minute, then said, "I'm not sure, Johanna. I just thought maybe you might need me."

Johanna's heart lurched. She dropped the letter as she ran to him.

"Oh, Ross!" She flung herself into his outstretched arms. As they closed around her, she rejoiced in their strength, in the safety and security she felt in his embrace. Why should she ever regret anything? She could not stop the tears, but now they were not tears of self-pity but of thankfulness. How lucky she was to have this love. How ungrateful to ever question it or doubt that it was meant to be.

It frightened her that even for a little while, she had allowed herself to waver as to whether she had made the right decision. Ross was real, not the romantic myth they had tried to describe him as. He was the reason she had resisted all attempts to persuade her to give him up.

That night, the mountains echoed with the first summer storm. It began slowly, with big raindrops pattering on the roof then quickly becoming a deafening thudding. Thunder boomed, echoing through the ridges and valleys of the mountains that surrounded the cabin. Great jagged forks of lightning crackled in the darkened sky. Awakened, Johanna moved closer to Ross, who slept on, as if used to this kind of nature's noise. He was of these mountains, Johanna thought, born and raised here. Nothing about them disturbed or frightened him. Without waking, he drew her close. His nearness thrust away the uncertainties and doubts she'd had that day. Fear brought on by the storm disappeared as she moved closer to Ross, felt his lean, warm body. A warmth, a sense of security, took its place. This wonderful man who loved her, who understood her, to whom she was important, was her protection against foolish regrets. Here in his arms was safety, tenderness. She must value them, know how richly she was blessed.

Ross was her life now. She would prove her parents wrong.

❧

Johanna knew she needed something to help her cope with her new life. She didn't know what. She had not thought beyond marrying Ross, getting her heart's desire. She had not anticipated the standoffishness she had encountered in Millscreek. Other than Aunt Bertie, none of the women she had met had invited her to visit nor taken her up on her invitations. Not even Merriman's wife, Jenny. Every time they were all at Eliza's house, Johanna had asked her. Jenny seemed even shyer than the little girls.

Johanna's feelings about Ross's mother troubled her most of all. She did not feel Eliza really accepted her. No matter how hard she tried, Ross's mother maintained an aloofness that Johanna could not seem to bridge.

Help for her anxious heart came from two unexpected sources. The first was from Uncle Tanner, who happened to drop in at the worst possible time. Johanna was crying tears of frustration over a batch of burned biscuits when his knock at the door and his friendly "Howdy, anybody home?" came.

Johanna hastily wiped her eyes, banged down the tin, and hurried out onto the porch to greet him. She invited him in but he said, "I reckon just some water will do me, as Bertie's expecting me home right quick." Johanna walked with him up the stone path to the spring. While Uncle Tanner helped himself to two dipperfuls, Johanna's expression must have told him something, because he said gently, "I gotta 'spicion you're feelin' some sorriness. Anythin' I kin do might help?"

"Oh, it probably sounds silly, Uncle Tanner. I just burned a whole batch of biscuits." Tears filled her eyes again. "Sometimes it seems I can't do anything right, and"—before she knew it, she was unloading to him—"and nobody seems to like me here!"

"Now, girly, let me give you a piece of advice. Go slow. Mountain folk don't make up to strangers easy, but once they take you in, nobody in the world could have kinder kin. You mark my words. Eliza will come 'round. My Bertie'll show the way, but you'll see. You're one of the family now—"

Uncle Tanner's soft-spoken voice fell like soothing balm. She had longed for just such comfort. His words were as much a gift of love as the beautifully crafted rocker. His genuine warmth, his smile, and his gentle way touched her deeply. As she waved him off, she felt much better. She went back inside, tossed out the "burned offering," and started mixing up another batch of biscuits.

One morning not long after Uncle Tanner's visit, Johanna was out weeding in the small vegetable garden Ross had started for her, when she heard the sound of horse's hooves plodding up the hill. She sat back on her heels, one hand shading her eyes, and looked to see who her visitor might be.

A stocky man in a shabby swallow-tailed coat, battered hat, and dusty boots dismounted and nodded toward Johanna. He had a scruffy red beard, prominent nose, but twinkly, bright blue eyes. He took off his hat, showing a balding head, then grinned and greeted her. "Howdy, ma'am. A good day to you and praise the Lord! Nathan Tomlin here. I'm the circuit preacher. Come to pay you a call."

Johanna got to her feet, aware of the skirt she had tucked up, the sunbonnet that had fallen back from her perspiring face. Self-consciously she wiped her dirty hands on her apron.

"Good morning." She tried to sound welcoming. Meanwhile she was hoping she had left the kitchen tidy before coming outside, and wondering what-on-earth refreshment she could offer him.

"Mighty pleased to meet you, ma'am. I knowed Ross from the time he were knee-high to a grasshopper. Growed up to

166

be a doctor!" Preacher Tomlin shook his head as if in amazement. "Eliza told me he had hisself a peart wife, now. So I come up to see if it were true," he chuckled, "and to make your acquaintance."

"Please, won't you come inside?" Johanna asked, feeling flustered. She should be better prepared for company, she told herself, even if she rarely had any. Her mother was always prepared, serving without seeming fuss a dainty tea tray, whether it was a neighbor or their minister making a pastoral call.

"Thanky kindly, ma'am." He took out a red bandanna and made a swipe at his perspiring forehead. "Mighty hot morning, and something to wet my whistle would go down mighty fine."

Johanna untied her sunbonnet, stuffed it into the deep pocket of her apron, patted her hair, then ushered the preacher into the house. Inside, a quick look around assured her it didn't look bad. The floor was swept, the place neat. She was happy she had picked a bunch of wildflowers earlier and set them into a glazed pottery jug on the table.

Johanna picked up the kettle to heat water for tea, but Reverend Tomlin held up his hand. "Don't trouble yourself, ma'am. I got a passel of visits to make this day, so I can't stay long. Just a dipper of your spring water is all I need."

"You're sure?" she asked.

"Yes ma'am, thanky kindly," he nodded.

As she took out a tumbler and started to fill it, she saw his gaze sweep the room as if looking for something. After he took the glass of water she handed him, drained it, and returned it to her, he commented, "No Bible, young lady?" His eyes were kind, if curious. "In most mountain homes, it's in a place of honor, like yonder on the mantelpiece, or at the table so's it can be read mornin' and night."

At the mild reproach in his tone, Johanna blushed. Quickly she pointed to her small leather New Testament she'd had since school days, beside her prayer book on the hutch.

Preacher Tomlin shook his head and said gently, "That ain't enuf. Not by a long shot. Gotta have the *whole* Word, read it every day! The Prophets, the Psalms, and Proverbs. Next time I ride by, I'll bring you one," he promised, then he moved toward the door. "Now I'll bid you good day. Got places to go, people to see," he laughed. "Didn't mean to admonish you, but remember, 'Who the Lord loveth, he chastiseth.' The woman is the heart of the home, you know. Ross needs to hear the Scriptures every day to give him the strength he needs in his chosen work. You need to provide that for him."

Johanna stood on the porch and watched Preacher Tomlin mount his horse, turn around, and start down the mountainside. She felt strangely sobered by his visit.

As much a surprise to *her* as it might have been to Nathan Tomlin, a verse came into her mind just then—"Be not forgetful to entertain strangers, for thereby some have entertained angels unaware." Johanna almost had to smile in astonishment. Surely *that* was from Scripture! But from whatever unknown memory source it had come, Johanna knew it was important. However, she had no idea at the time how it would affect her life.

⚜

Johanna had never been what people call "religious"—she was certainly not "pious," as Aunt Hannah was—but there was a deep core of spiritual longing that she had never been quite so aware of as she was now. Although she had attended church with her family regularly every Sunday, whatever the subject of the sermon was, it was quickly forgotten. Johanna had never thought deeply about spiritual things. Lately, however, surrounded by the natural beauty of God's creation wherever she looked, Johanna was filled with awe and reverence. There had been no channel for it, no way she'd found to express it. Ross said a perfunctory blessing over their evening meal, but he was usually so tired when he finally got home that it was short. Often he hardly got through supper before his eyelids would droop, and not long after the meal ended he would kiss her good night and go to bed, exhausted by the rigors of his day. Many nights, Johanna sat by the fire long afterward, gazing into the flickering flames until they burned into glowing embers. It was at times like this when she most felt the emptiness within.

After Preacher Tomlin's call, Johanna felt chastened. She did not know exactly what to do about it. However, a few days later, true to his promise, he stopped by and brought her a Bible.

"You're goin' to find God's very close up here in the mountains, little lady," he told her before he rode off. Johanna soon discovered that as untaught as the disheveled-looking preacher seemed, as much as he altered the King's English, there was a goodness of heart, a genuineness, that she had never encountered before.

In the Bible he gave her, there were dog-eared pages, notations in the margins, verses underlined. She began to read it daily. First, the marked chapters, out of curiosity as to what Preacher Tomlin might feel was important. Then more and more she found her own favorites. On warm afternoons, she would sit on the small porch of the cabin, in the sunshine, the Bible on her lap. Gradually some of the verses became familiar, and she began to say them softly to herself, memorize them. Quickly Psalm 121 became a favorite. "I will lift mine eyes unto the hills—From whence cometh my help? My help comes from the Lord, the maker of heaven and earth." Johanna felt she needed help badly—to adjust to the loneliness of her new life, to become a good wife to Ross, the helpmeet he needed. She loved him more than ever, and she never wanted him to be sorry he had married someone not up to the challenge of being the wife of a mountain doctor. She often recalled Aunt Hannah saying, "You can't live on love, my girl." Well, *without* love it would have been impossible.

⚘

Church was only held if Preacher Tomlin was in the neighborhood over a Sunday. The announcement that he was going to conduct a meeting would be circulated by word of mouth up and down the mountain. Ross usually brought home the news, but if there was sickness or a baby to be delivered, he could not accompany Johanna that Sunday.

The service was informal. No set ritual seemed to be observed, and it did not have a certain time that it was over. People brought their children, went up for healing prayers, commented with "amens" during Reverend Tomlin's sermons, which were apt to ramble and get diverted when his eye found someone in the congregation he wanted to address. Often he would break off in the middle of a sentence to say, "Good to see you, Sister Anna. How's your rheumatiz? Do say? Well, come up for prayer." Although this rather startled her the first time she attended, Johanna began to regard it as a real, down-to-earth way of reaching people—perhaps even the way Jesus might have done it when folks gathered around him and he talked, touched, and taught them. The hymns were sung without benefit of an organ. Someone would start and others would join in. The same verse might be sung over and over, and finally just fade away. "On Jordan's stormy banks I stand / And cast a wishful eye / To Canaan's fair and happy land / Where my possessions lie" or "O brother, it's how will you stand / And it's how you will stand on that day?" or "Sowing on the mountain / Reaping in the valley / You're going to reap just what you sow."

Johanna could not help but compare the services here with the formal services of the Hillsboro church she had always attended. There an air of solemnity reigned—the measured tones of the organ, the ritual that never deviated for that particular day of the church calendar designated by the prayer book. Here the small, frame church rang with hands clapping, feet tapping, spontaneous "hallelujahs," and joyously sung hymns. When Johanna looked around at the smiling faces, even the little children swaying to the rhythms, she thought that as different as the forms of worship were, maybe both were equally pleasing to God.

One Sunday when she and Ross had gone to church together, outside afterward Aunt Bertie had urged, "You-all come along home with us." Johanna always enjoyed being with the old lady, who she found was a fount of wisdom, humor, and good advice.

Ross went outside with Uncle Tanner to his apple press. It was soon going to be time to make cider and for Aunt Bertie to make her apple butter. The smell of biscuits baking and sausage frying crisply filled the cabin with delicious odor. "Can I do anything to help?" Johanna asked.

"No, thanky kindly, not this mawnin', but come time for me to make my apple butter, I might need some help a-stirrin'. You see, it's a daylong job. Them apples gotta be stirred every single minute. If a body don't stand right over the iron pot and keep that paddle moving, the apples'd burn and the apple butter would be plum ruined. A heap of folks ruin their apple butter by not doing so. There's nothin' worst than scorched apple butter."

Aunt Bertie went to the door and called out to Uncle Tanner and Ross to come in and eat. Coming back to the table, she said to Johanna, "Apple butter makin's not for a lazy-body or a weakly person. That's what I meant by mebbe you could come help me the day I do mine. Take turns a-stirrin."

Johanna said, "I'd be glad to, Aunt Bertie," having no idea what she had let herself in for.

Chapter Fifteen

❦

One evening when Johanna stepped out on the porch to hang up the dishpan, she called to Ross, "Come out here and see this!" She pointed to a new moon, a pale, thin crescent in the dark cobalt sky. "Have you ever seen anything so beautiful?" Standing behind her, he put his arms around her waist, bent his cheek against hers.

"Yes ma'am, many a time," he said softly. "Mountain moons are the prettiest, and I'm glad you're beginning to appreciate them."

"Oh, but I do! Did you think I wouldn't?"

"I guess I thought that come fall, you might miss all those parties, dancing, and taffy pulls." There was a hint of laughter in his tone.

"Not when I have *you* and the moon," she smiled in the darkness, snuggling against him. "It's very romantic."

He laughed. Then, stifling a yawn, he murmured, "I'm off to bed, darlin'. Must've rode a hundred miles up and down the mountain today." He kissed her cheek and went back inside. For the tiniest moment Johanna felt deserted. But she realized his days were long, arduous. He would be up before dawn, upon his horse, and on to making his calls. He needed his sleep. Still, it was so lovely out here, not a bit cold, and the moon was so beautiful. She didn't want to go back inside. But such beauty ought to be shared. It was the kind of night to be with some-one you loved, maybe quoting poetry to each other....

Johanna sighed. Suddenly she felt a little lonely. Her thoughts wandered. What were they doing at home tonight? Was Cissy getting ready to go to a party? Or were they all playing a parlor game together—snap-rattle or charades? Irrationally she wished she were there—and then, almost immediately, she knew she didn't want to be. That part of her life was over. She had what she wanted. It was just that there was a void that nothing here had quite filled for her yet. Not that Ross wasn't enough. He was everything to her. It was just that a girl needed a friend. Someone her own age. Another girl to laugh with, someone to share secrets with, someone to talk to....

Ross was completely at home here. He moved confidently where she felt so strange. She remembered how only a short time ago *he* had sometimes seemed awkward where she was so at ease. It was that very awkwardness that somehow had seemed so endearing to her, made her want to reach out to him, make him comfortable. His shyness and inarticulateness around her parents only made her love him more, made her feel protective. Her thoughts grew tender as she thought of her husband. His gentleness undergirded his strength and skill. He'd gone away to learn "doctoring," but he still belonged— he'd come home to heal and help them. She had seen the looks of awed affection that followed him, the respect in the eyes of people as they greeted him with "Howdy, Doc."

Now it was *she* who was in a different environment. What was that Scripture verse? Hadn't the captive Israelites com-plained that they couldn't sing in a strange land? That's how she felt sometimes, "a stranger in a strange land." She wanted so much to be liked, to be understood. Would it ever happen?

174

One sunny morning early in September, Johanna had taken her mug of coffee out onto the porch steps to drink in the sunshine. Ross had left before daybreak and had not wakened her. Since he usually returned at night exhausted from the long, work-filled days, mornings before he set out were the only real time they had together. Johanna cherished that time, and today they had missed that. A long day alone stretched out before her.

Suddenly a piercing scream caused her to jump up, spilling her coffee. She looked around to see where it was coming from. Then, stumbling out of the brush, Ross's sister Sue came running. "Oh ma'am, ma'am, Miss Johanna, ma'am!" she called when she saw Johanna.

Johanna set down the mug and hurried to meet the little girl rushing breathlessly toward her. "Oh ma'am, it's Katie. She's—" Sue stopped a few feet from Johanna, panting. "She's—she's—oh, please come help her!"

"Of course! Where is she? What's happened?"

Sue was sobbing. Her small, freckled face was flushed, tear-stained. She gulped and tugged at Johanna's apron. "Please, ma'am, come. Up yonder!" She pointed to the craggy hillside above their cabin. "We wuz out pickin' berries and started to crost the creek, over a log that had fell, and I got to the other side, but Katie, she—she got skeered, I reckon. Anyhow, she couldn't move no more. She jest sit down and started a-yellin'. I tried to git her to come. But she jest kept lookin' down at the water rushin' over the rocks, and—" She halted, gulping. "She cain't move!"

All the time Sue was talking, she was pulling Johanna by the hand up the hill. It was steep and rocky, and Johanna's own breath was coming fast and hard. From what Sue told her, she had a mental picture of what had happened. But she had no idea how bad the situation was until they reached the top. There she saw how high above the rushing mountain stream was the log where the little girl was stranded.

She had stopped screaming and was clinging to the rough bark of the log with both thin little hands. Johanna saw that the child's eyes were glazed and staring, a look of stark terror on her face.

"Why in the world did you try to cross there?" she asked Sue in a hushed voice. The child shook her head. "Dint know it was so high, I reckon. 'Til I got on it—then I knew I had to go on, but Katie got skeered and couldn't."

Sue, older by two years and having long, skinny legs, had probably made it across on sheer pluck. The younger, smaller Katie probably made the mistake of looking down, got dizzy, and panicked.

However it had come about, the situation was dangerous. Johanna tried to figure out how deep the water was, how she could get to the child to rescue her. First she had to calm her so she wouldn't get more frightened, lose her grip on the log, and fall off. The current was fast, the stream full of huge rocks. If Katie fell, she could hit her head on one of the jutting stones or be swept away in the swift waters. Johanna knew she had to act quickly.

"Don't worry, Katie," she called. "Don't be afraid. I'm coming to get you!"

She sat down on a large rock on the bank and untied her boots. She'd have to wade out to the middle, reach up, grab the child, and pull her into her arms, then carry her to shore. She had to do it fast, before Katie got dizzy, lost consciousness, tumbled into the water. From things Ross had told her, Johanna knew most accidents happened because people panicked.

Johanna's heart thundered. Her hands trembled as she loosened her laces, pulled off her boots and stockings. Standing up, she lifted her skirt, unbuttoned the waistband of her petticoat. Letting it drop, she stepped out of it and tossed it aside. Then, gathering up her skirt, she tucked it into her belt. The less she had on, the less chance that the water would soak it, weigh her down, drag her into the current.

Behind her she heard Sue sobbing, but she had no time to stop and comfort her. She had to save her little sister.

The first shock of the icy water on her bare feet made Johanna gasp. She would have to move quickly so that its freezing temperature would not hamper her progress. Hard rocks under the tender soles of her feet made her steps torturous. The cold water rose to her ankles and calves as she plunged forward. It was deeper than she thought and the current stronger. What if the water was even deeper in the middle, at the point on the log where Katie sat motionless, dazed with fear? Now she felt the water rushing around her knees, the edge of her turned-up skirt. Clenching her teeth against the onslaught of icy water, she pushed on. Nearing the fallen log, she almost lost her footing in a sudden drop of the riverbed.

"I'm coming, Katie. Hold on, honey," she called through her chattering teeth.

The water had reached her thighs, and she could feel the wet cloth of her soaked pantaloons chillingly against her skin. The rush of the swirling water made it hard to get a foothold. She stretched out one hand. The scaly bark scraped her palms. Gripping it desperately, she inched her way closer to Katie. *Please, God, help!* she prayed. At last she was just below Katie. In a voice that shook, she said, "Now, Katie, I want you to let go of the log, lean down, and put your arms around my neck. I'll hold you—just come slow and easy." Johanna put up one arm toward the child, holding on to the side of the log with her other hand to steady herself against the current.

"I cain't, I'm skeered!" wailed the little girl weakly.

"Yes, you can, Katie. Come on, honey. I'm here and I'll catch hold of you. Just let go."

Every minute the child hesitated was agony. Johanna knew she had to get through to the child, who was now numb with cold and fear. Time was of importance, the situation desperate. Johanna was losing the feeling in her legs from the freezing water, and she still had to make it back to the bank safely with Katie.

"Katie, come on!" she cried.

All of a sudden she felt the child throw herself forward onto her. The thin little arms went around her neck in a choking hold. Katie's trembling little body pressing against her nearly unbalanced Johanna. *Dear God, help us!* Words of Scripture Johanna didn't even know she'd memorized came pouring into her mind.

I have called thee by name, thou art mine. When thou passeth through the waters, I will be with thee and through the rivers, they shall not overflow thee.

Struggling with the added weight of Katie, Johanna turned, the strong current pressing against her, and made her way painfully back across the sharp stones, through the cold, rushing water, toward the bank. Finally, gasping for breath, her feet cut and bruised, she stumbled onto the grassy bank and fell on her knees, still holding the shivering Katie.

Sue hunkered down beside them, alternately sobbing and sniffling, "Oh, thanky, ma'am. Thanky." Then Katie began to sob. Johanna felt salty tears roll down her own cheeks. Then she started laughing. Both girls looked at her, startled, then gradually they too began to laugh. Johanna knew it was mostly hysterical. But it didn't matter. She'd rescued Katie. That was the important thing.

At last, breathless from laughter, she wiped her tears away, scrambled up. Her bare feet were beginning to have some feeling again. In fact, they felt hot and tingling. She picked up her stockings and boots, slung them over one shoulder by the laces, and threw her discarded petticoat over one arm. "Come on," she said, reaching out a hand to each of the girls. "Let's go back to my place and get dry and have a treat."

Johanna thought of the tin of powdered chocolate her mother had sent in her last box from Hillsboro. She guessed maybe Sue and Katie had never tasted it. She'd make some hot cocoa and wrap Katie up in a quilt, and they'd all feel better.

Without even realizing it at the moment, Johanna had crossed over whatever line Ross's family had placed between them. By coming to Katie's aid that day, she had definitely won over Sue and Katie. The very next day, Eliza came up the mountain to thank her personally, after hearing the children's story of Johanna's rescue. She brought a rhubarb-and-berry pie and shyly told Johanna that if she wanted the recipe, it was one of Ross's favorites. On a deeper level, something even more significant happened to Johanna after the day she rescued Katie. She realized that the Bible reading she had been doing lately had taken hold. She was not even sure from which chapter, what verse, she had drawn that passage she'd remembered. In the midst of panic but still with faith that she would be heard, Johanna had cried out for help. "I called on the Lord in distress, the Lord answered me and set me in a broad place." As Preacher Tomlin told her, "He does what he promises to do."

Chapter Sixteen

❧❧

*T*he whisper of autumn fell like a soft melody on the mountains. The air had a crispness in the mornings, a tart sweetness like a ripe apple in the afternoons. The hills were russet touched with gold, asters blue-gray swayed in the wind, goldenrod nodded on the banks of the winding road up to their cabin. In the October mornings, mist veiled blue hills, frost sparkled on the sumac in roadside thickets, hickory log smoke curled up from stone chimneys within the log cabins that hopscotched down into the valley, as breakfast fires burned on hearths inside.

Aunt Bertie sent word that she was going to start her apple butter. "You're to be there at dawn," Ross told her, his mouth twitching slightly, his eyes mischievous. Johanna's eyes widened. "Uncle Tanner gets the fire going before the sun peeks over the ridge. She's spent the last two days peeling and paring the choicest apples, and she'll be ready to start by sunup."

By the time Johanna ate a hasty breakfast and made her way down the hillside to their cottage, Aunt Bertie stood with a wooden paddle, stirring the boiling apples in a big black iron pot over the hickory fire. Uncle Tanner was sitting on a bench nearby, whittling. They both greeted Johanna cheerily.

"You come in good time, girly. My arm gets wore out a lot sooner than it used to, so I'd take it kindly if you'd spell me once in a while."

"Of course, Aunt Bertie. Now?"

"Not yet. Look at this and I'll show you what's next." Aunt Bertie motioned her closer with her free hand. Johanna bent and looked into the pot, where the apples were boiling, bobbing and making little popping sounds. "I've poured in a jug of Tanner's fresh cider, and now it's 'bout time to put in sugar and spices," Aunt Bertie said. "You can take over, Johanna, whilst I add it in."

Johanna had never imagined it would be such hard work. After Aunt Bertie had poured in the sugar and spices, Johanna took the paddle and slowly began stirring. The sun climbed into the sky, time passed, and still the apples kept boiling, puffing and popping like soap bubbles. Wood smoke got in her eyes, and she shifted arms for stirring, wiping her forehead with the back of her arm and pushing back her perspiration-dampened hair. Still, it seemed, the apples weren't ready.

Uncle Tanner kept feeding the fire, and he insisted on taking a turn stirring, because as the liquid got redder and stickier, the stirring got harder and harder. When Aunt Bertie protested, he gently but firmly told her, "Now, Bertie, don't fuss. I do my share of eatin' your apple butter—'tis only fair I pitch in on the makin'."

Johanna knew it was his way of giving Aunt Bertie a needed rest. She herself found the stirring very tiring and wondered when this famous apple butter would ever be called "done and ready."

She soon offered to do her spell of stirring, and it was hard going. The wind rose and a cool breeze blew on Johanna's red, hot face. It seemed an age before Aunt Bertie came to her side, peered into the pot, took the paddle from

Johanna, then said to Uncle Tanner, "It's done. Lookahere, it's so nice and thick, you could cut it with a knife. Come on, you can move the pot offen the fire."

Aunt Bertie gave a couple of extra stirs, then lifted the paddle, tapped it on the side of the iron kettle. Holding it in one hand, she swiped some of the apple butter onto her finger and stuck her finger in her mouth. Her eyes brightened as she tasted it, then smacked her lips. "Umhmmm!"

"How is it?" Johanna asked eagerly, feeling she'd had some small part in making it.

"It'll do," was all Aunt Bertie said. "Right tasty. Not a bit burned. Try some?"

When Johanna got a sample, she knew that Aunt Bertie's comment was a vast understatement. It was absolutely the most delicious apple butter she had ever tasted.

⚜

A week later Uncle Tanner stopped one day to bring Johanna several jars of the product. Johanna felt a particular pride to have helped make it. "Won't you come in?" she invited.

"No, thanky kindly, but can't stay. Too much to do. Firewood to cut and store. Winter's a-comin', rhododendron leaves is rolled up tight as a tobacco leaf. Soon it'll be November, and the frost in the mornin's means cold weather ahead," he predicted. Then he went on his way.

Johanna stood on the porch for a moment, her arms holding a basket filled with Aunt Bertie's bounty, and watched gray squirrels rattle in the leaves under the hickory trees, stopping every once in a while, shoe button black eyes darting back and forth, bushy tails quivering, then scrambling up the oak tree. Shivering, Johanna went back into the house. Uncle Tanner was probably right, she thought. October was fast slipping away, and now in the mornings, the wind rustled the tree branches and whistled down the chimneys.

Very early the next morning, she was awakened to the delicate patter of rain. She raised herself on her elbow and sleepily looked out the window. She saw silver needles of rain falling steadily. She cuddled back down into the quilts and went back to sleep. By the time she woke up for the second time, it was raining hard. Afterward, she wondered if she had experienced some kind of premonition. For some reason, she felt reluctant to get up and start her day. It was as if somehow it held something to dread. However, it was a fleeting feeling, and she soon was out in the kitchen, where Ross had a blazing fire going and had made coffee. As he poured her a cup, he said, "I'm riding down to Hayfork to the store to see if the medicine I ordered has come in yet."

"On such a bad morning?" Johanna asked with a worried frown.

"Ain't goin' git no better," he told her, grinning. Sometimes when he was teasing her, Ross deliberately lapsed into "mountain speech."

After he left, Johanna got busy with her chores. But to her surprise, only a short time later she heard the sound of his horse outside. She hadn't expected him home before late afternoon. Puzzled, she turned from the stove just as he came in the door. He was dripping rain from the brim of his wide hat, the shoulders of his slicker. There was something about his face that should have warned her. But it didn't. At least, not until he brought a letter out from under his coat, held it out to her. "It's from your mother—addressed to both of us. So I opened it, and—"

Somehow Johanna knew even before he spoke the words.

"I'm sorry, darlin'—" Ross's voice wavered slightly. "Your father is dead."

Unable to speak, Johanna moved stiffly toward him, then went into his arms, closing her eyes against the awfulness of those words, leaning against him.

"No," she murmured. "No. *No!*"

They stood holding each other wordlessly for a long time. Then Johanna looked up at him, asking numbly. "How? What happened?"

His expression was one of infinite tenderness, pity. "He was only ill a few days. They didn't think it was serious, or they would have sent for you—he went very quickly."

Before he could say anything more, Johanna burst into tears. She gasped, "It's my fault. I caused it. If I hadn't disobeyed ... If I hadn't left home ..."

"Oh Johanna, you mustn't say that. Don't. Don't blame yourself." His voice broke and he just held her tighter, unable to find anything to stop the pain she was inflicting upon herself. It was a pain she had not known nor understood nor even knew existed, one she did not think she could endure.

Throughout that long, cold night, Ross held her. Outside, the wind howled around the house, moaned through the tall pine trees, sighing like the keening sound of mourners. Johanna shivered and he drew her closer. She felt the deeply buried aching, the longing, rise within her. *I want to go home. I must go home.* She lay awake through most of the night, unable to stop thinking. When the gray light of dawn crept through the windows, she eased herself out of bed, crouched in front of the hearth, where the one remaining log left burning when they had gone to bed glowed red, making a whispering sound. She felt cold clear through. Her hands were icy, and she held them out to the fire to try to warm them. Johanna's eyes burned watching it and filled up with tears again.

She heard movement behind her, and Ross was beside her, holding her in his arms, rocking her like a baby while she sobbed on his shoulder. After a while he carried her back to bed.

When she awoke, Ross's place beside her was empty. She heard him moving around in the kitchen. A fire already blazed in the hearth, and she heard the clink of pottery, smelled the scent of boiling chicory. After a while he came to the foot of the bed. "I let you sleep. You needed the rest. But I'm taking you to your mother's today. You must see your father buried."

The rain had stopped and there was the smell of wood smoke in the air, which had a touch of frost. They rode down to his mother's house to tell them they would be gone to Hillsboro for the funeral, to spend some time with Johanna's grieving family.

While Ross explained, Johanna sat huddled on a bench and stared into the fire, her mind pain-paralyzed. She was unable to speak. Eliza's voice was gentle as she said, "Of course you must go. Your ma needs you."

Johanna did not answer. She started to say something, tell the truth. Her mother did not need her. Her mother had never *needed* her. The truth was, *she* needed her mother. Or at least everything her mother symbolized—comfort, safety, childhood.

She felt Ross's tender gaze upon her, saw him exchange a glance with his mother, a bid for understanding. Johanna made an effort to speak very politely. She longed for sympathy but could not seem to respond to it. Eliza poured a mug of tea and placed it in Johanna's numb hands. "Drink this afore you go. It'll help," she said softly.

During the long, jogging journey along the trail that zigzagged down the mountain, Johanna was racked by grief and burdened by guilt. Was her stubborn, rebellious behavior in some way the cause of her father's death? Her mother had often mentioned in her letters,

> *Your father is often downcast and without his old cheerfulness. He misses you, Johanna, always having relied on your special companionship.*

Could such a thing have brought on a depression leading to illness? It didn't seem possible—her father had always been hearty and vigorous.

I deserve everything I'm feeling, Johanna thought bleakly. But even in her misery, she was reminded of Preacher Tomlin's exhortation—"Condemnation is not from God. In Christ Jesus there is no condemnation." She wanted to believe that. Why then did she *feel* so guilty? But could God forgive her if she couldn't forgive herself?

At last they came into Hillsboro. It was raining here as well. The roads were wet. On walkways, sodden clumps of leaves were piled under the dripping branches of the bare trees. As they rode through the familiar streets, past the familiar houses, out the familiar road that led to Holly Grove, Johanna felt as if she had been gone forever, much longer than five months.

On their way down the mountain, several times Ross had drawn his horse up beside Johanna's, asked anxiously if she wanted to stop, take a short rest. She had shaken her head. Her only thought was to get home.

At last they saw the road, fenced with split rails, that led up to Holly Grove. In the curving driveway were several buggies and one carriage drawn up in front of the house. At first that startled Johanna, until she realized that of course the aunties would all have gathered to do all the things caring relatives did in times of sorrow. She could just

imagine them flocking there in proper mourning attire, like
so many blackbirds.

Drenched in spite of her wool cape, and saddle weary,
Johanna put her hands on Ross's shoulders and let him lift
her down.

"I'll see to the horses later. I want to get you inside," he
told her. His arm supported her as they went up the steps of
the porch. Before they reached the top, the front door flew
open, and Elly flung herself into Johanna's arms.

"Oh Johanna, you've come! I *knew* you would! I've been
waiting and waiting. Oh Johanna, poor Papa—" And she
burst into heartbroken sobs.

Johanna leaned over her, smoothing back the silken curls
from the small, tear-streaked face, murmuring comfortingly,
"Hush, sweetie. I know, I know."

"Do come in. You're chilling the whole house," spoke
another voice with a trace of irritation. Johanna looked up
and over Elly's head and saw her other sister standing there,
holding the door open.

Cissy looked different, more grown-up even than a few
months ago. She was dressed in black taffeta, her hair held
back by a wide black velvet band. However, it was her expression that puzzled Johanna. She had a fleeting impression that
her sister was not all happy to see her. Quickly Johanna dismissed that thought. She was probably wrong. Her cool attitude must be Cissy's way of handling her grief, Johanna
thought, and she went forward to embrace her.

"Where's Mama?" Johanna asked. The words were no
sooner spoken than Aunt Honey and Aunt Cady appeared
from the parlor, followed by Aunt Hannah. Immediately
Johanna was smothered with hugs and sympathy. Ross was
taken in hand and led to the dining room, where, as Johanna
knew it would be, food was spread out in abundance.

"I must go see Mama." Johanna extricated herself from the lilac-scented embrace of Aunt Cady, who was handsome in an elegant mourning ensemble.

"Of course you must, my dear. I'll bring up some tea for both of you," Aunt Honey promised, and Johanna shed her hooded cloak and went swiftly up the stairway.

~⚹~

Johanna opened her parents' bedroom door quietly. Her mother, dressed in a wide-skirted black dress, was sitting in the wing chair by the window, her chin resting on one graceful hand. At the sound of the door opening, she turned her head. In that brief moment, Johanna thought again how beautiful her mother was. Her dark hair rose from a distinct widow's peak. When she saw who was standing there, Rebecca gave a little cry, "Oh, my dear!" and held out her arms, and Johanna went into them.

For a long moment, mother and daughter clung to each other. Rebecca was the first to let go. Drawing back, she regarded Johanna thoughtfully.

"He loved you so, Johanna . . . so very much." In those few softly spoken words, Johanna sensed something else. A reprimand, an accusation, a judgment? Without actually saying so, her mother had deepened Johanna's own feelings of guilt. It was almost as if she had said, "If you hadn't gone away, this would not have happened."

There was no time to think that through, because Rebecca gestured for her to sit on the tufted hassock beside her chair.

Rebecca was unusually pale yet composed and as exquisitely groomed as always, onyx pendant earrings set in silver filigree swung from her ears, and an onyx cameo was pinned at the throat.

"Oh Mama, I'm so—"Johanna's voice broke. Her sense of loss and sadness was too deep for her to express. Her mother patted her hand. "I know, dear, I know."

"How did it happen? Was he sick long? Was it a heart attack, what?"

Still holding her daughter's hand, Rebecca began, "He came home one evening, chilled. There had been a cold drizzle all day that turned to a freezing rain. He was thoroughly soaked, not having taken an umbrella with him. He refused my suggestion to change and get to bed immediately to ward off any possible effect. He wouldn't hear of it—just took off his boots and had dinner with us as usual. But the next morning—" Rebecca shook her head, her eyes moistened. "He awoke with a rasping cough, pains in his chest. I sent for Dr. Murrison, but he was out delivering a baby in the countryside and did not come calling until that evening—"

Johanna clasped her mother's hand. "Oh Mama, how dreadful—did he suffer much?"

"You know your father, Johanna, how he always makes—*made*," she corrected herself, "light of any physical problem he might have—" She paused. "I don't think any of us realized how serious it was. He did agree to stay in bed that day, however. He asked me to bring his writing tray, some papers from his desk. Although I protested he should rest, he insisted. He worked for some time, then said he felt tired and would sleep for a while. But by the time Alec—Dr. Murrison—came by, he was already far gone—the congestion had gone into his lungs, and he had a high fever. Dr. Murrison thought he might be able to fight it." Rebecca sighed. "But he never really rallied. Spoke only a few mostly incoherent words, then—slipped into unconsciousness."

"Oh, Mama." Johanna felt as if her heart were breaking. Tears rolled unchecked down her face. She put her head on her mother's lap, felt Rebecca's hand laid lightly upon it.

After a few minutes, Rebecca said, "I must go downstairs now, Johanna. People will be calling. People have been kindness itself, and I must receive them. That's what your father would want me to do." With a rustle of taffeta, she rose to her feet, then said to Johanna, "You don't have to come, not just yet, anyway. Tomorrow after the funeral, there will be those who will want to see you." Rebecca moved over to her bureau, peered briefly into the mirror to check her appearance. She lifted one of the two boxes on top, took out an envelope, then turned and held it out to Johanna. "He wrote you a letter."

Johanna got up and walked over to where her mother stood, and took it. Her mother was watching her with appraising eyes, the ones Johanna had always felt could see and judge beneath the outer shell of a person. Rebecca seemed to hesitate, as if to wait for Johanna to open it and read it while she was there. But Johanna simply stared down at the familiar handwriting, the classic swirls and loops of her father's Spenserian script. Her finger traced the wax seal imprinted with the familiar crest of her father's signet ring. Torn by wanting to read it and somehow dreading what her father might have written to her, Johanna hesitated. Rebecca waited only a few seconds before going out the door, saying over her shoulder, "We've put you and Ross in Elly's room, Johanna. Cissy took yours when you left, and Elly can sleep with her while you're here."

Those words sent a chill through Johanna that her mother surely could not have guessed or intended. Although Johanna had relinquished her privileged place as the oldest daughter at home to Cissy before she left, the fact that Cissy had taken over the room *she'd* had since she was born made Johanna realize that things had truly changed in this regard.

That explained the enigmatic look on her sister's face upon their arrival. It was the unspoken fear that by Johanna's coming, she might be displaced. The old instinctive rivalry. Johanna smiled ruefully. It was *she* who felt displaced.

Leaving her mother's room, she walked down the hall and opened the door to Elly's room, went in, and closed the door. She went over to the window, then with hands that shook broke the seal on her father's letter and drew out two folded pages and began to read.

My Dearest Daughter . . .

In the months that were to come, Johanna would read that letter again and again. Its pages became stained from the tears that fell as she read what her father had written. In these lines, Johanna discovered the parent's heart she had never known. His love, his dreams for her, his hopes, his disappointment, his loneliness for her. In spite of what had happened to cause their estrangement, her willful insistence on making her own marriage choice, his love for her had never changed. Now that it was too late, she understood it was that very love that had seemed so strangely cruel to her. This letter, written when he was so ill, perhaps when he knew it was a mortal illness, was undertaken to release her from any remorse or guilt. It was his last will and testament to a beloved child.

On the day of Tennant Shelby's funeral, the sky was overcast. In the church, Johanna sat in the family pew, beside Rebecca on one side, her sisters on the other. Behind them were all the aunties, their husbands. Johanna's eyes, swollen from all her weeping, were hidden behind the veil that one of the aunties had hastily sewn onto her bonnet the night before because Johanna had been too shocked to come prepared with the mourning attire expected to be worn by members of the family. Tears blurred the print as Johanna tried to read the words of the service in her prayer book.

The church was filled. Tennant Shelby had been an outstanding man of the community, revered for his integrity. However, none had known him as Johanna remembered—a kind, gentle, loving father. Why had she not appreciated him more? She had taken his sheltering care, his indulgence, his concern, for granted. She had stubbornly resisted his counsel, his advice. Johanna thought of the times she had turned away as he had tried to embrace her during those awful months when he had opposed her marriage.

If only she could go back—do it over. Not that she would have loved or wanted Ross less, but she could have been less selfish, tried to see her parents' side more.

Winter sunlight shone weakly through the arched window behind the altar but soon faded, leaving the interior of the church gray, full of shadows. Johanna shuddered. Elly, sitting beside her, glanced at her worriedly and slipped a small hand, wearing a black kid glove, into hers. Johanna gave it a reassuring squeeze. She must be strong and brave for Elly's sake, for Cissy's too. At least *she* had Ross, while her sisters were left without a wise father, a protector.

The service ended and Johanna, with the rest of the family, followed the pallbearers carrying the casket out of the church to the adjoining cemetery.

The aunties were all appropriately draped in crepe veiling, which flowed from their bonnets in the November wind. With their caped shoulders and black-gloved, folded hands, they looked like a flock of black-winged sparrows hovering around their cousin, the widow.

Johanna tried to concentrate on the minister's words.

The minister began reading the final words over the casket before it was lowered into the newly dug grave. "In the
midst of life, we are in death. . . ."

Standing among the granite crosses, the engraved head-
stones, the flowers and wreaths, Johanna knew a sense of
intolerable loss, of terrible aloneness. Frightened, she glanced
around and still felt apart.

She looked over at Ross for reassurance. But his head was
bowed. She felt separated from him too. *I am a stranger here.
Among my own people.* Involuntarily she shivered. She must
pay attention. She clenched her hands. She felt as if she
might faint and stiffened her body, willing herself not to.

The minister's words came again, intoning the words of
commitment, consigning her father to his heavenly rest.
"Most merciful Father, who has been pleased to take unto
thyself the soul of this thy servant, grant unto us who are still
in our pilgrimage and who walk as yet by faith . . ."

Something in Johanna's heart refused to be comforted.
Inside she was wrenched with a terrible need for her father.
She didn't want to let him go. *Not yet. I don't want you to go.
I have so much I want to say to you, so much to explain. . . .*

It began to sprinkle, large drops falling slowly. Umbrellas
opened up. The mourners huddled closer together, and the
minister's voice picked up speed.

"Thou knowest, Lord, the secrets of our hearts. Shut not
thy ears to our prayers but spare us, Lord by thy gracious
mercy. . . ." He hurried to the last part of the service. "The
Lord be with thy spirit. And so we say together, Our Father,
who art in heaven, hallowed be . . ."

The assembled mourners joined in the Lord's Prayer as
the rain began to come harder, the wind stronger. Johanna's
throat thickened and she could not get past the hard, painful

lump lodged there, to repeat the familiar words. "Forgive us our debts . . ."

Back at the house, the aunties bustled about, setting out the dishes, the cakes, pies, and other things they'd baked and brought for the funereal feast. *Feast!* What a name, Johanna thought bleakly. She sipped the tea Auntie Bee urged upon her, wrapping her icy hands around the cup, trying to warm them. She accepted condolences from family friends, nodding, murmuring thanks. All she could think of was her father out in the graveyard in the rain.

The afternoon lengthened painfully. Toward dusk, the last of the guests began to straggle to the door with last-minute expressions of sympathy, platitudes of solace, offering to provide whatever the grief-stricken family needed. Soon the aunties began gathering up their assorted dishes and containers, promising to replenish or refill them before they too departed.

Ross came to Johanna and led her into the small alcove off the dining room.

"I'm going over to Dr. Murrison's tonight, Johanna. I've already spoken to him. As a matter of fact, he came over to me at the funeral, asked me to come. I'll have to leave early in the morning to go back, anyway. As you know, I've got a lot of sick folks in Millscreek that need me. If I'm over there with him, my leaving won't disturb your family." His eyes showed concern. "You look exhausted, Johanna. You *all* need your rest. It's been a long, sorrowful day. But I think you'll be a real comfort to your mother if you stay here a few days. Whenever you feel you can leave her, just send me word and I'll come for you."

Johanna was a little taken aback by Ross's decision. Truthfully, she had made no plans. She had not even thought as far as the next day. However, she could see that his was the wisest course. Perhaps he was right—maybe her mother did need her, more than she had thought.

He held her for a long time, kissing her gently before he left. When she realized he was actually going, she felt suddenly bereft. Perhaps, in a part of her mind, she had thought how comforting it would be to be in his arms tonight— where he would kiss away the tears that all day had been near the surface.

But he was already putting on his coat, slinging a knitted scarf around his neck, reaching for his hat. It was too late to ask him to stay.

However, that evening her mother, accompanied by Cissy, retired earlier than usual, and Johanna found herself alone. Elly, worn out, had gone to bed before the company had all departed. In Elly's borrowed bedroom, Johanna found she was restless, too upset to sleep. She wished she had not agreed to Ross's leaving. She missed the feel of his arms enfolding her, comforting her.

The events of the day, and her father's letter, had been emotionally wrenching. Before long, Johanna began weeping uncontrollably, trying to smother the sound in her pillows.

The squeaking of the bedroom door startled her. She sat up in time to see a small, white-gowned figure, like a little ghost, slip into the room and with a rush of bare feet run to the bedside and jump up.

"Oh Johanna, I woke up and thought about Papa. I couldn't go back to sleep. Can I come in with you?" Elly whispered urgently.

"Of course!" Johanna said and threw back the covers. The two sisters clasped each other and, close in each other's arms, wept together for all they had loved and lost.

❧

One day followed the next. Soon Johanna realized she had been at Holly Grove for over a week and had not sent word to Ross. The flow of visitors continued, because Tennant Shelby, a man of wide acquaintance, had been well liked, respected, held in affectionate regard by a number of people. Johanna took it upon herself to act as hostess in her mother's place, greeting guests. This became sometimes tedious and stressful, given her own emotions, yet Johanna considered it a labor of love, deeply appreciating the esteem in which her father had been held. In spite of their shared grief, Cissy's attitude toward her remained guarded. Employing newly gained sensitivity and tact, Johanna tried to ease the tension between them, to show her in small ways that her coming home did not threaten her sister's place. Gradually Cissy softened. The two older daughters were able to divide the many varied tasks in the wake of Tennant Shelby's death.

There was much to be done. There were thank-you notes to write for all the gifts of flowers, food, and visits from neighbors, friends, and acquaintances. Their father's office had to be closed with all the moving of books, papers, files. There were meetings with his law partners, arrangements to be made, and matters to be decided concerning disposition of property.

With all this to deal with, two more weeks passed before Johanna realized that she had moved back into the rhythm of life at Holly Grove. Her life with Ross in the mountains seemed to have faded into the background.

It wasn't until she had been there four weeks that the full truth of this came to her. Dr. Murrison was called to the house because of Elly's earache. Johanna had been taking care of her sister and was in the bedroom with her when Dr. Murrison arrived. He looked surprised to see her. "You *still* here, Johanna?"

After he finished examining Elly, he left a small bottle of oil on the bedside table with instructions on how to administer it. "Heat it slightly and put two or three drops in each ear every few hours." Then he turned to Johanna and gave her a sharp look. "So when will Ross be down to fetch you back *home?*"

The blunt question and almost accusatory tone startled Johanna. Her cheeks got hot under his appraising glance. Busying herself smoothing Elly's coverlet, she replied defensively, "Soon, I suppose. Right now I'm needed here."

"Oh? Is that right?" was the doctor's only comment as he repacked his medical bag, patted Elly's hand, saying, "You'll soon be up and around, young lady. Won't need any more of your sister's fussin' and coddlin', I expect." With another glance at Johanna, he departed, leaving her indignant and confused.

Johanna spent another few minutes plumping Elly's pillow, then went to refill her water jug. Why had she let Dr. Murrison's remarks upset her? Wasn't she doing what she *should* be doing? Didn't her mother *need* her during this terrible time? After all, her mother had lost the husband on whom she had depended for over twenty years. Didn't Dr. Murrison realize she needed support, comforting? Maybe he was just not sensitive to such things.

Later, still bothered by what the crusty old physician had implied, Johanna knocked at her mother's door. At her answering call, she went in.

"Can I do anything for you, Mama?"

Rebecca was seated at her escritoire, writing replies to the many condolence notes she had received. She looked up at her daughter's entrance. For a moment, she studied the slim figure standing in the doorway. Johanna seemed fragile, vulnerable somehow—Rebecca had not missed her roughened hands. And she was thin, too thin. What had she been doing all these months to bring about these physical changes?

Rebecca bit her lower lip. Was her new life as the wife of a hill doctor in that primitive backwoods community too hard for her? Johanna was still lovely looking, the prettiest of all her daughters. But youth and beauty were fleeting, and a life of deprivation and hard physical work could age a woman too soon. Rebecca curbed her inclination to say something— something she might regret, something that might bring pain or, worse, remorse. Besides, there were other things she had noticed, all to the good—a patience, a gentleness, a genuine sweetness in Johanna that had not been there before.

Life teaches hard lessons. Evidently, Johanna was learning this. Rebecca sighed, then answered Johanna's question. "Nothing, thank you, dear." She went back to the note she was writing.

Johanna remained standing there. "You're sure?"

Rebecca signed her name to one of the black-edged note cards she was writing. "Quite sure."

Johanna still hesitated.

Rebecca looked up again. There was something in Johanna's expression that Rebecca had never seen there before. An uncertainty—a pleading in her eyes. Ever since she had returned to Holly Grove, there had been something about Johanna that puzzled Rebecca. It was utterly unlike Johanna. She had been at Rebecca's beck and call, interpreting a gesture, a glance, a word, anticipating her slightest wish, volunteering to fetch a shawl, a footstool, seeking to please, anxious to help.

"Wouldn't you like a cup of tea?"

All at once Rebecca understood. Johanna was "doing penance" for what she perceived was her guilt. Somehow she blamed herself for her father's death. As if her being here would have changed anything!

Rebecca knew in her soul that she had often been jealous of Tennant's closeness to Johanna. She had sometimes been stricter, perhaps, to counteract his indulgence.

Things had always come so easily to Johanna—love, popularity, happiness. Rebecca had told herself she didn't want her to be spoiled. But was it more than that? Had she wanted the intimacy Johanna shared with her father for herself?

With sudden clarity, she saw that it was possible for her to have what she had always longed for from her oldest daughter—closeness, companionship, dependency even. In this moment, Rebecca knew it was in her power to bind Johanna to her more closely than she had ever been with her father. It would be easy, because Johanna wanted it, too. She could keep Johanna here, keep her from returning to where she had never wanted her to go in the first place. It would be so easy—*too* easy.

Then came an image of the tall, young, awkward man who loved her daughter. In her mind, Rebecca saw his compassionate expression, his thoughtful eyes, the way he looked at Johanna with unselfish love.

Pain slashed Rebecca's heart. That kind of love was no longer *hers,* but it was Johanna's. And she could not rob her of it. Johanna was a married woman, with duties that took precedence over any need her mother might have. Johanna must be made to see that. Johanna must go home to a husband who loved her, missed her, longed for her, wanted her *home.* The home he had made for her, the home that was theirs to live in together! It would be dreadfully wrong of Rebecca to delay Johanna any longer here at Holly Grove.

"Mama?" Johanna ventured hopefully. "Isn't there *anything* I can do for you?"

"No, dear, nothing," Rebecca said firmly and turned away from the eagerness in Johanna's eyes, back to her correspondence.

"Don't you need help with your notes?" Johanna persisted.

"I'm almost finished." Rebecca tapped the pile of black-rimmed envelopes with one finger. "Besides, Cissy can help me if there are any more."

Her mother's tone was definite. Of course Cissy was here to help her with anything that might come up, Johanna thought. Why hadn't she realized that? Johanna went out of the room, closing the door quietly behind her.

~✷~

At the click of the door being shut, Rebecca's hand clenched compulsively and a blob of ink dropped from the point of her quill pen onto the neatly written note. With a stifled exclamation of annoyance, she crumpled it up and tossed it into the wastebasket by the desk.

Rebecca knew she had hurt Johanna. However, she had deliberately sent her away. She also knew that when she was gone, she would miss her daughter dreadfully. Even with Cissy and Elly still at home, Rebecca knew she would be alone in a way she had never been before. Rebecca winced, placing her fists against her eyes.

Johanna was the child of her heart, the way the others were not. However, she had done the right thing—she had "freed" Johanna. A mother's sacrifices never end.

~✷~

Outside her mother's closed door, Johanna stood for a few minutes. Slowly the myth of her mother's need for her dissolved. The truth of her mother's self-sufficiency was obvious. Rebecca Shelby had not been prostrated, become unable to function, or fallen into a melancholic depression with her husband's death. She did not need Johanna here any longer. The household at Holly Grove hummed along as it always did, even without Tennant Shelby. Especially, it did not need Johanna to see that things ran properly.

The truth was, she had stayed longer than necessary, deceiving herself into believing that she was needed. The truth was that *she* had been the needy one. She had welcomed sliding back into the ease and comfort of her old home. Meals appeared on the table without her lifting a finger, hot water was brought upstairs for her morning bath by Bessie, fresh sheets appeared on her bed, and clean towels were there like magic when she needed them.

Why had she not seen what was happening? It had taken bluff old Dr. Murrison's words to turn the key. He had unlocked this truth in her mind by asking her when Ross was coming to take her *home*.

Hillsboro and Holly Grove were no longer her home. Home was with Ross, in the mountains, his beloved mountains—*her* beloved mountains. In her heart, understanding burst like a bud opening into a beautiful blossom.

That very day she wrote a letter to be sent in the next day's post. That night she packed her things.

When at the end of the week Ross came, no word was spoken. None was needed. They rushed into each others arms as if it were the first or the last time they ever embraced.

❦

When Johanna caught sight of the cabin, her heart gave a lurch. It stood there as if waiting for her return. *What an imaginative ninny I am*, she said laughingly to herself. Then she turned to smile at Ross, who was looking at her as if anxious to see her reaction.

"I'll take the horses down to the barn, rub them down, and feed them, then I'll be in directly," Ross said as he helped her out of her saddle.

When Johanna walked up the porch steps, she saw firewood neatly stacked at the far end. Often people paid Ross back with such things—suddenly there would be split logs piled beside the barn, with no clue as to who had left it there in payment. Or jugs of cider would be left outside the door. It was the mountain folks' way. No money but too proud to accept charity. These evidences of how much Ross was appreciated touched Johanna. She wished her relatives in Hillsboro who still thought she'd married beneath her could know this.

Opening the door, she walked inside the cabin. Immediately she breathed in mingled delicious smells—pumpkin pie, apple, cinnamon. Over the stove hung strings of red peppers, dried onions, pods of okra, striped gourds, rainbow-colored Indian corn.

"Aunt Bertie's doings, I expect," she said to Ross when he came inside.

"And Ma's too," Ross said quietly.

Johanna felt stricken that she hadn't thought of Eliza first. Ross's mother had not been nearly as forthcoming and friendly to her as Aunt Bertie.

"When she heard I was going down to bring you home," Ross added, "she said she'd bring up supper so you wouldn't have to cook when we got back. She knew you'd be tired. I think there's beans and ham and bread. Probably other things as well."

"How kind," Johanna murmured, making a mental resolution to make a real effort to get to know her mother-in-law better.

Chapter Seventeen

❦

*T*hat winter seemed long and cold and lonely to Johanna. Although Ross had suggested she might want to spend Christmas with her family in Hillsboro, Johanna felt a strange reluctance. Without her father's jovial presence, there would be a terrible void.

As it turned out, there were heavy snows, and with the mountain trails impassable, traveling was out of the question. It was hard enough for Ross to trek to the isolated homes in Millscreek Gap to make necessary sick calls. There was a great deal of illness that year—children with whooping cough, the older people with severe rheumatism and colds. Ross came home late most evenings, exhausted, too tired and chilled to do more than eat and fall into bed.

The snow kept away even her rare visits from Aunt Bertie and Uncle Tanner, as well as Sue and Katie, who had become frequent visitors since the rescue. Left much alone, Johanna experienced some melancholy about her father, thinking about what she might have said or done differently. She thought of the letter she had procrastinated about writing to him after her marriage, a letter expressing her love, her sorrow at having hurt him, her assurances that her choice had been the right one. She wished she had told her father that Ross was a good and loving husband. However, she had put it off time and again, not sure of exactly what to say. Now it was too late.

Little by little, Johanna gained peace of mind. With her newfound faith, she believed her father *did* know.

With the coming of spring, the mountains burst into glorious beauty. The air was filled with lovely smells—damp moss, sweet clover. There were warm, lovely days, longer afternoons, lavender evenings.

It was in these first weeks of April 1841 that Johanna knew she was going to have a baby.

After her first excitement at the prospect, Johanna had most of the same nagging little worries of any about-to-be mother. Tears came and went like April rain. *I'm as bad as we used to tease Elly about*, she admonished herself, *crying at the drop of a hat!* She knew it was the early stages of her condition. She had heard that expecting a baby sometimes made a woman fanciful and silly. After those first few weeks, a marvelous calm overcame Johanna, and with it a lovely glow.

Ross was deeply happy and proud and couldn't wait to tell everyone. Johanna wanted to wait to first share the news with his mother. Johanna felt somewhat shy about confiding some of her qualms about her approaching motherhood. Eliza was so strong and capable, she probably wouldn't be very understanding. After all, she had birthed four of her own with no seeming problem. However, Johanna instinctively felt it was the right thing to do to tell her mother-in-law first, before Ross, in his own happy pride, blurted out the information to someone else.

The path down to her mother-in-law's house was steep, winding its way precariously between the dark woods on one side, the rocky cliff on the other, with a sheer drop down to the glistening river snaking through the cove below.

Eliza's thin, lined face broke into a wide smile at the news Johanna shyly confided.

"I'm right pleased for you, Johanna. Havin' a baby, becomin' a mama—why, I reckon it's one of the happiest times in a woman's life. I 'spect Ross is beside hisself, ain't he?" Eliza nodded. "He'll make a fine daddy. He was always so good with the younger ones. Patient, kind to 'em. Even Merriman, who could be ornery," she chuckled. "He's got all that from *his* pa, and that's what makes him such a good doctor, I reckon."

In that afternoon she spent with Eliza was the first time Johanna began to feel close to her mother-in-law. Telling her about the coming baby seemed to have narrowed the gap between them.

"Now, of course, you're going to have to have quilts for the young'un. And it'll pass your waitin' time to be makin' some."

"I'm ashamed that I don't really know how to put one together," Johanna confessed. "I guess I was too impatient, too restless, always wanting to be doing something else."

"Well, you'll be sittin' plenty in the next few months and the further along you git. It's a nice, peaceful thing to do, sittin', dreamin' 'bout the baby to come. It was fer me. I musta made a half dozen each time I was expectin'."

Eliza went over to the blanket box and opened the lid. The smell of cedar rose as she did so. Inside were neatly folded quilts. She brought one out, smoothed it with her gnarled, work-worn hands, then unfolded it to show it to Johanna. "This here is one like I'd made for Jenny's last little 'un. I had some pieces left over, and I dunno why, I jest made up another one. It was even 'fore you and Ross got married. Mebbe even 'fore I knew about you."

"Oh, it's beautiful—*Ma*," Johanna said softly, using the name for the first time, then reaching out a hand tentatively to touch the quilt.

"You gotta be right careful about what pattern you use for a baby cradle," Eliza went on, warming to her subject. "It's just not the color or a pretty design you're lookin' for. There are some old tales about quilt patterns. Not to say I believe all of 'em. . . ." She shrugged. "I've always called this here one Turkey Tracks, that's the way it was taught to me. But some of the old women say it used to be called Wandering Foot, and nobody would use it for a child's bed."

"Why ever not?" Johanna was curious.

Eliza shook her head. "Oh, there's lots of old stories about it—things like iffen a child sleeps under it, it'll grow up discontent or with a roaming mind. You hear lots of things like that. Not that I pay a lot of mind to them. But there's lots of other pretty patterns to pick from."

"My mother quilts and so do all my aunties."

Eliza looked somewhat taken aback. "Then mebbe when they know about the baby, they'll all be sending you one they'll make up special. You won't need this 'un." She started folding the quilt up, as though to put it back in the cedar box.

"Oh, please no, Ma. I *want* this one," Johanna protested, then added shyly, "I think for our baby's first quilt—it should come from his daddy's ma."

For a minute Eliza almost seemed startled. Her eyes glistened and she turned her head quickly. "Well now, iffen that's what you want—"

"Yes, it is," Johanna assured her, then hesitantly asked, "Ma, would you teach *me* how to quilt?"

"You really don't know how?"

"Not really. I was never much interested, I'm afraid. I've made a few patches but never put together a whole quilt."

"Well, now." Eliza sat back on her heels, her expression thoughtful. "I've got a pattern—," she said slowly. "Made up a few patches but haven't got 'round to finishing it. Mebbe you could start on it. It's simple enough for a beginner." She leaned over the cedar chest again and brought up a brown paper package and slowly unwrapped it. Inside were layers of folded cloth, some cutout patterns, and other pieces of material. On top were two or three finished blocks on cream-colored cotton, each banded with deep pink. In the center of each block was appliquéd three stylized, pink-petaled flowers accented with green stems and leaves.

Johanna smoothed her hand over the delicately sewn pieces. She imagined Eliza bent over her quilting frame, taking the tiny stitches painstakingly by firelight after all her chores were done. It was a thing of simple beauty, crafted out of the creativity within her that needed expression.

"Oh Ma, it's truly beautiful," Johanna said softly. "What do you call this pattern?"

"Hit don't have any right name. I jest always admired the mountain lilies that bloom along in July. I didn't have a pattern—I just drew it off on paper from looking at it, then used that to cut out my material."

"Mountain lilies, of course," Johanna smiled. "Carolina Mountain Lily. That's what we'll call it."

She slipped her hand over Eliza's worn, rough one, awed that it could make something so exquisite as well as chop wood, churn butter, hoe corn.

On her way back up the mountain, the package containing the quilt pattern and materials strapped behind her saddle, Johanna felt excited, as if she were launching into a whole new phase of her life. It was funny, actually. Back at Holly Grove she'd had to practically be dragged to the quilting frame, constantly be made to pull out her indifferent stitches and do her part over. Now she was looking forward to learning how to make a quilt of her own. For the first time,

Johanna felt a real bonding to Ross's mother and to the mountain community that was now her home.

◦✎◦

The news spread fast among the extended Davison family up and down the mountain. Aunt Bertie and Uncle Tanner were the first to come visit and congratulate them, bringing a cradle made by Tanner's own skilled hands. As Ross and Johanna stood around it admiringly, Bertie told them, "Tanner's cradles are the best. Made out of buckeye log. He worked on it like he was makin' something fit for a king. He likes buckeye 'cause it's light and hollows out so easy and it's a pretty wood. He pegged it with oak pins to two hickory rockers, curved just so. His rockers never creep. It's somethin' I never saw in no other cradle." She gave the cradle a gentle press of her foot. "See there, it jest rocks so nice and easy. I always called Tanner's cradles a lullaby of buckeye."

Trying to look indifferent, Uncle Tanner beamed at his wife's praise.

Later the men went up to check the few apple trees on the hillside, and Johanna brought sassafras tea for Auntie Bertie and herself to drink out on the sunny front porch.

"When your time comes, honey, Tassie Rector's the one," Aunt Bertie said. "She's been bringin' babies for nigh on forty years, I reckon. Never lost a baby nor a mother in all that time. Iffen I wuz you, I'd go make her acquaintance, let her know you'll be needin' her," Aunt Bertie advised.

"But Ross is a doctor, Aunt Bertie. He knows all about babies. He's already delivered dozens since we came back up here," Johanna said.

"Doctor or not, he's a man, ain't he? I think you'd be glad if you go see Tassie and talk to *her*. A woman needs another woman at a time like that."

208

"I'm sure Ross's mother, Eliza, will come," Johanna said tentatively, wondering if maybe there was more to having a baby than she realized. She had a sudden longing for her own mother or Aunt Honey.

"You jest take my advice, Johanna, and go see Tassie," was Aunt Bertie's last word to her before she and Uncle Tanner took off.

⁓❧⁓

One Sunday after service, outside church Ross got into a conversation with Merriman, and Johanna was left standing with Jenny. She had always felt a little awkward with her sister-in-law. Jenny was one of the few people her own age—at least, one of the few girls—whom Johanna had not been able to win as a friend. She didn't know what made her feel so awkward around Jenny. She never seemed to be able to bring up a subject Jenny would respond to. Although Johanna told herself the girl was probably just shy, she had begun to feel that somehow Jenny disliked or resented her. This made it almost impossible whenever they were in each other's company. Most of the time, that was when they were all together at Eliza's. Then there was always so much to do, helping set food on the table or doing the clearing away or washing up. But sometimes, like now, Johanna found herself with a blank mind and a silent tongue.

Jenny seemed just as ill at ease as Johanna. Shaded by the broad-brimmed sunbonnet, her eyes were cast down, and her thin mouth worked nervously. At home, her father used to tease Johanna that she "couldn't stand a moment's silence," and this proved true at this awkward instant. Johanna surprised herself by impulsively bursting out, "Jenny, I'm really pretty scared about having this baby. You've had two—I wish you'd come up to visit me one day

209

and talk to me about it. It would really help to talk to someone else—I mean, someone my own age."

Jenny's face flushed and she looked startled. She opened her mouth and started to say something, then swallowed and seemed too taken aback to go on.

"Please, Jenny, I mean it. I'd really like you to come. Will you?"

"Yes, yes. Shure I will," Jenny finally murmured.

Just then the two brothers sauntered up to where their wives were standing. Ross smiled at them both. "What're you two ladies gossiping about?" he asked teasingly.

"Babies!" Johanna laughed and glanced over at Jenny merrily. To her surprise, Jenny had blushed beet red. Belatedly Johanna realized that maybe mountain women didn't talk openly about such things, even in front of their husbands, even when one of them was a doctor. She was sorry if she embarrassed Jenny, and she leaned toward her and gave her a reassuring touch on her arm, saying, "Now don't forget, Jenny—I'm looking forward to your visit."

Two days later Jenny did come, still shy, still pretty untalkative. She did, however, bring a gift of a beautiful little knitted baby shawl. She also endorsed Aunt Bertie's recommendation that Johanna go see Tassie.

"She helped brung both my boys," Jenny told her. "None better in all the mountainside."

~❧~

Some weeks later Johanna decided to follow both Jenny's and Aunt Bertie's suggestion. On a beautiful early fall morning, she saddled her horse and went down the mountain. The air was clear, with a definite sharpness to it. There was the smell of ripening apples, burning leaves, and she noticed the sharp-tanged fragrance of chokeberries.

210

"Tassie's home is easy to find," Aunt Bertie had told her. "If you get lost, ask anyone you see. Everyone knows her, will tell you how to get there." She was right, and soon Johanna came in sight of a weathered frame house on the side of the hill. As she got off her horse, leading him by his reins up the rest of the steep path, Johanna saw a woman sitting on the porch on a rush-seat rocking chair.

"Howdy," the woman called.

Johanna gave an answering wave. "I'm Johanna Davison," she said as she walked up to the porch. When she came closer, she saw the woman's strong, sensitive face, wreathed in wrinkles and a welcoming smile, and her deep-set, kind eyes.

"Well, I'm right happy to meet you. Doc's wife, ain't ye? Come and sit a spell."

For the next hour or so, Johanna felt as though she had been warmly hugged and comforted by this dear lady.

At once offered refreshment and the other rocker, Johanna was soon hearing the story of Tassie's life. "Was born right here, only a stone's throw from where we're sittin'. Married at twenty and had ten young'uns, all healthy, alive to this day. Now have thirty grandchildren and eight great-grands and brought 'em all into the world." She rocked and smiled with satisfaction. "I began midwifin' while my own was still little. It jest seem to be my callin' in life." She nodded. "We all come into this world with a mission. The Lord saw fit to give me this one, and so he was present with me all the time, at every birthin'. God give me the talent to bring babies safely, and that's what I've tried to do. I take no credit myself, you understand? I've had no real trainin' but what God give me. I jest always put my trust in him, and as Scripture says, "My grace is sufficient.""

When the sun was getting low, Johanna stood up, ready to leave. Tassie said, "I know your man is a doctor, and from what I heard, a fine one. But if you want me, jest send word and I'll be on my way."

"That's very kind of you," Johanna said as she tied her sunbonnet strings. She didn't think she'd really need Tassie, not with Ross there, but she didn't want to hurt the old lady's feelings.

On her way back up the mountain, Johanna wished she'd paid more attention when she still lived in Hillsboro, wished she'd listened when the aunties were discussing some friend's confinement or a birth in their circle of acquaintances. Then marriage and motherhood had seemed something in the distant future. Now that it was soon to be her own experience, she realized she knew next to nothing about it. Of course, Ross would be with her and certainly knew what to do when the time came. He was well trained and capable. And Eliza would also be on hand. She wouldn't have to rely on a backwoods midwife, thank goodness.

～εჯ←

Eliza helped Johanna begin her quilt. Uncle Tanner willingly made her a frame to set up. Once she got started, Johanna discovered she actually enjoyed doing it. She liked arranging the pieces of bright calico material and pinning them into the design more than the actual stitching. However, gradually and with Eliza's patient instruction, her stitches got smaller, neater, and after Ross moved the frame up to their own cabin, she found she could work while daydreaming about how life would be once their baby arrived. Being pregnant made her less active, and often Johanna found herself getting sleepy after only a half hour or more at her quilting frame, so it went slowly. She would often have to lie down and take a nap on the long afternoons as fall turned into winter and the wind blew around the cabin corners, sending the cedar boughs sighing against the windows, making the sound almost of a lullaby.

Chapter Eighteen

~❦~

Johanna felt her shoulder shaken gently and heard Ross whisper, "I've got a nice fire going, honey, but you stay in bed until the house gets good and warm. I've got a few visits to make, but I should be home early afternoon."

Johanna murmured something drowsily, felt Ross kiss her cheek, his hand smooth her hair, then she snuggled deeper into the quilts and went back to sleep.

She wasn't sure how much later she woke up. A fire was burning brightly but low in the big stone fireplace. Slowly she roused herself, pulled on her voluminous flowered flannel robe, got awkwardly out of the high bed. Six more weeks and she wouldn't be able to sleep in late like this, she thought with a smile. Neither would she have all this extra weight to carry around with her. She slipped her feet into slippers and went to the window. Outside the sky was a chalky gray. Snow? The edges around the glass pane were frosted slightly.

The kettle Ross had left hanging on the crane over the fire was sizzling. Johanna put a few spoonfuls of herb tea into a mug, poured in water, and stirred it into a fragrant brew. As she leaned over to replace the kettle, she felt a strange sensation in her back. Straightening up, one hand went to the curve of her spine. Had she imagined it? Probably pulled a muscle slightly when she reached for the kettle, she thought. Her body wasn't familiar to her anymore. She had all sorts of queer aches and pains now, in places she could never have imagined before. Sitting down at the table, she cupped her hands around the steaming mug, inhaling the spicy aroma of the tea. The room was pleasantly warm, the tea delicious. Johanna glanced around, thinking how happy and content she had felt in recent weeks.

Everything about the little cabin pleased her—the polished gourds on the mantel, the blue and white dishes on the pine hutch, the rocking chair, which she had enjoyed more and more these last months. Then her gaze rested on the cradle and the quilt folded over its side. Soon their precious baby would be nested within that. *Their* child, hers and Ross's. She didn't care whether it was a boy or girl, either way she would love it.

She looked out the window again. To her surprise, she saw a few snowflakes floating lazily down. If it snowed, it would be the first of the season. Autumn—or Indian summer, as they called it here—had lingered longer than usual in the mountains this year. It wasn't until way into November that the mornings had become really frosty and the evenings chilly.

Johanna got up from the table to go over to the window, when a quick, darting pain traveled down the back of both her legs. She gasped, clutched onto the edge of the table. What in the world? Had she slept in a cramped position so that her muscles were stiff? A fleeting worry passed through her mind. It couldn't be anything to do with the baby. Or could it? She took a deep breath. She put her weight back on her feet and straightened up. Nothing happened. It was all right. Just a twinge of some kind. Nothing more.

She walked over to the window, leaned on the sill, and watched the snow fall slowy, as if it were not in any hurry. Still, it was sticking, she saw, watching the steadily falling snow cover the ground with a light powder.

It looked beautiful. The sweeping branches of the pines and hemlocks that rimmed their property were dark green under the fluffy fringe of white, the rail fence like dark rickrack against the drifting snow.

Johanna moved back over to the stove, where the oatmeal she had set on the back burner the night before was now thickened, ready to eat. She started to dish herself out a bowl, when she again felt another strange little clutch in the middle of her back. This one lasted longer than the first one. She frowned. She waited a full minute. Nothing happened. She filled her bowl, poured milk and honey over her oatmeal, and went to sit by the fire and eat.

She hoped Ross would get home before the snow got any deeper. It was hard enough traveling the narrow ridges on the mountain to out-of-the-way cabins in good weather.

Finishing her breakfast, Johanna decided to work some on the quilt she was making for the baby. Then she wouldn't worry about Ross. Eliza had been right—making the quilt was a pleasant, "mind easin'" experience. Johanna enjoyed it more than she ever imagined. Wouldn't her mother and aunties be amazed? It used to seem a pointless occupation back when she would rather have been doing something else. Now, anticipating a baby, Johanna found it enjoyable. Working on the quilt, she dreamed of all sorts of happy things. With the baby, she felt that the life she and Ross shared would become even happier, more complete.

Johanna shifted her position. She seemed to become uncomfortable sooner than usual as she sat in the straight-backed chair at the quilting frame. She started to get up to get a pillow to wedge behind her back, when a sudden pain struck her. It was longer and stronger than either of the others. This time it traveled swiftly from the middle of her back down the length of her legs, causing her knees to cramp. She sat down quickly, holding on to the chair arms.

For a long while she remained absolutely still. What was going on? It *couldn't* be the baby. *Could* it? The last time Tassie stopped by, she had looked Johanna over with a practiced eye, declaring she had a good six weeks yet to go. Over a month.

Alarm coursed through Johanna. Was something wrong, then? Oh, if only Ross were there. She waited tensely but nothing else happened. Reassured, she got up and walked over to the window again. It was now near noon. The snow was coming down with a driving force. The ground was covered and the wind was blowing the snow in drifts along the fence and against the windowsills. Johanna put her hand on the pane and felt the cold.

Where was Ross? He'd better get home before it snowed any harder. She watched with increasing anxiety as the snow continued falling steadily.

Restless and unable to go back to her quilting, she felt suddenly chilly. She went over to the wood box, got a few smaller logs out, and threw them on the fire, sending up a spiral of sparks. She got down her shawl and wrapped it around her shoulders. Drawing the rocker closer, she sat down near the fireplace.

Suddenly a grinding sort of pain gripped her. She gave a startled cry. Was that the kind of pain that signaled the start of labor? Oh, no! Surely it was too soon. It couldn't be happening. Not now! When she was there alone! It couldn't be starting, could it? Please, God, no. A deep shudder went all through Johanna. She knew that once it started, there was no stopping it. What was it Tassie had said? "When a baby's ready to come, it comes!" Could this be how it begins? Slowly, so that you're not sure, then more often, harder, with sensations unlike anything else you've ever felt?

Holding the shawl close about her, she made her halting way back over to the window. The day was darkening quickly, clouds heavy with still more snow hovered, the boughs of the pines and hemlocks surrounding the cabin were now burdened with clumps of snow, and the wind-blown snow was now banked along the rustic fence along the horse trail down the mountainside.

Ross had better get home soon, or the way would be impassable. Fear stirred in the pit of her stomach, tightening her throat. If this *was* the baby coming, she couldn't go through it all by herself. She *couldn't*—dear God, she just couldn't! She felt her eyes fill with tears of fear and frustration. It just couldn't happen like this. Her body seemed almost apart from her mind, which became surprisingly clear. If this *was* the baby—and she was getting to the point where she *knew* it was—she should do something, get ready somehow to handle this alone, if she had to.

Before she could move or turn around, another slow pain clutched her, making her bend over and cling to the window sill, causing an involuntary groan. There was no mistaking it. This was it!

She closed her eyes for a minute, prayed frantically. *Please, God, make me brave, show me what to do. But please send someone! Bring Ross home!*

Boil water! That somehow tugged at her memory as something to do. She wasn't sure quite why, but she filled the kettle anyway and hung it over the fire. The fire was roaring, crackling, and the smell of apple wood was pungent as it burned. Still, Johanna could not get warm. She shivered and braced herself for another pain.

It came and she held her breath until it passed. Fifteen minutes later another one began. Between pains, Johanna heard the ticktock of the clock. She counted the time, clenching her hands on the arms of the rocker, waiting for the pain she knew would soon overtake her. Between those times, she prayed, *Please, someone come.* Outside the steady, silent snow continued.

The wind howled around the cabin, sounding like a hundred screeching owls. Johanna gritted her teeth, set her jaw, shuddered. How could this have happened to her? To the pampered daughter of well-to-do town folk? To be up here all alone in an isolated log cabin in a snowstorm that was gradually shutting her off from any help? At a time like this, she should be surrounded by loving, comforting, caring people— people who, for heaven's sake, knew what to do!

Panic set her heart to pounding. She hugged herself and moved closer to the fireplace, shivering in spite of its warmth.

She thought of the day Liddy Chalmers had come to see her before she got married, begged her to reconsider marrying Ross. "You *can't*, Johanna, you just can't!" Liddy had cried. Johanna thought of that scene in detail now. "To go so far away, to live on the edge of nowhere," Liddy had said.

Well, that's exactly what she *had* done. If she'd gone to Hillsboro months ago to have the baby there, as her mother had written to suggest, she wouldn't be in this awful situation. But Johanna had refused. *This* was her home now, she'd insisted in her letter back to her mother. Was she now paying for her stubbornness, her self-will, her pride?

Johanna imagined how it would have been for her now if she'd accepted her mother's invitation. A picture came to her of her own bedroom, with its slanted ceiling, the dormer windows looking out onto the garden, the four-poster bed, her little desk and white-paneled fireplace, her bedside table with her favorite books. She remembered how when she had some slight childhood illness, trays were brought up to her with cinnamon toast or lemon pudding, and if she had a fever, her mother's cool hand would be on her forehead. Ruefully she knew she'd never appreciated it enough.

Just then another wave of pain swept over her. Johanna clamped her teeth together, accidentally biting her tongue. Tears rushed into her eyes. Finally the pain passed and again Johanna made her way haltingly over to the window, peering out. Snow piled up on the window ledge and around the small panes shut off any view. Johanna saw that the trail was almost obliterated by the drifts. And it was still snowing. There was little hope that Ross would come now. He might be caught somewhere up the mountain. Perhaps he'd stayed too long at some remote cabin with a patient. Ironically, maybe even to deliver a baby!

First babies often took a long time, Tassie had told her. On the other hand, she'd said, some babies were in a hurry. What this baby would do, Johanna had no idea. She bit her lower lip as a strong spasm gripped her again.

She tried not to think of some of the horror stories she'd heard whispered among the girls at boarding school. Of course, none of them *really* knew anything about it. All they circulated were old wives' tales passed from one ignorant girl to the next. However, she *did* know that sometimes women died having babies. What if she died here all by herself? What if they came and found her dead, and the baby too?

If she died, how sad everyone would be. Even Cissy. The idea struck her that when people died, they always left a will. To distract herself from the next pain, which she knew would be coming soon, Johanna thought of what she would bequeath to her sisters in her nonexistent will. She really should have made a will, she thought. Facing what she was now, there was always the possibility of dying. If she *were* to make a will, she'd leave Cissy the cameo pin Grandmother Shelby had given *her* on her sixteenth birthday. Cissy had been really put out about that. She had always admired the delicate Grecian profile carved in ivory on a pale lavender background, framed in gold, circled with seed pearls. And Elly. What could she leave to her youngest sister. What would Elly want of hers?

That was as far as Johanna got in her melancholy thoughts. She perked up suddenly. Didn't she hear something? Above the wind, beyond the pattering of the icy snow against the windows—was that the sound of voices? Oh, dear God, was someone actually coming? She got up from her crouched position, staggered to the door. It *was!* She heard shouts! It wasn't her imagination. Someone was actually coming. Thank God.

Pressing her face to the window, wiping away the frost that veiled her view, she looked out. Stumbling through the blowing snow, the piled-up drifts, were two bundled figures, hanging on to each other, making their way toward the cabin.

With all her strength, Johanna slid back the wooden bars on the door. The wind pushed against it, and she was hard pressed to hold the door open enough for the two people to come inside.

Woolen mufflers around their heads hid their faces, and Johanna could only see their eyes, which were fringed by snow-crusted lashes. The tips of their noses were red with cold. Heavy shawls stiff with frozen snow were wrapped around them, disguising their shapes. Then as they began unwinding the long knitted scarves, she saw who they were. The first face revealed was Tassie's, the second that of Ross's mother, Eliza.

"Oh Ma, I'm so glad you came," Johanna gasped, clutching Eliza's arm. "I think the baby's on its way! But how did you know to come?"

"Tassie come by, told me she'd seen Ross up on the ridge near the Coltons' cabin early in the day. She heard tell that

Milt had broke his leg felling a tree, and thought Ross might have trouble gettin' down the mountain agin iffen it kept snowin' so heavy. We both decided you shouldn't be up here alone in case—well, just in case. So we come."

"Thank God you did!" Johanna said fervently. "But what about Sue and Katie?"

"They'll be fine. Took them over to Jenny and Merriman's 'fore I set out," Eliza told her. "Now, don't you worry 'bout nuthin' but bringin' this here baby into the world."

Even as her mother-in-law spoke, Johanna felt another pain coming. She nodded and braced herself. Her fingers clutched Eliza's arm. Immediately she felt the swift support of both women holding her firmly. When the pain had passed, Johanna let Eliza help her over to bed. There quilts were tucked around her, pillows piled beneath her head, shoulders, back. She could hear Tassie moving around in the cabin. Soon she brought Johanna a mug of steaming herbal tea, a mixture of red raspberry and chamomile. "Here, you sip on this, honey. It'll ease you and make you feel better."

After that, things became blurred. There was the rhythm of pain, each one closer and harder. Always in the background were the comforting voices of the two women, who held her hand, rubbed her back, soothed her with quiet, calm instructions.

Outside the day darkened. Between pains, Johanna asked, "Ross? Is Ross here?"

"Not yet, honey. Now, you jest quiet yourself. Everything's goin' fine. Your baby'll be here 'fore long."

Johanna couldn't remember just when she lost track of time—possibly hours passed. Everything centered on the cycle of ever-increasing pressure, Tassie's encouraging voice. Then she heard the slam of the cabin door as it was thrust open and banged against the wall. The next thing she knew, her hand was covered by two large ones, her name whispered. "Johanna, darling, I'm here."

She opened her eyes. Ross's face bent over her, his keen eyes worried. His cold cheek pressed against hers, and he said huskily, "It won't be long now, honey."

Relieved, reassured, Johanna clung tightly to his hand and gave herself up to the business of giving birth, feeling safe, secure, and completely comforted by his presence.

It seemed endless. Then, as if from a long distance off, Johanna heard the strong, unmistakable sound of a baby's cry! It was over. She'd had her baby. She fell back against the pillows, filled with a tremendous joy, a sense of accomplishment.

~✦~

Johanna awakened to the sweet aroma of spice wood tea boiling, then the stirring of the little bundle tucked into the bed beside her. Her baby! she realized in dreamy surprise.

She looked down into the pink, crumpled little face. The baby's eyes were closed. Gently she touched the downy crest of hair on the small, round head, let her finger trace the cheek. How sweet, how dear. She was in awe of this perfection. This is what she had waited for all these months, their child. Johanna felt an emotion new and deep move within her. "Thank you, God," she whispered.

Slowly she became aware of other movement in the room, and then she saw Eliza come to the side of her bed, holding a cup from which a spiral of fragrant steam arose.

"You're awake, Johanna. Let's see if we can sit you up some so's you can sip this tea. It'll give you strength, then mebbe later you can eat somethin'." She paused, then asked hesitantly, "Kin I hold the baby for you?"

Johanna smiled up at Eliza, turning back the edge of the blanket so she could see the little face better. "Isn't she beautiful?"

Eliza beamed. "Yes, she shure is a right peart little'un," she replied, nodding her head. "Ross sez you're namin' her Johanna—that's the custom in your family for a first girl."

"Yes ma'am, but we're going to call her JoBeth—Johanna *Elizabeth*."

Johanna watched as her mother-in-law's face underwent a change of expression, from a startled look to a softness she had never seen there before.

"'Lizabeth?" Eliza repeated softly.

"Yes ma'am, after *you*." Johanna said.

Eliza struggled not to show her emotion, but her eyes brightened suspiciously and her lips worked as if trying to say something. At length, not being able to express what she was feeling, she simply lifted Johanna's fingers and pressed them to her cheek. "I—well—thanky," she managed to say at last.

Chapter Nineteen

Johanna's third September in the mountains seemed particularly beautiful to her. Coming out onto the porch one afternoon, she lingered. High in the tall trees surrounding their cabin, the wind sang. Listening to its music, Johanna realized it was a melody she had learned to hear and love. She felt a part of all this now—these hills, the scent of wildflowers, wood smoke, the special light in summer evenings, the sweet scent of honeysuckle, the clean smell of freshly cut pine. She felt the satisfaction of belonging. A feeling that had been long coming.

Sometimes, Hillsboro and her own girlhood seemed a hundred years away. Her life now was centered here in the mountains, on the baby, and on Ross.

After her father's death, Ross had been her strength, her comfort. She had never before realized the depth of his love, the generosity of his soul, the strength of his devotion, the selflessness of his being. Johanna felt sure her father would be glad to know how beloved she was, how cherished, protected.

The baby was napping and Johanna was tempted to stay, enjoying the sunshine, but there were still chores to be done. She sighed and reluctantly went inside.

Her glance fell on the quilting frame Uncle Tanner had made for her before the baby was born. There was an unfinished quilt stretched upon it. She hadn't worked on it for weeks. Somehow there was always something else that needed doing. Besides, this one wasn't coming out as she had planned. Maybe she was too impatient, or maybe she didn't have the skill—it didn't seem to have a theme. Johanna went over to it, stood looking down at it. Shouldn't a quilt have some sort of theme, a message—shouldn't it represent something? Something was missing. Something was wrong. The colors? The pattern? The pieces she had selected? It was a daily reminder of something lacking in her—the will to continue, to complete. Whatever the problem, somehow it didn't please her. Something seemed to be missing, but she didn't know just what.

Johanna had finished two smaller ones for the baby. Eliza had sewed the tops to the matting and flannel backing, and JoBeth slept sweetly and soundly, wrapped up in their warmth. This quilt was supposed to be Johanna's showpiece, to exhibit the skills she had learned through much struggle, much ripping out and redoing, a masterful work to be displayed proudly. And yet it wasn't right. Why? Not feeling inclined to work on it, she went on to do other chores.

She still had trouble juggling everything there was to do. The baby took up most of her time. Johanna found her a source of endless delight. She knew she neglected other things to spend time with her baby.

JoBeth was a daily miracle to her. Everything about her seemed extraordinary to Johanna. She could hardly put her down or stop watching her. She loved caring for her, cuddling, feeding, rocking, admiring the rosebud mouth, the startlingly blue eyes, the way her silky dark hair was beginning to curl around her forehead and shell-like ears.

Hearing the sound of stirring from the cradle, Johanna hurried over and, greeting JoBeth with soft, cooing sounds, she lifted the baby. It was just too pretty to stay inside, Johanna decided. Then, taking one of the quilts Eliza had given her, she carried her outside. Spreading the quilt on the grass in the mellow gold of the autumn sunshine, she placed JoBeth on it. The baby was just about ready to crawl. She would get up on her fat little hands and knees and rock back and forth, as if she hadn't quite figured out just how yet.

Johanna never tired of watching her. She felt that time with her baby was precious, and she didn't want to miss a minute.

The afternoon lengthened. JoBeth had now been placed on her back, kicking her little legs, waving her arms. Her round, blue eyes watched a cluster of birds flying back and forth between the oak tree overhead and the fence nearby.

Above them, purple-shadowed mountains arched against the sky. Johanna realized how much she had come to love them. They no longer seemed threatening or ready to close her in, isolate her, but instead seemed to protect and surround her with love.

The light began to change, the wind began to stir the pine boughs. Ross should be coming home soon. Johanna picked the baby up and walked to the fence overlooking the trail, peered down to see if Ross might be making his way up. At a long distance on the mountainside, she saw him coming. Her heart lifted with a little thrill she astonishingly recognized as being much the same as the very first time she had seen him at the Chalmerses' Christmas party.

He sat somewhat slouched forward in his saddle, his shoulders bent as though he'd had a tiring day, his hands easy on the reins. Johanna felt a rush of tenderness.

Coming near, he saw her and waved one hand.

226

"'Evenin', honey," he called, then smiled at the baby. "Evenin', Miss Johanna Elizabeth."

At the top of the hill he dismounted. Taking off the horse's bridle, then the saddle, he placed them on the top of the fence, opened the gate, and turned the animal into the pasture.

Ross walked toward Johanna and held out his arms for the baby and placed her against his shoulder. Then he put his other arm around Johanna, and together the three of them went into the house. Inside, Ross leaned down, gave Johanna a long, slow kiss, then sighed, "It's good to be home."

Joy surfaced in Johanna. It *was* good to be home. *Their* home. She remembered hearing it said, "Home is where the heart is, where your treasure is." *Her* treasure was Ross and the baby. She felt a deep thankfulness for all that was there and for all the years ahead of them.

Johanna glanced at the quilt on the frame. She went over, stared down at it critically. Suddenly she began to see its design. She saw the pieces all coming together in a harmonious pattern. What she wanted it to represent was her life here with Ross and the baby. All the things home meant to her—love, laughter, devotion, belonging.

All at once Johanna knew what she wanted her quilt to say. There was still much of their life that was yet to come, just like the quilt. There was more to work on, more to bring forth. But the pattern was there underneath. Nothing was missing—not from her quilt nor from her life.

American Quilt Series Bonus Section

❧❧

How to Make Johanna's Quilt

Appliqué allows you to create your own design by stitching bits of fabric on a foundation material. The Carolina Lily quilt is easy to make if you follow the step-by-step instructions. Allow your creativity to blossom by selecting your favorite colors for your own lilies. No two lilies are the same on the Carolina Lily design, but our instructions will allow you to make the flowers look symmetrical to each other.

First, sew two diamonds. Stitch from the bottom of the diamond to the top seam. Second, sew two pairs of diamonds together making one Carolina Lily blossom. Be careful to sew from the bottom of the diamonds to the top—do not sew through it. Now, sew the long side of a triangle to the base of the blossom. You may need to trim the ends of the petals within 1/8 of the sewing line, while gradually tapering the points. Next, make the stems by folding green strips along each long edge. Put the center stem on top of the side stems. You may need to trim the side stems where they meet the center stem to avoid bulk. Hand-baste or pin the Lilies onto the foundation. Trim the stems, allowing 1/4" under the flower. Finally, using small slip stitches, appliqué the stems and the Carolina Lilies. If you prefer to work with felt, wool, or non-woven materials use the buttonhole embroidery stitch instead.

Now to assemble the quilt top, trim the sides of the appliquéd block so they are all equal in length. Make three vertical rows of four blocks, joined with long sashing strips. Press each seam toward the sashing strips. Each of these rows should have the same measurements too.

Now you are ready to layer and quilt. The backing fabric should be divided into two equal lengths.

Sew the two sides together. Outline-quilt around all the flowers and stems. Lastly, quilt the marked designs.

Finally, to complete the quilt sew the strips together in a continual diagonal seam. Stitch through all the layers around the quilt. When you reach the starting point overlap the ends.

Your Carolina Lily quilt will forever bloom the fruit of your needle art.

Acknowledgments

⊷≫⧸⊷

The author would like to acknowledge the following authors for their books, which proved to be invaluable in the research and writing of this book.

Dennis Duke and Deborah Harding, *America's Glorious Quilts*

Wilma Dykeman, *The Tall Woman*

John Parris, *Roaming the Mountains*

Suzy Chalfant Payne and Susan Aylsworth Murwin, *Creative American Quilts Inspired by the Bible*

Lillian W. Watson, editor, *Light from Many Lamps*

Part One

Prologue

❦

Johanna Elizabeth Davison sat at the small maple desk in her bedroom, writing a letter to Wes, when she heard her aunt's voice calling, "JoBeth, come down here at once! Harvel's brigade is marching by. Do hurry!"

She tucked a stray dark curl behind her ear, then put her pen back in the inkwell. Before getting up, she slid the half-written to Wes letter under the blotter. Hurrying into the hallway, she met her mother, Johanna, just coming from her sewing room. They exchanged glances. Although full of understanding, her mother's eyes held a message that JoBeth dared not ignore. JoBeth nodded and together they went down the winding stairway to the hall, where Aunt Jo Cady stood at the open front door.

"Come along, you two!" she called over her shoulder as she went out onto the porch, down the steps, and along the flagstone walk to stand at the gate. JoBeth and her mother followed.

The May morning was warm, bright with sunshine. Residents from the houses on the street were rushing out to the strip of grass on either side of the road. In the distance, they could hear the drums beating, the brisk sound of marching feet, the clatter of horses' hooves. Then the line of gray-clad soldiers rounded the bend and came into sight. People began to shout hurrahs and wave small Confederate flags.

Where had they got them so soon? JoBeth wondered. North Carolina had only seceded a few days before. Although, of course, secession had been discussed for months, ever since South Carolina's secession and Fort Sumter. When President Lincoln called for troops from North Carolina to subdue the sister state's rebels, Governor Ellis's response had been immediate. "I can be no party to this violation of the laws of this country and to this war upon the liberties of a free people. You can get no troops from North Carolina." The state had enthusiastically rallied to the Confederate cause.

After that things had happened with lightning speed. JoBeth's uncle Harvel Cady had immediately formed a brigade, and there had been no lack of men ready to join up.

As the soldiers marched by, everyone began to clap. The officers were mounted on splendid horses and crisply uniformed with shiny braid and buttons, sash fringes streaming in the wind, sabers glinting. Harvel, leading astride his gleaming, roan-colored mount, did not look at his relatives nor show any sign of recognition. It would have been unsoldierly to do so. But as he went by his mother, he seemed to sit a little straighter, jutting out his chin with its bristle of mustache and well-trimmed beard.

Among the rows of erect soldiers were many JoBeth knew—boys she had played with, had gone to school with as children, later had danced with, flirted with, teased. Now they were almost unrecognizable with their military bearings and their new, serious expressions, eyes straight ahead, not looking to right or left.

As she looked at the passing parade of familiar faces, JoBeth felt an enormous sadness. Only one person was missing. For her, the most important one: Wesley Rutherford, who was at college in Philadelphia. And even if he were here, he would not have been in the group. Wes had already expressed his deep doubts about the division among the states, saying, "Both North and South fought to create the United States; we shouldn't break apart now."

Next month, when he graduated, Wes would come back to Hillsboro, where he had made his home with his relatives, the Spencers. JoBeth worried about what would happen then. Will and Blakely, twin cousins his own age, had already gone to Raleigh to enlist.

In spite of the warmth of the day, JoBeth shivered. She had a feeling of impending trouble, a kind of premonition. The bright day seemed to darken. Suddenly, even though surrounded by family, friends of a lifetime, she felt cut off from everyone else. All at once JoBeth realized that she was the only one in the crowd not happily cheering.

Chapter One

~≈≈~

After supper, JoBeth helped Annie, the Cadys' elderly cook, in the kitchen, drying the dishes and putting away the silver, one of JoBeth's regular household chores. It wasn't until JoBeth went back upstairs to her bedroom that she had a chance to complete the letter she had started earlier.

She was more aware than ever, from the evening's dinnertable conversation, that war was now inevitable. Hillsboro was a hotbed of anti-Union sentiment. This was what Wes would be returning to in a few weeks. What would be his reaction? More to the point, how would they respond to his reaction? All his talk of brotherhood, settling differences peacefully, not taking up arms—all part of his Quaker grandmother's influence and his years at college in Philadelphia—was in direct opposition to what had been discussed among her relatives.

JoBeth pulled her half-finished letter out from under the blotter on her desk and began to write.

> *Everything here is talk of war. My uncles were here for supper, and the whole evening was spent in blaming President Lincoln for bringing about all this trouble. Uncle Madison kept pounding on the table and booming, "States' rights." Of course, Harvel and Munroe agree. They say,*

"If we're invaded, we'll defend ourselves." Would the president really send troops into North Carolina?

JoBeth paused, thinking about what had led up to all this. All the previous fall and winter, JoBeth had witnessed the growing resentment against the government in Washington. Every Thursday evening, friends and associates of her Uncle Madison gathered at the Cady house. Before the country's present crisis, it had been an evening of convivial fellowship, friendly conversation, congenial company, sometimes a game or two of cards. More recently it had become increasingly political. Often voices rose in not-so-gentlemanly confrontation. Most of the men present believed strongly not only in states' rights but also in the Union, and roundly put down the idea of secession as seditious and not to be considered.

The ladies of the house were never a part of the discussions, although they heard Madison's own opinions the next morning at breakfast. No one offered any comment. It would have been useless to do so, because naturally Uncle Madison never expected any difference to be voiced in his own household. However, JoBeth knew that Wes's views were almost directly opposed to her uncle's. This troubled her a great deal.

She dipped her pen in the inkwell and started writing again.

I wish you were here. All this would be so much easier if you were here to explain it to me. I miss you. I can't wait to see you.

JoBeth hesitated. Her pen hovered uncertainly. How should she sign this? Would "Love" be too bold? Although she *did* love Wesley and was pretty sure he loved her, too, they had not said those words to each other. Although they had nearly done so the day before he had left last Christmas.

240

JoBeth wished she had some small piece of poetry or something she could send with her letter, as Wes sometimes did with his. She reached into the pigeonhole in the desk, brought out his last letter to her, and read the poem he had enclosed.

Never seek to tell thy love,
Love that never told can be;
For the gentle wind doth move
Silently, invisibly.

Certainly that said *something*, she thought as she read it over. Through their correspondence this year, they had become much closer. It had been easier somehow to write about feelings than to speak about them. JoBeth tapped the end of the pen thoughtfully against her chin. Finally deciding that "discretion was the better part of—" she simply wrote

As ever,
JoBeth

She sealed the letter and again slipped it under the blotter. She would take it herself to the post office the next day and mail it.

As she got ready for bed, JoBeth thought of last summer. It had been a wonderful summer, a perfect one. At eighteen, JoBeth was an accepted part of the lively circle of young people in Hillsboro. Parties, picnics, dances, church socials, barbecues, and outings at the river. Wes spent half the year with his grandmother in Philadelphia while at college, but his summers were spent with his cousins in Hillsboro.

Of course, they had known each other long before that. In fact, Wes Rutherford was JoBeth's first friend in Hillsboro. JoBeth, her mother, and JoBeth's little brother, Shelby, had come back to live there after her doctor father, Ross Davison, had died. Her mother's family had lived there for several generations, and there were lots of aunts, uncles, cousins. Still, JoBeth had felt forlorn.

She missed her father, their mountain home, Granny Eliza, her cousins, and the life she had known. Life with her great-aunt Josie and great-uncle Madison was as different as could be from their life before. Here there was order, discipline, and nonnegotiable times to do everything from morning prayers before breakfast to wearing starched petticoats and high-button shoes that pinched little feet used to going bare six months of the year.

At first she was desperately homesick for the mountains, her freedom to roam, to wade in the streams, to pick berries and wildflowers. Gradually, with the natural resilience of children, she and her brother adapted to life in town, Shelby sooner than JoBeth. A quiet, handsome little boy with a naturally sweet disposition, he quickly became the household pet. Aunt Cady declared he reminded her of her own two boys, now both grown-up men.

JoBeth was entirely different. She was restless, imaginative, stubborn, often a trial to her mother and frequently the despair of Aunt Cady, who had envisioned bringing up a perfect, ladylike little girl.

In spite of their differences in personality, JoBeth and Shelby were very close. They played, read together, shared each other's secrets, and were each other's confidantes.

JoBeth blew out her lamp, climbed into the high, poster bed, recalling her first meeting with Wes.

That fall she had been enrolled in school. Shelby was too young, so JoBeth had to go alone. In a small town where everyone knew everyone else, she had felt lost and lonely. It was agony for her to sit quietly among a roomful of strange children.

One day soon after the beginning of school, JoBeth had been making her way slowly homeward, limping from a blister forming on her heel from the new shoes, when she met John Wesley Rutherford.

Wes, as he had told her he was called, was the Spencer twins' cousin. JoBeth had heard about him at the Cady dinner table, where all local news was discussed. His mother— Mr. Spencer's younger sister, who had "married North"—had recently died. Wes, her only child, had been sent to stay with his Hillsboro kin.

That day, Wes had offered to carry her books so she could slip off her shoes and walk the rest of the way on the soft grass. In that unusual gesture of compassion, JoBeth knew that Wes was different. Different from most boys their age, whose delight was teasing and tormenting girls. He was certainly different from his cousins, the boisterous Will and Blakely Spencer. Those two rode their ponies to school, then raced each other home with wild whoops, scattering dust and stones in their wake.

Wes had shown her a stream that ran under a stone bridge near the churchyard, where she could soak her burning foot in the cool water to ease its soreness. He had sat there with her on the bank, and they had talked easily. The fact that they had both lost a beloved parent gave them an immediate bond. From that day they had become friends.

Why was she so drawn to Wes? JoBeth wondered. Perhaps he reminded her in some ways of her adored father, had those same qualities she admired: loyalty, idealism, and personal honor.

Wesley was not particularly handsome, although JoBeth liked his looks—the sandy-brown hair that always seemed tousled, the strong, straight nose, the slow smile. He had a sensitive face with an intelligent expression and candid eyes. What JoBeth found most appealing about him was his generous nature, his honesty and openness. There was no shallowness at all in Wes Rutherford.

Was what she felt love? A kind of love, certainly. They had been friends for what seemed like forever. She felt more comfortable with Wes than with anyone else. She could share things with him, even the not-so-nice things, as when she was feeling upset or angry with someone or had had her feelings hurt. Wes always seemed to understand whatever her mood was, glad or down in the dumps. He could always make her laugh, too, jolly her out of the doldrums. Over the years, Wes and JoBeth's friendship had remained strong. Last summer it had reached another level. Both eighteen, they had discovered new things about each other. When Wes returned to college in Pennsylvania, they had written to each other. When he came for the Christmas holidays, they had spent a great deal of time with each other, and things had taken a decidedly romantic turn.

She had missed him terribly when he left, and through their letters that winter, they had become closer. Now JoBeth was counting the days until Wes came home.

Was this what love is? She would just have to wait and see.

Chapter Two

~❧~

Madison Cady, home for his midday dinner, was a solidly built man in his early fifties with graying blond hair, kind blue eyes, a pleasant expression. A successful merchant, he had the self-confident look of someone secure in his position in the community and in his role as head of the household. Seating himself at the head of the table in the dining room, he glanced around with satisfaction. Nodding to his wife at the other end, her widowed niece, Johanna, on his right, and her pretty daughter, JoBeth, on his left, he greeted them, then bowed his head and intoned the family grace.

Annie, in a crisp turban and white apron, came in from the kitchen and stopped beside his chair, holding a tray on which were two bowls. As he helped himself generously to a serving of rice and then some okra and tomatoes, he casually remarked to JoBeth, "By the way, missy, I ran into a friend of yours as I was coming out of my office. Young Wesley Rutherford."

JoBeth nearly dropped her fork. Her heart beat excitedly. She looked at her uncle expectantly as he went on.

"Just off the noon train, as a matter of fact. Told me he'd graduated college."

JoBeth held her breath, waiting for more information.

A smile tugged at the corners of his mouth. "Oh, yes, he sent his kind regards to you, madam"—he inclined his head to his wife—"to you, Johanna"—he nodded at JoBeth's mother, then paused, chuckling, and turned back to JoBeth—"and he said he hoped to come in person to give his regards personally to you as well, young lady! I told him I thought you'd be mighty happy to hear that, seeing as how you've just about worn out the rug on the staircase, and the path to the postbox, near every day lookin' for a letter from Phil-a-del-phi-a."

"Oh, Uncle Madison!" she exclaimed in amused indignation.

It was a family joke how the letters arriving from Philadelphia came at a rate that caused Aunt Cady to raise inquisitive eyebrows when the post was delivered and JoBeth came running down the hall.

"Did he say when he'd come by, Uncle Madison?" JoBeth tried to keep her tone light.

"Well, no, honey, now that you ask," Uncle Madison said solemnly. "I didn't inquire, either. I thought it might not be in keeping with how young ladies like to keep young gentlemen guessing. Maybe you might be entertaining some other young beau this afternoon. So I just told him he was always welcome to come visit." Uncle Madison's tone was level, but his eyes were twinkling with merriment.

"Oh, Uncle, you are a tease!"

JoBeth always tolerated Uncle Madison's teasing. He enjoyed doing it and she didn't mind. But if Wes *was* coming by this afternoon, she wanted to change into her new dress.

"What does Wes plan to do, Madison?" Aunt Josie asked him.

"Well, a few months ago his uncle told me he planned to ask Wesley to read law in his office with him. But I reckon that's all changed now. Wes'll probably join up with the same regiment as his cousins."

The conversation went on past the subject of Wes's return to Hillsboro. At least for the others. JoBeth, distracted by her own excitement at the prospect of seeing Wes again, was filled with nervous anticipation. *How would it be after all these months? Half a year with nothing but letters? Had she said too much? Or too little? Did he still care about her? Or had he changed?*

After the meal was over, Uncle Madison went back to his office, Aunt Josie for her nap, and JoBeth's mother to her quilting frame. JoBeth hurried upstairs to her bedroom. From the armoire, she took out the dress she had saved to wear for Wes's homecoming. It was a pale pink French lawn, sprigged with tiny blue flowers, its waist sashed in blue moiré, its flounced skirt made to billow out over the three starched petticoats she would wear underneath.

Dressed, she sat down in front of her mirror and tried a half dozen hairstyles. Not an easy task, for JoBeth's hair was naturally curly, thick, and inclined to be stubborn. Finally, flinging down her brush in exasperation, she impatiently tied her shoulder-length curls back and secured them with a blue satin ribbon at the nape of her neck.

Then she settled herself at the window, where she had a good view of the street, of the corner at its end, where, coming from the Spencers' house, Wes could be seen walking toward the Cadys'. As she waited, she was filled with uncertainty. What did Wes think about the secession of the states, including North Carolina? The firing on Fort Sumter and its aftermath had happened while he was at college in Pennsylvania.

JoBeth was more knowledgeable about current events than some of the other young women her age in Hillsboro. One of JoBeth's chores was to tidy and dust the parlor and

Uncle Madison's study. Although newspapers were not considered proper reading material for young ladies, JoBeth had a curious mind. As more and more reports of the raging debate between the states made bold headlines, JoBeth found herself picking up the daily papers her uncle discarded and reading the fiery editorials. It had all sounded ominous. Now the war was a reality.

Holly Grove, the spacious house at the end of a lane of holly trees, had once been her mother's childhood home. There the Cadys' son Harvel now lived, and there the latest events had been discussed at length for months. At first the sentiment was mainly for states' rights, although most present were opposed to secession.

Every time the family gathered, their lively dinner-table talk often became a heated discussion of the crisis hovering over the country. JoBeth had heard all the points her relatives argued, and knew they were not Wes's convictions. So when Uncle Madison suggested what Wes would probably do, JoBeth knew he was wrong. No matter what the Spencer twins did. Wes was still as different from his cousins as night and day.

JoBeth had been around the three enough to know that whenever the cousins had a difference of opinion, Wes was always able to diplomatically, logically, and sensibly settle it. However, *this* time she was not sure he would prevail. War fever was burning rampantly throughout the South, and the usually conservative state of North Carolina had caught it as well.

JoBeth remembered a conversation Wes and her uncle had had when Wes was here during the Christmas holidays. Wes had come to escort her to the McKennas' party, and since she had not been quite ready, Uncle Madison took him into the parlor to wait for her. She was just coming downstairs when she heard their voices. To her surprise, their tone of voice was not casual or jovial but tense. Halfway down, she stopped to hear what they were talking about.

She heard Wes say, "I'm sorry, sir, but I was taught that slavery is wrong. To go to war over something like that— well, I just can't agree that it's the right thing to do."

"It's not so much slavery that's the point here, Wes. How many people do we know personally who own any?"

Listening outside the door, JoBeth thought of Annie. Annie had already seemed old to her when JoBeth came to live here. Now the mahogany face was webbed with wrinkles, and her movements slow. But Annie still ruled the kitchen, and it seemed to JoBeth that both her mother and aunt were a little in awe of the venerable cook. A slave? She had never thought of Annie as a slave.

She strained to hear what else Uncle Madison was expounding upon.

"No, that's just the flag those Northerners are waving! They want to dominate us, because they outnumber us in the Congress! What it is, is a matter of principle. States' rights, my boy."

"But states' rights over the Union, sir? That doesn't seem right. Both my great-grandfathers fought the British to form the Union. I was brought up to believe that to be loyal to that is every citizen's duty. . . ."

"Well, Wesley, I reckon you got filled with a lot of Northern thinkin' up at that Pennsylvania college. Folks up north think and feel differently about things than we do. All I can say is, you're going to bring a heap of trouble down on yourself and your family if it comes to war." There followed a long silence that, to JoBeth, seemed to stretch endlessly.

"I hope it won't come to that, sir."

"You might rightly hope so, Wesley." Uncle Madison's voice had been solemn. Had it also been threatening?

"Yes, sir, I do." Wes's voice sounded strong.

Outside in the hall, JoBeth let out a long breath and hurried into the parlor. At her entrance, both men stood up.

249

"Well, now, lookahere!" Uncle Madison had exclaimed. "If this isn't the prettiest young lady I've seen in a month of Sundays. I'd say she was well worth the wait, wouldn't you, Wes?" He beamed at his niece, thinking what an attractive, graceful young lady JoBeth had become from the gypsyish tomboy she had been.

It was in that aura of pleasantness that they had gone happily off to a wonderful evening.

However, JoBeth hadn't forgotten that overheard conversation. So much had happened since. What they had all dreaded had happened. They *were* at war with the North. What was Wes thinking now?

She didn't have a chance to guess at the answer to her own question, because she saw Wes rounding the corner. JoBeth jumped up and ran down the steps to the front door before the doorbell might wake Aunt Josie or rouse Annie, who was probably nodding in her ladder-back rocker on the sunny back porch.

As he came up the steps, JoBeth caught her breath. He looked different somehow—taller, broader through the shoulders, handsomer. In spite of all the letters they'd exchanged, the things they'd written, she felt suddenly shy.

"Wes!"

"JoBeth!"

He stood there looking at her through the screen door. Then she opened it and stepped out onto the porch. "It's so good to see you," she said, holding out both hands.

He took them and held them tightly. "It's been so long. I can't believe I'm really here and seeing you," he blurted out, then blushed. JoBeth was pleased. His words seem to evaporate that first awkwardness.

One of the things she loved most about Wesley. He was so open, so without guile or pretense. He said what he thought, spoke what he felt.

"Would you like to sit down?" She gestured to the white wicker furniture on the porch. "I can have Annie bring us some iced tea or lemonade?"

"I'd really rather take a walk—to our favorite place, JoBeth. Past the churchyard, down by the creek that runs under the old stone bridge. I have so much to talk to you about, and"—he hesitated—"all the way down on the train, I kept remembering how we used to go there and talk."

"Then, wait till I get my bonnet and parasol and run upstairs to tell Mama I'm going," she said and went inside. Lifting her skirts and crinolines, she skimmed up the stairway and down the hall, then tapped on her mother's sewing room door.

Johanna Shelby Rutherford was known for her beautiful quilts, her original designs. Mountain Star and Carolina Lily were two of her most popular patterns. When she had returned as a widow to Hillsboro to live with the Cadys, Aunt Josie had fixed up a small room—once a dressing room adjoining one of the large bedrooms upstairs—for her. Here a permanent quilting frame was set up for Johanna's use. Soon she had a thriving business, which enabled her to send JoBeth to a good female academy, and Shelby to a fine boy's boarding school.

Some of JoBeth's earliest memories were of her mother bent over her quilting frame, her face rapt with concentration, her hand moving gracefully as she plied the needle in and out in a smooth, gliding motion.

JoBeth opened the door put her head inside. Her mother looked up questioningly.

Johanna Davison retained a youthful beauty—only tiny lines around her wide blue eyes and tender, vulnerable mouth traced the passage of years. She could have remarried. Upon her return to Hillsboro, several men had been eager to court the lovely young widow. But Ross Davison had been the love of Johanna's life. No one could ever replace him. Her life had centered on her two children. At the sight of her daughter, a smile softened her expression.

"What is it, dear?"

"Wes is here, Mama, and he wants to go for a walk."

"That's fine, dear. Go along then. Be sure to tell him hello for me and that Aunt Josie wants him to stay for supper."

"Yes, Mama, I shall." JoBeth turned and hurried back down to the porch, where Wes was waiting.

Opening her ruffled parasol, she took his arm and they went down the steps, out the gate. They both knew the way to the path that led past the church where both their families worshiped and up the hill to the arching stone bridge. Below flowed the broad stream where JoBeth had soaked her blistered foot the first day they had become friends.

The fact that Wes was here seemed like a dream to her. After all the months of writing to each other and waiting, to actually be together at last made JoBeth euphoric.

For the first few minutes, they talked about mutual friends. But the more news JoBeth told him about their acquaintances, the quieter Wes became. Gradually she sensed his thoughtful demeanor and stopped. She felt a little twinge of uneasiness. She and Wes had never had any trouble finding things to talk about before. In fact, one of the things she loved about their relationship was that they never ran out of things to say to each other. They delighted in each other's company, preferring it to the many social events they were invited to. That's why the sudden silence that fell between them frightened her. Was something wrong? Maybe Wes's feelings for her had changed and he didn't know how to tell her.

On the bridge, they paused for a few minutes, looking down to where the clear water rushed over the rocks. Then Wes turned gave her a long, searching look, smiled and said, "You're so much prettier than I remembered."

JoBeth felt her cheeks warm. She had hoped he would mention how becoming her dress was or how her blue bonnet ribbons matched her eyes, but this was much better. His words made *her* happy, but she wished *he* looked happier.

"You look troubled, Wes," she said rather uncertainly. "Is anything wrong? What did you want to talk about?"

"I'm sorry, JoBeth. I don't mean to worry you. I didn't mean to bring it up—at least, not right away. Not on my first day home."

"You look awfully serious."

"I guess I do. I guess—well, it *is* serious."

She pretended a pout. "Not about the war, I hope. That's all we seem to hear nowadays." She tilted her head and looked up at him quizzically. "What is it? You might as well tell me and get it over with. Then maybe we can enjoy the rest of the day!"

"I always could talk to you, JoBeth. The trouble is, I have to decide something. Uncle Wayne has asked me to come into his law firm to read law there—"

"Oh, Wes, how wonderful!" Impulsively she reached out, put her hand on his arm. "Then you'll be staying in Hillsboro. People said you might go back to Philadelphia, since your grandmother is there and you went to college there. Now everything you wanted, worked for, has come true, hasn't it?"

"Yes, everything has come true—except that everything else has changed."

"What do you mean?"

"The war, JoBeth," he said sadly. "Our country is at war."

"I know that. But people say—at least everyone here says—that it won't last . . . that it will all be over in a few skirmishes, maybe . . . then the politicians will settle things." She broke off impatiently. "Oh, Wes, do we have to talk about this now? You've just come back! And I'm so happy. Please don't spoil it with all this gloomy talk."

"I'm sorry. All right, I'll stop for now. But I can't avoid *really* thinking about what I am to do." He leaned toward her and took one of her hands. "Eventually you and I must talk about it. Because it affects us."

"The war? *Us?*"

"Yes, JoBeth. Sooner or later everyone's going to be affected. You, me." He hesitated, then said, "It's because I love you, JoBeth."

Wide-eyed, JoBeth gazed at him.

"I mean, *really* love you. I hoped you'd come to know that through my letters. I guess I've loved you for a long time. Last Christmas I *knew* it. I just felt I couldn't say anything until I had finished my education. I had to have a way to support a wife before I could ask you to marry me. Now all that's changed."

She took a deep breath and said, "I love you, too. So how has it changed, Wes?"

"Oh, JoBeth, don't you see?"

"No."

Wes shook his head, and his mouth tightened into a firm line. "This war, it's changed everything. I *know* how everybody in Hillsboro feels. Your relatives *and* mine. It's not that simple. In fact, it's very complicated."

She frowned, looking puzzled. "Why is it?"

"Because I guess you could say *I'm* not simple." He sighed. "Uncle Wayne wants an answer. Either I stay and go into law practice with him or I join up. Blakely and Will are all het up, ready to go."

"Well, you've never played 'follow the leader' with *them!*" she declared. "So what does what they do have to do with us? Oh, Wes, can't we just be happy?" JoBeth asked, knowing it was a silly thing to say, but she couldn't help it. Wes had just told her what she'd been longing to hear, and now he was ruining it by bringing up the war and all the things she'd rather forget.

"Because people have to choose. And it's splitting our country in two. Splitting families. That's what I'm facing. That's what I had to talk to you about. I don't think secession is right. To take up arms against our government. But I know what's probably going to happen if I make these kinds of statements here, to my uncle, to your folks."

JoBeth felt an awful tightness in her throat, the feeling that she was going to cry. She looked back down into the stream, wishing all her dread of what was going to happen would go away.

"Believe me, JoBeth, I wish we didn't have to talk about all this," Wes said earnestly. He leaned on the stone ledge, clasped his hands together, stared down into the water. After a long moment, he said quietly, "I felt I had to—*wanted* to— talk to you before I talked to Uncle Wayne. I had to know how you feel, whatever I decide."

JoBeth felt as if all the sunshine had gone out of the afternoon. "We may as well go back," she said plaintively.

Wes caught her hand, brought it up to his lips, kissed it.

JoBeth looked up at him, his face suddenly blurred because her eyes were full of tears. She couldn't speak.

"I love you, JoBeth."

"Love is supposed to make people happy, Wes," she said forlornly.

"I know. I'm sorry."

Slowly they retraced their steps back to the Cadys' house, not saying anything more. JoBeth's mother and aunt were sitting on the front porch as they came up the walk. They greeted Wes cordially, then Aunt Josie asked, "You will stay to supper, won't you, Wesley?"

"Thank you kindly, Mrs. Cady, but this being my first night home, Aunt Alzada's expecting me there."

"Well, certainly I can understand that. You've been away such a long time. But another night, surely. Tomorrow, then?"

"Yes, ma'am, that would be a pleasure. Thank you."

"Then, we'll look forward to seeing you tomorrow evening. Madison will be eager to talk to you about how things are up north."

Inwardly JoBeth shrank. She knew Wes was too respectful of his elders to argue with Uncle Madison. However, he was not a person to sit quietly and let his silence give consent if he disagreed with what was being said. Now, with his new determination to follow his conscience, JoBeth dreaded to think what might take place at the supper table the next evening.

She walked back to the gate with Wesley.

"Tomorrow I'll have my talk with Uncle Wayne," Wes said in a low voice.

"I'll be praying everything will go fine, Wesley," she said, not knowing what that meant exactly. Fine for whom?

He squeezed her hand. "However it turns out, JoBeth, I love you," he whispered.

"I know," she said over the lump in her throat. After he left, she stood for a minute at the gate before going back up to the porch. Preoccupied with her own heavy heart, JoBeth didn't notice that her mother and aunt exchanged puzzled glances.

Chapter Three

❧❧❧

The next evening, Wes arrived almost at the same time that Uncle Madison arrived home from his office. Greeting Wes heartily, Uncle Madison invited him into the parlor. JoBeth hoped Wes wouldn't bring up anything controversial and upset Uncle Madison. At least not until after supper. She knew Wes had determined to make clear his feelings about the war, and there was nothing she could do about that. She just wanted them to have a pleasant meal.

With a lingering glance at the two men, JoBeth went into the kitchen. Annie had asked for the evening off to visit her sick sister, so her mother and aunt were going to serve the dinner Annie had fixed ahead of time.

Johanna was busily spooning spiced peaches into small, cut-glass condiment dishes. Sniffing appreciatively the savory smells of baking ham and candied sweet potatoes, JoBeth asked, "What can I do to help?"

Her mother smiled at her. "You can get the extra silver servers out and fill the cream pitcher."

Aunt Josie, her cheeks flushed from the heat, closed the oven door and turned from the stove. JoBeth looked at her aunt admiringly. Even in the kitchen, the woman managed to look elegant, not a hair out of place, sapphire drop earrings twinkling. Aunt Josie untied the strings of a blue cotton apron that covered her lace-trimmed flowered dress and asked, "Are Madison and Wes having a nice chat in the parlor?"

"Yes, ma'am," JoBeth answered, sincerely hoping so.

Aunt Josie's brow puckered slightly. "Hope they're not arguin'."

"No, ma'am." JoBeth looked at her aunt warily. "Why should they be arguing?"

"Well, I'm sure it's nothing to be fussed about. It's just that I saw Alzada Spencer's sister in town, and she told me she'd heard that Wesley was going back up north—that he'd refused his uncle's offer to come into the law firm. That they had some bad kind of falling out. It's probably nothing, just one of those rumors that fly around."

JoBeth felt a sinking sensation in her stomach. How quickly word spread in Hillsboro! She held her breath as Aunt Josie continued.

"But then, everybody knows that Wayne Spencer's got a hot temper, and"—she shrugged—"sometimes young men pick up ideas that don't really fit into the lives they're going to live after they graduate, but they like to test them out. Of course, some folks couldn't figure out just why the Rutherfords let him go to *Philadelphia* to get his education. When there are several good colleges around here."

"Well, his grandmother lives there, for one thing," JoBeth began, but at her mother's almost imperceptible headshake, she halted.

"Well, you know Madison—he always feels he has to set a young person's head straight," Aunt Josie said. Picking up a quilted hot pad, she opened the oven again and peered into it. As she lifted the lid of the roasting pan, delicious clove-scented steam filled the air. "The ham's done, and the sweet potatoes are just right," she said with satisfaction. "Go tell the gentlemen they can come to the table, honey," she directed JoBeth.

JoBeth left the kitchen and hurried down the hall. As she neared the parlor, she heard raised voices. In his best lawyerly tone, almost as though he were addressing a jury, Uncle Madison was saying, "But Wes, there're North Carolina brigades starting up. *Your* friends, some of your schoolmates, chaps you've known all your life—couldn't you see your way to joining up with these troops?"

JoBeth held her breath for Wes's reply. There was a pause. Then he said, "No, sir, I couldn't fight for slavery."

Her stomach in knots, she moved closer, placing her head in the crack of the door in order to hear her uncle's response. She knew her uncle and she was afraid. It was not long in coming.

"Well, Wesley, I'm sorry to hear this." A pause, and then, "I'm sure you know that my wife and I set a great store by our niece, and it hasn't escaped our notice that you and JoBeth have fond feelings for each other." Uncle Madison cleared his throat before continuing. "I wouldn't want to see her burdened by your decision and brought to divided loyalties and unhappiness."

"No, sir. I wouldn't want that, either," Wes replied. "I do love JoBeth. Under other circumstances—I mean, if things weren't so uncertain—I would ask you and her mother for the privilege, the honor, of asking her to marry me. I have no intention of bringing her any unhappiness."

JoBeth pressed her hands tightly together. She didn't know whether to tiptoe back to the kitchen and let Aunt Josie call them to dinner or to retrace her steps and then make some warning noise to let the men know she was approaching the parlor. As it turned out, Aunt Josie called from the dining room, "What's keeping those men? Madison! You and Wesley come along while everything's nice and hot."

JoBeth dreaded the meal. However, when both her uncle and Wes joined them at the table, the conversation seemed pleasant enough. Everyone seemed to be making an effort to avoid controversy. As sensitive as JoBeth was, both to Wes and her uncle, she felt decidedly tense throughout the meal. JoBeth had the distinct feeling that the truce between her uncle and Wes was simply for courtesy's sake. It seemed to her that when Wes said he must leave, Uncle Madison's goodnight was untypically cool.

She walked out to the porch with Wes when he left. They stood for a minute at the top of the steps. She felt instinctively that Wes was about to tell her something she didn't want to hear.

"Blakely and Will have already joined the Confederate Army. Uncle Wayne assumes I will, too."

Surprised, she turned to him. Had he possibly changed his mind? Hope flared up. "So will you? Is that what you've decided?"

Wes shook his head. "No, of course not. I can't. I couldn't fight for something I think is wrong." He clenched his hands in a double fist. "I don't know whether I can even fight for what I believe is right."

"Is that because—I mean, are your feelings, like everyone says, because you went to school up north?"

"Yes, that could be a part of it. It influenced my thinking. But it goes even deeper than that. Ever since I was young, even when I was a little boy, eight or nine, I had these feelings ... about slavery, about folks owning other human beings. I couldn't put it into words then. It was just an uneasiness that it was wrong—"

"I don't think of *Annie* as a slave," JoBeth protested. "She's always been with us, as long as I can remember, but ..." Her voice trailed off weakly.

"That's just it, JoBeth. It's a way of life we've all just accepted. Until now. Now people have to decide. Do what their conscience demands."

"I know what you've told me the Quakers think about war, what your grandmother taught you about taking up arms." She frowned, genuinely puzzled. "But in the summers, when you're here, you go to *our* church. And they never say anything about slavery or about fighting. Everyone here feels it's only honorable to defend yourself. I guess I just don't understand. If it's wrong to fight at all, why do you have to choose sides?"

"That's the dilemma, JoBeth. I can't answer for anyone else. It's my own conscience I must answer to. My own belief. I never became a Quaker, although I attended their meetings when I was with my grandmother. Probably unconsciously absorbed their teachings." He sighed. "That was when I was a child, JoBeth. Remember the Scripture 'When I was a child, I thought as a child'—First Corinthians, thirteen, eleven? 'I spoke as a child, I understood as a child, I thought as a child, but when I became a man, I put away childish things.'" He paused. "Now, however, as a man with my own convictions about what is right or wrong, I have to choose." He sighed again. "And I don't think that the Union should be broken apart. I think it should be protected. Much as I hate the thought of fighting people I know and love, I have to make a choice and go with my own conscience."

"You mean—"

"I'll have to leave Hillsboro, JoBeth. Go back to Pennsylvania. Then I'll—"

"Oh no, Wes!" Her voice sounded almost like a sob. "Please, isn't there some other way?"

"I don't see that there is, JoBeth." Wes's voice grew husky. "I can't stay, feeling as I do, knowing how others will view my decision."

"You've told your uncle, then?"

"Yes. Of course he's furious. We had a terrible row. Aunt Alzeda went to bed with a terrible headache. The whole

261

household is in an uproar. The sooner I can make arrangements to go, the better for everyone." He gave a harsh laugh. "I'd better be gone before the two conquering heroes arrive back from Raleigh."

"Blakely and Will?"

"Yes." Wesley turned and drew JoBeth into his arms. "Oh, JoBeth, forgive me for what I'm doing to you." His words were muffled against her hair as he drew her even closer.

She clung to him, her cheek pressed against the starched, ruffled shirt. *This should be one of the happiest moments in my life*, she thought. *So why do I feel as if my heart is breaking?*

Just then Aunt Josie came to the door, holding an oil lamp.

"Oh, is Wesley still here, JoBeth?" she asked, of course knowing he was. They broke apart guiltily. "My, what a lovely night. Looks as if a new moon is coming up," Aunt Josie said. "Do give my regards to Alzeda, won't you, Wes, dear?" Then to JoBeth she said, "It's getting rather cool, isn't it, JoBeth? Either get a shawl, dear, or come inside."

There was no mistaking the subtle reprimand in her aunt's voice.

"Yes, Auntie," she replied, then whispered to Wes, "I guess I'd better go in."

"I'll come by tomorrow and let you know my plans," Wes said.

"No, maybe it had better not be here. Let's meet at the bridge instead. We can talk more freely there."

"Yes, that's a good idea. Tomorrow, then. Say, three o'clock," he replied. Raising his voice slightly, he said, "Good night, Mrs. Cady. Thanks again for supper." He started down the porch steps. JoBeth watched his tall figure walk through the gate and disappear into the shadowy night.

What tomorrow or the day after would bring, she had no idea. She had only a feeling of dread that her life was going to change drastically.

She'd had that same feeling once before, long ago.

Even at age seven, JoBeth had been old enough to remember the day of her father's funeral clearly. As they lowered the simple pine coffin into the ground her father had loved all his life, Reverend Tomlin, his voice breaking as he spoke the words, read from Matthew 25:34.

"'Come ye blessed of my Father, inherit the kingdom prepared for you from the foundation of the world. For I was sick and ye visited me. Inasmuch as ye did it unto one of the least of these, my brethren, ye did it unto me.'"

JoBeth had understood how much Ross Davison had been beloved by the members of the mountain community that he had served so faithfully for so many years. With no thought to his own comfort, he had traveled the hills in any kind of weather to bring aid to the sick, treating injuries and all sorts of illnesses.

His dedication had been unquestioned. At great risk to his own health and safety, he had given generously of his skill, his knowledge, his determination, and it was in treating a dangerous and deadly disease that he had at last succumbed himself.

But what JoBeth hadn't fully understood was why they had to leave Millscreek Gap.

She and her five-year-old brother, Shelby, had listened while Johanna explained that they were going down to live in Hillsboro with their mother's relatives. All JoBeth really heard was "leaving the mountains." But *why* must they leave? she had asked stubbornly. Why couldn't she stay with Granny Eliza?

"Johanna Elizabeth," her mother had said sternly. "You must not complain and whine and carry on like this. Your daddy is gone—we can't stay alone up in the mountains. You and Shelby have to go to school. That's what your father would have wanted. I must make a living there for us. Aunt Josie and Uncle Madison have been kind enough to offer us a home, and we should be grateful. I will work, making quilts to sell, in order to give us money enough to be independent— but Shelby must have his chance. A *man*, nowadays, needs to be educated. Maybe he'll become a doctor like your daddy, or a lawyer like Uncle Madison ... but he's got to have his opportunity. This is the only way I could make sure that he does."

JoBeth hadn't said any more. But it was with a sense of hopeless loss that she helped pack up their belongings, said good-bye to her beloved grandmother and to her mountain cousins, climbed up on the wagon seat alongside her mother— with Shelby wedged in between them—and started the torturous trip down the narrow, winding road to Hillsboro.

"Will we stay at Holly Grove?" she had asked once they came into town.

"No, honey. Grandmother Shelby lives in Charleston with Aunt Cissy now. Our cousins Harvel and Marilee live at Holly Grove these days. We'll be going to the Willows, to the Cadys' house."

JoBeth had nodded, not really sure if she knew just who the Cadys were. Her mother had so many "town kin," so many aunts and cousins, that JoBeth had found it hard to keep them straight when they came down to visit. That hadn't been often. In winter the mountain roads were impassable, and in the summers—well, there was always so much to do on the long summer days.

As they finally came to a stop in front of a large, white, pillared house just at dusk, JoBeth's memory had been stirred. She had suddenly remembered that Aunt Johanna Cady was the "fussy" one of her mother's aunties. Just then she had felt a sharp sense of loss over her father's death. She had recalled his deep, kind voice, the way he would swing her up in front of him onto his saddle, cuddling her in his strong arms, leaning down and asking affectionately, "Well now, Miss Johanna

Elizabeth, what kind of a day did you have?" Tears came stinging into her eyes. It was at that moment, in some indescribable way, that she knew in her child's heart that her life was forever changed.

Now, remembering that, JoBeth felt again the sensation of being on a road whose end she could not see.

Wes had warned her, *It's not that simple*. But she was yet to discover the full price of their love, their commitment to each other.

Chapter Four

❦

*W*es had been right when he said that things were complicated, JoBeth thought on her way to meet him the next afternoon. Everyone had his own opinion about the war. First the argument had been whether or not North Carolina should have seceded, then they debated what kind of president of the Confederacy Jefferson Davis would make, now it was a disagreement about what the generals were doing. Even within JoBeth's family, there were sharp differences.

In the mountain community, there were few hotheads for war, she found when she visited. Granny Eliza Davison had spoken for many when she said, "'Tain't our fight. Why should I send my grandsons to die for someone I don't even know to keep their slaves?"

Shelby, now in his first year of seminary, seemed to be having some private inner struggle. He had been unusually quiet since coming home this summer.

JoBeth saw Wes waiting for her and quickened her step. The very sight of him made her heart turn over. Everything she had imagined feeling about him as she wrote to him and received his letters was real. It set her pulse pounding and made her lightheaded. This was the love she had always dreamed of knowing.

The sad part of it was that the kind of idyllic, romantic time she had imagined for them when Wesley came home had not come true. When she reached Wes, it was evident from the look on his face that things were not any better at the Spencers'. In fact, Wes's expression, the sadness in his eyes, told the story, without JoBeth's asking for details.

"If it hadn't been for Aunt Alzada, I think my uncle would have ordered me out of the house right then and there," Wes said dejectedly. "There's no going back. All affectionate exchange between us is gone. He said he was bitterly disappointed in me. *Ashamed*, actually, that I was willing to go against my own people, my state." He shuddered. "He doesn't realize just how painful it is for me. Everything would be fine if I'd recant"—he snapped his fingers—"if I'd say I was wrong, he was right. But I don't believe that."

"What is he most angry about? Is it your view of slavery?" JoBeth frowned. "The Spencers only have house servants, just as my aunt and uncle do—"

"It's not just over slavery, whether a man has a right to own slaves or not. More importantly, it's whether a state can leave the Union at will. It's about how important the union of *all* the states is."

She had heard this argued among her relatives for months. So much so that she had begun to deliberately stop listening and instead to think about other things while the discussions went on. She had not really believed it would affect her life. Now she realized she had been mistaken. Still, she wanted—*needed*—to be convinced.

She gestured impatiently. "Yes, yes, I know all that. But what does this really have to do with *us?*"

"Everything. People are taking sides. No one can remain on the fence, JoBeth. We're all going to have to stand up for what we believe or what we're against. It's going to get people angry and bitter, and it's going to go on for a long time."

JoBeth felt as if a cold wind had blown over her, chilling her to the bone.

"There's no point now in asking permission to marry you. Now that your uncle knows where I stand, he as much as told me it was impossible."

"Oh, Wesley, did you have to be so *honest?*" she demanded with mock despair.

"Would you love me if I weren't?"

She threw out her hands helplessly. "I suppose not."

"Then you *do?* You do love me?"

"Yes, of course!"

He frowned deeply. "You have to be prepared. Now that they *do* know, they may forbid us to ever see each other again—"

"Oh, Wes, don't say that. Don't even *think* that."

"You still don't truly understand, do you? How deeply emotions about this war run? I wish to God you didn't have to, JoBeth." There was a desperate edge to Wes's tone.

"I'm trying to understand," she hastened to assure him. "I guess I just didn't want to understand. It hurts too much. To think your aunt and uncle would let something come between their love for you and what you believe. I mean, you've been like another son to them both."

Wes looked so sad. She knew how much Wes loved the Spencers, respected them, had always wanted to please them. She understood how much their approval meant to him. Impulsively JoBeth reached up on tiptoe and put her arms around his neck, kissed him on the lips. He drew her close, and the kiss deepened into a long, tender one, full of sweetness, tenderness, and tentative hope.

"I love you, Wes. Nothing else should matter."

"I love you, too, JoBeth. But I'm afraid other things *do* matter. At least at this time, in this place." He kissed her again, then gently released her, saying, "I'm also aware that what I'm going to have to ask you to do will take more than love. It will take everything either of us has within us. And we can't do it by ourselves. We're going to need God's help, JoBeth. It won't be easy. In fact, it might be the hardest thing we've ever been called on to do."

❧

That evening, JoBeth found out just how hard it was going to be, when she timidly approached her uncle. "Uncle Madison, I know Wesley has told you how he feels, and though I know you don't agree with him, I hope—"

Before she could finish, he cast aside his newspaper and declared vehemently, "It's not the government's place to tell us what we can do with our own property—"

"Uncle Madison, can't you try to see it from Wes's viewpoint? He's an idealist, and—"

"How many idealists do you find in history books? Not many, I'll tell you. It's the doers like Andrew Jackson we remember, the kind of men that stand up for what they believe."

"But that's exactly what Wesley is doing! Don't you see that?"

"I see that you're a foolish young woman who doesn't know dreams from reality," he said coldly. "Reality never measures up to anticipation, and expectation is usually the precursor of disillusionment. You're heading for a cruel disappointment, my girl."

JoBeth felt a rush of antagonism that he should dismiss Wes's beliefs so harshly. But she would not allow anyone to snatch away her dreams so ruthlessly. Even though she had to remain under this roof and accept that she and her mother were living here mainly at the largesse of their relatives, she was determined not to be defeated by her uncle's attitude nor to doubt Wes's staunch convictions.

JoBeth glanced away as if examining the silver epergne in the center of the table. She knew it was useless to argue further, to plead Wes's case. Uncle Madison's mind was closed. In his way of thinking, Wes had become a traitor.

That night, JoBeth thought long and hard about everything that had transpired in these past three days.

From being a romantic figure of fantasy and imagination, Wesley had become the central person in her life. Someone on whom so much revolved. In the matter of a few hours, everything had changed. There would be no long summer in which their romance would progress at a leisurely pace. All the things she had dreamed of doing when Wes came home—strolls by the river, long talks, reading poetry together—had been eclipsed by the need to make life-changing decisions. Suddenly they were living out a real drama. One for which there had been no rehearsal, she herself in a role she had never sought to play.

Wes had said everyone had to take a stand. He was right. She was being forced to choose sides: Wes or her family.

For her mother's sake, for the peace of the household, she had to keep her thoughts, her feelings, to herself—and yet she would not betray her loyalty and her love.

Because she knew now, without doubt, that she loved Wes. Something in him drew her irrevocably. A few days ago, even a few hours, she would never have had this certainty.

Remembering Wes's words "We're going to need God's help," she threw herself on her knees beside her bed. JoBeth prayed. But no peace came. Her soul was still in turmoil.

The serene, safe world she had known, the circle of love and acceptance, of affection and hospitality and shelter, had cracked. Hostility, resentment, anger, had been thrust into its quiet warmth. All the things she had taken for granted seemed to be slipping away.

Burying her face in her hands, she saw a mental picture of Wes standing alone outside the circle. In that moment, she knew she could not let him stand there alone or turn and walk away from her. *I'm mad about him*, she thought. *I'm half sick with it.* She was quivering. Life was so scary and unpredictable.

It's not that simple, Wes's words came back to her. No, it certainly wasn't. It wasn't like deciding to accept an invitation to a party, choosing a dress pattern, selecting the color of bonnet ribbons, the simple kind of choices she had made easily most of her life. This choice was different and not simple at all. One choice meant she might never see Wes again. If his conscience demanded he sacrifice everything, his hometown, cousins, family, friends, his love, then she had to decide if she would support that conviction. It was not, after all, debatable.

She knew she could not let Wes leave without telling him she was willing to stand by him. She got up from her knees, strengthened but trembling.

JoBeth did not realize she had entered a battle of her own making: the battle between loyalty and love. She had no intention, no matter what the opposition or provocation, of giving Wes up.

> I never spoke that word "farewell" but with an utter-
> ance faint and broken;
> A heart yearning for the time when it should never more
> be spoken.
>
> Caroline Bowles

Chapter Five

❦

Three more days passed. Days of anguish and silent misery such as JoBeth had never spent before in her entire life. JoBeth was well aware that the whole Cady household seemed to be walking on eggshells as they tried to avoid mentioning the subject of Wesley Rutherford around her.

Finally a note from Wes came, asking her to meet him. Heart racing, she slipped out of the house at a time when no one would miss her and hurried to their favorite place.

Although she had prayed, hers had been rather undirected prayers: for courage, for strength. She had not dared pray for Wes to change his mind. In her heart of hearts, she knew that the parting she dreaded was about to come. Even knowing that this was inevitable, she had no way to prepare herself for it.

When she reached him, they clasped hands silently. Was it her imagination, or had Wes aged overnight? He looked pale and there were dark circles under his eyes, as though he had not slept. JoBeth's heart winced in sympathy, as if his pain were her own. Only she fully understood how heart-wrenching it was for him to leave the home that had been his own since childhood, to say good-bye to the aunt and uncle he cherished. Worse still was the way of the leave-taking. In disgrace. As a turncoat. A traitor.

For a minute, they simply looked at each other word-lessly. Then Wes said brokenly, "I'm so sorry, JoBeth. The last thing I ever wanted to do was hurt you."

"I know."

"I thought it would all be so different—our future, I mean. I even dreamed we might be married this summer. Now that's out of the question. Your relatives would never let you marry me now."

Impulsively JoBeth burst out, "Oh, Wes, I'd marry you tomorrow, with or without permission."

He looked at her with a slight smile. "I wager you would, JoBeth. That's your sweet, generous nature. But I wouldn't ask that of you. It was wrong of me to even—"

"No, it wasn't. I love you, Wes. I say yes, now or when-ever," JoBeth rushed on, knowing it was unseemly, unlady-like, unheard of, but she didn't care. What did all that matter now? There was so much more at stake here than that.

"Bless you for saying that. If it weren't for you"—he paused—"I would feel totally alone, abandoned. I hope to God I'm doing the right thing, that it's worth all the people that are being hurt by my decision."

His sorrow was too deep for tears. Anything she might have said to ease his suffering would have seemed shallow, banal.

They walked along in silence, holding hands. There was so much they wanted to say to each other, but it was difficult to speak. Each was locked into a private sense of desolation. Memories still fresh of the past, dreams of the future they had hoped to share. They were both conscious of the heavy shadow hovering over them, the good-bye that must be said.

They climbed to the top of the hill, where they could look over the town. A soft summer dusk began to fall, and as it deepened, here and there a light winked on. People were setting their oil lamps at the window to welcome others or on a table ready for a family dinner. A kind of timelessness stretched over the scene. From where they watched, it all looked so safe, secure, almost like a toy village. It seemed impossible that such a picturesque scene could harbor hostility, anger, and flaming antagonism.

Reluctantly JoBeth said, "I'd better be getting home, Wes. There'll be questions. . . ."

"Yes, I know, we have to go. But first . . ." He drew her close, pressed his cheek against hers. Gently stroking her hair, he said, "Before we do, I have something to show you." He drew a small chamois bag from his pocket. "I guess I was too optimistic—took too much for granted. Here, look for yourself." He pressed the bag into JoBeth's hand. She untied the string that closed it, and shook out the contents. Two rings fell out into her palm. Each was a narrow band with two sculpted clasped hands. "Press it gently on the back," Wes instructed in a low voice. JoBeth did and the tiny hands sprang apart, revealing a heart.

"Oh, Wes!" she breathed softly. "How lovely!"

"I had them especially made from a twenty-dollar gold piece, by a Philadelphia goldsmith. One for you and one for me. The smaller one is yours. I intended to give it to you at the end of the summer, when I planned to ask you to marry me. Like a betrothal ring."

"They still can be, Wes. Betrothal rings."

"You mean that? You still would marry me, in spite of—"

"Of course, and not in spite of, Wes—*because of*. I admire you so much. I respect your courage." She hesitated. Then, with a catch in her throat, she said, "I love you."

He drew her into his arms, held her hard against his pounding heart. "JoBeth, it's *you* who is brave. How did I ever deserve you?"

She clung to him, feeling her heart throb wildly, feeling dizzy with the enormity of what was happening. After a minute, he released her and took one of her small hands in his. "Here, I'll put yours on, then you can put mine on."

She tugged her hand away. "But Wes, I can't wear mine on my finger, where everyone will notice—" Her voice faltered. "I wish it could be for all the world to see."

"Of course. I should have thought of that myself."

"I'm sorry—"

"No, I understand. It's better, safer that way," he said quietly.

"I'll wear it around my neck on a chain. That way it will be closer to my heart."

"What a girl you are, JoBeth," Wes said softly, taking her tenderly into his arms again. They kissed and in the kiss was tenderness, sweetness, commitment, and promise. Finally they drew apart and, arms around each other's waist, started back down the hillside.

As they passed the churchyard, Wes paused, looked at the old brick building heavily hung with ivy. He glanced at JoBeth as if for consent. She nodded, understanding what he meant. He agilely hurdled the stone wall and then, putting his hands around her waist, lifted her over it. Winding their way through the cemetery with its monuments, crosses, and stone lambs, they moved into the arch of the entrance to the church.

Wes took out his ring and handed it to JoBeth, and she gave him hers. Then he took her left hand and said solemnly, "JoBeth, if anything should happen, or if I shouldn't come back, I don't want you to feel that this is binding—"

"Don't!" With her right hand, she placed her fingers on his mouth, stopping whatever else he was going to say. "Never! Don't even think it!"

"All I meant was, if—if that did happen, I would want you to feel free to find someone else—"

She slipped her hand down from his lips and placed her palm against his heart.

"Wesley, let's pledge ourselves to each other for now. No one knows what's ahead. What we feel at this moment is what counts."

"You're right." Wes's voice was husky as he slipped the ring on her third finger.

"I, John Wesley Rutherford, pledge my life, my faithfulness, my enduring love, to you now and forever. Now you," he coached gently.

"I, Johanna Elizabeth Davison, pledge myself to keep this promise to love and wait for you. However long the separation, however long the war lasts, I will be true."

Wes leaned down to kiss her and discovered that her cheeks were wet with tears. He wiped them away gently with both thumbs. "Oh, darling, don't cry." Then they were in each other's arms again. She heard the drumbeat of his heart where her ear was pressed against his chest. At length Wes said gently, "It's getting dark. I'd better get you home."

"When will I see you again?"

His mouth tightened. "I didn't want to tell you, but I'm packed, ready to go. I could see that things were not going to get better. Too much has been said that can't be unsaid. The sooner I leave, the better, the less unhappiness and resentment I'll cause." He hesitated. "I've decided to leave tomorrow. On the morning train."

"So *soon?* Oh, Wes!" she exclaimed, then said, "I'll come to see you off."

He pressed her hands, shook his head. "No, I don't think that's a very good idea," he said slowly. "To be seen with me might—well, it would get back to your family. They would be angry. It would just make things harder—"

"Oh, it's so unfair. So cruel!" she cried. They stood there in the darkness, heart to heart, both fighting to hold back tears. After a moment, hand in hand, they walked on, not talking.

On the porch post of the Cadys' house, a lantern had been lit and shone out, illuminating the way from the gate. They walked up the path with lagging steps. Just before they reached the porch, Wes pulled her gently back. Turning so the light shone on her face, he took it in both his hands, lifted it, and looked down into it. "I want to remember how you look, so after I'm gone, I can close my eyes and see you."

"I'll send you my picture," she whispered.

"Yes, do that," he said huskily. Then he took one of her shiny dark curls, wound it gently around his finger. "Goodbye, darling JoBeth. I do love you so." He drew a deep breath. "Maybe it won't be long, and after the war, when I come back, we can marry"—he halted, adding in a voice that shook a little—"and live happily ever after."

Before she went in the house, JoBeth took off the ring Wes had placed on her finger and put it back inside the small chamois bag, then into her pocket. All evening long, every once in a while, she would put her hand down and touch it as if to see if it was there and if what had taken place between her and Wes that afternoon had really happened. She amazed herself that even while her thoughts were on Wes, she was able to carry on a conversation at supper, help Annie clear the table and assist her in the kitchen, then hold her aunt's skein of yarn while she rolled it into a ball. Was he packing, making his sad farewells, meeting coldness and disapproval as he prepared to leave? Not once did she give way to her feelings. Perhaps this was preparation for what lay ahead of her in the time she and Wes would be separated by this cruel war.

It wasn't until later, when she was alone in the privacy of her own bedroom, that she took out the ring. Inside the little bag, she found a piece of paper folded in tiny squares. Unfolding it, she saw that Wes had written something on it. Taking it closer to the oil lamp by her bed, she read it.

My Darling JoBeth,

In medieval times, the exchange of rings in betrothal was made in church. I found this and thought it appropriate for us. It's from Hosea 2:19–20: "I will betroth you to me forever, I will betroth you in loving kindness and understanding, I will betroth you with faithfulness."

Ever your loving,
Wesley

JoBeth reread the Scripture several times. She wasn't familiar with it. However, Wesley was right. They were pledged to each other. Whether anyone else knew it or not, she intended to keep the promise she had made that day *forever*.

Chapter Six

❧

*W*es was gone. And there was a void in JoBeth's life that she could not freely share with anyone. Any voicing of how much she missed Wes would bring cold stares, even some remark—perhaps unintentional but pointed—expressing the speaker's personal viewpoint. That would cut her to the quick. Was there no one in all of Hillsboro who shared Wes's abhorrence at the thought of war, of the dissolution of the Union?

Neither of them could possibly have imagined that a shot fired at Fort Sumter would resound throughout the land and like a cannonball shatter all their lovely plans.

Less than a week after Wes declared himself and left town, Alzada Spencer came to pay a call. Her intention for doing so was soon made clear, as was her opinion about her nephew.

She was seated in the parlor with Aunt Josie and Johanna. When JoBeth joined them, bringing in the tea tray and setting it down for her aunt to pour, she realized that Wes was the subject of the conversation. She quietly sat down and listened intently.

Mrs. Spencer gave a dramatic sigh and declared, "None of us can understand it, I declare—we simply cannot. It's all because of Grandmother Blakely, who, bless her soul, cannot help that she was raised by the Philadelphia branch of Lewis's family and adopted the Quaker religion. Wesley has absorbed it all, ever since his own folks died and he was sent up there to live. Then, of course, he went to that Quaker college— and the damage was done. It's hard to blame him, but he *is* a grown man *and* also a North Carolinian by birth. Wayne has tried to explain it to me"—she shook her head until all her clustered blond curls danced—"and I do try to take a Christian attitude about it, but my dears, if he goes into the Union Army, he will be, the Lord forbid, perhaps someday aiming his gun . . . at one of his cousins. . . ." She took a dainty handkerchief out of her velvet purse and brushed the tip of her small nose and sighed again.

"But Mrs. Spencer, I don't think Wes intends to fight, to carry a gun. That in itself is against Quaker beliefs. . . .," Johanna tried to gently suggest.

JoBeth, her hands locked in her lap, said nothing.

But she didn't escape Mrs. Spencer's lugubrious glance and direct comment, "I do feel sorry for *you*, darlin'. You know, Wes confided in me last Christmastime his hopes about you." She whisked the handkerchief again, sighing. "It's such a shame. I know what you and Wes were plannin', and we couldn't have been more pleased, and I'm sure you, Josie and Johanna, felt the same." She paused with a sniff and shook her head again. "But of course, now it is all just ruined—"

JoBeth sat up straight and her mouth opened to protest, but just then she caught her mother's warning glance and stopped. It would have been unthinkable to contradict Wes's aunt, rude to argue with a guest. JoBeth pressed her lips tightly and clenched her hands but thought, *Oh, no! No! Everything's not ruined. We're not giving each other up, no matter what. I love Wes and he loves me, and it will, please God, work out.*

"I can only be thankful that my own boys knew their duty and did it without question," Alzada continued.

Of course! Her sons, Blakely and Will Spencer, were reckless and wild, JoBeth thought indignantly. They'd do anything to avoid books, classes, or lessons. They had been among the first to join up. A few days after the April attack on Fort Sumter, they and some of their classmates from the university had gone up to Raleigh to enlist. They had come home saying they couldn't see sitting in classrooms while the threat of invasion from the "Northern aggressors" was a possibility. Only days later they had come over to the Cadys' house to show off their officers' uniforms. JoBeth had to admit they looked dashing, all spit and polish, complete with sashes and high boots.

JoBeth had to bite her tongue as she listened to Alzada's bragging about them. As far as JoBeth could remember, neither them had ever had a serious thought in their lives! Much less had they developed a philosophy or conviction about anything. Having known them since they were boys, JoBeth knew they weren't fighting for some cause they believed in. For them, riding off to war was an adventure, like so many of their other escapades.

Politeness kept JoBeth quiet, but she was relieved when Aunt Josie asked her to freshen the teapot and she was able to leave the parlor. In the kitchen, while waiting for the kettle to boil, she had a chance to get control of her feelings.

Where was Wes? Back at his grandmother's home? She hadn't heard from him. He had promised to write as soon as he knew his plans. Already the days he had been here were beginning to grow vague, faded. The conversations they'd had were becoming mixed up. What had they talked about and when? Had he actually asked her to marry him? Or was it she who had spoken first of love and commitment? Oh, she had been shamelessly bold, she knew. JoBeth felt her cheeks warm at the things she had said, the kisses exchanged. It had seemed so real then. Why was she losing hold of it? *Please, Wes, write.*

She measured the tea, poured the boiling water into the teapot, and carried it back into the parlor. However, Alzada was putting her bonnet back on, saying she had to be going. As she moved to the front door, she patted JoBeth's cheek, saying, "Now, don't you worry, darlin'. There are plenty of fine young men ready to serve North Carolina who will find you a mighty sweet girl to court. I know it's a great disappointment, and my heart is truly heavy, but we must all go on—somehow."

JoBeth knew that Alzada meant well and that she was doing the best she could to bolster her own sadness over Wes. However, her words fell on deaf ears. At this moment, JoBeth could not imagine being interested in any other young man—especially not one in the gray uniform of the Confederacy, who might consider Wes the enemy.

Her mother gave her a sympathetic glance, and Aunt Josie raised her eyebrows, but neither added anything else to Mrs. Spencer's words. While the two of them saw their guest out, JoBeth carried the tea things back to the kitchen. She left them there on the table for Annie to deal with and went out the back door, through the garden, and out the back gate.

She needed to be alone, to think her own thoughts and avoid any discussion with her aunt or mother about Wes.

～⚘～

There are few secrets in any small town. Hillsboro was no exception. The Spencers' dismay at Wes's defection to the North was common knowledge.

In the weeks that followed, for the first time JoBeth felt the full brunt of being associated with Wes. She had not realized how her name had been linked to the name Wesley Rutherford, which was now anathema to many. After he left, JoBeth began to feel that people were watching her, looking at her with curiosity. In the social circle to which they belonged, everyone had assumed that once Wes graduated from college and returned to Hillsboro, their wedding would soon follow.

She was the target of curious glances. At first, comments were made behind her back. Then, as time went on, they were said to her face as well. JoBeth knew that people expected her to denounce Wes's decision openly. She refused to do that. Not even to make things easier for her relatives. She was sure that both the Cadys had received their share of questions and criticism. Was their niece actually engaged to that Yankee sympathizer? Gossip fed by rumor was confirmed by fact. Alzada made no secret of her own distress over Wes's reason for leaving.

Even at home, JoBeth felt constricted. She went silently about her household tasks, avoiding any confrontation. Discussions about the war took place unabated at the Cady dinner table, where Harvel and Munroe were frequent guests. At family gatherings at Holly Grove, events of that summer were usually the topic of general conversation.

The war permeated the town in every way. Local men in small militia units drilled daily in the town park. War fever was everywhere. No one could avoid it! It was epidemic, infectious, and contagious.

The women had their own kinds of activities. There were fund-raisers of all sorts, bazaars, fetes, with booths selling palmetto pins in support of South Carolina's "gallant defense" of states' rights, and other Confederate symbols. Sales of the new red-white-and-blue Stars and Bars flag to display on porches or in yards were high. News of more states' seceding every day bolstered the patriotic fervor. Most of the girls JoBeth had grown up with boasted of sweethearts rallying to the call for volunteers to the cause.

JoBeth avoided her friends as much as possible. Why should she try to explain Wes to anyone? Let people think what they would. JoBeth kept a proud silence and walked with her head high in spite of it all.

It was only to her brother, Shelby, that JoBeth confided her own feelings. "Oh, Shelby, it's so hard. I am trying to understand why Wes did what he did. Why he felt he *had* to. But people are so cruel. They say such horrible things about him. And how can they? They've known him all his life. They know how honorable he is, how much things matter to him. He's following his conscience. . . ." Eyes bright with tears, JoBeth flung out her hands in a helpless gesture. "Uncle Madison makes it sound like—I don't know. He calls him an idealist, as if it were something contemptible."

Shelby was serious beyond his sixteen years. His deep-set eyes regarded his sister with sympathy. "I've always liked Wes. He's an idealist, sure, but he has convictions. People should admire him for that."

"But they don't! All people around here want is for everyone to feel and think and be the same way they are."

Shelby's expression showed his concern. His light-brown eyebrows drew together over gray eyes filled with compassion. "It's the same way at school," he said. "Everyone there thinks we had the right to secede. Freedom of dissent, they call it."

"Isn't that exactly what Wes is doing?" she asked in despair.

"I'm sorry, Sis. I really am."

"I know you are, Shelby. You're the only one I can talk to about this. Mama feels so obligated to Aunt Josie and Uncle Madison—well, you know how it goes." She sighed. "Oh, I wish this horrible war was over and everything was back to the way it used to be."

"I don't think it ever will be," Shelby said sadly. "Oh, eventually the war will be over—I didn't mean that. But I don't think things will ever be the same again."

JoBeth looked sorrowfully at her brother. How tall he'd grown since Christmas, how lanky. His face had lost its round boyishness and was becoming that of a young man. Would he too, before long, have to go into the army? Boys as young as sixteen and seventeen were joining up. Her heart lurched in loving fear. Ever since he'd been born, JoBeth had adored her little brother.

They had always been close. Especially since they came to live in town. They shared the same childhood and recalled a world no one else in Hillsboro knew, a world of tall pines, shadowy glens, mountain streams.

JoBeth longed to hear from Wes. To learn what he had done. Had he joined one of the Pennsylvania regiments that were forming as fast as the ones in the South, in defense of the flag, the country, the Union? It seemed so long since he had left, and she'd had no word. JoBeth wondered if her letters from him might be being withheld. She quickly dismissed that as a possibility. This family prided itself on its honor and would never stoop to anything like that, no matter how they felt. Wes must just be busy with all his plans and with all the decisions that he faced.

She tried to be the first to get the mail, and at last one day she was rewarded. Her first letter from Wes arrived one morning early in July. She ran upstairs with it to her bedroom and there eagerly tore it open.

My Dearest JoBeth,

I apologize for not writing sooner. It is not because you haven't been in my thoughts constantly since I took sad leave of Hillsboro and all that was dear and familiar

to me. But ever since my return here to my grandmother's home, my time has been occupied with making
my plans. I have found that here reactions to the declaration of war differ greatly from those in Hillsboro. Here
there seems to be a profound sadness at the thought of the
dissolution of the Union. There are no firebrands, no
fiery statements. At least none I've heard. My grandmother wept when I told her why I had returned and
about Blakely and Will already joining up. She said,
"Oh, my poor Southern kin! God forbid that it should
have come to this, brother against brother. It will bring so
much suffering to all of us. That I should have lived so
long as to see this happen."

There is here, however, a determination to prevent a
long war, and after much consideration and prayer, I have
decided to join a local unit headed up by a longtime friend
of our family. He is as fine a character as one would want
for a leader and will make a good captain of our mostly
unmilitary group—most of the men have never handled a
rifle or firearm of any kind. My summers in the South—
riding, hunting with my cousins—have made me at least
able to do this. We will be deployed to muster into Federal
service in a matter of weeks. Just now we are drilling
daily. When we wear our uniforms and march, people
come out to cheer us as we pass. Sentiment here seems to
be supporting our intention. Rumor has it we will be heading south into the Shenandoah Valley.

I know you are anxious about the future. I cannot
promise anything, as we both knew before I left. However, remember I love you and hold you in my heart,
whatever happens. I will write as often as I can.

Ever your devoted,
Wes

He enclosed a poem by one of his favorites, Robert Burns, the Scottish poet.

Ae fond kiss, "One fond kiss" and then we sever,
A farewell and then forever.
Deep in heart-wrung tears I'll pledge thee,
Banish Fate's power to grieve thee
Hold high the star of hope shining
While cheerful and ever glowing light
No dark despair can him benight.

Hungrily JoBeth read and reread the letter. There was no one with whom she could share her feelings, a mixture of relief, pride, love, and anxiety.

JoBeth had to keep the letter, its contents, and her feelings to herself. However, it was with a sense of doom that she learned that Harvel and Munroe's regiments were heading out to go north. There they would join a regiment under General Thomas J. Jackson, who was massing reinforcements for a threatened Union invasion into Virginia.

Upon hearing this news, JoBeth felt a sinking sensation in the pit of her stomach. Her hands turned clammy with dread. Was it only a premonition, or was it possible that in Virginia her uncles and their men would meet and engage in terrible conflict the Union troop of which Wes was a member?

Sick with secret dread, JoBeth stood nearby the day her uncles came to bid their parents good-bye. Uncle Madison struggled valiantly to control his emotions as he embraced his oldest son and said with a choked voice, "I only wish I were young and able enough to go with you, Son." He clasped Harvel's hand tightly, then turned to Munroe. "You two are brave, and we are more than proud of you both."

JoBeth felt like an intruder at this farewell scene. Her own heart felt as if it were split in two, divided in love and loyalty. She watched in a kind of frozen agony as Johanna embraced both cousins and gave them each the gift she had made for them. How much Harvel and Munroe knew of her own relationship to Wesley, JoBeth was not sure. However, both were too gentlemanly to betray anything, by word or gesture, that would indicate any resentment. They kissed her good-bye as tenderly as they had the others.

Then both men gave a last hug to their mother, saluted their father, and left the house. Everyone followed them out to the porch. In front of the house, their horses, held by their aides, waited. Before mounting, Harvel turned for one last look, brandishing his wide-brimmed hat in a kind of flourish. As they moved forward down the road and out of sight, Aunt Josie broke into sobs, and Uncle Madison put his arm around her, saying, "Now there, my dear." Together they returned into the house, heads bowed in mutual sadness.

Left together on the porch, JoBeth exchanged a glance with her mother, who was wiping away her own tears. Seeing that, JoBeth had another image, that of Wes's grandmother weeping as she kissed him good-bye. All the women, North and South, were going through this same heart-wrenching experience. Sending their men off to fight in a war that would last who knew how long, not knowing if they would ever see their beloved ones again.

~≈~

It was a silent meal that evening. Under the circumstances, it could have been expected. Everyone seated around the table had his or her own personal sadness, and yet there were no mutual words of comfort to exchange. The Cadys were openly grieving the absence of their two sons. Unable to share her own sorrow at Wes's departure, JoBeth sat quietly, yet she understood more than anyone what pain they were experiencing. She had told her mother of Wes's decision to join the Union Army, and she was conscious of Johanna's frequent anxious looks during the meal. JoBeth understood her reluctance to express sympathy for her daughter, because she knew it would offend her aunt and uncle. But she was not surprised when later her mother came into her bedroom. JoBeth didn't try to hide the tears she had been shedding. Johanna sat down beside her on the bed, cradling JoBeth's head against her shoulder.

"It's so hard, Mama," JoBeth sobbed. "To love someone as I do Wes and to have nobody care. He's in as much danger as Harvel and Munroe will be, and he believes in what he's doing as much as they do."

"I know, and I wish there were something I could say or do to make it easier for you, my darling."

"You can give us your blessing!" challenged JoBeth.

"That I do. All is in God's hands, anyway, JoBeth. Whether it happens or not, whatever the outcome of this war is, nothing comes to us but what is ordained. If you and Wesley are to be together, then it will come about."

Johanna knew what it was like to love so completely and have others oppose that love. She understood the ache of loneliness, the pain of being separated—perhaps forever.

Chapter Seven

❧

When the news of the battle of Manassas arrived, Uncle Madison came rushing home from the telegraph office at the train station that hot July day, red-faced and excited. It was the first major battle of the war, and the Confederates claimed victory. There was wild, triumphant reporting that the Yankees had turned tail and run. And there was pride that the Confederates had held their position unwaveringly, bringing acclaim to their commander, General Jackson, now nicknamed "Stonewall."

A wave of dizziness swept over JoBeth. Had Wes been among the routed Union troops? How would she know? JoBeth prayed for news yet dreaded hearing it. If he had been killed or wounded, would the Spencers be notified as next of kin? Or was his grandmother considered a closer relative, so that she would be the first to know? JoBeth could not enter into the victory celebration. It was all too awful. She concealed her anxiety as best she could and rejoiced with the others that neither Harvel nor Munroe had been injured or worse.

A letter finally reached JoBeth, informing her that Wes had not been in the battle of Manassas—in fact, he had not seen any action yet. She was relieved for a time. However, as summer turned into fall, letters were few and far between, and JoBeth spent much time wondering where Wes was or what he was doing.

Before the end of the summer, JoBeth and Shelby rode up to Millscreek Gap to visit their grandmother Davison and their father's relatives. In the first few years after they had moved to Hillsboro, their mother used to take them for a week's visit every year. As children, they had looked forward to a degree of freedom they had in the mountains, freedom they didn't enjoy in Hillsboro. They played, swam, and fished with their cousins Jesse and Reid, who were Uncle Merriman and Aunt Jenny's boys and just a few years older. Granny Eliza delighted in how they'd grown and in how much they'd learned, and she spoiled them with her special dishes. Her daughters—Aunt Sue, now the postmistress, and Aunt Katie, a schoolteacher—who were home for the summer, also took great pleasure in their adored older brother's children. It was always a time of special pleasantness for all of them.

This year, war talk had reached even this remote mountain community. Jesse and Reid, now grown men, helped Uncle Merriman on his large tobacco farm. They seemed eager to hear what news their town cousins brought but were reluctant to leave home to join up. Granny Eliza held to her staunch belief that it wasn't mountain folks' fight. "Let them as has sumpin' to protect, go. We'd have more to lose than gain. 'Sides, I don't hold with killin' for somebody else's purpose."

JoBeth spent many hours with her grandmother on this trip. Eliza seemed to have aged a great deal since the summer before—she was a little more bent, a little slower in her movement, though still sharp, with a dry, ironic wit. She still was at her quilting frame a good part of every day, and JoBeth was more interested in the skill than she had ever been before. She marveled that Eliza's gnarled, rheumatic fingers could yet ply a needle so deftly, making tiny stitches.

"What do you call this pattern, Granny?" JoBeth asked one day as she sat beside her at the frame.

"This here's called Jacob's Ladder. But there's other names for it. Most quilters change things in a pattern to make it their own. Your Mama's real good at that! She's done fine with her quilts, she has. Earned enough to send Shelby off to that fine school to get his education."

JoBeth nodded. "She's doing more than ever. Besides the quilts people order, she's making quilts for the soldiers too. She and Aunt Josie and the other aunties meet once a week to quilt."

"And what about you, missy?" Eliza turned a sharp glance at her granddaughter.

"I help, cutting out patches. I'm not really that good at quilting." She didn't add that she'd never been much interested. JoBeth was too active, too impatient, to spend hours perfecting the skill needed to produce the beautiful quilts her mother did.

Turning back to her work, Eliza said, "My next quilt will be for you. What kind would you like? What shall it be? The Double Wedding Ring pattern or"—she chuckled—"the Old Maid's Puzzle?"

JoBeth laughed ruefully. "Maybe it had better be the Old Maid's Puzzle!"

"What? No young man beatin' a path to your door?"

Before JoBeth had to answer, Aunt Katie came in from the garden with a basketful of ripe corn and enlisted JoBeth's help in shucking it so they could have it for supper.

※

When Shelby returned to school early in September, JoBeth felt lonelier than ever.

That autumn seemed particularly beautiful. But its beauty made her even more melancholy, reminding her of

292

how she and Wes had walked the hills, glorying in the winey, crisp weather, the smells of burning leaves, and the scent of ripening fruit in the orchards. Those weeks and months she walked a lonely path. Not a day went by that JoBeth did not think of him, long for him. She would close her eyes and try to remember his face, those clear, blue, truthful eyes, the hair that never seemed to stay put, the kind, gentle mouth.

In addition to JoBeth's anxiety about Wes and his safety, she also began to worry about Shelby. His letters to her were very different from the ones he wrote to their mother, the ones Johanna so proudly read aloud to the rest of the family. Those were filled with descriptions of his classes, his instructors, his fellow seminarians. But to JoBeth he told of his feelings that he was a "slacker."

While other fellows my age are out on the firing line, putting themselves at risk every day, I am poring over translations of Greek gospels. It seems wrong that I am safe behind these "ivy walls," tucked away in an "ivory tower" for that faraway day when I may be of some possible use to someone. And don't write and tell me that I've been called. I know that—I felt that (unless I've been deluded and self-deceived). However, might not the question be asked, Would I not be even better able to serve my fellow man if I'd been tried in the crucible so many of my peers are facing now? If I'd had my "dross burned away into silver"? You and I have always been able to tell each other our real feelings—I long for those heart-to-heart talks we used to have. I hope that when I come home, we can find a way to go to one of our old haunts. I need to confide in one I know will not only listen sympathetically but also help me find some answers. Don't think I don't know and understand that you, too, are going through your own troubled time. As we struggle together, may we both find the right path.

JoBeth thought long and hard about what should she write back. It was all too much to put into words in a single letter. As he had suggested, their real confidential talk would have to wait until he was home. But she wanted to send him some reply, even if it was inadequate. She wrote, reminding him how hard their mother had worked, making and selling her quilts to pay his school tuition and fees, how disappointed she would be if he gave it up and joined the army.

All of us have our own purpose in life, Shelby. Yours may be of greater value than taking up a gun and going out and fighting. No one should doubt your purity of intent, and no one could ever call you a coward.

Before she signed and sealed the letter, JoBeth had an inspiration. She wanted to add something that would speak to Shelby's heart in a special way. She got out her little concordance and, whispering a prayer for guidance, thumbed through it to look up the reference she wanted. When she found it, she quickly copied it onto the bottom of the page.

Jeremiah 29:11: "'For I know the plans I have for you,' declares the Lord, 'plans to prosper you and not to harm you, plans to give you hope and a future.'"

I can't wait till Christmas, when you'll be home and we'll have a chance to talk.

Always your loving sister,
JoBeth

December 1861

The family Christmas was to be held at Holly Grove. Both Harvel and Munroe had secured leave. The war that

294

was supposed to be over by Christmas cast its dreadful shadow still. In spite of that, Marilee, Harvel's wife, declared they would have a party just like in the old days.

JoBeth tried to enter into the preparations with the same anticipation the others had, doing her best to hide her own downheartedness. She wrapped presents with her mother, welcomed Shelby home for his school holidays, went with Aunt Josie to help decorate the church for Christmas services.

Her mother had made her a new outfit—a bright-red merino wool skirt and short Spanish jacket trimmed with black braid, and a popular Garibaldi blouse of black satin to wear under it. It was enormously becoming, but JoBeth's first thought was that she wished Wes could see her in it.

Two days before Christmas, she received a letter from Wes. It was on the hall table when she came in from shopping one afternoon. No one mentioned that it had arrived, nor asked her about it afterward. Wes was a subject never brought up, never referred to, in the Cady household.

JoBeth took the letter upstairs to read it in private. The battered envelope looked as though it had passed through many hands, had endured a hard journey before reaching her.

Dearest JoBeth,

I have started several letters to you, then stopped. There is so much to say, and I don't know where to begin or how to say it.

Being in the army is not at all what I thought. I imagined that everyone fighting for the Union would have the same high resolve as I did coming in, that the spirit among my fellow soldiers would be high, the ideals and conversation lofty. I'm afraid it is not at all that way, at least among us common soldiers. To say I have been sadly disillusioned is to put it mildly. Not that there aren't good-hearted men among us, but most seem not to know what it is we're supposed to be fighting for, and there is a great deal of coarse talk that, without my taking a superior attitude would be resented, I have to hear.

If I didn't have you to think about, this life would be unbearable. At least after a day's march (no encounters with the "enemy" as yet), I can carry my bedroll apart from the others, lie down on my blanket by my fire, and concentrate all my thoughts on you. What we had together, how lovely you are, how sweet and pure, and how much I love you.

I hope we have made the right decision, the right choice. Others who oppose this war, I've heard, simply took themselves and their families away, to Europe or England or out west. But I don't think you can run away, escape from your responsibility. This is my country, and I have to believe it is worth fighting for. That you have to suffer is a great sorrow to me. At least I am among those who have chosen to fight on this side—you are daily among people who despise your allegiance to a man whom they consider a traitor. God willing, we will soon have peace and both sides will be reconciled.

That, I fear, may be a long time coming. Longer than either you or I thought. It all seems such a waste— of time, men, and of the beautiful country our Creator gave us to live in and enjoy. As yet I haven't been in any battle, not even a minor skirmish, but I have seen troops returning, seen men with wounds that defy description, and listened to horror tales from veterans. I do not relish when my time comes to face—I cannot even call them the "enemy." My nightmare is that as we rush at each other from either side—and there is much hand-to-hand combat, I'm told—I will see the faces of men I know!

Reading this, JoBeth felt her heart wrench. Not only was Wes suffering the hardships of army life but his sensitive soul was in agony. There was a second page, more hastily written, and she realized from its date that it had been added later.

This may be my last opportunity to write for a while, so I want to have a chance to say this, for I know not what may befall. I love you, JoBeth. I pray God it will not be long until we are together again. But I fear the worst. No one talks anymore of an early victory or a peaceful settlement.

She couldn't hold back the tears that streamed down her cheeks. She read it over and over, the tears falling on the pages so that they became blotted.

The thought of going to the party at Holly Grove the day after next and pretending things she didn't feel seemed impossible. But she knew she had to. There was no alternative. No one would understand if she stayed away. She would have to go.

Determinedly she buried her heartache and joined the family for supper, keeping up her end of the conversation by sheer willpower. Only Shelby seemed aware that all was not well with her. He did his bit by turning the attention from her so that her unusually subdued manner was not noticed or commented upon by their uncle, aunt, or mother. He rendered stories of schoolboy pranks and other events, lightening the hour for everyone. JoBeth was grateful. When Shelby suggested a chess game with Uncle Madison afterward, she was able to slip away without any trouble.

On Christmas morning, after attending early church service, they came home to breakfast and to open their presents, then drove over to Holly Grove. Marilee had carried out her promise to have the kind of Christmas party that Holly

Grove was famous for. Evergreens tied with gilded ribbons were arranged on mantels and windowsills, candles glowed, and the long table in the dining room, spread with a Battenberg lace cloth, was beautifully set with gleaming silver, sparkling glassware, and a pyramid of cloved oranges and pine cones as a centerpiece.

The house was festive, as was the company. The Cady grandchildren were a lively bunch and had the run of the place. Their father, home for such a brief time, had suspended all discipline, so no one tried to stop the shouting, the tooting of tin horns, or the beating of toy drums, all of which were presents they'd been given. The mood among the military men was buoyant. Harvel and Munroe and the friends they had invited as guests were all in some branch of the Confederate service. As JoBeth listened to them talk, she heard a far less sober perspective of the war than she had read in Wes's letter. They were sure of victory, sure of their superiority in spirit and fighting skills.

Quite suddenly JoBeth could bear it no longer. Listening to all the bravado, knowing it was all directed against the man she loved and what he represented, she felt the blood rush up into her head. The room seemed to become stifling, the fire burned red-hot, the walls tilted dangerously. She thought she might faint. She had never before fainted in her life, but she now felt very much as if she were about to. *I must get out of here, get some fresh air*, she thought. She stood up, edged toward the parlor door, murmuring some excuse, and slipped out of the room. She rushed down the long hall, knowing that at the end there was a door leading out to the back porch. She pushed it open, went out into the darkening evening, and leaned on the railing, gulping the cold air. The pounding in her heart, the throbbing in her temples, mercifully slowed. Then the chill air penetrated her clothing and she shivered. She knew she had to go back, get through the rest of the evening, not let on that anything was wrong.

But it *was* wrong, horribly wrong. And she didn't know how long it would be going on. Wes didn't know, either. It was so hard to live in a house where Uncle Madison did nothing but talk about the war and what they were going to do to those Yankees. She shivered again. *I feel torn to pieces,* she thought, closing her eyes and hugging her arms around her shoulders. *I love Wes. I want to believe that what he is doing is right. But what about the others? Uncle Harvel and Uncle Munroe are both good men. Even the Spencer twins. And maybe Shelby will have to go if the war lasts any longer. Wes thinks it will—Oh, dear Lord, help me! I don't know what I think or feel or even who I am anymore. What will become of me?* Tears rose into her eyes, and she wiped them away. She couldn't go back if her eyes were all red. They would all wonder why she was crying when everyone else was celebrating. *Dear God, help me be brave like Wes. Bless and keep us both, please.*

In a few minutes, JoBeth felt calmer. Resolutely she went back inside. There she rounded up the children and got them into a rollicking game of blindman's bluff, much to the relief of their mother and aunties. The gentlemen had removed themselves to the study for brandy and cigars, so the ladies settled down for a nice chat. Shelby joined JoBeth and later gathered the little cousins around him in a storytelling that quieted them down enough so that eventually they could be put to bed.

Driving back to the Willows in the winter dark, JoBeth realized with a twinge of sadness that this was the first time in her life that she was glad that Christmas was over.

299

Part Two

A quilt, woven of love, dreams, and threaded with
grief, joys and laughter sewn into its patches, tells of life
beyond the shadows of hidden love, secret messages.
Carrie A. Hall

Chapter Eight

❦

*A*gainst all predictions, the war edged into a second
year. No one had dreamed it would last this long.
Both armies had been camped through the winter months,
with little action on either part. However, with the coming
of spring, everyone on both sides braced for the battles that
inevitably would happen.

JoBeth wasn't sure just when or how the idea of the quilt
came to her. *Of course!* she thought. It would be so simple, so
subtle, so innocuous, that no one would guess, no one would
suspect. Every young woman made quilts for her hope chest.
No one would think anything of one she would design for herself. The secret would be her own. The hidden truth. She
would keep working on the quilt all the time Wes was gone, as
a kind of talisman to their promise, their pledge to each other.

She took out a sheet of paper and, with a pencil, began
sketching her idea. Each square would have a dove in the
corner, an olive branch in its mouth, and in the center would
be clasped hands holding a heart!

Her mother seemed mildly surprised at JoBeth's sudden
interest in quilting and readily told her to rummage in her

scrap bag or among her many various lengths of cloth to select material for her design.

Her choice for the center of the square was a blue-gray calico with a tiny pattern. The dove shapes were white, the clasped hands she cut from pale-pink cotton, and the heart was red, as was the binding of each square. The olive branches she would embroider in brown and green thread after the patch was completed. Satisfied with her selection, she began work with high hopes. Perhaps it wouldn't be too large a quilt—perhaps the war would be over soon.

JoBeth's optimism, however, was short-lived. There was too much evidence to the contrary. Harvel's letters were full of the hardships the Confederate forces were suffering, camped as they were in winter weather that most of the Southern men were unused to. There were difficulties in reaching the troops with supplies and food as well as medical necessities. All this was discussed and worried over at length in the Cady household. JoBeth, who knew that Wes was suffering the same kind of discomfort, distress, and deprivation, had no one with whom to vent her own anxieties. When Aunt Josie enlisted Johanna's help in packing boxes with warm quilts, homemade jellies, knitted scarves, and gloves to send to her sons, JoBeth's desire to do the same for Wes had to be suppressed.

It was so unfair, yet she could do nothing about it.

The days were long and the work on the quilt went slowly. JoBeth started diligently enough, but then her thoughts would wander, bringing Wes dreamily to mind. Was he cold, hungry, weary? The long marches, the battles he might be fighting, the danger, all played on her vivid imagination. If only she would hear from him! Mail was slow and irregular, especially that coming through the lines from the North. All such mail was probably considered suspicious, she thought, and was more than likely opened and read to see if it contained any information that could be used or could be damaging to the enemy.

JoBeth had also started keeping a journal into which she poured her thoughts, her feelings, her fears, her hopes, her dreams. It was a place where all their secrets could be safe. JoBeth hid both the growing stack of letters from Wes and her journal under a loose floorboard under the rug in her bedroom.

She often echoed the plaintive question that Wes had written in one of his letters that spring.

> *Why are we killing each other? We are all the same, descended from the same band of brave men who founded this country in the first place. If we have such differences, why can't we settle them peacefully? What if men on both sides simply refused to fight, demanded that the politicians settle this some other way?*
>
> *Forgive me, my darling, for burdening you with all this. But I have no one else to talk to who would understand, who knows my heart, mind, and soul as you do. I miss you more than I can say. Pray that this wretched war comes to a speedy end with victory for the Union, saving our wonderful country. I long for the day I can come back to you, kiss your sweet mouth. I love you, JoBeth. Pray for me.*
>
> *Ever your devoted,*
> *Wesley*

If only Uncle Madison could read what Wes was feeling, maybe he would understand and forgive him. That was impossible, of course. JoBeth could not show this letter to anyone. As she read his letters, she realized that Wes was thinking deeper, becoming more mature, more spiritual. She had never heard any of the men in her family—for that matter, any of the men she knew—express such feelings. Her one comfort was the pledge quilt she was making. Hiding all in her heart, she stitched on her quilt, counting the finished squares as milestones until she could be with Wes again. Strengthening herself, she would think over and over, *No matter what anyone says or thinks, I love him and he will come back! We will be together.*

One day Aunt Josie asked, "Aren't you ever going to finish that quilt, JoBeth? Seems to me you've been working on it quite a spell."

"Yes, ma'am, I know," JoBeth answered noncommittally. No one knew her secret pledge not to complete it until the war was over and Wesley returned safely.

Spring arrived and the war picked up momentum—battles fought, battles won. First the Confederates seemed to be winning, then the Union forces. Elation or depression came and went like the tide. Letters from Wes were rare. Sometimes JoBeth would get two or three at once, and other times weeks would pass before she heard from him. The letters she received did nothing to lift her spirits.

She herself was surrounded on every side by those who are all "hurrah for the South." Of course, she understood. *Their* dear ones were in danger, fighting for what they believed was right. Sometimes it was hard to take so much talk edged with mean-spirited comments about "Yankees" as though they were an alien people. Did not people on both sides of the conflict bear a similar appearance, pray to the same God?

November 1862

With the bleak November weather, JoBeth experienced an eerie sense of doom. The war was never going to end. It would go on and on, just as her pile of patches grew. How many would she have to make before the war was over, before Wes was home? She began to feel like some kind of prisoner condemned to piecework, turning out a required number of units day after day. Each new one she cut out and started sewing added to her sentence. A self-imposed sentence. She would go on making them—she didn't care how long or how big the final quilt became. Sometimes she almost lost heart, but something—fear as much as anything else—doggedly compelled her on. *It isn't superstition*, she told herself. Wasn't she praying constantly all the time she worked on it—for Wes's safety, for the war to end? As the patches accumulated, so did the days and months drag by. She continued writing to Wes. Even if she wasn't always sure he got the letters, it helped her to write them. It relieved some of her tension to express the feelings she had to suppress in her daily life. The fall dragged into winter, and JoBeth dreaded facing another Christmas without Wes.

Chapter Nine

❧

*I*n an unspoken agreement, everyone seemed determined to follow Dickens' suggestion to celebrate Christmas. In spite of the war, in spite of shortages, in spite of worry and deprivation, all bent every effort to appear cheerful and optimistic.

Harvel was due home for a leave, so Holly Grove was again going to host the holiday dinner. It was the largest home in the family circle and thus could easily accommodate everyone in the family, as well as the few extras who were always welcome. Besides, it would be the right place for Harvel to spend his homecoming—among his young children. Each family group could bring some special dish, cake, or pie. Nowadays no single larder had the abundance of the past, so every contribution would add to the feast.

A few days before Christmas, JoBeth went over to help Marilee decorate the house. She was on a stepladder, arranging festoons of evergreen boughs on the mantelpiece, when Alzada Spencer stopped by. Not noticing JoBeth at first, she announced that the twins also had obtained leave and were coming home, bringing one of their fellow officers with them.

"It will be just like the old days—all of us together!" she declared happily. Marilee cast a quick glance at JoBeth, and Alzada, suddenly aware of her, gave a little gasp and flushed. Still she did not mention Wes, and she soon left.

Even as JoBeth continued at her task as casually as she could manage, her thoughts were bitter. She bit her lip to hold back the quick tears at the dismal thought of where Wes might be spending Christmas. Would he even receive a Christmas box, other than the small one she had been able to smuggle out of the house and post to him? It seemed such a heartless thing for the Spencers to ignore the boy who had spent every Christmas of his growing-up years in their house as part of their family. She had heard of families disowning their sons. How could Wayne Spencer—or especially, tenderhearted Alzada—so coldly cut Wes out of their lives?

JoBeth knew there were many others in Hillsboro who held deep feelings about a North Carolinian who would desert the Southern cause, join the ranks of the "enemy." Only a few weeks before, she had been over at her great-aunt Honey's, helping her put together a quilt. JoBeth's job was simple, consisting of basting the top onto the cotton batting, then whipstitching the flannel-back top to its underside. While she was there, a longtime family friend, Patsy Faye Wrightman, dropped by for an impromptu visit. JoBeth had gone on stitching while Aunt Honey, always the gracious hostess, urged Mrs. Wrightman to stay for a cup of tea.

JoBeth, concentrating on keeping her stitches straight, had paid little attention to the murmur of conversation behind her in the room. That is, until she heard Mrs. Wrightman say furiously, "I simply can't abide him. A hometown Yankee sympathizer." Aunt Honey gave a small warning cough, which was followed by a moment's silence. Without turning around, JoBeth felt sure her auntie was sending some kind of signal to her guest. Evidently it didn't matter to the lady, nor did it diminish the "righteous indignation" she was expressing. Instead, Mrs. Wrightman wiggled her plump body like a ruffled hen puffing up her feathers, shot JoBeth a scathing glance, and said sharply, "Oh, I pretty near forgot. *Wesley Rutherford* is one of them Unionists! I'm sorry, Honey, but maybe if *you* had three nephews and goodness knows how many dear friends' sons fighting for *our* safety and well-being, you'd feel the same way I do! I can't abide *any* of them turn-coats." Without an apology to JoBeth, Mrs. Wrightman picked up her shawl, gloves, and purse and stood up, saying haughtily, "Well, I'd best be on my way. I'm rolling bandages this afternoon for *our* poor wounded boys. . . ."

The echo of the remark hung in the air in the hollow quiet after the front door closed behind Mrs. Wrightman. There was no sound other than the ticking of the mantel clock, the rustle of Aunt Honey's skirts as she came back into the parlor, the clicking of the cups as she began gathering up the tea tray. At last she cleared her throat and said, "Don't pay her any mind, JoBeth. Patsy Wrightman never thinks before she speaks. I'm sorry if she hurt you, dear—"

"It's not your fault, Auntie. I know that plenty of people feel the same way. It *does* hurt. Especially when I know how hard it was for Wes to make the decision he did, knowing no one would understand." She added sadly, "But that's the way it is. It happens even at home."

She heard Aunt Honey sigh, then the rattle of teacups as she carried the tray back to the kitchen.

She continued working on the quilt, wishing she could share with Aunt Honey the letter she had received from Wes just a few days before.

> *Received your letter of the 25th. It arrived somewhat the worse for wear, having passed through who knows*

*how many hands to reach me. I read it hungrily. Seeing
your handwriting brought tears to my eyes. I had taken it
aside to read it so that none would be witness to whatever
unconcealable emotion it might evoke within me. Not
that my fellow soldiers are so hard of heart that they
would not understand—all here long for loved ones as
deeply as I—but there are some things a man wants to
keep private and precious, as I do my feelings for you.*

*Until recently we had not had a regular chaplain and
consequently no religious services. About three weeks ago
one was assigned to this regiment, at least on a temporary
basis, and conducted a meeting. The Scripture from
which he drew his sermon was very much on the same
order as you described.*

*Second Chronicles 20:15–17: "Thus saith the Lord
to you: 'Do not be afraid nor dismayed of this great mul-
titude, because the battle is not yours but God's. Position
yourselves, stand still and see the salvation of the Lord,
who is with you.'"*

*The men seemed to take great heart from that.
Although I cannot say there is great religious fervor
among soldiers, without this kind of preaching we would
all grow lax and weary with the dreary routine of daily
life in the army. I must not, however. Since we have had
the chaplain, there is a stirring within the troops, and
small groups are meeting for prayer. We all need the
Almighty so as not to lose sight of the real purpose of this
fight, to free men from bodily bondage, as we have been
freed from spiritual bondage.*

*Our unit got its orders to pack and be ready to move
out in the morning. It has been raining for days, and we
all live in mud, sleep in mud, and almost eat in mud. I
have no idea where we are headed or to what battlefield*

*we may be called upon to do what we have come to do. I
don't think they want to kill me anymore than I want to
kill them! More and more, I understand my grandmother's abhorrence of war. It is madness.*

The very next Sunday, JoBeth was seated in church. She
was not being too attentive to the sermon. That summer,
their old minister retired, one who had been an inspiration
to and was so fond of Shelby. In fact, he had encouraged
Shelby to go to seminary. His replacement was as fiery a Confederate as the most militant general would ask for. Suddenly
his forceful words brought JoBeth to quivering attention.

"Listen, church, to what the Scripture is saying to all of
you. Recently we have heard with awe the number of men
and weapons the enemy is gathering to come against us. So I
say to you, search for your answer, your strength in our cause,
in the book of Nehemiah, chapter four, verse fourteen. It is
as true today as it was then: 'So I arose and said to the noble,
to the leaders, to the rest of the people, "Do not be afraid of
them. Remember the Lord great and awesome, and fight for
your bretheren, your sons, your daughters, your wives and
your homes."' Amen?"

There was an enthusiastic round of "Amens" from the
congregation, which was usually known for its quiet and
decorum. In fact, some of the gentlemen rose out of their
seats and applauded. If they had not been restrained, JoBeth
would not have been surprised if the famous "rebel yell" had
been shouted to the rafters. Instead of feeling enthusiastic
and aroused by this, JoBeth's heart sank. As Wes had said,
"We all pray to the same God, the Creator of us all." So
whom was God listening to?

❧

Christmas afternoon, JoBeth dressed to go to the family
party at Holly Grove, wishing Wes could see her in the new

dress her mother had made for her. It was red poplin, and it had a molded bodice with a froth of white lace at the throat, and wrists banded with black velvet ribbon. She gathered her hair into a crocheted black silk snood tied at the top of her head in a wide black velvet bow. As she slipped in her small freshwater pearl earrings, she tried not to think about where Wes might be spending this Christmas. She just prayed it wasn't somewhere cold, miserable, and that he wasn't in any danger. He had sent her a small picture of himself in uniform. He looked wonderful, manly and brave. She had spent hours studying it, but of course she could not show it to anyone. The blue uniform was hated by everyone she knew.

The Cadys left for Holly Grove earlier than the three Davisons. Their carriage had been so crowded with goodies and gifts for Harvel and his large family that there had hardly been room for Aunt Josie's skirt, let alone Johanna, JoBeth, and Shelby. The Cadys then sent their driver, Jonas, and carriage back for the trio.

It was always a nostalgic trip for Johanna to visit her childhood home. As the carriage rounded the bend of the road and started up the holly-tree-lined driveway, dusk was just falling. They could see the candlelight from the windows of the house, glinting on the snow.

"Oh, look, children! My, it looks lovely! Just like old times!" Johanna exclaimed, clutching JoBeth's arm.

JoBeth tried to put aside any melancholy thoughts and strived to join into the spirit of the day when she entered Holly Grove. The sound of laughter, children's voices, and general merriment almost drowned out the greetings of Marilee, Harvel's pretty wife, as she met them at the door. She looked like a happy bride instead of a wife of sixteen years with a half dozen children. Her radiance was due, JoBeth was sure, to the happiness she felt at her soldier husband's homecoming. All her anxiety for his safety was put aside for one

313

glorious evening. Harvel, looking fit and ruddy in his tailored gray uniform and sporting newly acquired gold captain's bars, came out to welcome his cousins.

"Happy Christmas!" he said heartily, kissing the cheek Johanna turned to him and pumping Shelby's hand vigorously. Turning to JoBeth, he winked. "Just what we needed— a pretty girl to liven up the party for some of my bachelor officers. Come in, have some eggnog, and meet our guests."

The parlor was gaily decorated, the windows festooned with red bows and swags of evergreens. Red candles shone from candlesticks on the mantelpiece, between garlands of galax leaves and gilded pine cones. The Cady children and assorted cousins were running in and out, dodging and playing among the booted legs of the men and the billowing skirts of the ladies as people clustered in congenial chatting groups.

The merry scene before her dismayed JoBeth instead of pleasing her. The parlor seemed to be filled with gray uniforms!

She took a deep breath, willing herself to smile just as Blakely Spencer, hardly recognizable with a just-grown, curly beard, came up to her, gave her a hug and kiss, then grinned mischievously, "Rank has its privileges, and I'm doing the honors for our—dear *departed one*."

Startled by his words, JoBeth stared at him in confusion. Then, realizing what Blakely meant, she smiled. Blakely was always a cutup, never took anything seriously. Remembering this, she felt both relief and a new warmth for him. At least *he* did not harbor any animosity for Wes, no matter how the rest of the family felt. She knew Wes considered his twin cousins "almost brothers."

Blakely leaned closer and whispered, "How is the old scalawag?"

She made a small grimace. "It's a long time between letters," she told him in a low voice. "I hope and pray he is all right."

"Probably having a jolly old Christmas for himself in Yankee land." Blakely gave her a wink and squeezed her hand. "Now come along, JoBeth, I want you to meet someone." Taking her by the arm, he led her toward the piano, where Dorinda, Munroe's wife, was playing familiar carols that could hardly be heard above the din in the room. A gray-uniformed man, his back to them, was leaning on the piano. Blakely tapped him on the shoulder and announced, "Here she is!"

The soldier turned around. A direct gaze from intensely blue eyes momentarily stunned her. Blakely introduced them.

"JoBeth, may I present my brother-in-arms, Lieutenant Curtis Channing. Miss Johanna Elizabeth Davison."

The man introduced bowed slightly. "A pleasure, Miss Davison." She acknowledged his greeting and murmured something she hoped was appropriate, thinking that surely this was the most handsome man she had ever seen.

He might have stepped out of the pages of the romantic novels she used to ridicule. Tall and slim in his superbly tailored gray, he had coal black hair that fell in a wave across a high forehead. His features might have been considered too perfectly molded face too handsome, if it had not been for a tiny scar on his cheekbone. When he smiled, he revealed teeth that were very straight and white.

"What did I tell you?" Blakely demanded, gleefully nudging Curtis Channing with his elbow. Then he said to JoBeth, "I kept telling Curtis that Hillsboro has the prettiest girls in North Carolina—for that matter, in the entire Confederate states."

Never taking his gaze off JoBeth, Curtis replied gallantly, "Indeed you did, sir, you most certainly did. But you *understated* the matter."

"Curtis is from Georgia, JoBeth, and had too short a leave to make it home, so I brought him along so he could see for himself. Now I guess you believe me!"

"I certainly do," Curtis smiled.

Almost immediately the evening she had dreaded JoBeth began to enjoy. It had been such a long time since she had been with people her own age, exchanging light conversation, being flirted with, and even flirting a little herself. She almost felt guilty that she was having such a good time. Every once in a while during the evening, that thought would flash into her mind. In those fleeting moments, JoBeth hoped desperately that Wes had been fortunate enough to get leave and had perhaps gone to his grandmother's home in Philadelphia.

Actually, JoBeth hardly had time but to be in the present. Curtis Channing scarcely left her side for the rest of the evening. He was so attractive and charming, was such an amusing raconteur, that she was completely dazzled and entertained.

He seemed eager to tell her about himself, as if to make up for their short acquaintance and the brevity of his time in Hillsboro. When she attempted asking about his army life, he dismissed it as unimportant.

"It will all be over by summer," he said loftily. "The Yankees are no contest. Not for men like us, born in the saddle and knowing how to hunt! Most of them are clerks, farmers, shopkeepers, schoolteachers," he scoffed. "Most never held a gun or rode a horse."

He was much more eager to tell her about his family, his home, the life he loved and was anxious to get back to, a life of riding, hunting, socializing. He told her he had two younger sisters, Melissa and Anadell, whom he adored, a mother and father he loved and respected, two sets of grandparents, and an assortment of cousins, aunts, and uncles.

"Sounds like *us*!" JoBeth laughed, gesturing to the room full of Shelbys, Cadys, Hayeses, and Breckenridges.

"That's what makes Southerners strong," Curtis nodded, not arrogantly but with complete assurance. "We have unbreakable bonds of loyalty. We stick together, have pride in our land."

He talked about his horses, two fine thoroughbreds he'd brought with him into the brigade that he'd volunteered to join, and he added in a nonchalant aside, "I also brought Jericho, my groom."

His casual reference to his manservant after his horses jarred her. Later when she recalled her reaction, she wasn't sure why that had bothered her so much. Then she decided it was because she could imagine Wes's reaction. Putting a human being *behind* a pair of prized animals. At the time, she didn't have a chance to analyze it or question Curtis about the reference, because there was a general stir around them. Harvel called for everyone's attention. They were going to play "the farmer in the dell" for the sake of the smaller children, who would soon have to be put to bed.

The ensuing chaos chased away any serious talk for the rest of the evening. When the children were shepherded off to their rooms upstairs, the grown-ups went into the magnificent dining room, where a bountiful buffet was spread out. After that, the evening quieted down. People sipped coffee and ate fruitcake while Dorinda played softer melodies on the piano for all to listen and enjoy.

Gradually some of the guests began to depart, among them Uncle Madison and Aunt Josie. At this, Blakely and Will, with Curtis adding his pleas, begged Johanna to let JoBeth stay longer. They were going to roll up the rugs, declared another cousin, Ted Hamlett, and dance. They all promised her mother that they would escort JoBeth safely home later. Smiling, Johanna gave in to the chorus. Shelby decided to accompany his mother home and went to get her cape. JoBeth helped her mother on with it, and Johanna patted her daughter's cheek, saying, "I'm glad to see you having a good time, darling."

One by one the Munroe Cady children got droopy-eyed and cross, and reluctantly Dorinda and Munroe declared they had better take their children home, as they were dropping like flies and getting into little squabbles. Dorinda stood up regretfully to close the piano lid. Surprisingly, Curtis offered to replace her. At that the dancing gradually turned into a songfest, with the lingering guests gathered around the piano. JoBeth discovered that Curtis had a rich, true tenor voice and knew all the words to most of the popular songs.

Finally, at a little after midnight, everyone agreed it was time to depart and leave the household in peace and quiet. The last remaining quintet of Will, Blakely, Ted, Curtis, and JoBeth bade their hosts thanks and good night and went out into the starry December night. Outside, they linked arms as they walked, singing merrily some of the marching songs the young men had learned since enlisting. It was a short distance back to the Willows, and the crisp air and lively company made the trek seem short.

In the Cadys' wide front yard, Blakely, Will, and Ted succumbed to the temptation of an impromptu snowball fight, and Curtis walked with JoBeth up onto the porch.

"I can't tell you, Miss Davison, how glad I am that I accepted Blakely and Will's invitation to spend my leave here in Hillsboro. I cannot remember a recent evening when I have enjoyed myself so much."

The light from the porch lantern that was left burning for her return illuminated his expression as he spoke, and it was flatteringly sincere. Instinctively JoBeth stepped back from it so that he couldn't see the sudden blush that warmed her cheeks. She felt inordinately pleased and then immediately guilty. Why should she care that any other man besides Wes enjoyed her company?

"May I see you again? My leave only lasts three more days, and they will go very fast. I find myself not wanting to miss any possible time with you."

JoBeth hesitated. This evening had been enormous fun. Was it wrong to feel lighthearted and happy for a change? Was it a disloyalty to Wes? But then, she was sure *he* would be the last one to mind if she had a good time.

Curtis asked, "Is there something wrong?"

"No, it's just that I don't know whether it's such a good idea."

"Why not? Blakely tells me there are several other events planned for our time here—a ball tomorrow night, I understand, and if the temperature continues to drop, he says, the ice on Bedlow Pond may be solid enough for a skating party. Surely you're not going to miss those? Come now, Miss Davison, isn't it your duty to provide a brave soldier some respite from the war?" There was a teasing challenge in his question. "Besides, *I* want it very much, so please don't refuse."

How could she hold out against such persuasion? And what harm could it do to spend a few hours in such delightful company? Surely it would all be innocent enough. Besides, it would be hard to explain to Blakely and Will why she wouldn't accommodate their house guest. It would also be difficult to explain to her aunt and uncle, who, she could tell, had taken quite a liking to Curtis Channing.

"Yes? You will, won't you?"

She laughed. "Well, yes then. If it freezes tomorrow, I'd be happy to go skating."

"And even if it *doesn't*, may I call?" Curtis persisted.

She laughed again. "Yes, you may. And now I must go in, or else those fellows will wake the whole house!" She pointed to the other three, who were still scuffling and throwing snowballs at each other on the lawn.

She turned to open the front door, but Curtis caught her hand.

They both now stood shadowed by the porch columns, hidden from the frolickers in the front yard.

"Good night, Curtis," she said softly and gently tugged her hand, which he pressed and then very slowly released. Her heart gave a little warning flutter, as if alert to some unexpected danger. Quickly she went inside. After closing it, she peered through the glass panels on either side and saw Curtis leap buoyantly down the porch steps, join his comrades. Then the three of them, arms around each other's shoulders, went down the path, out the gate, whistling "Dixie" and singing at the top of their voices.

<hr />

To her surprise, a light was shining out from the small parlor. Who might still be awake and up? Tiptoeing toward the stairway, she glanced in through the half-open door and saw her brother sitting by the fireplace, his sandy head bent over a book.

"Shelby? What on earth? Do you know what time it is?"

"Couldn't sleep," he explained with a smile as she came over to join him.

JoBeth tucked her skirt under and sat down on the low hassock opposite Shelby, asking, "Problems?"

"I suppose you might say that. Mostly what I've already written you about."

"Enlisting?"

"I'm torn between what's my duty and my calling," he sighed.

JoBeth put out her hand and covered his to convey her understanding. "I know. It's the same here. Bugles blowing, flags flying. Anyone who isn't in uniform gets a scorching glare or a questioning look or even worse! It's almost as if those people who don't go, no matter if they have good reason or whatever, are supposed to walk around with a placard tied around their neck telling why in bold letters."

Her mockery brought a slight smile to Shelby's lips.

"There're only ten left in our class of thirty-five. Of the ones who all started out together."

"But you're so close to being finished," JoBeth reminded him.

"I know, but it all seems so pointless with fellows my age out there on the battlefield. Wouldn't it make more sense for me to be out there, ministering in some way—not carrying a gun, necessarily, but taking God's message?" He halted, then gave an ironic shake of his head. "That is, *if* God goes out on the battlefield—*any* battlefield."

"You sound like Wes," JoBeth told him.

"I thought Wes was convinced *he* had chosen the right thing to do."

"Oh, yes, I'm sure he believes he has. But he doesn't think war is right, no matter what. The longer he's in it, the more bitter, the more disillusioned, he sounds."

"You've seen him? He's been here?"

"Oh, no! He couldn't come." She gave a harsh laugh. "He'd be shot as a spy! Uncle Madison would probably meet him with a shotgun himself!"

It was Shelby's turn to comfort. "I'm sorry, JoBeth. It must be doubly hard for you. A divided heart."

She nodded. "Oh, Shelby, you always put it so right. Yes, that's what I have, a divided heart, and sometimes I feel as if I'm bleeding to death."

The two siblings turned to the fire and were lost momentarily in their own dark thoughts. Then Shelby said firmly, "Don't worry about me anymore, JoBeth. I'll go back. I'll finish out this term, at least. Then we'll see what next summer brings. Maybe the war will be over by then—"

"Please, God!" she said fervently. "I think you've made the right decision. At least for now. Mama would be so disappointed if you left. She's so proud of you, Shelby."

"I know. And I realize how hard she's worked, making quilts, selling them to pay for my tuition, room, board, books. I know that. Above all, I do want to do the right thing."

"You will, Shelby. I trust your judgment." She got to her feet, leaned down, and tousled his hair softly, "You're a wise old owl for seventeen!"

"Sometimes I feel more like Methuselah!"

"Well, I'd better get to bed, get some sleep," JoBeth said.

"Good night, then. Thanks for listening." Her brother raised his hand in a saluting gesture. "See you in the morning."

"Yes, I'll be up bright and early. I've promised to go skating if the pond is still frozen. Will and Blakely's house guest has unlimited energy!"

"Good! You deserve to have some fun."

"Want to go with us?"

Shelby shook his head. "As Proverbs says, 'Do not boast about tomorrow, for you do not know what a day may bring forth.'"

"Spoken like a true seminary student!"

"Or 'Out of the mouths of babes . . .,' right?" Shelby said, laughing.

"I'd better get out of here before you shame me any more with your Scripture quotes," she said. "Good night, Shelby." She waved her hand as she went out the door.

"Good night, Sis."

Chapter Ten

⁓⁊⁊⁓

The next day, instead of dropping, the temperature rose. An unseasonable warmth melted the light layer of snow that had fallen before Christmas, so there was no skating party on Bedlow Pond. However, the Spencer twins and their guest arrived at the Cadys' house to call upon JoBeth the following afternoon. Warmly received by Aunt Josie, they stayed, enjoying Uncle Madison's special holiday punch and the congenial company. The Spencers, always known for their exuberant personalities, were true to form and in high spirits. The visit ended after a round of singing, with Curtis again doing the honors at the piano.

When it was at last time to go, Curtis lingered a little behind as the others stood at the door, thanking the Cadys for their hospitality. He asked JoBeth, "May I call again tomorrow? On my own?"

"Tomorrow is the bazaar, a fund-raiser the Ladies Auxiliary is holding, and I've promised to help my aunt at her booth."

Disappointment clouded Curtis's handsome face momentarily, then quickly disappeared as he asked, "An event, I presume, that is open to the public?"

"Of course! Provided you bring lots of money to spend," she teased.

"Done." He saluted her. "And if I empty my pockets, may I have the honor of escorting you to the ball tomorrow evening?"

She laughed. "That sounds very mercenary."

"Anything for our cause, right?" He raised an eyebrow and smiled.

When Curtis departed with the others, JoBeth realized, with a guilty start, that she had not thought about Wes all afternoon.

～✂～

The bazaar to raise money to send needed supplies for "our boys in gray" had been planned for a long time. All the proceeds would go to various relief services. Hospitals, soldiers' widows and orphans, people who had left their homes in fear of Yankee invaders, and other charitable groups were listed as recipients of the money to be earned. For the past several months, all the Hillsboro ladies had been busy making handiwork of all sorts to sell. JoBeth's mother, aunt, and other relatives in the family had been involved from the beginning. Aunt Josie, known for her organizational ability, headed up the committee, assigning the different booths, each with specialized items for sale. Homemade delicacies, preserves, jams, jellies, baked goods. Embroidered pillowcases, tea towels, spectacle cases, slippers, floral potpourri and sachets, scented bath salts. Several booths were planned that would offer practical knitted garments, such as mittens, scarves, gloves, wrist warmers, socks, havelocks for foraging caps. There would also be booths tapping the varied creative talents of Hillsboro "artistes," exhibiting and selling such works as hand-painted china, watercolor greeting cards, and sentimental quotations in small frames. There would be a booth devoted to displaying dainty baby accessories, which were much in demand and would prove to be a popular item. (As would infant apparel—at one of the first organizing meetings, Patsy Faye Wrightman had commented, "With all the many military marriages that have taken place since Fort Sumter, there should soon be a market for baby booties, bonnets, buntings, blankets, and the like.")

The Logan ladies, as JoBeth's great-aunties were sometimes called by those who knew them before they were married, combined their quilting skills to contribute a beautiful quilt for which raffle tickets would be sold. In order to finish it in time for the bazaar's grand opening party, they increased their "quilting bee" from one to five days a week. The pattern they had chosen to make was Star of Bethlehem in bright yellow, blue, and red, with pointed patches making the star, and the quilt bound all around with a band of orange.

Johanna made several crib-sized quilts. JoBeth put aside her own work on her pledge quilt to help her mother. On these days when mother and daughter spent time together on the project, a new closeness seemed to grow between them. There was something about the quiet task that initiated confidences and sharing. Often the sound of November wind or rain beating upon window or roof created an intimacy, shutting them off from the outside world. Sometimes JoBeth would ask her mother about the years in the mountains when she had first married Ross Davison.

"Oh, it was a wonderful time, such happy years." Johanna's voice grew soft. "Hard work, which you know I wasn't used to at first. But so rewarding, so worthwhile. Your father was so kind, so loving—such a fine man, beloved by all the people in Millscreek."

JoBeth had her own memories of the tall, rugged man who was her father. She remembered his coming home and swinging her up into his arms, times he had held her on his knee, read to her. She could still recall how his beard felt against her forehead when she leaned back on his shoulder, the smell of him, the scent of leather, balsam pine, the slightly medicinal aroma that clung to his clothes. She remembered the gentleness of his hands, and the sound of his deep voice.

Thinking back on those long-ago childhood days, JoBeth felt the sharp twinge of loss. Only when she closed her eyes and really concentrated could she bring back the smell of the pine woods that had puckered her nostrils, the feel of the brown-needled carpet on her bare feet when she would run down the path between their home on the hill and Granny Eliza's.

"Do you remember the gritted cornbread Granny used to make?" Johanna's question broke in on JoBeth's thoughts.

"Oh, my, yes!" JoBeth looked at her mother, eyes shining. "That was the sweetest, tastiest cornbread I ever had! Was it a secret recipe or something?"

"I'm sure not. She told me how to make it and I tried, but mine never turned out as delicious as hers." Johanna laughed and shook her head.

"As soon as the weather gets better, I must go visit Granny," JoBeth murmured. "Maybe when Shelby comes home in the spring, when the snow melts, we can ride up there together." She thought of the weathered cabin nestled under the cedars with a tender longing. It was a part of her life, a part of herself that somehow had got lost in the years since she was a little girl. She felt an urgency to recapture it, treasure it somehow. Everything about the past had taken on a special significance, because everything else was changing so fast. Holding on to happy memories was important.

❧

The morning of the bazaar, soon after breakfast, Aunt Josie supervised packing Johanna's crib quilts into large boxes, then directed Jonas to carry them out to the carriage. Then she said, "JoBeth, you come along with me now. I need you to help arrange the booth, help me to decide which ones to display first." Buttoning her fur tippet, she nodded approvingly to JoBeth's mother, declaring, "Your quilts are just the sweetest, Johanna. Doting grandmothers will certainly snap them up in a hurry. I'm sure they will all go like hotcakes."

JoBeth glanced at her mother, who seemed a trifle wistful at seeing some of her favorite baby quilts disappear. It was as though she hated to part with them. JoBeth knew that each one her mother made was special to her. She gave her a sympathetic smile as she kissed her cheek, saying, "You'll come over later, won't you, Mama?"

"Yes, indeed. Aunt Honey's picking me up in her carriage. We don't want to miss the raffling off of the aunties' quilt."

"Good! You've worked so hard, you certainly deserve a bit of pleasure," Aunt Josie said decisively, putting on her bonnet.

JoBeth was amused that sometimes Aunt Josie spoke to her mother as if Johanna were still a young girl. Maybe that was the price her mother paid for coming back to live in Hillsboro with a member of her family.

Not for the first time, JoBeth wondered what would have happened to them all if instead, Johanna had decided to stay in Millscreek Gap among her husband's people. What would their lives have been like, hers and Shelby's? Shelby might have become a farmer like Uncle Merriman, their father's younger brother. *She* certainly would never have met Wesley! But she could hardly imagine that.

"Come along, JoBeth. Don't stand there dawdling and day-dreaming. We must be on our way. So much to do—," Aunt Josie said over her shoulder as she swept out the front door.

JoBeth glanced at her mother, who rolled her eyes in affectionate understanding, then JoBeth followed her aunt out to the waiting carriage.

When they reached the town hall, where the bazaar was being held, the place was abuzz with women's voices and the

swish of their skirts as they bustled about. A cacophony of
sound echoed in the vast building. People were issuing directions for the setting up of booths, the draping of bunting all
around. Hammers banged as signs went up, and a large muslin
banner hung from the rafters, declaring in gilt-edged letter-
ing such heart-quickening words as "For Our Glorious Cause"
and "For Our Gallant Men in Gray."

Aunt Josie was greeted by everyone. Mrs. Herndon, a
portly lady in pink and mauve taffeta, the grand chairwoman
of the event, rustled up importantly to lead her through the
of maze of cardboard boxes, unfurled crepe-paper streamers,
stepladders, and clusters of women busily erecting and deco-
rating their individual booths. JoBeth tagged behind.

"We always look forward to you Logan girls outdoing the
rest of us!" Mrs. Herndon simpered. JoBeth stifled a giggle at
the referral to her elderly great-aunts by their maiden name
and as "girls."

"As my own dear mama used to say, the Logan sisters do
the finest needlework in town!" Mrs. Herndon said effusively.
Then, gesturing with a flourish to a flimsy wood frame, she
said, "Now here we are, Josie. I hope this position suits you?
It is just to the right of the entrance door and will be the first
thing anyone sees! I'm sure you will be sold out long before
any of the other booths." She smiled at Aunt Josie, but her
smile did not include JoBeth. Startled by this obvious snub,
JoBeth wondered why not. Mrs. Herndon had known her
most of her life. JoBeth had gone to school with the Herndon
children, Billy and Maryclare. Slowly she understood. Mrs.
Herndon was a neighbor of the Spencers. So of course she
knew about Wes! *Her* son had joined Lee's army of northern
Virginia. By ignoring her, Mrs. Herndon was expressing her
disapproval of JoBeth's allegiance to Wes.

Realizing that this might be the general feeling of many
of the ladies working at the bazaar, JoBeth, her face flaming,

immediately went behind the booth. There she busied herself unpacking one of the boxes. Maybe she should have been prepared for that kind of treatment. JoBeth bit her lower lip as she bent over the boxes, wishing she could develop a hard shell. As it was, she couldn't help feeling hurt. More for Wes than herself. She laid some quilts neatly on one of the shelves, thinking, *I hope some Yankee women are doing for their soldiers what we're doing for—*She'd started to say *ours* to herself, then stopped. A bleak, hopeless feeling washed over her. She remembered what she and Shelby had talked about. *A divided heart! That's what I have! No wonder it hurts so much.*

JoBeth was sure that her aunt had been too preoccupied to notice Mrs. Herndon's deliberate coldness to her. Determined not to let her wounded feelings show, she began winding crepe-paper streamers around the spindly poles of the booth. Soon their booth was transformed into a bower of ribbons and clusters of flowers.

"Oh, that looks lovely, JoBeth!" Aunt Josie praised her, adding, "You certainly have your mother's artistic touch!"

For the next hour, they worked steadily, arranging, rearranging, setting out the lovely handmade items. Several of the other women working in various booths came by to admire and compliment them. Having been alerted by Mrs. Herndon's behavior toward her, JoBeth tried to act busy so as not to embarrass her aunt if any of the ladies refused to acknowledge her. She kept reminding herself that most of them were probably mothers who had sons off fighting and were sick with worry about their safety, so she tried to understand and forgive their resentment.

By the time they had placed the last patchwork pillow and agreed on the best angle to show off their favorite quilt, the bazaar had opened and people started streaming through the hall. From the size of the crowd, it appeared sales would be brisk. Most people seemed to first make the rounds—circling through the giant hall, admiring all the booths, browsing, getting an idea of all that was available—and then turn around and proceed to buy.

After two busy hours, Aunt Josie collapsed on one of the stools provided for the sales force. "Mercy me, JoBeth! I'm about done in! Do me a favor, darlin'. Like a good child, run along over to the food booth and get us each a bit of lunch. I heard tell they've got all manner of good things to eat, and I'm simply famished. I think we could both use a restoring cup of tea and a sandwich or two."

"Of course, Auntie," JoBeth agreed. "You just sit and rest. Now, don't do another thing till I get back, hear?"

"I couldn't if I wanted to!" her aunt laughed as she waved a pleated newspaper as an improvised fan.

JoBeth made her way through the crowded building to the refreshment booth. A long line of people was stretched out in front. It looked like a long wait to be served. Resignedly she took a place at the end. Others joined the line behind her, among them four chattering young women. Seemingly oblivious to anyone else, they were making no effort to keep their voices down. It was impossible not to overhear their conversation, and suddenly JoBeth began to catch some of it.

"The nerve of her—"

"She must think nobody knows—"

"Most likely doesn't care—"

"It's absolutely brazen, I think."

"With almost everyone here having *somebody*—brother, father, husband, sweetheart—serving!"

"It's outrageous, if you want *my* opinion."

"I should think Mrs. Herndon would have asked her to leave—"

"Or to not even come in the first place!"

"She could hardly do *that*! After all, the Cadys and the Breckenridges and Judge Hayes are all her relatives—"

"Even so—it's the principle of the thing!"

JoBeth's ears tingled, her cheeks burned. They were talking about *her*! *She* was the subject of this spiteful conversation. For the second time that day, the gossip about her and Wes that must be circulating hit her. Her heart hammered so loud, she wondered that people standing next to her didn't hear it! It even alarmed her with its banging. What if she fainted?

Should she turn around and confront them? Or just never let on that she had overheard? Her impulse was to whirl around, face them. But what could she say? How could she honestly defend being here at a fund-raising for the Confederacy when the man she loved was considered the *enemy*? All this raced through her mind. Her fists clenched. Part of her wanted to escape, even if it meant going back to her starving aunt empty-handed. Undecided, she debated. Then JoBeth heard her name spoken by several male voices.

"Miss Davison!"

"JoBeth!"

Dazed, she turned to see Will, Blakely, Ted Hamlett, and Curtis Channing! Within a few seconds, she was surrounded by four attractive, gray-uniformed officers. As she looked on in amazement, Curtis made a sweeping bow to the nonplused girls, the very ones who had been talking about her, and said in his most ingratiating manner, "I am sure you lovely ladies will give way to us"—he gestured grandly to his companions—"being that we're all heroic soldiers honorably defending your lives, homes, and country. Will you allow us to slip in line here? Yes, I was sure you would, seeing as we must soon be away again to the battlefields."

JoBeth glanced at him in astonishment. There was laughter in his eyes, a bold sureness of his own powers to persuade. Like magic, the disconcerted quartet stepped back and made way for the four officers. There was an amused ripple of laughter from others in the line, and looks of approval at the men. Someone was heard to say, "That's our rebels for you."

Escorted by the four, JoBeth moved up the line. Beside her, each handling two plates apiece, they quickly had them piled with sandwiches, frosted cupcakes, slices of pie. Blakely wheedled a tray from one of the booth ladies and loaded it with steaming mugs of fragrant tea to take back to the quilt booth.

Out of the corner of her eye, JoBeth saw the four indignant deposed gossipers staring at her with open envy. However, knowing that her companions' food purchases had totaled up a nice sum for the benefit's coffers, she walked off with her head high. Certainly, she thought, by the end of the afternoon other booths would find their cash boxes filled with the young officers' money as well.

Back at the booth, after consuming the delicious delicacies they'd brought back, the four men persuaded Aunt Josie to allow JoBeth to be their guide among the myriad booths. That way, they said, they could spend more money for "the glorious cause."

If unfriendly eyes followed her progress as she guided the good-looking cavalry officers from booth to booth, JoBeth knew they could not argue with the fact that the four were clearing out great quantities of the merchandise displayed.

JoBeth was ironically amused by all this. Underneath, however, the overheard comments still stung. But she thought it a small sacrifice on her part—Wes had made the much harder one.

In spite of the constant chaperonage of his three fellow officers, Curtis had a chance to whisper in JoBeth's ear, "Do I qualify for the honor of taking you to the ball tonight?"

Looking at his armload of pot holders, doilies, china bud vases, knitted scarves, and other miscellaneous purchases, JoBeth widened her eyes and exclaimed dramatically, "I should hope so."

Chapter Eleven

⋙⋘

That evening, JoBeth got ready for the ball, with both her mother and Aunt Josie hovering like bees around a favorite flower. Each had suggestions to complement her appearance. Johanna got out her point lace scarf and insisted JoBeth wear it, draping it over the shoulders of her hyacinth blue velvet gown. JoBeth was just securing a high-backed comb into her swept-up hair when her aunt left the bedroom and returned, carrying a jewel case.

"Here's something that will set off your gown," she said, opening it and taking out amethyst-and-pearl earrings and a matching pendant on a gold chain.

"Oh, Auntie, they're beautiful!" JoBeth exclaimed. "But I couldn't!"

"Of course you must. I'll hear no argument. They'll be perfect," her aunt said firmly. "Here, let me fasten this around your neck."

Persuaded, JoBeth then slipped the earrings in while her aunt clasped the pendant's chain. Both Johanna and Aunt Josie murmured approvingly at the result of the added jewels.

"Thank you both!" JoBeth smiled, touching the lace then the earrings with her hand. "I feel like Cinderella in her borrowed finery and jewels."

"Except it won't all disappear at midnight!" Johanna laughed.

"Let's hope not!" declared Aunt Josie in mock alarm. "That set was Madison's wedding gift to me!"

Downstairs, Curtis, splendid in a dress uniform and polished black boots, waited for her. The gilt epaulets and the golden swirls on his sleeve cuffs gleamed against the fine gray broadcloth coat, the tasseled yellow silk sash a bright slash of color at his waist.

Curtis had brought a wrist corsage of hothouse violets for JoBeth to wear. As she held out her wrist for him to tie the purple and lavender satin ribbons, the admiration in his eyes was open and unabashed. It made her a little breathless.

Uncle Madison handed Curtis JoBeth's dark-blue velvet cape, and Aunt Josie said with satisfaction, "My, what a handsome couple you make!"

Catching a glimpse of herself and Curtis in the hall mirror, JoBeth felt elated and excited. It was a heady moment, and she needed to defuse it. She whirled around, shook her fan playfully at her aunt. "Oh, Auntie, you're prejudiced. But thank you." She slipped her kid-gloved hand through Curtis's offered arm. Then, kissing her mother, she said, "Thank you all, and good night."

"Have a lovely time!" her mother's voice followed them out into the crisp December night.

As they entered the ballroom, which was adorned with a random mix of Christmas decorations and patriotic symbols of the Confederacy and brightly illuminated by candles in brass wall sconces tied with gilt ribbons, the band was playing.

JoBeth felt her heart lift at the sound of the music, the slide of feet upon a floor sanded and waxed for dancing, the sight of whirling colors—cerise, orange, green, gold, pink— and the ballooning skirts of dancers circling. The gaiety of the atmosphere was irresistible. Suddenly all JoBeth's under-lying sadness melted magically away. She was caught up and into it all. Curtis held out his hand to her and swept her out among the dancers.

Curtis knew every type of dance and executed each with finesse. His skill spoke of much practice and social experi-ence. JoBeth had never felt so light on her feet as he guided her expertly in several intricate maneuvers so that she never missed a step. During the first part of the evening, she danced with many partners—with Blakely, Will, Ted, and a half dozen others. Many were hometown boys she knew and had grown up with but hadn't seen much of in the past several months. Most were in uniform, on leave, or coming or going to some military post or service. Although this was a military ball and had been given to honor and aid the cause, strangely enough nothing was mentioned about the reason for it all. For once in what seemed forever, the war was not the main topic of talk. Gaiety seemed the order of the evening, and JoBeth gratefully entered into it. She found it almost easy to forget what had been constantly on her mind for months. She slipped back into what had once been natural—carrying on banter of a light, silly kind. In fact, she had almost forgot-ten she was very good at it.

When intermission was called, Curtis led her to a table at which Blakely and Will and the girls they were escorting were already seated. When Curtis and JoBeth joined them, it made six crowded around it. JoBeth knew the two other girls, Trudie Hartman and Flavia Bates. Of late they had pointedly excluded her from the social occasions that previously she would have been invited to attend. Tonight they were con-scious that she was accepted as part of the group they were with, and they were superficially polite. However, most of their attention was turned to their escorts as the two girls flirted with fluttering eyelashes and fans, giggling at the twins' outlandish jokes and flattery. Since Curtis was devoting *his* full attention to *her*, JoBeth hardly minded being ignored by her former friends.

When the music began again, a childhood friend, Kenan Matthews, came over from another table to ask JoBeth to dance. She excused herself from the others. Kenan had also been a friend of Wes, and for the first time all evening, she was asked about him.

"I realize how hard that must have been for Wes—and for you, too, JoBeth," Kenan said when she told him Wes was now in the Union Army. "Wesley Rutherford was the most idealistic, most honest, person I ever knew. Although I disagree with his decision, I admire him for his integrity."

"Thank you," JoBeth murmured, feeling her heart swell with pride at hearing these rare words of praise for Wes.

When Kenan returned her to her table with a courteous bow, she found that the other girls had left for the ladies' "refreshing room." The three men had been joined by cousin Ted, and although they had all risen and politely acknowledged her return, they resumed what appeared to be a heated discussion.

Curtis was saying, "I can't see what all the fuss about slavery is about. My father has a lumber mill down home and has about twenty men working for him there, and out at my granddaddy's farm there are people who have been on the land as long as I can remember and before. They all seem happy as can be. You should hear them singin' out in the fields—"

JoBeth experienced a sick sensation, a rush of blood to her head. The drastic contrast between Wes's long, agonizing soul-searching and Curtis's casual offhandedness about the same subject struck her like a blow. Her fingers clutched her little fan so tightly that she could feel the edges of its spokes.

Just then Curtis, as if aware of JoBeth beside him, seemed to lose interest in the conversation. He leaned toward her, smiling, and said, "I missed you." Then, lowering his voice and with his appealing little-boy grin, he said, "Let me have your dance card. I'm putting my name on all the rest." Disarmed, she handed it to him.

Watching him scrawl his name through the line of dances still left on her card, JoBeth knew she shouldn't blame Curtis for his attitude. Wes had even understood that. Like so many Southerners, he was only speaking from what he knew, what he had grown up with, never having learned any other opinion. Why should she expect any more from this charming man than an evening of flattering attention? With his graceful manners, his wit and good humor, it was impossible not to like Curtis Channing—and it would be easy to fall in love with him.

Back on the dance floor, Curtis said, "You know I go back day after tomorrow. This has been too—" He checked himself, as though he would have used a stronger way of expressing his frustration. "This has been *way* too short. At any other time that you and I might have met, we would have had a chance to get to know each other better—spend long, leisurely afternoons strolling, swinging in a hammock under the trees, playing croquet on the lawn, going riding. There are so many things I can think of I'd like to do with you." There was amusement, affection, in his eyes as he looked down at her. Then quite suddenly his eyes darkened. "I hate that we're missin' all that, Miss Johanna Elizabeth Davison." He spoke her full name as though he delighted in each syllable. "This has been one wonderful two and a half days." His hand on her waist tightened as he circled and then reversed in the final strains of the waltz. "Days I shall never forget."

The music ended, but he didn't take her right back to the table. Instead he stood, still holding her hand so tightly that she finally wiggled her fingers to free them.

The orchestra began playing the final piece of the evening—"Goodnight, Ladies"—and Curtis led her into the slow steps of the song, making a slow circle of the dance floor.

As was customary these days, the evening ended with a rousing chorus of "Dixie," which was finished with a flourish of trumpets, followed by some spontaneous renditions of the famous rebel yell inaugurated at the Yankee defeat at the battle of Manassas.

The Spencers' large carriage had been commandeered for their party. When they came out, they found the horses stamping their feet and blowing frosty breaths in the cold night air. They had to rouse the sleepy driver, Felix, who was bundled in front. The two girls were taken to the door of the Hartman's house, since Flavia was staying overnight with Trudie. JoBeth and Curtis remained together in the carriage. They could hear the high-pitched laughter and low voices saying whatever frivolous and foolish things were being said besides proper good nights on the doorstep.

Curtis made no move to give JoBeth more room on the seat on which the six of them had all been squeezed so tightly on their way from the ball. JoBeth did not move either, because she was cold and also did not want to call attention to the fact that they were sitting so close together.

At last the twins came running back and hopped into the carriage, and they went on toward the Cadys' house. When they reached it, Curtis helped JoBeth down. He then surprised her by leaning back into the carriage and saying, "I can walk home from here. You fellows go along." Before she could utter a protest, Will shouted up to the driver to go, and the carriage moved forward, leaving her and Curtis standing at the gate. For a minute there was silence. JoBeth hardly knew what to say about his bold dismissal of his hosts and their carriage.

"Did you mind?" Curtis asked in a low voice, taking JoBeth's hand and drawing it through his arm. "I hate for this evening to end. For our time together to end."

"You're to come to dinner tomorrow," she reminded him. Uncle Madison had issued the invitation before they left for the ball.

"Yes, I know, but he invited Will and Blakely as well, and from what he said, there'll be a bunch of people. We won't be by ourselves at all. Funny thing, but I've always enjoyed being around people until—well, to tell you the truth, all at once I find I want to be alone with you, JoBeth."

"It's late, Curtis. I'd better be going in," JoBeth demurred, thinking the conversation might be getting dangerous. She pulled her hand from his arm and placed it on the gate latch.

Curtis put out his hand and kept the gate from opening. He lifted his head, looking up. The night sky was studded with stars. "What a beautiful night. I can't remember seeing one so beautiful."

JoBeth felt she had to take charge of the situation.

"Yes, Curtis, it *is* very beautiful, but it is *also* very late," she chided gently.

Curtis laughed softly. "I know. My delaying tactics are pretty obvious, aren't they?" He didn't seem offended and pushed open the gate. They started up the walk, but Curtis's step was slow.

When they reached the porch steps, Curtis took her arm, keeping her from going up. "At the risk of repeating myself, JoBeth, I wish I could make this evening last...." He paused, then almost in a whisper said, "I would like very much to kiss you."

Startled, JoBeth halted, staring up at Curtis. He hurried to say, "I know it's highly improper, as you may rightly say, since we have just met. Hardly know each other. But JoBeth, don't you get the feeling that these days, time is telescoped? Each day, each hour, each minute, counts." He paused, reached out with his other hand, turned her face toward him. "You have quite the most beautiful mouth I have seen in a very long time and—simply put, I want to kiss it."

She was stunned. She had not been kissed in months, and then by Wes. All other kisses before his had disappeared from memory, like figments of a dream. Now this handsome soldier's request stirred her.

"Since you haven't answered, I'll take the offensive as a good soldier should—" And Curtis bent and kissed her very slowly, sweetly. When it ended, both sighed.

"You are very lovely, Miss Davison, and I couldn't resist the temptation. Say you forgive me?"

He didn't sound at all remorseful, and JoBeth realized she wasn't sorry either. The kiss had been gentle, warm, and very satisfactory. It would be silly to *act* offended. Indeed, to *be* offended. Curtis was right—the days they were all living through were moving too fast, taking with them the time for leisurely courtships, old-fashioned restrictions of all kinds.

They went slowly up the porch steps. At the front door, he put both arms around her waist, interlocking his fingers so that he held her in a tight clasp from which she could not easily escape.

"Do you have a charm chain, JoBeth? One of those strings of buttons that girls collect?"

"How do you know about those?" she asked, surprised. She didn't know any man who was aware of the current fad that single girls had of collecting buttons. The legend was that the button last collected, if given by a male and placed on the chain, was from the one you would marry.

Curtis chided her gently. "Remember, I told you I have two younger sisters. I'm on to all sorts of feminine pastimes. They each have one of those chains, and they're always

340

lengthening them, afraid the wrong fella will give them the last one. Girls!" Curtis chuckled, shaking his head in amusement. "They're somethin' else. You just never know what they'll do next." He paused, then asked, "So then, do *you*? Have a chain?"

JoBeth used to have one, as most schoolgirls did. But after she and Wes had made their pledge, she hadn't even thought about the silly tradition. However, not wanting to explain all that, she just nodded. "I confess I used to have a button collection."

Slowly Curtis released her. His hand went to the front of his tunic, grasped at the double row of shiny brass buttons, gave a hard tug, and a button came off. He held his hand out to her, then opened it to show the button resting in his palm.

"Here, JoBeth, will you take it? Let it be the last one on your charm chain?"

JoBeth was taken aback. She drew in her breath.

"But—but I'm not superstitious."

"No? Well, *I* am! I believe in fate, destiny, and predestination. That nothing happens by chance. My coming home with Blakely and Will on this leave. Meeting you. It's all in the cards." He paused, took her hand, and pressed the button into her palm. "Please take it. I want to go back to camp believing it means something."

341

Chapter Twelve

~❦~

The December morning was cold. Under a gray sky, a chill mist drifted. At the Hillsboro train station, the families gathered to see the "boys" off again. A kind of false gaiety prevailed—everyone chatted about unimportant things, marking time until the train came. Underneath the forced optimism ran an undercurrent of apprehension. They were sending them back to their regiment, back to the war—and no one really knew what these young men were going back to, what they might be facing in the next weeks or months.

As the group huddled together, making innocuous small talk, JoBeth shivered. Inside her small beaver muff, her hands were nervously clenched. Uneasily she met Curtis's fixed gaze. For the first time since she met him, Curtis's smile was not visible, and his eyes had lost their mischievous sparkle.

The evening before, which was spent in the company of the Cadys, the Spencers, and the Hamletts, had not been a success as far as Curtis was concerned. Impatient to be alone with JoBeth, he had endured an evening with company. Dinner had been festive, with all the ladies contributing their tastiest dishes, their finest cakes and pies, as a grand sendoff to the boys, who were used to army rations. Afterward there had been games, songs, and general conversation. As the evening progressed, Uncle Madison drew the young soldiers into a military discussion. Sitting across the room from him, only JoBeth had been aware of Curtis's growing frustration. Eventually the evening had come to a close. Good manners required the hosts to see their guests to the door, so at the end they had still been surrounded by other people.

All this JoBeth read in Curtis's eyes as he gazed at her this morning in the midst of the awkward group of family and friends.

Finally Curtis reached the end of his patience. He came over to where she stood. "I *must* speak to you," he said in a low voice. Then, ignoring the exchanged glances of the others, he took JoBeth by the arm and walked her to the end of the platform.

There, apart from the rest, he no longer felt obliged to present a bravado. Curtis's expression turned grave. "I didn't mean to be rude. But time is slipping fast, and I had to talk to you privately," he said. "I couldn't keep standing there pretending it didn't matter, when it does." His tone was intense. "I hate to leave with so much unsaid. I don't want to go back. It's not just going back. It's leaving *you*."

"Please, Curtis, don't—," JoBeth protested, but he didn't let her finish.

"No, JoBeth. You may not want to hear this, but I want to say it—*have* to say it. So please listen." He rubbed his hands together as if from the cold. "I attended church with the Spencers this morning. But the sermon was so long and tiresome, I got bored and started thumbing through the Bible. I came upon some pretty interesting stuff." He halted, then asked with mock severity, "Are you familiar with Scripture, Miss Davison?"

Surprised by his question, she replied, "Not as much as I should be."

"Well, neither am I ordinarily, I'm ashamed to admit. But this morning I had a revelation of sorts—I think you might call it."

"What do you mean?"

"Simply this. It was in Deuteronomy. I chanced upon something I heartily recommend—I scribbled down chapter and verse so I wouldn't forget it. Deuteronomy 24:5—this is what's written down right there in the Good Book, as a law to the Israelites—'When a man has taken a new wife, he shall not go out to war, but he shall be free at home for one year and bring happiness to his wife.'" Curtis's voice took on excitement as he quoted the passage. Looking directly at JoBeth, he said, "Now, *that* is a law I believe we should adopt in the Confederacy." A faint smile lifted the corners of his mouth. "And therefore I fully intend to bring this to the attention of my commanding officer. What do you say to that, Miss Davison? A good idea?"

"I suppose so...." JoBeth smiled tentatively, as if waiting for the joke she expected would follow.

Yet Curtis seemed totally serious. "Should we not press for the enactment of such a law?" he demanded.

JoBeth looked at him in bewildered amusement. "I don't think I understand, Curtis."

"Miss Davison, would you consider marrying me? And let me spend one full year bringing you happiness?"

Suddenly JoBeth realized this wasn't one of Curtis's pranks or comical attempts to make her laugh. He meant it. He was proposing.

"Curtis, I—"

"Don't look so shocked, please. I've been very proper about it. I've spoken to your uncle who, I understand, is your guardian, and asked for your hand in marriage. And also received permission from your mother to address you. It took a good deal of maneuvering to do that last evening. I had to follow your mother into the kitchen, and I was forced to waylay your uncle early this morning. I was waiting at the gate when he went out for his walk. They were a bit taken aback, I admit, but they said it was up to you, so—" He rushed on. "I realize we haven't known each other long. Just met, in fact. But we've spent nearly three entire days together. I know I could make you happy! You'd love my hometown, my family—and they would love you. They're much like your family. We have so much in common, JoBeth. The same background, the same values, the same—"

"Stop, Curtis! I can't. Please, don't say any more. Let us part as friends. It's been a wonderful three days, but that's all it can be."

"*Why?* I don't understand."

In the distance, the thin sound of a train whistle pierced the winter air, startling both of them. A frown brought Curtis's eyebrows together over eyes full of dismay.

"JoBeth, there isn't any time. I love you. I know I can make you love me."

In his face, disappointment and possibility mingled. JoBeth had the feeling that Curtis Channing had been refused very little in his life. And nothing that he really wanted. She shook her head.

"No, Curtis, I'm sorry. There is someone else—I'm pledged to someone else."

He looked shocked, then angry.

"But you never said—you never gave any hint that—neither did your aunt and uncle nor your mother!"

"They don't know. It's a secret."

His frown deepened. "I don't understand."

"I'm sorry—truly I am," she said, and she meant it. She had not meant to mislead or hurt him.

345

The train rounded the bend and was clanking down the track, a spiral of smoke billowing out of its stack. With a hissing of steam, a screech of brakes, it pulled to a grinding stop. The small group at the other end of the platform started calling, beckoning, gesturing to them.

"I can't believe there's no chance," Curtis said forlornly.

"I'm sorry, Curtis. Perhaps if we had met some other time—"

Blakely was shouting to Curtis, motioning with wild, flaying arms. Hillsboro was what was called a "whistle stop." Even in wartime it had a schedule to keep.

Curtis grabbed JoBeth's hands, held them tightly.

"Isn't there anything I can say to change your mind? Can't you give me some reason to hope?"

"No, that would be wrong—it wouldn't be true." JoBeth's voice broke. "I'm sorry," she said again.

He pressed her hands so hard, they felt crushed.

"I respect loyalty, JoBeth. If you are promised to someone else . . ." His mouth tightened. "Another soldier? I can accept that."

Something inside JoBeth shrank from telling him. If he knew *who* the soldier was and *what* he was fighting for— would Curtis be so noble, so understanding?

"I'm sorry, "she said weakly, knowing it was inadequate.

The shouts grew frantic. "Curtis, come on! You're going to miss the train. Hurry up!"

"I will never forget you—nor these three days—for the rest of my life." Curtis's voice was hoarse, ragged, above the warning shrill of the train's whistle.

Impulsively JoBeth raised herself on tiptoe to kiss him lightly on the cheek. But before she could, his arms went around her, drawing her tight against him so that her feet were lifted off the ground. He kissed her with passion and desperation. When he set her back down, she was breathless, deeply stirred by his kiss. "Good-bye, darling JoBeth," Curtis said huskily, then he took one or two steps, backing away from her. "Good-bye." He started down the platform, then turned, took one last, lingering look at her before he began to run toward the train. The locomotive was sending up great clouds of steam and the whistle shrieked again.

JoBeth watched him swing up into the car even as the train started moving down the track. He leaned out, waving his arm. She raised hers feebly and waved back.

As the train disappeared around the bend, she shuddered. A rising wind tore at her bonnet strings, tugged at her skirts. Still she stared down the empty tracks, standing away from the rest of the people at the other end—standing apart, standing alone.

⚶

JoBeth got back into the carriage. On the way home, Aunt Josie leaned over and patted her knee. "What a lovely young man, honey. And so taken with you. I don't know when I've seen such an example of love at first sight. Why, I could tell the minute he laid eyes on you the other evening at Harvel's—he never looked at anyone else. It was clear as a bell to see."

"As fine a young man as the Confederacy could ever have to defend us," was Uncle Madison's comment. "Good stock, good breeding. You can't miss it."

"And beautiful manners!" chimed in Aunt Josie. "He was so easy and gracious, you can tell he was brought up well."

JoBeth did not know how to reply. She knew her family assumed that her downcast mood was because of Curtis Channing's leaving and were treating her with considerate deference. She *was* sorry—not so much that he was gone but that she had hurt him. She hadn't meant to, but it couldn't be helped. Should she let their assumption go on? How could they possibly think she had so quickly forgotten Wes? They seemed to. People often saw what they wanted to see. They had been upset about Wes, so no wonder they hoped she would be attracted to the charming Curtis. In their minds, who could be more acceptable as a suitor for their niece than a well-born, well-mannered, handsome Confederate cavalry officer?

Arriving back at the house, JoBeth immediately went upstairs to her room, shut the door. She needed to be alone with her guilty conscience. Ever since Wes left, she seemed to be living a lie, hiding her correspondence, never speaking his name. Mostly to please her aunt and uncle, she had outwardly participated in Hillsboro's social life. All the time, she had been hiding her secret. Now her family happily believed she was interested in Curtis Channing.

She knelt down on the carpet in front of the fireplace and poked the sputtering fire to life. The look in Curtis's eyes haunted her. If she had misled him, there was no way to undo the damage, to avoid the consequences.

She regretted that she might have inadvertently led Curtis to imagine romantic possibilities for them. Worse still was her remorse that in enjoying his delightful company, basking in his flattering attention, she had betrayed Wes. How could she have—even for a few days—forgotten what *he* had given up, what he was going through? She put her face in her hands and wept bitterly.

That evening she got out her neglected pledge quilt squares and sewed diligently. Tears fell on the cloth as she sewed, and at times blurred her eyes so that she couldn't stitch properly. Finally, exhausted, she prepared for bed. Hopefully, after a good night's sleep everything would seem clearer. But sleep refused to come. Obsessively her thoughts kept returning to the scene on the train station platform, and Curtis's good-bye.

Chapter Thirteen

❦

*A*ll the following week, the hints, the innuendoes, and the inferences from both Aunt Josie and Uncle Madison began to mount. JoBeth assumed that Curtis's supposed proposal had been circulated among the close-knit family. She was sure the consensus was that she had best not summarily dismiss the courting of such a gallant young man. It was as if the combined family were holding its breath and waiting for her to make the announcement.

JoBeth simmered under the covert glances sent her way. She could just imagine the discussions about her that were going on within the family circle. While they held an idealized image of Curtis, they seemed to have forgotten all Wes's fine, brave qualities—his integrity, his courage. What hurt her the most was the fact that Wes had grown up in this town. They had known him since he was a little boy. They knew his parents as friends. Wes had often been a guest in all their homes, and now they had all turned against him in favor of someone they had just met. And only because Curtis wore the right uniform! Finally JoBeth reached the end of her tether. She went to her mother and told her about Curtis's proposal.

"Of course, I told him I was pledged to another. I don't see why Aunt Josie and Uncle Madison presume I could forget

Wes like that." JoBeth snapped her fingers. "They *want* me to be engaged to someone like Curtis, for their own sakes. So they won't be embarrassed any longer by a niece promised to a Yankee sympathizer. I don't think they even realize that Wes has joined the Union Army!" She got up from the chair on which she had been perched near her mother's quilting frame and began to pace. "No matter what they want, I am in love with Wes, *pledged to him*! Nothing or no one, no matter how charming or attractive or eligible in their opinion, will change that. I wish they'd stop insinuating otherwise."

"Do you want me to speak to them, darling?" Johanna asked sympathetically.

"Would you, Mama? Please? I'm afraid I'd just get defensive and get into an argument." JoBeth sighed. "I love Aunt Josie and Uncle Madison. I don't want this to cause any more misunderstanding."

Since Wes's departure, there had been an unspoken rule in the Cady household never to mention him. It was a rule that no one had yet disobeyed.

That evening at dinner, JoBeth guessed that her mother had broken the rule. Her aunt and uncle's attitude spoke volumes. There was an unnatural stiffness in their very postures. JoBeth could not only feel the disapproval but see it in her uncle's face. Aunt Cady regarded her with hardly concealed impatience, her mouth pressed as though she were trying to keep from speaking her mind about JoBeth's stubborn and distressing stand.

Uncle Madison never could keep from expressing himself on any subject for long, and before the meal was half over, he addressed himself directly to JoBeth.

"I understand you turned Curtis Channing down, young lady." Uncle Madison's tone was bitter, implying that he was a man who felt he had been greatly wronged. "In my opinion, that was a very rash and unwise decision. You would do well to reconsider that refusal. A finer specimen of an upstanding Southern gentleman it has not been my pleasure to meet. And from what Blakely tells me, a fine officer as well, admired by his comrades and well-thought-of by his superiors. I understand he will probably make captain before long—you should be proud that such a man has asked you to be his wife."

It was too much. After all, Wes had been welcome here since he was a little boy. He had sat at this very dinner table, had brought flowers and his gracious manners to her aunt and mother. Yet now he had become anathema, as though he had never even existed.

"Yes, indeed." Uncle Madison was waxing eloquent as to Curtis's qualities. "That young man is certainly an outstanding example of what is best in a Confederate officer—"

But this time he got no further. JoBeth could stand no more, and she turned furiously toward her uncle and interrupted, "Curtis Channing doesn't have the remotest idea what the war is all about—or even what he's fighting for."

At first, Uncle Madison looked stunned at this startling outburst.

Then his face reddened and he banged his fist on the table. "Well, he damn well knows what's the *right* side to be fighting for!"

At this, tears threatening, JoBeth flung down her napkin and jumped up from the table and ran from the room.

JoBeth's outburst at the dinner table that night ushered in a dreadful period of strained relations with her aunt and uncle. Uncle Madison maintained a dignified silence as he came and went, and he kept his contact with his niece to a minimum. Aunt Josie fluttered between her husband and niece, begging them both to relent and resume their former affectionate relationship.

Both were stubborn. At last Johanna intervened with her daughter, saying it was *she* who should apologize. Uncle Madison had been like a father to her all these years, she reminded JoBeth, and she should honor and respect him, no matter their differences. JoBeth, knowing she had been wrong to react as she did, finally yielded. She went to her uncle one evening, upon his return from his office, and asked his forgiveness. Wes was not mentioned.

"We'll say no more about it, my dear," was Uncle Madison's stiff rejoinder. After that the household seemed to regain its balance. However, under the surface, all knew that things might never be the same again.

Part Three

Spring 1863

Chapter Fourteen

━━◦℘◦━━

*T*hree letters from Wes, all looking "battle scarred," arrived for JoBeth at the same time. One touched her deeply but filled her with a feeling of apprehension. There was something about it that sounded so final, as though it might be the last time she would ever hear from Wes.

> *Lying here on my cot in the tent on this dark night, my dreams are filled with visions of your dear face. Even though now it seems endless, I know our separation must someday end. And we will find our love and happiness again. I take your letters out and press them to my lips—it seems your perfume still clings to the pages, and I am most aware of the sweetness of your memory, the scent of your skin, your hair. How I long to hold you once more. Pray God it will not be too long until that happy day comes.*
>
> > *Ever yours,*
> > Wes

The letters had no dates, so JoBeth could not be sure when Wes had written them or where he might possibly have been at the time.

> *Long march today, feet aching, legs weary, shoulder burdened with heavy pack. All made light, easy, because*

*I let my mind wander to thoughts of you—the bright days
of summers we knew . . .*

*I had a terrible dream. I woke feeling suddenly des-
olate. I dreamed I could not remember your lovely face.
How could this be? At night when I lie awake waiting for
sleep to come, your beautiful eyes appear, smiling, and
gradually your image comes to comfort me. I think sometimes I can even hear your voice.*

*I do think of you as my bride. Then I consider the
price I've asked you to pay. My love for a life of sorrow?
Alienation from your family, from those you hold near
and dear? This cruel war that has parted us, that has sent
me away from you. For what? For home and country? I
have left the only home I've known, my land, my people.
I am an orphan, in truth. Except for your love, my dearest—that is all that holds me staunch. And I believe our
cause to be a just one.*

<hr />

Spring brought the war even closer. With the battle at
Chancellorsville in May, the Confederates won a remarkable
but costly victory against the Union Army. The losses were
heavy, something that the Southern forces, with less man-
power, could not easily bear. Worse still was the tragic death
of General Lee's right-hand man, accidentally shot by his
own pickets.

At the news of Stonewall Jackson's death, flags were
flown at half-mast in Hillsboro. Some even wore black arm-
bands, like Wayne Spencer, whose sons had fought under the
brilliant general. Still, the success of Lee's army lifted spirits
and gave a renewed hope that the Confederacy would eventually be victorious.

A letter from Wes came, and JoBeth sensed a difference in tone from the previous ones. There was a sense of fatalism about it that frightened her.

June 1863

My Dearest,

> *In the silence around this encampment, the tension is almost alive. We expect attack or some action any-time. . . . We know the Confeds are somewhere camped in the hills just beyond the ridge. We speak of the enemy, but all I can think is that these are my former playmates, my classmates, my fellow college students, my broth-ers. . . . Are we not all God's children? This horrible con-flict must soon be resolved. Oh, JoBeth, I can close my eyes and see your dear face, see your sweet smile, the dark, silky curls falling on your shoulders, hear your ten-der voice. I remember the words we spoke, and they echo in my despairing heart. Will they ever be said again? When I finally drift off to sleep, when I wake, your name is on my lips.*

No more letters came for three more weeks. Anxiety about Wes was JoBeth's constant companion. Yet she could share it with no one.

It was in July, however, that the tide of the war was about to turn dramatically. Ironically, it would happen on the national anniversary celebration of American independence.

Hillsboro on the first day of July was blistering, not a breath of air stirring. The ladies were out on the Cadys' front porch, waiting for Uncle Madison to come home for noon dinner. JoBeth was sitting on the steps, and her mother and aunt were in rocking chairs, fluttering palmetto fans and dis-cussing a new quilt pattern. All of a sudden Aunt Josie sat up straight, exclaiming in alarm, "Will you look at that! Walking so fast in this heat, he's liable to get a stroke. Madison ought to know better."

JoBeth turned to see her uncle striding briskly down the sidewalk toward the house.

Aunt Josie got to her feet and went to the porch railing, ready to rebuke her husband the minute he came through the gate. But something in his expression stopped her. He came puffing up the steps, mopping his red face with his handkerchief as he said breathlessly, "News has just come over the telegraph wires. A great battle is underway near a small Pennsylvania town called Gettysburg. And we're winning! Surely now Lee will bring about a glorious victory—whip those Yankees once and for all."

A worried Aunt Josie urged him to sit down and rest a bit while she brought him a glass of iced tea. He did, under protest, and eventually he caught his breath, and they all went into the house for a delayed meal. However, Uncle Madison could hardly eat a bite and left without taking his usual short nap. He wanted to return to his office downtown to be close to the telegraph office, where further bulletins would be posted as soon as received.

Soon after he departed, Aunt Josie put on her bonnet, saying she thought she'd go over to Dorinda's. Munroe's wife was expecting a new baby, she said, and it might be well for someone to be with her, in case ... She left the sentence dangling, but Johanna and JoBeth knew the fearful thought she had left unspoken. Both Harvel and Munroe were with Lee's army and probably in the midst of the battle now raging. *And was Wes too?* JoBeth wondered. She had to keep her dread question to herself.

That night at the supper table, Uncle Madison was still in an excited, optimistic frame of mind.

"Lee's invincible! Everyone says so. Harvel told me at Christmas that even the Union generals agree he is a military genius. This could be the turning point!" He slapped his hands together in obvious anticipation of victory.

Suddenly the tension that had been building inside her over the past weeks and months came to the surface, and JoBeth turned to him tearfully. "Men and boys are *dying*, uncle! Being killed! On *both* sides in this awful war, don't you know? There's nothing to feel good about!"

She shook off her mother's restraining hand and continued to face her uncle, tears streaming down her cheeks.

Uncle Madison visibly paled. He stared at her.

"You forget yourself, young lady," he said in a trembling voice. "I have two sons most probably in the thick of it. But they are fighting for a cause that affects us all—you, your safety, our life here even this far from it—I never forget that."

"JoBeth, dear, please." Her mother's gentle reproach went unheeded.

"And so is Wes fighting for what he believes. No one here, in this family, gives him credit for that. Except *me*. I love him! And he may be dying or being killed this minute, and nobody cares—" Her voice cracked hoarsely, and JoBeth ran sobbing from the room.

❧

When JoBeth woke up, she knew it was late. The house was silent. There was not a sound of movement downstairs or in the hallway outside her bedroom door. Had they all gone to church without calling her? She knew that her mother thought she was ill last night and had made excuses for her to the others. Why else the outburst, the tears?

She remembered running upstairs the night before, throwing herself down on her bed, weeping uncontrollably.

She vaguely recalled falling into an exhausted sleep and her mother coming in later, placing a cloth, dampened with cologne, on her burning forehead, drawing her quilt gently over her shoulders, tiptoeing out again.

How long had she slept? Was the battle at Gettysburg over? Who had won? Was Wes still alive? Or was he dead—had he made the ultimate sacrifice for his beliefs? A vivid picture of him lying, bloody, broken, in some forsaken place flashed before her. The image pierced her like a bayonet. *Oh, God, I hope it has all been worth it!* New tears rolled down her cheeks and into her mouth, and she tasted the hot saltiness on her lips.

She rolled over and buried her face in the pillow, wishing she could go to sleep again and not wake up until the war was over.

For three hot, humid, miserable days, people clustered around the telegraph office of the Hillsboro train station, awaiting the latest news of the battle being so fiercely waged.

Gettysburg—few had even heard the name, but afterward few would ever forget it.

August 1863

Chapter Fifteen

❦

My Darling JoBeth,

Such wonderful news, I can hardly contain myself as I write. I have been reassigned. My captain discovered my educational background—that I could read, understand Latin, and had read law. He called me into his tent and said I was wasted as a foot soldier and would be of more value to the Union as an aide-de-camp or secretary to a commander. He gave me a field promotion to officer, and I am to go to Washington and await assignment.

This means that we can soon be reunited. As an officer assigned to a noncombatant status, posted in Washington (possibly at the war department), I will be able to send for you. I will arrange papers of passage as soon as I am settled. We can be married at last. I will, of course, keep you informed and send details. I love you, long for you, want to spend the rest of my life with you. God be praised that this has been brought about.

Ever your devoted,
Wes

After receiving this letter from Wes, JoBeth had to take her mother into full confidence. Both mother and daughter

361

wept, knowing that this would mean an inevitable separation that both of them dreaded.

"Mama, you must help me get to Wes." JoBeth clutched Wes's letter to her breast.

Johanna gazed at her daughter and saw reflected in her eyes an intensity she recognized. She was no longer a little girl, someone to be told what she could or should do. She was a woman in love and determined to follow that love through, wherever it led.

"You will help us, won't you?" JoBeth pleaded.

"I'll do whatever I can," Johanna promised.

The next week, another letter from Wes brought a new urgency.

It would be too dangerous for him to come to Hillsboro, where he was so well-known, so a meeting place had to be decided upon. Richmond seemed the most logical place, being closer to Washington. It would be easier to slip across the guarded border there. Richmond was also the capital of the Confederacy. Careful arrangements must be made. No one must know of their plans. Secrecy insured Wes's safety.

Even though they were both convinced of the necessity, Johanna and JoBeth quailed at the duplicity this would involve. Especially the idea of keeping it secret from the Cadys, who had given them a loving home all these years.

Johanna wrote to Amelia Brooke, who had been her closest friend when they both attended Miss Pomoroy's Academy as girls and who now lived in Richmond. They had kept in touch all these years. Without going into details, Johanna asked if she would allow JoBeth to stay in their home until her fiancé could get the necessary travel pass to cross the line from Washington.

Many Southerners had been "stranded" away from home when the war broke out and travel became restricted. So it was not an unusual situation. Johanna did say they planned to be married and that JoBeth would remain up north until the war was over.

They waited anxiously for a reply. It was not too long coming. Amelia wrote she would be more than happy to have her friend's daughter as a house guest. In the same letter, Amelia gave them other information that was rather disquieting. Amelia's husband was now a high-ranking Confederate officer on President Jefferson Davis's staff. She went on, saying, "Needless to say, we are often hosts to a number of young officers far from home and on leave from their duties, so I believe JoBeth will find our household one that is lively and merry in spite of this dreadful war. Jacob and I are both looking forward to welcoming your daughter."

Reading the letter out loud to JoBeth, Johanna looked at her daughter with raised eyebrows.

"You realize we are taking unfair advantage of my long friendship with Amelia by not telling her the whole truth? What would she—or more important, her husband—say if they knew Wesley was a Union officer? I think they would have grave doubts about having you come." She paused, then said very solemnly, "You must be careful not to do anything that would risk them in any way."

"I wouldn't, Mama. I'm sure as soon as Wes knows where I am, he'll move heaven and earth to come, take me safely to Washington. We wouldn't put the Brookes in any kind of danger of exposure."

"This could be construed as giving aid and comfort to an enemy," Johanna said thoughtfully.

"But *I'm* not an enemy, Mama!"

"Yes, but you must understand that *Wes* is," her mother said sorrowfully.

"He only did what he thought was right. What he was *honor bound* to do."

"And that is in direct opposition to what Amelia's husband considers right." Johanna leaned forward and grasped JoBeth's hands. "Oh, my darling, I don't think you fully realize the risks both you and Wes are taking. If Wes should be, for any reason, stopped and questioned when he comes to Richmond to get you—he will be in *enemy territory*. He certainly won't travel in his army uniform, and if they detain him and check his identification and find out who he is— JoBeth, he would be arrested as a spy."

The full impact of what her mother was saying made JoBeth draw in her breath. She felt the blood drain from her head. She put both hands up to her suddenly throbbing temples. *What did they do with spies? They shot them.*

"Oh, Mama, we'll just have to pray."

"Of course we'll pray, JoBeth. But darling, maybe you and Wes should reconsider this plan. Wait until the war is over . . . be patient . . ."

There was a long moment as mother and daughter looked into each other's eyes, Johanna's bright with tears. "We can't wait, Mama. We've waited long enough already. Wes needs me, Mama. His family has abandoned him, and the Spencers act as if he never existed, even though at one time he was like a son to them. Of course, there is still his grandmother, but even she did not want him to join the army—*any* army! I am all he has," JoBeth said simply. "I must go to him."

"Yes, of course you must, my darling," Johanna said and held out her arms to embrace her. "I understand, JoBeth, even though I cannot give my approval. I have done the same as you in my day. Left mother, father, family, friends, all that was dear and familiar—for love. So how can I possibly tell you not to follow your heart?"

"And did you ever regret it, Mama?"

"I only regretted the hurt my going caused others. My father—*your* grandfather. I don't think he was ever reconciled to my marriage. Although he never spoke one word of recrimination to me. Of course, I'm afraid your uncle and aunt are going to feel that your action is a betrayal. But that cannot be helped. Perhaps in time they will understand. Anyone who has ever been young and in love cannot fail to." She sighed. "Much as I hate to part with you, I have no right to stop you."

When Johanna presented Amelia's letter as an invitation to her daughter from an old friend, Aunt Josie seemed delighted. It was not difficult to persuade the Cadys that JoBeth needed a change. It had been clear to them that over the past months, JoBeth had not been herself, so no further explanation was necessary. Even Uncle Madison agreed.

"Best thing in the world for the girl! Better than a tonic," he said gruffly when the matter was presented to him.

JoBeth's trip to Richmond would involve a train ride, and a traveling companion had to be found to accompany her. It would, even in wartime, be improper for a young single woman to journey alone. As it happened, Bernice Fulton, a middle-aged cousin of Uncle Madison, was going to Fredricksburg to visit a daughter-in-law and would be delighted to have JoBeth for company.

Aunt Josie entered enthusiastically into all the preparations for JoBeth's trip. She had been a popular belle in her day and thought a young woman's happiness was solely dependent upon having lots of beaux, lots of parties and gaiety to fill her life.

"With all the young men gone, Hillsboro is very dull for her. I hear Richmond is the hub of social life. And with Amelia being such a hostess, JoBeth will have many opportunities for some fun and frivolity in spite of the war," she nodded happily when Johanna told her what Amelia had written. "We must outfit her properly," she declared, and ordered an immediate evaluation of JoBeth's wardrobe, which had become sadly depleted for the last two years, having had no additions. Aunt Josie clucked her tongue. "Well, we must do something at once. We cannot have her outshone by some of those Richmond ladies. Luckily, I put away some material I purchased before the war and the terrible blockade. We'll have Mrs. Harversahll, my dressmaker, come and make JoBeth some lovely dresses."

Aunt Josie went to the trunk, where she had stored some yardage, among them a fine, soft, coffee-colored wool for a traveling suit, exquisite lace for trimming, and a length of shiny forest green taffeta. As she showed these to JoBeth, she never dreamed that one would become her niece's wedding gown.

Chapter Sixteen

❧

At last the train pulled into the Richmond station. It had been a long, arduous journey. There had been delays of all sorts—breakdowns of the worn-out engine, times when the passenger car had been shunted onto a sidetrack to let boxcars of military supplies and soldiers go through. Mrs. Fulton had been an irritating traveling companion, talkative and complaining. JoBeth had been glad to see her get off at Fredricksburg junction. She hoped the woman's daughter-in-law had more patience than she herself had been able to muster for the last hundred miles.

Alone and nearing her destination, JoBeth felt both excitement and exhaustion. The trip had seemed endless. A combination of nervous tension and discomfort had made it almost impossible to sleep. There were frequent unscheduled stops, and looking out the grimy window of the car, she had seen wounded Confederate soldiers helped onto the train. The sight was depressing—the haggard, hopeless faces, the stretchers being lifted, men missing arms or legs, others with heads bandaged, still others hopping on crutches or leaning heavily on canes. Obviously the South had suffered enormous casualties and heavy damage. JoBeth was confronted head-on with the terrible results of war.

It seemed almost selfish to close her eyes and send up a prayer of thanksgiving that Wes was out of the fire of battle, when her uncle and cousins were in the thick of it and probably on the losing side. But it was only natural, she knew, that whatever catastrophic events are happening in the world, it is only how they affect one personally that matters. Her prayer turned into an earnest plea that soon those in charge of such things on both sides would see the futility, the cost in human terms, of this conflict and, as Wes had once written, declare peace.

"Richmond! Richmond!" The conductor's shout brought both a relief and a tremor of nervousness. Here she was. For the first time completely alone. The enormity of what she had undertaken and what she planned to do made her almost dizzy. Life was scary and unpredictable, and for one awful moment, JoBeth wished she had never left Hillsboro. Thrusting back all those feelings, she gathered her belongings and made her way to the end of the aisle to the door.

Wearily, JoBeth descended from the train onto the platform and stood there looking around dazedly. She felt stiff and achy from the cramped coach, and she felt suddenly bereft. There was no one to meet her. Not that she had expected anyone. Amelia Brooke had no idea when she would arrive, just the approximate week. The station was filled with people, some saying good-bye, others greeting a variety of persons—women, soldiers, children. Voices raised all about her, sounds of children crying, women sobbing. People jostled by her, pushing their way toward the train, some elbowing their way out. She had to find a carriage to take her to the Brookes' house. Her heart was hammering. She had never had to do anything like this before, not on her own, not without someone to look after her.

Slowly she made her way through the crowd, the handle of her portmanteau in one hand, the wicker basket in the other cutting deeply into her palm. Breathing hard, she finally reached the curb of the street. This, too, was lined by a variety of people—civilians, soldiers, women with children—all looking for some sort of conveyance.

After seeing several possible vehicles taken by more aggressive types, JoBeth finally got the attention of the driver of a shabby rental carriage just as he was unloading his passengers. She was forced to share it carrying a woman with a baby in her arms and with a fussy toddler hanging onto her shirt. She had been standing helplessly alongside JoBeth, frantically waving at several passing hacks. The toddler was crying hysterically. So JoBeth, taking pity on the distraught mother, helped her get her luggage, valises, baskets, parcels, into the carriage.

Bunched uncomfortably inside, at least they were off the street and moving. Between sighs, the woman told her she was to be let off at the Spotswood Hotel, where she was to meet her soldier husband. Leaning her head out the coach window, JoBeth relayed this information to the driver. After getting rid of her fellow passenger, she would worry about getting to the Brookes' residence. There was nothing she could do about this delay. The woman looked drained and certainly had her hands full.

After they and all their paraphernalia were safely deposited at the hotel, which looked as war weary as everything else, JoBeth gave the driver the Brookes' address.

Richmond looked entirely different from the time JoBeth had accompanied her mother here on a visit before the war. Everywhere were the effects of war on the city. Everything looked shabby—the buildings, the streets, the people. They left the main part of town and soon were driving through a pleasant, tree-lined residential section of the city. When they came to a stop in front of an imposing red brick house, JoBeth peered curiously out the carriage window.

After checking the number on the black ornamental iron gate against the one on the small card in her hand, she alighted from the carriage. Almost as soon as she did, the front door opened and a lady in a bell-skirted lilac dress hurried down the steps.

"Well, well, darlin' girl, welcome!" she greeted JoBeth in a soft Virginia accent. JoBeth was immediately enveloped in a rose-scented embrace. "I'm Amelia, your mother's best friend, and I'm so happy to see you," she declared, then turned to direct the driver to set down JoBeth's luggage. In spite of JoBeth's murmured protests, Mrs. Brooke paid the driver and sent him on his way.

"You shouldn't have, Mrs. Brooke....," JoBeth began.

"Nonsense, honey. My pleasure. Now, come on along into the house. I declare, this has been one of the muggiest summers I can remember. We'll just get us some cool refreshment."

Used to the cooler climate of the Carolina foothills, JoBeth thought that Richmond was sweltering. It was a relief to step into the dim interior, where the closed window shutters kept the outside heat at bay. The house felt refreshingly cool, and the fragrance of potpourri faintly perfumed the air.

"Do take off that jacket and your bonnet, honey," Mrs. Brooke urged. "Then we'll go into the parlor and have some lemonade." She took JoBeth's biscuit beige bolero and hung it across the banister of the stairway, placed her bonnet on the hall table, then gave her a quick glance. "I do declare, you are so like your dear mother! I want to hear all about her and your dear little brother, Shelby. Although I reckon he's a big fellow now. Gone into the army, I've no doubt, like most all of our brave young men."

There was a sharp silence. Amelia put her fingers to her lips, smothering a tiny gasp. At first JoBeth wondered if she had forgotten what her mother had written about Wes. But a moment later Amelia apologized.

"Oh, my dear, I didn't mean anything by that! I am sure you know that I *do* understand." She moved hurriedly ahead of JoBeth into the parlor.

Whatever Amelia thought she understood, JoBeth realized that the woman had too much courtesy, too much tact, and too much affectionate consideration for her friend to ever express any disapproval. JoBeth whispered a tiny prayer that Wes would complete their arrangements speedily so she wouldn't have to impose longer than necessary on this gracious lady's hospitality.

"Sit down, honey." Amelia gestured to one of two wing chairs on either side of the fireplace. On the low table between was a tray holding a pitcher of lemonade, glasses, and a plate of thin cookies.

Amelia Brooke looked younger than her forty-plus years. She was slender as a girl, and her movements were graceful. She was sitting under a portrait of her that must have been painted when her doll-like prettiness was at its peak, and JoBeth saw that her once-golden hair had silvered, that there now were a few wrinkles around her eyes and mouth, but that she still was very attractive.

For the next twenty minutes, they chatted about inconsequential things, Amelia dwelling mostly on reminisces about her school days at Miss Pomoroy's with Johanna. At length, when JoBeth had refused a second glass of lemonade and another wafer-thin cookie, Amelia said, "Now, I know you must be simply *fatigued*, and I insist you take a little rest before we have supper. We eat late, because Jacob—Colonel Brooke, my husband—doesn't come home until after seven. He is on President Davis's staff, as your mama might have told you, and they work the most awful hours. I'm hoping he will be in good time tonight. He knew your mother, you see." Amelia gave a soft little laugh and said in a conspiratorial tone of voice, "In fact, I accused him of being smitten by Johanna Shelby first, when he met her at one of Miss Pomoroy's 'dansantes.'"

Despite the scarcities and ravages of wartime—the upholstery, draperies, and carpets being perhaps a little worn—the Brooke household had somehow retained its tasteful elegance. The guest room to which JoBeth was shown was equally charming, the bed's ruffled canopy and curtains crisply starched, a lovely bouquet of fresh flowers from the garden below daintily arranged on the bureau.

"There are fresh towels and an extra quilt if you should need it, which I doubt," Amelia said, darting around the room. "I hope you will find everything you need, and if not, you have only to ask," she assured JoBeth. At the door she paused to say, "Now, do have a little nap, honey. I'm sure you're worn out. I hear travelin' these days is deplorable. Of course, I have not moved an inch since this war began—and do not intend to, come the Yankees or high water." When Amelia left, JoBeth took a long breath. She was here at last. She walked over to the window and looked out, stretching her imagination farther than she could see. The Potomac River, which separated Richmond from Washington, was all that separated her from Wes! After all these months, they would soon be together.

Everything had worked out so much better than she could have hoped. Amelia couldn't have given her a more genuine welcome. Whatever she thought of JoBeth's reason for being here, it had not seemed to interfere with her spontaneous friendliness. How lucky it was that her mother had kept in touch with Amelia since their school days. How very convenient indeed. How fortunate *she* was to be in such congenial surroundings.

However, JoBeth had yet to meet Colonel Brooke.

❦

After Amelia's warmth, Colonel Brooke was like a dash of cold water. He was a good-looking man in his late forties, with an erect, military bearing. He wore a mustard-colored mustache and sideburns, and his eyes, a steely gray, were keen, penetrating. He gave the impression of a man used to giving orders and having them obeyed. He was an exact contrast to his wife. JoBeth was at first quite put off by his aloofness. But although his manner was rather stiff, he was still a courteous host. JoBeth wondered how much he had been informed about her reason for being there. However, from the triviality of the dinner conversation, she felt reassured he knew nothing of the real circumstances.

Johanna had told JoBeth that Amelia was the type of person that "once your friend, was forever your friend." Amelia never gave the slightest hint that JoBeth's visit was cloaked in mystery and secrecy. She treated her as she would have any young house guest—with the kindest attention. Within the first week, JoBeth became very fond of her and understood why her mother had said she was such a delightful person.

The Brookes entertained a great deal. For the most part it seemed unplanned. Many nights, extra plates were put at the dinner table, because Colonel Brooke often brought home fellow officers. It did not seem to perturb either Amelia or her placid cook, Delilah. There always seemed to be another a batch of biscuits ready to pop in the oven, and no shortage of garden vegetables.

The talk was usually general. When it turned to the war or serious topics, JoBeth—who had learned to receive Amelia's discreet signal—rose with the other ladies and left the table.

These evenings were not out of the ordinary. They seemed, even if unexpected, not to upset the smooth running of the household. Weekends were different. Sunday nights, JoBeth discovered, the Brookes always held an open house. These evenings were attended by not only the colonel's contemporaries but younger officers as well. Mainly single, young men far from their homes, lonely for family. It was to these especially the Brookes opened their hearts and home.

The first Sunday JoBeth was with them, Amelia explained what had become the custom. "So many of these officers are just boys, like *your* own friends in Hillsboro. But they're homesick. Most are here in Richmond on furlough, some are stationed here temporarily, many are recovering from some injury or waiting to be sent back to their regiments. My heart goes out to all of them." Amelia shook her head sadly. "Even though I was never blessed with children of my own, I can just imagine how their mothers feel, and I try to give them a taste of home here." She went on, saying, "I also invite some of the young ladies I know, girls your age, to help make things light and let them have a little fun. Where they've been and where they're going to is dreadful— so I want them to have pleasant and happy memories to recall when they do." Amelia's wistful expression changed quickly into one of her radiant smiles. "Now, wear one of your prettiest dresses, honey." She wiggled a playful finger at JoBeth. "I know the sight of you will cheer some of these fellows enormously."

JoBeth felt a little reluctant to play the role Amelia expected. She felt awkward to be entertaining Confederate soldiers while *Wes* was arranging for her to join him in *enemy* territory! But there was nothing she could do but comply with her hostess' request.

She had brought a few summer dresses with her, having been warned by her mother that even in early September, Richmond might still be hot. From these, she chose a yellow organdy with a portrait collar embroidered with small yellow daisies. When she was dressed, she went downstairs and out into the garden.

Summer weather lingered, but in the late afternoon Amelia's brick-walled garden was shadowed by leafy fruit trees. Curlicued white iron benches and chairs were placed in small groups surrounding a lily pond in which goldfish could be seen under the lily pads. It was such a tranquil place, seemingly remote from the war and whatever was going on only a few miles away. For a few minutes JoBeth was alone there, relishing the serenity.

Soon Amelia, a lacy cloth over one arm, bustled out, followed by Deliah, who was carrying a large glass punchbowl. As she passed JoBeth, Amelia said over her shoulder, "It's so lovely and cool, I thought we could have our refreshment out here before we go in to supper." JoBeth helped them use the cloth to cover a table at the far end of the garden, then helped set out rows of small cups.

It wasn't long before the guests began to arrive. A half dozen young officers, smart in pressed gray uniforms, were soon followed by four extremely pretty young women. The young ladies immediately embarked on a lively repartee with the officers, as if this sort of party were something they did by rote. JoBeth had heard that wartime Richmond was a constant circus for belles. Now she believed it as she watched them ply their artful coquetry.

JoBeth felt suddenly shy. She had been so long out of the social swing of Hillsboro—having been not invited, overlooked, or simply left out—that she had almost forgotten her social skills. Feeling inadequate to the occasion, she retreated to a bench half hidden by a huge magnolia bush. Here she could stay until she got her bearings, felt a little more at ease, she told herself.

It was from this vantage point that she saw a tall, slim officer, his right arm in a black satin sling, escorted by Amelia to the trellised entrance of the garden. Then Amelia was evidently called back into the house on some domestic errand, leaving him standing alone. In a moment of startled recognition, JoBeth saw that it was Curtis Channing.

Chapter Seventeen

~≈❀≈~

*A*gain JoBeth was struck by Curtis's extraordinary good looks. She noticed he had grown a mustache and that it suited him. He was perhaps leaner but still held himself with that combination of assurance and athletic grace shown to such advantage in his well-fitting gray uniform. There was something else about him, something not so familiar. His expression had a maturity and character that it might have lacked before.

As she stared, stunned by this unexpected arrival, his glance caught hers. For a full minute neither of them moved. Her heart gave a little leap. Before he had taken a step, she knew he was coming over to her. She half rose from the bench. A few seconds later he was standing there, towering over her. She saw he now had captain's bars on his collar. They looked at each other. Then Curtis said huskily, "JoBeth! What are you doing here? I never thought I'd see you again."

She swallowed, trying to find her voice. When it came out, it sounded high and rather shaky. "I'm staying with the Brookes. I've been here about a week."

His eyes swept over her, moving from her dark hair to her eyes, lingering on her mouth, where her lower lip was now trembling.

"I'm so—glad to see you," Curtis said slowly. "I could hardly believe my eyes. For a minute, I thought I might be dreaming—could it really be *you?*"

JoBeth found relief from her tension by laughing lightly. "Yes, it's me. No illusion." She was trying hard to regain her composure, to stop feeling so dizzy, so at a loss. She gestured toward the sling. "What happened? Were you wounded?"

He shrugged, dismissing her concern. "Nothing more than a flesh wound, actually. My shoulder took a slight hit." With a cynical smile, he said offhandedly, "Those Yankees are damn poor shots." Immediately realizing he had cursed in front of a lady, he quickly said, "Sorry. Now tell me about you. How do you happen to be in Richmond? I thought travel was difficult, nearly impossible, these days."

How much she should say without telling a lie? She sat down again on the bench, shifting her crinolines to make room for Curtis beside her, and said, "Actually, Mrs. Brooke is an old school friend of my mother's, and everyone agreed it might be a good idea for me to visit."

It seemed a plausible enough explanation, but JoBeth could see from the slight frown between Curtis's dark eyebrows that it didn't satisfy him. She might have been pushed into saying more, except at just that moment Amelia came upon them and greeted Curtis effusively.

"Ah, I see my hero has found my house guest! How lovely. He won't tell you, I'm sure, my dear, but Curtis is one of the bravest of our young men. With no thought to his own safety, he returned not only once but twice into the line of fire to rescue two of his badly wounded men." She smiled dotingly upon him, patting his shoulder fondly. "Now, you must give him special treatment this evening, JoBeth, since he is just out of the hospital and deserves our attention and care."

With that Amelia floated away in a swirl of ruffles to circulate among her other guests.

JoBeth looked at Curtis. "So you are distinguishing yourself in battle."

"Nothing more than any of us would do under the circumstances." His frown got deeper. "Enough of that. What interests me is, How long are you going to be here?"

"I'm not sure just how long," JoBeth answered. "What about you?"

"Until the doctors certify I can go back to my regiment. I have day passes from the hospital now. But the doctors want me to be out and exercising, getting back on my feet, starting to ride again, before they release me back to duty."

JoBeth glanced at the sling. "Can you do that? Ride, I mean, with one arm?"

Curtis shook his head slightly, indicating how unimportant he considered this. "It's almost completely healed. I have to get the strength back into it. Thank God that my horse survived. Both of my horses are stabled here in Richmond, and my man is looking after them."

The garden was filling up with new arrivals. The buzz of voices, laughter, the clink of punch glasses, began to flow around them. Curtis bent toward her. "The important thing is, When can I see you again? I mean, alone." Then he asked abruptly, "Do you ride?"

She looked startled. "Yes, of course, but—"

"What if I come tomorrow, then? You can ride my other horse. She's a lovely, sweet-tempered mare." He looked at her eagerly.

"I'm not sure, Curtis. I don't know if Mrs. Brooke might need me or have other plans . . ."

He dismissed her protest. "Never mind about that. I'll clear it with her. It would be a real favor. Zephyr needs exercising."

"Come along, you two," Amelia's voice reached them. "We're going in to supper now."

"Tomorrow, then? Say, two o'clock." It was more of a directive than a request.

JoBeth hesitated a split second. Perhaps it would be better to see Curtis alone and, without revealing to him the complete truth, tell him she had come to Richmond to meet her fiancé. He need not know who it was or that Wes was a Union officer. The bare facts were all that were necessary. This evening, among all this company, would be an inappropriate time.

"All right, tomorrow," she murmured. "Now I must go help Amelia serve," she said and hurried away.

At the supper table, she was seated between two of Colonel Brooke's junior officers and so did not have another chance to talk to Curtis. However, she was often conscious of his eyes upon her during the meal.

JoBeth was surprised that there was less war talk there in the immediate vicinity of the conflict than there had been in similar gatherings in Hillsboro. Perhaps here they purposely avoided speaking of the current Southern situation, being anxious for some respite from the constant pressure of campaigns, looking for a relaxing evening of enjoyable company.

The evening progressed pleasantly enough. However, even while she chatted with some of the other officers, JoBeth was aware of Curtis's eyes upon her. Anytime she happened to look his way, she met his gaze. There was both admiration and hope in it. Again she prayed she had not made a mistake by agreeing to go riding with him alone.

When all the party had left and JoBeth was helping Amelia gather up the empty glasses, the napkins, and the coffee cups, she told her about Curtis's invitation.

"I couldn't be more delighted, my dear!" Amelia glowed. "Jacob considers Curtis Channing one of the most outstanding young officers he's ever known. Not a shred of fear in him, not a timid bone. He's all man, all courage." She rushed on, saying, "I'm so glad you can make his leave a happy one. I'm afraid he's pushing his superiors to let him go back to his regiment. Maybe too soon." She clucked her tongue, and a sad, worried expression shadowed her face. "We've lost so many of our wonderful young men—" She halted, as if remembering JoBeth's particular circumstances. Then she gave a small shudder and, quickly picking up some more cups and saucers, bustled off in the direction of the kitchen.

JoBeth stood there for a minute, looking after her, holding two plates of crumbled cake in her hands, thinking about what an awkward situation she had put everyone in.

Chapter Eighteen

❧❧

*T*he next afternoon, JoBeth, dressed in the dark-blue riding habit she had borrowed from Amelia, stood at the parlor window, waiting for Curtis. Since last night, she'd had all sorts of second thoughts about going riding with him. First of all, she worried that by accepting, she might have given him some kind of false hope, given him reason to think she might have changed her mind. After all, he *had* proposed to her. Secondly—and this was what bothered her most—she wondered if she was being disloyal to Wes. Perhaps it would have been more honest to have somehow found a private moment the night before and simply refused Curtis's invitation. Well, it was too late now. Whatever happened, she had to go through with it.

Just then she saw Curtis, on horseback, looking splendid in his gray tunic, sporting a black felt hat with a jaunty plume, coming around the corner. He had another horse, a sleek, cinnamon-colored mare wearing a sidesaddle, on a lead. In spite of herself, JoBeth's heart beat a little faster.

She heard the doorbell ring, footsteps along the hall, the door opening, then Amelia's lilting voice greeting Curtis. Next Delilah came to the parlor door.

"Miss Davison, yo' genemun is here to fetch you."

382

"Thank you, I'll be right there," she replied. Nervously she pulled on her leather riding gloves.

Taking a deep breath, JoBeth hooked her riding skirt to the loop on the side and went out into the hall, where Curtis was waiting. She couldn't miss his pleasure at seeing her. His eyes shone, his mouth lifted in a broad smile.

"Ready to ride?" he asked.

Amelia beamed at them both, like an approving mother. "I think it's just delightful you're taking JoBeth out into the countryside, Captain. It will do her a world of good—and you too, I've no doubt." As they went out the door together, she called after them, "Have a lovely time now, do."

JoBeth stepped up on the mounting block at the curb while Curtis held her horse's bridle. He assisted her into the sidesaddle, then handed her the reins. As he affectionately patted the horse's neck, he said, "Easy now, Zephyr has a sensitive mouth. You'll do just fine together."

Satisfying himself that she was comfortably settled, Curtis swung up onto his own horse, a feat he accomplished smoothly, even with his one arm still in the sling. They started off at a walk, then moved into a trot further along. There were other riders out, mostly men in uniform who saluted Curtis. He returned their salute smartly with his good arm while holding the reins loosely with the other. *What horsemanship*, JoBeth thought admiringly. Surely Curtis was as at home in a saddle as he would have been in a rocking chair on somebody's porch.

He had been right about Zephyr—an easy ride, a gentle mount. It took only the slightest touch of her rein or pressure of her knee to guide her.

Curtis looked at JoBeth, smiling, and pointed ahead. "We take a right turn down here at the crossroads."

Following Curtis, she soon found herself away from the main thoroughfare and on a beautiful stretch of road. All along the roadside, Queen Anne's lace and wild purple asters bloomed. The day was pleasantly warm but had lost the humidity of the last week. In fact, JoBeth sensed a hint of fall in the air.

She was riding alongside Curtis now, as there was no other traffic in the road. He glanced over at her with such open admiration that it sent a blush soaring into her cheeks and she had to turn away. Only a minute later Curtis reached for her bridle and brought both their horses to a stop.

"I can't help it, JoBeth. I could hardly sleep last night, thinking of what a happy chance seeing you again was. Remember, I believe in destiny. I told you that last Christmas."

JoBeth started to protest, but he shook his head and went on, saying, "I've never gotten over you. I've thought of you ever since—since I left you at the train station in Hillsboro. Thought about if we'd had more time, how things might have been different—"

"Please, Curtis, stop." JoBeth put up her hand as if to stem the flow of words. "Don't go on—"

"It's no use, JoBeth. Can't you admit that the two of us meeting again has some meaning?"

"I can't listen to this, Curtis. Please. Nothing's changed. The only reason I came out with you today was because I felt I had to try to make you understand."

"Understand what? I can't help loving you. What could you possibly say or do to change that?"

"I told you in Hillsboro and I'm telling you now, Curtis. There's someone else. I'm pledged to someone else." He *had* to know, she *had* to tell him, so she rushed on, explaining, "Last evening you asked me what I was doing in Richmond. Curtis, I'm here to meet him."

There. It was out, she'd said it. She watched for his reaction.

"He's a soldier, then." It was more a statement than a question.

"Yes," she nodded. Her breath was shallow, her heart pounding. He didn't need to know more. She prayed he wouldn't ask for details. Like information about his regiment, or what his commanding officer's name was.

Curtis frowned and stared over his horse's head at some distant point. Then slowly he turned back to her. A smile parted his lips under the mustache, showing a glimpse of his even, white teeth. He spoke softly, almost jokingly.

"Well, all's fair in love and war, isn't it? Even if I'm competing with a fellow soldier. *I'm* here and *he* isn't—at least not yet. Don't I have a chance to plead *my* case, try to win you?"

"There's no contest, Curtis," she said seriously. "This is someone I've known and loved most of my life."

"There's love, and there's *being* in love," he reminded her, still smiling. "Do you know the difference?"

She blushed. Had he read her mind? Had he somehow been aware that in spite of herself, she had felt excited, breathless, a little dizzy, at seeing him last evening? Had she inadvertently given him encouragement?

He leaned over, and she shrank back in her saddle, afraid he was going to touch her. The horses were getting fidgety at being held still.

"What are you frightened of, JoBeth? Your own feelings?"

"Of course not!" she said indignantly. Then she said firmly, "If you are going on like this, Curtis, we'd better turn around and go back."

He lifted his hand from her horse's bridle immediately.

"No, I apologize. I want us to go on. There's a spot up here I want you to see. It's by a stream, and the horses can get a drink and we can . . . talk." He flicked his reins, and his horse started off. Zephyr was glad to follow. The winding road, bordered with trees that were golden with the first touch of autumn, stretched before them. Enjoying her mount's easy gait and the beauty of the Indian summer afternoon, JoBeth relaxed a bit.

When Curtis left the road to go down a grassy path, she turned her horse in the direction he was heading. She soon found herself in a glade where willows bent over a rushing stream. Curtis dismounted and led his horse to drink. JoBeth did the same. Everything seemed stilled. The sounds of the busy city had been left far behind. A light breeze rustled the willow branches, and there was a scent of pine and of sun-warmed wildflowers. They sat down on a fallen log overlooking the stream, where sunshine glistened on the water as it rushed quietly over the rocks. For a few minutes the serenity of the place seemed to envelop them.

Feeling warm, JoBeth took off the riding hat and untied the attached velvet snood. She shook out her hair from where it had been clubbed under the net and lifted it to cool off the back of her neck.

"It's lovely here!" she sighed contentedly.

"I thought you'd like it," Curtis said. "I discovered it one of the first days they let me ride. A respite from the pandemonium of the hospital."

They sat there listening to the woodland sounds—an insect buzzing among the ferns, the sound of a woodpecker. At length Curtis broke the silence.

"Peaceful, isn't it? Hard to believe that a few miles from here, men are killing each other." The edge of bitterness in his voice startled JoBeth. She glanced at him. His expression was grave. He reached over and took her hand.

"That's why every moment counts, JoBeth. Time is so important now. None of us knows how much we've got, what the future holds, or even if we have a future."

JoBeth gazed at him, wide-eyed. In a flash of insight, she realized she had been wrong about Curtis Channing. He wasn't as shallow or unthinking as she had assumed. Or at least he'd changed since Christmas. Then he hadn't seen battle. It had all been an adventure he was embarking upon. Since then he'd fought and been wounded, seen it all firsthand. He knew what war was all about now, when he hadn't before.

His fingers tightened around her hand. "That's why telling you that I love you seemed important to me, JoBeth. I know that this man you say you love and are pledged to is a soldier, and maybe I should have some loyalty, some respect for that. But right now *I'm* here and he isn't and you're not sure, can't be sure, if he'll come—ever. He has just as much chance of getting killed as I do or anybody does." The pressure on her hand increased. "I'm sorry. I know I promised not to say any more, didn't I? It was a promise I shouldn't have made, one you shouldn't have asked for. Because I *do* love you, JoBeth. I don't think I ever really knew what love was until I met you."

"Oh, Curtis, love is so much more than what you're feeling now." JoBeth halted, then, daring to be truthful said, "Or even what *I'm* feeling. The reason I asked you to promise is because the person, the solider, I'm waiting for, who I'm here in Richmond to meet, deserves more than this—he deserves my loyalty to *our* pledge. So please understand." Her tone was pleading. "I know you're an honorable man. That you value honor. Honor my asking you not to say any more."

"That's the hardest thing anyone's ever asked me to do," he said, looking directly into her eyes for a long time. Then he raised her hand, turned it over, and kissed her wrist. His

387

lips were warm on her skin, and in spite of the sun on her back, she shivered.

Curtis released her hand, then stood up. "I'll get the horses. You're right—we'd better go back."

He held her stirrup while she remounted. But when she leaned forward to give Zephyr a reassuring pat, Curtis placed his hand on hers. From her saddle, she looked down into his upturned face and saw such unabashed love there that it took her breath away. She withdrew her hand from under his, and he made the pretense of arranging the edge of her skirt over her boot.

"I shall try to keep my promise not to speak of it, JoBeth, but I cannot stop loving you." Curtis moved over to his own horse and mounted.

They rode back into town side by side, not speaking, but every so often JoBeth felt his eyes upon her and was irresistibly drawn to turn and meet his gaze.

Back at the Brookes' home, upstairs in her bedroom, she took off the riding outfit, thinking, *I should never have gone. What has come over me? What am I doing? Whatever it is, it's dangerous. Of course Curtis is attractive, of course his obvious, adoring attention is flattering. But it isn't right. It isn't right for me to enjoy it. I shouldn't allow it.* She closed her eyes and put her balled fists up to her temples, pounded them lightly.

It's only because I miss Wes so terribly. It's been so long! It's Wes I love, Wes I want. To substitute what Curtis is willing to give would be betrayal, nothing less.

Chapter Nineteen

❦

Curtis did keep his promise not to *speak* to her again of his love, but that did not prevent his sending notes, flowers, calling with candy and bouquets. Amelia thought him enormously charming—chivalrous, she declared—because she, too, was included in the gifts he never arrived without. He was always among the other young officers at the regular Sunday night suppers, but Amelia made him feel welcome anytime. She never tired of singing his praises to JoBeth. "Oh, honey, if I were a young lady, I would be swooning at having such a gallant young man courting me."

JoBeth hardly knew how to reply. Surely Amelia knew she was pledged and that all of Curtis's charm would not change anything. However, Amelia *did* try. During the next ten days, Curtis's visits became more frequent. Perhaps this was what prompted Amelia to tap at JoBeth's bedroom door one afternoon and ask if they could have a "wee chat."

"I hope you will take what I'm about to say in the same spirit as I shall say it. But I do declare, I'm worried sick about what you are planning to do, JoBeth." As JoBeth was about to protest, Amelia held up her hand. "Yes, I know—your Mama has written quite frankly about your situation. I know that this young man you love is a someone you've known all your life—but JoBeth, do you really agree with what he has done? Left home, family, his own people, to fight with the *Yankees*! If you knew what they've done—why, some of my friends in Winchester and Petersburg are *homeless* because of them!" She stopped. "Well, there's no use to go into all that! I know things because of Jacob's position that aren't common knowledge. Enough to say, I have some serious doubts about the wisdom of what you are planning to do." She paused, shaking her head. "Don't you understand? Once you go with him, *you* will be turning your back on your own family, too." Her eyes misted as she looked with real concern at JoBeth. "Oh, precious child, *think* of that!"

JoBeth's own throat was sore with distress at Amelia's putting into words what she had avoided thinking herself. All she could say was, "Wes is doing what he thinks is right. Surely when the war is over, people will forgive and forget and go on with their lives."

"Oh, child, you are so naive! The war has gone on longer than anyone imagined. This war has cost too many people too much to be over. The wounds dealt are deeper than one could have foreseen, will never heal, and the scars will last forever. At least for our lifetime."

JoBeth felt terribly depressed after Amelia left the room.

Her argument, like Uncle Madison and Aunt Josie's, was so one-sided. They were all talking against Wes as if he were not every bit as committed to *his* cause as they were to theirs. They ignored everything but the fact that in their opinion, he had chosen the wrong side to fight for.

That night, JoBeth took out the picture of Wes she kept hidden in her handkerchief case. She studied his face, so intelligent, so kind, so candid. As she went to slip it back into its hiding place, her fingers struck something round and hard. Curious, she pulled it out and saw it was the shiny brass button Curtis had yanked off his tunic and given to her last Christmas. She held it in her palm for a minute, thinking that everyone would be so happy if it were Curtis she loved instead of Wes. Everything would be so simple then. But as Wes had said, nothing about this war was simple. And it was Wes she loved, Wes she was waiting for.

Oh, Wes, write soon. Come soon! Before anything more happens.

<hr />

Then one afternoon Delilah came to tell her that Captain Channing was waiting to see her in the parlor. The first thing she noticed was that he wasn't wearing his sling. He wasted no time telling her why he had come.

"I'm rejoining my regiment. I'm leaving tomorrow. I've come to say good-bye. I also came to say how much these last several days have meant to me. I cannot dare to think they have meant the same to you." He paused, holding up his hand to keep her from speaking. "But I can hope—pray— that when you remember them, you will think kindly of me and consider me to have been an honorable man. I kept my promise not to speak to you again of . . . love."

He frowned and walked over to the bow window and looked out for a few minutes before turning back into the room and saying, "I wish you loved me, JoBeth. I wish I could go back to whatever I'm facing and know that you did, know that I had something, someone—some reason to come back to."

"But you do, Curtis, you must. You have a family, parents, sisters who adore you, and you will have someone in your life—"

"The trouble is, it won't be you, JoBeth," he said flatly. "That is, unless—" He stopped, as if he wasn't sure whether he should voice his thought. "If anything should happen to change your plans—would you let me know?"

"Nothing's going to change, Curtis. I thought you understood that."

"Life is unpredictable. In wartime, more so. Just don't forget what I'm saying." He walked over to her. "I will never forget you as long as I live," he said solemnly. With that he put his hands on her waist and drew her closer. "Kiss me good-bye, JoBeth?"

Before she could demur, he caught her to him, pressed her against his jacket. His face buried in her hair, he whispered, "Please, JoBeth."

How could she not? She lifted her head and his warm, soft mouth was upon hers. The kiss was hard and there was something in it almost desperate. "Darling, JoBeth," she heard him say, felt his hands on her upper arms in a bruising grip, and then he released her and was gone. She stood there, shaken by the intensity of his kiss, listening to his booted footsteps on the hall floor, the click of the front door closing. Slowly JoBeth straightened herself. Fighting for control, she raised one hand to her lips and then to her cheek and found it wet with tears.

<hr/>

After Curtis's departure, JoBeth's mood was melancholy. She was wracked with guilt and her own ambiguous feelings.

Even though she was preoccupied with her own troubled thoughts and impatiently awaiting word from Wes, JoBeth was not unaware of the tension her presence caused in the Brooke household. The longer she was their house guest, the more she could feel it. She had the distinct impression that Colonel Brooke was unhappy with her prolonged stay. She noticed it mostly in Amelia's nervousness when her husband was home. At the breakfast table or at dinner, there was an undercurrent in the careful conversation they conducted. While she understood the reason for that, it made her acutely uncomfortable. If only she would hear from Wes and she could leave.

Coming down to supper one evening, JoBeth inadvertently overheard a clash between her hostess and her husband.

"I know you don't want her here, Jacob, didn't want her to come—" Amelia's voice held anxiety.

"You knew that at the outset. I made my feelings quite plain at the time."

"But how could I refuse? Besides, I never expected it to be this long. Her young man is in a position where a privilege should be granted—"

Not allowing her to finish whatever she was about to say, Colonel Brooke cut her off. "I don't want to hear about her 'young man.' I don't want to know anything about him, their plans. . . . To me, *he* is the enemy."

JoBeth fled back upstairs feeling both humiliated and helpless. She had never not been wanted anywhere before in her life! She had tried so hard to be pleasant, amiable, to Amelia's taciturn husband. She had thought it was the pressure of his duties, his position, that made him seem so uncommunicative, almost surly sometimes. Now she knew he resented her presence in his house. More than that, he detested the whole situation his wife's accommodating nature had placed their household in.

It was all she could do to maintain a semblance of naturalness that evening at supper. Fortunately, the colonel was called away by an emergency at his headquarters office and left when the meal had just started. Sitting alone at the table with Amelia was also difficult. She did not want to embarrass her hostess by letting her know she had overhead the sharp exchange between her and Jacob.

What could she do but wait to hear from Wes? And pray that word would come soon and she would no longer have to strain Amelia's goodness and hospitality, as well as her marriage.

Chapter Twenty

❦

The next morning, JoBeth came down for breakfast, murmured, "Good morning," then took her seat quietly. Amelia, looking as though she hadn't slept much, nodded and smiled absently. The colonel was drinking his coffee and reading the newspaper when Delilah brought in the mail. She laid it beside Amelia's plate, and distractedly Amelia sifted through it. Suddenly she came upon an envelope that caused her to jerk slightly. With a quick look down the table at her husband, then at JoBeth, she slid a letter over to her. At the same time, she signaled with her eyes and an imperceptible shake of her head. Immediately JoBeth was warned and slipped the envelope into her sleeve. In an agony of impatience, she had to wait until the colonel finished his breakfast and bid them both good-bye for the day and left the house. She then pulled out the letter and ripped it open with her knife.

It was the long-awaited letter from Wes. A direct answer to her prayers, and a much more prompt one than she had any reason to hope for. Hungry for details, she skimmed rapidly down the page. Although he could not give her the exact day and time, it *would* be within the week, sooner rather than later, so she must be packed and ready to leave at a moment's notice.

JoBeth looked up from the letter in her shaking hands. "Oh, Amelia, it's come! It's from Wes. He's coming to get me."

Amelia's reaction was a mixed one. She seemed both relieved and a little sad. "You have become very dear to me, JoBeth, even in this short time. And now you will be leaving." Her eyes brimmed with tears. "I worry about what you are going into and what may become of you."

JoBeth was too happy, too excited, to hear the note of sadness in the older woman's voice. Nothing could darken the elation she felt. "You mustn't worry, Amelia. I'll be fine. And I'll be so happy. You'll see. Wait until you meet Wes. You'll understand why I love him so. You'll see he's everything I told you."

⚜

Two days later another brief note came. He would be there within the next forty-eight hours. Almost two more days to live through! How could she bear it? The two days of waiting passed with agonizing slowness. Then in the late afternoon of the third day, Delilah knocked on the door of the bedroom, where JoBeth was packing. "Miss JoBeth, this jest come fo' you." JoBeth dropped the shawl she was putting into her valise and eagerly took the folded slip of paper the maid was holding out to her. "Oh, thank you. I think it's what I've been—," she said breathlessly and tore it open.

She read what she had so longed to know, in Wes's dear, familiar handwriting.

My Darling,

I'm in Richmond but of course in hiding. I cannot come in daytime, because of where you are staying. I'm sending this by a trusted servant in the house of a Union sympathizer. I'll be there this evening after dark. I have our passes and we can travel back to Washington as sister and brother going to see a sick relative. Not entirely true, I know, but of necessity. Be ready, be brave. Soon we will be together.

Hardly able to contain her joy, JoBeth ran down the hall to Amelia's room and knocked gently. To the answering "Come in," she entered.

Amelia was lying on the chaise, resting before dinner. She had a book on her lap but looked up as JoBeth approached her and said, "I hate to disturb you, but I have wonderful news."

"From the look on your face, I can only guess what it is," Amelia replied, unable to hide the tinge of regret in her voice.

Breathlessly JoBeth told her the contents of Wes's note.

While they discussed just how his arrival and her departure should be handled, they heard footsteps on the stairway. Colonel Brooke had arrived home unexpectedly early. The two women exchanged wary glances. Amelia squeezed JoBeth's hand and mouthed the words "Leave this to me."

After greeting the colonel, JoBeth excused herself and went back to her bedroom and in breathless excitement continued happily packing.

However, down the hall the scene was anything but that of happy anticipation. In her anxiety, Amelia's voice was unconsciously raised. "But what else could I do, Jacob? She is the daughter of my dearest girlhood friend. We were at school together."

"Perhaps it is a case of choosing between loyalties," came the stern rejoinder.

"My dear husband, I beg you, don't put it that way."

"What other way can I put it? This is wartime, woman. We should have no choices like this to make. Our allegiance is to the Confederacy. I have taken an oath on it, and as my wife, you—" His tone was harsh. "You expect me to stay calm when you propose harboring an enemy in my household?"

"Surely you don't consider *JoBeth* an enemy."

"No, I consider her a foolish, uninformed young woman who does not realize the hazards—not only the risk she is taking but the danger she has put us in."

"Danger? What possible danger?"

"If it were known that there is to be a rendezvous of a Union sympathizer and her Yankee lover *here*, in the house of a high-ranking Confederate officer—why, I might even be court-martialed."

"But who is to know?"

"Richmond is full of spies. They are everywhere."

"But I can't refuse to help now, Jacob. Plans have already been made—"

"Plans? What plans?" he demanded. Then, as if understanding had suddenly burst upon him, he exclaimed angrily, "No! Don't!" He got up and stalked over to the window. With his back to her, he stared out into the street for a full minute before speaking again. "Whatever it is, I don't want to know about it, you understand? Whenever the time comes, give me some signal, and I will go back to my headquarters for a meeting—that evening."

⁂

Ecstatic with anticipation, JoBeth was only vaguely aware of the high drama being enacted in the Brooke household as the hour of Wes's coming grew nearer. However, the undercurrent was high. Only someone totally insensitive to the electric atmosphere could have remained unaware of it. Late in the afternoon, Colonel Brooke came home briefly and left again after curtly telling Amelia to send word when it would be safe for him to return to his own home. Outside, the autumn dusk gathered quickly. In her bedroom, JoBeth ran back and forth from the window, where she watched anxiously for some sign of Wes's arrival, to her bedside, where she fell on her knees in frantic prayer that nothing would prevent Wes's coming.

Just after dark a tap came on the door, and Amelia stuck her head inside. In a whisper, which was no longer necessary, she said, "Your young man is here."

JoBeth's feet barely skimmed the steps as she flew down the stairway. In the hall stood a tall figure illuminated by the oil lamp on the table. Wes! Before she reached the last one, he was at the bottom holding out open arms, and she flung herself into them.

She pressed her cheek against the coarse greatcoat, smelling the damp wool smell, breathing in the fresh scent of rain and cold air. "Oh, Wes! Wes!" she cried, her voice smothered as he held her in a crushing embrace. "I can't believe you're really here!"

"Well, I am, my darling. Believe it!"

She hugged him tight, then drew back. "Let me look at you, see if you're real!" she exclaimed. "Oh, my goodness! You've grown whiskers!" she giggled.

"You don't mind, I hope!" he laughed. "I thought it gave me more dignity, made me look more like an officer and a gentleman." He grinned, then added quickly, "I'll shave it off if you don't like it."

"Let me see." She smiled and kissed him on the mouth. Their kiss was long, tender, infinitely sweet. Then JoBeth laughed softly. "It tickles. But I think I like it!" She hugged him.

Wes gave a low chuckle. "It's so wonderful to be with you again. To see you smile, hear you laugh. You don't know how I've missed that. Missed *you!*"

"*I* think I do know, as I've missed you," she said. "Oh, Wes, it's been so long. I didn't think it would ever happen!"

"Well, it *has*," he said almost solemnly.

For a long moment they simply looked at each other. Then she lifted her face and they kissed again. There was a difference in this kiss. It was the fulfillment of what had been only a hope, a longing. When it ended, Wes said, "Now, dearest, we will have to leave as soon as possible—you have your papers and I've brought your pass. It is best we leave when the sentries who have been on duty all night may not be as alert. There won't be too many questions when we show our passes. There is always a risk that if my true identity as a Union soldier should be discovered, I'd be considered a spy in enemy territory."

His words fell like heavy stones on JoBeth, briefly blotting her first happiness at their reunion. Stark reality of what they were facing hit. This was wartime. He was the enemy. They must flee under cover of darkness, like fugitives. Her heart thundered.

"How soon can you be ready?" he asked.

"Right away. I've most of my things packed."

Amelia, who had been standing at the top of the landing and had watched their meeting, overheard Wes's anxious question and came down a few steps, saying, "Come along, JoBeth. I'll help you get everything together. There's no time to waste."

Although Amelia had many doubts about this elopement—and was worldly enough to know that love did not conquer all, in spite of all the poems written, the ballads sung—she still felt exhilarated. These two star-crossed young lovers had excited her romantic imagination. JoBeth hurried back up the stairs and with Amelia's help put the last items into her valise. They both had to sit on her trunk to get it closed. Amelia held the gray melton cape for her to put on and hooked the corded frog fastenings under her chin. JoBeth pulled the hood over her hair. "Well, this is it!" she said breathlessly.

Suddenly tears sprang into Amelia's eyes as she looked at JoBeth. Then she placed both hands on the girl's cheeks, gazed at her for a moment, then kissed her fondly, saying, "Dear child, I wish you the best, all the best, and as much happiness as it is possible to find. God bless and keep you, my dear."

Impulsively, JoBeth put her arms around Amelia. "Thank you, thank you, for everything! I shall always remember your kindness and be grateful."

There was no more time to say anything. JoBeth went to the top of the stairs and called Wes. He took the steps two at a time and came into the bedroom to shoulder her small trunk. Quickly they went down the stairs and out into the night.

⁓ঌ৯⁓

Wes helped her into the carriage, then carefully arranged the rug over her knees. The sound of the carriage wheels against the wet pavement mixed with the hollow clip-clop of horse hooves. As she looked out the window of the cab, the whole world seemed wrapped in the mysterious yellow light from the street lamps. As the Brooke house faded into the rainy mist, JoBeth felt the same farewell she had the morning she left Hillsboro. Who knew when she would ever see it again?

Chapter Twenty-One

❧

*A*s they reached the city limits of Richmond, Wes took JoBeth's hand in his and said, "Now, don't be afraid and don't act frightened. This should go quickly. Our papers are in order, and there shouldn't be any problem. Just act naturally, answer any questions with yes or no. I'll do most of the talking." He squeezed her hand. "Don't worry, it will be fine."

The carriage came to a jolting halt. Even before it came to a full stop, Wes's hand was on the door handle. He opened the door and jumped out.

JoBeth could hear men's voices. Her stomach muscles knotted painfully. What if their passes—or at least Wes's—were found to be counterfeit? Would they be arrested, thrown into prison? All the horror stories she had ever heard about Yankee treatment of spies rushed into JoBeth's mind. She shrank back against the carriage cushions, holding her breath. She shivered, but not from cold. It was more the involuntary type of quiver that old Annie used to call "somebody walkin' 'pon ma grave." It was that same sort of childish fear of the unknown, fear of whatever might be going to happen.

Oh, dear Father God, let us get through safely, she prayed desperately. She leaned close to the carriage's open window. Wes was talking to the sentries, and she strained to hear what was being said. Wes's voice had taken on a distinctly South-ern drawl—more pronounced than it was naturally. Most native North Carolinians' accents were never as noticeable as that of someone from Georgia or South Carolina. If she had not been so tense, she might have smiled. She realized Wes was intentionally trying to distract the sentries as their passes were being examined. And it worked. In a matter of minutes, their passage into Washington was approved and they were again on their way.

Back in the carriage beside her, Wes took off his hat, wiped his forehead, and said, "Whew!" Not until then did she realize what a strain the encounter must have been for him. She'd had no idea how worried he'd been about getting by the Virginia border. She shuddered, remembering Amelia and Jacob talking about danger. It was wartime. Danger was everywhere. But surely they would be in no danger as they passed through the Union lines, JoBeth thought to herself. She shuddered again.

"Are you cold?" Wes asked with immediate concern. He put his arm around her shoulders and drew her close. "It won't be long now, dearest. Washington's actually not far. Ironic, isn't it, that the seat of the government and that of the rebellion are located so close together." He sighed deeply. "Only a few miles apart in distance, yet a million in purpose." His arm tightened around her.

The combination of emotional excitement, the wakeful-ness of the night before, and the rocking motion of the car-riage gradually lulled JoBeth to sleep. Her head cushioned on Wes's shoulder, his arm supporting her, she was hardly aware as they traveled through the night.

Grayish light was seeping through the slits in the carriage curtains when JoBeth stirred. She came slowly awake.

"We're almost there," Wes told her gently as she sat up, blinking sleepily. "We're safe now. We're coming over the bridge into Washington."

JoBeth rubbed the back of her neck, moved her shoulders to ease their stiffness, and peered out into the misty morning.

"We'll be stopped again, and our passes checked, but there'll be no problem here." Wes was getting out the leather folder containing their papers, so he'd be ready to get out at the checkpoint.

No problem? Why not? she thought drowsily, remembering how nervous Wes had been as they had approached the Virginia border. Then she realized why. They were no longer in the South, where Wes would have been in mortal danger, branded as a traitor, if caught. A Union officer traveling out of uniform with false credentials would have been considered a spy there. If they had been found out, Wes would have been dragged off, thrown into prison, shot without a trial! Of course there'd be no problem *here*, because now they were in what her relatives considered *enemy territory*.

Before Wes got out, he reassured her, "This shouldn't take long." He got out as soon as they stopped, shutting the carriage door behind him. Minutes passed. He did not come back. Concerned, JoBeth looked out into the murky morning to see what could be delaying him. She saw him conferring with two soldiers. He was gesturing back to the carriage with the hand that held their passes. What could be wrong?

She did not have to wait much longer to find out. Wes opened the carriage door and put his head inside, saying, "I'm sorry, darling, but they insist you get out of the carriage and present yourself." He lowered his voice. "I tried my best to convince them this was not necessary, that I could send to Major Meredith for confirmation of who I am and why I am escorting you into Washington. Of course, it's too early for the major to have arrived at his office. And I don't want to disturb him at home. If we don't comply, they tell me we will have to wait until such time as they can receive clearance and let us pass."

"I thought you said there would be no problem," she protested.

"I didn't think so. Evidently, security has been tightened. Lately there have been a number of occurrences of Confederate spies getting through, carrying secrets, vital military information. Unfortunately, these recent incidents have involved ladies. Hiding messages on their person." He hesitated, as if embarrassed. "I apologize, but it seems unavoidable. Unless we want to sit here for a couple of hours while they send for validation of our passes and wait for confirmation." He paused. "I promise, you will not be subjected to any indignity. They just want to make sure you are who our papers say you are, that you match the physical description. They'll ask you a few questions, that's all."

JoBeth had heard some of the stories relayed through the Richmond ladies' "grapevine." She had listened, appalled, to tales of female travelers being stopped and interrogated, the linings of their bonnets being ripped open, muffs torn apart, parasols cut to ribbons. Worse were other stories of some being required to remove their hoops as they were searched for possible contraband being carried to the enemy. Now she had to face such a possibility herself!

However, there was nothing to do but get out and do as they had been requested. The two young guards seemed a little uncomfortable, but they bluffed it out. They shuffled through her papers, asked her date of birth, her mother's maiden name, and a few more innocuous questions. Then the corporal, who seemed to be in charge, gruffly asked her to swear that all her answers were truthful, upon the possible charge of perjury. Never before having had her honesty challenged, JoBeth drew herself up and replied with cold indignation. "Of course."

She was then required to take the oath of allegiance, which with Wes's prompting she managed to do.

"You may proceed," mumbled the sentry to Wes, handing him back the sheaf of papers containing their passes.

Once they were back in the carriage and moving, Wes apologized. "I'm sorry, darling, but the fellow was only doing his duty."

JoBeth gave a little shudder. "Horrible," was all she could say.

"Soon all this will be over—a bad dream, a nightmare. We're safe. Nothing more to worry about," he said confidently. "Everything's going to be fine now."

JoBeth wished she could feel as sure.

All the happy excitement of their elopement had drained away, leaving her feeling shaken. What had she done? Come all this way, gone through so much, for this?

She looked out the carriage window. What she saw alarmed her and disgusted her. As they rolled along, she saw acres of makeshift shacks, dilapidated tents, lean-tos, set up on a stretch of swampy ground. It was too early for the poor dwellers of these pitiful shelters to be up and about—still, it struck her to the core that human beings could possibly be living in such squalor. She had never seen anything like it. Wordlessly she turned to Wes for some explanation.

Seeing her expression, Wes sensed her reaction. "It's one of the degrading facts of wartime life. People have poured into Washington since the war—doubling, tripling, the population. They are of all sorts: freed blacks hoping for work, the families of enlisted men who have followed them here and can't afford even the cheapest place to live. There are others, I'm afraid: rogues, thieves, camp followers, pickpockets—disreputable types you always find in any big city when normal life is overturned."

"But it's dreadful!" JoBeth exclaimed. "Can't something be done about all this? Can't better places be found for them to live?"

"The local officials and the metropolitan police try, but the problems are overwhelming—and of course, Congress and the army are occupied with the war." His arm went around her, drawing her closer as if to comfort her. "Try not to be too upset, JoBeth. This is all on the outskirts, terrible as it is. Farther along, it is different. I've found rooms for us in a quiet residential section of the city. In a lovely house. The home belongs to Mrs. Caroline Hobbs, a Southerner but loyal to the Union. She is a widow of only a few years and has been lonely living by herself. That's why she's renting us rooms. She is looking forward to meeting you, and I believe you will find her delightful company when I'm away on duty."

"But that won't be too often, will it? We will have time together? You won't be gone all the time, will you?"

"No, of course not. I should be home every evening unless Major Meredith has some special assignment for me." He smiled at her tenderly. "What is a few hours apart now? It will seem like nothing after all these months." He looked at her lovingly, almost as if he couldn't believe she was really there.

She rested her head momentarily against his shoulder. She knew Wes was happy, wanted her to be happy—and she wanted to be. But just now she felt unsure, frightened.

After a while, the carriage pulled up in front of a stone house. "Here we are," Wes said. He got out and turned to help her down. The morning was still rather dark, clouds overhead threatening rain. While Wes saw to her valise and hatbox, and the driver got down her small trunk, JoBeth looked up at the place that was to be her new home. There were lights on in the downstairs windows. As she stood there waiting, she saw the edge of a lace curtain lift in one of them, then drop. A minute later the front door opened and the portly figure of a woman was framed in the entrance.

"Come in, come in! Don't stand there in the chill," a genteel Southern voice urged.

"Good morning, Mrs. Hobbs," Wes called back, then said to JoBeth, "Come, meet our landlady." He took her arm, and together they went up the walk to the house.

Mrs. Hobbs was a handsome woman in her mid-forties, with salt-and-pepper hair under a lace-ruffled cap trembling with bows. She was wearing a black bombazine dress with a white collar. She shook JoBeth's hand warmly, studying her with quick, curious dark eyes. "Oh, my dear, I am so happy to meet you. I knew you must be a very special young lady, because your young man was very particular about everything being just so for you. Such devotion, such attention to every detail in your rooms. Come along, let me show you," Mrs. Hobbs invited, leading the way up the stairway. JoBeth murmured something she hoped was polite and followed.

The rooms were quite nicely appointed. In the small sitting room, a fire burned cheerily, lighting up the corners. There was a love seat and two comfortable armchairs. In the center was a round table with a ruby-glass-globed lamp. Flowered chintz tie-backs over unpleated lace curtains hung at the three-windowed bay. Watching for JoBeth's approval, Mrs. Hobbs pushed open the door to the adjoining bedroom. The high-backed, heavily carved mahogany bed was piled high with pillows and covered with an appliquéd quilt. In one corner stood a chaise, of the type that was popularly called a lady's "fainting couch."

"Everything is very nice, Mrs. Hobbs," JoBeth said appreciatively.

"I did so hope you'd like it!" beamed Mrs. Hobbs, seeming satisfied.

For a few more minutes Mrs. Hobbs fluttered about the rooms, touching antimacassars on the furniture, shifting the china dogs on the mantelpiece, stopping to rearrange a knickknack on one of the tables, before finally leaving.

JoBeth looked at Wes, not sure what to do next. At last, after all the conflict, all her stubborn resistance, her determination to come at all costs, she was here. And there was Wes, the reason for all of her rebellion, her refusal to listen to the pleas, the threats, the warnings, of her family and friends. A wave of doubt left her cold and shaking. Suddenly, what she had given up flashed before her. Should she have come?

Wes stood at the door, remaining there after having closed it behind the departing Mrs. Hobbs.

"Our appointment at the church is for four o'clock. I thought that would give you time to have a rest after our journey. It's been pretty intense, I know." There was concern in his eyes. He hesitated, as if waiting for her to say something. When she didn't, he went on, "I've made all the arrangements. My commanding officer, Major Meredith, will meet us at the church. He has agreed to stand up with me. I wanted him to meet you anyway. He is a fine person and very sympathetic to us. His sister is married to a Southerner, so they have experienced some of the same conflicts we have endured." He paused again, looking anxious. "Are you all right, darling? You look pale."

"Just a little tired and"—she smiled wanly—"a little hungry."

"Of course. I should have thought of that. I'm sorry." He turned, put his hand on the doorknob. "I'll go right down and ask Mrs. Hobbs if she could bring you something to eat."

"If it's no trouble?"

"I'm sure that would be no trouble at all. I think Mrs. Hobbs is the motherly type, don't you?" A smile brightened his face for a minute. "Would you like some tea, or would you rather have coffee?"

"Coffee, I think. I've not tasted real coffee for some time. The blockade, you know. . . ."

A rueful look passed over his face, but he did not discuss whatever he was thinking. "I'll be back in a few minutes," Wes promised and went out the door.

He was back before JoBeth had time to do more than remove her cape. As he came in, carrying a tray, he grinned. "Didn't I tell you Mrs. Hobbs was the motherly type? She had already prepared this. I met her coming up the stairs as I went down." He set down the tray on the table in front of the green velvet sofa. He poured two cups of coffee from the silver server and handed one to JoBeth.

"Mmmm." She held it, inhaling its fragrance, before taking a sip. "What a treat! It's delicious." The pungent taste immediately seemed to revive her. She took one of the small, triangular-cut chicken sandwiches and bit into it.

With the food and coffee, JoBeth's fuzziness began to disappear. She didn't feel quite so overwhelmed by all that had happened.

"I really must report to my office and let Major Meredith know we've safely arrived. I will come back here at three-thirty. Does that give you enough time?"

"Oh yes, that's fine." She made a funny little face and said, "Everything seems to be moving so fast."

"Yes, I know, but all these horrible long months of waiting are over. That's what I'm grateful for, what I thank God for," he said earnestly.

"Yes," she nodded, wishing she felt more certain. He finished his coffee, set down his cup, and got up. He took her hand, raised it to his lips, and kissed it. "Good-bye for a little while." He picked up his coat and hat and moved over to the door. There he turned back, as if he had just remembered something. He looked at her with a broad smile.

"I almost forgot. Our rings, JoBeth. We must exchange them so that we can use them in the ceremony." He drew his from the finger of his right hand and brought it over to her. He waited while she detached hers from the chain she had worn hidden around her neck for all these months. As she handed it to him, he leaned down and kissed her.

The kiss was sweet, reassuring. A warmth went over her. Wes was right: everything would be fine now. For a few minutes after he was gone, JoBeth remained motionless. She looked around uncertainly. She was really here in Washington, with Wes, and this was where she would be living. In just a matter of a few hours they would be married. At last all her dreams were coming true.

Chapter Twenty-Two

※e9※

After Wes's departure, JoBeth stretched out on the sofa and tried to rest. But she was too excited, too nervous, to sleep. She lay there looking around the unfamiliar room. Everything seemed unreal. Pictures of the last forty-eight hours flashed in her mind like images in a stereopticon. Everything that had happened since they fled through the night came back in vivid detail.

Too restless to lie still, she got up, inspecting the rest of the apartment. She went into the adjoining bedroom, pleased it was so nicely furnished and tastefully decorated as was the parlor.

She did not want to bother Mrs. Hobbs to ask for hot water for a bath. So she poured water from the pitcher into its matching pink china bowl and, using the lavender-scented cake of soap she was delighted to find in the dish on the washstand, bathed as best she could. Afterward she soaked a small linen hand towel with some precious cologne she had brought with her, patting it over her neck, shoulders, and arms.

Clean and refreshed, next she brushed out her hair until it crackled, then sat down at the dressing table to wind it into a figure-eight chignon. As she started placing the tortoiseshell pins into her hair to secure it, she saw herself in the mirror.

411

Her brush still in hand, she stared at the girl in the glass as if at a stranger. In the unfamiliar setting, she hardly recognized herself.

The chimes of the ormolu clock on the mantel began to ring. Two-thirty. In an hour Wes would return. *I must dress. Wes will be here soon, and then we will go to the church, and then*—her imagination took her no further. Everything seemed unreal. She was here by herself, with no loving relatives to get her ready for her wedding. She pushed away any regrets. This was what she had chosen to do. This was what she wanted.

She unpacked the jade taffeta dress, made from the beautiful material given to her by Aunt Josie, who had never dreamed it would be worn as a wedding gown—*to marry a man of whom they do not approve!* JoBeth thought guiltily.

She shook out the tiered skirt and stepped into it. Then she slipped on the bodice, which was embroidered with darker-green soutache braid. Starting to fasten the tiny hooks cleverly concealed under a narrow placket, she recalled instructing the seamstress to put the hooks down the front. She had known there would be no one to help her dress on her wedding day.

Lastly she slipped in her small pearl pendant earrings, then got out her hatbox and opened the lid. Unwrapping her bonnet from the tissue paper in which it was swathed, she took it out. She held it in front of her for a moment, admiring it. It was the prettiest one she had ever owned. Lined with fluted pink chiffon, it was trimmed with green velvet leaves in which nestled a single pink silk rose. Aunt Josie had selected the trimmings herself at her milliner's, declaring it perfect to wear with the green dress. Tying the wide green satin ribbons under her chin, JoBeth fervently hoped her aunt would eventually forgive her for eloping.

She was just buttoning on her gloves when a knock came at the door. It had a jubilant sound, as did Wes's voice announcing, "JoBeth, I'm here."

Her taffeta skirts swishing, she crossed the room to open it to her smiling husband-to-be.

~ಆ~

The interior of the church was dim and drafty. To JoBeth it had a strange, almost mysterious aura with its curved nave and shadowy arches. Entering, she felt the full impact of this solemn occasion. Wes covered her trembling hand with his, smiled down at her while they walked together down the long aisle. In the vestibule, JoBeth had been introduced to Major Meredith and to the regimental chaplain's wife, who were going to serve as their witnesses. Major Meredith was exactly as Wes had described him. His face, with its strong features and determined expression, revealed much of the qualities and character Wes had attributed to him. There was also an unexpected compassion in the deep-set eyes as he looked at them. Why? she wondered as they took their place and the chaplain opened his prayer book to begin the ceremony.

It was certainly not the wedding of her girlhood dreams. There was no organ music playing the traditional marches, nor was there a chosen soloist to sing her favorite hymns, nor did she know the clergyman who officiated. He read the ritual in what Wes told her later was a New England accent.

The ceremony was brief, but they both gave their responses in clear, sure tones, gazing happily at each other. JoBeth felt slightly delirious, as if her head were floating somewhere up over them and she were looking down on the scene. The words of the ceremony seemed natural to her. She had memorized them by repeating them each night after her bedtime prayers. She used to take out her pledge ring, hold it, and say the same promises she was making today. Ever since Wes had told her about betrothals in the olden days, she had cherished the idea. Speaking the words out loud "before God and this company"—although the church was empty except for them—was only a confirmation of the promise she had already made in her heart. Of course she would love, cherish, and obey Wes, in sickness and in health, for richer or for poorer, keeping only to him however long they both should live. There was no question, no doubts. All the uncertainty she had felt earlier had disappeared. This was a sacred moment. These were sacred promises, to be kept forever.

Exchanging their rings was only a repetition of what they had done in the Hillsboro churchyard, the fulfillment of all their hopes, prayers, dreams.

After they had all signed the register, Wes and JoBeth thanked the chaplain and his wife, then left the church with Major Meredith. As they came out onto the steps, they saw that a light drizzle was falling. The late afternoon sky was dark, heavy with clouds. Standing on the church steps, Major Meredith said, "You have a few more days of leave coming, don't you, Lieutenant? If I weren't required to report back to duty, I would insist on treating you two to a wedding supper at one of the city's finest restaurants. As it is, I have done the next best thing. I've taken the liberty of ordering a catered hamper from that same restaurant to be delivered to your address with my compliments. Perhaps it is even better this way. I know you both have waited a long, worried time to be together." He gave a brisk salute to Wes and bowed to JoBeth. "So I will not delay you. I admire your bravery and render my best wishes for a long and happy life together."

He saw them into their hired carriage waiting at the curb and bid them good-bye. By the time they arrived at Mrs. Hobbs's house, it was raining steadily. Wes held his military cape over JoBeth to protect her bonnet, and they ran up the steps. They had been given a key to the front door, and they let themselves in, then went quietly upstairs to their apartment.

JoBeth moved to the center of the room and stood for a minute, idly picking up a porcelain bird figurine, examining it. She could hear the rain pounding on the roof, giving the cozy little parlor a feeling of sheltered intimacy. Slowly she turned around and smiled.

Wes walked over to her, placing his hands gently on her shoulders, then very carefully untied her bonnet ribbons and removed her bonnet. He tossed it on the nearby table, then smoothed back her hair from her forehead, regarding her with infinite tenderness. Cupping her face in both his hands, he said softly, "Welcome to our home, darling wife."

"Oh, Wes, *wife*! That sounds so wonderful, so special."

"It is wonderful, and *you* are special. I thank God for you, JoBeth. I want always and only to make you happy, make you glad that you went through all you did and married me."

"Married. It hardly seems possible."

"But it is, my darling," he said, then kissed her. It was a long kiss but very gentle. "I love you, JoBeth, more than I can ever tell you." He took her hand and led her over to the sofa, eased her down to sit beside him, took her into his arms, and began to kiss her.

His kisses were slow and sweet, as if they had all the time in the world. He whispered her name over and over, kissing her again and again. An unspeakable joy surged all through JoBeth. The promise of their dream had been fulfilled. Their pledge had held, their wait had not been in vain, their faith had been rewarded.

Just then a discreet knock sounded at the door, and reluctantly they moved out of their embrace. They looked at each other questioningly. Then Mrs. Hobbs's voice came from the hall. "Lieutenant Rutherford!" Wesley gave JoBeth a helpless shrug, then got up, went to the door, and opened it to an apologetic Mrs. Hobbs.

"I wouldn't have disturbed you, but this was just delivered." She held out a wicker basket, its handle tied with a silver-edged white satin bow. There was a card on which was written, "Best Wishes to Lt. and Mrs. Wesley Rutherford."

"Thank you very much, Mrs. Hobbs. We were expecting it. A gift from my commanding officer." Wes took the basket from her.

Mrs. Hobbs peered around Wes at JoBeth. "Is there anything more I can do for you? I thought perhaps Mrs. Rutherford might not be used to our Northern weather—a hot water bottle, maybe?. . ." Her voice trailed away as if she suddenly realized the ridiculousness of her statement.

"That is most kind of you, Mrs. Hobbs. JoBeth—Mrs. Rutherford—*is* tired, of course, but we shall be just fine. Thank you." Wes stepped back, ready to close the door, but she stood there for a few seconds longer.

"Good evening, Mrs. Hobbs, and thank you again," he said firmly.

"Ah yes, Lieutenant. Well, if there should be anything—"

"That is indeed most kind—" Wesley again made an attempt to shut the door and this time succeeded. He turned around, made such an exaggeratedly bewildered face that JoBeth smothered her giggles with her hand. However, the ludicrous incident somehow broke through whatever stiffness either might have felt. As they unpacked the wonderful gift basket of delicacies—roasted squab, shrimp salad, dinner rolls, pears, grapes, chocolate eclairs, and a split of French champagne—they laughed and talked like old, carefree times.

Part Four

Chapter Twenty-Three

❦

*J*oBeth awoke in the depth of the feather bed alone. Dazzling October sunlight spilled in through the bedroom window. Wes was already gone. She must have slept through his departure. She felt disappointed to have missed fixing him at least a cup of coffee before he left, as a proper wife should. She sat up, yawning. Then she saw the note he'd left on his pillow beside hers.

Dearest One,

As you're beginning to find out, soldiers reveille early. Did not want to disturb you. Love you and will miss you all day until I return this evening.

Ever your devoted husband,
John Wesley Rutherford.

She smiled fondly, kissed the signature, saying softly, "And *I* am *Mrs.* John Wesley Rutherford." Saying it still thrilled her. They had been married nearly six weeks, and Wes still treated her as a bride.

She stretched out her left arm, gazing proudly at her hand, on which the gold pledge ring circled her third finger. The ring she had worn on a chain next to her heart for so long. How lucky she was, how blessed! All the partings, all the sadness, all the heartache, for them was over.

She tossed the covers back, got up, and dressed. She boiled water on the little spirit burner and made herself a cup of tea. Sipping it, she went to the window and looked out. The day promised to be delightful. The leaves on the elm tree outside had turned golden and were dancing in a brisk wind. Perhaps she would go for a walk.

When she had first come to Washington, Wes had cautioned her about where she should go on her own. Washington was a dangerous place these days. All sorts of unsavory people had come to the Union capital for all kinds of reasons, many of them nefarious. Crime and vice were rampant, and certain streets no sane person would risk going into. The police tried to keep the most flagrant lawbreaking in check, and the newspapers were full of floridly written accounts of raids on gambling dens and houses of ill repute.

However, this neighborhood was filled with other homes like Mrs. Hobbs's and was pleasant and safe. Although in the beginning JoBeth had felt somewhat timid to venture out by herself, she no longer felt at all that way. Washington was a cosmopolitan city and a stimulating one, and she very much enjoyed exploring it. She liked to stroll on the tree-lined avenues, and she especially liked window-shopping along the streets of fine stores displaying all sorts of luxuries and commodities unavailable in the blockaded South. Here was no visible shortage of anything. Certain items that Southerners had long been deprived of having were displayed in abundance.

Sometimes it appeared as if there were no such thing as a war going on. People on the streets were smiling, fashionably dressed women promenaded, others drove by in barouches. Children, often accompanied by black nurses, rolled hoops along the sidewalks or wheeled velocipedes. There were also soldiers in many kinds of uniforms: whole regiments who had rallied to the Union cause, colorful Zouaves who looked as if they were on their way to a costume ball. Vendors of all sorts plied their trades: there were ice-cream dealers in small booths, chestnuts being roasted on small portable stoves, flower stalls, an Italian organ grinder playing melodies as his little pet monkey held out a tin cup to passersby.

All this was fun and entertaining diversion for JoBeth, who, in spite of her new happiness, had times of homesickness. She was often alone, because Wes's duties in Major Meredith's office required his putting in long hours, working late. If she had not followed her own inclinations of curiosity about her new surroundings, coupled with her sense of adventure, time might have often hung heavily on her hands.

The letter that JoBeth had both waited for and dreaded receiving came.

Dearest Child,

You may be sure there were mixed reactions here to the news of your marriage to Wes. Although Aunt and Uncle Cady, after their initial shock, were tactful enough to refrain from expressing what I am sure they must have discussed—and certainly how they feel—in private. You know Uncle Madison, and it is understandable when you realize how strongly he feels about the Cause, and of course, they have two sons fighting on the opposite side from Wes. I realize there are other families divided like ours, only none that we personally know of. I truly believe it was mostly dismay that by this you have cut yourself off from the rest of the family—at least for the duration of this horrible war. Aunt Josie came to me later and asked me point-blank if I knew about it before you left. I could honestly tell her only that I felt somehow your love would show you a way to be together. Truthfully, even when you left here to go to Richmond, I wasn't sure what would be the outcome. I did get a letter from Amelia, which I now enclose so you can read for yourself.

JoBeth unfolded the other letter and read it.

Dear Friend,

I sit down with hammering heart and trembling hand to write to you. I have just seen your precious daughter off into the night with the man she loves. I pray we can trust him to protect and love her as she deserves to be loved. I can only commend you, Johanna, on the job you have done in rearing this lovely young woman. She is a credit to your training, nurturing, and caring love. She is not only accomplished in all the ways our society demands but has an inner goodness that shines out through her outer self. A fine, sweet, true heart and soul. I feel sure by the time this reaches you, you will have received word from her. May God be kind to these two young people who love each other so dearly and face such hard times ahead.

She turned back to her mother's letter.

Of course, I agree with all that she says about you, my darling. I just hope Wes appreciates the jewel he has now in his possession. God keep you and bless you both. You have chosen a hard road to walk together, but I am sure our Lord will be an unfailing source of strength for you both.

> *Always your loving mother,*
> *Johanna Shelby Davison*

JoBeth finished the letter with mixed emotions. She was not surprised either at her aunt and uncle's reaction to her elopement or at Amelia Brooke's dire predictions. Both were to be expected, considering the circumstances. Especially Aunt Josie and Uncle Madison's response.

The feelings of her relatives could have only been deepened and hardened by the news her mother sent in a later letter.

> *It grieves me to have to add the news received here that Harvel was badly wounded in the terrible battle at Chickamauga in September. He is in a hospital in Chattanooga, and we hope for the best.*

This war was a scourge on the whole country, North and South. JoBeth had seen the trainloads of Union wounded, the lines of ambulances rumbling through the city on the way to the soldiers hospitals. Fatalities on both sides were heavy. Nobody escaped, no family was spared. She felt almost guilty that Wes was safe in his noncombatant duty. However, he had known the horror of the battlefield, although he refused to talk to her about it. When she allowed herself to dwell on it, JoBeth's heart was wrung with pain. When would it be over?

"Going out, dearie?" Mrs. Hobbs called to her from her parlor as JoBeth came down the stairway.

"It looks like a lovely day, and I need some fresh air," JoBeth replied, pausing at the door while she pulled on her gloves.

"What a good idea," Mrs. Hobbs nodded approvingly. "I'm a great believer in fresh air and exercise, even for females."

Her statement rather amused JoBeth, since the good lady rarely seemed to move farther than from her comfortable chair by her fire to the front gate for the evening paper.

"I've been meaning to speak to you, my dear," Mrs. Hobbs continued, setting aside her sewing, rising, and coming to the parlor door. "To see if you'd be interested in joining me for a project. I make quilts for the soldiers hospital. Of course, they're not intricate designs or unique in any way. But they are warm and seem to comfort the dear boys. Reminds them of home, I believe, and their own mothers tucking them in at night."

"I suppose I could, Mrs. Hobbs. My mother makes beautiful quilts. In fact, she's famous for hers. As are all my great-aunts. It's a kind of family skill. However—" She hesitated. "I've only made one of my own. I've helped finish quilts—that is, stitch the tops to the under padding, but—"

"Well, then, that's good enough. These quilts for the soldiers don't have to be works of art. I'm sure you'll do just fine. I've made so many of these, I'll be glad to show you. There's nothing to finishing. Just a matter of diligence," she chuckled. "And working with someone else makes it go fast. You know what they say, 'Many hands make light work.' We'll make a fine team, you and I," she said with a satisfied smile.

They began working one or two afternoons a week on the quilts for the hospital. JoBeth discovered that in spite of the difference in their ages, spending time with Mrs. Hobbs was enjoyable, and they became good friends. On one of the long rainy afternoons they were together, JoBeth told Mrs. Hobbs about the pledge patches she'd made during her separation from Wes.

"And did you complete the quilt then?" Mrs. Hobbs asked interestedly.

"No. I mean, I kept making the patches I'd designed, collecting them. But I didn't know when Wes would come home—to Hillsboro, I mean. I assumed it would be after the war. I'd made a kind of bargain with myself that I'd continue making them until the war was over and he was home safely." She paused, took a few stitches before going on. "I guess none of us dreamed it would last so long—*this* long."

Mrs. Hobbs nodded her head in sympathetic agreement.

"Anyway, then I went to Richmond, and then Wes came for me and—well, I just never have put it all together. I'm not sure I know how to do it myself."

"I'd be happy to help you, if you'd like?" Mrs. Hobbs offered.

"Would you? That would be wonderful. Wes has never seen the patches. It would be fun to have it all put together and then show him."

"A lovely surprise—your work of faith and devotion!" Mrs. Hobbs's bright eyes sparkled. "He'd be so pleased."

A few days later JoBeth got the patches out from the bottom of her trunk and laid them out over her bed to see if she had enough to make into a quilt.

When Mrs. Hobbs saw the squares with their unusual original design, she exclaimed, "Why, you're quite an artist, my dear. I'm sure your mother was happy to see you follow in her footsteps, wasn't she?"

JoBeth looked sad. "Well, not exactly—she never saw it. I had to keep it a secret, even from her. You see, ever since my father died when I was a little girl and we went to live in Hillsboro, it's been difficult. At least, since the war. All my relatives supported secession. Almost everyone I know is for the Confederacy." She paused. "So when Wes made *his* decision, everyone there turned against him, and I just didn't want to make it any harder for Mama, since she had to continue to live there."

"I think I understand, dear," Mrs. Hobbs nodded, then said briskly, "Well, I see we have work to do, but in no time you should have a beautiful quilt—one that you and the lieutenant will always cherish for its meaning."

Mrs. Hobbs was patient as she showed JoBeth how to complete her quilt. She was generous in her praise of JoBeth's design, her tiny stitches. Mrs. Hobbs's romantic soul relished that the theme had stemmed from their secretly exchanged pledge rings.

After that their friendship seemed to blossom. "Do call me Caroline," Mrs. Hobbs urged JoBeth. Together they pieced the pledge quilt together and attached it to a cotton under-pad filled with fluffy cotton batting. The finished quilt was indeed "a thing of beauty whose joy would last forever," as Mrs. Hobbs quoted admiringly.

As fall moved into a stormy early winter, there were many afternoons working on the soldiers' quilts together before a cheerful fire in Mrs. Hobbs's sewing room. Although Mrs. Hobbs dismissed these quilts as "necessity quilts," their joint endeavor brought back some of JoBeth's happiest childhood memories. As a little girl, JoBeth had loved sitting on a low stool by her mother's chair and going through the overflowing scrap bag, finding colorful material from which her mother would select appropriate pieces for the squares that would be put together for the top of a quilt. Next there would be the length of flannel for the lining, to be stretched onto the frame and held by small nails all along each side. Usually Johanna whipstitched the lining onto the frame, because these quilts were done quickly so that she could get on with the quilts for which she had orders and that people were waiting to have delivered.

The quilts that JoBeth made now with Mrs. Hobbs were like the ones her mother had made for their own personal use when they still lived in the mountains, before JoBeth's father died. Those were most often made from clothes that no longer could be mended, pieced, or turned or the many tidbits and pieces left over from the designs of patterns for the ones she made for sale.

JoBeth could shut her eyes and nostalgically feel the warmth of those quilts, remember their smell, recall the feeling of being caressed with love, security, warmth. No wonder

Mrs. Hobbs's quilts were so welcomed at the hospitals by wounded soldiers sick of heart and body, a long way from the comfort of their own home and mother.

Caroline Hobbs had fulfilled Wes's early prediction that JoBeth would find her delightful company. Their friendship provided JoBeth with the feminine companionship she had known at home and missed. Mrs. Hobbs kept JoBeth entertained with her recital of the daily events of Washington society. She was an avid reader of the society pages of the daily newspaper, and she recounted the social doings of the capital city as though she had attended every fete and levee.

She was a great expert on the president's wife, Mary Todd Lincoln, a controversial figure, the subject of much gossip ever since she arrived from Springfield, Illinois. "She is a woman of unpredictable temper, apt to explode at the tiniest thing." Mrs. Hobbs made a clucking sound with her tongue at this deplorable trait. "An implied snub or a gesture is enough to send her into a fury. Those who have been witness to such tirades say they are frightening to behold. It's said she is insanely jealous of her husband and has caused terrible scenes as a result."

Mrs. Hobbs's favorite personality on the social scene was Miss Kate Chase, a popular belle who was the daughter of the secretary of the treasury, and she read every scrap written about her. She served as her widowed father's official hostess and did a great deal of entertaining, as was required of a member of the president's cabinet, reaping inches of complimentary newsprint.

"She is a stunning creature," Mrs. Hobbs assured JoBeth. "Holds herself like a queen, has skin like snow, marvelous hazel eyes, and glorious bronze hair."

The fact that Mrs. Hobbs had never seen the lady in person did not diminish her knowledge of the details of the beautiful socialite's life. "She's being courted by the young senator from Rhode Island, William Sprague."

Eventually her wedding was the social highlight of the winter and became the topic of Mrs. Hobbs's monologues to JoBeth for several days. Having avidly read the accounts, she could give JoBeth a full report, as though she had attended the wedding along with the president (but *not* Mrs. Lincoln: "It's said she's extremely jealous of Kate and wouldn't want to be where *she* ain't the center *herself*—which of course she wouldn't be, with its being, after all, the bride's day").

Mrs. Hobbs relayed almost word for word the newspaper-article description of the elaborate reception following the ceremony, telling JoBeth that "the beautiful bride was a vision in white velvet, lace veil, and the matched set of diamond-and-pearl jewelry that was the gift of the bridegroom."

Listening, JoBeth could not help but compare this glittering affair with her own wedding—which no one attended or wrote about or deemed in any way special. A wedding far from girlish imagination. But JoBeth was sure the bride of Mrs. Hobbs's extravagant description could be no happier than she.

Sometimes JoBeth had to pinch herself to believe her own happiness. It seemed strange that she *could* be so happy, having been cut off so completely from family and friends. But then, she had felt even more isolated and lonely in Hillsboro without Wes. Any doubts that she might have had that she had been foolish to follow her heart vanished entirely. Wes lived up to her idealized image of him: his brilliant mind, his absolute integrity, the sweetness of their intimate relationship. All they had been through to be together had been worth it.

Chapter Twenty-Four

◦═╍◦

*A*t long last, JoBeth's large trunk, battered, badly handled on its circuitous journey, finally arrived from Hillsboro. That it had come at all Caroline Hobbs declared a minor miracle, considering the "fortunes of war." It was scuffed, scratched, its leather straps worn, the brass locks rusted. Luckily, it had been well-made, and the contents were all safely intact.

JoBeth spent the day unpacking and putting away the embroidered petticoats, dainty camisoles, handkerchiefs, the peach dressing gown with its lace ruffles. She took a long time going over each dress before hanging it up in the armoire, contemplating where and on what occasion she might wear it. She lingered especially over the hyacinth blue velvet ballgown, fingering the folds. As she held it up to herself in front of the mirror, she remembered the last time she had worn it. It had been last Christmas, and she had danced with Curtis Channing.

Where would she ever wear it again? Perhaps a military ball here in Washington. For sure, if she ever *did* wear this gown again, she would most certainly dance with a soldier in a uniform of another color.

That possibility seemed dim. Wes worked long hours, came home weary. He often came home dejected from all the gloomy news he heard during the day, and it took all JoBeth's efforts to cheer him. The idea of any kind of social life for them seemed out of the question. Besides, just now a period of pessimism hung over the capital city. Things looked dark. The war was not going well. The North had lost its easy optimism about winning. Rumors were rife, morale was low. The draft for men was digging deep, dragging the bottom of the barrel for soldiers, taking all comers, including Irish and German immigrants straight off the boat who couldn't even speak English. The president was criticized at every turn, the generals were fighting among themselves, the Congress was in disarray.

The chance for any social occasion that would call for such a dress seemed remote. JoBeth sighed, putting the gown carefully away.

However, sooner than she could have imagined, an unexpected social opportunity came. To her complete surprise, Wes announced that they had been included in an invitation with Major Meredith's staff to attend one of Mrs. Lincoln's receptions. They were also invited to dinner at the Merediths' home before going to the White House.

JoBeth was beside herself with excitement. To think she would actually meet the president! Until she came to Washington, he had only been a shadowy figure to her, someone whose name she had heard denounced and vilified almost daily. Since then she had seen his name, headlines and articles about him, caricatures or cartoons of him, with regularity in the city's newspapers.

Mrs. Hobbs revered him greatly. When JoBeth told her of their invitation, she was as excited as JoBeth had ever seen the lady. Hearing his praises sung by Mrs. Hobbs when they worked together on the quilts had given JoBeth a different view of the president. She was curious to see him firsthand and form her own opinion.

JoBeth would have liked writing to her mother about all she was seeing, observing, doing. But since delivery of letters to the South was uncertain at best, she decided to start keeping a journal again. That way after the war, she would have a record of the places she went, the people she met, the things she could not tactfully or safely put in her letters. Certainly, going to the White House would be one such event she would have liked to share with her mother. JoBeth knew that Aunt Josie would faint if she knew to what "special occasion" her niece would wear one of the lovely outfits her own seamstress had made for her.

"Be careful not to outshine Madame President!" Mrs. Hobbs warned JoBeth when told of the invitation. "She don't like to be outdone in fashion—or anything else, for that matter. Especially by a pretty young woman like yourself."

Privately JoBeth doubted that the First Lady would give her a second look or a second thought. However, she did choose her dress carefully. A simple dusty rose silk, over which she wore a deeper-rose velvet jacket with a fan-shaped collar.

When Wes and JoBeth stepped into the entry hall at the Merediths' townhouse that evening, their wraps were taken by a rosy-cheeked Irish maid in a ruffled cap and apron over a black dress, just as Major and Mrs. Meredith came to greet them warmly. The major's wife, Frances, was equally as gracious as he. Taking JoBeth by the arm, she led her into the drawing room, where several well-coifed, elegantly dressed ladies and an impressive group of officers in dress uniforms shining with medals were already assembled.

She introduced her to a lady in purple taffeta lavishly trimmed with Belgian lace, who was seated on a satin-upholstered sofa. Then the major's wife called to welcome another group of arriving guests and left JoBeth there.

"What a lovely home," JoBeth remarked—a safe opening line she had been taught to use when starting a conversation with a fellow guest who was a total stranger.

The woman turned ice blue eyes upon her. "Do I detect a slight Southern accent?"

A little taken aback, JoBeth answered, "Yes, I am from North Carolina."

The woman moved her skirt an imperceptible inch. "How unfortunate! I've heard the city is filled with 'secesshes.'" With that the woman unfurled her fan and turned away, picking up the thread of the conversation she had been conducting with the woman on the other side of her.

JoBeth did not know whether to be insulted, amused, or grateful. Had the comment meant she was unfortunate to be from the South and far from home? Or unfortunate to be from the South when her husband was a Union officer? Or simply unfortunate on general terms? She certainly had not expected such blatant rudeness in such elegant company. She did not have a chance to either think of an appropriate retort or get up and move, because just then a splendid-looking officer bowed before her, saying, "I must be addressing Lieutenant Rutherford's charming bride?"

His flattering manner and the frank admiration in his eyes as he bent over her extended hand made JoBeth forget the enigmatic remark of the lady beside her. "May I introduce myself?" the officer said. "I'm one of your husband's fellow officers, Lieutenant Marsden Carlyle. May I have the honor of escorting you in to dinner?" He added with a smile, "I have your husband's permission."

At the table, JoBeth was seated between Lieutenant Carlyle and another officer. Wes was seated across from her, far down the other side of the table. Every so often he glanced approvingly over at her. It had been such a long time since she had been out socially, but JoBeth soon got the knack of it again. She recalled the advice Aunt Josie had given her before her very first dancing party: "If you can't think of anything to say, just tilt your head to one side, gaze intently at whomever happens to be speaking, look interested. It never fails. It is flattering to people to think you actually care about their opinions. Whatever they are."

As it turned out, JoBeth needn't have worried. Both men proved to be amusing conversationalists and flatteringly attentive.

After dinner, carriages rolled up to the front of the house, and the party divided into groups of four and left for the White House. Wes's approving look and smile as they left their hosts assured JoBeth that she had "passed muster" at her first Washington dinner party.

JoBeth felt as if she had swallowed a bunch of butterflies when they drove up to the imposing white mansion. Alighting from the carriage in front of the porticoed entrance, Wes held out his arm, and together they went up the steps, into the foyer, then on into the grand drawing room.

❧❦❧

Late that night, JoBeth could not go to bed until she had written about her evening in her journal. She did not want to forget a single detail.

> *I feel like the cat who went to visit the queen in the old nursery rhyme. Although we are a republic and not supposed to be in awe of royalty, I suppose going to the White House is as close as I'll ever come to such magnificence.*

*The White House has been newly refurbished, I was
told, and there has been much malicious gossip about
"Madame President's" extravagant expenditures for new
velvet drapes and Italian carpeting. But the Green Room,
where the reception was held tonight, is truly splendid.*

*Mrs. Lincoln, in comparison to her tall, rangy hus-
band, appears very small indeed. Her gown was quite
lavish—grenadine over silk, the bodice trimmed with
point lace—and her hair was dressed with artificial roses.
She may have been considered attractive as a young
woman—her coloring is very vivid: bright blue eyes, rich
mahogany-brown hair—but I found her animation
forced, her manner of speech affected. What once might
have been a "pleasing plumpness," at age forty-three has
grown to fat. I thought her flushed face and rather petu-
lant expression most unattractive.*

Here JoBeth paused and reread what she had just written.
She hadn't meant to be unkind, just truthful. There was
something about Mrs. Lincoln that she couldn't quite define.
An artificiality, a buried hostility she could not quite conceal,
as though she viewed everyone—mainly young, attractive
women—with slight suspicion. JoBeth had felt quite chilled
as those blue diamond eyes fixed themselves upon her for a
few seconds, and then the president's wife had given a prim
little smile and held out her gloved fingers to JoBeth, who
pressed them lightly, murmuring, "Good evening, Mrs. Lincoln," then moved down the line.

Although JoBeth knew that Mrs. Hobbs's unfavorable
opinion was drawn largely from journalists who did not like
the First Lady, she remembered Mrs. Hobbs's comment. After
observing Mrs. Lincoln in person, JoBeth could not help but
agree that there might be some truth in the rumor.

Her impression of the president was quite different. She looked into a face that was gaunt, deeply etched with lines, the eyes deep-set and dark, the expression of wisdom, sorrow, giving him the appearance of both determination and vulnerability. In the midst of all the music, the merriment, that flowed around him, he seemed to be troubled, brooding. She was too much in awe to do more than touch his hand briefly and move on. For some reason, she had felt drawn to turn and look back at him and was moved to instant sympathy. What burdens must be his to carry, what responsibility—the lives of so many to be lost or spared at his command.

JoBeth continued to write.

> *It was the person of Kate Chase Sprague (our landlady's "ideal"), the daughter of the secretary of the treasury, who quite outshone Madame President, in my opinion. A truly beautiful young woman with a slender, graceful figure, magnolia white skin, hair glinting with bronze lights, she was dressed in a lovely apricot satin dress and seemed always to be surrounded by admiring gentlemen.*

Chapter Twenty-Five

❧

*J*oBeth did not keep a daily diary. Her journal entries were sporadic. Sometimes days passed, even weeks, without her writing in it. However, there were times when something unusual happened during the otherwise rather uneventful passing of her days, and then she would write at some length.

November 1863

President Lincoln issued a proclamation declaring that the last Thursday in this month be set aside as a national day of Thanksgiving. Mrs. Hobbs invited Wes and me to have dinner with her and a group of her friends to celebrate the event. She told me it was a holiday long observed in her husband's native state of Massachusetts, and I guess it is celebrated in other New England states also. The Pilgrims' landing at Plymouth Rock is as great a cause for celebration as almost any other.

We dined on roast turkey, mashed potatoes, several kinds of vegetables, salad, and both pumpkin and apple pie. I could not help but contrast all this abundance with the probable fare of my relatives in the South. Even before I left, they were experiencing shortages of all kinds, due to the successful blockade of ports along the Southern coast.

436

Oh, that all this would soon be over and we could be one country again! That was the fervent prayer in all hearts, I'm sure, as we bowed our heads for grace before that festive meal.

❦

December 8th

President Lincoln offered amnesty to any Confederate who would restate his allegiance.

Would that it were that simple. He doesn't understand or realize the strength, determination, resentment, of most Southerners, who are fighting for what they believe are their states' rights.

❦

December 1863

The early days of the month passed by pleasantly enough, even though JoBeth had to fight back nostalgic thoughts of bygone Christmases in Hillsboro. This third year of the war, she knew that Christmases back there must be much different now than those she recalled so pleasantly. She was sure the Northern blockade of Southern ports intensified all the hardships, shortages, that had already begun to affect the lives of her family and friends before she left. Naturally, she missed her mother and Shelby terribly. Nevertheless, she was determined to make her first Christmas with Wes especially happy.

JoBeth was giving him her pledge quilt as a Christmas gift. For the first time, Wes would see her labor of love, the record of her constancy all during their separation. She worked in Mrs. Hobbs's apartment so that it would be a surprise. JoBeth spent hours stitching the squares onto the under-

437

cover batting and binding the whole with yards of blue trim the color of Wes's army uniform. When that was done, she carefully embroidered her name, the date of his departure, and the date of their wedding in one corner patch.

She planned to have a small trimmed tree, a new holiday custom popularized by Queen Victoria's German husband, Prince Albert, who had introduced it to England. Americans quickly adopted the idea, integrating it into their own Christmas decorations.

Besides giving Wes the now finished pledge quilt, she could afford only a few small gifts for him. A lieutenant's salary was small, and everything was so expensive. Still, she enjoyed being out among the bustling shoppers, who evidently had money to spend. JoBeth was sure that Washington was in sharp contrast to most cities in the South at this time. Downtown stores were blazing with lights until evening, windows displaying all sorts of attractive merchandise. One afternoon while mostly window-shopping, JoBeth happened to catch a glimpse of the newly wed Kate Chase, now Mrs. William Sprague. The woman was getting into her shiny, gilt-trimmed carriage outside one of Washington's most expensive department stores. She was extravagantly elegant, wearing a moss green brocade jacket with a pale mink collar and cuffs, a graceful skirt, a bonnet laden with shiny black and green feathers. JoBeth found herself gawking like a pauper viewing a duchess. She couldn't wait to tell Mrs. Hobbs about it.

JoBeth's time with Mrs. Hobbs was always amusing and diverting, and their conversations were not as gloomy as the war news Wes reluctantly brought home. The war seemed a seesaw: First, one side seemed to have the advantage, achieving some strategic objective; the next time the other won a decisive battle, claiming victory. However, Wes expressed the general feeling in Washington about the final outcome of the war, that the North would eventually emerge victorious.

JoBeth had mixed feelings—a Union victory meant a Southern defeat. She sometimes did not want to hear the latest news of battles. Perhaps she was acting like an ostrich, she thought. But if there was nothing she could do about the situation, what harm was there in being entertained by the reports Mrs. Hobbs related about the chaotic private lives of those in the White House?

Mrs. Lincoln's extravagance was notorious. Her frequent shopping sprees to the New York emporiums were widely reported. But even more interesting to JoBeth was the strange "behind the scenes" melodrama. It seemed that since their little son Willie died, Mrs. Lincoln had been consulting spiritists and attending seances. Although fascinated by these bizarre stories, JoBeth could not help being sympathetic toward this woman.

Christmas Eve afternoon JoBeth felt restless and a little homesick. She didn't want Wes to come home and find her melancholy, so to offset her mood she decided to go out for a while and mingle in the holiday crowds to try to capture some spirit. It worked. After browsing through a succession of shops, she made a few impulsive last-minute purchases. Some scented candles, a book of Browning's poetry, a pair of house slippers for Wes to wear when he kicked off his boots at night. Feeling better, she came out into the street to find it had begun to snow. She hurried home through the wintry dusk, anticipating the evening ahead. The snow was still falling when she let herself into Mrs. Hobbs's house, grateful for its welcoming warmth.

Upstairs in their apartment, she drew the curtains against the growing dark, looked around the cozy, firelit parlor with satisfaction. She fitted the spruce-scented candles into the brass holder on the mantelpiece.

Mrs. Hobbs had insisted they have Christmas Day dinner with her and some friends. But tonight was to be just for the two of them. Soon Wes would be here and they could have a candlelit dinner before the fireplace. From one of the small catering establishments that flourished in this city, she had bought a small roasted chicken, salad, a plum pudding she could heat on the spirit burner. They planned to attend the Christmas Eve service at a nearby church, then open their presents.

JoBeth wrapped the poetry book and the slippers and had just placed them under the tree when she heard the sound of Wes's voice speaking to Mrs. Hobbs on the landing.

She turned to greet him with a welcoming smile as he came in the door. But one look at his expression stopped her. Something was wrong. Something had happened. She opened her mouth to speak. Then, without knowing why, her heart chilled.

"What is it, Wes?"

"I'm sorry, darling. A telegram. Your Uncle Harvel died of his wounds in Tennessee."

JoBeth felt her knees buckle, and she had to hold on to the table to steady herself.

Poor Uncle Madison and Aunt Josie—and all those poor, adorable little children. She felt dizzy. She swayed and Wes was beside her in a minute, holding her, supporting her over to the sofa.

JoBeth's gaze moved to the tiny trimmed tree, with its paper chains and gilt candleholders. It looked so gaudy, so bizarre, taunting, in the face of this tragedy.

In her mind she was transported to Holly Grove. Remembering the gaiety of that last Christmas scene, the merry laughter of Harvel's children as they ran through the rooms festooned with evergreen boughs, holly, and mistletoe. Everyone had been so happy—

JoBeth closed her eyes against the pain.

In wartime everything is on the precipice. No one is guaranteed even a full day of happiness. . . .

Chapter Twenty-Six

❧

February 1864

Access to the president and to the White House still amazes me. People seem to wander freely in and out, with very few being stopped or questioned about their intent or errand. Does it not seem strange that the man most responsible for the great struggle to reunite our nation is so open to whosoever would come?

I suppose it particularly affects me because of the difference between Lincoln and the Confederate president, Jefferson Davis. He is almost a recluse. When I was in Richmond awaiting my pass to Washington, he remained a mysterious presence. Rarely did I hear of anyone, outside his immediate circle of trusted advisors or army officers, having an audience. Occasionally he could be seen riding out in the afternoons with General Lee or one of the other generals, ringed by a protective guard on horseback. But it was also said that because the threat of Unionist spies meant possible danger to his person, his route was often altered and his driver took him for airings on back roads and country lanes.

Here it seems to me that no such caution is taken for President Lincoln's safety, although secessionist sentiment runs high. He and Mrs. Lincoln are often easily viewed taking carriage rides with only a few mounted soldiers in escort.

I suppose this is much on my mind because of an encounter I had today. Wes had asked me to meet him at the White House, where Major Meredith's headquarters are located. We were to go to a late afternoon levee, held at the Merediths' home, for some new officers on his staff, and it would be easier and save time if I met Wes there.

As I was seated in the corridor, waiting for Wes, I observed the constant parade of people from the desk of the president's secretary to his office. How could he see so many people, hear so many petitions, answer so many questions, make so many decisions? One would have to be almost superhuman to handle such a load of demands.

Suddenly I became aware of a young girl, hardly taller than a twelve-year-old child, carrying a large artist's portfolio. She came down the hall toward me, juggling a sketch book that almost seemed too heavy for her slight build. There was an empty chair beside me, and she asked me timidly if it was taken. At my negative reply, she sat down.

At closer view, I reversed my estimate of her age and guessed her to be about sixteen, not more than seventeen at the most. She was quite pretty, her features regular, and her dark hair fell in ringlets to her waist. We acknowledged each other with a smile and a nod. I had no idea who she was and what on earth her business with the president might be. However, after a few minutes she introduced herself and enlightened me as to her purpose in being there.

Her name, she said, was Vinnie Ream, and she was an artist and sculptor. Shyly, not bragging or a bit arrogant, she then proceeded to tell me she had been given permission to station herself in the president's office and make sketches of him from life with the ultimate goal of sculpting a statue of him.

I was completely taken aback by this statement. She looked so young, looked to be barely out of the schoolroom. Quite unaffectedly she filled me in on her background. She had attended Christian College in Missouri, studying art and especially interested in sculpting. She told me her father had moved the family to Washington, where he was employed as a government mapmaker. She told me that on her very first day in the city, she had caught a glimpse of the president, and the nobility of his face had made a profound impression. Even then it became her ambition to sculpt him.

She went on to say it was a "miracle" how her deep desire came to be, how she was allowed to sit in the president's office and sketch him "from life." She may consider it a miracle—however, from listening to the account, it might well have also been her own persistence. What I've learned from being here in Washington, close to the political hub, is that it is also a matter of "whom you know" which most often is the way of accomplishing your goals. And so I believe it to be with Miss Ream. She went on to tell me that through the Missouri congressman James Rollin, she was apprenticed to a well-known Washington sculptor, Clark Mills. Eventually, through her connections, she was able to gain her long-held dream of actually drawing the president from life, with the object being a bust or statue of him.

She was very sincere in telling me what a privilege it was, how intimate the sittings became with Mr. Lincoln. That he shared with her the grief he felt for the loss of his little boy (his son Willie died tragically of typhoid fever), for whom he still mourned so deeply. She recounted to me how he would sometimes stand at the window looking out on the White House lawn, where he used to watch his children at play. Tears brightened her eyes as she told me how his head would bow, great tears would roll down his hollow cheeks, his shoulders would shake, even as he tried to control his sobs.

About this time she was motioned forward by the lift of the appointment secretary's hand. It was time for her to go, the girl whispered, and she quickly rose and, almost like a will-o'-the-wisp, slid quietly down the hallway and disappeared through the door of the president's office.

How much of all she told me is true, how much her dramatic rendition, I cannot say. However, I did feel that putting down this encounter might someday be of historic importance, should this young woman's dream of sculpting a statue of the president be fulfilled.

⤙᠅⤚

April 1865

Appomattox! Lee surrendered. The war is over!

From the pictures I've seen of General Robert E. Lee, stately and silver-haired, and the glimpse I once had of General Grant, the commander of the army of the Potomac, when he was in Washington—short, stocky, his uniform unpressed and rumpled—it's hard to imagine two more different men. Victor and vanquished. One could imagine that if they were actors in a play, their roles would be reversed. *I wonder how this news is being received at home? Certainly not with the church bells ringing, celebrations in the streets, as is here.*

✧✧✧

JoBeth heard that some of the still staunchly loyal Confederates were moving their families to South America, to Brazil, to escape living under what they feared would be harsh treatment from the dreaded Reconstruction government.

She knew the heavy price many persons dear to her had paid. They had lost all, then had been deprived of the victory that would have made their sacrifice worthwhile. She grieved for them. Again—it was as true now as it had been at the beginning of the war—she had a divided heart.

Dearest Mama,

Good news. Less than a week since the surrender was signed, and the travel bans between North and South have been lifted by presidential decree, so it should be possible soon for me to come home for a visit. Do you think Aunt Josie and Uncle Madison will welcome me? Or are they still angry and bitter about what I did? I would come alone and Wes would join me later. Perhaps I can lay the groundwork for reconciliation before he comes? After all, the president is advocating that the country come back together as one nation again. Surely our family can do no less? Let me know as soon as you can how you feel my plan will be received.

Give them all my dearest love, for it is still as true and strong as ever. Give Shelby especially a hug and kiss from his sister. I long to see you all.

Ever your loving daughter,
JoBeth

Chapter Twenty-Seven

❧

*O*ut on the streets, hawkers passed out the handbills that had been hastily printed to announce the special performance that would be held that evening.

FORD'S THEATER TONIGHT !! APRIL 14, 1865
Special Performance ** Farewell Appearance
of
Miss Laura Keene
In the Celebrated Comedy by Tom Taylor,
Our American Cousin
We will be honored by the attendance of
President Lincoln

Wes came home early that evening. Smiling broadly, he held up two theater tickets. "Guess what, Mrs. Rutherford? Tonight we are going out! Compliments of Major Meredith. He and Mrs. Meredith were unable to use them for some reason. So we are the lucky holders of dress circle seats to see *Our American Cousin* playing for one performance only at Ford's Theater tonight."

"How absolutely marvelous, Wes! How kind of the Merediths."

"And the president himself will be attending."

"Oh, good heavens!" JoBeth struck her forehead theatrically. "How can I stand it? I am most overcome with our good fortune!"

Wes laughed. He always enjoyed JoBeth's antics. Playing to her nonsense, he held up his hand, declaring, "Wait, you haven't heard all—General and Mrs. Grant will be accompanying them."

At this JoBeth staggered toward the sofa in a mock swoon. "Spare me, kind sir. I can stand no more!"

"What's more, afterwards"—Wes took a declaratory pose—"we'll go to supper at an elegant restaurant." He followed her over to where she sank back onto the cushions.

"And to whom do we owe *that* luxury?"

"To your husband!" he told her, laughing as he gathered her into his arms, cuddling her to him.

JoBeth struggled up from his embrace. "Good heavens, what shall I wear?"

Frowning fiercely, Wes relaxed his hold and, pretending to be outraged, demanded, "Here I am, kissing you—and *you're* thinking about clothes!"

"Well darling, after all, this is quite an occasion. I must dress appropriately. The dress circle certainly requires my most elegant gown. I know—my blue velvet!"

She dressed with much excitement. It had been so long since she could look forward to an evening like this, so long since she had felt free to enjoy herself. She had not had a chance to wear this beautiful gown yet in Washington. This was the *right* event. Anyone who was anyone in Washington would be there tonight. The city had been exuberant since victory. And tonight both the president and the victorious general would be in attendance.

Her elation enhanced the honey-rose glow of her skin, deepened the sapphire sparkle of her dark-lashed eyes. The

Shelby Italian cameo set—brooch and earrings of pale carnelian stone set in filigreed gold with their creamy carving of a Grecian lady's profile—were perfect accessories.

Wes was ready first and sat on a chair beside her dressing table while JoBeth fixed her hair.

"We'd better leave a little early, at least forty minutes before curtain time. They've got posters out announcing the fact that the president is going to attend this evening. So crowds will be forming for a glimpse of him as he comes into the theater," he told JoBeth as she twisted her hair into a chignon. "Poor fellow, he deserves some relaxation and entertainment after all he's been through. You know, he's aged even in the two years since I came here to Washington. The war has taken its toll on him as well as the country. But now, thank God, it's over and we can rejoice along with the president."

As Wes suggested, they left for the theater a little earlier than would ordinarily have been necessary. He was right about the publicity surrounding the president's attendance that evening. True to his prediction, the streets were jammed with carriages, buggies, hansom cabs. The crush of vehicles all vying with each other to dispatch their occupants as close to the theater entrance as possible clogged the thoroughfare. It was so crowded that after making futile attempts to get them nearer, their cab driver gave up and let them out a block from Ford's Theater. Already two lines on either side were pushing toward the ticket booth. The whole front of the theater was crowded with hopeful last-minute ticket-buyers and scalpers vending tickets to latecomers. Gawkers, waiting to see the president when he arrived, pushed against the queues of theatergoers.

Holding JoBeth's arm firmly, Wes managed to get past the shoving crowd and into the theater at last. He handed their tickets to one of the harried ushers in the foyer. The lobby was full, glowing with the flickering gas lights of the chandeliers, bright with the colors of women's hoop-skirted dresses, the flash of jewelry. In the snatches of conversation buzzing all around JoBeth, there was a mixture of exhilaration and relief. The victorious end of the war had brought a special excitement to this gala occasion.

JoBeth squeezed Wes's arm as they followed the usher down the plushly carpeted aisle, found their row, and settled into their seats. She was thrilled to discover that from where they were seated, she had a very good view of the presidential box.

Draped with red-white-and-blue bunting, it was one of two at the upper right-hand tier and was decorated with flags and flowers. The interior was wallpapered in dark red and hung with Nottingham lace curtains. An upholstered rocking chair with a carved frame had been provided for the president.

Suddenly a hush descended as the house lights mysteriously dimmed, and the rustle of the curtain being raised could be heard in the quieted theater. JoBeth's surreptitious glance up at the presidential box showed no occupants.

Act one began. The star, Laura Keene, a well-known comedienne, was well into the humorous dialogue when a definite stir rippled through the audience. For a moment everyone was distracted and turned to see Mr. Forbes, the theater owner, lead the presidential party down a side aisle. As they went up the stairs and into their box, a murmur circulated. Everyone immediately became aware of the arrival. There was a general shifting. People began to stand up and applaud. Miss Keene immediately halted in her lines and also began to clap her hands.

Then the whole audience got to its feet and the place rang with enthusiastic applause. The orchestra leader tapped his baton, and the first notes of "Hail to the Chief" rang out. The shadowy, tall figure of the president, half hidden by the draperies, could be seen standing as he acknowledged the recognition. Then he seated himself beside Mrs. Lincoln.

JoBeth had only one swift glimpse of the president himself, the unmistakable profile, the noble brow, the long nose, the dark beard. But she could see Mrs. Lincoln quite clearly as the lady fluttered her fan, turned to chat with the couple sitting behind them, who were definitely *not* the Grants. They were much too young, much too handsome. Who were they? JoBeth wondered. While the actors resumed the play, Mrs. Lincoln fidgeted. She patted her hair, adjusted her skirt, leaned forward with her small opera glasses to her eyes to look down at the orchestra seating, then touched her husband's arm as if to draw his attention to something or someone below.

JoBeth debated whether she dared draw her own tiny mother-of-pearl opera glasses from their velvet case and focus them on the presidential box. She had only seen Mr. Lincoln once: as she passed through the reception line at the White House. This was a chance to study him more closely. She couldn't let it go by.

Cautiously she took them out. Surely she could pretend to be viewing the stage. Discreetly she put the glasses up to her eyes, moved the tiny wheel to focus the lenses, slowly turned toward the pivotal box. A single second and she saw his face, and in that moment its expression etched itself indelibly on her memory.

She thought of all the times she'd heard him derided, spoken of with scorn, anger, hatred! And even worse, his physical appearance had been cartooned and described as "apish," "ugly." Yet what *she* saw was infinite compassion, conviction, and courage. She lingered on that face. Then, fearful to seem too obvious, she moved her glasses to view the two other occupants of the box. An extremely good-looking officer in dress uniform and a strikingly attractive young lady sat directly behind the president and Mrs. Lincoln. Whoever they were would probably be in tomorrow morning's society news. And surely Mrs. Hobbs would inform JoBeth.

Perhaps they were relatives of Mrs. Lincoln's, decided JoBeth, putting down her glasses. The First Lady had often had family members visiting and staying at the White House, even though it had caused vitriolic press attacks. Especially when her younger sister, the widow of a Confederate general, had been a guest there over a long period of time. That fact had even brought allegations that Mrs. Lincoln was a spy! *Poor lady,* JoBeth thought, turning her attention again to the stage. Mary Lincoln was probably more glad than anyone that the war was over and she would no longer be the target of such scurrilous rumors.

Those thoughts lingered in JoBeth's mind as she tried to get back to the gist of the play. For some reason it did not seem to hold her interest. It was a tired comedy of manners, and the acting was overdone. Still, it was amusing and brought a few chuckles and murmured laughter from the audience. It was, after all, a farce. Not to be taken seriously. She might have preferred a drama, a Shakespearean play for which the dramatic family of the Booths was famous. Perhaps another time.

An actor blared out his lines. "Don't know the manners of good society, eh? Well, I guess I know enough to turn you inside out, old gal—you sockdologizing old mantrap!"

As appreciative laughter ran through the audience, at almost the same time, there was a loud, cracking sound, like a storm door banging closed. Suddenly there was a scuffling noise and raised voices that seemed to be coming from the president's box. JoBeth turned her head just in time to see two figures wrestling, and she heard several piercing screams. The figure of a man scrambled to the ledge of the balcony, then leaped to the stage. There he sprawled for a minute before scrambling to his feet and running across the stage. A hoarse shout from the president's box rang out, "Stop that man!" Onstage, the actors seemed frozen in their places, their startled looks turning to horror as hysterical shrieking shrilled out from the presidential box. A young woman leaned over the railing and cried pleadingly, "Water!"

The audience rose to its feet. A protesting roar swelled into a crescendo. Exclamations, cries, gasps, screams, echoed throughout the building. There was a rush to the aisles. People pushing and shoving each other, clustering below the president's box. Then the horrible word circulated among the stunned theatergoers: "The president's been shot!" "Someone tried to kill Lincoln!"

JoBeth felt her knees weaken. She slumped against Wes, who was standing behind her. His hands tightened on her bare arms.

"Oh, dear God!" she heard him whisper. "This is what we've all been afraid of—he wouldn't listen to tighter security. And now, dear God, it's happened."

JoBeth felt a wave of nausea sweep over her.

The heart-wrenching screams and broken sobs could still be heard coming from the president's box. They watched in helpless shock as uniformed men clambered into the Lincolns' party box. Confusion reigned. People waited underneath the flag-draped balcony, with raised, questioning voices.

Wesley grabbed JoBeth's cloak, dropped it over her shoulders, leaned down, and spoke into her ear so as to be heard. "I should report to headquarters, in case—whatever. I should be there until—until anything happens. You must go home. I'll try to get you a cab. If there are any available. Otherwise, we'll make it back to Mrs. Hobbs some way. But then I must return, get to headquarters. God knows what this is all about. You understand?"

"Of course," she said, shuddering from shock and fear.

The cries and sobs rose all around them as the dreadful event took hold of the crowd. JoBeth bit her trembling lower lip.

"Poor, poor Mrs. Lincoln! Isn't there anything we can do?"

"Nothing, I'm afraid—*pray*. That's all that's left—but it may be too late." Wes's hands gripped her shoulders, firmly manipulating her through the dense crowd. "I have to get you out of here."

<hr />

JoBeth was only aware of the confusion, bordering on panic, that surrounded their exit from the theater. To get a cab, of course, was impossible. They walked all the way back to Mrs. Hobbs's. JoBeth's feet, in her thin satin slippers, became sore trying to keep up with Wes's longer stride. They were both breathing hard when they finally saw the night lantern on Mrs. Hobbs's porch. Wes handed JoBeth the key, then kissed her. "I have to leave now, get to headquarters. There's no telling what this means. Perhaps it's some kind of conspiracy, some plot to assassinate not only the president but others in the government. It may be a full-scale insurrection."

"Oh, Wes." She clung to him, trembling.

"Be brave, darling. I'll send word or come home as soon as I can." He took the key from her and opened the door. "Now go inside—and pray for the president and our country!" he said tensely. Then he was gone.

Almost staggering, JoBeth climbed the stairway up to their apartment. She paused briefly outside Mrs. Hobbs's door, then decided against waking her. Tomorrow would be soon enough for her to learn the news.

The night seemed endless. She moved restlessly from room to room, unable to settle down, praying for the president. The hours ticked away, spinning out into eternity.

~~❦~~

Outside, dawn was breaking. Its cold, misty light crept in between the curtains that JoBeth had pulled together the night before—as if to shut out the terrible truth, the inevitable news she dreaded.

Stiffly, JoBeth roused herself from her cramped position on the couch. From sheer emotional exhaustion, she had finally drifted off into a troubled sleep. She sat bolt upright. Wide awake. Her heart throbbed as if she were awakening out of a nightmare. Then memory struck with new impact and she remembered. It wasn't a nightmare. It had really happened. She had been there. She shuddered violently.

Almost at the same moment, she heard footsteps on the stairs and stiffened. Wes? The tread was slow, dragging. Outside the door they stopped, as if hesitating reluctantly. She watched the doorknob as one mesmerized. Slowly it twisted. Then the door opened.

Wes stood there on the threshold, his shoulders drooped, his face haggard, drawn. JoBeth held her breath. Her eyes, riveted on him, begged the question her lips dared not ask.

"The president is dead." Wes's voice was like lead.

"Oh, no!" JoBeth gasped. "Dear God, no!"

Wes walked over to her, then half fell onto the sofa beside her. He put his arms around her waist as she laid her head against his chest. Neither spoke for a full minute. Finally he asked, "You've been up all night? Not slept?"

"I couldn't. At least not for hours. And you?"

He shook his head. She put both her hands on either side of his face, searched it. His eyes were bloodshot, circled with dark shadows. His expression bore the signs of the night's vigil.

"What was it like—waiting there?"

"We were all locked into a kind of desperate trance. Hoping against hope. Nobody spoke much. Everyone prayed."

"Mrs. Lincoln?"

"Prostrated. They took her home to the White House. Poor woman. Out of her mind with grief."

"Poor, poor woman. This will break her." Tears of sympathy rolled down JoBeth's cheeks.

Wes sighed deeply. "The poor *South*." He shook his head sadly. "There'll be no magnanimity now ... nothing but revenge. Everyone blames the secessionist sympathizers. When I was coming home, there was already talk in the streets that it was a Southern conspiracy. Vengeance—" Wes put his head in his hands. His words were muffled as he said, "It's tragic. All *he* desired was amnesty, binding up the wounds, reconciliation...."

JoBeth wondered briefly how the news would be received in Hillsboro. In the Cadys' home. Many had hated Lincoln. But she knew Wes was right—the South would bear the brunt of the nation's anger at the killing of the president.

"Come, you must get some rest." Wes took both her hands and drew her gently up. The fire in the hearth had long since gone out and she shivered. Wes's arm went around her, supporting her as he led her toward the bedroom. She leaned heavily against him, feeling that all the strength had gone out of her. He eased her down to sit on the side of the bed.

"Here, let me help you." He proceeded to unbutton her long kid gloves, now streaked and stained with tears. His fingers fumbled with the pearl buttons, but she seemed to have no energy to assist him. Finally he pulled them off, finger by finger, then took her hand, lifted it to his cheek, pressing it there for a few seconds. Slowly he turned it over and kissed her palm. He laid her gloves on her lap. She smoothed them out and placed them in the long, narrow box he held out for her.

Then he knelt and took off the satin slippers with the silk rosette on each toe. For a moment, he held her feet in his palms, tenderly rubbing each instep.

"You must get into bed, darling." He helped her to her feet. She held on to the carved bedpost while he unfastened the hooks on the back of her bodice, unbuttoned the waistband of her skirt. The beautiful velvet dress slid to the floor. He picked it up and hung it carefully on the front of the armoire. But JoBeth knew she would never wear it again.

Wes turned back the quilt and covers for her. She sat down on the edge of the bed.

"Aren't you coming?" she asked wearily. "You need rest, too."

"I've been ordered home to get a few hours' sleep. However, we have a full day's work ahead, arrangements to be made, and ..."

The last of what he said faded as, sighing deeply, JoBeth fell back upon the pillows and closed her eyes.

～❧～

JoBeth didn't know how long she'd slept when she was aroused by movement in the darkened room. Struggling out of her heavy sleep, she squinted her eyes and glanced around. Then she saw Wes's figure silhouetted against the light seeping in through the draperies.

"Wes!" she called to him. He turned, then came over and sat down on the bed beside her. "Why are you up? Didn't you sleep at all?"

"I couldn't. I can't believe the president is dead."

"Oh, Wes!" JoBeth held out her arms to him. He leaned toward her and she held him, his head on her shoulder.

"It all seems so pointless," he said hoarsely. "He tried to make a difference. To bring this country back to its beginnings, hold the Union together. And now ... I thought it was all over—the hatred, the killing ... but it's not. It will begin all over again, and there will be no end to it—" His voice broke.

She could feel his body shake with deep sobs.

"Darling, darling," she crooned as if soothing a weeping child, her hands stroking his neck. She felt his tears dampening her shoulder through her nightgown. Her embrace tightened and she drew him down to her and they wept together, embraced in their mutual sorrow.

She could feel his body shake with deep sobs.

When JoBeth awakened again, Wes was gone. He'd left a note for her. He'd gone back to report to Major Meredith to see if he could be of any use.

Her head throbbed. She felt shaky and ill. Her eyes were burning, her eyelids swollen from all the tears of the night before. Her hair was tangled, for in all this time, she had not even removed her hairpins or the ornamental comb she'd worn to the theater.

The remembrance of the tragedy made her shiver, and she pulled on her quilted robe. She had been witness to murder. Had seen the alleged assassin jump onto the stage in front of her very eyes! She would see that scene over and over for the rest of her life, hear Mrs. Lincoln's piteous screams echoing down the years.

JoBeth moved stiffly over to the spirit burner, struck a match to light it, but her hand was shaking so badly that she had to do it twice. She'd feel better when she had some tea, she told herself hopefully. She waited impatiently for the water to boil, the tea to brew. Hot tea should bring some warmth into her unnaturally cold body. She got a fire started in the fireplace, then huddled in the chair in front of it, sipping the scalding hot tea.

Over and over she relived last night's horror. The scene played itself out on the stage of her mind, as if she were again viewing it in all its tragic drama.

She would never forget it. Never, never!

Chapter Twenty-Eight

✤

*R*emembering Wes's dire prediction about what would happen to the South in the wake of the president's death, she tried to imagine the mood in her own home when word came of the assassination. Lincoln had publicly stated his policy of rebuilding the nation. Even against the advice of some of his cabinet, and despite the fact that members of his own political party did not agree with him, he had advocated "malice toward none, and charity toward all." *Now* what would be the South's fate at the hands of its vindictive conquerors?

It seemed ironic that Lincoln's death should come on Good Friday. The great humanitarian, the emancipator of slaves, the president who had preserved the Union—struck down on the same day as the Crucifixion. Both Savior of the world and savior of the nation killed by their enemies.

She must do something—something personal—to mark this terrible deed, create something to memorialize this historic event. . . .

JoBeth began to visualize the design for a quilt—perhaps the outline of three crosses rising across a field of lilies. It would be her personal reminder that she must hold on to the belief that as senseless and devastating as this death seemed, it had some purpose in God's mysterious plan. It would say, in a very individual way, that there was hope beyond the crosses of life. The design formed very clearly in her mind. Excitedly she took out a piece of paper, a pencil, and began to sketch it.

The very act of doing this seemed to bring her mother very close to her. It was the tragedy of her father's early and unforeseen death that had been the motivation for her mother's lifework of making quilts to sell. Johanna had painstakingly disciplined herself to learn a craft for which she had no particular talent. She had done it out of necessity at first. She had gone back to her hometown a penniless widow with two small children, to live with relatives. Even though they welcomed her with love and generosity, she hated being a "poor relation" in the household of her affluent aunt and uncle. Johanna prayed for some way to support herself and her fatherless children. The answer came with her creativity. She soon became known for her beautiful quilts. Her skill and the demand for her work provided the education she wanted for her daughter, and her son's college tuition and seminary fees. JoBeth felt a surge of energy, a rush of elation. As her mother had done before her, *she* would make something beautiful out of this tragedy.

Later in the morning, an ashen-faced Mrs. Hobbs tapped at JoBeth's door, holding the latest edition of the newspaper with its black-banner headlines. She told JoBeth that they had almost certainly identified the assassin as the actor John Wilkes Booth.

Of course, JoBeth had heard of John Wilkes Booth. He was a matinee idol, adored by young lady theatergoers. She had seen his pictures, and he had once been pointed out to her in front of the theater. Tall, handsomely built, an Adonis with curling dark hair, high color, white teeth, features as finely sculptured as those on some Greek statue. Mrs. Hobbs had read extravagant raves about him in theatrical reviews of plays in which he had appeared in Washington. He was known as quite a "ladies' man," and it was even rumored that Bessie Hale, the daughter of Senator John Hale, was infatuated with him.

As more was learned about the assassin, the profile of a vain, arrogant man seething with a murderous hatred of the president emerged. Imbalanced, his weakness of character led him to believe he could commit murder and get away with it.

Three days later, his death—he was ambushed and shot as he hid from his pursuers—seemed almost judgmental, and few mourned him.

~~≈⋙~~

In the days that followed, the assassinated president drew the most mournful expressions of loss. A poem by the well-known author Herman Melville was published in the newspaper, and reprints were offered.

Spontaneous expressions of sorrow, grief, and respect began to appear in front of Ford's Theater. Garden bouquets, floral wreaths, formal funeral arrangements—sprays of lilies and other spring flowers—seemed poignant reminders of the one who would never see another spring.

Drawn by some irresistible impulse, JoBeth also trod the pilgrim's way there. Because she had been in the theater when it happened, she felt some inexplicable bond to the slain president and to his widow. She had heard her screams, felt her pain like a knife through her own heart. Although her own short life had known few losses, her sensitive nature suffered deeply with the mourning wife of the slain president. She could only imagine what she would have felt had it been Wes. Her sympathy was very real as she moved forward and, her bell-shaped skirt swaying, knelt and gently laid her small memorial bunch of flowers with the others.

～εϟ～

Easter Sunday, April 16, 1865

JoBeth attended service alone that Sunday, because Wes had to be at Major Meredith's side in case he was needed to facilitate any of arrangements for the funeral. As she walked the few blocks over to the church, the bright sun and the sound of birdsong in the blossoming trees seemed a bitter counterpoint to the dejected churchgoers. How could it be, when the dark cloud of national tragedy hung so heavy?

A pall of foreboding gloom hovered over the city. On Tuesday, Wes escorted JoBeth to where the president lay in state, so she could pay her respects. Her heart ached remembering the last, festive occasion on which she had come to the White House. Long lines stood patiently to file past the catafalque, draped in black silk, that had been erected in the East Room. At the head and foot of the casket—braided, studded, and starred with silver—in which the body of the slain president lay, uniformed officers stood at attention. Sepulchral light filtered in from windows hung with black drapery, and the veiled mirrors added to the somber atmosphere. The heavy fragrance of lilies and roses permeated the room.

The funeral on Wednesday was limited to six hundred guests. Two days later the president was to be taken by railroad car back to Illinois.

Friday morning, tolling bells awakened JoBeth to another day of sorrow. There would be a final, brief service conducted for the president in the Rotunda of the Capitol before the last solemn march to the depot.

From Major Meredith's office window, JoBeth watched the sad, solemn procession from the White House to the train station, where the body of the president would be placed in a special car for the journey back to Springfield, Illinois, to his final resting place. Black plumes adorned the

heads of the six gray horses pulling the hearse, which was festooned in black crepe, as they moved along the street in slow,
measured steps. Behind was the president's horse, his boots
placed in the stirrups. People lined four-deep along the way,
many openly sobbing.

The newspapers had been filled with eulogies. Even the
great Confederate general George Pickett, the nephew of
Andrew Johnston, and years before a partner in Lincoln's Illinois law firm, was quoted as saying, upon hearing the news of
the assassination, "My God! My God! The South has lost its
best friend and protector, the surest, safest hand to guide and
steer her through the breakers ahead. Again must we feel the
smart of fanaticism."

❧

After the mournful scene, returning to their rooms,
JoBeth removed the black satin ribbons from her bonnet,
sadly folded them, and put them in a box. As she did, an idea
for another way of marking this particular time in her life
formed. These years she had lived in Washington made up a
period separate from all the others in her life. In the space of
less than two years, momentous things had occurred. Unfor-
gettable things. Besides her journal, which she'd written in
only intermittently, how could she keep some sort of record?
No matter how sharp they are at first, memories often fade.

She remembered Mrs. Hobbs' telling her about a new
kind of quilt that was becoming popular. An elaborate, fancy
kind, a "memory" quilt made up of pieces from special gowns,
such as a wedding dress, or clothing worn at other special
occasions. The material was not cut into patches but in a
variety of shapes fitted together in any sort of pattern—thus
it was also called a "crazy quilt." Trimmed with lace or satin
braid, it was more a quilt to be displayed than used.

JoBeth had already decided she could never again wear the blue velvet she had worn to Ford's Theater that night. It held too many horrible memories. Yet it had been worn on a historic—if tragic—occasion, and as such should be kept. A crazy quilt such as Mrs. Hobb had described would be a way to memorialize her time in Washington, all the things that had happened to her during this historic era. She recalled Mrs. Hobbs' saying, "As yet in my life, nothing very important or dramatic has happened that I could make a quilt about!" But JoBeth realized that her experience had been different. Hers would be worth remembering.

Chapter Twenty-Nine

❧❦❧

*J*oBeth flitted from armoire to trunk, from bureau to portmanteau, back and forth, happy and rather distracted at the thought that she was at last going home—well, to Hillsboro. In this last week of May, Washington was already sweltering. She looked forward to being once more in the cool foothills town, surrounded by the mountains, sheltered by the tall pines.

It would be such a relief also to be away from the ferment of the capital city. Ever since the president's assassination, the air literally breathed of fiery speeches, of excoriating vengeance, of speeches swearing retribution for the murder. Wes seemed to grow more weary and worn each day from handling the bulk of correspondence flowing into the major's office.

Wes had insisted JoBeth go to Hillsboro as soon as travel became possible, promising he would follow as soon as he received his discharge.

At first she had refused to leave him. But as both the weather heated and his persuasion increased, she gave in. She was anxious to see her mother and Shelby. It had been over two years. In the last, desperate months of the war, Shelby had left his classes at the seminary and joined a local unit to make the final, hopeless stands against Sherman's irrevocable advance through the South. He had, however, contracted typhoid and become dangerously ill—he'd been sent home to die, in fact. Thankfully, with good nursing and heartfelt prayer he had slowly recovered and was planning to go back to resume his studies in the fall.

However, the deciding factor in JoBeth's decision to go was her happy suspicion. One about which she was not yet sure enough to tell Wes. By the time he could join her in Hillsboro, she hoped to be able to share the exciting news that they were to become parents.

JoBeth hummed happily as she packed. Then, hearing a familiar footstep on the stairway, she halted for a minute, her face turned to the door to welcome her husband home. She was eager to share with him the letter she had received from her mother that morning saying that everyone was happily looking forward to her "homecoming."

All her own doubts about not being welcome faded with this reassurance. But one look at Wes's expression gave her pause. She knew that since the murder of the president, Wes had been depressed. He had idealized and admired Lincoln for his noble purpose. She had thought recently that he was coming out of his deep melancholy, but today he looked solemn, almost sad.

After greeting her, he slumped into one of the armchairs and surveyed the packed boxes, the valises, and the open trunk thoughtfully. In an attempt to cheer him, JoBeth declared gaily, "I'm afraid we are going to have to make you some new clothes, Wes. You must have grown an inch in height and several wide in the shoulders and chest since you were a civilian!"

He made no comment, nor did his tired face lift in a smile as it usually did to her lighthearted teasing. Immediately she sensed something was wrong.

"Do you have a headache, Wes?" she asked worriedly. "Could I fix you some tea or a tisane?"

He shook his head. "No, thank you, but I do need to talk to you, JoBeth."

"You sound serious. What is it?" she asked, alarmed.

She put aside the garment she was folding and went over and knelt down beside the chair in which he was sitting. She took his hands, which hung limply, and looked anxiously up into his eyes. They were haunted, miserable.

"I can't go to Hillsboro," he said heavily.

"I knew that, Wes. Not right away, of course, but you'll come later. Mama says—," she began, but he cut her off.

"No, I don't mean just *now*. I mean *ever*." A muscle in his cheek worked, as if he were trying to control his emotion. "What I mean is, we can't *live* there. I know that's what we've talked about, what we've planned, but—" He took an envelope from the inside pocket of his tunic. "I've done some testing of the waters, so to speak. I wrote to Cousin Will, asked him to tell me frankly what the climate would be in Hillsboro should we return to make our home there once more."

"And?"

"This is his answer." He tapped the envelope on the palm of his other hand. "He says resentment runs very high. North Carolina feels especially bitter, not being a large cotton-growing state nor a large slave-holding one and yet having lost more men per capita in the war than many of the states in the Deep South whose property they were defending. They've suffered a great deal. They're very much afraid of the new reconstructionist policies now being discussed in Congress. This is what he wrote: 'They're not satisfied in bringing us to our knees—they want to place their foot on our neck, grind our faces into the dirt.'" Wes looked up and into JoBeth's eyes. "So you see how impossible it would be for us to go back—to try to live among people who would despise us?"

JoBeth drew her breath in a little gasp.

"I know Will wouldn't lie. He's telling me the truth. Because he cares about us"—Wes's smile was ironic—"loves us even." He sighed deeply, his jaw set, and he told her, "If we go back to Hillsboro, hate will surround us like a thick, smothering cloak. We won't be able to breathe. We'll suffocate. We cannot—I *will* not stay in such killing atmosphere, in an environment where love cannot overcome, survive."

"Then what, Wes? What do we do?"

"I don't know. At least, I'm not sure. I don't think we have many alternatives. But I do have an idea I want you to think about—"

"Tell me."

"I say we go west—a new life, a clean slate."

"Where out west?" She tried to keep her voice from shaking.

"California, that's where."

"California?" she gasped, then asked, "Not the gold fields, Wes. You don't plan to mine—"

"No, no, darling. There are all sorts of opportunities. And land and all kinds of things we can do once we're there."

"Oh, darling, but it's such a risk!"

"Life is a risk, JoBeth. The person who risks nothing does nothing, has nothing, is nothing, becomes nothing. He may avoid suffering and sorrow, but he simply cannot learn, change and grow, and live. He has forfeited his freedom. Only the person who risks is really free."

"It seems like you've already thought about this a great deal."

"I have. I didn't want to say anything until I'd investigated it more on my own." He took both her hands in his, raised them to his mouth, and kissed her fingers, saying tenderly, "I know how hard it would be for you to leave your family—"

JoBeth's heart recoiled from another parting with her dear ones. It had been hard enough the first time. But her own experience confirmed the resentment Will described. Even the warmth and closeness and love of her family hadn't been able to protect her before. How much worse it would be now if Wes, a veteran of the hated conqueror's army, returned and tried to make a home, earn a living.

She had always hoped that when the war was over, she and Wes could settle down happily in the town they both loved, where they had grown up among their family and friends. But everything had changed now. Nothing would ever be the same for them. Old friends had become cold, doors once opened to them were now closed, warm greetings had become outright rejections. The homes where they had always been welcomed would not receive them. Hillsboro was no longer a place where they would feel comfortable, happy, or wanted. Peace may have come to the country, but the South only knew unforgiveness and vengeance.

The truth was bitter and hard to accept. But she couldn't deny it. Wes was right.

JoBeth remembered her mother's saying, "When we love, we place our happiness in the happiness of another." If this was what Wes wanted—*needed*—to do, if this was what he felt was the best thing for them and for their future life together, then there was no question she would agree and go. His happiness meant everything to her.

"Oh, Wes, it will be hard. But don't you know that we promised each other never to be separated again? Wherever you are, that's where my home is, my heart." She thought of the long separation, how she had yearned for him. No matter what happened, they belonged together. Wherever he went, she would gladly follow.

"California." She said the word tentatively, as if trying it out. "California!" she repeated. She felt a prickle of excitement. Looking up, she met his steady gaze and smiled.

The Crazy Quilt

~⚬⚬~

Sewed points and squares form a pattern like life's cares—old garments, old memories—and what is life? A crazy quilt, sorrow, joy, grace and guilt, a scrap of silk, a piece of velvet, a length of ribbon, a square of scarlet, here and there an edge o' lace to enhance the commonplace, and so the hand of time will take fragments of our lives and make out of life's remnants in patterns fall, to make out of our life a thing of beauty after all.

Douglas Malloch

469

American Quilt Series
Bonus Section

❦

How to Make the
Heart-in-Hands Quilt

❦

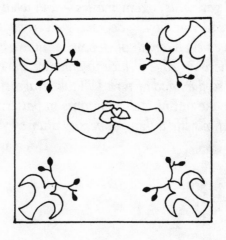

Unlike the "Carolina Lily" quilt pattern portrayed in *The Pattern*, Book 1 of the American Quilt Series, this "Heart-in-Hands" design is not traditional. It was designed specifically for this book by author Jane Peart, and she offers it as a way of thanking the many readers of her books. She would like to extend a special thanks to master quilters Connie Chapman and Liz Miller for their instructions and for the execution of the actual quilt.

Supplies needed for a 10-3/4-by-9-3/4-inch patch

Background Fabric: gray/blue, small print or plain
Doves: white fabric
Border Trim and heart: red fabric
Outer Border: blue fabric
Hands: peach or flesh colored fabric
You will also need: Fusable fabric or Wonder-Under

Copy the overall design onto paper to make the basic template. (You may trace the design by hand or enlarge the above design several times in a photocopier until it is the correct size).

Cut and fuse the fabric squares according to the manufacturer's instructions. Then trace the pattern design onto the fused fabric squares. Cut out designs and place them in the desired places on the patch background fabric. Then embroider the olive branches that are held by the doves.

When everything is in place, remove the paper backing, and with a hot iron, fuse the design to the background.

Sew on the blue border. Place the square on the backing, which is layered as follows: 1. Fabric. 2. Batting. 3. Muslin.

Stitch down the various pieces of the designs (the doves, the hands, and the heart—with running stitch, button-hole stitch, or pin stitch).

For the 1-1/2-inch border, cut 4-1/2 feet of red fabric two inches wide. Fold it in half lengthwise and press it to the width of 1 inch. Sew around front of patch, turn it over, and hand stitch it down.

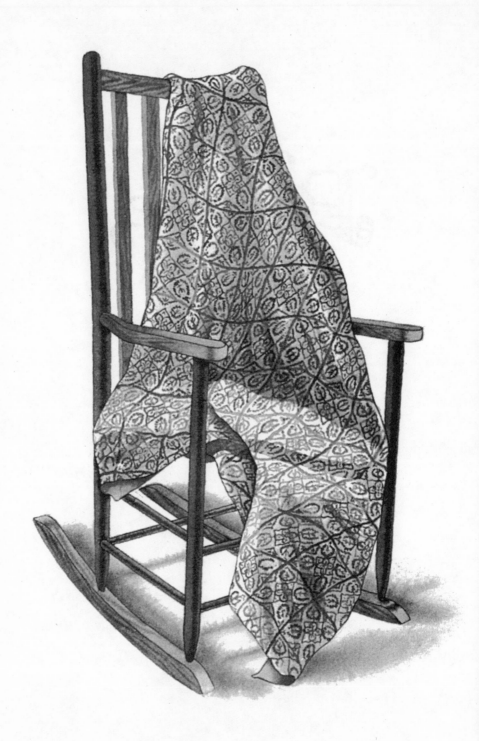

Part One

Prologue

❧❧

Jana Rutherford stood looking out from her window at the familiar scene she loved, one she never tired of viewing: beyond the rim of beach, the distant blue line of ocean. As she watched, along the horizon moved a single boat, its sails billowing against the orange-pink sky.

She would never forget her first sight of the Big Island. She had been ten years old and standing at the railing of the steamer coming from Oahu when her father declared, "There it is! Hawaii, the biggest of all the islands."

She had looked in the direction he pointed. The Big Island seemed to emerge out of a sea of turquoise water. Lush green walls of dark tropical vegetation rose steeply above the scalloped beach, onto which the foam-edged surf swirled.

"That's where we're going to live, Jana. That's our new home," he had said. "We're all going to be happy there."

And they had been. Especially Jana. From the beginning, she had loved everything Hawaiian. She even liked her name better in Hawaiian. *Koana.* It sounded softer, more musical, than Jana or Johanna, her christened name.

A gentle wind rustled the fronds of the palm trees surrounding the house and stirred the curtains. Sighing, she reluctantly turned away, back to her bedroom. She still had much to do before tomorrow, when she would leave for Hilo, travel by steamer to Honolulu, and then board the ship that would take her to the United States.

Only one thing left to do, something she had left to the last. This task would seem in some way to tie up the loose ends of her life here in the house where she had lived for the last ten years.

She had to go through the contents of the rectangular koa wood box at the end of her bed. The chest had come with her from Oahu. It held her childhood, and the disposition of all the things stored within would have to be decided upon. It was a job she dreaded and so had procrastinated doing.

Kneeling in front of it, she raised the top. The collection of a lifetime was piled haphazardly within: old dolls long since put away; worn books; toys; a ragged, one-eyed plush bear, too scuffed and limp to be passed along to some other child, yet too beloved to part with; a cardboard portfolio she had fashioned to hold some of the first drawings and water-colors she had done at school; and in one corner, a battered shoe box. When she picked that up, a fine drift of sand spilled over her hands. Inside was an assortment of seashells. Immediately a whole parade of happy days on the beach swept through her mind. It was then that she saw what lay underneath, at the bottom of the chest: her memory book, a little warped, mildewed on the edges, its original pink cover turned brown, the spray of pansies that had been painted diagonally across it, faded.

Taking the book out, Jana sat back on her heels and placed it on her lap. Slowly she opened it and read the first yellowed page.

THIS MEMORY BOOK BELONGS TO
JOHANNA RUTHERFORD

*born on Oahu in the Hawaiian Islands, on the occa-
sion of her twelfth birthday, given to her by her loving
Grandmother, whose fondest wish is that these pages may
only record sunny hours, noble thoughts, joy-filled days,
and happy memories.*

Johanna Shelby Davison

November 1881

My grandmother, who lives in North Carolina on
the mainland, sent me this book. In it I am going to write
all the important things that happen in my life. Then
when I am old, I can look back and remember what it
was like to be a child. Grown-ups seem to forget.

Some important things have happened to me this
year. First, I have a baby brother, Nathan. Alani, his
nurse (she used to be mine), mostly calls him Nakana or
keiki, which means "baby" in Hawaiian. He was such a
surprise. When my mother arrived from Honolulu, she
was carrying him. He is the most beautiful thing I've ever
seen. Like a little doll, with plump rosy cheeks, a little
button of a nose, and a tiny round head covered with soft
golden hair.

I had another brother, born in California where
Mama and Papa lived before they came to the islands.
But he died of scarlet fever when he was only a few
months old. Mama says he's a little angel in Heaven
now. That's why Mama was so happy to have me after
they came to Oahu. And now we have another little boy
for our family. Isn't God good?

The second important thing is that we moved to the Big Island. My father, Wesley Rutherford, is now principal of a school in Waimea. My father and I came here first. We came by ship and landed in Hilo, then rode in a wagon over to the home of Mr. Caldwell, the superintendent of island schools, where I am to stay until Mama and the new baby come with all our household things.

The next important thing that happened to me: I met Akela and Kimo. They are cousins. They live with their tutu—that's the Hawaiian name for grandmother. She was in Kohala, at the other end of the island, so they were boarding there, too. I mention this because Akela is now my best friend.

Akela will be in my class when school starts. She is very pretty and very sweet. Kimo is twelve, and two years ahead of us. At first I didn't like him at all. He seemed kind of stuck up. Later I found out they belong to the Kanakui family, known by Hawaiians as the alli. They are considered nobility, because they are descended from the ancient chiefs of the islands. I did not know this until Kimo informed me.

Summer 1882

Akela, Kimo, and I go to the beach together most every day. Kimo likes to be the leader in our games. We climb on the banyan trees, build sand forts, and look for shells in the tide pools. We swim in the shallow water. Kimo has a board on which he paddles out beyond the breakers, then catches a wave and rides it in. He showed me how to do it, too. But I kept falling off. I wish I could go barefoot all the time.

❧❦❧

September 1882

Summer is over. I hate for it to end. I love being free of lessons and homework, and only going to the beach all day. School started today. Edith Preston, the daughter of Colonel Preston of the big Preston Ranch, enrolled this year. She was put in our class, since she is the same age as us. She has been tutored at home until now. Her father wants her to go to regular school and have friends on the island. She has dark eyes but golden blond hair, because she is a hapa-haole. Her mother was a Hawaiian princess, Akela's tutu told us. Akela and I haven't decided yet if she will be our friend.

❧❦❧

September 25th

We've decided to be friends with Edith Preston. Her Hawaiian name is Ekika, which we have shortened to Kiki. That's what we call her. She is fun and friendly. I think we're going to like her, even if she is very rich. We have formed a friendship club: Akela and Edith and me.

❧❦❧

October 1882

Kimo is an awful tease. Sometimes I hate him! He does this really maddening thing—he'll pull the ribbon out of my hair and hold it out of my reach while I try to snatch it back. Then he'll recite a terrible singsong:

"Johanna, banana, tee-legged, toe-legged, bow-legged Johanna!" I don't know where he got it, but it makes me really angry.

Tutu Kipola says not to pay any attention to him. "He's just trying out being a man." We had so much fun all summer. Kimo went with us most of the time. At school he hardly speaks to us. He stays with the boys. It isn't mana to talk to girls there except to tease.

~~❦~~

December 1882

Akela and I went up to the Preston Ranch the day after Christmas. Edith showed us all the things she got for Christmas. I never saw so many presents for one person. Edith's big brother, Bayard, is home for Christmas from the school on the mainland. He never paid any attention to us at all till he heard me call Edith by her Hawaiian name, Kiki. Then he yelled at me. He is so stuck up and bossy. Anyway, we got to ride horses and have fun.

~~❦~~

September 1884

I haven't written in here for a long time, because nothing important has happened. This is very important. Kimo is to go to a boarding school in Honolulu, to the Hawaiian Heritage Academy. The fees were provided by a trust fund set up by a wealthy Hawaiian, for pure-blooded Hawaiians only. Akela cannot attend, she told me, because her father was Chinese. Even though I hated Kimo's teasing, I know I shall miss him.

❧❧❧

January 1885

Kimo came home for the Christmas holidays. He has grown a lot. At first we were shy with each other, because it seemed he had been gone such a long time. But after a while it was all right. We will always be friends, I think. At least, I hope so.

❧❧❧

Summer 1885

I haven't written all summer. I've been too busy. So much has happened. Kimo was back on the island from school. He is helping his uncle in his carpentry shop in Kona during the week, and he's only at Tutu's on the weekends. He graduates from Heritage Academy next year and has applied for an apprenticeship to a famous cabinetmaker in Germany! If he gets it, he will be gone two years!

❧❧❧

September 1885

Kimo left for Oahu today. He came to see me last evening to say good-bye. He gave me a beautiful koa wood jewelry box he'd made. He said it was for my birthday, since he won't be here when I turn sixteen. We walked down to the beach together. Kimo wrote in the sand, Kua kau makamaka. In Hawaiian that means, "Forever friends."

The rest of the pages of the memory book were blank. Idly Jana turned them. So much had happened since that last entry. And it all seemed so long ago. Nearly four years. . . .

When had she stopped writing in this book? More to the point, why? Could it be because of her grandmother's wish that only "sunny hours, joy-filled days, and happy memories" be recorded here?

Jana sighed and slowly closed the book. She held it for a minute against her breast, then thoughtfully replaced it and closed the koa box lid.

Was it the Christmas of 1885 when everything had changed for her?

Chapter One

❦

I have something so exciting to tell you two!" declared Edith Preston as she, Jana, and Akela left school one afternoon the first week in December. "I've been dying to tell you."

"What is it, Kiki?" Jana asked, using her friend's Hawaiian name. "Do tell. I love secrets."

"Well, it's not exactly a secret, but I had to wait until everything was arranged. Bayard is bringing home some friends for the Christmas holidays. Papa says I am to invite you both to come stay over New Year's. It will be a *real* house party, the kind Papa and Mama used to have in the old days. Papa says he wants to have the house filled with young people, music. There will be a ball and a rodeo. It will be ever so fun."

Jana looked at Edith. Even in her school uniform of shirtwaist and khaki skirt, she was strikingly beautiful. The combination of golden hair, tawny skin, and dark-brown eyes revealed her mixed heritage. Her mother had been a Hawaiian princess, and her father was the owner of the largest ranch on the island.

"So you will come, won't you?" Edith demanded. She halted, her hands on her slim hips, facing her friends.

485

"I don't know," Jana replied uncertainly. She wasn't at all sure if her parents would allow her to attend such a house party. It might sound too sophisticated.

Bayard Preston, Edith's half brother, was a student at Yale on the mainland. His classmates, the guests he was bringing home, would all be his age, sophisticated college men. Details of Colonel Preston's lavish parties, which were attended by wealthy friends from Honolulu and as far away as San Francisco, fed the gossip mills of Waimea. The Prestons moved in a social world unknown to the conservative Rutherfords.

Although her parents had never done anything to discourage the girls' friendship, Jana's father, Wesley, was the exact opposite of the flamboyant Colonel Preston. She knew that her father disapproved of some of Colonel Preston's projects. His buying up of land and developing it the way he did was one example. Her father often expressed his concern that the very things that seemed to expand the economy also destroyed some of the old ways, the customs of the Hawaiian people. He believed that as more people went to work at the Preston Ranch and other such enterprises, fewer maintained their own small farms and businesses and remained independent.

Her mother's objections would be more personal. She regularly cautioned Jana not to be too impressed by what was taken for granted at the ranch. "Money can't buy happiness, you know." That statement totally bewildered young Jana. Edith, Bayard, and Colonel Preston seemed perfectly happy to her.

These thoughts passed quickly through Jana's mind. Edith looked indignant at her hesitation. She stared at Jana wide-eyed. "Of course you're coming! It's going to be marvelous. Why ever *wouldn't* you come?"

"I'll have to ask," Jana hedged.

By this time, they'd reached the hitching post where Edith, who usually rode to school, tethered her horse, Malakini. As Edith swung herself easily up into the saddle and picked up the reins, she said confidently, "Don't worry. Papa will come and speak to your folks. He can persuade anyone to do anything."

Jana and Akela exchanged a knowing look. Both the other girls were used to their friend's self-assured manner. Rarely did Edith Preston fail to get what she wanted. And no wonder. She had everything: money, position, beauty. Edith rode off, and as they continued walking, Jana asked, "Will you go?"

Akela shook her head. "I don't think so. Our whole family will be celebrating Christmas together in Kona."

Of course, that was to be expected. Immediately the word *ohana* came into Jana's mind. Ohana, the Hawaiian word that symbolized family. A beautiful word, a beautiful reality, which the Kipolas reverenced. But it meant much more. It meant an unbroken circle of relationship that extended beyond the immediate family and included many others. Ohana meant a bond of love that surrounded, protected, the individual so that no one ever needed to feel alone. Jana envied that closeness she'd glimpsed within the ohana. Her own father was an orphan, and her mother's family lived far away in the southern part of the United States.

"But couldn't you even come for a few days?" Jana persisted. "Over New Year's, like Kiki said?"

"Well—" Akela blushed slightly as she said, "Pelo's family will be there, too."

At the mention of Pelo Kimura, Jana gave her a sharp glance. Were Akela's feelings for Pelo more than friendship? They had known each other from childhood, been playmates. Just as *she* and Kimo, Akela's cousin, were.

They had reached the fork of the road where they turned to go to Akela's grandmother's house. No more was said about the Prestons' house party as they started up the winding hill that led to the home. It stood high on a windswept cliff, overlooking a stretch of white-sand beach and a crescent of blue ocean. Through an arched gate, they passed into a garden lush with color—purple, orange, yellow, pink—and fragrant with the mingled scents of hibiscus, gardenias, and plumeria.

They sat down on the porch steps to take off their high-topped boots, as it was Hawaiian custom to remove one's shoes before entering a home.

Unlacing her shoestrings, Jana asked, "What do you want to do when we finish school, Akela?"

Akela looked startled. "Do? I don't know. I haven't thought."

"I want to be an artist."

"You're very good. Your paintings of flowers and all."

"I want to do more than just pretty pictures. I mean *really* paint. My parents want me to go to teachers college in California. They want me to start sending out applications." Jana made a face. "Ugh! I don't want to teach! All I really want to do is stay right here and have my own little studio where I can see the sky and the sea, and paint!"

Akela smiled. "That sounds nice."

"So when we *are* finished with school," Jana persisted, "deep down, what do *you* want to do?"

Akela's expression became dreamy. "I suppose—something like you—stay on the island, be happy."

Just then they heard Akela's grandmother's voice calling, "Is that you, girls? Come in, I've poured some guava juice, and there are fresh cookies."

"Coming, Tutu!" Akela called back.

488

Any further discussion of the future interrupted, they pulled off their stockings, ran up the steps and into the house. Mrs. Kipola, tall and silver haired, stood at the door waiting, holding herself like a duchess.

Pekila Kipola's regal bearing came rightfully. The Kipolas were descendants of an ancient clan of royalty called the *alli*.

Inside it was dim and cool. The girls settled down on the floor on straw mats to sip their juice and munch on crisp macadamia nut cookies while Tutu, seated nearby on a fan-backed rattan chair, picked up one of the quilts on which she was working.

Jana glanced at Tutu, then over at Akela. Hawaiian women were all so beautiful—velvety eyed, satin skinned. Kipola had an unusual face, but one of rare beauty. Her full lips seemed lifted in a perpetual smile. Her nose was strong, the nostrils slightly flared, and her dark eyes shone with an inner light. Akela's beauty was more delicate. Her dark, wavy hair framed a perfect oval face. Her hands were slender, graceful. Beside Akela, Jana was always aware of her own *haole* appearance. She took after her father, having sandy brown hair, hazel eyes, skin inclined to freckle.

"So how was school today?" Tutu asked in her low, melodic voice.

"History!" both answered in unison. Then Akela said, "We're learning about the Civil War and President Lincoln." She looked over at Jana. "Tell Tutu what you told me about your mother and father being at the theater the night Mr. Lincoln was shot, Jana."

Tutu looked up from her quilt, shock replacing her usually serene expression. "How dreadful."

"Yes, it was terrible," Jana nodded. "Mama has a quilt she made—not like the ones you make, Tutu, but one they call a memory quilt or crazy quilt. It's made out of all sorts of different materials and fabrics cut from dresses or cloaks that have special meaning in their lives. Mama was wearing a blue velvet dress that night to the theater. And after the shooting and President Lincoln's death, she vowed she would never wear that dress again. So she cut it into scraps and pieced them together for a quilt. She bound the whole thing with black satin ribbon from the bonnet ribbons she wore to his funeral." Jana paused. "It was all very sad."

"It sounds like a sad quilt, a sad memory to keep," Tutu said mildly.

"Well, it's not *all* sad. The whole quilt, I mean. She also has pieces of her wedding dress in it, and the cloak she wore when she traveled through enemy lines with my father when they were eloping."

"Eloping?" echoed Akela, looking puzzled.

"Yes, isn't that romantic? They had to run away to get married, because Mama's family didn't approve."

"Oh, now *that* is sad," murmured Akela. "To be married without your family! How awful."

Jana looked from one to the other. She saw at once they did not think it romantic at all, but tragic. To be married without your family, your ohana, was truly a tragedy. The bonds of the Hawaiian family were very strong.

They went on to talk of other things, until at length Jana got to her feet reluctantly, saying, "I'd better be going."

"Will you stay and eat with us, Koana?" Tutu asked, using Jana's Hawaiian name. "Uncle Kelo's coming, and there'll be plenty of 'tell story,'" she promised with a throaty chuckle.

"*Mahalo*, Tutu, thank you. I wish I could, but Mama's going to her mission circle this evening, and Papa is over in Kohala at a school board meeting, so I have to be there with Nathan."

Jana's regrets were sincere. She liked nothing better than to be in the midst of the Kipola family. Even an ordinary time there was like a party to her. There was always such relaxed congeniality and laughter, and Tutu's brother was an excellent storyteller. He held them all spellbound with his tales and legends of old Hawaii. He liked best to tell stories about the *menehuenes*, the mysterious "little people" of the islands. They were the Hawaiian equivalent of the brownies, elves, or Irish leprechauns.

After Jana said good-bye, she walked down the hill and along the road past the school, deep in thought.

She was truly sorry to miss what promised to be an entertaining evening. She loved the feeling of being accepted as one of them as she dipped *poi*, the starchy mixture of mashed taro that Hawaiians are weaned to and most *wahines* can't tolerate. The first time she had taken a meal at Tutu's, she hadn't liked it, either. But with Kimo's eyes challenging her, she had defiantly stuck her finger into the calabash, twirled it, and taken a mouthful. Truthfully, she had hardly been able to swallow it, but she had refused to give Kimo a chance to make scornful fun of her. Nowadays she managed to take one or two fingersful just to feel part of the family.

The Kipolas represented what to Jana was truly the best of Hawaii: the *aloha* spirit. She had heard that term used so often by her father that one day she had asked Tutu what it meant.

"What is the aloha spirit? Well, little one, I can only give you my interpretation. The first *a* stands for *akaha'i*, meaning kindness expressed with tenderness. The *l* stands for *lokai*, meaning unity expressed with harmony. The *o* stands for *olu'olu*, meaning agreeableness expressed with pleasantness. The *h* stands for *ha'aha'a*, meaning humility expressed with modesty. The last *a* stands for *ahounu'i*, meaning patience expressed with perseverance. This is the philosophy passed down to me from my ancestors."

Jana understood Tutu's explanation, for it was what she herself found most appealing about the Hawaiians she knew: their warmth, charm, and sincerity.

Why had she hesitated to question Akela about Pelo? For all their closeness, there was a reticence about Akela, an invisible line over which Jana had never crossed.

Jana's friendship with Edith was entirely different. They'd had frequent "falling outs." Both were strong-willed individuals, which led to arguments. They had times when they weren't speaking. Jana found her uncomplicated relationship with Akela much easier. Edith, used to having her own way, tended to be bossy, which Jana refused to tolerate. Edith was independent, impatient, restless—but she was also generous, kindhearted, high-spirited, and fun loving, with an adventurous streak that matched Jana's own. When they were in one of their "spats," Jana found she missed her, so their fights usually did not last long.

One thing they quarreled over was when Edith brought up her royal heritage, haughtily reminding Jana that *her* mother was a Hawaiian princess. Edith would declare that her mother's heritage made her more Hawaiian than Jana. In turn, Jana would furiously argue that *she* had been born on Oahu, while Edith's mother had gone to San Francisco for *her* birth. That made Jana the more Hawaiian of the two. This argument usually ended in a stalemate, with neither girl giving an inch. A few days might pass before they would make up and the old argument would be forgotten.

As they grew up, Jana realized that some of Edith's snobbishness was Colonel Preston's fault. From a prestigious eastern family, the Colonel had come to the island as a young man and made his fortune in cattle ranching, a new enterprise on the island. He had built his hilltop mansion, married an American heiress, and had a son, Bayard. Widowed a few years later, Preston had remarried. She was Edith's mother, who had tragically died two years later.

Edith was the adored, cherished child of this brief, blissful second marriage. Surrounded by luxury, Edith had grown up without discipline, lavished with love. Once Jana accepted that Edith's behavior was not entirely her fault, she overlooked the flaws and loved her wholeheartedly.

Kiki, as she preferred to be called, was so much fun, and going to the ranch such a treat, that it was hardly worth it to stay angry at her long. At the ranch, Jana got to ride, and enjoy the life lived by the Prestons. They were allowed almost unrestricted freedom by Colonel Preston. Wearing wide-brimmed sombreros and split skirts, they rode along with the *paniolos*, Preston's hired cowboys, and watched them herd cattle. These men were colorful characters, with their multistriped ponchos and their boots with jangling spurs. They adored Edith, treating her with a combination of courtesy, respect, and loving indulgence. They showed the girls rope tricks, tried to teach them to lasso and how to cut and herd the cattle.

Yes, Edith Preston's friendship was one Jana valued in spite of their differences.

Within a few days, Edith's prediction proved right. Colonel Preston—big, handsome, jovial, attired in a white linen riding coat, polished boots, and a wide-brimmed Panama plantation hat—cantered up to the Rutherfords' house. Dismounting from his sleek white mare, he marched up the porch steps, carrying an armload of gifts—a bouquet of the spectacular red-gold bird-of-paradise flowers, a basket of fruit from his orchards, bags of macadamia nuts. He then proceeded to charm Jana's mother. His gallantry reminded her of her southern male relatives as she recalled her own North Carolinian background. It took only a half hour's visit to win her approval for Jana to attend the house party. So it was settled that Jana would come up to the Preston Ranch after Christmas to stay over New Year's.

Chapter Two

❧❦❧

The Wednesday before Christmas, Jana took her Sunday school class—children ages five and six who had learned carols in both Hawaiian and English to sing at the midweek evening service—into the small red frame church.

They filed up crooked steps into the little choir loft. Stationed there, she could oversee her charges as well as lead the singing. She also had a view down into the sanctuary.

They had been practicing for weeks, and now the children's clear voices rose sweetly. "O come all ye faithful, *E he-le-mai ou-kou-ka,* joyful and triumphant, *po-e ma-nao i-o . . .*" The beloved song was familiar to her in both languages. It had been sung to her in her cradle by her Hawaiian nurse when they lived on Oahu, and her mother had sung it to her in English. Almost as soon as she could speak, she had sung it, too. Listening to it now in the church, which had been built by some of the earliest missionaries to the island, she sang along with the children.

All at once the words halted in her throat. She saw *him* enter the side door of the church. Kimo!

Akela had told her he was expected home for the holidays, but somehow she hadn't been prepared to see him. Not quite like this. Her heart skipped a beat, and she lost her place in the

495

hymnal. She had not seen him since last summer when he left for his last year at the Heritage Academy in Honolulu.

Memories of their childhood days flashed into her mind: running barefoot along the sandy shore together; swinging on the low limbs of the banyan trees that fronted the missionary compound; eating the bananas and the soft, tangy mangoes and licking the juice from their fingers; building forts and sandcastles and playing pirates at the cove, their own private stretch of the beach. A flood of recollections swept up in her like the rushing tide. Now her childhood playmate was a grown man.

Jana watched his tall figure as Kimo moved into the Kipolas' pew, sat down beside his grandmother, kissed Tutu's cheek. From Jana's viewpoint, his shoulders looked broader. She couldn't seem to stop looking at the back of his head, at how the dark hair grew in waves and clustered at his neck.

It was with a start that she realized the service was over. Quickly she rose with the rest to receive the benediction and join in the closing hymn. The children around her stirred restlessly, eager to be out in the balmy evening. The congregation began its leisurely exit down the aisles of the church, stopping to exchange greetings and hugs with each other. Suddenly Tutu and Kimo seemed to have disappeared in the slow-moving crowd. Jana hurried to the door, shepherding her little group outside. There she had to control her impatience until each child in her charge found a parent. She looked around, frowning. She hoped she hadn't somehow missed the Kipolas. They couldn't have left already, she thought, searching the clusters of people to see if she could spot Tutu's flower-wreathed straw hat. Tall as Kimo's grandmother was, it might be easily seen. But no, there was no sign of her or Kimo. Disappointed, she gave a deep sigh and turned to leave. Just then she heard a teasing voice behind her say, "Johanna, banana—"

She spun around.

There he was. Tall, taller than she remembered. He must have grown at least two inches. His face might have lost its boyish contours, but the mischief was still in his dark eyes, and his grin was just as wide, his square teeth white against his bronze skin. "Kimo! I thought—," she began, then said, "It's been a long time."

"Too long," he said softly. "Aloha, Koana." He put his hands on her shoulders and kissed her on both cheeks. It was the traditional Hawaiian greeting. Jana wondered why it had brought her tinglingly aware of him. Was it the *way* he had said her Hawaiian name that had taken her breath? They stood there in the lavender dusk, looking at each other as if with new eyes.

Jana struggled to regain her sudden loss of composure. "Tutu must be so happy. She's missed you." Her voice didn't sound like her own at all. It was high pitched and shaky.

"I missed her. I missed everything about the island. Every*one*." He paused as if to let the emphasis on the last word register. "We're going to Kona for Christmas, but I'll be back for New Year's. I want to come to pay my respects to your parents. Then we can spend some time together. I have so much to tell you."

Jana was dismayed to find out that Kimo would be gone the entire week. The Prestons' party was planned to start on the twenty-ninth. That meant she wouldn't be at home when Kimo returned from Kona.

"Oh yes, and I . . . The only thing is that—" She broke off. "What?"

"Well, what day will you come? I mean, be back in Waimea? You see, I may not be—" Jana stumbled, flustered. For some reason, she didn't want to use the Prestons' party as an excuse. But there was no other explanation. "You see,

Bayard Preston is coming home for Christmas, and he's bringing some of his friends with him, and ..." Her words sounded
awkward. That wasn't what she wanted to say at all. What
she wanted to say was, "Can't you come to see *me* before you
go to Kona, or come back sooner?"

But as she was speaking, she saw Kimo's expression
change. "In that case ..." He shrugged with a show of indifference, leaving his thought unspoken. Then, tossing back
the lock of silky hair that had fallen forward on his forehead,
he said, "Well, it was nice to see you, Jana. Please give your
parents my regards."

"Thank you, I will," Jana replied lamely.

Wishing her a merry Christmas and a happy New Year in
Hawaiian—"*Mele Kalikamaka* and *hau'oli Makahiki Hou*"—
Kimo turned from her.

"Mele Kalikamaka, Kimo," she repeated through numb
lips. Helplessly she watched him walking away. In desperation, she called after him, "Give Tutu my love."

He looked around, hesitated a second, then nodded,
waved his hand, and was swallowed up in the crowd of congenial people still gathered in front of the church.

Slowly Jana walked home. All her happiness at seeing
Kimo again drained away, leaving her feeling let down.

The change in him had taken place when she mentioned
Bayard Preston's name. Suddenly she wished she weren't
going to the Prestons' house party. Now she would miss Kimo
when he came to pay his duty call on her parents. She
wouldn't be there to walk with him down to the beach or
down to the valley of the twin waterfalls. Somehow she had
managed to ruin their meeting, the one she had looked forward to all these months.

When she reached home, she let herself in quietly, still
feeling subdued by the puzzling encounter with Kimo. As she

made her way down the hall to her own bedroom, she passed her little brother's room and paused.

She could hear her mother's voice with its southern accent, talking to Nathan as she got him ready for bed.

"And when I was a little girl, just about your age, on Christmas Eve we would hope and hope for it to snow."

"And did it?" Nathan's eager question came.

"Sometimes, but not often. Even if it didn't snow in town where we lived, we could see it up on the mountains—"

"Like on Mauna Kea?"

"Well yes, sort of like that. Except that for us the mountains weren't away far in the distance but were all around the town, like encircling arms." A tinge of nostalgia now crept into her mother's tone. "But the air was as crisp and cold as you can imagine. So much so that our noses and cheeks would be as red as cherries. Best of all, if it *did* snow, Uncle Myles would get out the sleigh and it would be getting dark and all the stars would come out, twinkling, and we would go skimming along the icy roads over to Holly Grove...."

Holly Grove. The very name seemed to have a certain magic. Jana remembered her mother telling *her* the same Christmas memories when she was Nathan's age.

"The house would be all decorated, with candles in every window and a fire roaring in the fireplace...."

Jana could imagine Nathan's eyes getting big with wonder by now. He had not the slightest idea what a fireplace was. It was all like a fairy tale to him.

Jana realized, perhaps for the first time, that talking about Christmases back in North Carolina was important to her mother. Jana suspected there was still a longing in her mother's heart for the place she had left long ago, the people she would never see again. The place that was her "heart home," even now that her home was with all of them here in Hawaii.

Jana could sense that her mother longed to see the pine trees and the dogwoods on the distant mountains that surrounded her North Carolina home, longed to enjoy the autumn colors that blazed scarlet, bronze, gold, and longed to hear the soft cadence of southern voices. Now especially, at Christmas time, those yearnings took form and shape in the telling of the stories to her children. That was the reason, Jana thought, that her mother tried to bring to life for them what was still real for her. Her "tell story" was exactly like what Hawaiians did to keep the old times, the traditions, the customs, alive for the next generation.

Jana smiled. Her mother was not that far removed from Tutu or the other Hawaiian mothers.

For Jana, Christmas was not the sound of sleigh bells ringing out in the frosty evening air, or snow-clad fields, or frozen ponds on which steel blades made their sharp clink against the ice. It was the brilliant red of anthuriums blooming by the roadside, the clusters of poinsettias growing wild, the whisper of palm fronds in the soft sigh of the wind, the singing of the surf, and the music of the ukulele and guitar strings.

Jana knew she had a "heart home," too. But it would always be Hawaii. She was sure that if she were ever away, she would be soul-sick for the seamless blending of blue sky and sea. In her deepest being, she would never be quite happy away from the Big Island.

Chapter Three

〜❧〜

he Rutherfords' Christmas was full of traditions, ones
JoBeth had brought to Hawaii from her childhood in
North Carolina. Stockings were hung up the night before
and magically filled in the morning. The Quaker background
of Jana's father precluded too much emphasis on Santa Claus.
But her mother's persuasive plea—"After all, Nathan is still
only a baby"—had won over his mild objections. So everyone agreed to perpetuate the myth for his sake.

Of course, the religious significance of the day was reverently observed. After the gaiety and laughter of emptying the
stockings and exchanging small gifts, the family went to the
morning church service.

Entering the sanctuary, Jana looked around hopefully to
see if Kimo by some chance had not gone to Kona. But there
were other people sitting in the pew usually occupied by the
Kipolas. With a resigned sigh, she seated herself and opened
her Bible to Luke 2:1: "And it came to pass in those days that
a decree went out from Caesar . . ."

She tried to concentrate on the sermon. The minister
drew some parallels between that long-ago event in Bethlehem and life on the island. "Although pictures sometimes
portray the scene of a snow-shrouded stable," he said, "in

truth the weather in Bethlehem the night Jesus was born was probably more like that of the Big Island." He suggested, "We Hawaiians should feel particularly close to the Savior in this beautiful place so abundantly blessed with God's creation."

Jana responded to that and felt momentarily uplifted by it. However, her mind wandered. How was Kimo spending Christmas? Had he gone to one of the other small frame churches whose twins dotted the whole island? Then, as she joined in the singing of the familiar ancient melodies in Hawaiian—"Hark the herald angels sing, glory to the new-born King, *Ha-mau e na ka-na-ka, mele mai na a-ne-la*"—it struck her that all over the world, in some places at this very same moment, voices were raised in songs of praise. To God, she thought, the world must seem like one gigantic patch-work quilt with all sorts of colors, textures, patterns—but all one as they sing of his glorious birth, of the new birth possible for all those who believe. Jana's heart was all at once full, bursting with happiness, as she sang the chorus: "Joyful all ye nations rise, *Malu no ko la-lo-nei*."

On the way home, she swung Nathan's hand as they hurried along the road, singing the merry secular holiday song she had taught him—"Jingle Bells"—until they were both breathless and laughing.

The rest of the day was spent quietly and happily. She helped Nathan build with the block set he'd received, helped her mother set out the punch, and decorated cookies for the open house they usually held for friends in the afternoon. But all the time she half hoped that maybe Kimo had come back early from Kona and still might drop by to see her.

By late afternoon she had given up. By evening, after a sleepy Nathan had been put to bed clutching his new toy boat, she kissed her parents good night and, taking the book they had given her, went to her bedroom. However, her eyes merely skimmed the pages, and she found herself reading the same paragraph over and over. Finally she put it aside. It was no use. She kept thinking of Kimo, of that brief encounter, wishing she had it to do again, wishing she hadn't told him about the house party, wishing even that she wasn't going.

No, that was silly. What difference would it make whether she went or stayed home? Kimo had never been a special friend of the Prestons. Why should he feel hurt that he had not been included in the invitation? No, she knew it wasn't that. Had he expected her to just sit around and wait for him to come by? She thought of all the letters she had written him when he was at the academy in Honolulu. From him there had been only a few postcards, pictures of the Iolani Palace, the gardens, a few lines scribbled, nothing personal. What had he thought of some of the things she had enclosed in her letters? The quotations, the bits of poetry, the small sketches or paintings she had done?

But after all, hadn't *he* written on the sand the same words she had written in her letters? Of course, the ocean had washed up on the beach, erasing those words. Had Kimo also wiped them out of his mind, his heart?

Hawaiian men were stubborn, proud, reluctant to express emotions, Tutu had told her. They were afraid to seem weak or womanlike. But there was exquisite expression in the songs they composed or in their beautiful crafts. Jana took out the koa wood box Kimo had made for her, let her fingers move across its smooth surface. Giving it to her had meant something to him *then*. Did it still?

She put it back in her drawer again. Her mouth pressed into a straight line. Well, she wasn't going to let worries about Kimo spoil the rest of the holidays. She was going to the house party at the Prestons' and would have a good time, in spite of Kimo.

Chapter Four

~e~

$\mathcal{J}$ana could hardly contain her excitement as her father drove their small buggy up the winding driveway hedged with hibiscus and oleander bushes ablaze with blossoms, past groves of coconut palms. Beyond the gates and the arched sign that read "PRESTON RANCH," at the top of the hill stood a sprawling, white frame ranch house. Its architecture was a mixture of traditional Hawaiian plantation and New England–style farmhouse.

Mr. Rutherford had just pulled to a stop in front of the wraparound veranda, when almost immediately one of the Prestons' Chinese menservants came running out of the house. Dressed in a uniform of immaculate white duck coat and trousers, he smilingly greeted them. He took Jana's suitcase and valise and motioned them to precede him up the porch steps while he followed, carrying her bags.

Through the screen door, they saw a large woman coming down the center hall, seeming even larger because of the ballooning of her *mumu*—the Hawaiian "at home" dress—made of flowing, lavishly flowered pink, yellow, and green material.

Jana recognized her at once as Meipala, the housekeeper. She had been Edith's nurse when she was a baby and a little girl, then had stayed on to run the household.

"Aloha!" the woman called to them as she approached. Meipala was handsome, with polished mahogany skin and a halo of crystal-sparkled silver hair. "Aloha! Welcome, Mr. Rutherford, Jana." She pulled the screen door wide for them to enter. "Come in and have some refreshment," she invited. "The Colonel and Edith are out riding, showing Bayard's friends around the ranch. But they should be back soon."

"Mahalo, thank you, but I cannot stay." Mr. Rutherford made his refusal of the offered hospitality—a Hawaiian ritual—gracious yet firm. "Duties, you know. Please give my kind regards to the Colonel, though, and thank him for having my daughter as his guest."

"Oh, *this* one!" Meipala gave Jana a hug. "*She's* like part of the family."

"Good enough. Then, I'll be on my way. Jana, have a nice time and be a good guest."

"I will, Papa."

"Don't worry, Mr. Rutherford," Meipala told him. "I'll keep my eye on both young ladies. And it's Edith, not Jana, who has to be reminded of manners!"

"I'm glad to hear it." He smiled, then leaned down, kissed Jana's cheek. "Good-bye, dear. Have a good time."

After the Rutherfords' buggy disappeared around the bend of the driveway, Meipala put her arm around Jana's shoulders. "Well, now, *kaikamahine*," she said, using the affectionate word for "girl-child," "I have to tell Cook something, and then I'll be right back and we'll go upstairs and I'll show you which room you're to have."

"I won't be in Edith's room with her?" Jana asked, surprised.

"No, not *this* time. You'll be in one of the guest rooms— that way you two won't stay up and gossip half the night." Meipala pretended to look stern—an impossible feat, since any movement of her generous mouth showed deep dimples. "But it's right next to Edith's room, so you two will manage!" she chuckled. Then she said, "I'll be back *wikiwiki*," and she waddled off to the back of the house.

Left alone in the wide front hall, Jana gazed about her in awe. No matter how many times she visited the ranch, entering the house always seemed like walking into a palace. Overhead was a huge rock-crystal chandelier hanging from the ceiling. It might have looked out of place in most ranch houses, yet here it belonged. The Prestons' house was filled with such contrasts. Chinese rugs on polished floors of native wood, teakwood furniture, and carved screens mingled with ornately carved Victorian chairs and settees upholstered in red flocked damask.

Through open louvered doors, Jana could see into the drawing room that opened onto the lanai. A huge painting framed in heavily sculptured gold took up most of one wall. Edith had once pointed it out to Jana, telling her that at one time it had hung in a French museum. Her father had seen it on one of his trips abroad, wanted it, bought it, and brought it home. Imagine!

Along the other wall were glass shelves displaying artifacts of Old Hawaii. Above a wide, handsome, native stone fireplace, an antique Austrian mirror reflected the rest of the room's splendor. In the center of the room stood a round koa wood table with intricately carved legs, holding a glass bowl of pink, red anthuriums.

The sound of Meipala's heavy tread on the polished floor signaled the housekeeper's return. "Everything fine in the kitchen. Getting ready for *pa'ina*, dinner party, tonight. Bayard's pals here." She rolled her dark, merry eyes. "Big doin's." She picked up Jana's suitcase and motioned with the other plump hand. "Come along, I'll take you upstairs."

Jana followed with her valise. "Where are Bayard's guests staying?"

"Colonel put 'em out in one of the cottages." There were three guest cottages located under the kukui trees behind the house. They were self-sufficient, complete, small units—consisting of two bedrooms, a sitting room, a bath, and a lanai—where Colonel Preston's guests could stay for months at a time, and often did. "I think Colonel figured that out there, away from the main house, those boys could make much *kulikuli*, high jinks, and not disturb anyone else." Meipala laughed, a deep laugh that shook her whole body, as if she thought that young men having a loud good time was a great joke.

At the top of the stairs, Jana caught up with Meipala and walked alongside her down the long hall. "Here you are," Meipala announced, opening the door into a large, airy room. "I got plenty to do," she told Jana, "but you can settle yourself until Edith gets here, *pono?*"

"Right. Yes, I'll be fine," Jana assured her.

❦

After Meipala hurried off, Jana looked around with delight at the luxurious room she was to occupy. Sheer curtains billowed at the floor-length windows, which opened up to a second-story circling porch overlooking the lawns and gardens. Dominating the room was an enormous bed with turned railings and carved pineapple posts. It was covered with a beautiful Hawaiian quilt, a design of pale green breadfruit leaves appliquéd onto a creamy background.

Compared to her simply furnished room at home, this was ultimate luxury. *I feel like a princess!* Jana thought as she began unpacking her suitcase, hanging up her clothes in the armoire.

She heard Edith before she saw her. There was no mistaking that gay, laughing voice calling her name, the sound of bare feet running down the hall.

"Jana!"

In the next minute, Edith burst into the room. Grabbing Jana by the arms, she whirled her around a couple of times.

"Oh, I'm so glad you could come! We are going to have a glorious time. Just wait till you see. And just wait until you meet Bayard's friends!" Edith stopped breathlessly and looked around her. "Let me see what you've brought!" She dashed over to the armoire, where Jana had just hung up some of her dresses. Edith held out the skirt of one of the dresses. "Oh, your mother is so clever. You are so lucky, Jana. All my things are store-bought. Aunt Ruthie did send me some dresses from San Francisco. I'll show you later."

As if she had suddenly lost interest in clothes, Edith tossed her hat carelessly off, not noticing that it landed on the floor. Then, shaking out her tangle of golden curls, she plopped down on the bed.

"Bayard's friends are incredible, Jana. One is the captain of the debating team, the other of the tennis club, and the other one—oh, I forget, but something interesting. We are going to have such a good time. We shall be included in everything. I made that crystal-clear to Bayard." Her tone turned severe. "He promised. We are *not* to be sent upstairs or pushed out of sight like babies, as we used to be—this time, we are *in* the party!" She laughed gaily. "In fact, we *are* the party. At least until some of Bayard's Honolulu crowd gets here. They've taken practically a whole deck of the steamer from Oahu. But," she declared, "by the time they get here, we will have them all eating out of our hands! Now all we have to do is plan our strategy."

Amid peals of laughter, Edith outlined for Jana their plan of action. Since she had met the three young men, she gave Jana a brief description of each one. "I've only had a chance to look them over after they first arrived, because of course

Bayard was in his usual form. In total control. But they are all attractive. I've already picked out *mine*. Greg Amory." She giggled. "But he'll not have any idea of it. Instead, I shall act indifferent to him and interested in someone else—Tom Markham. Really a quiet, serious type—I can't think why Bayard would be friends with him. Maybe he coaches Bayard on economics or math!" She picked up one of the pillows, bunched it up, flipped over onto her stomach, and hugged it, laughing.

Amazed, Jana looked at her friend. "Where on earth did you learn all this?" she demanded.

"Oh, I've been doing my homework!" Edith reached under the bed and brought out two glossy magazines and held them up so Jana could read the titles—*Metropolitan Ladies*. "These are full of all kinds of articles, from the latest hairstyles to how to use 'complexion enhancements' subtly, to examples of witty dinner table conversation, to the latest dance steps, to rules of flirtation!"

"You mean, they have *rules* for such things?" gasped Jana.

Edith rolled her eyes. "We have been living in kiddieland, Jana. Girls our age on the mainland go to tea dances and evening parties all the time. To *college* proms! Bayard and his friends are *used* to girls who know their way around—not only how to dance, but how to flirt and how to tease and talk to men. It's all a sort of game, you see. Not at all like we're used to—but we can *learn*." She flipped open one of the magazines, then handed it to Jana. "Just look at that."

Jana's eyes traveled quickly down the page, which was headed "Be Interested in Whatever He Is Interested in." She threw the magazine back at Edith. "That sounds stupid to me. Dishonest! Why should we pretend, like this is some kind of childish game of make-believe? Surely you don't believe all this drivel?"

Edith looked indignant. "Well, it's worth a try! I don't intend to be ignored, as we usually are when Bayard is here." Flinging back her hair, she lifted her chin defiantly, her eyes flashing. "*You* can suit yourself, but I'm sure going to try it." Edith shrugged. "And *tonight*."

Jana shook her head. "I don't think I can change that much. Be any way but just me."

"I don't mean *change*, Jana. I just don't want to be treated like a child anymore. Not by Bayard and not by his friends. *You* can do what you want."

Jana stared at Edith with a mixture of dismay and admiration. Edith was so pretty, so confident. She seemed charged with joyous energy at the prospect of waging a campaign to capture one of her brother's classmates. For her it *was* a game.

Suddenly Jana realized it was a game that she had no idea how to play.

Chapter Five

❧

That evening Jana was dressed first. She was waiting at the top of the stairway, ready to go down to dinner, when Edith came flying out into the hall. Her hair, swept up in a new style, had not been secured properly, and hairpins went scattering in her wake.

"Uh-oh! I'd better go back and fix it!" she exclaimed and went running back to her room.

Jana, who was wearing her hair in the usual way—tied back with a bow—smiled resignedly. There was no use complaining. Kiki was determined to present a grown-up image tonight. And that evidently meant pinning her hair up, however inexpertly.

Jana wandered over to examine the life-size portrait of Edith's mother that hung in the alcove of the landing. Jana had seen many photographs of her. They were all over the house. She had never really studied this gold-framed painting. In it, Ketura Preston, although she was dressed in a gown designed by a famous Parisian clothier and was holding an ostrich-plume fan in one graceful hand, looked every inch the Hawaiian princess she had been.

Looking at it closely, Jana decided that Edith looked more like her mother than she had realized. Except for their coloring. Edith was blond, while Ketura's hair was a gleaming black. However, their features were very much alike. Both had a small, delicate nose, dark eyes, a full, curved mouth. Gazing at the portrait, Jana felt a twinge of pity for her friend growing up without a mother. No wonder Edith was the way she was sometimes.

"All right, I'm ready now. How does it look?" Edith put a tentative hand to the French twist she had managed to achieve, if imperfectly. "Do I look at least eighteen? Twenty?" she asked hopefully.

"You look lovely!" Jana laughed and tucked her hand into her friend's arm and pulled her toward the stairway. "You'll be the star of the evening."

Jana didn't realize how true her teasing prediction would prove to be.

Reaching the last step, they heard the murmur of male voices coming from the lanai, through the drawing room doors. Outside, a purple dusk was just falling. Tiki torches on the lawn illuminated the lanai, where Bayard and his guests were gathered with Colonel Preston. Edith dropped one eyelid in a conspiratorial wink. "Come on, let's make our grand entrance."

"Wait, Kiki," Jana protested mildly, feeling suddenly shy about meeting all these strangers. But it was no use. Edith pulled her relentlessly forward.

"Good evening, gentlemen," Edith announced gaily.

Three white-linen-jacketed backs were to the doorway, and Colonel Preston and Bayard were facing it. At Edith's voice, all three turned with eager smiles. Colonel Preston's face was immediately wreathed in an indulgent smile of welcome.

"My daughter, Edith, and her friend Jana Rutherford, gentlemen," he announced. "Welcome, ladies."

Jana caught Bayard's surprised and rather disapproving expression. Why? she wondered. Didn't he like to see his little sister in her new grown-up appearance? That first impression of Bayard's reaction to their entrance lingered. Did his disapproval include her as well? Was he annoyed that the two girls he remembered as children were being admitted to the grown-ups' party?

She recalled the first time she had seen Bayard Preston. She had been an eleven-year-old girl, he a seventeen-year-old prep-school boy home for the summer. To Jana, in a way, he had always seemed like a royal prince out of the pages of a fairy tale. Tall, athletic, he had the same tawny gold hair that Edith had inherited from their father. Bayard's manner had been a combination of arrogance and condescension, all characteristics she attributed to royalty.

Even though he had treated Edith and her friends with lofty indifference, it was no more than the young Jana expected of a prince. The Preston Ranch was like a kingdom, with its own rules, activities, behavior. Although Bayard had mostly ignored her, Jana had observed *him*. He seemed as at ease among his father's friends as he was among the *paniolos*. He could ride with the best of them and was fearless in the saddle.

All three of Bayard's guests were tall, well built, nice looking. They did, however, look pale. Of course, they would be, having come from the mainland, where it was midwinter. They were introduced to her as Joel Matthews, Tom Markham, Greg Amory. Then Edith said to Bayard, "You remember Jana Rutherford, don't you, Bayard?"

Bayard lifted an eyebrow. "Not looking like *this*." He moved forward and took Jana's hand, his eyes amused. "Not all grown up. When did this happen?"

513

"It's a natural process, I'm told," she replied, not meaning to sound clever or flippant. But everyone laughed, including Bayard.

His steady gaze made her feel uncomfortable. She turned away from him to address Joel Matthews, whose boyish good looks and nice smile were less threatening and who seemed eager to talk to her.

"How do you like the island so far?" she asked him.

"It's beautiful. I had no idea. It's my first trip to the islands, you see. . . ." This enthusiastic response was all that someone who loved Hawaii as much as Jana could hope for. They immediately fell into conversation, which was interrupted eventually by the mellow sound of the dinner gong being struck.

Joel offered Jana his arm, and they started into the dining room. On the way, she showed him the brass Chinese gong, suspended between teakwood posts, used by one of the servants to signal that dinner was being served.

Ceiling fans whirred over the beautifully set table, making the large dining room refreshingly cool. Each place held gold-rimmed, hand-painted china settings, crystal goblets.

Seated next to Jana, Joel immediately resumed their conversation.

"After Bayard's invitation, I read everything I could find about the Hawaiian Islands, and I must say, they've more than lived up to my imagination. I hope you realize how lucky you are to live here. What a climate, what gorgeous flowers, what colors. My mother is an avid gardener, and she fusses and hovers over her flowers constantly, but her best prize blooms don't compare with what I've seen here. She'd go out of her mind to see what grows wild on this island."

"I guess we're so used to it, we don't realize how it must seem to *malihinis*."

"Malihinis?" Joel looked puzzled.

"Oh, sorry! Malihinis. Tourists, mainlanders. That's Hawaiian."

"So you speak the language, too?"

"Of course. I was born here."

"Good grief. I didn't realize. What I mean to say is, I hadn't thought of people like you—like *us*—actually being *born* here. Being natives, so to speak."

"Bayard was. Didn't you know?"

"Bayard? Well yes, I guess so. Just never thought. I mean, he's so typically a Yaley! I guess with Bayard having gone to prep school in New England and then on to college there, like we all did—Greg, Tom, and me—I never actually thought of *him* as being Hawaiian."

"Of course, his parents were both *haoles*. Mainlanders. Both the Colonel and Bayard's mother are not of Hawaiian ancestry. But Bayard was born right here. Now, *Edith's* mother, the Colonel's second wife, *was* Hawaiian. From a royal family, actually—the alli, the clans of ancient chieftains who were here before the white men came."

Joel shook his head. "Fascinating."

Suddenly Jana was conscious that Bayard was regarding her intently. Her cheeks grew warm. She wondered if he had overheard her giving Joel the background of the Preston family. And if he had, did he mind? Flustered, she turned back to Joel. However, now Joel was engaged in a conversation with Edith, who was on his other side, and Jana was left momentarily to her own thoughts.

She chanced another quick look at Bayard. Elegantly dressed in a white linen dinner jacket, starched shirt, and black tie, he looked even more handsome than she'd remembered. At the ranch, where she usually saw him, he wore the rough clothes of the paniolos with whom he rode.

She knew he was a daring rider. Once, she and Edith had overheard a tongue-lashing that the Colonel was giving him for some reckless stunt. They had been in the hall outside the library when the sound of the Colonel's voice, raised angrily, reached them.

"What are you trying to do, break your neck—or worse, get yourself killed?" Colonel Preston had shouted. "Don't you know that this ranch, everything, will someday belong to you? That is, if you don't land in a ditch, or down a cliff, with your fool stunts. Listen to me, young man. I don't ever want to hear of you risking yourself so foolishly again, do you understand?"

Edith, startled, had clutched Jana's arm so tightly that it had left marks. Subdued, shaken, they had tiptoed down the hall and run upstairs, not wanting to be caught eavesdropping.

For some reason that incident came back to Jana now. It took Joel's touching her arm and repeating something to bring her back to the present. "Tell me about the language," Joel urged. "It sounds so musical when it's spoken."

"The Hawaiian language has only a dozen letters. The five English vowels plus *h, k, l, m, n, p,* and *w*. Sound every letter, even in a string of vowels. Usually you put the accent on the next-to-last syllable."

"Amazing," Joel said with honest awe. "We struggle with Latin at college, but none of us speak a second language. I think it's the American arrogance. Even when traveling in Europe, nobody seems to bother to learn the language of the country in which they're traveling. Instead, we rely on phrase books. Actually, it's insulting to the people of that country."

Listening to Joel's comments, she was impressed by such sensitivity in a man so young. How did he happen to be friends with Bayard Preston, who was about as indifferent to others' feelings as anyone she knew? She glanced across the table at Bayard now. He was telling a long, wild tale about some college prank in which he and a friend had been involved, making it sound hilarious rather than relating how humiliating it must have been for the poor student on whom the practical joke had been played. But that was Bayard— only concerned with himself.

As dinner progressed, the room came alive with gaiety. Colonel Preston could be the most gracious of hosts. The conversation was spirited, punctuated with cross-table quips and laughter. Once or twice more Jana caught Bayard's gaze upon her. There was something challenging in it. Like a dare of some kind. She was reminded of Colonel Preston's warning to his son about his irresponsibility. What reckless venture did Bayard have in mind?

It wasn't long until she found out.

After dinner, back in the drawing room, Colonel Preston suggested that Edith play the piano. When she demurred, he insisted. Edith knew better than to argue further. Throwing a resigned glance at Jana, Edith took her place at the grand Steinway. While everyone was finding seats, Bayard came up behind Jana, took her by the arm, and quietly led her out onto the lanai.

"Isn't this rude?" she whispered.

"I've heard Edith play before—dozens of times—and you must have, too," he said. "I've heard her practicing for years, for heaven's sake. Besides, I wanted to talk to you, and Joel has been monopolizing you all evening."

Jana tugged at her arm and he dropped his grip. The lanai was silver swept with moonlight. The fragrance from the gardenia bushes that bordered it sweetened the night air with a heavy, exotic scent.

Bayard drew a long breath. "You forget about all this when you're gone. It's like learning about the island all over again when you come back. Things change and yet this place remains, somehow, strangely the same." He turned toward her. "Except you. *You've* changed. You're all grown up. I can't seem to get over it. How much you've changed."

Jana didn't repeat the retort she'd made to that same remark earlier.

"Sorry, that was quite blunt for me to say. I don't mean to offend you. My only excuse is that I had the same reaction when I saw Edith. You see, she's always been my little sister to me. I've thought of her that way, talked about her that way. It never occurred to me when I brought home my friends that—well, you see what I mean? I find she's become a young lady. Pretty, beautiful even, and too flirtatious for her own good. Certainly attractive to my friends. Did you notice how Tom was drawn like a moth to a flame? And how Edith was enjoying every minute?"

Jana was amused that Bayard seemed genuinely bewildered by his little sister's transformation. She wondered what Bayard would think if he knew this was exactly how Edith had planned it. Of course, she would never betray her friend.

"Not to say that Joel isn't equally taken with *you*," was his next comment.

"Me? Oh, you're mistaken. He's just very interested in learning about Hawaii, so—"

"Don't be naive," Bayard scoffed. "He could find all that out in a travel book. He is getting immense enjoyment out of hearing it from you."

Astonished, she nevertheless couldn't help being a little pleased at this. Especially to have Bayard notice. Still, she had not consciously used any of the "feminine wiles" Edith had been lecturing her on before dinner.

"You have no idea how very attractive you are, do you, Jana?" Bayard asked, looking at her with his head to one side, as if contemplating her. He took a step toward her, put his forefinger under her chin, tipped it up, studied it in the moonlight. "Know what went through my mind when Edith introduced you? I thought, 'Impossible. That skinny, freckle-faced, long-legged tomboy? Turned into this lovely creature?'"

Jana took a step back from him.

"I'm sorry," Bayard apologized. "I didn't mean to—" He halted. "You *are* quite lovely, but thank God, you don't realize it. At least, not yet. Heaven help us when you do."

He moved away, walked to the edge of the lanai, looked out toward the sea. "I forget how beautiful it is here. I go for weeks at a time—forgetting how I feel when the ship moves into the harbor and I see those steep green cliffs, the rim of blue water rolling up on the beaches. My heart twists in my chest." He turned around, almost glared at Jana. "Do you know what I mean? No, of course you don't. You've never been off this island, and neither has Edith."

He spun around suddenly and said abruptly, "Don't mind me, Jana. I'm always like this my first week back on the island." He changed the subject. "So tell me, what are you planning to do when you finish at the island school? Go to the mainland?"

"I want to be an artist. I'd really like to go to some art school, but my parents think—well, they want me to go to teachers college, which is probably the right thing to do."

"Not follow your own heart?" There was an edge of discernible bitterness in Bayard's voice. "Is that wise, little Jana? There's a quote from somewhere—I don't know where exactly—that speaks of the 'long eternity of regret.' Have you thought of that? No, probably not. Don't mind me. I'm probably transferring some of my own frustration to you." He paused. "You don't have a clue as to what I mean, do you?"

Before Jana could comment, the piano music inside stopped abruptly. Edith's impatient voice reached them, saying, "Oh, that's enough, Papa. Our guests' polite patience has been taxed enough with my playing. After all, I'm not a concert artist!"

A few minutes after that, their mingled voices and laughter floating ahead of them, the rest of the group joined them on the lanai.

Later Jana wondered how her strange conversation with Bayard would have gone if they hadn't been interrupted. Part of what Bayard had been saying touched her. She thought she understood, but she did not know how to express that understanding.

After the others joined them on the lanai, Bayard became once again the genial host. Tom borrowed Edith's ukulele, and the fellows regaled them with college songs. To everyone's surprise, it was Edith who made the first move to end the evening. With an exaggerated yawn, she said, "I'm calling it a night. Tomorrow we go on a sunrise ride and picnic at the head of the valley, remember. Knowing Papa, he'll have us up at dawn. Come on, Jana. Let's tear ourselves away from this fine company." Edith grabbed Jana's hand and playfully dragged her toward the house. "Good night, gentlemen. See you all in the morning."

There were murmurs of protest, but finally the good nights were said and the girls left.

The minute they were inside, Edith rushed Jana across the hallway, up the stairway, and down the corridor till they reached their rooms. There she clapped one hand across her mouth and burst into giggles.

"Didn't I tell you it would work?" she demanded. "I believe I've made a conquest in Tom! And Joel is certainly smitten with *you*," she declared. "Oh, this is such fun! I didn't realize how much fun it would be!"

Jana didn't say anything. She was still thinking about her conversation with Bayard, which was far from "fun." In fact, it had been quite disturbing.

Why had he chosen her to confide in, to pour out such deep feelings to? Although his words had touched something deep within her, how could he have known that they would?

Chapter Six

❧❧❧

The next morning, when Jana and Edith came down dressed for riding, the sun was just barely tinting pink clouds with gold. Through the open front door, they saw that Colonel Preston was outside, overseeing the loading of the wagon that was to follow them down into the valley, packed with food for their picnic breakfast. Bayard and his friends were out on the lanai, gathered around a table presided over by Meipala, who was pouring glasses of pineapple juice and dispensing fragrant Kona coffee from a silver urn.

Bayard brought a cup over to Jana. "How do you manage to look so fresh at this hour?"

"Spotless conscience," she smiled, taking the cup from him. "Mahalo."

He raised an eyebrow, then said, "Lucky you. Greg maneuvered us into a card game, and we didn't break up until after 2 A.M."

"No willpower?"

Bayard grinned. "I was winning. Can't pull out then."

Joel came over and joined them. "Your father says that only experienced riders should go down into the valley." He looked at Jana. "Are *you?*"

"Of course she is," Bayard answered for her. "She's an islander, after all."

"I haven't been on a horse much lately," Joel said hesitantly.

"Then, maybe you'd better not," Bayard said with a shrug.

"Colonel Preston's horses are all well trained. If you just sit back in the saddle and hang on, you'll be fine," Jana assured him. She gave Bayard a reproachful look. He shouldn't have been sarcastic to his guest. There wasn't time for any more discussion, because Colonel Preston clapped his hands and declared, "Saddle up, folks. We're ready to ride."

In front of the house, two of the ranch hands had brought up saddled horses, and the Colonel assigned a mount to each of Bayard's friends. Edith swung expertly upon Malakini, and Jana was helped to mount the sweet-tempered mare she usually rode when at the ranch.

Jana knew that Waipi'o Valley was considered by islanders to be one of the unrecognized wonders of the world. It was where the menehuenes were supposed to live, in the deep rain forests. The valley featured great soaring cliffs with waterfalls that fell a thousand feet and glittering lava beaches that looked like acres of black diamonds. Orchids bloomed, and the white-blossomed coffee plants called "Kona snow" grew.

She also knew that the way down on horseback, an almost perpendicular trail to the bottom, was a frightening test of courage, at least the first time. She could not help but wonder if it had been such a good idea to take these mainlanders on such a scary trip. Of course, that was Bayard and Colonel Preston's decision, not hers. She realized that Bayard and Edith had done it often, challenging each other. The competition between brother and sister had always been fierce.

She had not been down into the valley this year. Her schoolwork—including her extra studies in math and science with her father, who was preparing her for college entrance exams next fall—had taken much time. Time she used to spend with Edith at the ranch.

As the group started out in the beautiful morning with its fresh, flower-scented air, Joel fell back to ride alongside her.

"Bayard says this valley is special. Spectacular views, that sort of thing. True?"

"If you've thought Hawaii beautiful thus far, you're going to be really impressed. The valley *is* spectacular."

"I'm sure it has a story," Joel smiled. "Like everything else here."

"Of course," Jana nodded. "It was once called the Valley of the Kings. It is where the great Kamehameha was taken for safety after his birth, to become the great warrior king who defeated all the other chiefs and united the islands into one sovereign state."

The pace picked up, with Edith and Bayard at the head of the group as the riders thundered through the small, sleepy town of Waimea, their horses' hooves pounding the dusty streets. Waimea looked like a transported New England village, with its brightly painted wooden houses decorated with gingerbread on porches and roof peaks. As they rode by, the cool wind held mingled smells of the rich countryside, as well as the briny smell of the ocean. On the way to the valley, they passed hillsides of macadamia nut orchards, sugarcane fields. At last they came to the head of the valley.

Even though she had made this trip a number of times, there was always that heart-chilling moment when they reached the top of the torturous path. They would have to go single file down the steep, wooded hillsides stretching down to the valley half a mile below, where a river wound its way between patches of taro, the plant from which poi is made.

First Colonel Preston and Edith started down. Bayard had pulled to one side, letting his guests go next—he would follow, going last. Jana heard him say, "Your turn, Jana. I'll be right behind you."

She held her breath. Her hands tightened on the reins as her horse stepped off the cliff and began the descent. Her heart pounded. Once started, there was no turning back. She always forgot how steep it was, but she never dared look over the sheer drop into the valley. She was conscious of Bayard behind her, saying, "Lean back in your stirrups, Jana." Instinctively she shut her eyes and leaned forward, putting both arms around the horse's neck. Her horse, Palani, was as surefooted as a mountain goat, and before she knew it they were at the bottom. Finally, hearing his hooves splash into water as the group crossed the edge of a narrow stream, she opened her eyes. She had to blink at the glorious scene bursting upon her. The walls of the valley rose majestically. The tops, etched against the pale blue sky, were purple. Jana drew in her breath. It was like a painting on a Japanese screen. There were dark koa trees on the shady side, and yellow-green kukui trees on the other.

Deep down, surrounded by the sheer cliffs, were taro fields. All sorts of fruits and vegetables grew abundantly here as well: passion fruit, guava, and tiny, sweet bananas.

The double waterfalls were most breathtaking. Cascading like a filmy veil over green ferns and rocks, their beauty was otherworldly. From Tutu's brother, Uncle Kelo, Jana had heard the "tell story" represented by the beautiful twin falls. It was the sad yet romantic island legend of two separated lovers. Dismounting, she led her horse over to the stream to drink. Bayard sauntered over to where she and Joel stood.

"Well, was it worth it?" Bayard asked rather sardonically of Joel. However, his eyes were on Jana as he asked the question, and she felt it was her answer he wanted.

525

"Yes. Well worth the trip," Joel agreed quietly. Jana glanced at him, realized he was almost too moved to speak. Then Bayard strolled away and Joel turned to Jana. "I wish I had longer to stay. There is so much I'd like to explore and discover about Hawaii."

"You must plan to come back."

"Would you be my guide if I did?" he asked. Although it was spoken lightly, Jana had the feeling that there was more meaning in Joel's question. In spite of the fact that she hadn't tried any of the flirtatious suggestions outlined in the magazines Edith read. Could Edith be right? Was Joel "smitten?" Joel was very nice, but—

Wherever her thoughts were going, they were interrupted by the mule wagon rumbling down the path and Edith calling everyone to come eat.

The Prestons' Chinese cook and his helper turned the buckboard into a bounteous buffet table. The riders, their appetites sharpened by their early morning expedition, did justice to the delicious food.

Luscious pineapple spears, crescents of papayas, mangoes, bananas, an assortment of rolls, sweet breads, and creamy mounds of scrambled eggs, sausage, and bacon kept hot in a small hibachi were heaped on plates, and mugs of fragrant, hot coffee were poured.

Edith looked charming in a boy's blue cotton shirt, suede weskit, a wide-brimmed straw hat banded with a wreath of fresh flowers—the Hawaiian touch—her head thrown back, laughing and joyous. She was having the time of her life. How had Kiki learned to be so comfortable among Bayard's sophisticated college friends, to be so adept at banter and flirting, wondered Jana. Those magazines?

Jana walked a little way down the black-sand beach, and in a few minutes she heard footsteps behind her, turned, and saw that Bayard had followed her.

526

"A penny for your thoughts?" he offered.

"Not worth it. Just enjoying this lovely place. Wishing I had my paint box and sketch book! All this beauty. I'd like to capture it somehow. Correction—*try* to capture it. I'm not nearly good enough, of course. Still, I'd like to."

They walked along together in silence for a while. Then Bayard said, "What did you think of my little outburst last night?"

Jana stopped walking and turned to look at him.

"Just that you were being very honest. About your feelings, I mean."

"I seldom do that—or I should say, get a chance to do that." He paused, glanced at her. "It was an impulse, maybe, but somehow I thought you might understand. Did you?"

"I'm not sure. I've never been off the island, you see. Well, not since I came here from Oahu when I was eleven. So I've never had the kind of experiences you were talking about."

Bayard stooped and gathered some small stones in his hand, then stood and tossed them one by one ahead of them.

"It is different on the mainland," he said. "You can't imagine some of the stupid questions I get. It usually starts when I'm introduced at a party or somewhere. And you know how it goes, those stiff, clichéd openings to conversations. What I hate most is always explaining myself. 'Hawaii? You're from *where—Hawaii?*' I get so sick of hearing that sort of appalled tone in people's voices. Like you're from outer Mongolia. They look you over, almost as if to see whether you're wearing shoes—or a loincloth." He shook his head. "I'm like a man wearing two hats or standing with a foot in each world: the United States, the rock-bound New England of New Haven, the bastion of conservatism, where everyone wears a mask to conceal their emotions—then *this*. All this lushness, these soft-spoken, velvet-eyed, kindhearted people, generous, gracious—" He broke off. After a pause he said tightly, "That could be good or bad. It's kind of a homesickness. Island sickness, actually. On the mainland, I think I play a kind of part, all the while having a terrible yearning to be back *here* where I *know* who I am, how I'm supposed to act, what I'm supposed to say and do." He halted. Facing her, Bayard threw out his hands in a kind of hopeless gesture. "Do you understand at all what I'm saying?"

She saw a sort of desperation in Bayard's eyes, a need to be understood, and she instinctively responded to it. "Yes, I think I do."

"Wait up, you two!" a voice behind them called, and Joel came running down the beach to catch up with them.

Bayard muffled a groan. "Oh, no." However, when Joel reached them, Bayard was the affable friend again.

Jana was sorry yet relieved that they had been interrupted. Bayard's sharing left her confused. Why was he choosing *her* to tell his innermost thoughts to? She was moved by his honesty, touched that he trusted her with such intimate revelations. Yet what was she to say or do about it?

But the moment was past. Bayard again was the smooth, slightly mocking young man she had always believed him to be. If he had allowed her a glimpse behind his polished facade, it was over. And there wasn't anything she was supposed to do about it. Instinctively she knew that certainly she was never to bring it up.

❧

Back at the Prestons' that afternoon, the girls bathed and rested while Meipala rubbed them both with kukui oil, kneading their muscles so all the stiffness of the long ride was massaged away. They both fell asleep and didn't awaken until the evening shadows crept into their rooms and they had to hurry to get dressed for dinner.

As Jana had anticipated, Bayard completely ignored her. It was as though the time on the lanai or in the valley had never happened. It stung a little, but Joel and Tom were so flatteringly attentive that Jana was diverted and did not notice when Bayard excused himself and left the party before the others.

Tired from the valley excursion, everyone decided to call it an early evening. The next day would be even more full. Tomorrow was the rodeo and then that night, the New Year's Eve ball. Jana felt somewhat let down as she and Edith went upstairs. But Bayard's behavior should not have surprised her. That was simply Bayard's way. She blamed herself for being so vulnerable.

Chapter Seven

❧

A buffet luncheon was to be held before the rodeo, scheduled to start at one o'clock. Colonel Preston's guests from Kona and Hilo began arriving in their carriages at eleven. As each one entered, they were given a *lei*—a garland of flowers, white or pink carnations, plumeria or hibiscus—which was placed around their necks. The women were dressed in pastel-colored ensembles, carried matching parasols, and wore large-brimmed hats to shade their faces from damaging sunlight during the rodeo. These were the ladies who graced the society pages of the local newspapers, and Jana found herself observing them with awe. They looked like some of the fashion models in Edith's magazines. Her own simple cotton frock looked decidedly plain in contrast.

Colonel Preston was in his element, expansive in his favorite role of jovial host. He welcomed his guests, ushering them into the dining room. There was spread a lavish feast served by uniformed servants. Platters of fresh fruits, several kinds of salads, hot dishes of shrimp and *mahi-mahi*—a tender, white fish—steaming platters of rice and baked chicken papaya, as well as some traditional Hawaiian food made for the special occasion and to tempt the guests, such as *kulolo*, a delicious pudding of taro and coconut cream, were laid out on the fully laden tables before them.

Colonel Preston's voice boomed over the others as he held forth about the rodeo, an annual event on the ranch, bragging about his paniolos. "There'll be some local lads competing, too. But *my* men are the best. I only hire the finest. Good with horses, fearless riders. You're going to see stunts today you'd never see in a rodeo stateside, not even in California or Texas."

Jana caught a skeptical glance pass between Greg and Tom, but Joel said enthusiastically, "I can't wait, sir. Hawaii continues to amaze me. Somehow I never connected it with rodeos. I never imagined a real cowboy Wild West show put on here—in a tropical *paradise!*"

Colonel Preston looked smugly pleased. "You've never seen anything like it. You're in for a *real* treat, I'll tell you."

At this statement, Jana saw Greg Amory suppress a supercilious smile. Immediately she felt a rush of resentment. Of all Bayard's guests, she liked Greg the least. He had a superior attitude that made her feel defensive. What *did* Kiki see in him? Why not pick Joel, who was so open and seemed to love the island, the ranch, and everything?

Just as she was thinking about him, Joel came over to Jana, saying, "Tell me, what's the history of this? I can't help saying that this ranch, the cattle, and the rodeo here in Hawaii has me totally baffled. The rodeo isn't just to show off Colonel Preston's cowboys, is it?"

"It's more than that," Jana explained. "The cattle were brought from California as gifts to King Kamehameha. Before there were any ranches, they ran wild in herds, eating forests, trampling taro patches. So cowboys from Spain and Mexico were brought here to teach natives how to ride, rope, round them up, keep them on fence-bound ranges. From that, the ranching business began here. Now there are several cattle ranches on the island. Colonel Preston's is one of the largest."

"How did the rodeos get started?"

"It seemed to just develop naturally out of the paniolos' competitive spirit. Their rivalry with each other. It became a real challenge to see who could ride and rope the best. They started having different kinds of races and competitions. I guess you'd say it just evolved and became an annual event here at the Preston Ranch. As you can see, people come from all around to see it. There are parties everywhere afterward—and before too, I guess. It's a really special time."

Overhearing Jana's explanation seemed to have caught Greg Amory's interest. Standing nearby, he leaned toward her, asking, "So these Spanish and Mexican cowboys stayed on in Hawaii?"

"Some did, but the Hawaiians they taught their skills to took to it right away. They loved everything about it: the high-horned saddles, long spurs, and braided lassos. It was just the sort of thing that appealed to them. The excitement, the style, the danger, the risk, the daring of the buckaroos. They have their own version of all they have learned," she laughed, "which is even wilder, more reckless, than anything they were originally taught."

"And the name *paniolos?*"

"It's a kind of 'pidgin' translation of the word *Español*, which of course means Spanish, which most of them were, originally."

Greg seemed about to ask something more, when Colonel Preston went to stand in the dining room arch and waved his hands for silence, then announced, "All right, folks, we should be on our way. Ladies and gentlemen, your carriages are being brought around. You'll ride down to the far pasture, where the rodeo ring is set up. A grandstand and bleachers will accommodate you there. For you young people, the large ranch wagon will service you. It's a little rough, but

532

it's a short ride. Let's get going. You young people, don't delay. When *I* get there, the rodeo starts."

Evidently Edith had decided to ride her horse and go ahead of the rest with her father. Jana saw her touch Greg's arm, tip her head coquettishly, and whisper in his ear. He laughed and she looked back over her shoulder at him as she went out of the room. So she was now making Greg her open target, Jana mused, hoping her friend hadn't over-played her hand.

Bayard rounded up his friends, and Jana found herself escorted by both Greg and Joel. The large wooden wagon, with three rows of seats and drawn by four of the ranch's dray horses, was waiting for them out front. Greg Amory helped her up into the wagon, then took a seat beside her. Joel sat down on the other side. Bayard threw her an amused glance and sat down across from them with Tom.

Arriving at the high pasture, they saw that the wide corral had been turned into a rodeo ring. The rustic fencing was now festooned with bright banners. Multicolored streamers tied from each fence post blew in the wind.

Most of the bleachers were filled by townspeople who had ridden up from Waimea for the show. Colonel Preston had a box of seats in the front for his guests. Edith met them and immediately linked arms with Greg and Tom, and they took their places in the front row. Joel and Jana followed. Bayard seemed to have disappeared for the moment, and Jana wondered if he had decided to ride after all. She noticed that Edith seemed to be concentrating on Tom. For effect, she was also waving and greeting people she knew who were sitting around them. Was she trying to impress Greg? If so, he didn't seem to be paying much attention to her. In fact, he looked rather bored.

As they settled in, Jana saw groups of men on horseback assembling at the far end of the field. Those were the riders who would be competing. She pointed out some of the events on the program to Greg and Joel—neither of whom had ever been to a rodeo before—explaining what they could expect. She had decided not to be put off by Greg's aloof attitude. It was a kind of challenge to get him actually interested. The excited expectation that was tangible in the air would be contagious.

"It's really fun," she told him. "You'll find yourself yelling your head off!"

"*Me?*" he protested. "I doubt it."

"Wait and see!"

Colonel Preston, mounted on his handsome white horse, circled the center of the ring, waving his arm and shouting instructions to the rodeo riders lining up at the starting gate. Then he cantered up in front of the bleachers, took off his wide-brimmed, white felt Stetson, and bowed—as did his horse—to a burst of applause and cheers.

"Ladies and gentlemen, our rodeo riders will now promenade so that you can pick your favorites," he announced dramatically. "Then the games will begin!"

Loud applause mixed with "yahoos" greeted this pronouncement. Jana heard Greg Amory murmur to no one in particular, "What a ham!" Jana bristled. Such a rude comment to make about his host, she thought. For all his so-called background, she was beginning to think Greg Amory was a boor. Accepting the Prestons' generous hospitality obligated him to be at least respectful. She gave him a withering glance to let him know that his remark had been overheard. But he wasn't looking, for at that moment the thundering of dozens of horses' hooves pounded over the dusty ground as the festively attired paniolos galloped into the ring one after the other. The spectators rose, cheering and screaming.

The paniolos wore sombreros of woven palm, leis of fresh flowers, red sashes around their waists, high leather leggings over white duck pants. Braided leather lariats wound in circles hung from their saddles, and spurs jangled from their boots.

As they passed by the grandstand, each horseman slowed his horse, whipped off his hat, bowed in his saddle, and then, touching his mount's foreleg with his sombrero, made the horse also do a semblance of a bow. One gleaming black horse cantering up to take its turn particularly caught Jana's eye. With a flourish, the rider removed his hat and revealed what the shadow of the brim had hidden. Jana gasped. It was *Kimo*! Spontaneously she jumped up, clapping her hands. He breasted his hat, shook back the thick, dark waves from his forehead. His eyes held laughter, his smile was broad. He was enjoying his surprise. Had he planned to be in the rodeo all along? Or was this a last-minute decision? Either way, Kimo was here and would compete with the best the Preston Ranch could offer. Her heart thrummed excitedly. She knew him to be a superb rider. She had seen him on horseback many times. No question—*he* was her favorite paniolo for today's competition. He gave his sombrero a cavalier twirl, then whirled his horse around and was gone in a clatter of hooves, a cloud of dust.

After that the rodeo took on a much more personal interest to her. In every event, she eagerly awaited to see if Kimo was going to participate in it.

One by one the events of cutting, barrel racing, calf roping, and steer throwing were called. Waiting to see if Kimo was entering, she sat on the edge of her seat. She remembered that the Heritage Academy maintained a livestock ranch to partially support itself. Most probably, Kimo had worked there to earn the tuition and fees not included in his scholarship.

The only event in which he didn't compete was the bucking bronco contest. This always brought the audience to its feet, screaming, yelling, and rooting for the daring ones who entered the event. Hardly any survived longer than a few minutes. The crowd shouted and cheered for their favorite, groaned when one "bit the dust." Buckled on, the riders bounced, flipped, and circled as the horse tried to get the burden off its back and everyone roared encouragement.

Jana was glad Kimo was not entered in this one. She had already gripped her hands into fists as he did the cutting, the relay, and the barrel racing. Her nails bit into her palms, which now were burning and stinging. Her throat was raw, her voice hoarse, from all her shouts.

"You really go in for all this, don't you?" a sarcastic voice beside her asked. She turned and saw Greg Amory's cynical smile.

"Yes, I guess I do. You'd have to be dead and embalmed *not* to!" she retorted. Then she turned around, feeling suddenly foolish. She shouldn't have lost her temper. Greg wasn't worth it. Had she made a spectacle of herself with her show of enthusiasm? No! Everyone else was doing the same thing, shouting, cheering, yelling. It was *Greg* who was out of step. *He* was the one.

It took Joel to really call him on his attitude. "What's wrong with you, Greg? Come on, show a little life. Remember the saying 'When in Rome, do as the Romans do'?"

"I guess so. It just seems—well, I can't believe this is taking place in Hawaii. You'd think it was some one-horse town in Montana or Wyoming. To think Bayard comes from all this—it seems odd somehow."

"Didn't he tell you he lived on a ranch?" Jana asked coolly.

"Oh, I suppose he did. But it was never—well ..." Greg shrugged, not finishing whatever he was going to say.

"If you'd ever seen him ride, you wouldn't think it so odd!" she flashed back, wondering why was she defending Bayard against his friend.

Just then Colonel Preston's voice came through the megaphone he was holding. "And now, ladies and gentlemen, the grand finale. Each paniolo will ride by and give his talisman to the lady of his choice."

Jana watched eagerly as the parade of colorfully dressed paniolos in full regalia began. Keeping their horses beautifully in control, the mounted men trotted into the ring. Moving with precision and pacing the high-stepping horses, each approached the grandstand.

One by one they came, waving their hats as the crowd applauded, cheered. In front of the reviewing stand, as a mark of special gallantry, each paniolo halted his mount, bowed, and tipped his hat. Then, unfastening the broad ribbon he wore across his chest, he handed it to his special "fair lady" among the spectators. At each presentation, there was more applause and cheering as each lady rose to receive her talisman. Sometimes a bold paniolo would lean from his saddle and plant a kiss on her cheek.

When Kimo came riding up, Jana's heart almost stopped beating. He drew his horse to a stop in front of her, swept off his sombrero and bowed to her, then held up his yellow satin ribbon with its cluster of ribbons for her. Joel nudged her. "Jana, he means *you*," he prompted. "Go on. He intends for you to accept it."

Hoping that in her excitement she wouldn't stumble, Jana got up and made her way to the edge of the box, held up her hand to receive the honor. Kimo smiled. Using her Hawaiian name, he handed her the talisman. "Aloha, Koana."

"Mahalo," she said huskily.

He tipped his hat, replaced it, then flicked the brim with his hand and rode off while she stared after him.

Her heart was pumping. Her breath caught in her throat. Kimo, her knight in shining armor. It was as if all the old fairy tales, all the romantic legends, all the poetry and music, all the dreams she had ever dreamed, had suddenly come together in this magic moment.

Chapter Eight

❦

The New Year's Eve ball was to be a gala event. Edith was wildly excited at the prospect of her first "*really* grown-up party.*" For Jana the best part of the house party was Kimo's surprise appearance at the rodeo. Whatever she had felt in their meeting outside church before Christmas, all that strangeness had melted in the warmth of his smile as he handed her his trophy. Nothing could match that moment. Jana packed the ribbon carefully into her suitcase to take it home with her. She was already looking forward to when Kimo would come to see her.

New Year's Eve at the Preston Ranch was always widely attended, and talked about for weeks afterward. Detailed descriptions of the music, the food, the gowns, the decorations, and the flowers would usually take up columns in the society section of the local paper.

In the past, Jana and Edith were relegated to the balcony overlooking the entrance hall, and would peer through the koa balustrade, watching the guests arrive. Meipala called it *okolehaeo*, a good-time kind of party. Of course, in the days when Edith's mother was alive, she told the girls, there had been many of those types of parties.

Tonight's affair was special not only because *they* were going to attend it, but because it would also be the send-off for Bayard and his guests. The next day, they would leave on the steamer to Honolulu, then take the ship back to the mainland.

The ball would not begin until ten, but Edith and Jana started their preparations much earlier.

When she had returned from the rodeo late that afternoon, Jana took out the party dress her mother had made, examining it critically. It was one of the prettiest and fanciest she had ever owned, a blue voile with faceted lace seams, a bowed sash, and a ruffled skirt. At home it had looked fine, but here it somehow didn't look right. After observing the elegant gowns the other guests had worn to the rodeo, Jana could only imagine what their ball gowns would be like.

She knew that Edith's Aunt Ruthie in San Francisco had sent her a dress from some exclusive shop there. Jana felt guilty finding fault with something her mother had spent hours making. Yet it just wasn't right for a grand ball.

Well, there was nothing to be done about it. She would have to make the best of it.

Just then she heard Edith call her. "Jana, come here for a minute, please. I want to show you what I'm going to wear."

Trying to hide her dissatisfaction about her own dress, Jana called back, "Coming."

When she walked into the adjoining bedroom, to her complete surprise she saw Edith standing in front of the full-length mirror wearing a turquoise blue *holoku*, a long, one-piece gown styled after the type the missionaries had first made for the native women, but now fitted, with a yoke and a train.

"What do you think?" Edith half turned for her friend's reaction.

"It's gorgeous! But where did you get it? Surely that's not what your aunt sent from the mainland, is it?"

"No, it belonged to my mother! Meipala has kept all Mama's Hawaiian dresses. It fits me perfectly. And I'm going to wear it tonight!"

Jana had never seen her friend look so lovely. "Oh Kiki, you look beautiful!" The dress itself was breathtaking. The color perfectly set off her apricot tan skin, her dark, shining eyes, and her golden hair.

Still viewing herself critically in the mirror, Edith pointed to two gowns spread on top of the quilt on her bed. One was a scarlet velvet, the other a blue green silk. Jana tentatively touched the material. It felt luscious.

"Those are the gowns my aunt sent. But I've decided to be my Hawaiian self tonight. Why don't you wear one of them? Either one should fit."

"Oh Kiki, I couldn't. Not possibly. Your aunt meant them for you—"

"Of course you can. Go ahead, pick the one you like best!" ordered Edith. "You *are* going to wear it."

Jana stared at her friend incredulously. She shook her head.

"You *must*, Jana. Think of it as a dress-up occasion. Playing pretend, the way we used to. Going to our first ball. It will be only this once. The *blue* would be perfect for you. Do take it and try it on, Jana!" Edith gathered it up and thrust it at her. "Here!" She took Jana by the shoulders, turned her toward the full-length mirror.

Jana held the dress up to herself and looked at her reflection.

"See for yourself! It could have been made for you," Edith declared triumphantly.

Jana *did* see. It *was* very becoming.

"There are slippers to match." Edith brought out a shoe box. "And I know we wear the same size." She rustled back tissue paper and brought out narrow blue satin pumps with French heels and rhinestone-sprinkled bows. She held them out for Jana to admire. "Now, I won't take no for an answer. You *must*, Jana."

Jana had come up against Edith's indomitable will before. Once Edith had made up her mind about something, it was useless to protest. This time Jana didn't really want to. She had never wanted anything so much in her life as to wear this beautiful dress. "Well," she said slowly, "if you *insist*."

"I *do!* So it's settled. Go ahead, put it on," Edith commanded.

Back in her room, Jana placed her own dress back into the armoire with a brief pang of guilt. But, she told herself, this *was* after all a very special occasion. She felt like Cinderella, whose fairy godmother had provided her with an undreamed-of chance to go to the ball in a beautiful gown. Besides, her mother would never know.

Meipala came to see them before they went downstairs. Her dark eyes misted as she regarded Edith. "So like your mama," she murmured. She had brought a wreath of fresh flowers that Edith wanted to wear on her hair, which she had brushed out to hang in shimmering waves to her waist.

Jana needed some help with the fasteners and tiny buttons on her borrowed dress, a designer creation. She had never seen a dress constructed such as this. Lined in satin, the skirt was gathered to the back in a modified bustle falling into graceful folds. The bodice was separate, tapering to a point at the waist. There were huge, puffed sleeves and a portrait neckline. The blue dress deepened the color of Jana's eyes. Edith was right: the dress could have been made for *her*.

At last it was time to go downstairs.

The lower part of the house had been transformed into a fairyland of flowers and light. Ferns were everywhere—giant

542

tree ferns stood against the wall, *lehua* in natural green were wired with red flowers, baskets of *kupukupu* fern hung from the ceiling, garlands of fern crisscrossed against the ceiling, pillars were woven with *palapalai*, *wawaeiole*, and *uluhe* ferns accented with spikes of *ieie*, a form of *pandanus*. In the wide entrance hall, long tables were set with red cloths, huge platters of fresh fruit, and bowls of punch. Outside, the wide veranda was festooned with lit paper lanterns, and lehua sprayed with white and bright with red blossoms framed the entrance.

As the girls came down the stairway, Colonel Preston was in the center hall, giving directions to one of the manservants. When he looked up and saw his daughter, he stopped midsentence. For a moment he seemed stunned. He shook his head as if in disbelief. Then slowly a smile broke across his craggy face. He came to the foot of the steps and held out his hand. As she reached the last step, Edith took it and he spun her around a couple of times, declaring, "Darling girl, you are a vision to behold."

Jana halted a step or two behind Edith, saw the Colonel's eyes moisten. She knew he must be thinking of the young wife he had loved so much and had lost when Edith was a baby. An interesting reversal; the Hawaiian lady in a Paris gown and her daughter, a *hapa-haole*, who longed to claim her Hawaiian heritage.

Colonel Preston quickly controlled his momentary emotion and turned to Jana to graciously compliment her as well. "You two will have the young gentlemen battling to be your dance partners," he teased. "Jana, you'll have to excuse Edith for a while. She must do her duty in the receiving line with Bayard and me. I'm sure you won't find yourself alone for long. Bayard's guests have been impatiently waiting for you to appear." Jana watched as Edith gracefully picked up her train, took her father's arm, and went with him to greet the guests, who were arriving in a steady stream. Bayard was already standing at the door. His eyes swept over his sister. An enigmatic expression passed over his face. One Jana couldn't read. Disapproval? Amusement? Before she could interpret his gaze, he turned to her. He gave a nod and smiled. Again it was hard to know what his look meant.

Nor did she want to try. Bayard was someone she would never understand. Where had he been throughout the rodeo? She had seen him later with his father in what appeared to be a heated argument. Had Colonel Preston expected his son to ride and been disappointed he hadn't? It was hard to tell. Whatever it was, their discussion had ended abruptly, with both men walking away from each other, shoulders stiff.

Jana walked toward the drawing room, which had been transformed into a ballroom. Most of the formal furniture had disappeared mysteriously, the rugs had been rolled up, and the floor had been highly polished for dancing. The women guests were beautifully dressed. The parade of jewels and finery was overwhelming. There were enough ruffles, flounces, bows, bustles, ostrich feathers, fine laces, ivory fans, and ornamental combs to tax the vocabularies of the island's society page editors.

The sounds of the party swirled around Jana: the clinking of glasses, the murmur of conversation, the small bursts of laughter. It was a dizzying montage of movement and color. Menservants in bright, flowered shirts and white pants circulated with trays of iced tea or poured sparkling wine into crystal glasses never allowed to empty. A band of Hawaiian musicians in floral shirts and wearing *maile*—a fragrant, leafy vine—and leis were seated at one end of the large room. Their mellow guitars, backed by muted drums and the plink of ukuleles, provided a background of soft, melodic sound.

It was a dazzling scene that gave Jana a feeling of unreality, as though she were watching a colorful pageant, not being part of it. Then a voice at her side spoke.

"Good evening, Miss Rutherford." It was Joel. "You look lovely."

"Mahalo, thank you. It's borrowed. A fairy godmother waved a magic wand over me and—poof!—here I am," she laughed.

Joel shook his head. "You amaze me. You're so natural, it's refreshing. Most girls simper when paid a compliment and start to fuss and fiddle with their hair or dress. I find it totally charming."

"To be honest, I have no idea how other girls act under these circumstances. It's the first time I've ever been to such a ball. I *do* feel like Cinderella."

"Would you like to dance?" he smiled.

"Yes. Edith and I have been practicing for weeks for just such a chance," Jana replied and let him lead her out onto the dance floor.

With a few false starts they got in step, and within minutes Jana was having the time of her life. Every once in a while she caught a glimpse of herself in the wall mirror. It was like looking at someone else. As Joel whirled her around in time to the music, the dress caught the light, and its fluttering ruffles edged with beading sparkled.

She and Joel were chatting between sets when Bayard's stint in the receiving line was evidently over, and he came up to them. "Come now, Joel, you cannot monopolize Jana all evening. Give someone else a turn, old fellow."

"Reluctantly," said Joel good-naturedly and left. When the music began again, Bayard held out his arms and Jana moved into them.

He danced as well as he rode, she thought, with skill and confidence. They circled the room three or four times, then reversed. But before she realized what he was doing, he had smoothly danced over to the open French windows and out onto the lanai. The night air was warm, balmy, scented. His hand circling her waist dropped to capture her hand. They walked to the edge, where the camellia bushes rimmed the terraced wall. He plucked a creamy blossom from its stem and handed it to her.

Jana took the flower, lifting it to her nose and inhaling the heavy sweetness of its fragrance. The only noise was the distant sound of the surf, the whisper of palm fronds crackling softly in the wind. Then Bayard spoke.

"Just one question. Was the gallant paniolo just playing a role this morning, or is he truly your cavalier?"

Surprised at his directness, Jana hesitated. Her truth might be one-sided. She had not yet talked to Kimo since the incident at the rodeo, had not yet discovered what he had meant when he handed her his ribbon. She couldn't be sure it meant what she hoped. Why did Bayard want to know? Why should she tell him? As her hesitation lengthened, Bayard gave a short laugh. "So is the old saying true? 'Silence gives consent'?"

"Not exactly. I don't know how to answer," she said quietly. "That paniolo was Kimo Kipola. Akela's cousin. I think you knew him—at least, as a boy. He's been away. On Oahu, at the Heritage Academy."

"Oh, an alii, then. Not just a cowboy. He rides like a seasoned paniolo."

"But then, so do *you*."

"We islanders—," he began, but a peal of laughter broke in on them as Edith and Tom and several other couples burst out from the ballroom. It was intermission, and the dancers were flocking out to the lanai to enjoy the cool ocean breeze.

There was no opportunity to continue the conversation. Actually, it had not been so much a conversation as an *interrogation* of her by Bayard. She was glad it had not continued. Why should she expose her heart to his razor-sharp wit? Why hand over her secret for him to examine, maybe ridicule? No. Jana had no intention of confiding in Bayard Preston.

The waiters followed the dancers out, bringing trays holding cups of cool punch for refreshment between dances. Joel had again engaged Jana's attention, and she was soon chatting with the others. When the music started playing again, Joel claimed her for the next set.

As the dancing continued, Jana had many partners. Even Greg Amory asked her to dance, and she found he was more pleasant than she had previously thought.

Ten minutes before midnight, the band stopped. Colonel Preston held up his hands for silence. "Time to see the new year in. Everyone is invited to come outside, and we'll see the old year out with a fine farewell, and the new one in with a howdy-do. Come along, we'll give 1886 a rousing welcome."

Jana knew from past years that Colonel Preston always put on an extravagant fireworks display that lit up the sky in celebration.

As brilliant, colorful bursts of scattering lights spun out in beautiful arcs against the dark sky, there were oohs and aahs of wonder. Then everyone joined in the slowly chanted countdown to midnight, until at last came the exuberant shout, "Happy New Year!"

Jana had been so entranced watching the fireworks, she did not notice that Bayard was standing behind her until the new year was announced. All around her, happy wishes and kisses were exchanged. She felt his arm go around her waist, and he turned her around, drew her close. *"Hau'oli Makahiki Hou,"* he whispered. Before she could draw back, his lips had found her mouth, in a kiss far more intense than a friendly New Year's greeting.

Jana was too startled to react at first. Besides, Bayard was holding her too tightly for her to easily escape his embrace. Underneath the happy voices and laughter, he said, "I had no idea you would grow up to be so irresistible."

Jana gave him a gentle push and stepped back, breathless, a little dizzy. Before she could think of a reply, Joel came up, said, "Happy New Year, Jana," and kissed her lightly. When she looked, Bayard had slipped away into the group around her. Tom and Greg and Edith followed, all laughing and happily exchanging kisses and greetings. Minutes later, Colonel Preston was inviting everyone to go inside again and toast the new year with a freshly uncorked bottle of champagne.

Although on the surface Jana joined with the others in the lighthearted chatter, inside she was a little shaken. Maybe when she was twelve or so, attention from Edith's older brother might have sent her head whirling, her heart thudding. Now it only troubled her. Now Kimo was back on the island. She had yet to discover if he loved her. Until she knew how Kimo felt toward her, she could not have any romantic feelings toward anyone else.

～❧～

By one o'clock the party had dwindled. Most of the guests had departed after being served a sumptuous buffet. A few remained, gathered in clusters of conversation, some continuing to dance until the sleepy musicians packed up their instruments and prepared to leave.

Edith, as effervescent as each new bottle of champagne that Colonel Preston opened, was still dancing with a succession of partners.

Bayard had left to escort some of his father's guests who were staying over down to the cottages. Jana and Joel sat near the open lanai doors, enjoying plates of fluffy scrambled eggs, banana nut bread, and cups of black, steaming Kona coffee. Greg Amory joined them. He looked around the room, commenting, "Look at this place! What a mess."

The other two followed his glance. Everywhere were the scattered remains of the party. The confetti that had been tossed out at midnight lay in crumpled streams of colors on the floor, wilting flowers hung limply where they had been festooned, the ribbons draped above the windows drooped gaudily in the light edging in through the windows.

"I'd sure hate to be on the cleanup committee," Joel laughed. "That's usually where I land after dances at our fraternity house."

"But you're in Hawaii," Jana reminded him. "Maybe the *menehuenes* will come and do it all."

"*Menehuenes?*" Greg echoed.

"Yes. The legendary 'little people' of the islands. You know, like Irish leprechauns or the trolls in Scandinavia? You've heard of *them*, haven't you?" Joel asked, eyes twinkling with the newly gained authority he had from Jana's coaching. "Well, the *menehuenes* are something like that. They build, do all sorts of mysterious things. They're said to appear only at night—but many claim to see them even in broad daylight."

"Come on!" Greg gave Joel a withering look. "Where did you get that kind of foolishness?"

"From an expert on Hawaii," Joel grinned.

Greg glanced at Jana. *"You?"*

"Yes, *me!*" she retorted. "And I get my information from the people who should know—the old ones, the *Kama'aina*." She looked Greg square in the eye. "There is so much about Hawaii that people don't know and outsiders don't understand," she said, hoping to beat him at his own game with her dismissing tone. However, it seemed to just whet Greg's appetite for baiting.

"You don't really believe all this stuff, do you?" Greg asked skeptically. "I mean, about Pele and the volcano and these—what did you call them, menehuenes?" Without waiting for her answer, Greg went on. "It's positively uncanny how primitive it all is under the surface." He halted, daring Jana to respond. "You seem like an intelligent girl. How can you stand—don't you ever want to see any place else? I mean, it's so limited here, so provincial—aren't you curious about the rest of the civilized world?"

Jana was ready to launch into a heated defense, when Colonel Preston walked over to make sure they were getting enough to eat, having a good time. The argument was immediately dropped.

In the absence of the band, Edith and Tom were seated at the piano, playing a lively tune, singing a duet. Some of the others, who'd thought they had run out of energy, now gathered around the piano.

Colonel Preston studied his daughter with pleasure. She was impetuous, stubborn, but also completely charming. There were only brief flashes when he saw his beautiful second wife in her. A momentary twinge of sadness and regret tugged at his heart as he remembered the serene, lovely, dark-eyed beauty who had been Edith's mother. The woman who had given him nothing but joy had left a daughter both headstrong and reckless who might one day be a problem. Still, his pride in his daughter was boundless.

"Edith lights up any room," Colonel Preston remarked almost to himself, then turned to Jana. "You've heard of people who march to a different drummer. . . . Edith dances to a melody no one else can hear."

It seemed a surprisingly lyrical observation for such a pragmatic man to make. Yet it was true. Edith had something quite unique, both the look of an American girl and the exotic beauty inherited from her Hawaiian mother.

Colonel Preston got to his feet. "I hope nothing changes her, takes that glow. I know that's wishful thinking. Whether we like it or not, whether we want it or not, life is a constant change. As the saying goes, 'One cannot hold back the dawn.'" He smiled at Jana. "And speaking of dawn, I have to admit that my old bones have just about had it. I'll leave you young ones to see in the first morning of the new year. I'm going to call it a night."

With a courtly bow he left, walking as steadily and straight as if he had not consumed a great quantity of the vintage champagne he had been urging on everyone else. The three of them watched him leave. Greg nodded his head in the direction of the piano, where Edith was still holding forth. "*She's* certainly the apple of his eye, isn't she? His little princess that nothing's too good for, right?"

"Well, I suppose so," Jana replied. "She *is* his only daughter—naturally he would dote on her."

"Oh, that's obvious. And she *is* a stunner. Especially in that Hawaiian outfit she's wearing tonight." He squinted his eyes slightly. He turned to Jana and said seriously, "There are subtle dangers in being brought up to believe you're special. There's danger for others as well—being lured into so much brilliance. Like moths drawn to the flame, there's a real possibility of being consumed."

It seemed a strange comment, when Jana knew *he* was the object of Edith's shining. Was he actively resisting her flame?

Suddenly she felt very tired. "I think I'll say good night," she said and stood up. Joel stood up, too, and walked with her out to the hall.

At the bottom of the staircase, he said, "I've enjoyed being with you. You've made this vacation special, Jana. I hope we'll meet again—sometime."

"You'll come back to Hawaii. People usually do."

"I hope to."

He seemed to be about to say something else, but Jana said good night and went quickly upstairs.

She took off her borrowed finery, returned the gown to Edith's room, and replaced the dancing slippers, a little worse for wear. Edith's bed had been turned down, her nightgown and robe laid out for her, a thermos jug placed on the bedside table. Her every need, every wish, anticipated, taken care of—a princess indeed, just as Greg had commented. Looking around for a moment, Jana became newly aware of the difference between Edith's home life and her own. She had been here only a few days, and yet she realized how easy it would be to be seduced by all this luxury. When you were with the Prestons—any of them, the Colonel, Bayard, or Edith— there was this feeling that life was to be enjoyed fully, with no thought of tomorrow. It was such a contrast to how life was lived in her own home. Her parents, while not at all stuffy or overly strict, were both idealistic and high principled. They believed that the purpose of life was not merely to be happy, but to contribute something, to do something worthwhile, something that mattered. To find God's will for your life, was the important thing.

In his own words, all Colonel Preston wanted was for Edith to be happy. And what about Bayard? Did Colonel Preston expect more of his son? Probably. One day all this would belong to Bayard. A crown prince to take over the kingdom.

Back in the guest room, Jana put the gardenia Bayard had given her into the small crystal vase beside the bed. She thought of the intensity of his kiss. . . . What should she make of it?

This room overlooked the lanai, from which the murmur of voices and the laughter of the group who still lingered rose. Someone was singing a familiar Hawaiian melody, accompanied by the sweet plink of a ukulele. The sounds mingled dreamily as she drifted off.

For her the party had ended. The holidays were over. It had been an exciting interlude. But that's all it had been.

Chapter Nine

❦

$\mathcal{J}$ana was not sure how long she had been asleep when suddenly, slashing through her dreams, came Bayard's harsh command, *"Get to bed, Edith!"*

Instantly awake, Jana sat bolt upright in bed, every nerve tingling. She strained to listen for what might follow. But she could hear nothing more. Only dead silence. The loudest sound was her own heart hammering. She reached for the small clock on the bedside table. After three! She had left the party little more than an hour ago. What had happened since then? What had Edith done to cause her brother to shout at her like that?

She only had to wait minutes to find out. She heard running feet along the corridor outside her room, and then the door burst open and Edith ran in, flung herself, sobbing, onto Jana's bed.

Jana put her arms around her friend's violently shaking shoulders. Frightened, she held her while the wrenching sobs went on and on. Bayard adored his little sister, treated her with affectionate indulgence. What kind of quarrel had erupted between them to bring on *this*?

Gradually the gulping sobs lessened, the ragged breaths became gasps. Finally Edith sat up, wiping her eyes with her fists like a child, and found her voice.

"I'll never forgive him! Never!" she said fiercely between clenched teeth.

"Kiki, tell me! What happened?"

"I'm furious! How could Bayard humiliate me that way? I didn't do anything wrong! He just . . . just *assumed* . . . oh, I don't know what! It was beastly of him."

"Calm down, please. Just tell me what happened."

Edith gulped. "I need a hankie."

"Here, use this!" Jana lifted the bud vase in which she had put her gardenia and slipped the lace-edged doily from under it and handed it to Edith. "Now *tell* me."

"Well. . .," she began, then sniffled and blew her nose before going on. "Only a few of us were left—actually me, Greg, Tom, and Joel. You know how interested *he* is in everything about Hawaii, asking all sorts of questions—about the native customs and so on. He asked about Hawaiian music, so I picked up a ukulele and was playing some of the tunes we all know. He liked one particularly and I told him it was one the *hula* was danced to. Well, one thing led to another, and I decided to show him what a hula was. I took off my shoes"—Edith pulled up her skirt and stuck out her legs, wiggling bare feet—"and I began to dance for him. I was telling one of the island legends, the way Akela's mother taught us, and I was just doing it, when all of a sudden Bayard came thundering out onto the lanai and shouted at me!"

"And that's all? That's *it*?"

Edith nodded. "I don't know what got into him or what he thought I was doing—but I've never seen him so angry. I was shocked. Totally stunned. I dropped the ukulele and ran into the house." She sniffed again. "I don't know what the others thought. Or how Bayard will explain himself to his friends." Edith thumped a fist on the edge of the mattress. "Oh, it was unspeakable! I'll never forgive him for shaming me like that—in front of everyone. Especially *Greg*!"

"Oh, Kiki," Jana said, attempting to soothe her. "It will probably all blow over. In the morning, everyone will have forgotten it."

"I won't have," Edith said stubbornly.

"Bayard will be sorry," Jana assured her. "I'm sure he would never intentionally hurt you." Then she added as an afterthought, "You know, everyone had a great deal of champagne...." This, she knew, was rather a lame excuse. She had the feeling it wasn't too much champagne that had made Bayard lash out at his sister. It was more probably his own internal conflicts.

It was a long time before Edith stopped railing at her brother. After a while she seemed to go limp.

"Things will look better tomorrow. You'll see, Kiki."

"I don't know how," Edith sighed.

"I'm sure Bayard will apologize and everything will be fine."

"Maybe," Edith said doubtfully. "I hope you're right."

At length she got off the bed, said a sleepy good night, and went listlessly into her adjoining bedroom.

Jana had trouble getting back to sleep. What a shame, she thought, that the beautiful party and the celebration of the start of a new year had ended so badly.

After Edith left, Jana lay awake. She realized there was deeply felt bitterness in Bayard Preston. He was caught between two cultures. As Colonel Preston's son by his marriage to an American woman, he was ever considered by Hawaiians as a *haole*. No matter that he had been born here on the island. His was a love-hate relationship with the island. Half the year, he lived in the United States, where Hawaii was considered a foreign country, its traditions trivialized, its legends and lovely customs vulgarized. He managed to keep his anger controlled and suppressed—most of the time—but it cost him.

Jana understood that under his outburst at his sister's dancing was his fear that his friends would consider the hula something pagan, uncivilized. After all, the first missionaries had banned it at one time. They had missed the significance of the graceful, legend-telling native dance. He had impulsively acted in defense of what he held dear—Hawaii and Edith.

It was a long time before Jana's troubling thoughts allowed her to go to sleep again.

~e9~

The sun streaming in through the latticed screens awoke Jana. She lay there for a moment, reluctant to come into full wakefulness. The bed felt soft, comforting, like a cocoon from which she did not want to pull herself. But slowly the events of the ball and the aftermath pulled her into consciousness. She hoped there would be no repercussions from the upsetting scene between Bayard and Edith last night. She slipped out of bed and went over to the windows to see what kind of day the weather promised for the garden party planned as the last event of the holiday. Stepping out onto the balcony, she heard Bayard's and Colonel Preston's voices from the lanai below. Bayard was speaking earnestly.

"Father, I know it would be hard for you to let her go. But Edith needs exposure to another culture, to the society in which she should learn to move, behave. You must see that, Father. She's grown up almost wild here. She knows nothing but this island, the provincial attitudes. She needs polishing. She needs a whole other environment, different friends, other influences—she needs to associate with people of our own class, not just Hawaiians."

Jana stepped back as if she had been slapped. Bayard's words, "not just Hawaiians," stung. Did he include *her* when he said Edith needed a different kind of friends?

The night before, she had felt compassion for his uncertainty about his life, had felt she understood it. Now she had only resentment, anger. Jana started to go back inside, but something held her. Colonel Preston was protesting.

"I can't let her go so far away."

"I'm not talking about England or a French finishing school, Father. There are many fine finishing schools in New England near New Haven, where she could be close enough to Yale so I could see her. Every weekend, if it came to that. And you could visit often. You make at least one trip to the States every year as it is." Bayard paused, then said more forcefully, "Believe me, Father, it's for Edith's own good. At least promise you'll think about it, won't you?" Another pause. "In the meantime, I'll do some checking into some of the schools for young ladies in the States."

Suddenly Jana wished she had not overheard this conversation. The bright promise of the day ahead faded. She wished she could leave the ranch. Right away. Go home. She was hurt. Words were weapons that could wound. The cuts Bayard's words had inflicted were deep. And they were ones from which she might not recover.

The two men's voices faded as they left the lanai. Later she heard the sound of their horses' hooves as they rode down the drive for an early morning horseback ride together. Jana dressed quickly and went downstairs. No one else seemed to be up or around except Meipala, who told her with a wink that the other guests were still sleeping, adding with a chuckle, "It musta been some *okolehao*." Silently agreeing and secretly glad to be alone, Jana took her coffee out to the lanai to drink, in case one of the young men took it into their heads to come up to the big house for breakfast. She wasn't in the mood to socialize.

The prospect of the garden party loomed ahead. It was Colonel Preston's annual open house to his local friends on

New Year's Day. New year, Jana thought, sighing. What did
this new year hold for her? By this time next year, she would
be almost through high school, and maybe even accepted at
some mainland college and selected to receive a scholarship,
if her parents' hopes were fulfilled. The prospect filled her
with sadness. She didn't really want to go to the mainland.
Unlike Bayard, she loved her life here—she didn't want anything to change. His words to his father came back to her
now, and she felt the slow rise of resentment again. There was
still the garden party to get through. She would make it a
point to avoid Bayard at this afternoon's party. If she didn't,
she might lose her temper and tell him what she thought of
his attitude about Hawaii and Hawaiians!

Jana finished her coffee and went back inside and
upstairs. Edith was awake and last night's trauma seemed to
have dimmed sufficiently for her to be her usual cheerful self.
She had always been able to throw off moods, dismiss
unpleasant situations. Surprisingly, she seemed to hold no
grudge against her brother. In fact, she did not even mention
what had happened the night before. She was flitting around
her room like a butterfly, trying on one dress after the other
to wear to the afternoon party.

While Edith seemed to be looking forward to it, Jana
dreaded it. But there was no way to escape. She just hoped her
father would come early to pick her up and take her home.

That afternoon, the garden was soon filled with ladies in
pastel gowns and gentlemen in white linen suits, arriving
from Hilo and Kona in their splendid carriages. While Edith
moved gaily about among the guests, laughing and chatting
and showing off one of the flowered organdy gowns her aunt
had sent, Jana tried to be as inconspicuous as possible.

Her effort to avoid Bayard proved impossible. She was
hovering near the punch bowl, thinking herself safe, when

she felt a hand on her waist gently but insistently turn her around and she was face to face with him.

"Why are you running away from me?" he asked.

Disconcerted, Jana demanded, "What makes you think that?"

"It's pretty obvious."

Remembering how Edith had often told her Bayard was *pursued* by young ladies in the most blatant fashion, Jana wanted to say something to deflate his smug assertion. "You're pretty self-important to think I would go to the bother."

For a minute he seemed taken aback. "I was under the impression that we were *hoalohas*, friends, that we understood one another." He frowned. "Was I wrong?"

"I don't know, I'm sure," Jana shrugged.

"I thought your lack of artifice, flirtatiousness, was very attractive. I don't like to see you playing the usual feminine games."

"Don't be so patronizing," she flashed back at him. "Not every girl in the world wants to fall at your feet."

Bayard's eyes narrowed, his mouth tightened. Then he did a surprising thing. He reached his hand under her chin, tilted it upward with his fingertips, gazing into her eyes.

"I'm disappointed in you, Jana. I thought you were different. I guess I was mistaken."

She felt her cheeks burn. Her first indignation began suddenly to dissipate. A smile touched Bayard's lips, as if he had read her thoughts or had found out what he wanted to know. His hand dropped away from her and he stepped back.

"It's all right, Jana. Forget what I said. Forget everything." With that he turned and walked away.

Jana got through the rest of the afternoon trying to follow Bayard's suggestion. To forget the whole incident. Still, it cast its shadow. She was relieved when her father arrived earlier than expected to take her home.

Chapter Ten

❧

$\mathcal{J}$ana was glad to be home. The house party had been like indulging in too much rich food—she was happy to be back in her familiar surroundings, eating the plain fare of her regular life again.

Most of all, she hoped the Kipolas were back from Kona and that Kimo would come to see her. After being exposed to Bayard and his college friends, it would be wonderful to be with someone like Kimo. So natural, so honest, so completely who he was.

Remembering how his eyes had lit up when he first greeted her outside the church that evening before Christmas, and the way he had looked at her as he handed her his scarf at the rodeo, had sent her hopes soaring.

Her mother wanted to hear all the details of the house party. Jana tried to give her a full report, except she left out the part about the borrowed designer gown she'd substituted for her own to wear to the New Year's Eve ball. She didn't want to hurt her mother's feelings, so to distract her from questions about what *she* had worn, Jana went into great detail about Edith's Hawaiian dress. She also left out her strange encounters with Bayard. Jana had the impression her mother would not have approved at all of any of it.

Her mother seemed satisfied with the account. "Well, I'm glad you had a good time, dear."

Two days later, Jana took Nathan down to the beach to play.

She was helping him build a sand fort when she happened to look up and see a tall, familiar figure coming along the beach toward them.

"Look, Jana. It's Kimo!" exclaimed Nathan, dropping his little shovel and waving his hand.

Kimo waved back. He came up to them as casually as if he had never been away at all. "Aloha." His gaze met Jana's over Nathan's head. Then, smiling, he squatted down on the sand beside Nathan, started scooping sand, packing it along with him. In a minute he looked up and grinned at Jana.

"Like old times, eh?"

"Yes," she smiled, "like old times."

It was as simple as that. Even Nathan seemed to accept Kimo's presence, as if it had only been a matter of days since they were all together. Later, when Nathan was busily running back and forth to the shallows to fill his sand bucket with water and bring it back up to fill the moat they had constructed around his fortress, Kimo and Jana began to talk.

"I loved getting your letters," he told her. "It was like receiving a piece of home. I could almost see, hear, and taste Hawaii." He smiled. "Mahalo."

"I'm glad. I liked writing them." She paused, hardly daring to meet his gaze, and then she said shyly, "I missed you." She quickly asked, "How did you happen to come to the rodeo?"

"One of my cousins is a paniolo, works for the Preston Ranch." There was a slight sharpness to his saying of the name Preston—or was it her imagination? "He told me about it, said there were always prizes, that it would be fun. So I thought, why not?" Kimo shrugged. "Truthfully, Akela told me you would be at the ranch for their New Year's celebration, so I decided to come along, hoped I might see you."

Ah, what she had longed to know, but to hide the color she felt flaming into her cheeks, Jana ducked her head as though to dampen down a crack in one of the fort's turrets with water Nathan had just dumped into a hole at her feet.

"Well, you did," she murmured.

"Yes, and it was wonderful," Kimo said quietly.

Jana raised her head and looked straight at him. This was how it should be. No games, no teasing, no subtle playing. Kimo didn't know the meaning of subterfuge. What a relief. He was telling her he missed her and that he cared. Now she was free to do the same.

"Oh Kimo, I'm so glad to see you. How long will you be here?"

"Another week. You know this is my last year at the academy. My teachers have suggested I apply for an apprenticeship to a famous cabinetmaker in Germany—"

"Germany!" Jana gasped. She had forgotten all about the possiblity that Kimo would receive the apprenticeship. She vaguely remembered him talking about it. But that had been long ago. So many other things had happened since she had first heard about it. But no...She blinked. The thought of Kimo's leaving struck with a sharp pain.

"Yes. He is very well known. One of the finest. It would be a real honor to be accepted. He only accepts a limited number of apprentices."

"But it's so far away! So far from Hawaii."

"Yes, I know. But it would mean so much. Everything. For the future. If I get the opportunity, when I come back I can start my own business."

Over the hard lump rising in her throat, Jana managed to ask, "How long would you be gone?"

"Two years."

"*Two years?*" she repeated, her heart sinking.

Kimo met her startled eyes.

"You would care? That I was gone?"

"Yes, of course." She lowered her eyes, afraid he would see the sadness and the fear in them. Fear that if he were gone that long, he might forget her. . . .

"No, Koana," he said softly. "Don't look so sad. It is such an opportunity for me, for the future. If I get to go—well then, I must go." He paused. "You'll be going off to school next year, too, won't you? Akela tells me your parents want you to go to teachers college in the States."

"Yes, but I—" Jana made a sweeping fan in the sand with one hand, saying almost defiantly, "I don't want to go! All I ever want is to stay here and paint!"

Nathan, who had kept busy building his fort, suddenly looked up and said, "Jana's an artist. She paints really good. Did you know that, Kimo?"

Kimo laughed and reached his hand out, tousling the little boy's hair. "Yes, I knew that, *keiki*. She sent me some of her paintings when I was away." He turned back to Jana. "That's what you will do, Koana. First you will do what your parents wish, and then you'll come back here and paint." He added softly, "Maybe we both have to go away—to come back."

For a moment Jana looked into Kimo's eyes and knew that what had passed between them was real, binding, and a promise. A promise that couldn't be spoken of yet, but one they both understood.

Kimo got to his feet. "I'm taking Tutu over to Aunt Peula's this evening. But could we spend tomorrow together? Take a picnic somewhere?"

"Oh yes, I'd like that," Jana answered, feeling her heart rise happily.

"Well then, I'll be on my way," he said. "Aloha, Nakana."

The little boy looked up and grinned. "Aloha, Kimo."

"Aloha, Koana," Kimo said to Jana, who echoed, "Aloha."

Kimo left then and walked back down the beach the way he'd come, stopping halfway, turning back to wave his hand. Waving hers in return, Jana felt happiness flood all through her. Kimo was back. He'd come home and to her. Just as she'd dreamed, just as she'd prayed.

The next day when Kimo came, Jana was waiting. She had to check her impatience while he carried on a leisurely conversation with her parents. He answered her father's questions—about school, his classes, his woodworking, life at the Heritage Academy—seemingly in no hurry.

At length Jana picked up the picnic basket she'd packed early, and moved to the top of the porch steps. Her mother took the hint and said, "Well, you two have a nice day." As they went down the steps, she cautioned, "Jana, be sure to keep your hat on. You know how freckled you get with too much sun."

Inwardly Jana winced. Why did her mother have to remind her—and Kimo too—that hers was not the sun-loving skin of a Hawaiian girl?

"Yes, ma'am," she replied.

Kimo threw her a teasing glance, then said to her mother, "I'll see that she doesn't get sunburned, Mrs. Rutherford."

They took the path behind the house that led to the beach. Jana remembered the days when she and Kimo had raced down this same way when they were children. So many shared times, so many happy memories.

"Akela should be here!" she said impulsively.

"She's with Pelo. She stayed over in Kona for a few days so that she could be with him some more."

Jana stopped in her tracks, surprised, and looked questioningly at Kimo. He smiled. "I think they're in love," he said matter-of-factly.

"Oh?"

"Yes. Don't look so surprised. It happens."

"Of course. I know, it's just that—"

"Akela didn't say anything to you? Well, she's shy. It's easy to tell when they're together. They have eyes only for each other."

When they got to the beach, they found a nice sheltered spot under a banyan tree, surrounded by dunes, and set down the basket.

"So did you have a good time at the Prestons' house party?" he asked her.

How to describe all that had happened? "It was all right. But—" Suddenly Jana decided this might be the time to ask him about the night outside the church when he first came home. Hesitantly she told him how she felt, saying, "I thought you were angry at me."

"Angry? No, I'd never be angry at *you*, Koana. I guess I was just disappointed that you'd be away when I got back from Kona. Besides, maybe I resent the Prestons a little. For a lot of reasons that have nothing to do with you. *Kala mai ia'u*, I'm sorry, if you misunderstood."

Relieved, Jana said impulsively, "I'm glad. I was afraid something had happened that we wouldn't be—well, friends anymore."

Kimo reached for her hand, held it for a minute. "We'll always be friends, Koana, remember?" Then he leaned forward and with his finger wrote something in the sand—*kau a kau maka maka*, forever friends.

Reading what he had written, Jana felt a warmth spread all through her until her very fingertips tingled. "Mahalo," she said, smiling.

"Let's walk down where the rocks are, look for tide pools," he suggested, getting to his feet, then reaching down to take her hand and pull her to her feet.

"Wait!" she said and bent to unlace her shoes, pull off her stockings. Kimo had already kicked off his sandals. Together they walked to the edge of the water and waded along the shallows, letting the incoming tide curl around their bare feet.

"Tell me about Honolulu," Jana demanded. "Did you ever see the king?"

"The 'Merry Monarch'? Not often. We hear a great deal about him. The Iolani Palace is beautiful—at least, that's what people say. I can't, because I've never been invited there myself."

"You're entitled, though, aren't you? I mean, being that you're a descendant of one of the chieftains of Hawaii?"

"So are many students at our school. Queen Kapiolani attended the graduation and awards day at the academy. But I was sitting too far away to get a good look at her. The girls said she was gorgeously dressed, silken trains swishing, jewels sparkling. The king is supposed to be something to see, too," Kimo laughed. "He has so many medals on his uniform, people have to shield their eyes, because the sun makes them dazzling."

"That sounds so exciting. Seeing royalty and all. Tell me more," Jana begged.

"I've heard other things about the king, but I don't know whether I should tell you or not. You're such an innocent," he teased.

"I am not!" she retorted indignantly. "Tell me, please. You must," she pleaded.

"Well, you've heard that the Scottish poet Robert Louis Stevenson is a great friend of the king's. He visits the palace often, and they spend lots of time together."

"That's all? Why shouldn't you tell me that?"

"You interrupted me. I was going to say that rumor has it he puts away four or five bottles of champagne in an afternoon. However, Stevenson says the king is none the worse for it. If you can believe that. Stevenson also declares that King Kalakua is very fine and intelligent. You knew he was an accomplished musician and composer, didn't you?"

"All Hawaiians are talented," Jana said. "*You* are."

"With my hands," Kimo conceded. "That's not like hearing music in your head and being able to put it into notes so other people can play it on instruments or sing the words."

"You make beautiful things out of wood. Just like poets make something beautiful with words," Jana insisted. "Poetry in wood."

"Mahalo," Kimo said quietly. "I'll remember that."

That day together was one Jana would treasure for a long time after Kimo had returned to Honolulu. She was so happy, in a way that was different from other times of happiness. With Kimo she was more truly herself than with anyone else. There was no need for explanations, not even for words.

In the week that followed, they saw each other almost every day. When Akela came back from Kona to Tutu's, they made a threesome, often taking Nathan along with them on their picnics and sometimes sailing. Kimo was teaching Jana's little brother to swim and surf, and those were wonderful days.

Then at last it was time for Kimo to return to Honolulu. The afternoon before he was to leave the next morning, Kimo came alone to walk with Jana along the ocean.

They both knew that something had happened, something had changed in their relationship. They were not children, not playmates, any longer—they were something more than friends. What they were now to each other, neither was quite able to say.

There was a certain poignancy to that last afternoon they spent together. They didn't talk much, just held hands and walked along the beach. As the wind off the ocean grew cool, the shadows long, they knew it was time to go. Before leaving the beach, Kimo halted by the surf's edge, sat down on his heels, and wrote something else in the wet sand. Jana leaned over to read the words *Aloha ka-ua,* Let there be love between you and me.

He stood up, looked at her with dark, serious eyes. Then he took her hand and they walked slowly up the path back to the Rutherfords' cottage.

At the gate Kimo asked, "Will you write to me, Koana?"

"You hardly ever answer," she pretended to pout.

"They keep us pretty busy at school. After classes there's workshop. Then we all have other duties around the grounds and buildings. Lots of work, not many hours to yourself. But I'll do better this year, I promise," he laughed softly. "I like getting your letters on that pretty pink stationery. I get a lot of joshing from the other fellows when they see those envelopes with the flowers you paint on them."

"Do you mind?"

"No, it makes me feel proud. Someone cares enough about me to take the time and trouble to write." He paused. "You do care, don't you, Koana?"

He had to bend his head to hear her reply, "Yes, I do."

Then Kimo put his hands on her shoulders, leaned forward, and kissed her on both cheeks, the traditional Hawaiian way. "Aloha, Koana."

Impulsively Jana put her hands up, captured his face in them, held it for a moment, then kissed him on the mouth.

"Aloha, Kimo."

The day after Kimo left for Oahu again, Jana felt lonelier than she had ever remembered. The possibility that the next time Kimo left the island it might be for Germany made her desolate. Something had happened between them during this vacation, something new, something different. *Aloha kaua a kau maka maka.* She wrote those words over and over, on scrap paper and on the margins of her lined school tablet "may we be friends forever."

When school started again, Jana was shocked to learn from Edith that her father, acting upon Bayard's advice, was investigating schools on the mainland for her to attend next year. Dismayed, Jana exclaimed, "Then, you won't be graduating with Akela and me?"

"I know, I'm sorry about that. At first I told Papa I wouldn't go! Then he kept persuading me"—she dimpled—"*bribing* me, you might say. Adding things he would do if I'd agree to go. He's even promised to ship Malakini to Walnut Hills for me to ride when I'm there. And Bayard says that's near enough to New York to go to the theater and go shopping at the big stores, and there'll be all sorts of interesting places to go and see. Besides parties and balls at the nearby men's college." Edith's eyes sparkled with excitement at the promise of a new life.

Jana did not say anything. She remembered Bayard's voice coming clearly to her from the patio on New Year's morning: ". . . she needs to associate with people of our own class, not just Hawaiians."

Part Two

Chapter Eleven

❧

*E*dith left for the mainland to the fashionable boarding school she would be attending in Virginia. Jana and Akela accompanied her and the Colonel to Hilo to see them off on the steamer to Honolulu. The friends embraced and said tearful good-byes. Although Edith shed copious tears when she hugged them both, there was an unmistakable excitement in her farewells. As eager for new experiences as Edith was, this was the ultimate adventure for her.

As they stood on the dock watching the steamer move out of the harbor, a sense of melancholy hung over the two girls left behind. Riding back in the Prestons' carriage, they were somberly aware of the fact that the two of them would be starting their last year of high school without the third member of their trio. Although they didn't put it into words, both girls felt that something would definitely be missing in their lives.

The months that followed Edith's departure were even harder for Jana than for Akela. Jana felt Edith's absence more keenly than Akela did. Akela was always surrounded by the large, supportive Kipola family, with their frequent gatherings. Then too, she now had Pelo to love and comfort her. Almost every other weekend, Akela went to Kona to be near him.

Edith proved a poor correspondent. A month after she left, Jana and Akela received a letter addressed to them both, in which she described her life as "hectic" and said that the school kept them "hopping":

> *There are classes in everything you can imagine! Fencing! Dancing! French! Weekends, we have all sorts of social activities, such as the dansants (that's French, but means that young men from nearby schools come, stand against the wall, and gawk at us, then clumsily ask some of us to dance, and we all drink fruit punch). I live in a suite of six rooms. There are two girls to a room, and we share a sitting room. My roommate's name is Vinnie Albright.*

That was about the extent of correspondence from Edith. She did, however, send picture postcards from many of the "educational" field trips the school took to "historic sites"— one a view of Mount Vernon, another of Jefferson's Monticello, yet another of the Washington Monument.

With both Edith and Kimo gone, Jana felt lonely. She missed Kimo especially and more than she had expected to. He had been gone all summer, working at a woodworker's shop in Manoa on Oahu. After their brief, idyllic reunion at the beginning of the year, she thought his feelings for her had changed, deepened, become more than just affection. Why hadn't he written? But then, why should she have thought he would? He had told her he wasn't good about writing.

However, it was a terrible blow when Jana learned that Kimo had been accepted as an apprentice by the German cabinetmaker. When Akela told her he would leave for Germany without returning to Hawaii, Jana was stunned. What had only been a possibility had become a reality. Germany was a world away. She couldn't share with anyone, not even Akela, how much it hurt that Kimo hadn't written to tell her himself. Her feelings for Kimo were buried deep in her secret heart.

Jana tried to fill up the emptiness she felt by concentrating on her studies and her painting. Still, her days seemed long and lonely. She took Nathan with her to the beach and sketched while he played, she helped her mother with household tasks, and somehow time passed.

Another disappointment came with the news that Edith would not come home for Christmas as they had all hoped. Instead, the Colonel would travel to the mainland, where Bayard would meet them in New York for a holiday of parties and theatergoing. Edith had sent a hasty note of explanation along with presents for both her friends—a chiffon scarf for Akela, and a beaded evening purse for Jana. What possible use she would have for it, Jana didn't know. To make matters worse, Akela would be gone to Kona for the Kipolas' annual family gathering. As a result, Jana was hard put to pretend she was looking forward to Christmas. For Nathan's sake she tried.

As if to lighten her sagging sprits, a few days before Christmas she received a package in the mail. It was heavily wrapped in brown paper, with lots of strings and stamps. From Germany, from *Kimo*! Excitedly she unwrapped it and found a book of reproductions of lovely watercolors, pictures of Rhineland castles and cathedrals. Inside was a short letter saying that he was living with a German family, managing to learn enough of the language to get along, and that the cabinetmaker to whom he was apprenticed was a hard taskmaster and kept them working long hours.

I've never been good at putting thoughts into words, as you know, Koana, but I do think of you every day. I miss you. I miss our talks, our times together. I miss everything in Hawaii. It is so strange to be so far from everything I love and understand.

Jana read these few lines over and over. Was she included in those things Kimo loved and understood? In the note, Jana sensed the deep loneliness Kimo must be experiencing, and she wept sympathetic tears, feeling his heartache.

Spring 1887

With graduation only a few months away, Jana filled out several applications to a number of women's colleges. Her parents suggested one in San Francisco that offered a two-year course to earn a teacher's credential. There was a need for elementary teachers on the island, and finding a position would be almost guaranteed. Obediently but halfheartedly, Jana filled out the forms. She didn't want to teach—she wanted to be an artist. She had sent for the brochure of a California art school and had learned that there were scholarships available.

She had discovered Psalm 37, and it had become her favorite. Especially verses 3 and 4, which she said over and over to herself: "Trust in the Lord . . . Delight yourself also in him, and he will give you the desires of your heart." Why would the Lord have planted the desire to paint so deeply, given her the talent she had, if he didn't mean to "bring it to pass"?

The thought of going away from the island to the mainland was frightening. There had been so many changes in her life in such a short time—in the space of a year, actually—with both Edith's and Kimo's departures from Hawaii. Jana didn't want to leave the island, didn't feel ready for such a change. To be in a strange surrounding, among strangers, didn't appeal to her. Only if she could win a scholarship to an art school might the idea be more acceptable. Then she could come back to Hawaii and fulfill her dream of being an artist, even if she had to teach to support herself.

To qualify for one she had to submit a portfolio of her art-work, with one main piece on which her chances for a schol-arship would be decided. Both parents were full of suggestions. Her father liked many of the watercolor seascapes she had done, her mother favored copies she had made of famous paintings. Jana knew it should be something entirely original. She wanted to do something that would stand out from other entrants. Something that expressed her in a unique way. Something that spoke of Hawaii, that came from her heart, expressed her feelings. A personal statement. That was what she felt would attract the judges, the people who decided who got the scholarships.

Jana walked the beach, stared out her window, prayed about it, thought, sketched, and tore up many attempts before at last she got an idea. She would design a quilt, a pat-tern, blending both styles, Hawaiian and American, into one beautiful, complete design. Just as she herself was a blend of both cultures. Excited as she was about her idea, she knew she needed to learn more about the Hawaiian quilts. She decided to go talk to Tutu, who was always working on a quilt, and share her idea and find out about the "secret" hid-den in Hawaiian quilts. She wanted her design to have its own secret meaning as well.

Tutu welcomed Jana as usual and was eager to share her wisdom and talent with her.

"We take quilt making very seriously in Hawaii," she began. "It is considered an art, an individual, creative expres-sion of each woman," she said in her soft voice. "The mis-sionary ladies taught Hawaiians to quilt and showed them how to cut out the patterns and sew them on the cloth. Gradually, instead of copying the designs the missionaries gave them, Hawaiian ladies began to create their own." Tutu's capable brown hands moved slowly, taking precise, small stitches. "My mother made beautiful quilts. She was a very spiritual lady. She prayed over her quilts, blessing the persons who would receive them as a gift, sleep under them." She paused, then went on thoughtfully. "Her designs were often the result of a vision or dream. An idea would come and she would cut it out from memory, with no pattern.

"The cloths used by the missionary ladies for bedcovers were much different from the ones Hawaiians used. In the olden days, people slept on mats woven from the *lauhala*, the ribbonlike leaves of the *pnadanus*. They were soft and fine, almost like silk to the touch. Before the missionaries came, Hawaiian women were skillful in making tapa cloth from the inner bark of the *wauke* plant. They wet it and shaped it into size, dried it in the sun, pounded it. It was a long, tedious process. Tapa cloth was then used for everything, for clothing as well as for bedcovers."

"But the quilts you make, Tutu, are constructed much like the ones my mother has, like the ones my grandmother makes. A padded undercloth, then the design part on top."

"Yes, I know. The basic quilt is the same. All of us who attended the missionary schools learned how to cut and sew and make quilts like we were taught. The difference is in the design. For some reason, we were quick to learn the skill of handling needle and thread and stitching the appliquéd patterns. The art was in creating our own designs."

Jana watched, fascinated, as Tutu's needle weaved in and out around the pattern she was applying to the quilt. It was the shape of a pineapple.

"Hawaiians took to quilt making very easily," Tutu went on. "Hawaiians love happy occasions and any reason to celebrate. They love to make gifts to give loved ones at special times, such as weddings, birthdays, new babies, and other joyful happenings. Quilts are perfect for this. My mother made wedding quilts for all her daughters and daughters-in-law, and many, many baby quilts." Tutu laughed her deep, throaty laugh.

"But what about the secret, Tutu? Tell me about them," Jana asked. She was curious about this element, which made the Hawaiian quilts different from the ones her mother's aunties had given her.

"Well, there's a code of ethics about the quilts. The person who creates a design keeps it a secret. To exchange an original design is a sign of a deep bond of friendship and is rarely done, but when it is, the person who receives the design alters it slightly to put her own stamp upon it and to respect the originator." Tutu halted, holding up the part she was working on, putting her head to one side, and studying it for a minute before continuing. "Even the giver of an original design does not necessarily confide the hidden inspiration of it to the person receiving it—that is her choice. Sometimes it is too personal or has such intimate meaning that she wants to keep it to herself. Often it could be a particular event, or a meaningful episode in her life, that she does not want to share with anyone."

Jana could understand that. In her mind, an idea for her "secret" message in her design was forming, and it was something she knew she wanted to keep private.

"What about the quilt you're making now, Tutu? Does it have a secret?"

"Aha, Koana—if I told you, it would no longer be a secret, would it?" she chuckled. "But no, this is one I'm making by request. My sister wanted me to make this one like one I made before. It's a more common design. Hawaii has so many beautiful flowers and fruits, most of the simpler designs are drawn from pineapple, breadfruit, and anthurium shapes. One of my personal favorites is a quilt I made after I was baptized."

"The one hanging in your bedroom on the wall opposite your bed?" Jana had often admired the colorful design of that one. With its orange-colored fruit, red flowers, and green foliage on a white background, it looked like a garden in full bloom.

"It reminds me of one of the happiest days of my life," Tutu smiled reminiscently. "I hung it there so I can see it every night before I go to sleep and it's the first thing I see in the morning when I wake up."

Jana knew that Tutu's religion meant everything to her. She could remember waking up early sometimes during the nights she spent with Akela and hearing Tutu praying. The cottage had an open floor plan, and from where Jana slept on a mat in Akela's bedroom, she could see Tutu standing at the window in the front of the house, looking out over the valley, holding her big, floppy Bible in both hands. Later, when both girls were awake, Tutu always led them in grace before breakfast and always ended it with, "Today, Lord, I ask that you bless our day and let us be a blessing to others."

Jana had incorporated that thought into her own prayers.

"So, little one, have you heard enough about quilts for now?" Tutu asked, starting to fold up her work, signaling it was time for her to stop for the day.

"Yes. Mahalo, Tutu, you've helped me so much." Jana rose, then kissed Tutu's soft cheek and left.

On her way home Jana felt excited. She could not wait to get home, get out her drawing board, her sketch board and put the idea for a quilt design on paper.

Actually it was only after several sketches made, torn up, and begun again that finally Jana traced her design onto a sheet of fine watercolor paper and carefully outlined it.

Hawaiian quilts were always given a name as well as a secret title known only to the quilter. She wanted to choose an appropriate one for her design. That was a little longer in coming. As she selected the colors, she prayed to get just the right name, the one that was meaningful and true to what she wanted to express. The colors were easier, she used the yellow of the royal hibiscus, the violet blue of the jacaranda blossoms, and the pale pink of the anthuriums to represent what she found most beautiful about Hawaii—the flowers that grew here wild, as purely God's creation on this special island.

Hour after hour as she painted in the design the Scripture verse that came to her was Matthew 6:28. "Consider the lilies of the field...even Solomon in all his glory was not arrayed as one of these."

She didn't show it to anyone, didn't want anyone to see it until it was finished, until she was satisfied that it was the best work she could do.

At length as the deadline for submission for scholarship consideration neared, she allowed her parents to see it.

"It's lovely, darling," her mother said. "Just beautiful."

"Very fine, Jana. I'm proud of you, my dear," her father nodded. "And what do you call it?"

She told them she was going to letter in the Scripture verse with an explanatory note that the flowers depicted were all indigenous to the island.

"Good. I think the judges will take note of that." Her father seemed pleased.

The secret title she kept to herself, not sure anyone else would really understand. She called it *The Gift*. Because she felt being born in Hawaii was a gift, growing up here was a gift, her talent was a gift. And she wanted the design, whether it won a scholarship or not, to be her gift to God, her thank you for living as close to paradise as it was possible on this earth.

Jana recalled an afternoon when she had asked her mother about *her* quilts. She wondered if they had a "secret" like the Hawaiian ones did. Was it possible that her mother had more in common with the island ladies than she thought?

Her mother had opened her cedar chest and brought out a tissue-paper-wrapped bundle, placed it on the bed, and unwrapped it carefully, displaying a beautiful cover. "This is what we called a "crazy quilt," she told Jana, "They were very popular twenty years ago, all the rage. It's a different sort of a memory quilt as well. You take pieces of clothing you wore on some memorable occasion and cut it into squares, they don't all need to be the same size, then piece them together and make a quilt. They're more for display than use. I made this when we lived in California. This was after we left Washington, where your father was stationed with the Army. Here is part of the skirt of the ball gown I wore to my first White House levee. I was so excited at the thought of meeting President and Mrs. Lincoln. And this was a gown I wore to attend a Military Ball." She pointed to triangles of peach satin embroidered with apricot suttachi.

Jana was intrigued, listening entranced as JoBeth talked and pointed out the different materials that had once been a dress or jacket or bodice, from which it had been cut and woven into this unique coverlet.

JoBeth started to refold the quilt, wrapping it carefully in tissue paper, then she pointed one slender finger to the patch of azure velvet. "See this, Jana, this piece of blue velvet? That was part of a dress I wore to the theater the night the president was murdered. I vowed I'd never wear it again. And I didn't. But I did cut it up and sewed it into the memory quilt. See, I bound it with black satin, those were the ribbons on my mourning bonnet, the one I wore to the Capitol Building where Lincoln lay in state—" JoBeth's eyes moistened and she shook her head. "It was such a sad time—still, I wanted to mark it as something very significant that happened in my life." Her hand moved over to some squares of jade taffeta. "And this was my wedding dress, Jana—"

"You didn't wear a white gown and veil, Mama?"

"No, darling, perhaps if we had married in my home-town. . . ." JoBeth looked pensive then she quickly brought out another quilt, spread it out so Jana could see it.

"This is my Friendship Quilt. I started it on our wagon train journey across the country and finished it when we got to California. You see, after the War, feelings still ran high between North and South, there was much bitterness and unforgiveness toward people still considered enemies on either side. Since your father had fought for the Union, we felt we could not return to the south to make our home, to build our life together. So we decided to come west. We joined a wagon train of thirty-five other families. It took us eight months and in those months I made many friends among the women. We all were boded by the excitement, the adventure of heading into an unknown place to start new lives. There were many hardships on the trail and so it was necessary and wonderful to have other women as friends, to support and help, to comfort you in case of sickness and yes, sometimes, in death." JoBeth paused, her eyes expressing some of the sorrowful memories. "See, this is a patchwork quilt, four squares to a patch and the center one has a special design. Each woman created her own patch to exchange with the others, embroidered her name, the date, where she was from, and where her family were headed." JoBeth held the quilt out so Jana could see.

"Millie Hartshorn, 1867, Bridgeville, Kentucky, Ho, for California." Jana read out loud. "Ruth Alice Webster, 1868, Dayton, Ohio, California." She looked at her mother. "How come they weren't all going to California like you and Papa?"

"There was what you call a turnoff point, those wagons going to Oregon went one way, the California group another.

That's what makes this quilt so special. We knew when we exchanged our patches that we might most likely never see each other again. But all I have to do is look at one of these autographed patches and that face comes right into mind. I can almost hear a certain laughter, a voice, a cheery word, remember a funny incident, or a sad one, or a time of sharing—I can never forget any of these ladies."

"Do you know where they are now? Do you ever hear from any of them?"

JoBeth shook her head. "No, none of us knew exactly where we'd be, or had an address where someone could write to us." She sighed. "That's the hard part, but, the good part is I'll always remember the happy times, where we were all young and looking forward to the future. Before anything bad happened to any of them or before any of us got old."

"I guess all quilts tell a story, don't they, Mama?"

"Yes, dear, I suppose they do." her mother replied

And her mother could weave as fascinating a yarn about *her* quilts as any of the Hawaiian quilters could, Jana decided with satisfaction.

"How did you and Papa happen to come to Hawaii?" Jana asked.

"We hadn't planned that at all. But after our little baby died, your brother Ross, named after *my* daddy, I was sad and not well for a long time. Your father thought a milder climate and change would be good for me. For both of us." She smiled at Jana. "And so it was. Not long after we went to Oahu we had *you*! So it was a happy move indeed." She put both hands on Jana's cheeks and kissed her. "See, 'all's well that ends well.'"

Chapter Twelve

❧⚜❧

O ne early April afternoon, Jana was in the stationer's
store shopping for art supplies. Busy examining a variety
of brushes, she was startled to hear a familiar voice behind her.

"Well, if it isn't Miss Rutherford."

She turned around, brush in hand, and saw Bayard
Preston. Completely taken by surprise, she exclaimed, "What
are *you* doing here?"

"Home for spring vacation," he replied, regarding her
with that look she had always found disconcerting.

"Did Edith come, too?" she asked hopefully.

Bayard shook his head. "No, she'll not be coming until
June. She's spending her vacation in Newport, visiting one of
her classmates. All sorts of parties and other exciting events
were planned, and it proved too enticing to turn down for a
mere trip home." His smile was slightly cynical. "My sister's
become a social butterfly and also something of a belle. A few
fellows you and I both know have been making weekend pil-
grimages to Virginia to pay court to her." He paused. "Does
that surprise you?"

"Not really," Jana said, but turned away so that her disappointment wouldn't be seen. Actually, it didn't surprise her.
It was just what she'd been afraid would happen. Edith was

growing away from Hawaii and her old friends. All in the space of less than a year. Jana continued to look through the display of brushes, saying casually, "That will be fun for her. But I'm sure your father will miss her."

"Father is on a business trip in Honolulu. I just returned from seeing him off in Hilo," Bayard said. "I'm to hold down the fort at the ranch for a few weeks." He added, "I hope you won't let me get too lonesome. How about going riding with me some morning?"

Jana took her time selecting two brushes before replying. She needed a moment to absorb the fact of the invitation. She remembered unpleasantly their last encounter. Turning around, she said coolly, "Mahalo, Bayard, but I'm very busy right now. I'm studying for final exams, and I've a painting project I'm working on that has to be finished by the first of the month."

Bayard raised a skeptical eyebrow. "It can't take *all* your time, surely? Besides, if you're working that hard, you deserve an hour or two off."

Jana moved to the next display and picked up a watercolor pad, opened it, and rubbed a page with her fingers to test its quality. Her experience with Bayard during the house party still rankled. She also resented the conversation she'd overheard between Bayard and the Colonel, the one that had persuaded Colonel Preston to send Edith away to school.

"I really don't think so, Bayard." Jana moved toward the cash register.

Bayard followed. "Come on, Jana, you know what they say about all work and no play," Bayard coaxed. "A ride? Take a picnic down to the valley?"

She remained unconvinced. "I don't think so."

While the clerk rang up Jana's purchases, Bayard stood beside her. After she had paid for them and received her change, he adroitly took the package.

"I'll carry these for you," he said ingratiatingly. "May I drive you home?"

"Mahalo, but no. I can walk."

"I *know* you can walk, Miss Rutherford," he teased. "I would be honored if you'd let me escort you home, either on foot or in my gig, which is just outside."

For some reason, Jana felt she would be more in control of this chance meeting if they walked. "It's only a short way," she said. "I can manage that, thank you." Jana put out her hand for her package.

Playfully he held it out of her reach. "No, you don't. Why are you being so independent, Miss Rutherford? Can't you tell I want to talk to you? Let me walk you home."

It would have seemed silly to continue to refuse or make a fuss, since Bayard seemed so determined. So she simply shrugged and they fell into step, walking together down the street. At the corner, they turned onto the road that led to the Rutherfords' house.

"What have you been doing with yourself since I last saw you?" Bayard asked.

"Studying mostly, painting," she replied. "Nothing very exciting. Tell me more about Edith."

"Oh, I don't keep track of all her doings. But I can tell you, there's not much studying going on at that fancy school. The most that the young ladies learn there is how to flirt, dance, and order from a French menu."

But that's exactly what you wanted for your sister, wasn't it? Jana was tempted to say. *Making good social contacts, mingling with people other than "just Hawaiians."*

"Evidently, Edith is at the top of her form, enjoying every minute. At least, that's what I gather by the amount of traffic that departs our campus on weekends," he laughed. "Quite a few keep the railroad tracks clacking between New Haven and Washington. I think Greg Amory is the most frequent traveler."

Aha, Jana thought, *so Edith is succeeding in achieving her goal.*

"Enough about my sister," Bayard said. "Tell me about yourself, Jana. What kind of plans are *you* making? What is this mysterious art project that you claim is taking up so much of your time that you can't go horseback riding?"

With some reluctance, but since she had given it as her excuse for having little free time, Jana told Bayard about her plan to try for an art scholarship.

By this time they had reached the Rutherfords' gate. Jana hesitated, wondering whether to ask Bayard to come in or not. While she debated, he glanced at their house. It was a gray and white Hawaiian-style bungalow built on stiltlike pillars, with a wraparound veranda. Surrounded by palms, lime trees, and banana trees, the yard was blooming with all sorts of flowering bushes.

"I've always loved Hawaiian cottages," Bayard said softly. "Their simplicity, their design—how they exactly fit right into the landscape. They're not an intrusion. I've often thought I'd like to be an architect...." He gave a rueful smile. "However, of course, I'm destined to be a rancher." He sighed. "Aren't you going to invite me in, Jana? I've never been inside your house."

Embarrassed, Jana stammered, "Yes, please, do come in. I'm sure my mother would be happy to see you."

"Another time, maybe." He started to hand her the package but then held it just out of her reach and asked, "Will you think about going riding with me?"

Flustered by her lack of hospitality and eager to make amends, she impulsively answered, "Yes. I haven't ridden in quite a while. Since the Christmas before last, in fact, at the house party—" She broke off, wishing she hadn't brought it up.

Bayard looked thoughtful. "Ah yes, *that* Christmas. The house party. New Year's." He gave her a rueful glance. "As I remember, I wasn't in a very good mood for one reason or another. Did I somehow—" He halted, frowning. "We ended up rather badly, or am I mistaken?"

Jana put her hand on the gate latch, but Bayard put his hand out so she could not lift it and asked, "Did I do or say anything to offend you? If so, I'm sorry. Please accept my apology?"

"It was nothing. I have to go in now."

"All right." He gave her the package. "May I come by sometime?"

"Of course." She pushed open the gate. "Mahalo, Bayard."

"My pleasure." He tipped his Panama hat. "My regards to your parents."

When Jana came into the house, her mother was in the kitchen, slicing *pumelos* to make marmalade.

"Who was that with you, dear? I didn't recognize him."

"Bayard Preston, Mama."

"Edith's brother?"

"I met him in town."

"Oh, is Edith home, too?"

"No, she won't be coming anytime soon. He says she quite loves it on the mainland."

"You will, too, dear, when you go."

Jana pursed her lips but did not answer. Instead, she left the kitchen and called back, "I think I'll go down to the beach for a while. I want to do some sketching."

In her room, Jana gathered up her paint box and a small tin cup for water, then unwrapped the package containing the new sketchbook and brushes, put them in her canvas bag. The encounter with Bayard had upset her somehow. It had stirred up something that still bothered her. She felt they had unfinished business between them. Seeing him again had brought it all back.

Down at the beach, she settled herself under a banyan tree and, backed by the dunes, propped her sketchbook against her knees, wiggling her bare toes in the warm sand. She always felt happier, calmer, near the ocean. Its vastness, its blue stretch to the horizon, seemed to make whatever was troubling her seem smaller, less important. She squeezed out some blue from the tube, dipped her brush into the water in her cup and stroked a horizontal line across the top of the page. She squinted out at the sea and saw that there were at least three shades of blue to be somehow captured and translated to her picture. How could she ever make it look as beautiful as she was seeing it, as it really was? She bent forward, moving her brush across the rough, textured sheet of paper.

Looking up again, she saw a surfer riding the crest of a wave, his bronzed body glistening in the sun. Immediately she was reminded of Kimo. How he must miss Hawaii, long for the sun-streaked skies, the curve of beach, the blue swells of the ocean. Did he miss her?

Did he have drifting dreams of the Big Island, its valleys, bamboo forests, the beach where they had walked so many times together? She thought of the sandcastles they had built as children, and her throat swelled and tightened. She closed her sketchbook, rested her chin on her knees, and watched as the surfer came ashore in a shower of foam, then turned and remounted his board and began paddling out past the swells again.

Kimo had been gone only a few months, and yet those days spent together on the beach, the days of childhood, and even the days of the Christmas before last when he had come home seemed a long time ago. They were fading even for her, who was trying to hold on to them. For Kimo, they may have disappeared entirely.

Chapter Thirteen

School was closed for Easter vacation. Jana was sitting at her desk reviewing her notes for a book report when there was a light tap on her bedroom door and her mother's smiling face peered in. "Jana, Bayard Preston's here."

Jana frowned. What did *he* want? Probably just bored and lonely being at the ranch all by himself. With a sigh, she closed the book and got up. Passing her bureau mirror, she gave her hair a cursory pat. As she walked down the hall toward the porch, she heard her mother's voice and Bayard's deeper one. She hesitated a moment before joining them, determined to be cool, to not be taken in by his charm. Jana opened the screen door, walked out, and deliberately used the Hawaiian greeting. "Aloha."

Bayard rose from the wicker chair. He looked crisp and handsome in a beige linen suit, polished boots, white shirt.

"Hello, Jana. I was just telling your mother I have to drive over to Kamuela and would love to have your company. We could have lunch at the hotel. Will you come?"

Her mother smiled encouragingly. Jana could see that Bayard had already convinced *her* that it would be a good idea. His look challenged, as if he suspected she was trying to think of an excuse.

"Why not, dear? It would be a nice break," her mother suggested mildly. To Bayard she said, "Jana's been working very hard, getting ready for exams and finishing her painting projects."

"Then, an outing should be just what she needs," Bayard said.

"I have a book report to write...," Jana started to say, but that sounded indecisive and Bayard took the initiative.

"Do come, Jana. It will do you good."

"Yes, dear, why don't you?" urged her mother.

Caught between the two, she could think of no reasonable excuse. Nothing that wouldn't sound rude. So she gave in and went to put on a fresh blouse and get her straw sailor hat.

Within minutes she found herself in his surrey, with his high-stepping horse trotting along the beach road toward Kamuela. Glancing over at Bayard's handsome profile, Jana wondered again at the invitation. He was probably bored and at loose ends up at the ranch alone. She felt the same ambiguity about him she had felt at the Christmas house party. In the year since then, she had come to the conclusion that Bayard Preston was attractive but dangerous. She still thought so. Yet she had not forgotten how she had felt when he kissed her.

It was a perfect Hawaiian day. Cloudless blue skies, balmy breezes stirring the fringe of the surrey's canvas top. All along the road, flowers of every kind and description were in bloom. Hibiscus, ginger, plumeria, and the feathery blossoms of the jacaranda trees scented the air with perfume.

It was only a short drive to Kamuela, and they were soon in the center of the small town.

"I have to stop at the bank, sign some business papers for my father. Do you mind waiting? It won't take long, and then we'll have lunch."

"Not at all," she replied as Bayard pulled the surrey into a shady spot across the street from the bank.

As she sat waiting, Jana tried to remember why she resented Bayard so much. It wasn't that last angry confrontation in the Preston garden on New Year's Day. At last she realized what it was. She still blamed him for Edith's going away to finishing school. His urging his father to send her had really been a result of his own frustration, his ambiguity about his bicultural background.

Before she had thoroughly thought it through again, Bayard was back and they drove over to the oceanfront hotel. At the entrance, a hotel employee helped them from the surrey, then led the horse away. Bayard placed his hand under Jana's elbow, and together they went up the wide steps to the veranda. Here white rush-bottom rocking chairs lined the long porch, and varicolored hibiscus trailed from baskets hung along the fretwork.

Although she had often admired the stately dignity of the impressive, white-pillared structure, Jana had never been inside. The Rutherfords did not move in the same kind of circles as the Prestons and never dined out. At the entrance to the dining room, the waiter greeted Bayard by name and suggested they take a table on the screened porch.

"Would you enjoy that?" Bayard asked.

A little overawed by the luxurious setting, Jana simply nodded. They were led out to a screened-in area overlooking a terraced garden of palms and winding paths among brilliant flower beds. A cooling breeze wafted gently in from the ocean. The waiter seated Jana, pulling out a white wicker chair and handing her a large menu, then quietly departed to a discreet distance to await their order.

The tablecloth and napkins were pale pink linen, and the water glasses sparkled like crystal. Jana noticed fashionably dressed men and women at the other tables. This was a part of island life she had rarely seen at close hand: people of wealth and leisure who lunched expensively at this exclusive place as a matter of course. Bayard, perfectly at ease and assured, was studying the menu.

So many choices were confusing, so Jana let Bayard order. After bringing them iced tea with mint sprigs and slices of lemon, the waiter went away. Jana began to relax and enjoy this new experience. She took a sip of her tea and murmured, "The view is lovely."

"So is *mine*," Bayard said, regarding her with amused eyes.

She ignored the flattery, discounting it as automatic— he'd had lots of social practice at that sort of remark. Deciding that his sister might be a safer topic of conversation, Jana asked, "So exactly when *will* Edith be coming home?"

Bayard shrugged. "When she gets bored with Newport, I suppose. As you may have noticed, my sister has a short attention span. But to answer your question, more than likely Father will insist she come back with him in a few weeks, and she'll probably bring some of her friends." He pulled a grimace. "A bunch of sillies, if I've ever seen any. All giggles, flirting, game playing!" He rolled his eyes. "Deliver me. Not an intelligent statement in any of them."

"Ah, but isn't *that* what *you* wanted Edith exposed to?" Jana demanded, feeling a bit of spiteful pleasure in turning the tables on him. "If I'm not mistaken, you said, 'Edith needs to be with other kinds of people, not just *Hawaiians*.'"

Bayard frowned. "Now that I think about it, I admit I did say that—*think* that. I'd forgotten," he admitted. "And that was before I'd met any of the young ladies at Millvale Hall!" He paused, then leaned his folded arms on the table. "I'd forgotten how refreshing it is to be with someone like you, Jana. Someone who's forthright, natural, not afraid to have her own opinions."

"Then, you've changed your mind about *independent* women?"

His frown deepened. "Is that something else I said that you're quoting? Aha, I must have said something that really offended you, or you wouldn't be bringing up this. Did I?"

The waiter arrived with their order, so she did not have to answer Bayard's question. Perhaps it was all best forgotten anyhow.

Jana realized she was very hungry, and she picked up her fork and began to eat shrimp salad served in a melon shell garnished with pineapple spears and kiwi fruit. But Bayard leaned toward her. "You didn't answer. So if I did hurt your feelings or anything, I'm very sorry."

"It's all right, Bayard. It doesn't matter. I think I'm too sensitive sometimes."

"Then I did. Just say you forgive me. You're the last person I'd ever want to hurt."

"Yes, it's all right. I'm sure you have better things to think about than me."

"You're wrong, Jana. I've had a lot of time to think about it. About you." He lowered his voice. "When I saw you that Christmas, it was the first time since you were a little girl. Or at least it was the first time I'd *really* noticed you. I recognized something in you. I didn't know what it was that drew me, but I felt we had a bond I hadn't realized before. It's very strong, very powerful."

"And that is?"

"Hawaii."

She looked surprised.

"Down deep I have the same feeling you have. Born here but still a *haole*. It causes a kind of dual personality." Bayard gave a self-deprecating little laugh. "Not that I'm one of those new scientific fellows that talk about childhood influences on the adult character. Most of that, I think, is a lot of rubbish. But Father sending me to the mainland at an impressionable age *did* have an effect on me. I felt caught between two worlds, actually. He did what he thought was best. Wanted me to get the kind of education he didn't think was possible here on the island. For *me*, at least. Then I went on to Yale, still trapped in this dichotomy—" He halted suddenly. "I don't know why I'm rattling on like this. I must be boring you to death."

"No, you're not. It's very interesting—"

"You're sure?"

Jana did not have a chance to respond to Bayard's question, because the waiter came to check if everything was all right and if they wanted dessert.

At the same time, four gentlemen wearing white linen suits and Panama hats came out onto the porch and took seats at a table nearby. One of them, seeing Bayard, waved and then excused himself from his friends and came over to their table. Bayard introduced Jana, and the two men spoke for a few minutes about a business matter the man was arranging for Colonel Preston. When he left, Bayard and Jana did not pick up the thread of their conversation again. Jana was relieved. It was edging on too personal a tone.

Finished, they rose, and after Bayard had signed for the bill to be put on his father's account, they left. Back in the surrey, on their way to Waimea, Bayard gave Jana a sidelong glance. "You're not sorry you came, are you?"

"No, not really." Thinking that might have sounded ambivalent, she added, "It was very nice of you to suggest it, to think of me."

"I think about you a great deal, Jana. More often than you'd guess."

Again she felt that this was leading to an exchange that might prove to be too personal, so she skirted around the subject, remarking on some particularly lovely anthuriums. "Oh look, I'd love to try to paint those."

When they reached the Rutherfords' cottage, he helped her down from the surrey, "When may I see you again? Tomorrow?"

She shook her head. "Tomorrow's Sunday. I go to church and Sunday is our family day. I usually take Nathan to the beach, or we visit some of my parents' friends."

Bayard looked disappointed. "You said you might like to go riding? Remember?"

Jana hesitated. She wasn't sure seeing Bayard again was a good idea.

However, he persisted as he walked her to the gate. "I'll come by sometime in the middle of the week. We can make plans then. All right?"

"Mahalo," she said, again deliberately using the Hawaiian word. She didn't know exactly why, but it was almost as if she were testing Bayard.

"And you will think about going riding?"

"Yes."

"Good." He seemed satisfied. Bayard Preston was used to getting his own way. He turned and went whistling back to his surrey. Jana went into the house.

Her mother lifted her head from her sewing and looked at her daughter with thoughtful eyes. "Did you have a nice time, dear?"

"Yes, it was lovely. Lunch was delicious."

"Bayard is a handsome young man, isn't he? And a perfect gentleman. You can certainly tell he has been educated on the mainland."

"He says Edith won't be home for another month," Jana told her. "Bayard says Colonel Preston has gone to the mainland and they'll return together. She's visiting some school friends in Newport, Rhode Island."

"Newport?" her mother repeated. "That's a very fashionable resort for very wealthy people. Edith must be traveling with high society."

Jana darted a quick look at her mother. Was there a tinge of regret in her voice? Jana knew that her mother had come from a fine old southern family. She had left it all to follow her idealistic husband west—to California first, then to Hawaii. She had probably had all the luxuries and refinements of a gentle upbringing in an affluent home. Did she miss it? Did she want that kind of life for her daughter?

Jana did not realize *she* was the object of her mother's thoughtful speculation. Looking at Jana as she filled a glass of water from the cast-iron kitchen pump, JoBeth Rutherford thought about what a graceful, attractive young woman Jana was becoming. What exactly did the future hold for her here on the island? What did she hope for her daughter? Of course she wanted her to find love and happiness. But was it wrong to hope she would have a life easier than her own had been? She recalled her rather practical Aunt Jo Cady saying, "A woman can fall in love as easily with a wealthy man as a poor one." But was that true? It was for Aunt Cady, evidently— Uncle Madison had been a prosperous lawyer. JoBeth herself had given no thought at all as to whether Wes was rich or poor. It hadn't mattered. She had loved him with all her heart, and they had—in spite of everything—been happy.

But what about Jana? JoBeth felt sometimes that her daughter was a hopeless dreamer, impractical, romantic, given to fantasy. What would life hold for someone like her?

With a man like Bayard Preston, Jana would never lack anything. She'd have a beautiful home, clothes, every luxury, travel ... the things a talented person like Jana would enjoy. There would be no financial worries, no scraping or scrimping.

Was Edith's older brother becoming romantically interested in Jana? The question lingered tantalizingly.

Chapter Fourteen

❧❦❧

On the Saturday before Easter, Jana assembled all the
necessary implements to help Nathan dye three dozen
eggs for the Easter party the Rutherfords held every year.
They had hard-boiled them the evening before and let them
cool overnight.

"Now's the fun part!" the little boy said eagerly as he
watched Jana spread newspaper on the kitchen table, place
the bowls filled with food coloring in a row of red, blue, yellow, and green.

"That's right," she smiled, getting out two big spoons for
them to use for dipping the eggs. She had also brought her
paint box and brushes and a glass jar of water, to add designs
and finishing touches when the colored eggs were dry.

"The next fun part will be hiding them, won't it, Jana?"

"Yes, and Papa has promised to help so *you* won't know
where all the eggs are and get them all and fill your basket
before anyone else!" she laughed, tousling her little brother's
hair.

"That wouldn't be fair," he declared, but his eyes sparkled
and his grin was mischievous.

"No, it wouldn't."

The process of dyeing took both of them over an hour,
and Nathan soon tired of the tedious job.

"When do we get to paint on flowers and stuff?" he asked Jana.

"I guess you could start on some of the first ones we did. They should be dry by now." Jana tested the first half dozen with one finger. Satisfied that they were ready for the additional decoration, she got Nathan set up at one end of the table, then sat down beside him to get him started. She was painting some daisies on the shell of one, when Nathan suddenly flung down his brush in frustration, spattering paint.

"Mine are awful, Jana! Next to yours, they look terrible!"

"No, they don't! Not at all. Here, let me show you. You're doing just fine. You have to be patient, that's all."

"But yours are so much prettier. That's because you're an artist. Everyone says so."

"Well, maybe. I guess so, but *yours* are special, because *you* are doing them yourself. Mine are different, not better," she consoled him.

"Did you always know you were an artist, Jana? Even when you were little—my age?"

"I always liked to draw and paint," she replied.

"So you did know you wanted to be an artist when you grew up?"

"I guess so."

"I know what I'm going to be when *I* grow up," Nathan said firmly.

"What's that? A teacher like Papa?"

He shook his head vigorously. "No! A builder and woodworker like Kimo."

Surprised, Jana looked at him. "Like Kimo?"

"Yes. I miss Kimo. When is he coming back?"

"I'm not sure," Jana answered, thinking about how long Kimo had been gone and how long it had been since she'd heard from him. "Soon, I hope."

"I love Kimo," Nathan said matter-of-factly.

Jana gave him a hug, saying to herself, *I do, too.*

❦

Easter morning dawned brilliant with sunshine, the air sweetly fragrant with flowers and filled with the sound of church bells. Jana had a new bonnet, a new blouse, and a new prayer book. After an early breakfast and while her mother went to get dressed, Jana got Nathan buttoned into a white sailor suit. It was rather stiff and he squirmed uncomfortably, making the job almost impossible. However, in the end, with his curls slicked down and a blue silk scarf tied neatly, he looked almost cherubic. Then the whole family walked the short distance to the small church where they worshiped.

It had dozens of twins all over the island, with the same tiny porch, peaked roof, and bell tower. Pink anthuriums bloomed on either side of the steps leading inside, and cala lilies were clustered in profusion on the altar. The Rutherfords settled into their regular pew just as the choir marched in to the chords of the small organ. The congregation rose to its feet, joining in the opening hymn, which was first sung in Hawaiian, then in English.

"Holy, holy, holy, Lord God Almighty, heaven and earth are filled with your glory. Hosanna in the highest. Blessed is he of Israel who comes in the name of the Lord."

The voices lifted up, mellow and clear, and enveloped Jana in a lovely peace. The beautiful words swept her up into their meaning. *In whatever language the praise is sung,* she thought, *it must be a sweet sound in the Lord's ear. All over the world, in all different tongues, believers are greeting the risen Savior, King of Kings, Lord of Lords.*

Jana lowered her head so no one could see the tears that sprang spontaneously into her eyes.

The joyous service concluded with Communion and then a final hymn. The choir filed out, and the congregation followed them outside into the lovely morning, greeting each other with traditional hugs and kisses, saying, *"Ka la i ala hou ai ka Haku."*

To her astonishment, Jana saw Bayard standing in the churchyard. Dressed in a spotless white linen suit, ruffled shirt, and Panama hat, he came toward her.

"Good morning and happy Easter," he said, bowing slightly. His gaze moved over her admiringly. "That is one of the prettiest bonnets I've yet seen, and the lady wearing it is quite charming as well."

"What in the world are you doing here?" she asked.

Bayard placed one hand on his heart, with an injured look. "Don't tell me you suspected I was one of those Christmas and Easter Christians?" he demanded. Then, with an ironic smile, he added, "Which, unfortunately, I am. If I reform, will you forgive me?"

"You don't need to ask *my* forgiveness. I shouldn't have—" She broke off, embarrassed that he had surmised the truth. She *had* been surprised—in fact, astonished—to see him at church.

"Not at all. You're right."

"Whether you're a churchgoer or not is none of my business."

"I'd like you to make it your business," Bayard said in a low voice. "I can't imagine anything more pleasant than being reformed by you."

Jana blushed and was glad to be rescued when her parents and Nathan joined them. Bayard greeted them all graciously. To Jana's surprise, her mother said, "We're having an Easter breakfast party and an old-fashioned Easter egg hunt for the children, Bayard. You'd be more than welcome if you cared to join the fun."

"I'd be delighted," he accepted at once.

As they fell into step behind her parents, Jana could not resist saying, "I didn't know you went in for such things."

"Maybe there's a lot you don't know about me, Jana. If you'd give me a chance, I'd reveal some hidden qualities you may not even suspect." His tone was light but his eyes were serious.

"I'm intrigued," Jana murmured, but she was not sure she wanted a chance to get to know Bayard Preston better. It was like looking down a road that had danger signs all along the way, with a sharp curve in the distance so that you could not see where it ended.

There was no more time for Jana and Bayard to be alone. Friends had already begun to gather at the Rutherfords' for this annual event. Jana had to help her mother set out the fruit and banana nut breads, keep the adults' coffee cups filled, and pour pineapple juice. When the children began clamoring to begin the egg hunt, Bayard shed his jacket and enthusiastically joined Mr. Rutherford in supervising. Bayard seemed to have great fun running around with the children, pointing out hiding places to some of the smaller, slower ones.

At last all the eggs were discovered, and families with children, their baskets full of eggs and candy, began to leave.

Bayard retrieved his coat, said his thanks and good-byes to the Rutherfords, then found Jana.

"Will you come riding with me tomorrow?" he asked as she walked with him to the gate. "Remember what I said earlier? There's no telling how much I might improve if we spend enough time together."

"Oh Bayard, I'm not sure. . . ."

"There's no school, so you have no excuse. I'll come for you at nine. You can ride Palani. She's a gentle, copper-colored mare with a sensitive mouth. You'll love her. I guarantee it."

Chapter Fifteen

❧❧

True to his word, Bayard came by for Jana at nine the following morning, and they rode up to the ranch in a small, open buggy. At the Preston stables, one of the grooms brought out the horse Bayard had promised her, a lovely little mare with delicate legs, shining coat, and blond mane. Bayard patted her nose, murmuring something, then turned to Jana, smiling. "See, isn't she a beauty? You'll find her a dream to ride."

He checked the saddle. Then as the groom stood at Palani's head, Bayard helped Jana to mount. As he had promised, Palani was sweet tempered, with an easy mouth. As soon as Jana picked up the reins, she felt an instant response from the horse.

"Where's yours?" she asked.

"Come along, I'll show you," Bayard said. He took the tooled leather saddle and tack that the groom handed him. With long strides, he went past the corral and into the pasture. Jana, on horseback, followed at a walk.

At the pasture, Bayard whistled through his fingers, and a horse that had been grazing on the hilltop lifted its head, ears pricked up, and whinnied. Then, with a toss of its head, silver mane flying, the mixed gray horse galloped across the field. Approaching Bayard, he slowed to a kind of prancing trot, circled Bayard a couple of times, then stopped, one hoof pawing the ground.

Bayard ran his hand along the horse's back, stroking it gently, then leaned for a moment against its arched neck. Slowly he slipped the bridle over the horse's bowed head, adjusted the bit, then saddled him. Swinging lightly into the saddle, he came over to where Jana was halted on her mare, watching. Grinning, he said, "A paniolo at heart." He leaned forward in his saddle toward her. "If I'd been in the New Year's rodeo, would you have accepted *my* talisman?"

Taken aback, she countered, "Why *didn't* you ride that day?"

He shrugged. "Who knows? Maybe I was inhibited by my guests. Those *haoles*, strangers to our land and our customs, think we're wild enough. I didn't want to give them any more ammunition." He whirled his horse around, shouting over his shoulder, "Come on, let's go!"

He galloped off. Jana loosened her reins, and Palani followed in an easy canter. It was a glorious morning and an exhilarating ride. Bayard always kept a few lengths ahead of Jana, but she didn't care. She was not in competition with him, as Edith might have been. She was enjoying the rocking motion of Palani's gait, and the feeling of freedom engendered by the wind in her face, tugging her hat back, blowing her loosened hair. She had missed riding as she and Edith had often done, traveling over these hills together. Jana suddenly realized how much she missed Edith as well.

However, there wasn't time to indulge in nostalgia about the old days of comradeship, for Bayard had reached the top of the cliff and had halted there. As she came alongside and reined, she saw what Bayard was looking at: the rolling green hillside and, in the distance, the ocean, stripes of varied blue stretching out to a cloudless horizon. For a few minutes neither spoke as they absorbed the breathtaking view. Finally he said quietly, "Shall we go home now? Next time we'll ride down to the valley."

Next time? Jana thought. Bayard was assuming there would be a next time. She watched him turn his horse and start back toward the ranch. Following him at a slower pace, Jana recalled vividly her last ride down the precipitous, almost perpendicular path to the legendary Valley of the Kings. Gradually she caught up to him, and with both horses slowed to an easy canter, they rode back to the ranch.

At the stables, Bayard quickly dismounted, came around to Jana's side, held up his arms to help her down from her saddle. She stood for a minute smoothing Palani's mane, rubbing her nose, murmuring affectionate thanks for the lovely ride. Watching her, Bayard said, "She could be yours, you know. You two are kindred spirits."

Startled, Jana looked at him. She was not quite sure what he meant, but she did not dare ask. Bayard continued to confuse and bewilder her.

One of the grooms led the horses away to be rubbed down and fed, and Bayard and Jana walked up to the house.

"One day we should ride to the volcano side of the island. Would you like that?" he said.

"I don't know about that," she answered slowly. Hawaii still had two active volcanoes, Mauna Kea and Kilauea. Jana had been into the volcano country on the other side of the island. She had found it oppressive and forbidding, and when you got close, the smell of sulfur fumes was heavy. She knew all about the ancient beliefs regarding Pele, the goddess of fire, who was supposed to dwell within the volcano. In the olden days, native people tried to appease her with all sorts of gifts so that her anger would not erupt and send fiery molten lava flowing over their land, their homes, their crops.

"Well, you *will* go riding with me again, won't you?" Bayard asked.

"Yes, of course. And thank you for allowing me to ride Palani. She was wonderful."

They had reached the house, but before going inside, Bayard stopped and reached for Jana's hand, held it, and said, "I meant what I said back there. She could be yours."

Jana looked at him, puzzled. Before she had time to answer, Meipala came out onto the veranda.

"Mr. Bayard, there's a gentleman here to see you. A Mr. Pollard from the bank. He says he has a message from the Colonel."

Bayard frowned, then said to Jana, "This shouldn't take long. Probably more papers to sign. I have Father's power of attorney. You can sit out here on the porch. Meipala will bring you something cool to drink." He excused himself and went into the house.

A few minutes later Meipala brought Jana a glass of cool guava juice. As she handed her the tall glass, Meipala asked, "You hear from Edith?"

Jana shook her head. "Not much. She's not much of a letter writer. From what Bayard says, she's having a really good time."

"Too good, if you ask me," Meipala sniffed. "Did he tell you she bringing party of girls with her when she come home?"

"He mentioned something about it."

Then Meipala asked Jana about her family and her own studies.

"Akela and I will graduate in June. But we miss Kiki— we always thought we three would finish school together."

"You *should* have. Don't know what got into the Colonel to send her so far away." Meipala shook her head sorrowfully. "I thought she would miss the island more than she seems to."

Just then Bayard came out onto the porch, accompanied by Mr. Pollard, so they had no more time to discuss Edith. Mr. Pollard recognized Jana, whom he had met at the Kamuela Hotel when she was there with Bayard, and greeted her cordially. Then he said to Bayard, "Well, I suppose that's all for now. If you want to go over this further or discuss it later, I'm always available."

"Fine, sir." Bayard's voice seemed unusually crisp.

He walked Mr. Pollard to his buggy and saw him off. When he came back to join Jana, Bayard seemed preoccupied. She hoped the banker had not brought worrying news. However, his good humor returned at Meipala's suggestion that she have their lunch served out there on the veranda. She poured him a glass of guava juice, then left them.

Jana leaned back against the striped linen pillows of the white wicker rocking chair. She felt pleasantly tired from their ride and completely relaxed and comfortable. What a heavenly day, she thought. And how delicious it felt to just lazily rock and stare out at the lush gardens and the distant blue ribbon of the ocean. She didn't even feel the least bit guilty. At home, nobody ever sat around just doing nothing! This was pure luxury.

And to think that this was how the Prestons and their friends spent their days. They took this kind of leisurely life for granted. Doing whatever occurred to them—no chores, no duties, no time frame, people to wait on them . . .

Her dreamy thoughts were interrupted by the arrival of one of the uniformed Chinese house servants. He carried a large tray from which he set a low, round table with their lunch: a delicious assortment of fruit, small, hot shrimp-filled pastries, salad, a loaf of banana nut bread, and a pitcher of iced tea.

"I could soon be spoiled here," Jana remarked half jokingly as she helped herself to the appetizing array of food.

"And why not? It's good to see things appreciated and enjoyed. Isn't that what all this is for? To be enjoyed?"

"I don't know whether my father would agree with you, Bayard!" she laughed.

"Does he frown on people enjoying themselves?"

"Oh no, not that. But he does believe there is more purpose to life than just enjoying oneself. You know: life is real, life is earnest."

"That's a throwback to the early missionary days. They disapproved of almost everything about Hawaiian life and tried to change it." Bayard paused. "However, it worked in the reverse. The Hawaiians converted them to an easier way of life, a more relaxed style of living. That's what makes this island so special." He halted abruptly. "It seems we had this sort of conversation once before, and we ended up—how was it?"

"I think I just misunderstood, Bayard. I thought—well, that you were somehow ashamed of loving Hawaii."

"No, it wasn't that. It's just that I can't be completely Hawaiian. . . . I'm sort of torn in two. Maybe when I come back here to live for good, take over the running of the ranch . . . Maybe then it will seem more—" He broke off. "I guess I'm talking a lot of rubbish."

"Not at all. Kiki and I argue about which one of us is more Hawaiian than the other. At least, we used to. . . ." Jana's voice trailed off uncertainly. She wasn't sure what Kiki thought anymore.

"Of course, her mother *was* Hawaiian."

"Yes, but I was *born* in Honolulu—she was born in San Francisco."

"I was born here on the island," Bayard said. "That makes *us* technically natives, doesn't it? And gives us a special relationship." He gazed at her thoughtfully. "Wouldn't you say?"

For some reason, Jana felt a little tingling sensation. Somehow she couldn't pull her own gaze away from Bayard's.

Her heart fluttered erratically. Her hand holding the iced tea glass shook, and her fingers slipped on its frosty surface. She put it down quickly, afraid she might drop it. She wiped her mouth with the napkin and said, "I really think I'd better be going, Bayard. I've been gone all morning, and I promised Nathan I'd take him to the beach this afternoon." She brushed the crumbs from her lap, folded her napkin and placed it beside her empty plate on the tray, and rose.

"Must you go?" he asked, but he got to his feet also.

"Yes, I really must."

Bayard was quiet as he drove Jana home in the surrey. A thoughtful air had replaced his earlier lighthearted manner. Jana wondered again whether it was something Mr. Pollard had said. Or was it something in their own conversation that was bothering him? At the gate of her house, he said, "Mahalo, Jana, for making it such a pleasant time. Remember, you promised to go riding with me again. Palani will be disappointed if you don't."

"School starts again next week," she reminded him, feeling a little twinge of regret that she wouldn't be free to go on the kind of spontaneous expedition Bayard had suggested.

"Ah, that's right. You're still a schoolgirl, aren't you?" His eyes were teasing. "Well, we'd better make the most of this week, then, hadn't we?"

She watched Bayard's buggy, the fringe on its striped canopy swinging jauntily, disappear down the road. It had been fun today. More fun than she had ever anticipated having with Edith's older brother. She had been comfortable and at ease with him. No, not exactly that. Underneath, there had been a tiny bit of tension. As though she were on the brink of something. Something in the way Bayard looked at her, treated her, that was different from last Christmas. Something that was both exciting and a little frightening. . . .

That night, lying in bed and looking out her window at the shadow of the palm tree against the star-studded sky, Jana let her mind wander. . . . What would it be like to have the kind of life the Prestons had, a life of leisure and luxury and servants and trips and never worrying about money or what other people said or thought about you? What would that really be like?

She had never before really envied Edith Preston, had never thought much about what a contrast their families and lives were. Actually, it was Akela's family, the ohana, that Jana had looked at longingly. Now, however, there was a certain allure in the idea of being wealthy, free from worries about the future or about getting a scholarship. Edith had no such thoughts. She would always be taken care of. There would always be money for whatever she wanted to do, wherever she wanted to go. . . .

What was it Bayard had said? First about Palani—"She could be yours." Had he just meant she had ridden the gentle horse well and the mare had responded well to her? Or had he meant more than that? Had he meant it literally?

Then when he had looked at her and said, "We have a special bond, a special relationship, don't we?" They were both islanders. Born here but still of white parentage. It did give one pause. It did make one think.

Her eyelids felt heavy. It had been a long day, an interesting day, a day that in some ways seemed a turning point.

She was getting too sleepy to think it through, but as she drifted off, it was of Bayard Preston she was thinking. . . .

Chapter Sixteen

❦❧

School started again, and at first Jana found it hard to settle back down to the routine of studies and homework. The interlude of impromptu outings with Bayard had set her off track. It had been an interesting time but one that was also rather disturbing. Her long-held view of Bayard had altered, and yet she still wasn't sure she really knew or understood him.

One afternoon a few days after classes had resumed, Jana accompanied Akela into town on an errand for Tutu. Akela was to pick up some spools of thread that Tutu had ordered. Just as they came out of the fabric store, they practically ran into Bayard, who was coming down the street. Jana was surprised to be so glad to see him.

Bayard seemed equally surprised but pleased. "Well hello, ladies. Would you give me the pleasure of taking you somewhere for a cool drink?"

"Mahalo, Bayard," Akela said. "I'm sorry, I can't. I have to hurry home. Tutu's working on one of her quilts and needs these." She held up the small bag containing the thread.

"Another time, then. How about you, Jana? You're not in any hurry, are you?"

"No." Jana turned to Akela. "Do you mind?"

"Of course not. You two go ahead," Akela smiled. "Have a nice time."

"Do give my regards to your grandmother, won't you?" Bayard called after her, then held out his arm to Jana. "Come along, then."

Jana slipped her hand through his arm, and they walked down the street to a nearby confectionery store.

"Limeade?" he asked when they went inside.

"Lovely."

Bayard placed their order at the counter. He received two tall, frosted glasses and suggested, "Let's take these outside."

They went to one of the umbrellaed tables on the small lanai and sat down.

"You've changed my luck today," he told her.

"How's that?"

"Oh, I've just come from a long, boring session at the bank. My father's business. But while he's gone, I have to take care of some things. I was feeling very dull when I left there, and then—lo and behold!" He threw out his hand dramatically. "There you were! What a treat!"

Jana laughed at his foolishness but felt pleased. She held up her glass in a toasting gesture. "But it's I who's getting the treat."

"You'll have to pay for it, though," Bayard smiled. "I need you to help me select a gift for someone. A lady. Now, don't get any ideas. It's a hostess gift. For Mrs. Amory. You remember Greg, don't you? Well, I've spent several weekends with them over the last year or so, and I want to send her something special. But I don't know what, and I need your artist's eye to help me find something."

"Any idea what she might like?"

"I think something distinctly Hawaiian." He pulled a face. "You know how mainlanders are. They think anything from the islands is *exotic*."

"Well, that shouldn't be difficult. There's a wonderful shop not far from here that has beautiful things."

"Great. As soon as we finish here, let's go and take a look."

The store was one Jana had often lingered outside of, gazing raptly into the display windows at the merchandise. She had never ventured inside, because she knew that the prices were way beyond anything she could ever afford. It was even more marvelous than she had imagined. She wandered about, admiring the delicate porcelain vases, the intricate jade sculptures, the exquisite embroidered silk screens, the jewelry.

"Do you see anything that appeals to you?" Bayard asked.

Jana widened her eyes. "Of course! Half the store!" she answered in a hushed voice. Then, smiling, she led him over to a display of blue-and-white china and pointed to two graceful candleholders and a matching bowl.

"Yes, I think I agree with you," Bayard nodded. "I believe that would suit Mrs. Amory's taste very well." He gave Jana an approving grin. "You're a genius."

While his gift was being boxed and wrapped, they waited at the large jewelry display counter. Pearls and jade in all shades, shapes, and styles—rings, necklaces, earrings, pins, and pendants—were set out on dark velvet. Jana was totally entranced.

"Something here you'd like?" Bayard asked quietly.

"I've always loved pearls. They have such a quality of surprise about them. How they're found even seems romantic—out of the sea, like some lovely gift."

"I'd like to get you something. Pick something out."

Startled, Jana looked at him, stepping back from the display case. "Oh, I couldn't, Bayard. It wouldn't be—be proper."

"Why not? Just as a little thank-you for helping me today."

"That's not necessary, Bayard," she protested. "I enjoyed doing it. You don't owe me anything."

"What if I just want to do it? What's wrong with that?" His mouth twisted sarcastically. "Is it some kapu I never heard of?"

A *kapu* was an ancient rule of the Hawaiian culture, existing long before the white man came to the islands. There had been placed upon the people many restrictions that had to be obeyed. Certain things were forbidden. These included eating certain types of fish, which were reserved for royalty, or passing within the shadow of a king or his possessions.

A kapu breaker was severely punished. It was believed that if he or she went unpunished, some disaster, perhaps a *tsunami*—a tidal wave—or a volcanic eruption, might occur. However, if the culprit managed to reach a place designated as a refuge, the person was safe. All who sought entry there were admitted—vanquished warriors and noncombatants as well. It was a sanctuary in which offenders could stay as long as they wanted, but if they left, they were again subject to punishment. One such place, on the south Kona coast, was called City of Refuge.

Jana bristled slightly at his tone. She didn't like hearing jokes about the old Hawaiian culture. She felt that it should be respected, not ridiculed. "No, of course not. It's just that ... a young lady should not accept an expensive piece of jewelry from a gentleman unless they are—" She stopped short.

Bayard smiled as he finished her sentence. "You mean, unless they are engaged?"

Jana's cheeks flamed. "Well, yes."

"Wouldn't allowance be made if it was something quite small, given in friendship?" Bayard persisted. "For instance ..." He leaned forward and pointed down into the display case, to a small brooch, a pale pink, fan-shaped shell in which a tiny

616

pink pearl nestled. It was a delicate piece of jewelry, and Jana would have loved it. Still, it was out of the question. Her mother would have a fit! Reluctantly she shook her head.

"Mahalo, Bayard—it was a very nice thought, but no."

Just then the clerk returned with Bayard's package. Bayard peeled off several bills in payment and they left the shop.

"Could I talk you into going for a horseback ride along the beach this evening?" he asked.

"Oh, you certainly know how to tempt a girl!" she laughed. "I have a history test tomorrow. I have to really study hard tonight."

Bayard gave her a long, steady look.

"I never met a girl so honest or one with so much character."

Again Jana felt her face grow warm. When she was with Bayard, he often said things that made her react strongly.

For a moment a kind of uneasy silence tingled between them.

"Well, I have to go, Bayard," Jana said and took a few steps away from him.

"Could I give you a ride? My surrey is right across the park."

"No, thanks. I'll walk."

All the way home Jana thought about the afternoon, the time she had just spent with Bayard, and how much she would have liked the small shell pin with the tiny pearl.

Chapter Seventeen

❦

$\mathcal{D}$uring the next two weeks, there were other impromptu meetings, other little excursions, other unplanned outings, with Bayard. He would often show up with Palani on a lead and insist that Jana put aside her books and go riding.

It was getting near the end of school, and there were final exams and several special activities for the graduates. An open house was planned to which the island superintendent of secondary schools, magistrates, and other dignitaries had been invited. The seniors had been asked to bring samples of their artistic work or crafts to exhibit. The small island high school wanted to show off its students and their accomplishments.

Late one afternoon when Jana was going through her portfolio, trying to pick out some of her watercolors for the school exhibit, Bayard stopped by. She had spread some of her watercolors on the living room floor to look at them and decide which ones to submit. When she saw him standing outside the screen door, she called, "Come in, Bayard. Maybe you can help me decide."

He took off his boots and came in on stocking-clad feet. Jana, barefooted, was stepping between the pictures, moving them around for better viewing, selectively discarding some, leaving others. Bayard stood beside her. "You're very good, Jana," he said as he examined her work carefully. "I had no idea."

"Mahalo," she said rather absently. "I'm not so sure. These are not as good as I'd like them to be." She shook her head. "I've neglected my watercolors the last few months. I spent so much time working on the design I submitted for a scholarship to art school."

"You haven't heard yet, then? From the art school?"

"No, and I'm kind of losing heart. Maybe my entry was too different. It was a Hawaiian quilt design. I don't know. Perhaps I should have sent a seascape, like my father suggested, or a copy of some famous artist's painting, as Mama wanted me to do." She sighed.

Bayard looked steadily down at the paintings. "Want my choice?" he asked.

"Of course. Please."

Quickly he pointed out two. One was a scene at sunset, palm trees curved against a brilliant sky, a sailboat on the far horizon. The other was a small church surrounded by colorful red and pink anthuriums, the waxy, heart-shaped flower. "They show not only your skill but your emotion. The way you feel about the subject. Your heart. They *are* Hawaii."

Jana studied the paintings Bayard was pointing to. Immediately she knew he was right. She nodded. "Yes, I see what you mean."

"You really have talent, Jana. Scholarship or no scholarship, you should go on with it."

"Without one, I can't. Couldn't afford to go." Once the words were spoken, Jana could have bitten her tongue. She certainly didn't want to sound "poor mouth" to Bayard. However, he didn't seem to have even heard her. He had picked up one of the watercolors and was holding it at arm's length, examining it carefully.

"This is really good work, Jana. You can't give it up. Study abroad. You should go to France, to Paris."

"*Paris?* You are dreaming!" Jana gave him an incredulous look, thinking, *That's easy enough for you to say, Bayard*. People like the Prestons, people with money, never thought that the lack of it could make the difference between what you did and what you didn't do. Most of all, they didn't realize that money was necessary to fulfill dreams.

"But it would be a waste if you didn't continue." He caught her look, and a slow flush reddened under his tan. Still, he added seriously, "There must be a way."

"Oh sure, if you believe in Aladdin's lamp and have three wishes," she laughed, trying to lighten the moment.

"Could you leave this for a few minutes? Take a walk down to the beach with me? I have something to tell you."

His mood had changed abruptly. He had something on his mind. "Yes, of course. Just let me put these aside and stack the others. Mama is having her missionary society ladies' meeting here later."

Bayard was waiting for her outside when Jana came down the porch steps.

"Is something wrong?" she asked. "You look worried somehow."

"Not worried, exactly. Just sad. I have to go to the mainland. Father has arranged for me to take a position in a brokerage firm in New York. He wants me to learn investments so that I'll be able to take over when ... he's gone."

"When are you going?" Jana asked, surprised that the thought of Bayard's leaving dismayed her. During the past few weeks, they had seen a great deal of each other. Her old impressions of him as being arrogant, conceited, self-centered, had gradually disappeared. She had come to know another Bayard, one she had never suspected. The bond between them *was* there, stronger than she had realized, and true—the deep love they shared of Hawaii.

"As soon as Father gets back and I can get my things together—a few weeks."

"Will you be here for my graduation?" she asked. Then, afraid that might have sounded too personal, she amended, "*Our* graduation, Akela's and mine."

"I wouldn't miss it," he assured her. They were at the gate and Bayard opened it. Together they walked a short distance to the small grove of banyan trees at the start of the path that led to the beach. Here Bayard halted.

"I hate to leave all this." His voice sounded strange, tight. "I think only *you* would understand that, Jana. I don't want to go. But I have to. I can't escape my responsibility."

"But you'll be coming back, Bayard. I mean, your father wants you to run the ranch, after all, doesn't he?"

Bayard nodded.

Her heart wrenched empathetically. She *did* understand how he felt. She placed her hand on his arm and he turned toward her, then drew her into his arms, holding her tight against him. She felt his chin on her head as her cheek pressed against his chest. His hands smoothed her hair, and he murmured something she could not quite hear. Then he turned up her face and kissed her mouth. A slow, tender kiss. Sensing his need for comfort, Jana returned the kiss with a natural sweetness and sympathy. Bayard's arms tightened and he kissed her again. This time it was not gentle, but demanding—in it was a desperate longing that startled and then frightened her. Struggling out of his embrace, she stepped away from him, breathless. Her mouth felt bruised. Bayard dropped his arms and said, "I shouldn't have done that. I guess I want to hold on to something. You mean so much—symbolize all that I love. You're so special." He sighed heavily. "Now I have something else to apologize for, I suppose." The slightly sarcastic tone was back in his voice.

"No, not at all," she protested a little shakily. She wasn't blaming him, because she knew she had enjoyed his kiss. She had liked being held. For that moment, she had felt something wonderful. But was it for Bayard?

"I'd better go now," he said.

"Yes, and I have to get back home."

Silently they walked back up to the house. At the gate, Bayard took Jana's hand and held it in both of his for a moment. "Mahalo, Jana. For everything. For being you. I'll never forget the time we've spent together these last weeks."

Then he turned and walked away, and Jana went into the house. Inside she tiptoed down the hall, past the kitchen, where her mother was talking to Nathan, and to her room. She needed to be alone for a while to try to sort things out, analyze her feelings about what had just happened, about Bayard Preston.

She sat there on the edge of her bed, staring out at the darkening sky outside her window. The curve of the palm tree was silhouetted against a purple, mauve, and pink background.

The kiss had shaken her. Her response to it, even more so.

The time they had spent together these past few weeks had no reality, as if it were set apart from her normal life. It would be foolish to imagine a romantic relationship with someone like Bayard Preston. Who was under all that easy charm, the sophistication, the patina acquired by affluence and experience?

What would it be like to live within the magic circle of people like the Prestons? Bayard spoke so casually of going to Europe, and no expense had been too much for Colonel Preston to make sure Edith had her own horse at her prestigious school. Jana remembered the beautiful clothes Edith took so for granted, the lavishness of everything at the Preston Ranch. Her mind toyed with the idea of wealth, luxury, and travel.

Could she trust Bayard's enigmatic words? They were too vague, ambiguous. Had she been just a challenge, an interesting diversion? Yet there *was* something that drew them to each other, some strong attraction. But it wasn't love. Jana was sure it wasn't love. It couldn't be. Could it?

Fantastic daydreams invaded her thoughts. Dreams of being fashionably dressed, traveling to Europe, wandering through the vast halls of the great museums. . . . Bayard Preston could provide all this. If it was offered to her, would she turn it down?

Suddenly she thought of Kimo. It made her heart sore. Did he even remember what he'd written on the sand before he went away? In her heart of hearts she knew that no one else could fill the empty place he had left there.

"Jana!" her mother's voice called. "Come set the table for supper."

Jana got up. What foolishness she had been thinking. She could not expect anyone to fulfill her dreams for her.

~~~

Graduation night was a beautiful mingling of traditional stateside and Hawaiian ceremony. The graduates were all in white—the girls in their prettiest dresses, the boys in embroidered shirts, white duck pants. All wore leis of red carnations and white plumeria, the school colors. There was an invocation by a well-known minister from Kona, a welcome from the principal to parents and friends of the graduates, the salutatory, the prize giving, the valedictorian's speech, and then the diplomas were handed out, the school song was sung, and everyone was invited for refreshments at the reception in the decorated gym.

The graduates formed a receiving line at the gym entrance. Jana had won the art prize and was happy to see Bayard in the crowd, coming up to congratulate her. She was pleased that he had come, pleased that he brought another lei to add to the several she was wearing. The gift of a lei on special occasions was a Hawaiian custom.

"May I walk you home?" he asked as he dropped the lovely garland of white and yellow hibiscus over her head.

It was a starry night and blissfully cool after the warmth of the crowded reception, where the air had been heavy with the scent of mixed flowers.

"I'm leaving day after tomorrow, Jana," Bayard told her.

"So soon?" Her disappointment sounded in her voice. "Just when I'll be free, with no lessons, no deadlines to meet."

"Yes, I know. But . . ." Bayard shrugged. "But duty calls and all that nonsense." He sounded bitter. "I would have liked this time to go on, but Father has put everything into motion, and there's nothing I can do about it."

They walked back up to the house together in silence. At the gate Jana said, "The lei you brought is lovely, Bayard. Mahalo."

"I have something else for you, too," he said, putting his hand in his jacket pocket and bringing out a small, square package, wrapped and ribboned. He held it out to her. "I want you to have this."

She hesitated a moment, then took it. Her hands were already full with her diploma and her art prize.

"Don't open it now but after I'm gone. It's something I want you to have."

"Mahalo."

"Jana, I'm not sure when I'll be back. . . . I hate saying good-bye. I even hate saying good night." He laughed softly, then drew her into his arms, this time more gently than the other time. "I think I like the Hawaiian way best." He bent his head and kissed her the traditional way, once on each cheek. "Aloha." Then he was gone.

Jana stood there for a moment, looking into the darkness into which he had disappeared. In a few minutes she heard voices coming. Her parents were walking home with some friends and would soon be here. She wanted to be alone when she opened Bayard's gift, so she hurried into the house.

Once inside the house, she went straight to her room. She was trembling and didn't know exactly why. Excitement, probably. It had been a momentous evening. The end of a chapter in her life, the beginning of another.

It had been a wonderful evening. Only one important thing had been missing: Kimo. Her throat had ached when she saw all the Kipola family surrounding Akela, showering her with leis. Jana wished Kimo had been there. He would have brought her a lei, she was sure. But how could she be that certain? It had been so long, she could hardly remember what it was like when he had been here.

She understood now why she had responded to Bayard's kiss that evening. It was Kimo she had been longing to kiss when she was in Bayard's arms. She knew that was wrong. Unfair. But figuring that out had helped her put it into perspective.

That's why she wanted to open Bayard's present in private. She was afraid her mother would read too much into his gift. Perhaps, in a way, her mother might have liked to see her develop a romantic relationship with Bayard Preston. But Jana knew that would never happen. She was glad she had come to know Bayard in a different way, but it would never be that kind of love.

As soon as she unwrapped it and saw the name of the jeweler on the small silk box, she knew without opening it what it was. With shaky hands she lifted the lid, and there was the tiny shell pin with the one perfect pearl in its pale pink center. She drew in her breath. It looked even lovelier than it had when she first saw it in the display case.

Of course, she could not keep it. Not because her mother might think it improper for her to accept it, saying it was far too expensive a piece of jewelry for her to accept from a young man, *unless* ...

But Jana herself knew why keeping it would be wrong. She and Bayard had used that very word "unless" and understood what it might mean. And there would be no *unless*. Not now, not ever. Not with Bayard Preston.

Jana snapped the little box closed. Keeping it was out of the question. And Bayard Preston was out of the question as well.

⤙❧⤚

As Jana had expected, her mother said she must send it back. Jana rewrapped the present, wrote Bayard a note of thanks and regret, and mailed it to the Preston Ranch the next day. She did not hear from Bayard. Two days later she knew that he had left for Hilo.

Part Three

Chapter Eighteen

❧❧❧

When Jana heard that Edith Preston was coming home, she felt excited and yet a little anxious. She was afraid her own prediction that Edith would be drastically changed would prove true. Not only because of what Bayard had said about his sister but because of the fact that after her first few weeks at the Virginia school, neither Jana nor Akela had heard much from her. She seemed completely caught up in her new life on the mainland, her new friends, new activities. There had been a few notes, postcards, graduation gifts, but all the signs were that Edith's life had become a constant round of travel, theater, and weekend house parties.

The biggest shock and disappointment to Jana was that Edith had not seemed a bit homesick. In the two years she had been gone, she had not once come home to the Big Island. Instead, Colonel Preston had gone to the mainland twice, the last time for Bayard's graduation from Yale.

When Jana got the news, she confided some of her anxiety to Akela, hoping she might contradict her. "She'll probably be terribly changed," Jana said glumly. "She and her friends at that fancy school move in an entirely different world than we do. Edith could always afford to do things *we* could never do. But it's different now. She has friends with the same kind of money, who are able to do the same things she can. She spends time at *Newport, Rhode Island*—where only enormously wealthy people live, my mother says. They have *mansions* they call *summer cottages*! Edith will have nothing in common with *us* anymore."

Akela's smooth brow furrowed for a moment.

"Maybe not," she said complacently. "Maybe Kiki will be glad to be home. With *us*. Here where she can be herself. Not have to be something everyone expects. I imagine she has to 'pretend' a great deal with her friends over there. Especially because they don't know or understand anything about Hawaii."

"Maybe you're right, but I'm not so sure," Jana said doubtfully.

All her fears came to a climax a week later. Edith came tearing into the Rutherfords' yard on her horse, jumped down from her saddle, and ran up the steps onto the porch, calling, "Jana! Jana! Where are you? I'm home!"

Jana was sitting at her bedroom window, sketching. At the sound of that familiar voice, she jumped up, spilling her sketchbook to the floor, upsetting her brushes, overturning her water jar. Replacing everything in quick movements, Jana dashed out the door. She heard her mother's voice greet Edith, and Edith's enthusiastic response. In the hallway, Jana halted, feeling all at once strangely shy. Then Edith, standing just inside the front door, turned and saw her. "Jana!" she shrieked and rushed toward her.

The two girls hugged, then grabbed each other around the waist and danced together down the length of the hallway.

"Oh, Kiki! I'm so glad to see you!"

"Oh, I'm so glad to be back. You can't imagine!" screamed Edith, laughing merrily. "I'd forgotten what heaven Hawaii is!

I leaned over the ship's railing so far, Papa kept worrying I'd fall over as we came into the harbor."

Jana took a step back, still holding Edith's shoulders, regarding her speculatively. Dressed in a blue cotton shirt, a divided riding skirt, she looked just the same. The carelessly tied ribbon on her straw hat had loosened and had fallen back, letting her fair hair tumble about her shoulders. All Jana's apprehensions about a changed friendship faded. The old Kiki she remembered was back, just the same lovable, harum-scarum girl as ever.

They tethered Edith's mare in the shade of a sprawling banyan tree beside the Rutherfords' house, then trudged down the road and up the hill to Tutu Kipola's house to see Akela. On the way, Edith asked anxiously, "How is she? All the time I was away at school, I worried that you two would forget all about me. That when I came home, you would have changed, wouldn't want me as a friend anymore."

"How funny!" Jana stopped short and looked at Edith in amazement. "That's exactly what *we* thought might happen with *you*!"

"Really? Well, you two were always so close. I mean, before I came to school, you and Akela were best friends. I wasn't sure if you'd accept me, and then you did—" She shrugged. "But when I went away, I just thought—well, maybe I was afraid that after I was gone so long . . ."

Jana slipped her hand through Edith's arm. "No way! Never. Remember what we always said: 'A threefold cord is not easily broken'? We'll always be friends, no matter what."

"And how about Kimo?" was Edith's next question.

Jana's face got warm in spite of her not wanting to reveal too much to her sharp-eyed companion.

"Kimo is in Germany, didn't you know? He got a two-year apprenticeship with a famous cabinetmaker. He won't be home again for I'm not sure how long."

"I didn't know. I just remember him showing up at the rodeo at our house party that Christmas." She looked sideways at Jana. "You saw him that summer, didn't you?"

"No, he left for Germany right from Honolulu. It's a very long trip, you know." Jana tried to sound casual. "Kimo was always good-looking."

"You should hear what the girls at my school say about him when I've shown them pictures!" Edith laughed gaily. "They roll their eyes, pretend to faint, and giggle like crazy! They call him the 'noble savage,' from that picture of him dressed up as King Kahmehameha in our eighth-grade May Day pageant."

"How stupid!" Jana reacted indignantly. "I never knew anyone less like a savage than Kimo. He's the most gentle, kindest, most soft-spoken person in the world."

Edith looked at her with a startled expression. "Why are you getting your dander up? It was meant as a compliment—"

"Well, it certainly didn't sound like one," Jana retorted huffily. "What do those girls know about Hawaiians, anyway? To make such a remark."

"Jana! It's nothing to get upset about."

"It does upset me." Jana tossed her head. "Kimo is so intelligent and talented and well read. To make snap judgments about someone you don't even know seems—well, pretty *ignorant* of them."

"I'm sorry I said anything. I certainly didn't mean to offend you."

"It's not *me*, it's Kimo."

"But *you're* the one taking offense."

"Well, he's not here to defend himself. I should think *you* would have defended him when those silly girls made that comment."

Edith stopped walking, turned and faced Jana.

"Listen, Jana, I'm sorry. For whatever I said or did—or didn't say or do! Don't let's quarrel, for heaven's sake. It's my first day home. Please."

Jana felt ashamed and somewhat embarrassed by her outburst. "I'm sorry, too," she mumbled.

"Is there something you're not telling me?" Edith asked quietly. "Something about Kimo—and you? You love him, don't you?"

Jana met her friend's eyes slowly. "Of course I love him."

"And not like a brother, right?"

"Oh, I don't know, Kiki. He's been gone a long time. I don't know how he feels or—I suppose you'd say, as a dear friend."

"*More* than a friend?" Edith persisted.

Whatever more she was going to ask was interrupted by a voice calling to them from the top of the hill. Jana turned and, seeing a figure in a wide-brimmed straw hat and colorful mumu standing there, said, "There's Tutu. Let's hurry."

That afternoon, it *did* seem like old times. The three girls had a happy reunion. Edith left earlier than Jana, saying that she had to stop at the post office for the ranch mail and that her father expected her home for dinner.

After she was gone, Akela gently chided Jana. "See, what did I tell you? Wasn't Kiki just the same as she used to be? I didn't think she'd changed a bit."

Jana did not comment. She herself had sensed something different about Edith. She didn't talk much about her life at school, on the mainland, or with her new friends. Instead, she seemed happy just to do the things the three of them had always done.

Jana soon dismissed the idea that her friend had changed. But even during the occasional times they spent alone together without Akela, Jana felt there was something held back, something Edith wasn't quite ready to open up about, even to her close friend.

That is, until one afternoon when Edith arrived at the Rutherfords' house quivering with suppressed excitement. Her dark eyes were shining. "I have something wonderful to tell you, Jana. You first, because you were in on it from the beginning. But it hasn't been easy to bring off. I had to come clear home—but it worked! Look, *look*!" She thrust out her left hand and wiggled the third finger, on which a large emerald ring sparkled. "I'm engaged!"

"What?" gasped Jana.

"I couldn't wait to tell you. I can hardly believe it myself."

Jana glanced from the ring to Edith's radiant face.

"Yes, yes, it's true. I'm going to be married. To Greg Amory."

"Greg Amory," Jana repeated. Of Bayard's chums at the house party, Greg was the one she had liked least. She almost exclaimed, "Oh no, not *him*!" Then she remembered that Edith had set out to capture his heart, had mapped out a whole campaign. She must have continued to pursue him when she was on the mainland.

"Remember how *smitten* I was with him at the time? He was so ... so sophisticated, so aloof. I didn't want to make a fool of myself. But I played my cards just right. I told him that if he wasn't serious, I was going home to the island and not ever coming back to the States. I wasn't even sure when I left if it would work. But it did. I got letters, and then—it happened." Edith snapped her fingers. "He sent the ring. It came by insured mail this morning!" She laughed delightedly. "It's taken me a long time to catch him. But *persistence* won the day! Oh Jana, I'm so excited, so thrilled. He is so handsome—you do remember, don't you? Tall, blonde. He's captain of the tennis team at college and—oh well, so many things. And he thinks that"—she threw back her head, laughing—"I'm adorable. Can you imagine?"

"But isn't this all—well, awfully sudden?"

"Well, no, not really." She pulled a face. "I thought I'd better act quick. Before he changed his mind!" She laughed again, a laugh that sounded a little high and forced to Jana. "You see, he was planning to go to England for a year, travel on the continent. I was afraid he might meet someone going over—you've heard of those shipboard romances! Anyway, Greg's parents were sending him abroad and—well, you just never know. Well, Bayard and I were invited to their home on Long Island Sound. It was then that I worked all my magic." Edith looked down at her ring again, holding it out so it glittered. She admired it for a minute before she rushed on, saying, "But I also issued my ultimatum. . . ."

Jana found herself speechless, unable to think of anything appropriate to say. Somehow Greg Amory, at least the Greg she remembered, was not—*could* not be—right for Edith. Could he? Before she could think this through further, Edith said something that halted her cold.

"It was a romantic weekend all around." She glanced at Jana, her dimples showing. "No one was immune, including Bayard. Actually, Bayard has been seeing quite a lot of my roommate, Vinnie Albright, who is a friend of Greg's sister, Katherine. As a matter of fact, both she and Katherine will be my bridesmaids. And of course you and Akela will, too."

At this Jana felt her heart pinch. Bayard?

It was too much for Jana to take in all at once. She tried to listen as Edith went into the plans for the wedding, explaining that her Aunt Ruthie was coming from San Francisco to oversee the details. However, Jana's mind was like a phonograph record with the needle stuck in place. Edith's casual reference to Bayard being romantically interested in Vinnie Albright kept playing itself over and over. After all the things he had said to her—about Edith's mainland friends, about how different and refreshing he found *her*. Yes, Bayard had said a great many things. Maybe none of them should have been believed. But in spite of herself, Jana felt hurt.

If she had been taken in by Bayard's flattering attention those few weeks he was here in the spring, it was her own fault. The whole rather intense time might have been a combination of his own unsettledness and the fact that she had been there.

Edith's voice brought her back to the present. "We've set a date six weeks from now. Not much time to plan everything. But Aunt Ruthie will be here soon to help arrange it all. I've already decided that I'll wear my mother's wedding gown. It will have to be altered a little to fit me. Just wait until you see it, Jana. It's simply gorgeous—yards of Brussels lace over ivory satin, the train six feet long and embroidered with seed pearls. I've also decided on the bridesmaids' gowns—different pastel shades to suit each one's coloring. Yours and Akela's will be perfect for you both. Yours will be a lovely color of blue to match your eyes, and Akela's will be a deep rose...." Edith rambled on and on about the wedding while Jana only half listened. It still seemed incredible. A restlessness about this marriage stirred in her spirit. It was an uneasiness she couldn't explain, yet she felt it deeply. But Edith was so deliriously happy....

"Come, let's go over to Akela's. I want to tell her too and show her my ring," giggled Edith, flinging out her arm dramatically and wiggling her finger so that the stone's facets danced in the sun.

Later, after their visit with Akela, Edith and Jana walked back down the hill to the Rutherfords' house. On the way, Edith squeezed Jana's arm and said, "Isn't it thrilling, like something out of a dream or a romance novel? But all this is really happening to me. It's like a kind of fairy story, with a prince falling in love with me."

But Edith Preston was certainly not a Cinderella, even though she might have been treated like a princess all her life. Neither did Jana think Greg Amory was any Prince Charming. In fact, Jana thought he was a spoiled, self-indulgent rich boy. Could these two possibly find happiness together? For Edith's sake, she hoped so.

"We are going to Europe, Jana, on our honeymoon," Edith rattled on. "Just think, I'll see Paris, Florence, Rome! I'll visit all the galleries and museums for you!" She jumped up. "I must be going. Aunt Ruthie is coming, did I tell you? She'll be here until the wedding to see to all the details. Papa says I'm not competent now that I'm out of my head in love," she laughed gaily. "Greg won't come until the week of the wedding. Come up to the ranch tomorrow and you can sketch my idea for the bridesmaids' dresses so we can give them to Aunt Ruthie. She'll have her wonderful seamstress, who does the most exquisite work, make them."

How long had Edith secretly been planning this? Jana wondered. Greg Amory never had a chance. Once Edith set her mind on something, she either got her way or else.

"See you tomorrow!" Edith gave Jana an impulsive hug, and then she was gone.

Jana went inside the house, then decided to walk down to the beach. That was where she did most of her "heavy thinking." And today she had plenty to do.

She sat on the sand, her arms locked around her knees, looking out at the ever-rolling surf. As it usually did at the beach, time passed almost unnoticed. Her mind turned over all the changes that had happened in just the past two years. Kimo in Germany, Akela and Pelo in love, and now Edith planning to marry. And she would be going away herself, to the mainland. Either to teachers college or art school—she had not heard definitely yet.

Childhood was gone and with it her childhood friends, each taking his or her own path, leading to individual destinies. What would become of them all?

Jana thought about Bayard, what Edith had told her about him and Vinnie Albright. She remembered his kisses and what he had said that last night—"I'll never forget our time together"—and she thought about the gift he had wanted to give her, the lovely shell pin with the pearl.

After he was gone, Jana had rarely heard from him. There were no impassioned love letters to keep alive the flame that had briefly flared between them. Perhaps it had burned brightly for a moment in time and quickly flickered out.

Jana examined her own reasons for being caught up in that fleeting romantic interlude. Deep down she had never really believed anything would come of it. Perhaps Bayard could not help himself. Through Edith, Jana had always heard of Bayard's many romantic escapades. Every vacation that he was home, on his bureau were letters, a new framed picture of still another young lady he was courting.

She could explain her own attraction to Bayard. His easy charm was very appealing, and he had a way with words, an ability to make you feel you were the only person in the room—for a while. What girl would not be flattered?

However, in her heart of hearts Jana understood that someone like Bayard could never give her what she longed for—an enduring love, devotion, faithfulness. He wasn't capable of that kind of love. Maybe he realized that to Jana he would have to offer something more than he could give.

Jana truly believed that for some people, there is only one deep, passionate love in a lifetime. Whether that love is fulfilled or unrequited, the memory of such a love will give sweetness and strength to all one's days. That's the only kind she wanted, the kind she would wait to have.

Slowly the sun lowered, turning the sea to a gray-blue polished glass. It was time for her to leave, go back up to the house. She only wished she could feel happier about Edith.

~≈~

The day of Edith's wedding was perfect in the only way one can be in Hawaii. A soft ocean breeze wafted up gently, stirring the flower-scented air. The ranch could have been a stage setting. On the lawn, an expanse of green grass was like a velvety carpet rolled out from the house. White folding chairs had been set in semicircular rows before a flower-decked trellis, where the wedding was to take place. All through the trees that lined the driveway, decorated paper lanterns were hung to be lit after sunset. By noon the musicians began arriving, settling themselves on the platform stand, tuning their instruments in preparation for playing traditional wedding music during the ceremony and providing a background of island music for the reception that would follow. Colonel Preston had hired a well-known vocalist to sing some of the most popular songs, to the accompaniment of the soft strumming of guitar and ukulele.

In the house, servants moved quickly and quietly on the main floor, moving in trained competence as they arranged long refreshment tables, placed the floral centerpieces, polished the crystal glasses. Even though this was their young mistress' wedding party, their efficiency was unaffected by the special importance of the occasion, as Preston Ranch had held many grand fetes, had entertained royalty, both Hawaiian and European.

Upstairs, in contrast, was all hustle and bustle. Edith had invited Akela and Jana to come to the ranch to dress. The other bridesmaids—Katherine Amory, Greg's sister; Maevis Latham, one of Edith's suitemates at the Virginia school she attended; and Vinnie Albright, Edith's roommate—were staying in one of the guest cottages and would dress there.

Jana was glad of that. She'd had about all she could stand of the fluttery threesome from the mainland. Katherine Amory was very much like her brother—a cool blond with an aloof manner. Maevis was sweet but rather dull, the perfect foil for Edith's vivacious personality. What other type could have put up with such competition? Vinnie Albright was another matter. Jana was surprised at the sharp twinge of jealousy she felt when she was introduced. She grudgingly had to admit that the vivid brunette was extremely pretty. She had a witty tongue and a poise that could only come from a certain eastern shore background. Jana could see why she would be attractive to someone like Bayard.

At the prenuptial festivities, Jana had tried to avoid both of them. That hadn't proved difficult. Bayard had also seemed to be avoiding her.

Was he embarrassed or uncomfortable? That was his problem, she told herself. In a way, it made her feel superior. She was proud that she could handle an awkward situation with more grace than he could.

Bayard and Greg were occupying one of the guest cottages, and so when Jana had arrived at the ranch, she had gone through the house and upstairs without encountering either. As she reached the top of the steps, she could hear her friend's laughter ringing out, and Akela's softer voice. Unbidden, a lump rose in her throat. This would be the last time the three of them would be together in the same way. After today nothing would ever be the same. Determined not to let any feelings of sadness overshadow what should be a shining moment for Edith, Jana winked back tears. Just then Edith had come running barefoot down the hall.

She had greeted Jana enthusiastically with a hug and pulled her along by the hand to her bedroom. "You must see my gown!"

Gazing at the beautiful dress hanging from the armoire, Jana had given Edith the reaction she wanted. "I've never seen anything more beautiful!"

Edith's usual high spirits today were at their peak— sometimes her tendency to dissolve into giggles bordered dangerously on the brink of hysteria. Meipala's expression was concerned, her dark eyes worried, as she hovered anxiously. Jana, always sensitive to undercurrents, was aware that her friend was teetering on doing something reckless. She had the wild thought that maybe Edith would dash out of the room, out to the stables, get on her horse, and ride off. She quickly thrust that possibility away. She gave Akela a warning glance, and they both tried to exert a little calm.

"It's only natural to feel nervous," Akela began as they all sat on Edith's bed, enjoying the jasmine tea and thin ginger cookies Meipala had left on a tray before going downstairs.

"Why should I be nervous?" demanded Edith, tossing her head. "I absolutely adore Greg, and he adores me! We are going to be divinely happy!"

And why shouldn't they be? Jana asked herself. No two people were starting out together with more potential for happiness—they had youth, wealth, health. Why this nagging feeling that Edith's expectations were too high for her not to be disillusioned or disappointed?

Jana hoped this wouldn't happen, prayed it wouldn't. Edith had been so caught up in the elaborate preparations for the extravagant wedding—picking out the "exactly right" engraved invitations, selecting her china, her silver, the fittings for her trousseau—she'd had no time to consider what followed: the reality of living with another person for the rest of her life, day after day, year after year. Was the man she was marrying right for her? Jana still had her doubts. Jana could also not help wondering what was going through Greg Amory's mind at this point.

Meipala's head peered into the bedroom. "Time to get ready, girls."

They made a scramble to uncurl themselves from their perches on the bed. Akela and Jana left Edith to the ministrations of her old nurse and went into the adjoining bedroom.

"I hope—I hope she's doing the right thing," Jana whispered.

At the tone of doubt in Jana's voice, Akela's dark eyes widened. "She seems to be very much in love."

"I know, but—" Jana hesitated. "I wish I felt more sure."

"Tutu says that only the two people involved know. Everyone else looks on the outside—*they* know their hearts."

"It's easier for you, Akela. You and Pelo. You've grown up together, practically in the same family—you have the same kind of childhood, the same traditions, and you want the same kind of life." Jana shook her head slowly. "Greg Amory comes from an entirely different world. I just want Edith to be happy."

Akela reached out and pressed Jana's hand. "She will be, don't worry. Love between two people is very powerful. It can change things, make differences seem unimportant."

Jana wished she could share Akela's confidence.

There was no time to discuss it further. The wedding was scheduled for five o'clock. That time was especially picked because the garden would be golden with the glow of an early sunset, enhancing everything with glorious light.

Akela helped Jana with her hair, and then Jana did hers. Their dresses had been chosen in the most becoming color for each. Their picture hats were flattering, the curved brims lined with shirred pink chiffon. At last came a knock at the door and Meipala's voice reminding them it was time to go downstairs.

The other three bridesmaids were gathered in the library, whose French doors opened onto the lanai. As Akela and Jana joined them, there were exchanged murmurs of mutual admiration. Then a kind of expectant hush fell over them as they waited for Edith. When she appeared on Colonel Preston's arm, they all drew a collective awed breath. The Edith they knew had been transformed into a vision of a bride. Under the voluminous tulle veil that covered her face, they could see she was smiling. Her gown was a dream of shimmering satin, embroidered and outlined in tiny pearls. Before they had a chance to say anything, Colonel Preston declared proudly, "Was there ever such a beautiful bride?"

There were a few moments of emotional flurry, and then Meipala handed them their bouquets. From outside they could hear the strains of lovely Hawaiian music. Through the open doors, they saw that most of the seats were full. Between the rows was a path for the bridal party, which led to the flower-banked podium, where the surpliced and black-cassocked priest, prayer book in hand, waited. At his side stood Greg and Bayard, looking erect and handsome in white linen suits. Even though she had schooled herself against Bayard's charms and found it difficult to excuse Greg's superficiality, Jana had to admit that the two tall, blond young men could have modeled for a picture of a pair of Grecian gods from some Athenian temple.

The ceremony, the reception, even the fact that she had caught the bridal bouquet, did not lift Jana's spirits to the level such an event should have. She tried her best to enter into the festivities, to laugh, to chat, to join in the toasts to bride and groom, to dance with Greg's cousin, who seemed very attracted, and at the end of the evening to pelt the couple with flower petals as they ran hand in hand to the new carriage that would take them away on their honeymoon.

Later, when she was finally home, in her own room, easing her tired feet out of her blue satin slippers, Jana felt as lonely as she had ever been. She glanced at the beautiful bridal bouquet that, she was convinced, Edith had aimed directly at her, and sighed. Her emotions were a mixture of pleasure and pain. Jana had not mistaken the meaning of the distance Bayard had kept from her. It had really needed no explanation, because when she had entered the library where the bridesmaids were assembled, she could not miss seeing the small shell pin with the tiny pearl Vinnie Albright was wearing on the bodice of her bridesmaid's dress.

Today had been the end of one part of her life. She did not know what the next chapter would bring. All she could hope was that Kimo would be in it.

❧

Two weeks after Edith's wedding, in the island newspaper appeared the announcement of Bayard Preston's engagement to Vinnie Albright.

Part Four

Chapter Nineteen

━━❧❧━━

With Edith married and gone, Kimo far away in Germany, and Akela spending most of her time in Kona, preoccupied with Pelo and planning a December wedding, Jana found herself lonelier than she had ever been before in her life.

Because of the Rutherfords' financial situation, it was decided Jana would have to wait another year to go to teachers college on the mainland. Even if she was aided by a partial scholarship, there were other expenses to be met. Although her parents came to this decision regretfully, Jana actually did not mind. She still hoped that she might win a scholarship to art school.

Besides, she had been asked to be a bridesmaid in Akela and Pelo's wedding, the only one outside their immediate family to be included in the bridal party. The Hawaiian *ohana* was very intimate and close. Most of the other bridal attendants were Akela's cousins, so Jana felt honored to have been chosen.

Jana wondered if Kimo would return in time for the wedding. No one, not even Tutu, knew for sure when he would get home from Germany. Jana had kept all the postcards he had sent her, but two years was a long while. Sometimes their moments together seemed unreal—sometimes she could hardly remember what he looked like or what they had talked about. More and more, the romantic dreams she had after his last visit home gradually faded. Perhaps he had met someone in Germany he cared about. Perhaps . . .

In the meantime, she took a job clerking at the fabric store in Waimea, putting aside most of her small salary to save for college.

She kept busy with her job and helped her mother around the house, trying to make herself useful, and in her free time she painted. She took on Nathan's Sunday school class, since there was no one else in the small congregation who volunteered, and to her surprise found she liked it.

Not often, but once in a while, her thoughts strayed to Bayard Preston and the brief interlude they had shared. Had he really considered pursuing a romantic relationship with her? Or had he already decided that a prestigious marriage with a socialite like Vinnie Albright was more advantageous? She was happy she had not been dazzled too much by his charm and all he might have offered. In her heart of hearts she knew they were "unequally yoked."

She also tried not to put too much importance on her memories of Kimo. Perhaps she kept thinking of him because right now her life seemed empty. She tried not to envy Akela's happiness or Edith's glamorous life.

Maybe her life was going to be different from her friends' lives. Maybe she would never marry, just live in a cottage on a hillside overlooking the ocean, with a small studio where she could paint. While Edith toured Europe in style and Akela became a traditional Hawaiian wife whose duties were her husband's comfort and contentment, *she* would live alone and become a famous artist—a reclusive one!

The morning of Akela's wedding, Jana arrived at Tutu's house. She found a radiant Akela. Never before had she seemed so beautiful. Her inner beauty shone from her luminous dark eyes. The two friends embraced and Jana had to fight the lump rising in her throat. She remembered the first time she had ever seen Akela. She had looked like a small, exotic doll. Akela and Kimo had been fellow boarders at the Caldwells' house while Jana's parents were in Honolulu and Tutu was in Kohala at the bedside of a sick family member. Jana recalled how quickly she and Akela had become friends, and all the walks, the talks, the confidences shared, the secrets kept over the years. They had been like sisters. Now she was losing her. It would never be the same again.

Not wanting to spoil her friend's day, Jana held back tears, entering into all the last-minute activities with affection and enthusiasm.

Since Akela and Pelo were both Christians, there would first be a wedding ceremony in Tutu's church, where Akela had worshiped as a child and still did, except for the weekends she spent in Kona. This would be followed by a traditional Hawaiian exchange of vows, and a *luau* on the beach. That way, any of the bride and groom's friends who could not be squeezed into the tiny church would not feel left out.

Akela's bridal gown was an exquisitely embroidered white muslin dress fashioned with a high neck. The long, tapered sleeves were puffed at the top and had wrists that were edged in delicate lace. A train fell from the shoulders in panels of ruffles. She wore a wreath of fresh flowers. Her long, dark hair hung loose, and around her neck was the traditional ti-leaf lei.

When it was time for them to go to the church, a wagon decorated by the family with garlands of flowers and driven by one of the male cousins drew up in front of Tutu's cottage. Tutu helped settle Akela carefully in front, arranging her train, and then Jana and the four other bridesmaids, Akela's pretty, giggling cousins, climbed in, and they started off down the hill to the church.

As they stopped in the churchyard, a crowd was already waiting for the bride's arrival. Through the open church door, they heard the wheezing sound of the old organ playing some of the beloved old hymns. Now quiet, subdued with the solemnity of the occasion, they all got out of the wagon and went up the steps. At the top, waiting on the porch, was Uncle Kelo, who was to give Akela away. He greeted them all with an "Aloha" and a hug and kiss, then held out his arm to Akela. She took it but not before she turned and stretched out her hand to grasp Jana's, squeezing it hard. Then the squeaky notes of "The Wedding March" sounded. The brides-maids followed Tutu, then slowly marched down the aisle in the church, which was bedecked with flowers and crowded to the walls with smiling people.

During the ceremony, Jana had an entirely different reac-tion than she'd had at Edith's wedding only months before. She'd had so many doubts about Edith's happiness with Greg Amory—she had none at all for Akela.

Hearing the words of the vows her friend was taking, Jana knew they were promises she herself longed to make. But only with a man she could love and trust. Would it ever happen for her?

The ceremony over, the bridal party went out into the bright sunshine to gather on the church steps for the photog-raphy session. The jovial photographer kept rearranging them until all were laughing. Their laughter was a mixture of irri-tation and resignation, because they were all eager to get to the gala luau still ahead. Finally satisfied, he released them, and they all scattered among the assembled well-wishers in the churchyard. The bride and groom were swallowed up in the crowd, which showered them with congratulations and loaded them with leis.

Eventually, as if by some silent signal, everyone started on foot down the path to the beach below, where they could already smell the tantalizing aroma of the roasting meat being prepared for the upcoming feast.

Pelo's brothers and cousins had been up before dawn getting the pork ready to be roasted in the specially dug pit. A delicious herb-seasoned aroma rose with the spiraling smoke, prickling nostrils and whetting appetites. Tables were arranged in a large U-shape, decorated with piles of fruit and flowers, loaded with dishes of sweet potatoes, rice, and salads, and hovered over by colorfully mumu-clad "aunties" in flower-bedecked straw hats. Mats were placed on the sand, and groups of guests, friends, and families were settling themselves for the entertainment that would come later.

The scene might have been some exotic painting, Jana thought. She looked around at the gaily dressed company. Under the shade of the curved palm trees, their jagged-edged fronds languidly moving in the gentle sea wind, were clusters of guests happily chatting. Beyond the white-sand beach, the water of the lagoon stretched in rippling shades of blue, turquoise, jade. Down at the edge of the ocean, scores of little brown-skinned children played, shrieking as they chased each other, waded, and fell full length in the shallow waves. Their mothers and tutus sat not far away, watching them with tender tolerance.

Hawaiians were so joyous, so lighthearted, enjoying everything with a kind of happy nonchalance that Jana found most appealing. There was no stiffness, no studied awareness of social protocol to be observed—just simply living in the moment.

At last the meat was ready, and everyone began to serve themselves from the abundance set out: the tender white fish, freshly caught; the piping hot *laulaus*, seasoned meat wrapped in leaves and baked; and of course, inevitably, a huge bowl of poi set in the middle of the table for everyone to dip from. As Jana skipped putting any on her plate, she caught the eye of Uncle Kelo, Tutu's brother, who winked at her broadly. Although through the years, especially when Kimo was present, Jana had managed to take some of the gluey taro and swallow it, it was not her favorite Hawaiian delicacy.

While everyone ate and talked, the drums began to play softly. There were drums of all shapes and sizes, gourds, coconut shells. Gradually the beat began getting steadily louder, until it filled the air with an insistent rhythm impossible to ignore. A murmur went through the crowd. Soon the dancers would begin. Young men and women seemed to emerge as if by magic from the grove of banyans to a place in front of where the diners were seated. The girls were dressed in *sarongs*, lengths of flowered material in bold designs of red, yellow, and black, one end brought up over the shoulder, caught up and knotted at the hips. The dance was the traditional Hawaiian *hula-hula*, the slow, graceful telling of legends, the hand motions spelling out the story to those who understood the signs.

It was mesmerizing to watch, the music haunting. The spectators could not keep themselves from swaying or beating their hands on their knees to the rhythm of the drums.

Behind the dancers, the sun began dropping—a huge, orange ball—into the now glazed, silver-toned sea.

Jana hated to see this beautiful day come to an end. She wished it would go on and on, but the wind off the ocean became cooler, the shadows of the palm trees fell gently on the sand. It was time to go. Unnoticed, the wedding couple had slipped away, and the other guests were gathering up their children, baskets, belongings, preparing to leave the beach.

As the last plaintive notes of the guitars, ukuleles, and drums echoed in the balmy air, Jana felt a strange ache, her heart hungry, her soul a little lonely. Something within her yearned to belong to this culture, so simple, so sweet. As she reluctantly said her good-byes to Akela's family and turned to retrace her steps up the path to the church, a voice behind her spoke.

"Aloha, Koana."

Unbelievingly, she whirled around and saw Kimo.

At first she was speechless. Then words tumbled out, one on top of the other.

"Kimo! What are you doing here? When did you come?"

"Just now. I tried to make it for the wedding, but the steamer from Oahu was late. Then I had to get a ride from the dock, and—well, it looks like I've missed everything." He paused, then smiled broadly. "Except you."

"Why didn't you let anyone know? We could have met you—"

"I wanted to surprise everyone. Especially Akela and Pelo—" He stopped, looked around. "It seems everyone has gone."

Jana followed his glance. A few groups were left. Parents were collecting their children, some of whom were playing hide-and-seek and pretending not to hear their mothers calling them.

"I've seen Tutu. She's going home with Uncle Kelo. So may I walk you home?" he asked her.

Suddenly Jana's earlier melancholy vanished. Kimo was back and their meeting was just as she had imagined it, only better.

Chapter Twenty

❧❧❧

With the evening of Akela's wedding and Kimo's return, Jana's life took a decided upward turn. Kimo's first few weeks after coming back from Germany were spent visiting his large family of relatives. However, he found plenty of time to see Jana. He would come to the store at closing time, and they would walk home the long way, going down the beach. The awkwardness she had feared after their long time apart never materialized. They found they had much to say to each other. It seemed as if all the years of separation had been like waters dammed up for a long time but now let flow. Kimo told her of what it was like to be a hardworking apprentice in a foreign land, learning a new language, a new way of communicating with people, while learning all kinds of new skills.

"It was different than when I was at school in Honolulu," he told her. "There I was among my own race, other Hawaiians. Even though we all came from different towns, even from different islands—some were from Kauai and Maui—still we were all Hawaiians. In Germany it was different. Sometimes I felt very alone."

"I wish I'd known—"

"I didn't want to write, worry Tutu or anybody. It seemed better just to work hard. That way, the time would pass faster.

Push the loneliness back. Suppress it, get on with what I had to do."

"I'm so sorry, Kimo. If I'd known, maybe I could have helped somehow. Written to you about things here—"

He shook his head. "No, that would have hurt too much. It was probably better this way. I managed. Most people were kind, and my master's family tried to help. Actually, they were very kind to us—the apprentices. Had us to their house for dinner." Kimo made a face. "The food, though. Very heavy, very rich."

"It must have been really hard."

"It was. At least at first. But I learned a great deal. Not only in woodworking. I had to learn the language, of course, to understand directions, just to get along every day. And German is a hard language to learn." He laughed. "Maybe especially for a Hawaiian. It is very precise, very practical. Just like the Germans."

Jana recalled how she had once said that Kimo's woodwork was like poetry.

"No poetry, then?" she suggested softly.

He looked surprised that she had remembered that. "Of a sort. German woodworkers have their own poetry. Of course, it's different than mine. Poetry comes from the soul, and each country has a different kind of soul. Different doesn't mean inferior—just different. However, it was a valuable experience. I got a lot out of it. Things I intend to apply to my own work here."

"Then, you're going to stay here? Not go away again?"

Again Kimo seemed surprised at her question. "Of course. Hawaii's my home. Why would I want to go anywhere else?"

Jana's heart leaped. That was just how *she* felt.

"I don't plan to *ever* go away again," Kimo said definitely. "I will do my own designs, make them out of native wood, become a master woodworker here on the island."

"Oh, that's wonderful, Kimo. I'm so glad." Jana sighed. "I was afraid. People assumed you might either stay on in Germany or go to the mainland."

"I don't know why they'd think that. I'd never do such a thing. I was so glad to get home. To see Tutu, my family—" He paused. "And *you*, Koana. I thought about you all the time. I missed you more than you know."

As it turned out, within weeks Kimo and two other woodworkers formed a cooperative, opening a carpentry business together in Hilo. It would be slow going at first, but all three men did outstanding work. They were all ambitious and hardworking, and they hoped that soon more orders would begin to come in as their work became known.

It was only on weekends that Kimo and Jana could spend uninterrupted time together. They usually met after church and took long walks on the beach. They found they could talk to each other about almost everything. Sometimes their conversation turned serious.

Jana discovered that Kimo had become politicized. He and his coworkers often discussed the future of the Hawaiian islands. They were afraid, he told her, that little by little Hawaii was being taken over by foreigners, was losing its sovereignty. They felt that Hawaii should be for Hawaiians, not for the English or the Americans.

"I don't understand. Isn't it?"

"The Americans have too much influence, want power. Besides, Americans do not accept Hawaiians as equals."

"What do you mean? My parents are Americans, and so are the Prestons. They don't feel that way, I'm sure."

"Maybe not on the Big Island. But elsewhere. I've traveled in the States, on the mainland, Jana. I've seen things firsthand. Americans have prejudice against dark-skinned people. I experienced some of it myself. Nothing bad. Just a few curious looks. Still, I felt it."

Jana felt an inner rage. She knew enough history to be aware of the treatment of blacks that had led to the Civil War in the United States. But that was over now. It couldn't be that someone like Kimo, the descendant of kings, although dark haired and bronzed of skin, could be considered inferior by Americans or by *anybody*!

"I wish the queen had more Hawaiians as advisors," Kimo continued. "Right now she is surrounded by men who have their own influence to peddle. She has some powerful enemies."

"But if royalty cannot rule well, wouldn't it be better to have good counsel?"

"As long as their motives are pure." Kimo shook his head. "I don't have the answers—I just know we should have our own people deciding things for us. I don't like to see my country exploited."

Not all their conversations were of this depth. Something else was happening between them. It was on these walks, in this time they spent together, that their childhood friendship and youthful uncertainty with each other began to develop into something deeper. Perhaps Jana knew it first. She realized that the girlish attraction she'd had for Kimo was now much more. The handsome boy she had admired had become a man of strength, character, and integrity. The kind of man she could love with the kind of love that would endure for a lifetime.

With Kimo back, everything was just as she often had imagined it would be, had hoped it would be, only it was better. They seemed to have reached a new level of relationship. Jana did not yet dare call it love, because she was unsure of Kimo's feelings.

The cooperative kept Kimo very busy. The three men had to work very hard to earn enough to cover the rental of

657

their shop, pay supply bills, and meet other expenses. Orders were slow coming in at first, and they sometimes had to take other work, plain carpentry, to make ends meet. It seemed a shame to Jana for Kimo to work on ordinary things, when his own designs were truly "poetry in wood." However, Kimo remained optimistic about his future. His dream was to one day have his own shop in Waimea or Kona where he could create beautiful original furniture.

Sometimes he wasn't able to get home for the weekend. Other times he surprised Jana by showing up unexpectedly. A kind of telepathy developed between them. If he arrived too late to attend the Sunday service, she would often get a feeling of his presence, and when she came outside, she would find him waiting in the churchyard. The growing bond between them was difficult to explain but very real, and it grew stronger and stronger.

Jana was unaware that anyone else noticed how often they were seen together walking, talking, sharing coffee in one of the small outdoor cafes, or meeting after church to go down to their favorite spot on the beach. She forgot it was a small town.

Chapter Twenty-One

❧

One evening Mrs. Wantanabe, the elderly Japanese lady who owned the fabric store, had a toothache and left early to see the dentist, asking Jana to close and lock up. She had just stepped outside and was turning the key in the lock of the door, when she heard a familiar voice call her name.

"Jana."

She turned. "Bayard! My goodness, you startled me! I didn't know you were back. I thought—"

He sauntered toward her, a cynical smile lifting the corners of his mouth under a new, neatly trimmed mustache. "I'm a fugitive." He held both hands up in a surrendering gesture. "Escaped."

"Escaped? From what?"

"A fate worse than death," he said sarcastically. "Had to save my sanity. I had no idea it took so much planning to arrange a wedding. Edith's seemed simple enough."

"That's because you didn't do anything! You should have seen all the hard work Meipala and your Aunt Ruthie did behind the scenes. Even so, Edith rushed things so that she and Greg could go to Europe. I think his passage was already booked when they decided to get married before he went—"

"I think it was *Edith* who decided. That poor fellow didn't know what hit him."

"That's a fine way for her brother to talk," Jana chided him as she pocketed the store key and began to walk along the wooden sidewalk. Bayard fell in step alongside her. "And you certainly don't sound like a man planning to embark on the sea of matrimony himself."

Bayard didn't respond to her teasing bait. Instead, he plunged his hands into his jacket pocket and, head down, remained quiet for a few minutes.

"Do you have to go right home? Could we go somewhere and talk, Jana?" he asked her.

Surprised, she looked at him.

"Please. I really need someone—need to talk to you." He sounded serious.

"All right. We can take the beach road—that's a little longer. But if I'm not home at the usual time, Mama will wonder."

They strolled to the end of the street, then turned to take the narrower road that led to the beach.

"I must tell you, I've gained a great deal of information since I last saw you. About weddings. Things I never heard of before. Did you know that it takes six months to have a silver service monogrammed? Or that you have to order a full set of dinnerware from England a year ahead of time? Linens from France take almost as long. Did you know you cannot possibly get married without any of these?" His tone was sarcastic, with a tinge of bitterness.

Jana glanced at him. Bayard looked angry as he continued, saying, "And then there are endless parties, dinners one has to sit through, long lines of relatives to be introduced to, be ogled by, approved or disapproved by—"

"Surely Vinnie must know how you feel and can help you get out of some of these?"

"*Vinnie?* She adores all this. Revels in it. *She's* the one who's insisting on the whole shebang. I suggested eloping, even coming here to be married at the ranch—" He shook his head vigorously. "But oh no, not my darling fiancée. Besides, she has *always* spent the summer in Newport. She couldn't *dream* of being anywhere else. And of course, we will *have* to spend at least four months of every year on the mainland, besides a month in Italy."

Jana stopped walking and stared at Bayard, who also halted.

"Bayard, you don't sound very happy."

"*Happy?* Of course I'm not happy. I'm miserable. And furious. And I could kick myself every time I think of the mess I've got myself into."

Jana hardly knew what to say. At last she managed, "Does Vinnie know?"

"No, of course not. I was too much of a coward to tell her. I felt as if I were strangling. Trapped. All I told her was that I had to get back to Hawaii, to the ranch. I made some excuse about Father's needing me. It wasn't the truth, but—" He shrugged.

"I'm sorry," Jana said lamely.

Bayard turned toward her. It was fast getting dark, and his features were indistinct, but she could tell his expression was anguished.

"It was a mistake, Jana. An impulsive proposal. Blame it on too much champagne, the desire of the moment, the crazy feeling that making a decision about my future here on the island would somehow make things ... right. But I was wrong. A girl like Vinnie doesn't any more belong *here* than I belong in Newport."

He put his hands on Jana's shoulders and, clamping his fingers tightly, drew her close so that their faces were inches apart.

"I've made a terrible mistake. It's *you* I should have proposed to. You and I, we belong here on the island, both of us.

You understand. We could have—" It sounded like a groan. "I wish I'd had the good sense to ask you when I was home last year—" He broke off and pulled Jana to him. Before she could pull away or protest, he had drawn her into an embrace and was kissing her.

She was too astonished to resist. There was a desperateness in the kiss. It was neither tender, gentle, nor loving. Finally she found the strength to press both hands against his chest and break away. Breathlessly she said, "You shouldn't have done that, Bayard."

"I'm not sorry, Jana. All the way home, back here to the island, I've thought about you. What a fool I was not to recognize what we had last spring, what we could have—marry me, Jana. You won't regret it. Whatever you want, we'll do. But the island will be our home, our anchor. You love it as much as I do, but I want you to see the world. And I can take you there. And we can always come back to Hawaii, to home."

Jana listened with more understanding than she would have thought possible. What Bayard was saying echoed in her own heart. She knew the longing, the loneliness, he must have experienced on the mainland. She felt sorry for him. But that was all. You don't give your life as a gift to someone else—not for what it can bring you, nor for sympathy, not even for love. Your life is God's gift to *you*. To use for his purpose, not someone else's.

"I'm sorry, Bayard."

"What do you mean, sorry? Don't you care for me? Can't you see the possibilities of a future with me?"

"I do care for you, Bayard, but I don't love you. Not like you seem to want me to. I'm sorry you feel you've made a mistake. But mistakes can be corrected. It would be far worse for you to go on with Vinnie if you feel it's wrong for both of you."

"Didn't you hear anything I said, Jana? It's *you* I want, *you* I need."

"I'm sorry, Bayard," she said again. "There's someone else."

His shoulders sagged. "It's Kimo, then, isn't it?"

Strangely enough, as Bayard said the words Jana knew it was true. The name she had hidden in her heart for so long came singingly to the surface. Yes, yes, she *did* love Kimo.

"Well then, I wish you the best," Bayard sighed. "I don't think it will be easy for you or him. People will make it difficult."

They had reached the fork in the road. One side led down to the Rutherfords' house, the other up to another part of town.

"What are you going to do, Bayard?" Jana asked quietly.

"My duty, I guess. Whatever that means." He glanced at her. "It's too late to back out, I suppose. That seems to be the story. Too late. If I'd spoken earlier—before Kimo came back from Germany—would there have been a chance for me ... for us?"

Jana hesitated. Hadn't there been a time when what Bayard could offer her had some appeal?

"I'm not sure. Maybe. But now I know for sure that whatever I felt for you, it's not what I feel for Kimo."

"I wish I could wait for that kind of certainty."

"It's worth it. But then you would hurt a lot of people—" She wished she could say something more comforting. However, she had always been taught to speak the truth with love. Was it right for Vinnie Albright—regardless of the monogrammed silver, the English china, the French linens—to marry a man who didn't love her? "I wish I could say something to help, Bayard."

"Thanks anyway, Jana." He took a few steps away from her, then half turned and raised his arm in a farewell gesture. "Aloha!"

"Aloha, Bayard," she said gently. Then he started walking fast up the road and around the bend, disappearing from her sight.

Slowly she walked home alone. In her own heart, there was a joyousness. She had acknowledged her love for Kimo, and it spread a warmth all through her that simply blotted out Bayard's warning. A warning that she would remember later.

⚜

One evening Kimo met her after work. As she was leaving the store, she saw him coming toward her. Her heart lifted like it did once when she had tried surfing and a wave caught her at its crest, creating a soaring sensation, propelling her in a rush to shore.

Kimo seemed excited. His smile was broad, his eyes sparkling. "Wait till you hear what's happened, Koana!" he greeted her. "We have got the most wonderful order. A whole dining room set—table, six chairs, a sideboard—for a house newly built in Hilo! The owner had seen some of our furniture and admired it. It was *my* design, Koana. Isn't that wonderful? This is a prominent man. He'll be doing a great deal of entertaining. Others will see our work—it may mean we are really on our way."

"Oh Kimo, I'm so proud of you! Of course, I *knew* you would succeed. Your ideas are original, your work very beautiful."

"I feel like celebrating!" he laughed, throwing his head back. "But it's not just *this* order, Koana. This means I can make a good living. It makes everything possible."

He took her arm and they started walking. Almost without thinking, they took the path past the school yard, their old way down to the beach.

"Of course, it will mean lots of hard work, long hours," he continued. "I'll probably have to stay over in Hilo to fin-

664

ish the set in time. He wants it when he moves into his new house. But it will be worth it. He is very influential, has wealthy friends. It may be the beginning of our becoming well known and successful."

They had reached the beach by this time. It was the most beautiful time of the day, Jana thought, her favorite time. The ocean was a pale silver, gentle waves rolled onto the sand in glistening scallops of foam, and a peaceful quiet seemed to settle over everything.

"This is just as I dreamed so many times when I was in Germany," Kimo said softly. "Watching a sunset here on the beach—with you, Koana." He took her hand and held it.

Her heart began to pound heavily.

"This is what I've wanted to tell you for so long, Koana. All my life, maybe. Or at least since I came back from Honolulu after being away that first year. I love you. You are my dearest friend. More than a friend. More than a sister. More than that. Do you know that?"

"I think so. At least, I've hoped that. I love you, too, Kimo."

He put his arm around her shoulder and drew her close and kissed her. They watched the sun sink slowly until it was swallowed into the water, leaving the sky streaked with pink, orange. Arms around each other, they walked back up the path to the Rutherfords' house. At the gate they kissed each other again. Jana walked into the house as if in a dream. All that she had ever wanted seemed to be coming true. She could hardly believe it. It was too precious, too sweet, to share yet with anyone else. Hugging her secret close, she simply drifted back to her bedroom. There she knelt by her window, looking out into the night now studded with early stars. "Thank you, God," was all she could whisper, "for bringing my love to me."

Chapter Twenty-Two

❦

ost of the time Jana was happy, so distracted by her romance that she had almost forgotten about her quilt design, the possibility that it might win her a scholarship to art school.

So it came as startling news when she arrived home from work one evening and found her father and mother both standing out on the porch, her father waving an envelope as she came near.

"It's come, Jana. A letter from the scholarship committee! Hurry and open it. We can't wait to hear if it's what we've all hoped for you."

Jana hurried up the porch steps and, with both parents looking over her shoulder, tore open the letter. Inside was the news she had been waiting to hear for so long. A full scholarship!

But instead of being elated, a wave of shock and dismay swept over her. This meant there was no obstacle to her going to the mainland. She would be able to study at the art institute for a full year at no expense to her parents. She could follow her dream. It was coming true.

"Oh darling, we're so proud of you!" her mother said, hugging her. "You've been so good and patient, and now your talent is being rewarded."

Jana felt completely stunned, frozen by this news, while the excitement swirled all around her. Her parents' voices, interrupting each other, went in and out of her ears without Jana really hearing what they were saying. Nathan, who didn't fully understand what all the fuss was about, was skipping around the trio, blowing on his tin toy horn to add to the confusion.

Underneath it all, slowly the realization of what it meant to receive the scholarship came crushing down on Jana. This meant she would leave the island, leave Kimo. It was then she knew without doubt that she loved Kimo—and scholarship or no scholarship, she didn't want to leave him.

Jana moved through that night's impromptu celebration in a blur of mixed emotion. Her mind whirled. How could she tell her parents that she didn't want to accept the scholarship? How could she tell them, unless she and Kimo revealed their love, their hopes for a future together? Things were happening faster than she had expected. She must talk to Kimo first.

⚮

It wasn't until late the next afternoon, when Kimo arrived from Hilo, that she had a chance to tell him. She met him at the gate, before he could go into the house and have one of her parents give him the news.

They walked down to where the beach curved in a long crescent, a row of bending palms swaying toward the glistening sand washed by lazy swirls of foam-edged surf. The cry of wheeling seabirds, the roar of the surf, merged with their thundering hearts. It was always thus when they were together after days apart.

When they reached their favorite spot, she turned toward him. He took her face in both hands, looked down into her eyes. "Koana," he murmured before he kissed her upturned mouth.

"Oh Kimo, I have something to tell you," she began haltingly.

"What is it? You look . . . sad, worried." His dark brows came together over his concerned eyes. "Tell me," he whispered, stroking back her hair, loosening the hairpins that fell silently onto the sand as her hair came uncoiled. He listened as her words tumbled out.

". . . but now it's impossible. Even though Mama and Papa think I'm happy about it, I can't go, not now. I can't accept it."

Kimo's expression became serious, and then he said slowly, "Of course you must take it. It's an opportunity you can't turn down. It's like my opportunity to go to Germany. At first I didn't want to go, didn't want to leave family, the island, *you*. But I knew I had to go, so I went—and I'm glad I did. It was the chance of a lifetime, and I couldn't afford to pass it up. None of what's happened would have happened for me if I hadn't gone." He paused. "It's the same for you, Jana. You'll have to take it. Your parents would be terribly disappointed if you didn't, and later on you'd be sorry."

She shook her head. "No, I don't think so, Kimo. I wouldn't be sorry. When I think what it means. Gone—a whole year! I couldn't afford to come home. Twelve months away from my family, everything—*you*! What about us if I go?" Jana looked at him, bewildered. She had expected him to say she couldn't go. "I don't care about the scholarship. Let someone else have it. I mean, once I thought I wanted to learn to paint really well, be an artist, but not anymore. Not since—"

"I want you to go, Jana," he said quietly.

Her eyes suddenly filled with tears. "How can you say that? I'd be miserable if I went away now, left you. I love you, Kimo."

"*Makamae*, my darling. And I love you, Jana." He hesitated, then said, "I wasn't going to ask you until—well, until I was in a better position to do it, but . . ." His voice deepened. "I want to marry you."

"Oh Kimo, I hoped you'd say that! That's what I want, too. I don't want to go away. I won't."

"Your parents may blame me if you don't, and it will hurt them, Jana. They have such high expectations for you. What would they say if we went to them and said that instead of you accepting this wonderful chance, you want to get married. To marry *me*?"

"I believe they'd understand. You should hear *their* love story. Everyone was against them marrying—sometime I'll tell you about it. But they overcame all the odds, and they *eloped* when the families opposed it. Surely they *should* understand that when two people love each other—"

"I hadn't thought we could marry for at least a year, Jana, when the business is thriving. Right now the three of us divide what comes in, put it back into the shop, for tools, lumber, whatever. If we marry now, there wouldn't be much to live on."

"What do we need? A little house, a garden? We'd be together. It would be heaven, Kimo." She touched his cheek with her hand. He caught it and kissed her palm.

Looking at her with soft, loving eyes, he said gently, "It's too much to ask. One day, I know, the business will be good—but it takes time. If we wait, we can have a wonderful life. I will build us a beautiful house, on a hilltop, overlooking the ocean. . . ."

"I don't want to wait, Kimo. It might take years. I want to work with you for the future—that would be so much better!"

Again Kimo's handsome face looked sorrowful, his dark eyes even darker, as he shook his head. "I don't think so, Jana. I'm sure your parents won't think so."

"Let me handle it, Kimo. I'll try to explain how we feel, what we want. They love me and will want me to be happy."

Impulsively she threw her arms around his neck, pulled his head down close to her cheek, let her fingers tangle in his silky dark hair.

"Oh Kimo, I love you so much. We will be so happy. Just wait and see. Everything will work out."

❧

When Jana came into the house, her mother was in the kitchen. Jana stood in the doorway for a few minutes, trying to gather her thoughts together. She felt she might burst if she didn't tell her mother right away.

"Oh Mama, something wonderful has happened," she said.

Mrs. Rutherford raised her head, looked at her daughter. Jana's face glowed with happiness, her lips parted in a radiant smile. Some intuition chilled her mother's heart. One of the most endearing things about her daughter had always been her transparency, her openness, the truth that shone out of her eyes.

Her mother's hand, holding a knife, poised over the pineapple she was slicing. "What is it, Johanna?"

Jana should have been alerted. Her mother rarely used her christened name. But her own excitement was too high to pay attention to the serious tone of her mother's voice, the edge of caution in it. She went blithely on, saying, "Mama, Kimo has asked me to marry him, and of course I said I would. I can't go to the mainland now, Mama. We want to be married right away, or as soon as possible. Of course, he plans to speak to Papa and to you also, but isn't it a miracle? I've loved him for so long and never was sure—although I had hoped. But I always thought he'd fall in love with one of the beautiful Hawaiian girls—not someone like me. Oh, I'm so

670

happy, Mama." Jana twirled around a couple of times, over to the table, where her mother remained silent.

Something in her mother's face halted Jana.

"What is it, Mama? What's wrong?"

Slowly Mrs. Rutherford put down her knife and wiped her hands on her apron, shaking her head.

"Oh Jana, dear child. It cannot be. It's out of the question."

"What do you mean, out of the question? I don't understand."

"Isn't it obvious that it would be impossible? It would never be accepted. What would the Kipolas think? Don't you see that?"

"No, of course not. The Kipolas love me. Tutu thinks of me just like she does Akela and Kimo. I don't know what you mean."

"Then you're deliberately trying not to, Jana. You and Kimo and Akela grew up together, of course—you were childhood friends. But marriage. That's an entirely different thing. We and the Kipolas are from different cultures, different backgrounds. . . ."

"Mama, I can't believe you're saying this."

"The Kipolas are pure Hawaiians and proud of it. They don't want the members of their family marrying out of their nationality. That's why I say it's out of the question. Neither Kimo's family nor our family would agree to such a marriage."

Stunned, Jana stared at her mother.

Her mother tried to speak more calmly, less emotionally. "I know you are very fond of Kimo, that it's more than mere friendship, but that's what I'm trying to explain. Friendship is all that it can ever be."

"No! I love Kimo. Really love him. And he loves me. Why can't you be happy for us?"

"Because I know, I can see down the road, Jana. Life has taught me about the world, about mixed relationships. *I* see what *you*, blinded by infatuation, cannot see. . . ."

"It's not infatuation," Jana said stubbornly. "I can tell the difference. I know what love is, and what I feel for Kimo *is* love."

"Darling, you're going to the mainland—you'll have all sorts of new experiences, meet new people."

"I don't want to go now! I want to stay here and marry Kimo. That's all I want."

"You're still very young, Jana."

"I'm old enough to know what I want."

Her mother's tone was very patient. "Surely you can't mean you want to give up your scholarship? Your chance to go to art school? It's what you've wanted, what you've worked so hard for. . . ."

"None of that matters. Not if I have to leave the island, leave Kimo."

"Jana, dear." Her mother came around the table and reached out her hand to touch Jana's arm, but she jerked away.

"I don't understand, Mama. You've always liked Kimo. You've always said how considerate he was, how intelligent. . . . Why wouldn't you want me to marry him?"

Mrs. Rutherford sighed. "If you can't understand that, Jana, I don't know how else to explain it."

"I thought *you*, of all people, would understand, be glad for me, Mama. How many times have you told me about *your* mother marrying your father? How opposed her family was to the marriage, how they sent her away to forget him. Still they held out and finally got married. And you and Papa, too! Your family didn't want you to marry *him*, because he fought on the other side in the War between the States. But it didn't work. *You* eloped!" she said triumphantly. "Making me go to the mainland won't work either."

Her mother was silent for a minute, then she turned away, went back to the table, picked up the knife. "I think we should wait to discuss this until your father comes home, after supper." She began slicing the pineapple again, saying, "Now, if you'll please set the table."

They heard Nathan's voice calling to one of his friends as he came inside, letting the screen door bang behind him.

"All right, Mama. But discussing it with Papa isn't going to change my mind. Don't think that it will."

"Until you're twenty-one, Jana, you are under obedience to your parents, remember that," her mother said coldly. Then she turned to greet Nathan, who came running into the kitchen.

❧

Jana was too upset to eat. Feeling her mother's anxious eyes upon her, she stirred the soup, took a few spoonfuls, nibbled at a rice cake, ate part of a sliced mango. Her father, oblivious to the strain between mother and daughter, talked cheerfully about his day.

Jana glanced at him once or twice, thinking how kind he had always been, always interested in her activities, encouraging her talents. Would he turn against her now, side with her mother, agree that marriage to Kimo was impossible? She twisted her napkin nervously in her lap.

Finally the meal was over. Mrs. Rutherford rose from the table and said, "Wes, Jana has something to tell you. She has already told me—however, it is something we must all discuss together. As soon as I put Nathan to bed, I'll be back."

When her mother left, her father turned to Jana, his eyes filled with some amusement. "Well, Jana, what's this all about?"

She knew he had no idea of the seriousness of what she had to tell. She drew a long breath and poured out her heart.

He listened attentively. "Kimo will come and talk to you himself, tell you his plans, ask your permission. He is doing so well, Papa. His cabinet shop is thriving—they have several big orders. He will be able to support a wife, and I plan to keep on working at the store for a while, and—"

"What about your own plans, my dear, your dreams? Your scholarship? Surely you don't imagine to marry and then take off for a year on the mainland? Have you considered all these things before you make such a statement? Marriage is not to be entered into hastily, you know, but with much prayer, much thinking."

Her mother had reentered the room and took her place at the other end of the table. Jana looked from one to the other and then, near tears, said shakily, "I love Kimo, he loves me, and that's all that matters."

"No, my dear, that is not all that matters," her father said quietly.

Silence fell upon the room. Then her father continued, saying, "You are too young to make such a serious decision. To give up your scholarship would be foolhardy, something you would regret bitterly later. As your parents, we cannot allow you to make this mistake. You will go on with everything as planned, Jana. Your passage is booked, your living in Oakland arranged, and the school is expecting you to start with the next term." He paused. "As for marriage to Kimo, I believe you when you say you love each other. From what I know of Kimo, he is a fine, intelligent young man of character and integrity. I am sure he will agree with our decision." He paused again. "True love waits. If your love is such as you declare it to be, time apart will not weaken it—it may strengthen it. There is plenty of time to speak about marriage."

Jana pushed back her chair and stood up, her hands clenched, her breath short from trying to suppress sobs of grief and frustration. "I have to do what you say, Papa, Mama. But I don't understand. I think there's some reason you're objecting to our getting married. But I don't think I want to hear what it is!"

Jana walked across the room and yanked open the door, letting it shut behind her just short of slamming it.

Chapter Twenty-Three

~❧~

When Jana awoke, sunshine was streaming in through the window. The palm fronds of the tree just outside her bedroom shadowed her quilt with its own intricate patterns. It was as if the Hawaiian design were superimposed on the coverlet her mother had made. Mrs. Rutherford's quilts always reflected her North Carolina memories. The colors were the magentas and mauves of rhododendron and the pink and tangerines of mountain laurel. The colors of Hawaiian quilts were rich and vivid, the designs bolder, just like the landscape, rich and lush.

She knew she would be expected to appear for breakfast, for family morning prayers. She had gone to bed in such misery, she didn't know how she could face her parents, pretend everything was fine when everything seemed so wrong. For a few minutes she lay huddled there, unwilling to get up. She knew that the resentment she was feeling was not right. No two people could be more loving and compassionate than her parents. They just didn't understand. How could she convince them?

Finally she threw back the covers and got up. Stretching, she padded over to the window and looked out. Warm, sweet air was blowing in. The cloudless sky met the line of the

676

ocean like a paintbrush stroke of three different shades of blue. How could a day be so beautiful when her heart was breaking? It should be enough just to be alive. Yet Jana felt weighted by her own sadness.

As she stood there, she saw a mother and a little boy on the beach below, walking along the water's edge. The child ran ahead, dodging the frothy waves, then turned and ran back to his mother, gesturing, stopping every once in a while to look for shells. Jana's heart was suddenly wrenched. She remembered when long ago she had strolled with her mother along that same stretch of sand. They had been so close, mother and daughter. It hurt her that now this misunderstanding had come between them. Could they ever get back that old closeness? Did love always have to cause pain to someone?

Didn't her parents know that Hawaii was her home? She loved this little town, with its small, New England–style houses and their gingerbread porches and peaked roofs. Here she had grown up in view of Mauna Kea. Here the wind blew cool with the combined smell of the briny sea, the flowers, the orchards, the sugarcane fields, the coffee and orchid farms. The thought of going away was like a knife cutting deep.

And leaving Kimo. For a minute Jana closed her eyes, bringing his face into her mind—the dark eyes, so dense that sometimes they seemed impenetrable, then the smile that softened his expression and warmed her heart.... Long before they had declared their love, she had copied a quotation from the writings of Alphonse de Lamartine: "There is a name hidden in the shadow of my soul where I read it night and day and no other eyes have seen it." *Kimo* was that name for her.

Knowing now that he loved her too, made leaving Kimo seem impossible. "True love waits," her father had said. Was her father right? Fragments of a melody, words of a half-forgotten song, floated into her head. It was a famous Hawaiian love song: *Ke kali nei au,* "I am waiting," *Ko'u aloha.* She spoke the words softly to herself. Would it be possible to do? For a whole year?

Jana sighed. She dressed and left her room. The house felt strangely quiet. Empty. When she went out to the kitchen, she realized why. Her mother had left a note propped against the sugar bowl on the table.

> *I've gone to the missionary society meeting. Took Nathan to the Caldwells'. Be back about noon.*
>
> *Love, Mama.*

She glanced at the clock. It was after nine-thirty. But it was Saturday, and she didn't have to go to work today. She must have been worn out from crying and had slept heavily toward dawn. She poured herself some coffee from the pot still hot at the back of the stove, then wandered out on the porch to drink it.

There was so much to think about. Kimo would be coming from Hilo for the weekend, expecting to go to her father, ask for her hand. She would have to intercept him. She would have to explain what she could about her parents' opposition. She didn't want him to be hurt, to misunderstand.

She was convinced, though, that they were wrong— especially her mother, who'd explained about them being from different worlds. She and Kimo were more alike than any two people she knew. They were both Hawaiians. They had been born on the islands, had grown up together. More than that, their spirits, their souls, were in perfect harmony. Their love was deep and real. It would endure, no matter what. Of that Jana was sure.

She finished her coffee and went back inside. Coming down the hallway, she paused outside the open door of her parents' bedroom. Her attention was drawn to the quilt covering their bed. She had seen it a thousand times, had heard the story of its making. Now it seemed to hold some kind of message for her.

Jana walked slowly into the room and over to the bed, with its tall, carved posts. She stood at its foot, looking down at the neatly sewn quilt squares.

This was the "waiting" quilt her mother had worked on for all the long, dreadful years of the war that had divided the States, when her parents lived on the mainland. Her mother had created the design to disguise the "pledge" she and Wesley Rutherford had secretly made before he left to join the Union Army. Jana now realized that this was like the *huna* Tutu had explained to her, the hidden poetic meaning to a Hawaiian quilt's design, known only to the quilter herself.

With her forefinger, Jana traced the outline of the doves in each corner of every square, the clasped hands in the center holding the tiny heart. The quilt was larger than most, because her mother, JoBeth Davison, had kept adding to it for three long years. She had pledged to keep making it until the war was over and the two lovers were reunited.

No wonder her father could say that true love waits. He and her mother were living proof that love can last through every kind of trial, tribulation, separation.

But that had been wartime, and her mother's relatives had been vigorously opposed to the match, declaring Wes a traitor to his people for siding with the Union against the Southern Confederacy.

For her and Kimo it was different. Jana did not really understand why her parents seemed so much against their love, their wanting to marry. She thought of her father's words again. She was willing to wait if in the end she and Kimo could marry.

Why were her parents so concerned, so reluctant to give their consent, even their blessing, to a future marriage? She did not know how to prove to her parents that their love was true. Her plans were as vague and unformed as the drifting clouds overhead. But somehow she knew she would find a way.

She knew she needed assurance, help. Instinctively she went down on her knees, put her head into folded hands, and whispered, "Dear God, tell us what to do and we will do it. I want to be in Your will. I know that's all that matters. Please help us."

❦

Jana had been taught that asking for a sign from God was not something to do lightly. However, having also been taught that parents were His earthly representatives and were to be obeyed, Jana prayed to accept their decision. But she wanted to feel that it really *was* God's will for her.

The next day, she had her Sunday school class to teach but was distracted by her own turbulent mind. It probably didn't help when she went in to face fifteen restless, active, mischievous five- and six-year-olds. Singing always seemed to give them a chance to vent their energy, so she had them all join hands and form a circle and sing some of the hymns she had taught them. "Jesus Loves Me" was one everyone loved and knew the words to and sang at the top of their lungs. Round and round the little group went, singing it over and over. Then one little girl piped up with the first line of another hymn. Raising her voice above the rest, she sang, "Jesus loves the little children, all the children of the world. Red and yellow, black and white, they are precious in his sight. Jesus loves the little children of the world." All of a sudden, Jana's heart was struck as she looked around the circle at all the little faces, all the little mouths open, their voices singing with complete assurance that they were loved and accepted by the Creator of the universe. She was hard put not to start crying. She gazed at each child. Of course it was true. Hawaiian, Chinese, Portuguese, Japanese, or a mixture—they were all God's beloved children.

When the older girls came over to take the smaller children out to play in the churchyard during the service for the adults, Jana, deep in thought, walked over to the church. She slipped into one of the back pews. The choir was just filing out, and Reverend Homakaa was stepping up to the pulpit.

She had asked for a sign but had not expected to get such a clear one. She heard the minister's voice say, "I am taking my sermon today from Acts 10:34–35, where Peter states, "God is no respecter of persons. In every nation he whoever fears him and works righteousness is accepted by him." In both Galatians 3:28 and Colossians 3:11, that same theme is repeated: "In Christ there is neither Greek nor Jew, slave nor free, nor male or female. All are one in Christ."

To be truthful, Jana did not really hear much of Reverend Homakaa's sermon. She had opened her Bible and read and reread the passages he had quoted. *Thank you, Lord*, she said in her heart. *That is what I needed to hear.*

The doxology was sung in Hawaiian: "*Ho'o-na-ni-i ka Ma-ku-a-mau*, Praise God from whom all blessings flow," and Jana rose to sing it with a grateful heart.

During the closing hymn, Jana left quietly. She needed to be alone before joining her parents and telling them she had accepted their decision.

She could still hear the voices of the congregation raised in praise as she took the path that led down to the beach.

Suddenly she saw the day in its glorious beauty, the blue sky and sea merging almost seamlessly, the whisper of music in the palm fronds tossed by the soft wind.

God must see his world like a quilt, she thought, *made up of all different textures, colors, designs, sizes, shapes, all blending into a beautiful whole*. She smiled at her own imagery and then thought that perhaps God smiled, too.

Chapter Twenty-Four

❦

A few days before Jana was scheduled to leave for Honolulu and from there take the ship to the mainland, Tutu Kipola sent for her. Jana's heart was heavy as she went up the familiar path to the small house shaded by the wide banana tree leaves, through the garden lush and brilliant with flowers.

She found Tutu sitting at her frame on the porch, busy quilting.

"Aloha, Tutu," she said, embracing her.

"Aloha, Koana," Tutu replied, using her Hawaiian name. "Come sit down here beside me and tell me—are you all ready to go?"

Jana tucked her skirt up and sat down on a low stool at the side of Tutu's chair. "Yes, everything is packed," she sighed, then impulsively burst out, "You know I don't want to go. I'm just doing it for my parents' sake."

Tutu took a few tiny stitches more before raising her head and meeting Jana's soulful eyes.

"Respect for your parents is not a thing to be sorry for, Koana. You would regret it if you went against their wishes."

"I hate leaving. I'll miss . . . *everything* so much. It will all be so different."

683

"Yes, that's true, Koana. It will be different, but you will learn many new things, many new ways."

"I'm happy here. I don't care about new things." Jana hesitated, then rushed on, saying, "Oh Tutu, the *real* reason, the *main* reason, I don't want to leave is Kimo. You know we love each other. What I really want to do is stay here, be with him. I'm afraid—" She caught herself before finishing the sentence.

"Afraid, Koana? Of what are you afraid?"

"Of losing"—Jana thrust out her hands in a sweeping gesture—"this, all this. And maybe . . . of losing Kimo."

"But what you carry in the heart is never lost, little one," Tutu said gently. "If your love is real, true, it will last. Separation will not destroy love. It may even make it stronger."

"Please don't tell me that true love waits, Tutu. That's what my father says—that's why I'm going. He thinks this is some kind of test for Kimo and me."

"And maybe he is right."

"We've already been tested. First when Kimo went to the academy on Oahu, then all the time he was in Germany. My parents simply don't understand. They think we are too different, that we would not be happy, but they're wrong. We were children together—all my memories of my childhood include him. Kimo was the most wonderful playmate, full of fun and imagination, always ready to laugh and enjoy whatever the moment held. Even as a boy, he was sensitive to and tender toward animals, had an appreciation for the natural things—the shells, the tiny creatures in the tide pools, even the *gheckos*, the little lizards that are everywhere, the ones most people dislike."

Tutu laughed and nodded her head.

Warming to her subject, Jana went on, saying, "When he came back from Germany and I saw him again, every other man I had ever met simply faded into the background. Everyone else seemed smaller, paler, by comparison. Now that we're grown up, I know so much more about him, so many things that I admire and love. It's breaking my heart to leave."

Tutu put aside her needle and thread, carefully folded the quilt she was working on, got to her feet, and said, "Come inside, I want to show you something."

Jana followed her into the cool interior of the cottage. Tutu went to the large closet and opened its doors and pulled out one of the sliding drawers. Jana knew this was where Tutu kept her treasury of quilts, alternating them on her own beds or keeping them for when opportunities arose to give them as gifts. Now she carefully lifted one out, slowly unrolling it so that Jana could see it at full length.

It was exquisite. Pink and green on a paler green background, the elaborate scrolls around the scalloped edge surrounding interwoven wreaths of flowers, the circling design repeating itself, forming a medallion in the center.

Jana drew in her breath. "It's beautiful, Tutu," she whispered.

"It's for you. I made it for you. To take with you now so that every time you see it, use it, you will be reminded of the island and what the message of this quilt is. . . ."

Jana waited for Tutu to tell her what the secret of the design was, although she longed to ask.

"I call it *Ka Makani, Ka'ili Aloaha,* Wind That Wafts Love from One to Another. The encircling wreaths, with flowers you recognize by their shapes as being island flowers—plumeria, hibiscus—represent two winds that blow, meeting each other, wafting in opposite directions, then coming back together to meet in a perfect circle. You and Kimo are like that: one calm, steady; the other adventurous, going hither and thither; both unsure, then blending in one harmonious center. See? Understand?"

Jana nodded. "Yes, I think I do. We both have to find that center, even as we search in different directions?"

Tutu smiled and the radiance that was in her shone in her eyes and smile, making her brown, wrinkled face almost beautiful.

"Oh Tutu, mahalo from the bottom of my heart! How can I ever thank you enough?"

Tears came and streamed unabashedly down Jana's cheeks as she hugged Tutu.

Later as she carried the quilt, which was swathed in protective tissue paper, back along the road home, Jana's heart was full of tenderness. She knew that every stitch of the quilt had been an act of love. She had never appreciated Tutu's caring and wisdom as much. In the space of the afternoon, she had eased Jana's heartache, made her more fully understand that life sometimes requires sacrifice, effort, and time to make something beautiful of it, just as much as is required in the making of a quilt.

Jana knew she would cherish Tutu's gift all the time she was away, daily learning the lessons it taught. Then one day she would bring it back to the island—one day it would have a place of honor in the home Jana was sure she would share with Kimo.

When she got home, she did not show the quilt to her mother. She was afraid, somehow, that it might hurt her. After all, her mother had also made two quilts for Jana to take with her.

Her mother's quilts were beautiful. But they spoke of *her* home, her land—of the mountain laurel and pines of North Carolina, of the golden poppies and purple lupine of California, where she had lived before she came to Hawaii. It was Tutu's quilts that spoke to Jana's heart.

Carefully putting Tutu's quilt at the bottom of her trunk, Jana said to herself, *On the surface, I am doing what my parents*

want me to do, but I am my own person. My destiny is my own.
They will always be haoles, not of this island. I was born here,
belong here—this is my heart's home, to which I shall always return.

⟋⟍

The evening before she was to leave for Honolulu, Jana
went in to say a private good-bye to her father, since he
would not be there to see her off. She knocked softly at his
study door, waited for his answer before turning the knob and
entering.

He was at his desk, a pile of school reports spread out on
its surface. He turned toward her, smiling. "Come in, my
dear," he greeted her, holding out one hand. "Come, sit
down," he invited. "Well, Jana, so it's tomorrow then and
you're off—into the great world, is it? It's all come soon, so
much sooner than I—" He broke off. Still holding her hand,
he drew her closer. "Sit down, let me have a good, long look
at you." She sat and her throat tightened as her father's tender gaze lingered upon her. "You're very talented, Jana, and I
hope you realize it is a gift that you should cherish and
develop—I think you will. I feel confident that although we
may not have been able to prepare you for all you're going to
be facing in the future, at least we have given you a foundation that will stand you in good stead, whatever happens.
Your mother and I count on you, Jana, to make the most of
this opportunity." He looked at her for a long moment before
going on. "This is hard for you, I know, but hardships and sacrifices and separations from those you love are all part of life.
They are all part of what we each have to learn."

"Yes, Papa, I know." Quite suddenly Jana saw him as
through a stranger's eyes. Her beloved father looked worn, suddenly older than she remembered noticing before. Everything,
now that she was leaving, seemed to have added significance.

She had never given much thought to how wearing his job must be, the constant interisland traveling, staff, committees, school·board, student-teacher meetings, problems, complaints. Not wanting to cry, she got up and leaned down and kissed his cheek.

"Thank you, Papa, for everything."

"We'll miss you, dear, but it's the right thing, and the time will pass more quickly than you think it will now."

"Yes, Papa," she whispered. For his sake, Jana did not let him see the tears just under the surface, the heartache she was hiding. She would spare him that.

At the door she turned and looked back. His head was already bent over the papers on his desk. Quietly she tiptoed out. Kimo was coming and this last good-bye would be the hardest.

***

They held hands, fingers locked, palms together, and walked down the path to the deserted evening beach. A palm tree, uprooted by a recent storm, lay on its side. Its scattered dry fronds crackled under their feet as they picked their way among large pieces of bleached driftwood until they found one to sit upon.

Kimo was unusually quiet. Jana's departure was the dark cloud that had hung over them these past weeks. They had avoided facing it until now. Jana realized that he, more than anyone else, understood what her going away meant. He'd had the same kind of opportunity, and it had meant two years in Germany, away from Hawaii. Exile!

She knew Kimo was struggling against his own natural desire to keep her with him, so he could give her the courage she would need to say good-bye. A year, twelve long months—and then the future loomed uncertainly. The fear that lurked in both of their minds was that even then something might prevent their being together. Perhaps one of them might change—although Jana could not believe that would happen. Still, it lay heavily on both their minds, unspoken.

The clouds were turning pink, orange. For a few minutes the sky turned brilliant. Then the sun began its descent. Once, Kimo had told her that watching a sunset was to him almost a spiritual experience, so she was silent now beside him. The awe both felt was tinged with sadness. It would be a long time before they would share another sunset together.

If only, Jana thought wistfully, *it could always be like this, never change, remain this beautiful moment, caught in an eternity.* She put her head on Kimo's shoulder. His arm went around her waist, drawing her close, and his chin rested on her hair. She could smell the scent of wood, the faint fragrance of sandalwood and koa that sometimes clung to him.

Kimo began to speak to her in a low tone, in both English and Hawaiian, so that the words sounded almost like poetry.

"Someday we will build our home on the top of the bluff, overlooking the beach, where the wind blows the palm fronds, making enchanted music for only us to hear. . . ."

As Jana listened to his deep voice, melodic and soft in her ears, she was filled with happiness, knowing deep within her that this was the language of their love, the combination of two cultures, two minds, hearts, spirits, so closely joined that no translation was necessary. How many people in the world were lucky enough to have this kind of perfect understanding? In spite of her pain at parting, she was convinced that this was the person with whom she was destined to spend the rest of her life in this special place. They had pledged their love, just as her parents had, years ago, in the face of a long, dreadful separation, and it would last, whatever lay ahead.

Kimo put his fingers under her chin and turned her face toward him, then kissed her with infinite tenderness. "*Aloha, Mau loa, kau a kau,*" he said gently.

"Aloha, Kimo," she replied.

Chapter Twenty-Five

❧❧

Once aboard the steamer to Honolulu, the fact that she was actually leaving Hawaii and on her way to the mainland became real to her.

Things had moved so quickly. Her father had business in Kona that morning and so had said his good-bye, giving her a new Bible as a going-away present. Then, accompanied by her mother and Nathan and surrounded by her luggage, she went by wagon to the dock, where Akela and Kimo were waiting to see her off. Of course, she and Kimo had already said their private good-bye. Now the unspoken things lay too deep to share, but they understood their mutual silence. The things they *had* spoken, the promises exchanged, they both considered as sacred as though they had been said before an altar.

At last the small boat's whistle sounded. Eyes brimming with tears, Jana hugged Nathan, embraced her mother, and said her final alohas. Akela and Kimo both had leis for her. Akela's was of carnations and plumeria blossoms, Kimo's of yellow hibiscus. Knowing how far she was going and how long it would be before her return, it took every ounce of Jana's will to give Kimo the traditional kiss, whisper, "Aloha," turn away, and board the boat.

As the boat pulled out of the harbor, gradually her tears stopped. By the time she arrived in Honolulu, Jana had regained her composure. She realized that for the first time in her life, she was entirely on her own. Nervous but excited, she asked directions to the information office. There she was told that the ship SS *Umatilla* was already loading passengers, and she was directed to its moored place at the dock.

Clutching her ticket, heart thumping, Jana went up the gangplank. At the top she was greeted by the ship's officer, who then turned her over to a uniformed stewardess who led her through the passageway to the cabin.

"You'll be sharing it, dear. With one of the missionary wives going home on furlough. She hasn't arrived yet, so you can have your pick of bunk and chest," the woman said briskly. "When you've settled in a bit, you'll want to go back up on deck. The farewell is always interesting, band playing and all." She smiled, then leaned forward and said in a stage whisper, "You're going to have royalty for fellow passengers this trip." She gave Jana a wink and then went out the door.

Royalty? Jana thought. Who could she mean? It was all very mysterious and exciting. She would be sure to take the stewardess' advice and go back up on deck and see what was going to happen.

Jana explored the small, narrow cabin, then opened her suitcase and hung up the things she would need for the week's journey. Most of her clothes were packed in her trunk. She unpacked her toilet articles, put them away. Then she lifted out the lovely quilt Tutu had given her, from the bottom of the larger of her two suitcases. Before placing it at the foot of her narrow bunk, she smoothed its delicate design tenderly. It would always remind her of the loving acceptance Kimo's family had given her. It symbolized *ohana*, the Hawaiian word meaning family in the fullest sense of the word. Ohana, a beautiful reality. Because Kimo loved her, all the Kipolas loved her.

She shoved both suitcases under her bunk, then went out of the cabin, down the passageway, and up the steps. As she stepped out onto the deck, she noticed an audible stir among the passengers, a murmur that grew into a buzz circulating throughout the groups of people on deck. Aware that she was about to witness something unusual and exciting, Jana found a place at the railing just in time to see that it was the royal entourage coming up the gangplank. Jana could hardly believe her eyes. Princess Kaiulani!

Of course, she had often seen many pictures of the child who would one day be Hawaii's queen, but she had never dreamed she would ever see her in person. She recognized her immediately. At fourteen, the princess was exquisite with her satiny golden skin, her thick, curling black hair, her rounded nose, her sweet, vulnerable mouth. She held the promise of even greater beauty as she grew into womanhood.

The princess was accompanied by the tall, splendid-looking gentleman who was her father, the Scotsman Archibald Cleghorn, husband of the Hawaiian princess Like-like, the younger sister of King Kalakaua.

As they came on board, for a moment Jana found herself close enough to look into the small, beautiful face of the princess. There was an instant of eye contact. Their gaze locked. In that moment, Jana saw something she recognized within the velvety depths of the dark brown eyes. Something for which she felt immediate empathy. *Poor little girl! I know exactly how you feel. My heart aches, too. To leave this beloved land, to go to something strange, new, unknown. My heart aches for you.*

All around Jana another rippling murmur swirled. Following the princess and her father came a tall, lanky, spectrally thin gentleman, a *haole* whom Jana also recognized. She had seen him photographed with the king. It was the famous writer-poet, Robert Louis Stevenson! He was a good friend of the king and of the royal family and was often a guest at the palace. Hollow-cheeked, long of nose, the man nevertheless had eyes that twinkled, and his mouth, under a drooping mustache, had a humorous tilt. He seemed to enjoy the celebrity he had among the people clustered on deck.

He was escorting an elderly woman. His mother? She looked like an aristocratic Scotswoman. Her dark, austere clothing oddly contrasted with the rest of the colorfully dressed company and the lei of brilliant flowers she was wearing.

Loud whispers ran from one passenger to the other, all crowding to see what they could see yet keeping a respectful distance from the group, to whom the ship's crew were now showing decided deference.

Jana was thrilled to see, in person, the creator of some of her favorite stories. As the group passed out of view on their way to their suite of cabins, the other passengers thronged again to the railing to watch as the huge ship moved slowly out of the harbor. People leaned forward to get their last glimpse of Honolulu.

Jana felt the painful lump rise into her throat again as she looked down at the wake of cerulean blue waves taking them further out to sea. The scent of the plumerias and carnations in her leis rose fragrantly—she hated to part with them, and yet she was determined to carry out the tradition. According to the old legend, if a lei thrown from a departing ship floated out to sea, you would not return, but if it went instead toward the shore, that meant you would come back to Hawaii.

Gently she lifted the leis over her head and, one by one, tossed them over the railing as far as she could throw. Then she leaned forward, anxiously watching the direction in which they floated.

She held her breath, trying to keep her eyes on the strands of white, yellow, and lavender flowers riding on the surface of the water. First they bobbed this way and that. *Oh no!* she thought, as they seemed almost directionless. Then suddenly the yellow hibiscus lei seemed caught in a whirling wave and, like a skilled surfer, drifted *shoreward*.

The relief she felt brought tears to her eyes. The scene blurred and she blinked, trying to keep the lei in sight as it moved inland toward the beach.

Immediately the Scripture Matthew 6:21 came into her mind: "Where your treasure is, there your heart will be also."

"Yes, yes, I will come back," Jana promised herself. "Back to the land of my birth, of my heart, of my love.

"I will return. . . . *Aloha nui loa.* . . ."

American Quilt Series
Bonus Section

❧

How to Make
a Hawaiian Quilt

In the eighteenth and nineteenth centuries, Christian missionaries first brought the basic quilt-making techniques to the Hawaiian islands, and before long, a local tradition sprang up that diverged widely from that found in the continental United States. The nature of the Hawaiian quilt makes it nearly impossible to outline a simple method of making one, but those readers who are experienced in basic quilting will be aided in making a Hawaiian quilt by observing the following principles.

First of all, Hawaiian quilts do not rely on the building up of smaller repetitive square-and-diamond patterns in the way that many traditional quilts do. Rather, they display one large, overall design that can even look at times to the uneducated eye like a folded-paper cutting of a Christmas snowflake. Usually, a floral, vine, or other decorative pattern radiates from the center of the quilt, covering the entire surface with its pattern. The pattern repeats, in a sense, like a pie cut into four, six, or eight pieces, all radiating from the center. To get a sense of the traditional designs, we recommend that you study the designs in one of the books listed below.

Second, the Hawaiian use of color is different than in other quilt traditions. White is usually used for the background color, and the main pattern, which is frequently a silhouette motif, is usually rendered in a single bold color. This gives the quilt a brightly toned and high-contrast look, which is a reflection of the sunlit islands themselves. Sometimes other colors are added with smaller decorative pieces to the main pattern if more detail is desired.

Third, unlike most American quilts, every Hawaiian quilt is quite different. A Hawaiian quilt maker varies her design from quilt to quilt, developing a distinctive and recognizable style, but seldom repeating a pattern or element. This is different from Appalachian quilts, for instance, in which common forms and patterns are widely shared among quilt makers and repeated often from community to community. In a sense, the Hawaiians have a very strong tradition of individual expression in their quilt making, which makes this form especially appealing.

Aside from these differences, the techniques largely remain the same, from the designs being cut and appliquéd onto the layered white fabric to their final stitching together. For details of the actual stitching techniques and sample designs, you might want to refer to the following books, which can be ordered from your local bookstore: Elizabeth Root, *Hawaiian Quilting* (New York: Dover, 1989); Milly Singletary, *Hawaiian Quilting Made Easy* (Singletary Publications, 1992); and Reiko M. Brandon, *The Hawaiian Quilt* (Honolulu: Honolulu Arts, 1989).

Acknowledgments

The author would like to acknowledge and thank the authors and publishers of the following books, which proved invaluable in the research and writing of *The Promise*.

Joseph Brennan, *The Parker Ranch of Hawaii*
Albertine Loomis, *Grapes of Canaan: Hawaii 1820*
Ruth Eleanor McKee, *The Lord's Anointed*
Margaret G. Martin, Nattie Hammond Lyman, Kathryn Lyman Bond, and Ethel M. Damon, editors, *The Lymans of Hilo*
James Michener, *Hawaii*
Robert Louis Stevenson, *Travels in Hawaii*
A. Grove Day and Carl Stroven, editors, *A Hawaiian Reader*
Armine von Tempski, *Born in Paradise*